# FAILURE OF THE PUBLIC TRUST

proof of FBI and OIC cover-up
in the Independent Counsel's probe into the
death of deputy White House Counsel Vincent W. Foster

*Best wishes*

*Patrick Knowlton*

John Clarke     Patrick Knowlton     Hugh Turley

McCabe Publishing
www.FBIcover-up.com

ISBN 0–9673521–0–X

LAW OFFICES
# JOHN H. CLARKE
1730 K STREET, N.W.
SUITE 304
WASHINGTON, D.C. 20006

(202) 332-3030

ALSO ADMITTED IN VIRGINIA
AND MARYLAND

FAX (202) 822-8820

June 23, 1999

**United States Court of Appeals**
For the District of Columbia Circuit

**FILED** JUN 23 1999

UNDER SEAL

**Special Division**

The Honorable David B. Sentelle
The Honorable Richard D. Cudahy
The Honorable Peter T. Fay
UNITED STATES COURT OF APPEALS
    FOR THE DISTRICT OF COLUMBIA CIRCUIT
Division 94-1 for the Purpose of
    Appointing Independent Counsels

Re:   *In re: Madison Guaranty
      Savings & Loan Association*
      Report on the Death of Vincent W. Foster, Jr.
      Patrick Knowlton's motions -
      (1)  To amend the Comments & Factual Information
           included in the appendix to the OIC's
           interim Foster Report, pursuant to the
           Ethics in Government Act of 1978; and
      (2)  Motion to unseal proposed
           Comments & Factual Information

Dear Sirs:

In September 1997, the Court ordered the Office of
Independent Counsel ("OIC") to include Mr. Knowlton's
filing in the appendix to the OIC's interim Report on Mr.
Foster's death. That Report, inclusive of its appendix, is
available from any government printing office, document #
028-004-00095-8. Mr. Knowlton respectfully asks the Court
to order the OIC to substitute this work in the place of
his earlier filing, so that it too will be available as
document # 028-004-00095-8. Mr. Knowlton also respectfully
asks the Court to immediately unseal this filing.

The objects of the relief Mr. Knowlton seeks[1] are the same as those of our Ethics in Government Act[2] -- to ensure that (1) justice is done, (2) justice appears to have been done, (3) those named in a Report are afforded a measure of fairness, (4) reports are full and complete, and (5) the Independent Counsel is accountable.

---

[1] See pp. 2-4 of Motions of Patrick Knowlton, filed herewith: (1) For Leave to Amend Comments and Factual Information included in the Appendix to the OIC's Interim Report on the Death of Vincent Foster... (2) Unseal Comments and Factual Information Proposed to be an Appendix to the OIC's Report & (3) Compel the OIC to produce his grand jury minutes:

> Patrick Knowlton respectfully prays that the Court grant him leave to amend the Comments and Factual Information, attached as an appendix to the OIC's interim Report by Order entered September 26, 1997, and to substitute the enclosed Comments and Factual Information in its place... Because of the extraordinary public importance of the current debate on whether to reenact our Ethics in Government Act, and the need to promptly disseminate the information in the subject filing to the American people, movant respectfully requests that the Court consider the motion to unseal his filing on an expedited basis...

> Summary of argument: ...The OIC's reliance on § 594 in filing its interim, as opposed to a "final," Report, was in error. The OIC's interim Report is unknown to the Act and this Court therefore need adjudicate movant's rights under the Act. *** Patrick Knowlton [also] respectfully moves the Court to unseal his proposed comments and factual information. The common law, the First Amendment to the Constitution, and the traditional practice of this Court support the relief requested. Personal privacy interest in non-disclosure, if any, is outweighed by the public interest in the administration of justice. The Act specifically authorizes this Court to unseal... *** A grand jury witness has a general right to the transcript of his own grand jury testimony when sought in connection with a judicial proceeding.

[2] The Ethics in Government Act of 1978, 28 U.S.C. §§ 591-599 (1994) [hereinafter also the "Ethics in Government Act," the "Independent Counsel Statute," or "the Act"].

# Summary of Contents

# **Preface**

If the Court grants Patrick Knowlton's motion, this document will forever be available from any government printing office. This filing is for the public. It presents most of the available evidence of cover-up. We believe that it proves, beyond doubt, the existence of a conspiracy, a cover-up.

If a cover-up exists, Mr. Starr's Office of Independent Counsel is infected with the very corruption it is designed to fight. That is important. But more importantly, in light of the scrutiny we are told our government has given the matter, if a cover-up has survived now for almost six years, then the matter of the existence of the conspiracy raises larger issues. Two of the three branches of our government, the executive and the legislature, as well as the press, did not function as intended. In the pages that follow, we are examining whether our Constitutional system protects us from government corruption, as the experiment of our founding fathers envisioned. These questions about our democracy are not merely academic.

The records filed in two District of Columbia federal courts tell how Patrick Knowlton became embroiled in this case. One is his 20-page submission to the United States Court of Appeals, Special Division for the Purpose of Appointing Independent Counsels, filed on his behalf in accordance with the Independent Counsel Statute. The Court ordered Mr. Starr's OIC, over its objection, to include those 20 pages in its Appendix to Report on the Death of Vincent Foster, Jr., a nine-page letter and eleven pages of exhibits. On October 10, 1997, the OIC's Report on Mr. Foster's death, inclusive of its Appendix, was released to the public. Another Court in which Patrick Knowlton is proceeding is the United States District Court for the District of Columbia, where his civil rights lawsuit is filed.

Excerpts from these two Court filings appear below.

# Preface

Appendix to the OIC's Report on the Death of Vincent Foster, Jr., September 23, 1997:

**Facts.** While heading home in heavy traffic on the George Washington Memorial Parkway, and facing over a two-hour commute, Patrick Knowlton pulled into Fort Marcy Park at 4:30 p.m. on July 20th, 1993, to relieve himself. Patrick parked close to the main footpath entrance into the park, between the only two cars in the small parking lot, which were parked just four spaces apart.

To Patrick's left was parked an unoccupied mid-1980s rust-brown four-door Honda sedan with Arkansas tags (closest to the footpath entrance), and on his right was a late model metallic blue-gray sedan, backed into its parking space. A man was seated in the driver's seat of the blue-gray sedan. Immediately after Patrick parked, the man lowered the passenger side electric window and stared at him, menacingly. This unnerved Patrick as he exited his car.

As he started from his car toward the footpath, Patrick heard the blue-gray sedan's door open. Apprehensive, Patrick walked to the sign bordering the footpath entrance to the park and feigned to read its historical information while nonchalantly glancing to his right to see if the man was approaching. He saw the man leaning on the roof of the driver's side of his blue-gray sedan, watching him intently. Patrick then cautiously proceeded 75 feet down the footpath's left fork to the first large tree, in the opposite direction from which Mr. Foster's body was later recovered.

As he relieved himself, Patrick heard the man close his car door. Because the foliage was dense, he couldn't see the parking lot and hoped the man wasn't approaching. As Patrick walked back to the parking lot with a heightened sense of awareness, he scanned the lot but did not see the man. Patrick surmised that the man had either gotten back in his car or perhaps could even be crouching between the brown Honda and Patrick's car preparing to attack him.

In order to maintain his distance from the space between the two cars until he learned the man's whereabouts, Patrick walked directly toward the driver's side door of the brown Honda, and then around the back of it. As Patrick reached the driver's side door of the brown Honda, he looked through the window. He also looked into the back seat as he walked the length of the car. He saw a dark colored suit jacket draped over the driver's seat, a briefcase on the front passenger's seat, and two bottles of wine cooler on the back seat. As he reached the back of the Honda, Patrick was relieved to see that the man had returned to his own vehicle. The man was still staring fixedly at him.

Of the five things Patrick witnessed at the park ((1) the man and his car, (2) the suit jacket, (3) the briefcase, (4) the wine cooler, and (5) the mid-1980s Arkansas brown Honda), the Honda itself is the most relevant. It was not Mr. Foster's car. When Mr. Foster's body was discovered approximately 70 minutes after Patrick had left the park, Mr. Foster had been dead for well over 70 minutes. Mr. Foster therefore could not have driven to the park in his Honda, as claimed in the government Reports on the death.

The following evening, Patrick saw on the news for the first time that Vincent Foster had been found dead at Fort Marcy Park, so he telephoned the U.S. Park Police and reported what he had seen. Nine months later, FBI Special Agent Larry Monroe... wrote in his reports of those interviews that Patrick "identified this particular vehicle [Honda] as a 1988-1990...," and that Patrick "reiterated his description of this Honda as a 1988-1990." This information was false and known to be false.[fn2]

Eighteen months later, in October of 1995, Patrick was provided a copy of his then publicly-available FBI interview reports by a reporter for a London newspaper. He realized for the first time that Monroe had falsified his account of the car and other facts he had recounted during his FBI interviews. His true account, along with the contradictory information from his FBI interview reports, was reported in the London newspaper on Sunday, October 22, 1995.

Two days later, on Tuesday, October 24, the paper reached American newsstands. That day, Mr. Starr's office prepared a subpoena summoning Patrick to testify before the Whitewater grand jury in this courthouse on November 1, 1995. Two days after that, Thursday, October 26, FBI agent Russell Bransford served the secret grand jury subpoena.[fn2]

Beginning that same day he was subpoenaed, and continuing into the following day, Patrick was harassed... Experts tell us that the technique is known to federal intelligence and investigative agencies, and that its objects were twofold: (i) to intimidate and warn Patrick in connection with his grand jury testimony; and failing that, (ii) to destabilize him and discredit his testimony before the grand jury.

It worked.

---

**fn. 2:** Monroe tried for hours to get Patrick to admit that the Foster's 1989 silver-gray Honda "could have been" the car Patrick saw. Patrick steadfastly responded, "No," repeating the description he had provided to the Park Police by telephone. Monroe falsified his interview report, writing that Patrick had "identified" the Honda as a "1988-1990," despite the fact that during his second FBI interview, Patrick had picked out the same color he had seen on the mid-1980s Honda from the "browns" section of the car color panels in the FBI laboratory, and that color corresponded to one available only on 1983 and 1904 Hondas.

**fn. 3:** Agent Bransford had been detailed to regulatory Independent Counsel Fiske's investigation, where he worked with Agent Monroe. Bransford told Patrick he had been "kept on under Starr."

*   *   *

[P]rior to Mr. Starr's appointment to head the statutory OIC in August of 1994, the only substantive investigations into the case, with the sole exception of the U.S. Park Police investigation (conducted with FBI participation), were conducted by the FBI.[fn8]  The publicly-available federal government record upon which the Fiske Report is based is replete with evidence that the FBI concealed the true facts surrounding Mr. Foster's death.[fn9]

*   *   *

The fundamental purposes of our Ethics in Government Act are (1) to ensure that justice has been done and (2) to preserve and promote public confidence in the integrity of the federal government by maintaining the appearance that justice has been done.  In light of (1) the FBI's statutory mandate to exercise primary jurisdiction in July of 1993 in the event of foul play, (2) two prior FBI findings of no criminal activity, and (3) evidence of a cover-up by the FBI already in the public domain, the OIC's use of the FBI in this matter undermines both purposes of the Act.  No OIC can fulfill its mandate to preserve and protect the appearance of justice having been done when its investigation

---

fn. 8:   There have been no other official investigations.  The 1994 Senate Banking Committee was precluded by the limited scope of Resolution 229 from independently exploring the issue of how or where Mr. Foster died ("whether improper conduct occurred regarding... the Park Service Police investigation into the death..."). [Ranking Republican, Committee on Government Operations, U.S. House of Representatives, William F.] Clinger did not investigate and Senator D'Amato's Committee did not explore these issues.

fn. 9:   Much evidence of obstruction of justice by the FBI is documented in Patrick's lawsuit in this District Court (No. 96-2467) for inter alia, violation of 42 U.S.C. § 1985(2), "...Obstructing justice; intimidating... witness...

employs the very agency it is designed to be independent from, the Justice Department.[fn11]

Upon review of those excerpts of the Report provided by the OIC, it is manifest that the Report omits the information Patrick provided which refutes the FBI's repeated official conclusion of suicide in the park...

*     *     *

Moreover, the Report's purported reliance on grand jury testimony is an attempt to give the Report more credibility.  Indeed, the catalyst for Patrick's grand jury testimony was the appearance in U.S. newsstands of the October 22nd [1995] issue of the *London Sunday Telegraph,* in which Ambrose Evans-Pritchard described Patrick's reaction when he was shown the FBI report of his interview with two FBI agents detailed to Mr. Fiske's probe.  It was the first time Patrick had seen the report of the interview, which had been conducted eighteen months earlier.  Evans-Pritchard wrote that Patrick "was stunned." Referring to the FBI's assertion that Patrick stated he "would be unable to recognize the man" he had seen at the park, Patrick is quoted as saying "That's an outright lie."

---

**fn. 11:**  Under the Act, the OIC's use of the FBI is free, tempting the OIC to create a microcosm of the DOJ. (See Act of Dec. 15th 1987, Pub. L. No. 100-191, 1987 U.S.C.C.A.N. (101 Stat. 1293) p. 2172:  "Congress intended the Justice Department to provide independent counsels with the same assistance it provides to its other high-priority, federal criminal cases... federal agencies are instructed to discontinue... requiring reimbursement agreements..."

**fn. 12:**  See Exhibit 4. A USPP report notes that the autopsy doctor estimated that Mr. Foster died "2-3 hours" after having eaten a "large meal" "which might have been meat and potatoes."  Several people reported that Mr. Foster had finished his lunch of a cheeseburger and French fries by 1:00 p.m., therefore putting the time of death between 3:00 and 4:00 p.m. Also, the paramedic in his Incident Report estimates that based upon the "pooling of blood in the extremities," Mr. Foster had been dead "2-4 hrs" at 6:10 p.m...

Evans-Pritchard's article also states:

"They showed him a photograph of [Foster's] Honda... 'They went over it about 20 times, telling me that this was Foster's car,' said Knowlton. 'But I was quite adamant about it. I saw what I saw, and I wasn't going to change my story'... Starr's investigators have never talked to Knowlton. The federal grand jury has never summoned him to give sworn testimony."

*     *     *

On October 24, the same day that this newspaper reached U.S. newsstands, the OIC prepared a subpoena summoning Patrick to testify before the Whitewater grand jury. The secret grand jury subpoena was served two days later by an FBI agent who was formerly detailed to Mr. Fiske's probe, whereupon Patrick was harassed and intimidated... The Report omits all of this, even though Patrick submitted a report detailing the harassment to the OIC in March of 1996, which included reports of a polygraph examination, a psychiatric examination, witnesses' affidavits, photographs of two members of the harassment team and the names and addresses of two others.

**Conclusion.** Because Patrick did not heed the warning regarding his grand jury testimony and continued to tell the truth, including his account of the *bizarre* harassment he suffered, his testimony was discredited. Patrick was harassed in an effort to make him look unbalanced or dishonest. Since that time, he has been defamed by numerous individuals, most of whom are journalists. He has been attacked as a delusional conspiracy theorist, a homosexual, and as an outright liar. Patrick has been fighting to reestablish his credibility for the past two years. Patrick did nothing to deserve the outrageous treatment he received at the hands of the OIC and its FBI agents. He did nothing to deserve being yanked into this FBI debacle, having his life turned upside down, and having to endure this fight for his reputation. Patrick's only "crime" was reporting to the authorities what he had seen at Fort Marcy Park, consistent

with his understanding of his duties as a good
citizen.

Patrick respectfully asks that the Division of
the Court append this letter to the Independent
Counsel's Report on the Death of Vincent Foster,
Jr. to afford him a measure of fairness.  A
denial of this relief would augment the
appearance of justice having not been done and
would further frustrate legislative intent.
Patrick should not have to go through the rest of
his life labeled as a liar or some kind of nut.
He has no remedy at law for injury to his
reputation causally related to the subject
investigations.  Patrick Knowlton merely seeks to
establish that he is telling the truth and that
he is mentally stable.

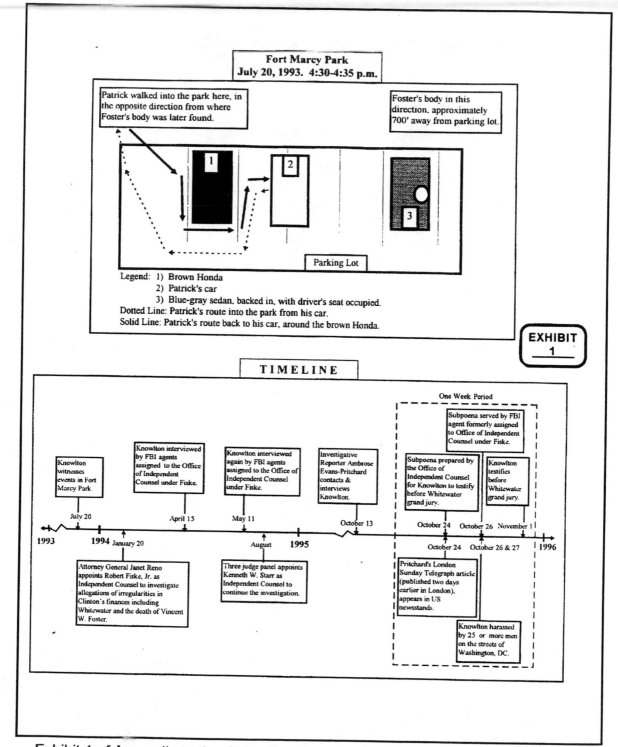

**Fort Marcy Park**
**July 20, 1993. 4:30-4:35 p.m.**

Patrick walked into the park here, in the opposite direction from where Foster's body was later found.

Foster's body in this direction, approximately 700' away from parking lot.

Parking Lot

Legend: 1) Brown Honda
2) Patrick's car
3) Blue-gray sedan, backed in, with driver's seat occupied.
Dotted Line: Patrick's route into the park from his car.
Solid Line: Patrick's route back to his car, around the brown Honda.

**EXHIBIT 1**

**TIMELINE**

One Week Period

Knowlton witnesses events in Fort Marcy Park.
July 20

Knowlton interviewed by FBI agents assigned to the Office of Independent Counsel under Fiske.
April 15

Knowlton interviewed again by FBI agents assigned to the Office of Independent Counsel under Fiske.
May 11

Investigative Reporter Ambrose Evans-Pritchard contacts & interviews Knowlton.
October 13

Subpoena served by FBI agent formerly assigned to Office of Independent Counsel under Fiske.

Subpoena prepared by the Office of Independent Counsel for Knowlton to testify before Whitewater grand jury.
October 24

Knowlton testifies before Whitewater grand jury.

1993  1994 January 20  August  1995  October 24  October 26 & 27  1996

October 24  October 26  November 1

Attorney General Janet Reno appoints Robert Fiske, Jr. as Independent Counsel to investigate allegations of irregularities in Clinton's finances including Whitewater and the death of Vincent W. Foster.

Three judge panel appoints Kenneth W. Starr as Independent Counsel to continue the investigation.

Pritchard's London Sunday Telegraph article (published two days earlier in London), appears in US newsstands.

Knowlton harassed by 25 or more men on the streets of Washington, DC.

Exhibit 1 of Appendix to the OIC's Report on the Death of Vincent Foster, Jr., submitted September 23, 1997, released to the public on October 10, 1997

**USPP REPORT. INTERVIEW BY USPP & FBI OF ASSISTANT IN WHITE HOUSE COUNSEL'S OFFICE: MR. FOSTER ATE LUNCH OF "CHEESEBURGER" AND "FRENCH FRIES."**

| United States Park Police | 0 7 2 0 9 3 9 3 -3 0 5 0 |
|---|---|
| NATURE OF INCIDENT Death Investigation | RECLASSIFICATION OF INCIDENT |

The first conversation she had with him was about lunch around 1200 1230 hours. He said he would eat at his desk. He ordered a medium rare cheeseburger, french fries and coke. She and Linda Tripp went to the cafeteria and ordered his lunch. She

**FBI INTERVIEW REPORT. EXECUTIVE ASSISTANT IN WHITE HOUSE COUNSEL'S OFFICE: MR. FOSTER LEFT OFFICE SHORTLY AFTER 1:00 PM AFTER HE ATE LUNCH.**

Continuation of FD-302 of ___Linda A. Tripp___ , On __4/12/94__ , Page __4__

from work. When he left the office at shortly after 1:00PM he did not have anything with him. TRIPP did not know where he was going and it was not appropriate for her to ask him. He did not have any appointments noted on his office calendars or that anybody knew about.

**USPP REPORT. DOCTOR WHO PERFORMED AUTOPSY SAID EATEN "MEAT AND POTATOES" "2-3 HOURS PRIOR TO DEATH."**

NATIONAL PARK SERVICE
SUPPLEMENTAL CRIMINAL INCIDENT RECORD     • JUVENILE CASE ☐

| GWY Ft. Marcy | 0 7 2 0 9 3 9 3 -0 3 0 4 2 |
|---|---|

Dr. Beyer stated that it appeared that the victim had eaten a "large" meal which he believed to have occurred within 2-3 hours prior to death. He was unable to state positively what type of food was consumed but stated the it might have been meat and potatoes.

**PARAMEDIC'S INCIDENT REPORT. AT 6:10 PM "HAD BEEN DEAD APPROX 2-4 HRS."**

This is certified a true copy of the actual field incident report in possession of the Fairfax County Fire and Rescue Department
Signed _Bonnie Diamonko_
Date _7-19-94_

EXHIBIT
4
Page 1 of 2 pages

| NARRATIVE REPORT | NARRATIVE REPORT |
|---|---|
| INCIDENT # R32011315 UNIT M01 SUPP 01 SEG 2 SITF 301 DATE 07/20/93 | INCIDENT # R32011315 UNIT M01 SUPP02 SITF 801 07/20/93 |
| HAD SET IN. POOLING OF BLOOD IN THE EXTREMITIES. PT HAD BEEN DEAD APPROX 2 | HAD SET IN. POOLING OF BLOOD IN THE EXTEMITIES. PT HAD BEEN DEAD APPROX 2-4 HRS. PT HAD A WEAPON IN HIS-RIGHTHAND |
| -4 HRS. PT HAD A WEAPON IN HIS-RIGHTHAND | |

Exhibit 4 of Appendix to the OIC's Report on the Death of Vincent Foster, Jr., submitted September 23, 1997, released to the public on October 10, 1997

**FBI REPORTS OF INTERVIEWS WITH PATRICK AND TWO OTHER CIVILIAN PARK WITNESSES**

**PATRICK ARRIVED 4:30 PM. CAR "BROWN... HONDA WITH ARKANSAS PLATE"**

parking area, he immediately noticed an unoccupied vehicle parked
front end in facing the park in one of the first parking slots on
the left hand side. He identified this particular vehicle as a
1988-1990 brown or rusty brown in color Honda with Arkansas
plates. He stated that he could not remember whether this
vehicle was a two door or four door sedan and outside of the

**MALE SAYS HE AND FEMALE ARRIVED AROUND 5:00 P.M. CAR "BROWNISH."**

They arrived at Fort Marcy Park at approximately 5:00
p.m. As they drove into the parking lot, he observed a vehicle,
possibly a small station wagon or "hatchback" model, brownish in
color, parked to his left. The vehicle was parked close to the
path leading up to Fort Marcy, with the front of the car pulled

**FEMALE SAYS THEY ARRIVED BETWEEN 5:15 & 5:30 PM. CAR "MID-1980s."**

Marcy Park in her white Nissan         , arriving at Fort Marcy
Park sometime between 5:15 and 5:30 p.m. To the best of her
recollection, she maintained that upon entering the parking lot
at Fort Marcy Park, she noted that the only vehicle in the
parking area was a relatively old (mid-1980's) Honda, possibly a
Honda Accord, either tan or dark in color, parked close to the
entry of the parking lot, adjacent to a path leading to the
Northern section of the park.          believed that this
particular Honda was parked with the front of the vehicle facing
the park area and to the best of her recollection, believes a

**SWORN TESTIMONY OF PATRICK KNOWLTON (ARRIVED FMP 4:30 PM)**

REGARDING: VINCENT FOSTER. SWORN STATEMENT OF PATRICK KNOWLTON
PRESENT:  CONGRESSMAN DAN BURTON   KEVIN BINGER   JOHN CLARKE

| 14 | THERE WAS TWO VEHICLES IN THE PARKING LOT -- ONE WAS A |
| 15 | BROWN, RUST-BROWN COLORED HONDA WITH ARKANSAS LICENSE |
| 16 | PLATES.  IT WAS AN OLDER VEHICLE. |
| 19 | SUGGESTED TO ME THAT THAT WAS THE AGE OF IT, AND, WHEN HE |
| 20 | SHOWED ME THE PICTURES OF A CAR THAT WAS AN '88 OR A '90, I |
| 21 | SAID, NO.  IT IS, OBVIOUSLY, AN OLDER CAR.  THE CAR THAT |
| 22 | YOU ARE SHOWING ME THE PICTURE OF IS TOO NEW. |

EXHIBIT
4
Page 2 of 2 pages

Exhibit 4 of Appendix to the OIC's Report on the Death of Vincent Foster, Jr.,
submitted September 23, 1997, released to the public on October 10, 1997

## Preface

On October 25, 1996, a year before the Court ordered that the OIC's Report on Mr. Foster's death be released to the public, Patrick Knowlton's civil rights lawsuit was filed in the US District Court for the District of Columbia, Case No. 96-2467. In it, he alleges violations of 42 U.S.C. § 1985(2), *Obstructing justice; intimidating... witness.* On October 21, 1998, he filed a motion to file a Second Amended Complaint. Excerpts of that amended lawsuit follow.

Patrick Knowlton v. Robert Edwards et al., US District Court for the District of Columbia, Civil Action No. 96-2467:

### SECOND AMENDED COMPLAINT (10/98)
### (Conspiracy to interfere with Civil Rights
### in violation of 42 U.S.C. § 1985(2), Obstructing justice;
### Intentional Infliction of Emotional Distress;
### Assault; Battery; Civil Conspiracy)

\* \* \*

### Summary of case

2. This case arises from an overall conspiracy to obstruct justice in connection with federal investigations into the death of deputy White House counsel Vincent W. Foster.

3. Upon learning that Mr. Foster's body was found in Fort Marcy Park, Virginia, Plaintiff reported to authorities what he had seen in the park approximately 70 minutes before the discovery of Mr. Foster's body.

4. In April and May, 1994, Defendant Monroe, then an FBI agent detailed to the Office of regulatory Independent Counsel Robert Fiske, interviewed Plaintiff... Monroe falsified Plaintiff's account and misreported that Plaintiff identified the car he saw as a "1988 to 1990" year-model, which coincided with Mr. Foster's 1989 car. Because Mr. Foster was dead by the time Plaintiff visited Fort Marcy Park, Plaintiff's information refutes the official conclusion that Mr. Foster drove his car there.

5. Shortly after Plaintiff learned from a reporter that Defendant Monroe had falsified his account, Plaintiff's account of what he had witnessed at Fort Marcy and contradictory information from his FBI interview reports were published in the October

15

22, 1995, edition of the *London Sunday Telegraph* newspaper.

6. On the same day that the *Telegraph* reached American newsstands, October 24, the Office of Independent Counsel, *In re: Madison Guarantee Savings & Loan*, prepared a subpoena for Plaintiff to testify before the Whitewater grand jury in this Court.

7. Two days after that subpoena was prepared, Defendant FBI Agent Russell Bransford served it. At the time of the service of that subpoena, Bransford was detailed to Mr. Starr's Washington, DC, Office. Bransford had been detailed to the Fiske probe.

8. Beginning the same day that Bransford served Plaintiff the secret grand jury subpoena... Defendants... harassed and intimidated Plaintiff before he appeared to testify before the grand jury...

\* \* \*

10. Wrongful acts alleged herein were violations of 42 U.S.C. § 1985(2), which prohibits, <u>inter alia</u>, attempts to deter witnesses by intimidation or threat from testifying freely, fully, and truthfully to matters pending before federal courts...

11. Overt acts directed at Plaintiff were part of a subsidiary conspiracy. Because that subsidiary conspiracy was the reasonably foreseeable, necessary or natural consequence of the overall conspiracy to hide the facts of Mr. Foster's death, each member of that overall conspiracy is liable for Plaintiff's damages simply by virtue of his being a conspirator.

\* \* \*

### Parties

13. Plaintiff Patrick James Knowlton is an individual presently residing at 2424 Pennsylvania Avenue, NW, Washington, DC. At the time of Mr. Foster's death in July of 1993, and when Plaintiff was contacted and interviewed by Defendant Monroe in April and May of 1994, Plaintiff resided in Etlan, Virginia.

14. Defendant Robert Edwards (hereinafter "EDWARDS") was at all times material hereto an individual employed by the United States Park Police, holding the position of Sergeant, assigned to the Second District station, 7300 MacArthur Boulevard, Glen Echo, Maryland. EDWARDS has since retired...

15. Defendant James C. Beyer (hereinafter "BEYER") is and was at all times material hereto an individual employed as Deputy Chief Medical Examiner, Northern Virginia District, 9787 Braddock Road, Suite 100, Fairfax, Virginia, and in that capacity performed the July 21st, 1993 autopsy on Mr. Foster.

16. Defendant John Doe Pathologist (hereinafter "PATHOLOGIST") assisted Defendant BEYER in the performance of the autopsy on Mr. Foster. BEYER refused to identify PATHOLOGIST to the Park Police at the autopsy and there is no public record of the PATHOLOGIST's identity. Plaintiff will seek leave of Court to amend his Complaint by inserting his true name in place of the fictitious name PATHOLOGIST when the same has been ascertained.

17. Defendant Robert A. Bryant (hereinafter "BRYANT") is and was at all times material hereto an individual employed by the Federal Bureau of Investigation ("FBI"). During the times alleged hereinafter that BRYANT committed overt acts in furtherance of the conspiracy, BRYANT served as the Special Agent-in-Charge of the FBI's Washington, DC, Metropolitan Field Office. BRYANT currently holds the position of Deputy Director of the FBI, and his business address is the J. Edgar Hoover Building, 10th & Pennsylvania Avenue, NW, Washington, DC.

18. Defendant Scott Jeffrey Bickett (hereinafter "BICKETT") is an individual whose residence address is presently unknown to Plaintiff. Upon information and belief, Plaintiff avers that BICKETT is and was at all times material hereto an individual employed by the Department of Defense, holding an "Active SCI" security clearance, which stands for Sensitive Compartmented Information, a top U.S. Government security clearance. Upon information and belief, Plaintiff also avers that BICKETT has been briefed at FBI headquarters, has served at the direction of FBI personnel, and was so serving when BICKETT committed the acts hereinafter complained of.

19. Defendant Lawrence Monroe (hereinafter "MONROE") is an individual who resides at 8128 Blandsford Drive, Manassas, Virginia. When MONROE committed the overt acts recited below, he was employed by the FBI as a special agent, and was detailed to the office of regulatory Independent Counsel Robert B. Fiske, Jr.

20. The captioned Defendant referred to as John Doe FBI Laboratory Technician is one or more laboratory technicians employed by the FBI's forensic laboratories, located in the J. Edgar Hoover Building, 10th & Pennsylvania Avenue, NW, Washington, DC. Because Plaintiff does not yet know whether all the FBI laboratory reports quoted below were authored by the same individual, nor his or their identities, the author or authors of these laboratory reports are hereinafter referred to in the singular as "FBI LAB." Plaintiff will seek leave of Court to amend his Complaint by substituting his or their true names instead of the fictitious name FBI LAB when the same has been ascertained.

21. Defendant FBI Agent Russell T. Bransford (hereinafter "BRANSFORD") is an individual who is currently and was at all times material hereto employed by the FBI as a special agent. BRANSFORD's business address is the FBI's Washington, DC Metropolitan field office, 1900 Half Street, SW, Washington, DC. BRANSFORD had been detailed to Mr. Fiske's office of regulatory Independent Counsel and, upon Mr. Starr's appointment in August of 1994 to serve as statutory Independent Counsel and the simultaneous dissolution of the office of the regulatory Independent Counsel's office, Mr. Starr's office retained BRANSFORD.

22. Defendant Ayman Alouri (hereinafter "AYMAN ALOURI") is an individual whose residence address is 2300 Pimmit Drive, Apartment 704 West, Falls Church, Virginia. AYMAN ALOURI was born in the country of Jordan and is a naturalized citizen of the United States.

23. Defendant Abdel Salem Alouri (hereinafter "ABDEL ALOURI") is an individual whose last known residence address is 5800 Quantrell Avenue, Apartment 1511, Alexandria, Virginia. ABDEL ALOURI was born in the country of Jordan. His citizenship is unknown to Plaintiff.

\*     \*     \*

25. Some of the conspirators joined the conspiracy at different times by pursuit of the common goal or overall conspiratorial objective, the particulars of which are not presently known to Plaintiff. As all conspirators are not presently known, Plaintiff will, should it become appropriate, seek leave to amend this Complaint to name other Defendants and to plead the particulars of their

functions in pursuing the overall or subsidiary
conspiracy.

## Facts

26.   On July 20th, 1993, between the time of
3:00 p.m. and 4:00 p.m., Vincent Foster died of a
small-caliber gunshot wound to his head, at the hand
of another.  The bullet entered his head from the
upper portion of the right side of his neck, under the
jaw line, passed upward through the body of the
tongue, pierced his brain and struck the skull
approximately three inches below the top of the head,
fracturing it.  The bullet remained in his head.
Blood drained from the entrance wound in the neck onto
his right collar and shoulder and was absorbed down
onto his right shirtsleeve.  Blood also accumulated in
his mouth.

27.   Also on July 20th, 1993, Plaintiff was
driving on the George Washington Memorial Parkway...

Paragraph 11 above alleges that the harassment that
Patrick suffered was part of an overall conspiracy to hide
the facts of Mr. Foster's death.  Under the law of civil
conspiracy, each member of that overall conspiracy is
legally responsible for the civil rights violation that
Patrick suffered.  That means that the issue of cover-up,
as well as its participants, is relevant to the prosecution
of Patrick Knowlton's civil rights lawsuit.

The first goal of this filing is to prove the
existence of a conspiracy, as alleged in the lawsuit, as
well as the named defendants' participation in it.

We will see the participation in the conspiracy of
Park Police Sergeant Robert Edwards while at Fort Marcy
Park on July 20, 1993.  We will see the role, just 15 hours
later, of Deputy Chief Medical Examiner James C. Beyer,
Jr., as well as the unknown "John Doe Pathologist" who
assisted him.  We will review the evidence of the knowledge
of the cover-up during the first 17-day FBI/Park Police
investigation by the Agent-in-Charge of the FBI's
Washington Metropolitan Field Office, Robert M. Bryant, who
now serves as the FBI's Deputy Director.  We will review
the evidence against FBI Agent Lawrence Monroe, the unknown
"John Doe FBI Laboratory Technician," and Scott Jeffrey
Bickett, all of whom participated in the cover-up in the
Spring of 1994, when the FBI conducted its second

investigation, under the auspices of the 5-month Fiske probe. And we will see that FBI agent Russell T. Bransford participated in the conspiracy in October of 1995, during Mr. Starr's probe. Finally, we will see how Ayman & Abdel Alouri and others harassed Patrick Knowlton on the eve of his Whitewater grand jury appearance, also in October of 1995, two-and-a-half years after the death.

If you have ever served on a jury, you probably recall being instructed to keep an open mind, and not to decide the case until you have heard all the evidence. Most of the available evidence is presented in this filing. Like a trial, reviewing the evidence can be work, tedious at times. But most of the chapters have factual summaries at the beginning, so you have the ability to read only the summary should you not care to read the body of the chapter. Because the same evidence is sometimes presented on more than one issue, you may occasionally see testimony or excerpts of FBI interview reports that you have already seen in another part of the paper.

Chapter I of this filing, *Background*, repeats what many of us have heard about the case, sets forth much of the record of the events preceding the death, relates the official version of the discovery of the body, and points out some anomalies in the official story of the body's discovery. Chapter II, *Authorities Arrive at the Scene*, sets forth the movements of the Park Police and Fire & Rescue workers ("Firefighters") at the park, and provides a synopsis of much of the evidence that we will review later.

In Chapters III through X, we compare the publicly available evidence in the case with the OIC's Report on the death. After Chapter III, *Overview of the Comparison of the Publicly Available Evidence to the OIC's Report,* we begin our review in earnest, a 250-page comparison of every substantive point in the OIC's Report to the available evidence in the case. The discovery process in Patrick's lawsuit has not yet begun, so we do not yet have subpoena power. We obtained all but a tiny fraction of the evidence we will review from the public record. It was generated by the federal government.

Beginning in chronological order, Chapter IV, *Evidence of Knowledge of the death before the Official Time of Notification*, looks at the OIC's claim that no authorities other than the Park Police knew of the death before 8:30 p.m. Next, to underscore the importance of the testimonial evidence of park witnesses recounted in subsequent chapters, Chapter V, *Evidence that the OIC concealed that Photographs Vanished*, reviews the OIC's claim that no Polaroid photographs of the body vanished, and that all of the 35-millimeter shots were "underexposed."

The next Chapter, VI, *Evidence that the OIC Covered up the Absence of the Official mouth Entrance Wound & head Exit Wound, and the Existence of a Neck Wound*, is the longest chapter, almost 100 pages. It compares all the records of all the witnesses who saw the body at the park and morgue to the OIC's claims and conclusions regarding the issues of the wounds and the blood. This chapter also reviews the record of the autopsy.

In the next three Chapters, we review the evidence regarding all the remaining issues in the case save one -- the claim of depression. These three Chapters are: VII, *Evidence that the OIC covered up that Mr. Foster did not own or fire the gun found at the park;* VIII, *Evidence contradicting the official claim that Mr. Foster drove to the park;* and IX, *Other Anomalies*.

The next Chapter, X, *Inferences to be drawn from the Facts*, takes the step of discussing the evidence in the case, as well as its interrelations -- how one anomaly in the case is related to others. We suggest that you ponder in Chapter X the question posed, whether there is in fact a cover-up of the facts of the death.

The three chapters which comprise the balance of this Court filing are XI, *State of Mind;* XII, *Investigative History;* and lastly, *Conclusion*. In the *State of Mind* Chapter, we do not attempt to prove that Mr. Foster was not depressed because we conclude that it is too problematic and, in any event, irrelevant. We do offer some compelling evidence that the OIC's expert psychologist's conclusion is unreliable. The *Investigative History* chapter explains that the FBI is almost the only entity that has investigated the case, three times in all.

The Court released the OIC's Report on the Death of Vincent Foster, Jr. 20 months ago, having been submitted at the conclusion of its three-year investigation. This filing took three people 17 months to research and write:

Patrick Knowlton, Hugh Turley, and the undersigned, all of whom are self-employed. Patrick is 44 years old. He has lived in Washington, DC, since he moved here in 1990 from his native Syracuse, New York. Having worked in the construction industry for seventeen years, he was a master carpenter and builder. Today, he is a part-time licensed tour director in Washington, DC, Philadelphia, and New York, and is a private investigator. Patrick is heterosexual, has never been charged with a crime, is a registered Democrat, and has no political agenda. Hugh Turley is a Washington area businessman who lives in suburban Maryland. Hugh took an interest in the case soon after the death.

Those witnesses who are discussed below, who are not named defendants in Patrick Knowlton's lawsuit, deserve the benefit of the doubt, and so we caution you not to hastily conclude that any one of them participated in the cover-up merely because his or her actions appear suspicious.

The Ethics in Government Act is designed to accomplish parallel goals of ensuring that justice is done and maintaining the appearance of justice having been done.[3]

---

[3]   Congress seeks to accomplish the special prosecutor's independence from the Department of Justice by, among other things, having the judiciary select and appoint Counsel upon request by the Attorney General, limiting the Counsel's investigative jurisdiction, and having the Counsel removable only by the Attorney General for good cause or by the Court upon the completion of the investigation. Counsel is required to file reports with Congress and the Court.

The 1978 Act was passed five years, to the month, since Watergate Special Prosecutor Archibald Cox had was fired by President Nixon in what is referred to as the "Saturday night massacre."

Use of special prosecutors predates the 1978 Act. Independent state investigations include Thomas Dewey's early twentieth-century fight against New York City corruption, Governor Nelson Rockefeller's 1972 investigation into New York's criminal justice system, and Maryland's creation of a special prosecutor after Spiro Agnew's misconduct was exposed.

Independent federal investigations predating the 1978 Act include President Coolidge's 1924 appointment of special

## Preface

"The purpose of the system is to ensure fair and impartial criminal proceedings when an administration attempts the delicate task of investigating its own top officials."[4]

In 1993, on the eve of the expiration of the last five-year term of the Act, then Senator William Cohen stressed the importance under the Act of investigations being independent from the Justice Department in ensuring that justice appears to have been done.

> The appearance of justice having been done is equally important as justice having been done. We can see this over a period of years where an investigation has been conducted by the Justice Department... questions have remained. They say, "Well, was it really an independent investigation or was it a coverup, a whitewash?" When those questions tend to linger... the cloud of doubt remains, and the cynicism remains... The law, however, serves two ends, both equally important in our democratic society. One is that justice be done, and the other is that it appear to be done. The appearance of justice is just as important as justice itself, in terms of maintaining public confidence...[5]

---

prosecutors in the Teapot Dome scandal (corruption by Interior and Justice Department officials in leasing of oil reserves), the Truman administration's investigation of the tax scandals in 1951 (tax fixing by the IRS and Justice Department), and in 1973, Watergate.
The three judges of the Special Division of the U.S. Court of Appeals, which appoints Independent Counsels, are appointed for two-year terms by the Chief Justice of the United States Supreme Court. There have been at least 20 independent counsels appointed under the Act, seven of whom were appointed during the Clinton administration.

[4]    S. Rpt. No. 100-123. Act of Dec. 15th 1987, Pub. L. No. 100-191, 1987 U.S.C.C.A.N. (101 Stat. 1293) p. 2151.

[5]    See 139 CONG. REC. S15846-01 & S15847-01 (daily ed, Nov. 17, 1993) (statement of Sen. Cohen). See also 139 CONG. REC. S15850-01 (daily ed, Nov. 17, 1993) (statement of Sen. Levin): "Here is what the American Bar Association said in its letter of November 17. As noted above, the principle underlying statute is that an independent counsel may be needed when there may be a conflict of interest in having the Department of Justice carry out a particular investigation and possible prosecution."

## Preface

The Act was renewed for another five-year term. It will expire on June 30, 1999, unless reenacted.

The question of whether there is a cover-up in this case is an important one. Our Constitution separates the governmental powers into separate branches, limiting the ways each can act, and provides that the branches shall exercise oversight over one another. The system supposes that this division of power would create an adversarial system, with each entity serving different interests. Another component of the system is a free press, which facilitates this adversarial process by reporting the truth that surfaces when adversaries battle. In sum, the separation-of-powers doctrine and having a free press are designed to keep our government honest. You are deciding if the system failed in the Foster case. If it did, you have a right to know.

The official version of the death is that on July 20, 1993, around 1:00 p.m., Mr. Foster left the White House alone in his own car, and sometime later drove into the Fort Marcy Park parking lot, and walked 700 feet up into the park. He is said to have then taken his own .38 caliber revolver, loaded with two high velocity cartridges, placed its barrel against his soft palate, and pulled the trigger, leaving an exit wound in the top of the back of his head about the size of a half-dollar.

It is time to review the evidence. You have never read or heard it before.

26

## Background

The OIC's Report on the death of Vincent Foster is cited below as the "Report" or "OIC." Excerpts from it appear in Italics, except where they appear in the footnotes. An asterisk* appears next to all exhibits that were not generated by the federal government.

## I.   BACKGROUND

### 1.   Introduction

Those who saw Mr. Foster most and knew him best, his friends and colleagues, disagree on whether he displayed signs of depression in the weeks preceding his death. Most failed to notice anything unusual,[6] a few did,[7] and a few changed their minds.[8]

---

[6]   **Exhibit 1**, Report of FBI interview with Deputy Attorney General Webster Hubbell, April 14 & 15, 1994: "Hubbell said Foster was a great friend... He did not notice Foster acting differently in the days or weeks before his death... Hubbell said that he was not aware of any problems or difficulties Foster was experiencing prior to his death."

**Exhibit 2**, Report of FBI interview with Executive Assistant to Deputy Counsel Deborah Gorham, April 19 and 26, 1994: She viewed him as reserved, not depressed or unhappy. He would share a joke with others in the office, but was a very hard worker and would ask people "to keep it down" if their talking disturbed him. The only time he seemed to be more agitated than usual was when he was under time pressures. He had a very long fuse, so it was a rarity for him to show agitation... Even in hindsight, Gorham did not see anything in Foster's behavior which would indicate a distressed state of mind.

**Exhibit 3**, Report of FBI interview with Assistant Counsel at the White House Beth Nolan, June 7, 1994: "She saw him Monday, July 19, 1993 for just a few minutes and he did not seem distracted and handled the exchange normally. She said that she did not recall anybody ever remarking about Foster holding up or not holding up, and she did not herself notice any weight loss." **Exhibit 4**, Report of FBI interview with Special Assistant to the President for Legislative Affairs Timothy J. Keating, June 12, 1994: "He said he dealt with Foster only on a "handful of matters... almost a daily basis... He described Foster as being 'very professional and a strong individual... together and on top of his game...'" **Exhibit 5**, Report of FBI interview with attorney John Phillip Carroll, May 17, 1994: "Carroll advised that Foster's suicide is a complete mystery to him." **Exhibit 6**, Deposition of Park Police Investigator John Rolla, July 21, 1994:

"...I remember asking her [Mrs. Foster], did you see any of this coming, and she stated no. Nobody would say anything about depression or that they noticed some signs, they were worried. There was no information given to us."

> Compare OIC, p. 99: Dr. Berman reported that "[m]istakes, real or perceived posed a profound threat to his self-esteem/self-worth and represented evidence for a lack of control over his environment. Feelings of unworthiness, inferiority, and guilt followed and were difficult for him to tolerate. There are signs of an intense and profound anguish, harsh self-evaluation, shame, and chronic fear..."

[7]    Exhibit 7, Report of FBI interview of Associate White House Counsel William Kennedy, May 6, 1994: "He said Foster was drawn and frowned and was working too many hours. Foster was working on the run and he was working under stress, as most in the White House were... You could see someone beaten down, but those seeing it also were beaten down."

> Exhibit 8, Report of FBI interview of Associate Attorney General of Legislative Affairs Sheila Anthony, April 28, 1994: In terms of changes in personal appearances, Anthony noted that Foster's face had become gray and drawn. *** Foster said that he was not yet ready to see a psychiatrist in Washington, D.C., but he told Anthony that he had called his physician in Little Rock and had gotten a prescription... To the best of Anthony's knowledge, Foster was not receiving any type of medical treatment. [redacted]

[8]    Exhibit 3, Report of FBI of interview with Associate White House Counsel Beth Nolan, June 7, 1994: "She realizes in hindsight that he must have been upset about something." Exhibit 9, Report of Park Police interview of Beryl Anthony, July 27, 1993: "Mr. Anthony stated that he and his wife had noticed a gradual decline in Mr. Foster's general disposition to the point of depression."

> Compare F. Murray, Foster Faced 'hard times' in Final Days, Wash. Times, July 24, 1993: "Close friends told him to cool things and relax and not take things so personal," the source said, citing Mr. Foster's ex-brother-in-law, former Rep. Beryl Anthony, as one who had talked to Mr. Foster about his depression. "There's not a damn thing to it. That's a bunch of crap," Mr. Anthony said yesterday, slamming down the telephone at his El Dorado, Arkansas home.

## Background

In the delivery of his speech to the graduating class of University of Arkansas Law School, given May 8, 1993,[9] nine weeks before his death, some reported he looked healthy, both physically and mentally,[10] while others thought he looked pale, distraught, and tense.[11]

Many Americans have read or heard that Mr. Foster committed suicide because he was troubled by Travelgate, Waco and two *Wall Street Journal* editorials, that he had lost weight, that he had just started taking medication for depression, that a note was found,[12] and that he was suffering from depression.[13]

---

[9]    Exhibit 10, Transcript of Mr. Foster's speech to the University of Arkansas Law School, May 8, 1993:  [360-3631] Following the bar exam, your most difficult test will not be of what you know but what is your character.  Some of you will fail. The class of 1971 had many distinguished members who also went on to achieve high public office. But it also had several who forfeited their license to practice law.  Blinded by greed, some served time in prison.  I cannot make this point to you too strongly. There is no victory, no advantage, no fee no favor which is worth even a blemish on your reputation for intellect and integrity...  The conviction that you did the right thing will be the best salve and the best sleeping medicine... Take time out for yourself.  Have some fun, go fishing, every once in a while take a walk in the woods by yourself. Learn to relax, watch more sunsets... If you find yourself getting burned out or unfulfilled, unappreciated, or the profits become more important than your work, then have the courage to make a change.

[10]    Exhibit 5, Report of FBI interview with Senior Rose Law Firm Partner John Phillip Carroll, May 24, 1994:  "[A]t a commencement ceremony at the University of Arkansas Law School, Foster gave a splendid delivery with no stress showing during the speech."  Exhibit 11, Report of FBI interview of Rose Law Firm Secretary Loraine Cline, May 25, 1994:  "He [Mr. Foster] acted excited and 'up' and he looked good."

[11]    Exhibit 12, Fiske Report, June 30, 1994:  "Sheila Anthony [Assistant Attorney General for Legislative Affairs] recalls that during his address Foster's voice was unnaturally strained and tense, reminiscent of their father's voice when he was distraught during the period before his death in 1991."

[12]    OIC, p. 106-107:  At some point in the last week of his life, Mr. Foster wrote a note [fn337] that he had "made mistakes from ignorance, inexperience and overwork" and that he "was

---

not meant for the job or the spotlight of public life in Washington. Here ruining people is considered sport."[fn338]

[13]     See R. Marcus & AA. Devroy, *Clintons Mystified By Aide's Death*, Wash. Post, July 22, 1993; F. Murray, *Foster Faced 'hard times' in Final Days*, Wash. Times, July 24, 1993; *Depression symptoms difficult to hide*, Wash. Times, July 24, 1993; M. Isikoff, *Foster Had List Of Psychiatrist, Search Discloses*, Wash. Post, July 28, 1993; D. Jehl, *Clinton Sought to Cheer Aide, Official Reports*, N.Y. Times, July 28, 1993; D. Jehl, *Clinton Aide Appeared Depressed Before Death His Associates Say*, N.Y. Times, July 29, 199; A. Devroy & M. Isikoff, Wash. Post, *Note Supports Idea that Foster Committed Suicide*, July 29, 1993; A. Devroy & M. Isikoff, *Handling of Foster Case is Defended*, Wash. Post, July 29, 1993; W. Pincus, *Vincent Foster: Out of His Element*, Wash. Post, August 5, 1993; S. Blumenthal, *The Suicide*, New Yorker Magazine August 9, 1993; J. Birnbaum, *Politics & Policy: White House Aide Listed Troubles in Shredded Note*, Wall St. Journal, August 11, 1993; M. Isikoff, D. Balz, *Foster Note Reveals An Anguished Aide Probe Concludes With Finding Note*, Wash. Post, August 11, 1993; David Von Drehle, *The Crumbling Of A Pillar In Washington, Only Clinton Aide Foster Knew What Drove Him To Fort Marcy*, Wash. Post, August 15, 1993; J. DeParle, *Portrait of a White House Aide Snared by his Perfectionism A Life Undone: A Special Report*, N.Y. Times, August 22, 1993; Michael Isikoff, *Probe Pursues White House Aide's Undisclosed Diary*, Wash. Post, December 18, 1993; J. Seper, *Clinton papers lifted after aide's suicide*, Wash. Times, December 20, 1993; K. Ball, *Hit Muckrakers They never doubted suicide of White House aide*, N.Y. Daly News, March 12, 1994; M. McAlary, *The Unfostered D.C. Suspicions, Aide's suicide is confirmed by heads-up cops*, N.Y. Daily News March 14, 1994; C. Sennott, *Foster 'Case Is Closed,' Parks Police Chief Says*, Boston Globe March 16, 1994; W. Styron, *'An Interior Pain That is All but Indescribable*, Newsweek Magazine, April 18, 1994; D. Jehl, *First Whitewater Report Pleases Clinton Advisors*, N.Y. Times, July 2, 1994; L. Hoffman, Scripps Howard, *Starr Apt To Second Ruling On Foster*, Wash. Times, January 6, 1995; E. Pollock & V. Novak, *There May Be Less to Whitewater Case than Meets the Eye*, Wall St. Journal February 22, 1995; M. Isikoff & M. Hosenball, *Picking up the Scent*, Newsweek, March 18, 1995; J. Stewart, *On the Road to Scandal*, Newsweek, March 18, 1995; E. Pollock, *Vince Foster's Death Is a Lively Business For Conspiracy Buffs*, Wall St. Journal, March 23, 1995; J. Seper, *Foster papers up first as Whitewater hearings open July*, Wash. Times, July 7, 1995; M. Isikoff, *The Night Foster Died*, Newsweek Magazine, July 17, 1995; M. McGrory, *Whitewater-Waco Weariness*, Wash. Post, July 20, 1995; James B. Stewart, Blood Sport; A. Lewis, *Ken Starr's Problem*, New York Times, February 21, 1997; Angie Cannon, *Whitewater Investigators Release Final Report On Suicide Of White House Counsel*, St. Paul Pioneer Press, October 11, 1997; LA Times Wire

## Background

The record, as we said, is ambiguous on the depression.  Mr. Foster was angry that Bill Kennedy was singled out for criticism in the Travel Office matter,[14] but did not appear to have feared Travelgate.[15]  There is a

---

Service, *Starr's Report Also Concludes That Foster Killed Himself,* <u>Minneapolis Star Tribune</u>, October 11, 1997;  M. Morrison, *In Re: Vincent Foster,* <u>Wall St. Journal</u>, November 25, 1997.

[14]   <u>Exhibit 13</u>, Report of FBI interview of Assistant to the President, Bruce Lindsey, June 22, 1994:  At the initial meeting regarding the Travel Office, Vincent Foster was most defensive about William Kennedy's participation in the matter.  Foster was very unhappy that Kennedy was reprimanded with regard to the travel Office matter... Foster was angry about the letters of reprimand.  Kennedy was also very unhappy and Lindsey said he thought he remembered that Kennedy was feeling as though perhaps he should resign.  Lindsey thought he remembered Foster's opinion being that if one person in the counsel's office received a reprimand then they should all receive letters of reprimand because they were all equally responsible and accountable for what occurred.  Lindsey could not remember anything else Foster found disturbing...

<u>Exhibit 7</u>, Report of FBI interview of Associate White House Counsel William Kennedy, May 6, 1994:  Kennedy was asked about Foster's view of Kennedy's involvement in the Travel Office matter.  Kennedy said that Foster was very upset that Kennedy got reprimanded.  Foster had been heavily involved and felt strongly regarding the FBI leaks in the case.  Foster came to the conclusion that he couldn't trust anyone in Washington D.C.  He was worried about Kennedy's emotional health.

<u>Exhibit 14</u>, Report of FBI interview with Associate Attorney General Webster Hubbell, June 7, 1994: "Foster expressed concern to Hubbell that he shouldn't have handed the matter off.  Foster wanted to take responsibility.  He was not happy that the FBI report had criticized Kennedy."  <u>Exhibit 3</u>, Report of FBI interview with Associate Counsel at the White House Beth Nolan, June, 7, 1994:  "She remembers that he was most upset about Kennedy having been reprimanded...  [S]he does remember Foster's feeling that it would have been easier if he had been reprimanded also."

[15]    <u>Exhibit 14</u>, Report of FBI interview with Associate Attorney General Webster Hubbell, June 7, 1994:  "Hubbell advised Foster to get outside counsel if that was what he needed.  Foster was trying to get Bernard Nussbaum, White House counsel, to hire

record of one witness saying he was upset about Waco.[16]  One witness reportedly said he was angered by the *Wall Street Journal* editorials,[17] but another said he joked about them.[18] While two of the eight who opined on the matter are said to have reported a weight loss,[19] most did not.[20]  Actually, his

---

outside counsel.  Foster was never concerned for his personal exposure on the issue."  Exhibit 15, Report of FBI interview with Director of White House Personnel David Watkins, June 22, 1994: "Watkins was much more emotional overall than Foster.  Watkins never heard directly or indirectly that Foster was distressed about it [Travel Office], or about anything else for that matter."

> Compare OIC, p. 106:  The Travel Office matter, in particular, was the subject of public controversy beginning in May 1993 and continuing through Mr. Foster's death. Criticism focused on the White House's handling of the matter before and after the May 19 firings...  During the week of July 12, Mr. Foster contacted private attorneys seeking advice in connection with the Travel Office incident.[fn336]

[16]    Exhibit 16, Report of FBI interview of Mrs. Lisa Foster, May 9, 1994:  "The other [redaction] occasions when Foster sounded choked up and tense were when the Branch Davidian complex near Waco, Texas burned..."

[17]    Exhibit 2, Report of FBI interview with Executive Assistant to Deputy Counsel Deborah Gorham, April 19 and 26, 1994:  "She saw him angry once, in response to the *Wall Street Journal* article..."

[18]    Exhibit 3, Report of FBI interview of White House Associate Legal Counsel Beth Nolan, June 7, 1994.

[19]    Exhibit 8, Report of FBI interview of Associate Attorney General for Legislative Affairs Sheila Anthony, April 28, 1994:  Foster began to lose weight during the last six weeks prior to his death and weighed much less than he had weighed in January 1993.  However, Anthony is unable to estimate the amount of weight Foster lost in terms of pounds.  Foster did not mention to Anthony any problems with headaches, loss of appetite, indigestion or vomiting.

Exhibit 7, Report of FBI interview with Associate White House Counsel William Kennedy, May 6, 1994:  "Kennedy replied that he knew Foster had lost weight but was unaware of any other

autopsy weight was three pounds more than it had been six months earlier, in December of 1992.[21] The claim that he had just begun medication for depression is questionable.[22]

---

symptoms." Compare Exhibit 12, Fiske Report, June 30, 1994: "[I]t was obvious to many that he had lost weight."

[20]     Exhibit 16, Report of FBI interview with Mrs. Lisa Foster, May 9, 1994: "[S]he believed that most of the weight which Foster had lost by that time had been lost prior to his arrival in Washington, D.C." Exhibit 18, Report of FBI interview with attorney Susan Thomases, June 14, 1994: "She noted no change in his demeanor or physical appearance..." Exhibit 3, Report of FBI interview with Associate White House Counsel Beth Nolan, June 7, 1994: "She said that she did not recall anybody ever remarking about Foster holding up or not holding up, and she did not herself notice that there had been any weight loss." Exhibit 19, Report of FBI interview with Deputy Assistant to the President Nancy Henreich, June 12, 1994: "She said that while she can recall seeing no changes in Vincent Foster's physical [or] psychological presence, she does not feel comfortable making such judgements considering that their relationship was not particularly close." Exhibit 20, Report of FBI interview with Deputy Assistant to the President Marsha Scott, June 9, 1994: "She said that she personally didn't notice any weight loss." Exhibit 21, Report of Park Police interview with Executive Assistant to the Counsel of the President Betsy Pond, August 22, 1993: "There was nothing unusual about his emotional state. In fact, over the last several weeks she did not notice any changes, either physically or emotionally. She noticed no weight lost [sic]."

[21]     Exhibit 22, Report of FBI interview with Dr. Larry Watkins, May 16, 1994: "His weight on December 31, 1992 was 194 pounds and Watkins made a note that he was on a diet and exercising." Exhibit 23, Report of Autopsy, July 21, 1993: "Weight 197" Compare S. Blumenthal, *The Suicide*, The New Yorker Magazine, August 9, 1993: "But Foster's disequilibrium wasn't so well hidden from those closest to him. By early July, his friends had begun to notice changes in his appearance... He had lost fifteen pounds."

[22]     Exhibit 24, Park Police handwritten note, author unknown, July 30, 1994: "7/30/93, Dr. Beyer Tox. Report ready... Trazadon[e] wasn't tested for and probably wouldn't show up." Exhibit 25, Virginia Division of Forensic Science Autopsy Lab Report, July 26, 1993, negative for presence of "tricyclic antidepressants" [includes Trazadone] "benzodiazepines" [includes Valium] OIC, p. 60: "The FBI Laboratory later conducted more sensitive testing and determined that the blood sample from Mr. Foster contained trazadone.[fn174]" OIC, p. 60, fn. 175: "The Lab

## Background

And some notable experts opine that the note, found torn up into 28 pieces six days after the death with no fingerprints on it, is a forgery.[23]

---

also detected diazepam [valium] and nordiazepam [Trazadone] below recognized therapeutic levels. FBI Lab Report, 5/9/94, at 8." Exhibit 27, FBI Laboratory Report, Washington Metropolitan Field Office: "[O]ne plastic vial containing twenty nine tablets [Trazadone], date received May 25, 1994 [year after death], by SA Russell T. Bransford."

[23]  *Exhibit 28, Opinion of Reginald E. Alton, Oxford University Emeritus Fellow and lecturer on detection of forgery (ruled on C.S. Lewis, Oscar Wilde, Donne, Shelley, and Christina Rosetti), September 18, 1995: Q 1 [questioned document – torn note] is a forgery related to K 1 to K 12 [exemplars]... Foster seems to have been a natural 'swagger'... The writer of Q 1 is aware of this habit but he fails to match Foster's usage or elegance... Even more revealing is... the word benefit, Q 1 (1.8 and 1.10) as compared... Foster is a habitual writer of counter-clockwise loops or circles... In Q 1 the loops in this ligature either do not exist or are a mere thickening of the ascender of h. The writer of Q 1 is generally uneasy about joining one letter to the next... This sort of failure is characteristic of forgeries... In contrast the hand of Q 1... imitates letters and words from the K group it fails to understand how they are made.

Compare OIC, p. 107, fn. 338: In this matter, Mr. Lesnevich compared the original note to four original pages of known writing of Mr. Foster that were in his office at the time of his death; to one other original page of paper that was known to have been written by Mr. Foster; and to 18 original checks bearing the known writing of Mr. Foster. Mr. Lesnevich concluded that the written text on the note "contained normal, natural and spontaneous writing variations. These normal, natural and spontaneous writing variations could be found in the letter formations, beginning strokes, ending strokes, connecting strokes, etc." Lesnevich Report at 2. He further concluded that "examination and comparison of the questioned written text appearing on the note with the known writing on the [known] documents has revealed that the author of the known documents wrote the note." Id. (reference numbers omitted). Mr. Lesnevich prepared a thorough 51-page comparison chart "that points out and illustrates a number of the normal, natural and spontaneous writing habits that were found common between the written text appearing on the questioned note and the known handwriting of Vincent Foster found on the [submitted known] documents. Id. at 3.

## Background

The majority of the state of mind evidence, reflecting what many Americans have read or heard, is set forth in the notes above. In light of the physical evidence in the case, whether the depression verdict is mostly fact or fiction (a problematic issue) is not relevant to the issue of whether Mr. Foster died at his own hand at the park.

---

Exhibit 29, US Capitol Police Identification Section Report, Sergeant Larry G. Lockhart, July 29, 1993 (failing to identify characteristics for conclusion): "Both the Known and Questioned Documents were completed by the same author/writer and that writer/author is known as Vincent W. Foster." *Exhibit 30, Affidavit of Reed Irvine re interview with Sergeant Lockhart, April 23, 1997 (Sergeant repudiated his July 29, 1993 conclusion when unknowingly given same words from both the exemplar and the note).

Exhibit 31, FBI Lab Report handwriting analysis, June 17, 1994: It was determined that the handwriting on the previously submitted note designated Q29 in the Laboratory report dated May 9, 1994 (Lab #40324038 S/D QV ZG WK UD AL QW ZT VY ZZ and AR) was written by VINCENT FOSTER, whose known writings are designated K4 (previously submitted and assigned Lab #40525017 S/D QV ZG UD and VY), K5 (previously submitted and assigned Lab #40602045 S/D QV UD) and K6 (assigned Lab #40617025 D UD).

*Exhibit 32, Opinion of Vincent J. Scalice, October 6, 1995 (re May 17, 1994 FBI Lab analysis above): [It is] an unsuccessful attempt to produce a credible forgery... The use of a single document and a series of checks alleged to have been written by Vincent Foster by the FBI's Questioned Document section is not consistent with standard forensic examination. *** Q-1 appears to be a forgery***

Compare [omitting May 17 FBI Lab Report] OIC, p. 107, fn. 338: At the request of the OIC, the FBI Laboratory compared the original note to four original pages of known writing of Mr. Foster that the OIC had obtained from the documents that were in Mr. Foster's office at the time of his death. The Laboratory determined that the note and these four sheets were written by the same person (Vincent Foster). FBI Lab Report, 11/9/95, at 1.

## 2. The record of events surrounding the death

### a. Before July 20, 1993

Mr. Foster arrived in Washington in January of 1993. He first stayed with his sister. After a few months, he rented temporary quarters and lived with his college-aged daughter. His wife, Lisa, arrived in June with the younger son, having both stayed in Little Rock for the completion of the son's junior year of high school there. His elder college-aged son also arrived in June. They lived in a Georgetown townhouse, 3027 Cambridge Place. "There were no domestic problems between Lisa Foster during the entirety of their twenty-five year relationship."[24]

Mr. Foster was part of the core group of longtime Clinton friends and supporters. They included Mr. Webster Hubbell, former law partner of Mrs. Clinton and then deputy Attorney General, and Marsha Scott, deputy assistant to the President. Associate White House Counsel William Kennedy worked at the Rose Firm, both before and after serving a stint as Counsel to the Senate Appropriations Committee under Senator John McClellan in 1977. David Watkins served as Director of White House Personnel. Bruce Lindsey was (and is) Assistant to the President. Mack McClarty served as White House Chief of Staff. Mr. Foster's sister, Sheila Anthony, was Assistant Attorney General for Legislative Affairs, and in 1993, her husband, former Arkansas Congressman Beryl Anthony, worked as a lobbyist.

Susan Thomases knew Mr. Foster for 17 years, since 1976. The FBI report of its interview with her reflects that she last saw him on Wednesday, July 13, when "they had lunch together with some other people from Washington. She recalls him mentioning he had planned to take a weekend trip to the Eastern Shore of Maryland. She noted no change in his demeanor or his physical appearance but was aware that he was working very hard and was under considerable pressure. His death came as a complete shock to her and she can offer no reason or speculate as to why he may have taken his life."[25]

---

[24] Exhibit 16, Report of FBI interview with Mrs. Lisa Foster, May 9, 1994.

[25] Exhibit 18, Report of FBI interview with Susan Thomases, June 6, 1994.

## Events surrounding the death

Associate Legal Counsel Beth Nolan's FBI interview report noted that as of Friday morning, "his mood had lifted a little in the last couple of days of his life and she bases that on some joking around that had occurred during the previous Friday [July 16] staff meeting."[26]

Before leaving his office for home shortly before 4:00 on Friday, Mr. Foster checked out a long-range beeper[27] to take with him for his weekend trip with Lisa to the Eastern shore of Maryland. (It may have been the same beeper that was clipped to his waist when his body was found four days later.[28])

---

Compare James Stewart, Blood Sport, 1996: On July 11, Foster was again complaining to his wife about the travel office... She [Thomases] was worried about Foster. As someone who saw him less, the change in his appearance and demeanor was more noticeable.*** Now [July 13] she tried to reassure Foster, but he said he needed to talk to her "off the campus," somewhere they wouldn't be seen. Thomases suggested 2020 "O" Street, a private rooming house where she herself sometimes stayed in Washington. When Foster arrived that evening, Thomases thought he looked a little better... But then he began to unburden himself. He mentioned how overworked he was and how he lacked the time and the support staff he was used to in Little Rock. If he didn't get more help, he said, he was afraid he'd "let the President and Hillary down... And he indicated he was homesick, not just for Little Rock, but for the quieter, predictable life he had there. But then the conversation took a curious turn. One thing he had not missed about his life in Little Rock was Lisa, his wife. The marriage had not been what he'd hoped for, and it hadn't been for years. He had to make all the decisions in the family. She was completely dependent on him, and this had become a burden. He found he couldn't confide in her. Lisa's recent arrival in Washington had brought this to the fore, just when Foster himself needed someone to lean on... Foster seemed... infinitely sad.

[26]   Exhibit 3, Report of FBI interview of White House Associate Legal Counsel Beth Nolan, June 7, 1994.

[27]   Exhibit 2, Report of FBI interview with Executive Assistant to Deputy Counsel Deborah Gorham, April 19 and 26, 1994.

[28]   Exhibit 33, Testimony before United States Senate by Park Police Investigator John Rolla, July 29, 1994: Well, let me explain it to you. You go on the scene, you observe the facts that are there, and the facts that are there was that

## Events surrounding the death

"Lisa Foster made all the arrangements for the weekend and asked Foster to be home by 3:00 p.m. that Friday, July 16, 1993. Instead, Foster arrived home at approximately 4:00 p.m., and she and Foster had to drive through terrible traffic to reach the Inn."[29]

*The Weekend.* The Fiske Report describes as "coincidence" that Mr. and Mrs. Foster were spending the weekend at the Tidewater Inn on the Eastern Shore of Maryland when Mr. and Mrs. Hubbell were staying fifteen minutes away with Nathan Landow and his son-in-law Michael Cardozo.[30] (Mr. and Mrs. Cardozo in separate interviews

---

this was an apparent suicide. Not one fact then or has ever come forward since then to this day to say it was anything other, anything sinister, anything other than a suicide. With that in mind, a pager, the White House credentials on the pager were recorded, at least the pager was. I do not remember if I recorded the White House credentials because obviously I am going to give them back to the Secret Service. They may have been Xeroxed. The pager brand was recorded, the name brand, the serial number was recorded, the pager was turned off. As far as any information on the pager, he could have turned it off at any time, and if anybody paged him while it was off, that does not tell me anything. If they paged him after he killed himself, it does not tell me anything. It does not tell me what time he turned it off because he could have had his last page 20 to 30 minutes before he turned it off. If it turned out something crazy, that it was a homicide, the FBI could have taken my report and the serial number to the pager company and subpoenaed the pager records and got all the calls that were paged to him that date. We turned it over to the Secret Service, yes, any property that belongs to the White House United States Government, the credentials and the pager, a matter of security, yes, it is proper procedure. I called them up, they wanted to come down and get it, and I turned it over to them after I recorded the information that I needed to get from it. I had no further use for it, because there was nothing to say that this was anything other than a suicide.

[29] Exhibit 16, Report of FBI interview with Lisa Foster, May 9, 1994.

[30] Exhibit 12, Fiske Report, June 30, 1994: "Coincidentally, Webster Hubbell and his wife were also on the Eastern Shore of Maryland for the weekend staying with friends, Michael and Harolyn Cardozo, who also knew the Fosters."

reportedly told the *Washington Post* that the weekend had been planned for more than a week.[31]) Mr. Cardozo had been Deputy White House Counsel in the Carter Administration,[32] the same position that Mr. Foster held at the White House. Mr. Cardozo had also had spent four months at the DOJ during the early days of the Clinton Administration.[33]

Evidence shows that Mr. Hubbell knew where the Fosters were staying from a telephone conversation he had with Mr. Foster on Friday, July 16, 1993.[34] The Fosters and the Hubbells spent Saturday and Sunday at the Landow Estate.[35] Other weekend guests at Mr. Landow's home included Nick Boliterri and Pam Shriver, who played tennis with Mrs. Foster. There is no record of Mr. Landow, the Cardozos or others present at the Landow Estate besides Mrs. Foster or Web Hubbell ever being interviewed about the weekend.[36]

---

[31] A. Devroy & M. Isikoff, Wash. Post, *Handling of Foster Case is Defended*, July 30, 1993: "In separate interviews yesterday, Harolyn Cardozo and Michael Cardozo said the weekend had not been designed to cheer up Foster, but had been planned more than a week before as a means for everybody concerned to get a break from the stress of their Washington jobs."

[32] Exhibit 1, Report of FBI interviews of Associate Attorney General Webster Hubbell, April 13 & 15, 1994.

[33] Exhibit 1, Report of FBI interview of Webster Hubbell, April 13 & 15, 1994.

[34] Exhibit 1, Report of FBI interviews of Webster Hubbell, April 13 & 15, 1994: Hubbell was asked about the weekend before Foster's death. He explained that he and his wife were supposed to go to dinner with the Fosters on Friday evening, but that Foster had called him (Hubbell) in Miami and said that he and his wife were planning to go to the Eastern Shore.

[35] Exhibit 1, Report of FBI interviews of Webster Hubbell, April 13 & 15, 1994.

[36] See Wash. Post, January 26, 1978: *DC Gambling Kingpin is Linked to Prominent Investors' Casino Deal*, January 26, 1978: Two prominent Washington investors [Nathan Landow and Smith Bagley] with connections to the Carter administration were involved in a proposal to build a hotel and gambling casino in Atlantic City, with Washington gambling kingpin Joe Nesline as a consultant. Nesline's involvement with the casino venture became known Jan 14

## Events surrounding the death

Webster Hubbell, close friend and law partner of Mr. Foster's at the Rose Law Firm, was the only person present who was questioned, other than Mrs. Foster. He mentioned the weekend only briefly.[37]

*Sunday.* Although Mr. "Foster had not made specific plans for the [following] weekend... [h]e had spoken with Lisa Foster about trying to go to Pennsylvania... but had not made any reservations..."[38] He told Jim Lyons, a Denver lawyer and advisor, who he spoke to on Sunday evening, that "he had a great weekend and agreed that he ought to do it

---

when federal and local police raided Nesline's Bethesda apartment... FBI agents seized a file containing and memoranda spelling out a proposed $85 million deal involving Bagley and Landow... [It] was not the only gambling venture in which Nesline had been involved with Landow... Involved in the St. Marten venture were Landow and Edward Cellini, a brother of Dino Cellini, a former associate of organized crime figure Meyer Lansky... In November... [t]he party at [the] Landow home was observed by Montgomery County plainclothesmen, who took down license plate numbers of guests' cars. Officers of the county's organized crime section have had Landow under surveillance for nearly a year. They learned from Florida police that Landow had an interest in a now defunct corporation whose concealed owners allegedly included an identified member of the Carlo Gambino Mafia "family." Secret Service agents who were at the party to protect the president's son, questioned the Montgomery County plainclothesmen who explained their interest in Landow. *** Landow said the meeting actually took place in the hallway outside the Senate Appropriations Committee chamber... [T]he committee's chairman [was] the late Sen. John L. McClellan... *** [The] business involvement of Landow that originally attracted the attention of Montgomery County's organized crime unit was an investment in Quaker Masonry... Florida law enforcement authorities reported to other police agencies in October of 1973 that Anthony Plate known to them to be an associate of the Gambinos, was believed to have a 25 percent interest in Quaker.

[37]     Compare: OIC, p. 100: "Dr. Berman said that Mr. Foster's "last 96 hours show clear signs of characteristic vulnerability."

[38]     Exhibit 16, Report of FBI interview with Mrs. Lisa Foster, May 9, 1993.

more often. They [also] confirmed that Lyons was coming to Washington, D.C. the following Wednesday, July 21, 1993."[39]

*Monday.* The FBI's report of its interview with associate Legal Counsel Beth Nolan reflects that "[s]he saw him [on] Monday, July 19, 1993 for just a few minutes and he did not seem distracted and handled the exchange normally."[40] Director of White House Personnel David "Watkins saw Foster at 11:00 am on Monday, July 19, 1993 as Foster was entering the White House. Foster stopped Watkins as they were passing one another to pass on regards to Watkins from Pam Shriver whom he had recently met. Foster's demeanor was cheerful."[41]

One of Mr. Foster's sisters, Sheila Anthony, called to ask how the weekend had gone.[42] Mr. Foster told her that he had a great weekend. Sheila served as Assistant Attorney General for Legislative Affairs in the Justice Department and lived in Washington with her husband former Arkansas Congressman Beryl Anthony. Mr. Foster's other sister, Sharon Bowman, along with her daughter, had just arrived for a visit from Arkansas, and was scheduled to have lunch with Mr. Foster on Thursday, July 22.[43]

Marsha Scott, longtime Deputy Assistant to the President and Director of Presidential Correspondence, told the FBI that her relationship with Mr. Foster was a

---

[39] Exhibit 35, Report of FBI interview of James M. Lyons, May 12, 1994.

[40] Exhibit 3, Report of FBI interview of Beth Nolan, June 7, 1994.

[41] Exhibit 15, Report of FBI interview with Director of White House Personnel David Watkins, June 22, 1994.

[42] Exhibit 8, Report of FBI interview of Associate Attorney General of Legislative Affairs Sheila Anthony: "Lisa Foster came to Washington, D.C. permanently in mid to late May 1993. On July 19, 1993, possibly in the morning, Anthony called Foster. Foster stated that he was feeling good that the weekend had gone pretty well."

[43] Exhibit 36, Mr. Foster's calendar, Park Police file: "July 22, 1993, 1:15 p.m., Sharon lunch"

"personal friendship,"[44] having known him since 1967. Ms. Scott's office was in the Old Executive Office Building.[45] She related that she met with Mr. Foster on July 19, 1993 in his White House office. That meeting lasted over an hour. Linda Tripp, one of Bernard Nussbaum's Executive Assistants, told the FBI this was "highly unusual."[46]

Ms. Scott first told the FBI that "[s]he does not remember what topics they talked about"[47] the last time she saw her friend of 25 years who died the next day, but that "he did not appear distracted or distressed."[48] She later told the FBI that she had stopped by to ask him how the weekend on the Eastern Shore of Maryland had gone.[49]

Webster Hubbell also stopped by Mr. Foster's office. He reportedly told the FBI he could not remember the

---

[44]    Exhibit 37, Report of FBI interview report of Deputy Assistant to the President Marsha Scott, May 12, 1994.

[45]    Exhibit 20, Report of FBI interview of Deputy Assistant to the President Marsha Scott, June 9, 1994.

[46]    Exhibit 38, Report of FBI interview of Executive Assistant Linda Tripp, April 12, 1994: Marsha Scott, Deputy Assistant to the President and Director of Presidential Correspondence, came to see Foster for a closed-door session that lasted over an hour, possibly as long as two hours. This was highly unusual, both her coming to see him and anyone taking up that much time with Foster.

[47]    Exhibit 37, Report of FBI interview of Deputy Assistant to the President Marsha Scott, May 12, 1994.

[48]    Exhibit 20, Report of FBI interview with Deputy Assistant to the President Marsha Scott, June 9, 1994: He loved being a lawyer and she along with others just couldn't believe that he would have taken his own life without having reached out to his friends. She said that during the meeting on July 19, he did not appear distracted or distressed. She explained that Foster could be very focused when he was involved in something and she knew that she had interrupted his train of thought when she entered the room but he didn't give her an indication that she came at a bad time, otherwise, she would have left. They did not, however, have a heart-to-heart talk...

[49]    Exhibit 20, Report of FBI interview report of Deputy Assistant to the President Marsha Scott, June 9, 1994.

"business matters discussed, if any, but does remember discussing the previous weekend the Foster and Hubbell families had spent together."[50]

Reportedly, at sometime around mid-day on Monday, Mr. Foster called his Little Rock physician and friend of fifteen years, Larry Watkins. The FBI's interview report of Dr. Watkins reflects that Mr. Foster complained of trouble sleeping, as he had confided to Web Hubbell.[51] Dr. Watkins prescribed Desyril, apparently for insomnia and not for depression. It is prescribed for both. The FBI's version is that it was for depression, but Dr. Watkins told the FBI that "[h]e did not think that Foster was significantly depressed nor had Foster given the impression that he was 'in crisis.' From what Foster told him, Foster's condition sounded mild and situational."[52] The doctor had prescribed Mr. Foster insomnia medication before, probably in December, seven months earlier.[53]

---

[50]    Exhibit 1, Report of FBI interview of Associate Attorney General Webster Hubbell, April 13, 1994.

[51]    Exhibit 1, Report of FBI interview with Deputy Attorney General Webster Hubbell, April, 13 and 15, 1994: "He said, however, that both he and Foster had confided in each other about sleep difficulties."

[52]    Exhibit 22, Report of FBI interview with Dr. Larry Watkins, May, 16, 1994: [W]atkins knew that it took 10 days to two weeks to take effect but helps with insomnia, sometimes the very first day. He felt it was very important for Foster to start sleeping better and thought if he got some rest that he would feel a lot better. He did not think that Foster was significantly depressed nor had Foster given the impression that he was "in crisis." From what Foster told him, Foster's condition sounded mild and situational. Watkins advised that he was only a little bit alarmed in that Foster had insisted on talking to him directly instead of discussing things through his nurse.

[53]    Exhibit 16, Report of FBI interview of Mrs. Lisa Foster, May 9, 1993: "In terms of other drugs which may have been prescribed for Foster in the past, Lisa Foster is aware of the sleeping pill Restoril having been prescribed. She also recalls that an antibiotic was prescribed for Foster in approximately December, 1992."

44

## Events surrounding the death

"On the evening of July 19, 1993 Lisa cooked dinner at home. When Foster returned home from work, he came into the house [and] smiled at Lisa Foster while saying that a quarter to eight was not bad. Lisa Foster responded to him that she was thinking he would be home at 6:30 or 7:00 p.m."[54]

The President testified that on the evening of Monday, July 19, he called Mr. Foster at home.[55] Hubbell and Lindsey were with the President when he placed the call.[56] Among the reasons for the call was that the President wanted to know, like Sheila Anthony and Marsha Scott, how the weekend in Maryland with Hubbell and "another couple" had gone. The President also claimed that he had heard Mr. Foster was "down" about the Travel Officer matter, and telephoned to invite him to watch a movie at the White House,[57] "In the Line of Fire," with Hubbell and Lindsey. (The normal "movie night" at the White House was Friday,[58] not Monday.) The President testified that "[i]t was a time of high stress for the Counsel's Office because of the White House travel office matter and other things."[59] Mr. Foster declined, according to Mr. Clinton, because he was home with his wife and wanted to stay there.[60]

---

[54] Exhibit 16, Report of FBI interview of Mrs. Lisa Foster, May 9, 1994.

[55] Exhibit 40, Deposition of President Clinton by Robert Fiske and deputy regulatory Independent Counsel Roderick Lankler, June 12, 1994: "Yes. When I called him, I thought he might still be at work but it was in the evening. I don't remember exactly what time it was, but it was already night."

[56] Exhibit 40, Deposition of President Clinton, June 12, 1994.

[57] Exhibit 40, Deposition of President Clinton, June 12, 1994: "But he said -- first I asked him if he wanted to come to the movie."

[58] Exhibit 13, Report of FBI interview of Assistant to the President Bruce Lindsey, June 22, 1994.

[59] Exhibit 40, Deposition of President Clinton, June 12, 1994.

[60] Exhibit 40, Deposition of President Clinton, June 12, 1994: "And he said that he would like to, but that he was already home with Lisa and he didn't think he should leave and come back to the White House. I understood that."

The President then requested to see Mr. Foster.[61] The two men scheduled to meet Wednesday, July 21, to discuss, according to the President, unspecified "organizational changes" being contemplated at the White House.[62] According to the President's testimony, if the organizational changes involved Mr. Foster himself, Clinton was unaware of it. He denied being among those who reported to have known that something was disturbing Mr. Foster, that he was depressed[63] or that he was considering resigning.[64]

---

[61]  Exhibit 40, Deposition of President Clinton, June 12, 1994:  Then I told him I wanted to talk to him about some matters relating to the White House and I wanted to ask his advice on some organizational issues, but that I could not see him the next day because we had the announcement of Mr. Freeh, the FBI Director, and several other things on my schedule, and could we please meet on Wednesday.  And he said, yes, I have some time on Wednesday and I will see you then.

[62]  Exhibit 40, Deposition of President Clinton, June 12, 1994.

[63]  Exhibit 40, Deposition of President Clinton, June 12, 1994:  "Q.  would you have heard from him or anyone else that he was depressed?  A.  No.  Not depressed.  Now again leading up to the day --  Q.  Right.  A. -- when I talked to him, I knew that he had been concerned about these things that I mentioned earlier.  But I wouldn't use the word 'depressed'."

[64]  Exhibit 40, Deposition of President Clinton, June 12, 1994:  Q.  We'll get there in just a minute.  Was there anything else that you heard, right up to that phone conversation on the 19th that -- [question interrupted]  A. No.  Q. -- might be disturbing him?  A.  No.  Q.  Had you ever heard that he was thinking of resigning his job?  A. No.

Exhibit 8, Report of FBI interview of Deputy Attorney General of Legislative Affairs Sheila Foster Anthony, April 28, 1994:  "At the last dinner which Foster shared with Anthony, Foster confided to her that he was considering resigning from his post at the White House."

Exhibit 7, Report of FBI interview of Associate White House Counsel William Kennedy, May 6, 1994:  Normal politics in RLF and feelings of abandonment were there but it didn't rise to the level where Foster thought he couldn't go back. Kennedy was asked if he observed any noticeable behavioral or emotional changes in Foster.  *** [H]e did not recall in conversations with Foster that he [Foster] wanted to go

## b.   Tuesday, July 20

As he left for work, Mr. Foster asked Mrs. Foster about her schedule for the day, which she characterized as an "unusual" question.[65]  It was the middle of the summer. He arrived at his White House office about 8:50 a.m.,[66] in time for the 9:00 Office of Legal Counsel staff meeting.

That morning in his White House office, Mr. Foster wrote a letter to his mother, and mailed it roughly six hours before he died.[67]  Mr. Foster's sister, Sheila Anthony, was with her mother when she opened it.  "The letter from Foster concerned oil leases which had been

---

back [to the Rose Law Firm]...  Kennedy did recall Foster making one comment to him in the second week of June saying "he (Foster) was thinking of finding a job with less pressure."  Another job in the administration with not so much distress.

Exhibit 1, Report of FBI interview with Associate Attorney General Webster Hubbell, April, 13 & 15, 1994:  [N]ewspaper accounts concerning the previous administration's removal of office items was determined by Hubbell as accurate. Hubbell said that he was not aware that Foster was experiencing any type of stress.  Foster never talked to Hubbell about missing the comfort zone of the Rose Law Firm where they had worked for more than 20 years.

Compare OIC, p. 99:  "Dr. Berman reported that...  He, furthermore, faced a feared humiliation should he resign and return to Little Rock."

[65]   Exhibit 16, Report of FBI interview of Mrs. Lisa Foster, May 9, 1994.

[66]   Exhibit 2, Report of FBI interview of Executive Assistant Deborah Gorham, April 19, 1993.

[67]   Exhibit 38, Report of FBI interview of Executive Assistant Linda Tripp, April 12, 1994:  Gorham told Tripp that the morning of his death, much earlier than his leaving, Foster placed three pieces of correspondence in the outgoing mail. The pieces were definitely personal, Foster having addressed them by hand and used stamps instead of officially stamped envelopes.  This was sufficiently unusual that Gorham noted it, and told Tripp who two of the items were addressed to.  Tripp was unable to recall one of the items, but said the other was to Foster's mother.

passed on to Foster's mother from her late husband's estate... In attempting to recall what was in the envelope, Anthony now believes that there was an extremely brief cover letter which had been typewritten, and which contained one or two sentences asking Foster's mother to sign the enclosed form and return it to the oil company."[68]

He attended the Rose Garden ceremony announcing the selection of Louis Freeh to replace William Sessions as the FBI Director, the first-ever FBI Director to be fired.[69]

---

[68]    Exhibit 8, Report of FBI interview of Sheila Foster Anthony, April 26, 1994.

[69]    See M. Isikoff, *Sessions Said Likely to Quit as FBI Chief Within Days*, Wash. Post, July 17, 1993:  An internal Justice Department report concluded that Sessions had committed numerous ethical abuses...***  Knowledgeable sources said that by the time she took office in March, Reno had concluded that Sessions had to leave. ***  At one point, Sessions suggested that he fly down to Waco, a city where he once lived, so he could personally negotiate with cult leader David Koresh.  The idea of an FBI director personally seeking to negotiate with a religious fanatic whom bureau scientists had already concluded was a madman alarmed FBI officials...

M. Isikoff, *Sessions Adopts Defiant Stance*, Wash. Post, July 19, 1993:  "Sessions — who has been under a cloud for months because of internal Justice Department findings of ethical lapses..."

M. Isikoff & Ruth Marcus, *Clinton Fires Sessions as FBI Director*, Wash. Post, July 20, 1993:  Clinton telephoned Sessions yesterday afternoon to inform him that he had been fired and then called back several minutes later to remind him that the dismissal was "effective immediately."  The President told reporters later that he acted after Attorney General Janet Reno reported... ***  Officials said the delay was partly to avoid any criticism that the FBI was being politicized... ***  Clinton yesterday named Clarke to serve as acting director until a successor is confirmed. On Saturday morning Sessions was summoned to a meeting with Reno and White House counsel Bernard Nussbaum and was told to quit by Monday or be fired. ***  Rep. Charles E. Schumer (D-NY), chairman of the House Judiciary subcommittee on crime, said that Sessions "has lost rank-and-file support and therefore his leadership effectiveness has been severely compromised."

## Tuesday, July 20

At around noon, Betsy Pond, White House Counsel Nussbaum's Executive Assistant, ordered Mr. Foster's lunch, a cheeseburger and French fries.[70] Because Mr. Foster's Assistant, Deborah Gorham, had already left for her lunch break, he asked Linda Tripp, the other of Nussbaum's Executive Assistants, to fetch the lunch he had selected off the daily menu of the cafeteria. A little while later, Mr. Foster dispatched Tom Castleton, a junior employee of the Office of Legal Counsel, to the cafeteria to see what was taking Tripp so long. When Castleton saw Tripp, she was on her way back with Mr. Foster's lunch and was surprised that Mr. Foster had sent Castleton to look for her because she had not been gone long.[71]

Tripp delivered Mr. Foster's lunch, a medium-rare cheeseburger, French-fries, a Coke, and some M&Ms, to his office. He relaxed on his couch and read his newspaper while he ate his meal.[72] At about 1:00,[73] as he left his office for the last time, Mr. Foster told Tripp that there were still some M&Ms on his tray if she wanted them. He also said, "I'll be back." Tripp told the FBI that "[t]here was nothing unusual about his demeanor and he did not seem distressed."[74]

Betsy Pond also saw Mr. Foster leave his office for the last time. "[S]he and Linda were in the office when he left... There was nothing unusual about his emotional

---

[70]   Compare OIC, p. 109:  "I talked to Vince on 7/19/93, at which time he complained of anorexia..."

[71]   Exhibit 38, Report of FBI interview of Linda Tripp, April 12, 1994.

[72]   Exhibit 38, Report of FBI interview of Executive Assistant Linda Tripp, April 12, 1994.

[73]   Exhibit 41, Report of Park Police interview with Executive Assistant Betsy Pond, by Captain Charles Hume, July 22, 1993: "At around 1300 hours he [Foster] came our of the office and stated 'I'll be back, there are M&Ms left in my office.'"   [2130

[74]   Exhibit 38, Report of FBI interview with Executive Assistant to Counsel Linda Tripp, April 12, 1994:  Shortly after she left him eating and reading the newspaper Foster came out of the office with his jacket on and empty handed. He said, "There are lots of M&M's left in there. I'll be back." There was nothing unusual about his demeanor and he did not seem distressed.

state. In fact, over the last several weeks she did not notice any changes, either physically or emotionally. She noticed no weight loss. She was unaware of him taking any medication or seeing any doctors. I asked her would she be surprised if I found out he was seeing a psychiatrist. She said yes. She was not aware of any depression problems."[75]

When his Executive Assistant, Deborah Gorham, returned from lunch, "Foster was gone... Pond told her that he had had his lunch, left M&M's for everybody, and left with his jacket slung over one shoulder, saying 'I'll be back.'"[76] Gorham reported that he "had never left in the middle of the day before," but that he "appeared relaxed and normal."[77]

After Mr. Foster left, a number of people tried to reach him by telephone. Brantley Buck, a Rose Law Firm partner, called twice from Little Rock, reportedly regarding the blind trust that Mr. Foster was handling for the Clintons.[78] (Buck described Mr. Foster's remaining duties concerning the blind trust as being merely

---

[75]     Exhibit 41, Report of Park Police interview with Executive Assistant Betsy Pond, by Captain Charles Hume, July 22, 1993.

[76]     Exhibit 2, Report of FBI interview with Executive Assistant to Deputy Counsel Deborah Gorham, April 19 and 26, 1994: Soon after he returned – about 11:40 – 11:50, Gorham entered his office and told him she was going out and did he need anything. He answered, "No _ I believe I have everything." He appeared relaxed and normal. Foster was gone when she returned about 1:20 – 1:30 p.m. He had left a couple of letters and a memo for her to type. She does not recall who the letters were to or what, specifically, the memo pertained. She also does not recall what was on his itinerary for the afternoon. Pond told her that he had had his lunch, left M&M's for everybody, and left with his jacket slung over one shoulder, saying "I'll be back."

[77]     Exhibit 2, Report of FBI interview with Executive Assistant Deborah Gorham, April 19 and 26, 1994.

[78]     Exhibit 12, Fiske Report, June 30, 1994. Exhibit 40, Deposition of President Clinton, June 12, 1994.

"ministerial."[79]) Gordon Rather, a Little Rock Attorney who worked at Bruce Lindsey's and the President's old firm, also called,[80] reportedly about the President's appointment of federal court judges. Maggie Williams, Ms. Clinton's Chief of Staff, also called, as did William Kennedy.[81] Betsy Pond paged him at Nussbaum's request.[82] When Mrs. Foster called around 5:00,[83] Deborah Gorham told her that Mr. Foster was unable to come to the phone, but did not reveal that he had left his office around 1:00 and had not returned, as he said he would.

That evening, Web Hubbell was beeped while having dinner at the Lebanese Taverna restaurant in Washington with his wife, his children, White House intern Janet Schaufele, and Marsha Scott. Hubbell, his wife, and Marsha Scott proceeded to the Anthony's nearby home to notify Mr. Foster's two sisters, brother-in-law and niece of the death.[84] Officially, Sheila, Sharon, and Web then went to

---

[79] Exhibit 42, Report of FBI interview of C. Brantly Buck, May 18, 1994. Exhibit 12, Fiske Report, June 30, 1994.

[80] Exhibit 43, Report of FBI interview of Gordon S. Rather, May 17, 1994: "He was impressed with the fact that the same day, possibly within an hour of his call [2:14 p.m.], someone from Foster's office called him back and asked if it were an urgent matter or if it was all right if Foster returned his call the following day."

[81] Exhibit 2, Report of FBI interview of Executive Assistant Deborah Gorham, April 19, 1993.

[82] Exhibit 2, Report of FBI interview of Executive Assistant Deborah Gorham, April 19, 1993.

[83] Exhibit 16, Report of FBI interview of Mrs. Lisa Foster, May 9, 1994.

[84] Exhibit 37, Report of FBI interview with Deputy Assistant to the President Marsha Scott, May 12, 1993: "Foster's other sister Sharon Bowman, was also visiting from Arkansas. Scott told the two sisters and the niece what had occurred. Scott was unable to say who was notified in what order among The White House staff." See also Exhibit 44, White House Chronology Memo by Jane Sherburne, May 15, 1996: "Marsha [Scott] and Web [Hubbell] found Sheila Anthony at home with Vince Foster's other sister [Sharon Bowman] and her daughter, who was visiting from out of town."

the Foster residence. Reportedly they arrived at the same time as Park Police investigators Cheryl Braun and John Rolla had, to notify the family. The whereabouts of Sheila's husband Beryl and the Foster sons that evening is unclear. The two Police Investigators spent 70 minutes in the Foster home where a dozen or so close friends and relatives gathered. According to Webster Hubbell, "everyone at the Foster residence that evening was trying to make logic out of the death, trying to pinpoint some event, but that they could not do so..."[85] Investigator Rolla testified about his interview of some of those there that night.

> Q. Did anyone at the notification mention depression or anti-depressant medication that Foster might have been taking?
>
> A. I mentioned depression, did you see this coming, were there any signs, has he been taking any medication? No. All negative answers.[86]

---

[85] Exhibit 1, Report of FBI interview with Associate Attorney General Webster Hubbell, April, 13 and 15, 1994: Hubbell said that everyone at the Foster residence that evening was trying to make logic out of the death, trying to pinpoint some event, but that they could not do so. *** Individuals present at the Foster residence on the night of Foster's death included the following: Bruce Lindsey; Bill Kennedy; Marsha Scott; David Watkins and his wife (Watkins was Operations for the White House); Mack McLarty and his wife Donna; Senator Pryor; Beryl Anthony; Foster's daughter, Laura; and then later the two boys were located, and on one of those nights [sic], President Clinton...

[Also present at the Foster residence that night were David Gergen, Sheila Anthony, Sharon Bowman & daughter, Craig Livingstone (outside), Helen Dickey, Vernon Jordan, Walter Pincus and Mrs. Pincus.]

[86] Exhibit 6, Deposition of Park Police investigator John Rolla, July 21, 1994.

> Compare A. Devroy & M. Isikoff, *Handling of Foster Case is Defended*, Wash. Post, July 30, 1993: Police who arrived at Foster's house the night of the death were turned away after being told Lisa Foster and family members were too distraught to talk. Investigators were not allowed to interview her until yesterday. "That was a matter between her lawyers and the police," [David] Gergen said, and the White House "had no role in it."

On July 21, Mr. Clinton spoke to the White House staff members who knew Mr. Foster well.

In the first place, no one can ever know why this happened. Even if you had a whole set of objective reasons, that wouldn't be why it happened, because you could get a different, bigger, more burdensome set of objective reasons that are on someone else in this room. So what happened was a mystery about something inside of him. And I hope all of you will always understand that... [Vince Foster] had an extraordinary sense of propriety and loyalty, and I hope when we remember him and this we'll be a little more anxious to talk to each other and a little less anxious to talk outside of our family.[87]

### c. No record of Mr. Foster's having left the White House complex

The White House itself is roughly a rectangular-shaped building with a wing on each end. It is bordered by Fifteenth Street on the East and Seventeenth Street to the West. Beyond the West Wing of the White House, running perpendicular to it, is West Executive Avenue. It is lined on both sides with end-in parking. Across West Executive Avenue from the White House, also within the White House campus, is the Old Executive Office Building (OEOB). A security fence surrounds the White House grounds, including the OEOB.

Prior administrations had housed their entire Counsel's office in the OEOB. The Clinton administration moved the offices of White House counsel Bernard Nussbaum and deputy Counsel Vincent Foster to the second floor of the West Wing. The majority of the White House Counsel's offices, where Associate Counsel William Kennedy and others were, remained in the OEOB. Mr. Kennedy reported to Mr. Foster.[88]

---

[87] Exhibit 45, Remarks by the President to the White House staff, July 21, 1993.

[88] Exhibit 46, Deposition of Associate White House Counsel William Kennedy, July 11, 1995: "Q. And did you report through Mr. Foster to Mr. Nussbaum or directly to Mr. Nussbaum? A. Usually through Mr. Foster."

The Office of White House Personnel Security, of which Craig Livingstone served as Chief, was also in the OEOB.[89] Mr. Livingstone reported mostly to Mr. Kennedy, and so was a regular visitor to the White House Counsel's Office in the OEOB. Livingstone was also a regular visitor to Mr. Foster's office in the west wing.[90]

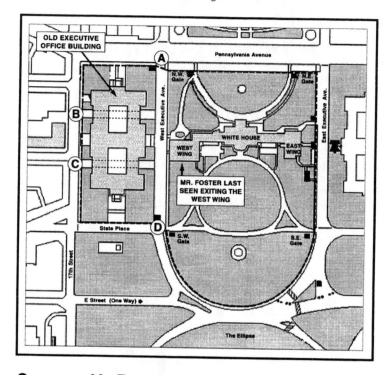

**White House Campus**: Mr. Foster's car was officially parked on West Executive Avenue between gates designated as A and D. His car would have exited the campus from gates designated as A, B, C, or D.

---

[89] Exhibit 47, Deposition Craig Livingstone, July 10, 1995: "Q. Okay, and you reported to Mr. Kennedy? A. That's correct... Q. Mr. Livingstone, in the White House complex, where is your office? A. I'm located in the Executive Office Building in Room 84."

[90] Exhibit 48, Deposition of Tom Castleton, June 27, 1995: Q. [W]ho were regular visitors to the counsel's [Foster's] office? A. ...Craig Livingston... Q. What was Mr. Livingstone's business at the counsel's suite in the west wing? A. Well, I think he worked for us. He was the director of security and the counsel's office, I believe, serves as an umbrella to that office. Q. He had a reporting relationship to Mr. Nussbaum? A. Yes, although I think he more directly reported to Mr. Kennedy... Q. Where was Mr. Kennedy's office physically located? A. In the Old Executive Office Building.

## Tuesday, July 20

On July 20, 1993, Uniformed Secret Service Officer John S. Skyles was posted at the exit in the West Wing, close to West Executive Avenue. He told the FBI he recalled that Mr. Foster had walked out of the West Wing "about lunchtime" on July 20. Officer Skyles "easily recognized Foster because he had seen him enter and exit the White House west wing on numerous occasions." Skyles "remembers this encounter in detail because, when he heard that Foster had died via suicide, he distinctly recalled that Foster did not appear to be at all depressed or preoccupied as he walked by. He said that he was therefore quite surprised to hear that Foster had committed suicide."[91]

The morning after Mr. Foster's death, FBI agents Dennis Condon and Scott Salter were dispatched to the White House to meet with FBI agent John Danna to investigate the death. They visited the OEOB. Agent Condon testified he

---

[91]  Exhibit 49, Report of FBI interview of US Secret Service Officer John S. Skyles, April 21, 1994: He explained that he easily recognized Foster because he had seen him enter and exit the White House west wing on numerous occasions when he (Skyles) was on duty. On July 20, 1993, Officer Skyles worked the 6:30 a.m. through 3:00 p.m. shift at post E-4. He described this as a rather routine day about which he could recall noticing nothing out of the ordinary. He advised that numerous White House staffers came and went through post E-4 on July 20 but that he could recall few specifics about these individuals. He advised, however, when he learned of Vincent Foster's death late on the evening of July 20, he remembered that he had seen Foster leaving the west wing of The White House through entrance E-4 earlier that day. Skyles said that he was approximately two thirds of the way through his shift on July 20 when he saw Foster leaving The White House. He said that while he cannot recall exactly when he saw Foster, he does distinctly recall that it was "about lunchtime." He said that as Foster walked pass [sic] the guard desk at entrance E-4 he (Skyles) asked Foster, "How are you doing sir?" He said that Foster replied, "Hello-fine" and nodded his head to Skyles with what Skyles remembers as a "half smile." Officer Skyles said that he remembers this encounter in detail because when he heard that Foster had died via suicide he distinctly recalled that Foster did not appear to be at all depressed or preoccupied as he walked by. He said that he was therefore quite surprised to hear that Foster had committed suicide.

could "not recall" why they went to the OEOB, what offices they visited, or to whom they had spoken.

> Q. Where did you go there [OEOB], what office in particular?
> A. I don't recall.
> Q. Do you know why you went there?
> A. I don't recall exactly, no.
> Q. Did you meet anybody there?
> A. I believe so, but I don't know...[92]

If these agents interviewed anyone at the OEOB, the interview reports have not been made public. So, we do not know who, other than Uniformed Secret Service Officer John Skyles, saw Mr. Foster around lunchtime.

Officially, Mr. Foster went to his Honda, parked in slot 16 on West Executive Avenue,[93] then drove off the White House campus and, hours later, into the Fort Marcy lot. There has never been any video or testimonial evidence produced that Mr. Foster did, in fact, leave the White House grounds in his car. Officer Skyles is the last publicly known person to have seen Mr. Foster alive.

## 3. Fort Marcy Park, discovery of body

### a. Fort Marcy Park

Fort Marcy National Park is about 25 acres in size. It is located about a mile from Washington in suburban McLean, Virginia. It is five-and-a-half miles from the White House. The park is preserved for historical reasons.

---

[92] Exhibit 50, Deposition of FBI Agent Dennis Condon, June 28, 1995: Q. At what point did Agent Danna meet with you? A. I believe we met with him almost immediately upon our arrival... Q. And then you went into the Old Executive Office Building? A. I believe that's correct. Q. Where did you go there, what office in particular? A. I don't recall. Q. Do you know why you went there? A. I don't recall exactly, no. Q. Did you meet anybody there? A. I believe so, but I don't know - I don't recall exactly who that might have been, possibly somebody from the Secret Service, but I'm not certain.

[93] Exhibit 16, Report of FBI interview of Lisa Foster, May 9, 1994.

It offers no view of the nearby Potomac River and is not scenic. The park is positioned between two busy arteries into Washington, Chain Bridge Road to the north and the George Washington Memorial Parkway to the south.[94]

The park contains no buildings. The Fort is simply earthen embankments, or berms, shaped roughly like a triangle. The Fort is located in the northern part of the park, with one side of the triangle running parallel to Chain Bridge Road, about fifty feet from it. Two sides, or berms, of the triangle are about 375 feet long, and one is around 300 feet. Except for the area inside the triangular Fort and the parking lot, visibility is very limited because most of the park is heavily wooded. The berms that form the sides of the fort are covered with trees and underbrush.

The park's small, banana-shaped parking lot is about 100 feet southeast of the southwest corner of the Fort. It parks 21 cars. The only paved vehicle access into the park is a 300-foot driveway into the lot, running due south to the Parkway. At the southern end of the parking lot, bordering the footpath leading to the Fort, is a sign with a description of the park.[95]

---

[94]  Compare OIC, p. 102: As to the Fort Marcy Park location, Dr. Berman stated Mr. Foster "was ambivalent to the end" and may have driven for a while before going to Fort Marcy Park.[fn324] He may have "simply and inadvertently happened upon the park or he may have purposely picked it off the area map found in his car."[fn325] Dr. Berman stated that Mr. Foster's suicide in Fort Marcy Park is "[s]imilar to the typical male physician who suicides by seeking the privacy of a hotel room, and a 'do not disturb' sign."[fn326]

[95]  With the outbreak of the Civil War, Washington turned into the training ground, arsenal, supply depot, and nerve center for the Union cause. To protect the city and vital supply routes from enemy hands, Union armies built a ring of earthen fortifications. The remains of those fortifications preserved by the National Park Service are now known collectively as the Fort Circle Parks. Taking command of and reorganizing the Army of the Potomac, Major General George B. McClellan appointed Major John G. Barnard of the Corps of Engineers to build many new forts. By the spring of 1865, the defense system totaled 68 forts and 93 batteries with 807 cannons and 98 mortars in place. Washington had become the most heavily fortified city in the world. Fort Marcy, perched high above the Potomac, protected against enemy attacks from northern Virginia land routes.

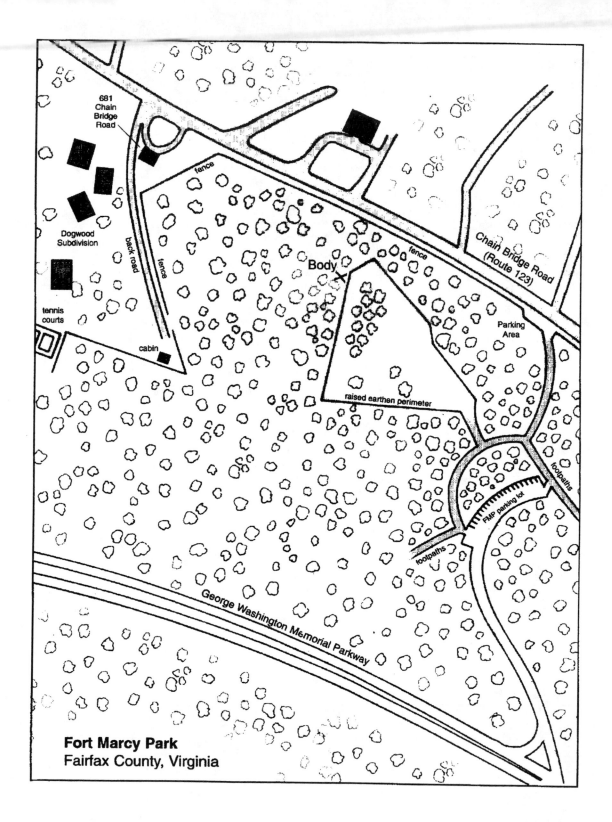

**Fort Marcy Park**
Fairfax County, Virginia

## Fort Marcy Park

Mr. Foster's body was found close to the northwest tip of the Fort, lying on a path on the outward side of the western berm around 100 feet from Chain Bridge Road and 300 feet from the closest house which is just on the other side of Chain Bridge Road. The next three closest homes are on the same side of Chain Bridge Road, from 470 to 550 feet from the body site. Four or more homes are 600 to 700 feet from the site, and the two Saudi Arabia Embassy buildings are 700 feet away the site.[96]

Another vehicular approach to Fort Marcy Park is an old dirt road around 600 feet west of the body site. This road runs along the western border of the park and the nearby homes. The hidden entrance to this old civil war road is a driveway to a house on Chain Bridge Road that abuts the park (681 Chain Bridge Road). The ground separating the body site from the old road is so heavily treed that the civilian who officially discovered the body testified that anyone entering the park via this road "would not be seen, period."[97] The fence separating this road from the park's border is collapsed for several yards, near an old unoccupied cabin located near the park's border. (There is not a single reference to this Civil War road in the entire investigative record, including the OIC's Report.)

In July of 1993, seventeen-year-old Leslie Rutherford lived near the park. The day before Mr. Foster's death, Monday, July 19, 1993, was an extremely hot and humid day. At around three o'clock that afternoon, Leslie was walking near the west border of Fort Marcy Park, having entered the park over or through one of the gaps in the park's fence bordering the old road. Although investigators did not

---

[96] Compare Exhibit 12, Fiske Report, June 30, 1994: "Saudi residence is the closest building to the park."

[97] Exhibit 51, Deposition of Dale [see below] by Congressman Burton, Mica, Rohrabacher, July 28, 1994: Q. But there is a private road that goes back to that cabin? A. There is a private road that goes right back to it from the housing development right next to it. Q. Okay. If somebody came back that road they wouldn't be seen? A. They would not be seen, period. Q. How far is that from the cabin? A. 150, 175 yards. Q. So they could have walked around that and come right up -- A. They are dead in the woods all the way, and there is a path that leads right straight through there, a very well worn walking nature trial.

canvass the neighborhood, she came forward during the initial investigation because she remembered seeing a man wearing a suit walking through Fort Marcy, and "thought it was strange."[98] The man she saw was in the section of the park where Mr. Foster's body was found the following day. When she looked in his direction, he immediately turned his head away. The only Park Police record of the strange man Leslie saw is found in handwritten notes of Investigator Renee Abt, recorded on July 24, 1993. The typewritten Park Police reports did not mention this man.

The FBI's Report of its interview with Leslie is dated May 17, 1994.

[A]t approximately 3:00 p.m. on July 19, 1993... [she] noticed at a distance of approximately 10 to 15 feet a white male walking by himself in a direction leading from the George Washington Memorial Parkway into the northeast section of the park. She stated what caught her attention was that this white male, in spite of the heat, was dressed in a dark suit, white shirt, and a red neck tie. [She] further described this white male as being in his early 40's, dark hair, approximately 180 pounds, and slightly over 6 foot [sic] in height... This white male had no facial hair nor was he wearing eyeglasses. She further stated that when she noticed this white male, he immediately looked away from her and therefore she could furnish no additional details relative to his facial characteristics. In a further attempt to determine the height of this white male, it was [the interviewee's] opinion that he was slightly over 6 foot [sic] tall, but did not approach 6 foot [sic] 4 inches in height. [The interviewee] was exhibited photographs of Mr. Foster but she was unable to make any determination as to whether these photographs resembled the white male she saw at the park on July 19, 1993.[99]

---

[98] Exhibit 52, Handwritten notes of Park Police Investigator Renee Abt, July 24, 1993: "Saw man walking thru [sic] park on Monday thought it was strange."

[99] Exhibit 53, Report of FBI interview of Leslie Rutherford, May 17, 1994.

Discovery of body

The FBI reported that she observed this man in the "northeast section of the park." Northeast is the opposite from where she had the man. But the handwritten notes by the FBI agent who interviewed Leslie reflect that she actually said she saw the suspicious acting man on the path on the park's "west border," where she had entered the park from the direction of the neighboring tennis courts -- and the side of the park where Mr. Foster's body was found.

"Location - by cabin by the tennis courts - west border of Ft. Marcy park - on path."[100]

The OIC omits any mention of Leslie Rutherford's account of having seen a man acting suspiciously by the back road the day before the death, wearing a suit in 90 degree weather.

### b.    Official version of discovery of body

Summary: The OIC reports that at 5:50 p.m., Dale stopped at the park to urinate, discovered the body, drove 3 miles and reported the death to two park workers. Eight months later, a New York daily newspaper reported that two park workers admitted that they had discovered the body, whereupon Dale decided to come forward, contacted G. Gordon Liddy, and the FBI interviewed Dale. Based on a "detailed" comparison of Dale's version of the conversation with the park maintenance workers', Fiske gave credence to Dale's account, yet these accounts differ in virtually every detail, including that the maintenance workers reported that Dale said the body had been shot. Dale saw no gun and believed death had been caused by a blow to the head.

The OIC reports that Mr. Foster's body was found by "C5", which stands for the fifth civilian witness at the park. His first name is Dale. The Fiske Report refers to him as "CW," which stands for "Confidential Witness." He had requested anonymity (Dale's full name has since been published in the Washington Times and its sister publication Insight on the News). Dale is the only one of the five civilian park witnesses whose name is wholly redacted in the government records of the case. Officially, he discovered the body, drove 2.75 miles on the outbound George Washington Parkway to the Park Headquarters

Discovery of body

---

[100]    Exhibit 54, Handwritten notes of FBI interview of Leslie Rutherford, May 17, 1994.

at the Turkey Run Maintenance facility, where he saw two uniformed off-duty Park Service employees. He told them about the body, whereupon one of them reportedly called authorities.

OIC, p. 22:

*C5 said that he exited his van, and while walking through the park, found Mr. Foster's body near the second cannon, the cannon closer to Chain Bridge Road.* **fn42** *C5 then left Fort Marcy and drove approximately 2.75 miles further outbound on the GW Parkway to a parking area near GW parkway Headquarters; there, C5 reported the dead body to two off-duty Park Service employees who called 911.* **fn43**

Aside from what is in the Fiske and Starr Reports, we learn of Dale's story from three sources. The first is the March 22, 1994 "Report of Interview," authored by radio talk show host and former FBI agent G. Gordon Liddy, to whom Dale had confided. Second, we have four reports of FBI interviews by FBI agents Monroe and Columbell. And third, we have Dale's deposition, taken at his home on the evening of July 29, 1994, by Congressmen Dan Burton, Dana Rohrabacher, and John Mica. Most of what we know is from this transcript. (Burton took Dale's deposition before the Fiske Report was released to the public. The Senate Banking Committee never deposed the Park Service employees or any civilian park witnesses.)

Dale reported that he stopped at the park because of an urgent need to relieve himself.[101] He backed into a parking space, took off his shirt and walked to the furthest end of the fort, around 750 feet, whereupon he urinated.

After he discovered the body, he said, he drove to the Turkey Run maintenance facility "to go to the nearest phone"[102] (it was not the nearest phone). Dale said he told

---

[101]   Exhibit 55, Report of FBI interview with Dale, April 14, 1994:  "[H]e had an urge to relieve himself and realized that the first pull off area where he could have some degree of privacy was Fort Marcy Park."

[102]   Exhibit 51, Deposition of Dale by Congressmen Burton, Mica and Rohrabacher, July 28, 1994.

## Discovery of body

a Park Service maintenance worker about the body. Dale did not make the call to authorities himself (or come forward for eight months) because, as he later told G. Gordon Liddy, he didn't "want to end up like that guy"[103] he found. Dale had inspected the body and was certain there was no gun in Mr. Foster's hand. Dale never explained why he feared he would "end up like that guy" simply by virtue of his having discovered the body.

Dale claims the catalyst for his coming forward was the appearance of an article in the March 14, 1994, issue of the New York Daily News. It began with puffery, reporting that although most of the investigation was still-secret, the New York Daily News had reviewed the Park Police Report. It then reported what Dale claimed was the cause of his concern, that one of the Park Service workers had discovered Foster's body at the park but had lied about it because, at the time, he had been drinking at the park.

> Most of what happened in Fort Marcy Park on July 21 [sic] has remained secret. The Park Police Report has only been reviewed once by the Daily News... The body was discovered by a park maintenance worker who had slipped into the area for a quiet midday drink. He reported finding the body, but then made up a story about having seen a white van. He has since recanted the white van story, admitting it was created to cover up his own behavior.[104]

Dale testified why he reconsidered.

> "[W]hat I knew would become public and if there was a threat to me, that, that possibility would be greatly, greatly reduced simply by the fact that what I knew would have been now made official."[105]

---

[103]  Exhibit 56, Report of interview of Dale by G. Gordon Liddy, March 22, 1994.

[104]  M. McAlary, *Aide's Suicide is Confirmed by Heads-up Cops*, N.Y. Daily News, March 14, 1994. See also J. Seper, *Foster death still a puzzle,* Wash. Times, July 19, 1994:  "The man told the FBI and Mr. Liddy that he notified National Park Service personnel of the discovery [of the body] and then left the park."

[105]  Exhibit 51, Deposition of Dale by Congressmen Burton, Mica and Rohrabacher, July 28, 1994.

Dale said he was worried because, he reasoned, if he officially did not exist, Foster's killers might kill him, too. He talked it over with his brother, who suggested that Dale contact former FBI agent G. Gordon Liddy because Liddy could be trusted not to reveal Dale's identity. Liddy took Dale's information, wrote a "Report of Interview," and forwarded it to deputy regulatory Independent Counsel Roderick Lankler.

Liddy's Report related that Dale had described seeing a white car, and in it, from the distance of twenty-five feet away[106] through the closed windows, a suit-jacket that "matched" the trousers he had seen on Mr. Foster, and a briefcase. Dale testified that on the passenger's side floor of the car he saw "a four-pack of wine cooler with two gone,"[107] and that the wine coolers had a light pink label "exactly like the bottle" he had seen beside the body.[108]

In his cover letter, Liddy concluded that Dale had described the interior of Mr. Foster's car, and wrote that "the report contains information about the scene and the

---

[106] Exhibit 56, Report of Interview of Dale by G. Gordon Liddy on March 22, 1994: "[O]bserved a suit coat [in the car] which matched... from approximately eight feet above and twenty-five feet laterally in distance."

[107] Exhibit 56, Report of Interview of Dale, by G. Gordon Liddy, March 22, 1994: He observed a suit coat which matched in color the trousers on the body he had found. The coat was light gray, appearing to be thrown, not neatly folded, over the back of the seat on the passenger's side. The coat was barely over the top of the seat-back. Witness thinks he saw a briefcase on the passenger's side on the floor, although he is not certain. He stated that he is certain, however, that there was a "Four pack" of "wine cooler" in there. Witness stated that he observed the interior of the Honda from approximately eight feet above and twenty-five feet laterally in distance.

[108] Exhibit 51, Deposition of Dale by Congressmen Burton, Mica and Rohrabacher, July 28, 1994: Q. And you said that you also saw a wine cooler pack on the floor? A. A four-pack wine cooler with two gone. The same color as - it was - it had a light pink label. Q. Okay. Did it look like the bottle that you saw beside the body? A. Exactly like the bottle.

interior of Mr. Foster's automobile that I, for one, have
never seen published."[109]

Liddy told Dale that he could trust the two FBI agents
who were to interview him, because, Dale testified, Liddy
said they were "old Hoover guys... not young kids... trying
to get a reputation or prove anything [and that] they can
be trusted."[110]  (Three weeks later, these same agents
interviewed Patrick Knowlton.)

The Fiske Report patently gave credence to Dale.

In order to test the veracity of the information
provided by CW, this Office performed a detailed
analysis of that information.  CW provided details
that have never become public, and that could have
been known by the person who discovered Foster's body.
These details include specific information about the
appearance and location of the body, the description
of the park maintenance workers, and the short
conversation held with them.[111]

Dale testified that he saw no gun, no "signs of a
gunshot on his shirt or clothes,"[112] and that he figured that

---

[109]   Exhibit 59, Letter from G. Gordon Liddy to deputy
regulatory Independent Counsel Roderick Lankler, April 5, 1994.

[110]   Exhibit 51, Deposition of Dale by Congressmen Burton, Mica
and Rohrabacher, July 28, 1994: A.  And I went to them
because after talking with Mr. Liddy the FBI was really
asking and begging and doing everything they could to get
in touch with me.  Mr. Liddy said these are two of the old
Hoover guys, they are not young kids and they're not trying
to get a reputation or prove anything.  I think they can be
trusted, I think you can help an investigation, would you
be willing to meet with them.  Remaining as a confidential
witness with their promise to do the same and they have
done that absolutely.  Q.  What are the names of the two
agents... A.  I prefer you all don't have them.  Q.  We are
not going -- they are going to testify tomorrow before the
Committee so their names will be known tomorrow.

[111]   Exhibit 12, Fiske Report, June 30, 1994.

[112]   Exhibit 51. Deposition of Dale by Congressmen Burton,
Mica and Rohrabacher, July 28, 1994:  Q.  Yeah.  Go ahead.
Tell us what you saw.  A.  I saw blood traces on his nose
and lips.  There was not streams of blood on the side of

65

Mr. Foster had been "hit in the head."[113]  Yet, according to the FBI's Report of its interview with one of the two park maintenance workers, Charles Stough, Dale told him the body had been shot.

> [Stough] stated that the driver of this white van specifically asked him if he would call the Park Police, further informing Mr. [Stough] that he had seen a body at Fort Marcy Park and that it looked like this man had been shot and that he looked dead.[114]

According to the FBI's Report of its March 30, 1994 interview with him, Stough had reported that he was "confident he would recognize"[115] Dale.  But the FBI waited for three more months, until June 21, nine days before the Fiske Report was issued, to ask Stough to identify Dale. After viewing him for about 10 seconds, Stough told the FBI it "possibly could be him" but could not "state positively."[116]  The other park maintenance worker, Francis

---

his face.  There was not trickles of blood as indicated in the Foster report.  I was looking straight down into the man's face and saw the blood.  That's when I said to myself hey, did somebody shoot this man?  I didn't see any signs of a gunshot on his shirt or clothes.

[113]  Exhibit 51, Deposition of Dale by Congressmen Burton, Mica and Rohrabacher, July 28, 1994:  A.  You see a somebody laying there dead, you go what happened here, did somebody shoot him?  No signs of it.  Was he in a fight? Was he hit in the head?  *** Q.  What did you think happened?  What did it look like?  A.  Well, when I started looking to see if he had anything in his hands, he had been hit in the head, what does that tell you?

[114]  Exhibit 60, Report of FBI interview of Charles Stough, March 30, 1994.  Exhibit 61, Handwritten notes of FBI Interview with Charles Stough, March 30, 1994: "crossing parking lot - white van - 'you need to call Park Police' - he saw a body at Ft. Marcy - 'looks like he is shot,' called USPP and informed that person was shot."

[115]  Exhibit 60, Report of FBI interview of Charles Stough, March 30, 1994.

[116]  Exhibit 61, FBI handwritten notes of interview of Charles Stough, June 21, 1994.  Exhibit 68, Handwritten notes of FBI Interview with Charles Stough, June 21, 1994

## Discovery of body

Swann, reportedly told the FBI that he "probably could identify" the driver of the van if he saw him again, but no such request was forthcoming.

The record demonstrates that Dale and the two park workers also disagree on almost everything else that occurred during their short visit.

Dale had told Liddy he saw the two park workers "leaning against the tailgate"[117] of a truck. Stough reportedly told the FBI he was "walking" across the parking lot when he encountered the driver of the van.[118] Swann had reportedly told the FBI that both he and Stough had been "sitting"[119] when Dale entered the lot.

Stough said there were no other individuals in the parking area the evening of July 20, 1993, according to the FBI's Report of its interview with him.[120] The FBI's report of its interview with Swann, on the other hand, relates that "a few park rangers" were at Turkey Run, and that neither he nor Stough told the rangers about the dead

---

[117]   Exhibit 56, Interview of Dale by G. Gordon Liddy, March 22, 1994:  "There he saw two males dressed in what appeared to him to be park service uniforms.  They were leaning against the tailgate of a truck."

[118]   Exhibit 60, Report of FBI interview of Charles Stough, March 30, 1994:  "[A] white van entered the parking area and the occupant of the van engaged him in conversation while he, [Stough] was walking from [Swann's] vehicle to his own vehicle." Exhibit 61, Handwritten notes of FBI Report of interview of Charles Stough, March 30, 1994:  "[Stough was] crossing the parking lot."

[119]   Exhibit 62, Report of FBI interview of Francis Swann, March 30, 1994:  "[A] white Chevy van pulled into the maintenance yard off of the GW parkway.  He estimated the time to be approximately 5:45 p.m.  The van pulled up to where he and [Stough] were sitting."

[120]   Exhibit 60, Report of FBI interview of Charles Stough, March 30, 1994:  "He stated there were no other individuals in the parking area the evening of July 20, 1993 who would be in a position to provide a further description of this van or the occupant."

body.[121]   Stough "thought he [Dale] stepped out of the van,"[122] and estimated he was 5'7" to 5'8" tall.  Swann said Dale's height was hard to estimate because "he never got out of the van."[123]  The caller to the Park Police, reportedly Swann, estimated the man was 5'11".[124]

After arriving at the Turkey Run maintenance facility parking lot, Dale said he looked both ways and did not see any phones in the small parking lot.[125]  He explained he had missed them because "the phones sat back behind the trees."[126]  However, the telephones are not obscured by any trees and anyone entering the small Turkey Run maintenance facility parking lot would have been hard-pressed to have missed seeing them.  Dale testified that he repeatedly asked Stough where was a telephone, and that each time, Stough replied, "Why?"[127]

---

[121]   Exhibit 62, Report of FBI interview of Francis Swann, March 30, 1994.

[122]   Exhibit 61, Handwritten notes of FBI interview of Charles Stough March 30, 1994:  "Thought he [Dale] stepped out of van."

[123]   Exhibit 62, Report of FBI interview of Francis Swann, March 30, 1994:  "Approximately 5'9"-5'10" (difficult to estimate because the driver [Dale] never got out of the van)."

[124]   Exhibit 63, Transcript of call to Park Police, July 20, 1993 at 6:03 p.m.:  "Sergeant Myers:  White male, how tall?  Park Service Employee:  Uh, he was sitting in the van (unintelligible).  Sergeant Myers:  Oh, he was sitting in the van.  Park Service Employee:  Five eleven, five something like that."

[125]   Exhibit 51, Deposition of Dale by Congressmen Burton, Mica and Rohrabacher, July 28, 1994:  "I was looking at them, drove by, still didn't see any phones, looked both ways and never saw them, backed up turned around, started back out and was going to ask them to use the phone..."

[126]   Exhibit 51, Deposition of Dale by Congressmen Burton, Mica and Rohrabacher, July 28, 1994:  "There is two phones there. I never saw them because I saw the guys there.  I was looking at them, the phones sat back behind the trees over here on the right side."

[127]   Exhibit 51, Deposition of Dale by Congressmen Burton, Mica and Rohrabacher, July 28, 1994:  "I asked him for a phone. He stated that, you know, 'Why?'  And I says, we, it's an

Dale, the witness who officially found Mr. Foster's body, testified that he drove into this parking lot to find a telephone. He claimed not to have seen them because "the phones sat back behind the trees."

emergency, I need to use the phone. Can you get me to a phone? 'Yes, but why?' And he says - I think he said it the third time."

Stough, however, reportedly told the FBI that he did not "ask any questions of the occupant of the white van."[128] There is no record of either Swann or Stough having related that Dale had asked any questions other than whether the Park Service employed them.[129]

Swann reportedly told the Park Police that Dale told him about the dead body.[130] Both Swann and Stough reportedly told the FBI that Dale had informed them both of

---

[128]    Exhibit 60, Report of FBI interview of Charles Stough, March 30, 1994:  "[Stough] advised that he did not ask any questions of the occupant of the white van which immediately departed the parking lot after furnishing this notification to himself and Mr. [Swann]."

[129]    Exhibit 62, Report of FBI interview of Francis Swann, March, 30, 1994:  [Swann] stated they both had 3 beers and were getting ready to leave the yard when a white male in a white van pulled into the maintenance yard off of the GW Parkway.  He estimated the time to be approximately 5:45 p.m.  The van pulled up to where he and [Stough] were sitting.  At the time, both he and [Stough] were still in their park service uniforms.  [Swann] advised that the van driver asked if they worked for the park service and they responded in the affirmative.  The van driver then stated words to the effect that "there is a body down at Fort Marcy..."

Exhibit 60, Report of FBI interview of Charles Stough, March 30, 1994:  [Stough] further advised that since there was unusually heavy traffic on this particular evening, [Swann] parked his vehicle directly opposite a public telephone and both proceeded to consume two or three beers apiece.  According to [Stough] sometime between 5:30 and 6:00 p.m., a white van entered the parking area and the occupant of the van engaged him in conversation while he, [Stough] was walking from [Swann's] vehicle to his own vehicle.  [Stough] stated that the driver of this white van specifically asked him if he would call the Park Police, further informing Mr. [Stough] that he had seen a body at Fort Marcy Park.

[130]    Exhibit 64, Park Police Report of interview of Francis Swann, by Park Police Detective James Morrissette, August 2, 1993:  "This operator advised Mr. Swann that there was a body in the area of the cannon in Ft. Marcy Park."

the dead body;[131] yet Dale told the FBI he had spoken only to the white park worker, Stough, and stated that the "black male [Swann] remained by the pickup truck."[132]

When Mr. Swann called the Park Police, he had two things to report, a car accident and a dead body. Swann reported the car accident first. Swann first called 9-1-1, then the Park Police. He, like Dale, refused to identify himself. There is no record of Swann's ever having been asked why he refused to give his name.

A car accident occurred just before 6:00 p.m. on the George Washington Memorial Parkway, just below its intersection with Route 123. Because its location was between Fort Marcy Park and the workers' reported location, Swann could only have known about it if he had driven by it or been told of it. They could not have driven by the accident if, as reported, they had been at Turkey Run for some time. Neither Dale nor the park workers related that Dale told them about it,[133] but Swann reported it to the police when he called to report the body.

The official version is that Swann and Stough had been drinking beer in their uniforms at Turkey Run maintenance

---

[131] Exhibit 60, Report of FBI interview of Charles Stough, March 30, 1994: "After receiving this information from the occupant of the white van, [Stough] called [Swann] over and believes that the occupant of the white van repeated the same information to [Swann]."

Exhibit 62, Report of FBI interview Francis Swann, March 30, 1994: The van pulled up to where he and [Stough] were sitting. At the time both he and [Stough] were still in their park service uniforms. [Swann] advised that the van driver asked if they worked for the park service and they responded in the affirmative. The van driver then stated words to the effect that "there is a body down at Fort Marcy up by the cannon and could they call the police.

[132] Exhibit 55, Report of FBI interview with Dale, April 14, 1994: "[T]he white male came over... the black male remained by the pickup truck... the white male responded to the effect that he would call authorities... [T]he black male did not come over to his van nor was he a part of any conversation."

[133] See Exhibit 62, Report of FBI interview of Francis Swann, March 30, 1994. And see Exhibit 60, Report of FBI interview of Charles Stough, March 30, 1994.

facility, which would have been in view of co-workers, Park Rangers, and supervisors.

The New York Daily News article cited the Park Police Report as its source that Swann and Stough had been drinking; yet that information is not in the Police Report. The first record that the park employees had been drinking appeared in the Reports of their FBI interviews, conducted March 30, 1994, sixteen days after the New York Daily News reported it.

There is nothing in any records, including the Park Police Report,[134] that the park workers ever changed their stories and admitted they were at Fort Marcy Park.

The Park Police did not contact Swann until August 2, 1993, thirteen days after Mr. Foster's death and three days before the conclusion of the first death investigation.[135] Only Swann was interviewed. Stough told the FBI "he was never interviewed by the Park Police regarding this particular incident."[136]

---

[134] Exhibit 64, Park Police Report of interview with Francis Swann by Park Police Detective James Morrissette: During the interview with Mr. Swann he stated that "Chuck" [Stough] (tree crew) and himself were sitting outside the Turkey Run Headquarters at approximately 1750 hrs. At this time a large white van, thought to possibly be a General Motors make, drove into the parking area. The van was best described as follows: 1987-1990, Chevy white in color construction writing on the side, Va. Tags unknown, no windows, described as "well used." The operator of the van was described as follows: WM, 47-50 yrs, chunky/heavyset, 220-225 lbs, mostly graying hair, light sun tan, clean shaven with whiskers, possibly gay. This operator advised Mr. Swann that there was a body in the area of the cannon in Ft. Marcy Park. Based on this notification Mr. Swann called the Fairfax County Police and reported the incident. Subsequent to this call he called the U.S. Park Police and made the same report. Mr. Swann stated that there was no other conversation with regards to the body.

[135] Exhibit 65, Deposition of FBI Agent Scott Salter, June 30, 1995. "We [FBI] were there to assist them in conducting the investigation which meant interviewing co-workers... [and] then proceed as the investigation, you know, called for."

[136] Exhibit 60, Report of FBI interview of Charles Stough, March 30, 1994.

The FBI's Report of its interview with Swann is four pages long. The entire last page, a fourth of it, is redacted. The FBI's handwritten notes of its interview with Swann have not been released. The first of Dale's FBI interview Report is eight pages long. Almost two pages are entirely redacted.

## II. AUTHORITIES ARRIVE AT THE SCENE

County and federal authorities responded to the scene. The Park Police are federal employees of the US Department of the Interior. The Firefighters and the medical examiner, Dr. Haut, are all employed by Fairfax County, Virginia. Almost all the Firefighters are Emergency Medical Technicians, or EMTs, and have medical training. The two Firefighters with the most medical training are referred to as paramedics.

Also in the park when authorities arrived were two civilians, a man and a woman. Although their identities do appear in the public record, they are referred to as Male Civilian and Female Civilian out of deference to their privacy.

The following is a list of those people who are known to have been present in Fort Marcy Park on July 20, after the official discovery of the body.

Park Police
Officer Kevin Fornshill
Inv. Christine Hodakievic
Officer Franz Ferstl
Sergeant Robert Edwards
Lieutenant Patrick Gavin
Investigator John Rolla
Investigator Cheryl Braun
Investigator Renee Abt
Officer William Watson
Intern with Officer Watson
Evidence Technician Peter
    Simonello
Officer Julie Spetz
Lieutenant Ronald Schmidt

Fairfax County
Firefighter Todd Hall
Firefighter Ralph Pisani
Paramedic George Gonzalez
Firefighter Lt. James Iacone
Paramedic Richard Arthur
Firefighter Jennifer Wacha
Dr. Donald Haut
Firefighter Corey Ashford
Firefighter Roger Harrison
Firefighter Lt. Wm. Bianchi
Firefighter Andrew Makuch
Firefighter Victoria Jacobs

Civilians
Dale
Male Civilian (continued)

Female Civilian
Tow Truck driver (to tow a Mercedes)
Dr. Haut's female driver
Tow Truck driver (to tow the Arkansas Honda)

Twenty-one people, 20 officials plus Dale, viewed the body. (The OIC claims that 19 witnesses saw the body[137] -- omitting Officer William Watson and the unidentified intern who accompanied Watson.)

The time that the first Police Officer officially arrived, simultaneously with Firefighters, is 6:09:58.

But there is evidence that Officer Kevin Fornshill, in an unmarked car or scooter, and Investigator Christine Hodakievic, were already in the park when Firefighters arrived.[138] Investigator John Rolla testified that police arrived before 6:00 p.m.[139] Fornshill appears to have met the Fire and Rescue workers in the park proper, not in the

---

[137] OIC, p. 20: Thirty-one witnesses, 19 of whom observed Mr. Foster's body, have provided relevant testimony about their activities and observations in and around the Fort Marcy Park area on July 20, 1993. They include:

> 6 private citizens (one of whom discovered and observed Mr. Foster's body);
> 13 Park Police personnel (9 of whom observed Mr. Foster's body);
> 11 Fairfax County Fire and Rescue Department (FCFRD) personnel (8 of whom observed the body); and
> Dr. Haut, the doctor representing the Medical Examiner's Office who responded to the scene and examined the body.

[138] Exhibit 66, Report of FBI interview of Firefighter Todd Hall, March 18, 1994: "Upon arriving at the park, Hall noted that officers of the U.S. Park Police (USPP) were already on site."

[139] Exhibit 6, Deposition of Park Police Investigator John Rolla, July 21, 1994: I have no idea why he [Dr. Haut] would -- unless he just meant the time he was pronounced. Perhaps that's what he meant, I am pronouncing him. He said, make that the time of death. I knew that wasn't the time of death, officers were there before 1800 hours. So if he decide [sic] at 1800 hours, somebody is in trouble.

74

parking lot, as reported.[140]  (There is no record of any
witnesses having seen Hodakievic arrive in the lot in her
civilian car, nor of her car being identified among the
vehicles there.[141])  Firefighter James Iacone heard that a

------

[140]   Exhibit 67, Deposition of Firefighter Todd Hall, July 20,
1994:  Q.  What did you see as soon as you got there?  A.
Nothing but a park.  Q.  Any cars there, any people there?
A.  Yes.  There were some cars parked there.  I don't
recall seeing any people, no.  I don't recall seeing any
people.  Q.  What did you do after you got to the park?  A.
We had a call that came in, suicide in front of a cannon,
so we searched the grounds for a body in front of a cannon.
I think we were met there by the Park Police.  Q.  You said
it was a call for a suicide?  A.  Yes, possible.  No, well,
somebody lying in front of a cannon, possible DOA.  I
forgot what the initial call was...  Q.  After you got
there, what did you do?  A.  We searched the grounds, we
split up.  Some of us went this way, some that way, looking
because I was worried.  There was only four cannons there
so we split up.  Me and one of the Park Police, we was
together, and I think he pretty much knew the vicinity of
the cannons.

[141]   Exhibit 76, Park Police Report, by Investigator Christine
Hodakievic, July 21, 1993. Exhibit 118, Handwritten notes of Park
Police Investigator Renee Abt, July 20, 1993.

    Exhibit 70, Report of FBI interview of Park Police Officer
    Julie Spetz, May 2, 1994:  As she drove into the park
    entrance, she noted a disabled vehicle off to the right on
    the ramp leading into the parking lot.  Driving into the
    Fort Marcy parking lot itself, she observed two cars; one
    to her left toward the front of the lot which she later
    learned was Foster's vehicle.  Officer Spetz cannot recall
    the color or make of the vehicle but does remember it had
    Arkansas tags on it.  Officer Spetz stated that a second
    car, white in color, was in the rear of the parking lot,
    but she is unable to recall any other identifying data
    regarding this car.  She stated that emergency vehicles
    (ambulance and fire truck) were also in the parking lot.

Exhibit 75, Park Police Report of Park Police Investigator Cheryl
Braun, July 21, 1993:  "[Male Civilian and [Female Civilian] were
driving a white Nissan with Maryland registration." Exhibit 76,
Park Police Report, by Investigator Christine Hodakievic, July
21, 1993:  "I observed a blue Mercedes 4 door displaying Va.
Tags... the vehicle was unoccupied and returned registered to
Jeanne Slade."

civilian directed rescue workers to the body site.[142]
Hodakievic was off duty[143] and dressed in civilian clothes.[144]
Hodakievic had viewed the body by the time Lieutenant Gavin
arrived at about 6:24 p.m.[145]

Because we have been unable to conclusively determine
when Fornshill and Hodakievic arrived in the park, the
official version of their arrivals is used in the timetable
below.

Proof of who was with the body, and when, is an
important aspect of the case. The body site is in a
secluded area of the park and cannot be seen from the
direction of the parking lot. When the timetable is
compared to witness accounts of the state of the body, it

---

[142]   Exhibit 77, Handwritten notes of FBI interview of
Firefighter James Iacone, March 11, 1994: "Directed by citizen"
Exhibit 78, Report of FBI interview of Firefighter James Iacone,
March 11, 1994:  "Iacone now believes that the crew of Medic 1
was directed by a citizen to a body, later identified as that of
Foster, but he knows no details regarding this citizen such as
whether the person was a male or female."

[143]   Exhibit 81, Report of FBI interview of Investigator
Christine Hodakievic, May 2, 1994:  "Officer Hodakievic advised
that shortly after 6:00 p.m. on July 20, 1993, while in an off-
duty status and while traveling North on the George Washington
Memorial Parkway in her personal vehicle, heard on her police
radio that a dead body had been located at Fort Marcy Park."

[144]   Exhibit 79, Deposition of Park Police Officer Kevin
        Fornshill, July 12, 1994:  A.  I went back to the parking
        lot.  There was a lot of confusion with other cars coming
        in.  My car, Officer Ferstl's car, the sergeant's car, and
        about that time the investigators would be rolling in.  I
        believe Officer Hodakievic, who at the time was a
        plainclothes investigator.  Q. And he's an investigator?
        A.  She, Christine, she was an investigator at the time.
        She's back in uniform now.  She's at the same station you
        can reach me at.

Exhibit 80, Handwritten notes of FBI interview of Lieutenant
Patrick Gavin, April 28, 1994: "Christine Hodakievic -
investigator off duty - P/C [plainclothes]"

[145]   Exhibit 80, Handwritten notes of FBI interview of
Lieutenant Patrick Gavin, April 28, 1994:  "Inv. Christine
Hodakievic met him in Pk [parking] lot, took up to scene, she'd
been there."

proves that the body was tampered with, and by whom. These issues are analyzed later in this paper. In the balance of this paper, in discussing those issues which relate to the state of the body at the park, the witness accounts are presented in the following order:

Civilian Dale
Officer Kevin Fornshill
Firefighter Todd Hall
Paramedic George Gonzalez
Paramedic Richard Arthur
Firefighter Ralph Pisani
Firefighter Lt. James Iacone
Firefighter Jennifer Wacha
Officer Franz Ferstl
Investigator Christine Hodakievic
Lieutenant Patrick Gavin
Investigator John Rolla
Investigator Cheryl Braun
Investigator Renee Abt
Evidence Technician Peter Simonello
Dr. Donald Haut
Firefighter Corey Ashford
Firefighter Roger Harrison

There will be no review of the records of the accounts of Sergeant Robert Edwards, Officer William Watson, or the unidentified Intern with him, because there are no public reports of interviews with them.

The times used below are estimated, except where obtained from radio dispatches and electronic logs. The time to walk from the parking lot to the body site is approximately 1 minute, 50 seconds.

Approximately 700 feet from the parking lot to the body site, about a two-minute walk at a brisk pace.

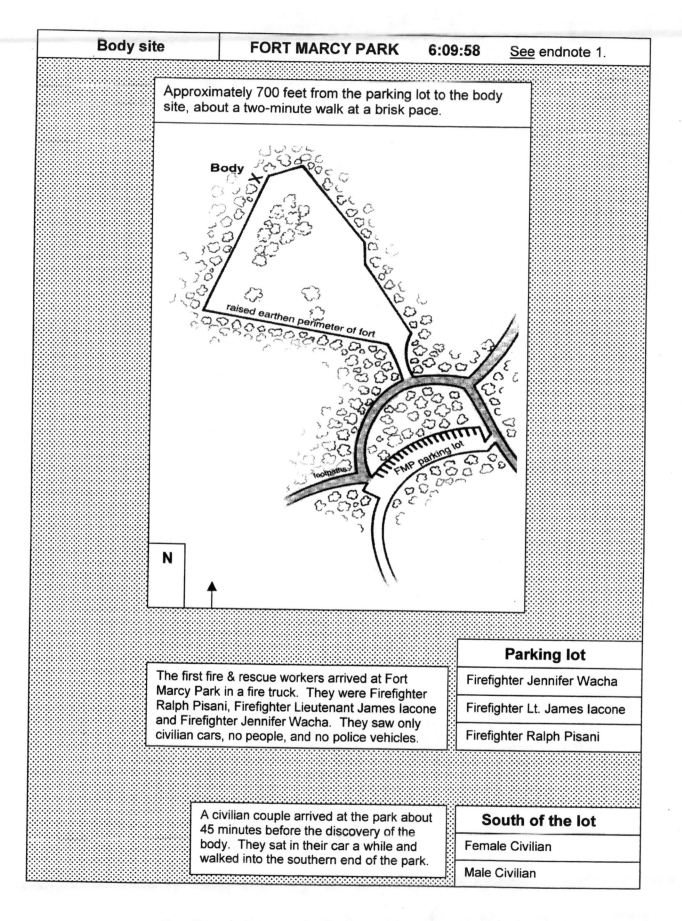

The first fire & rescue workers arrived at Fort Marcy Park in a fire truck. They were Firefighter Ralph Pisani, Firefighter Lieutenant James Iacone and Firefighter Jennifer Wacha. They saw only civilian cars, no people, and no police vehicles.

| **Parking lot** |
| --- |
| Firefighter Jennifer Wacha |
| Firefighter Lt. James Iacone |
| Firefighter Ralph Pisani |

A civilian couple arrived at the park about 45 minutes before the discovery of the body. They sat in their car a while and walked into the southern end of the park.

| **South of the lot** |
| --- |
| Female Civilian |
| Male Civilian |

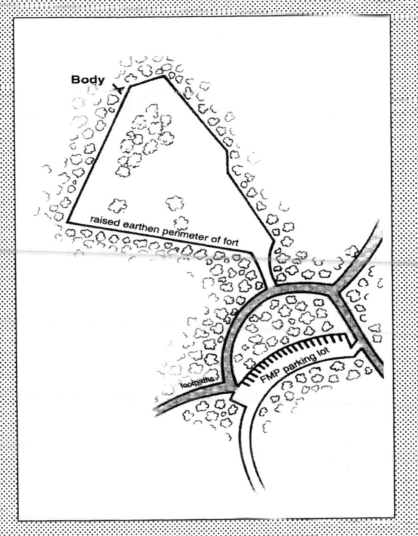

The second group of fire & rescue workers, paramedics Richard Arthur and George Gonzalez and firefighter Todd Hall arrived in an ambulance, joining firefighters Ralph Pisani, James Iacone and Jennifer Wacha in the lot. When these six rescue workers arrived, they saw at least two cars in the lot in addition to a Honda with Arkansas plates. One car was parked, unoccupied, engine running. One of these cars and its driver was not identified in any police reports. The six fire & rescue workers decided to search for the reported dead body by splitting up into two groups. One group of four searchers decided to go Southeast into the woods toward the couple. The group of two, Hall and Gonzalez, headed the opposite way, toward the fort and body.

### Parking lot

| |
| --- |
| Firefighter Todd Hall |
| Paramedic GeorgeGonzalez |
| Paramedic Richard Arthur |
| Firefighter Ralph Pisani |
| Firefighter Lt. James Iacone |
| Firefighter Jennifer Wacha |

| Female Civilian | Male Civilian | **South of the lot** |
| --- | --- | --- |

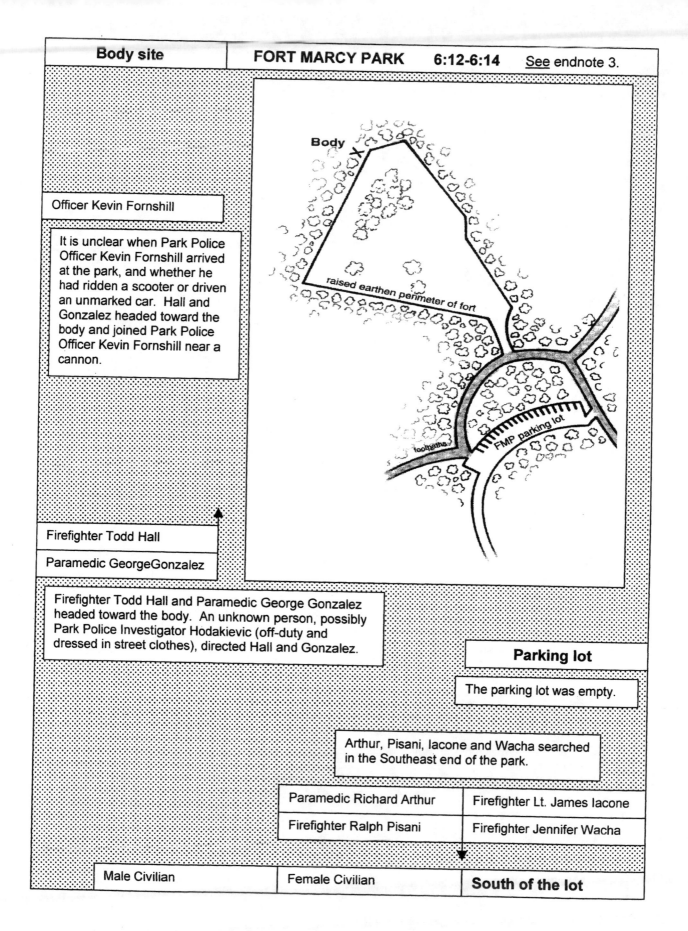

| Body site | FORT MARCY PARK | 6:12-6:14 | <u>See</u> endnote 3. |

**Body**

raised earthen perimeter of fort

footpaths

FMP parking lot

Officer Kevin Fornshill

It is unclear when Park Police Officer Kevin Fornshill arrived at the park, and whether he had ridden a scooter or driven an unmarked car. Hall and Gonzalez headed toward the body and joined Park Police Officer Kevin Fornshill near a cannon.

Firefighter Todd Hall

Paramedic GeorgeGonzalez

Firefighter Todd Hall and Paramedic George Gonzalez headed toward the body. An unknown person, possibly Park Police Investigator Hodakievic (off-duty and dressed in street clothes), directed Hall and Gonzalez.

**Parking lot**

The parking lot was empty.

Arthur, Pisani, Iacone and Wacha searched in the Southeast end of the park.

| Paramedic Richard Arthur | Firefighter Lt. James Iacone |
| Firefighter Ralph Pisani | Firefighter Jennifer Wacha |

| Male Civilian | Female Civilian | **South of the lot** |

| Body site | FORT MARCY PARK   6: 14:32-6:15   See endnote 4. |
|---|---|

Officer Kevin Fornshill

Firefighter Todd Hall

Paramedic GeorgeGonzalez

At Officer Fornshill's direction, Hall and Gonzalez searched another area of the park. Fornshill, searching alone, found Mr. Foster's body. He called Hall and Gonzalez over to the body, who radioed the other team of searchers. Hall immediately noticed a gun in Mr. Foster's hand and told Fornshill. Fornshill radioed to the Park Police who were en route to the park that the death was an "apparent suicide." At the body, Hall "heard someone else in the woods [and] subsequently saw something red moving in the woods."

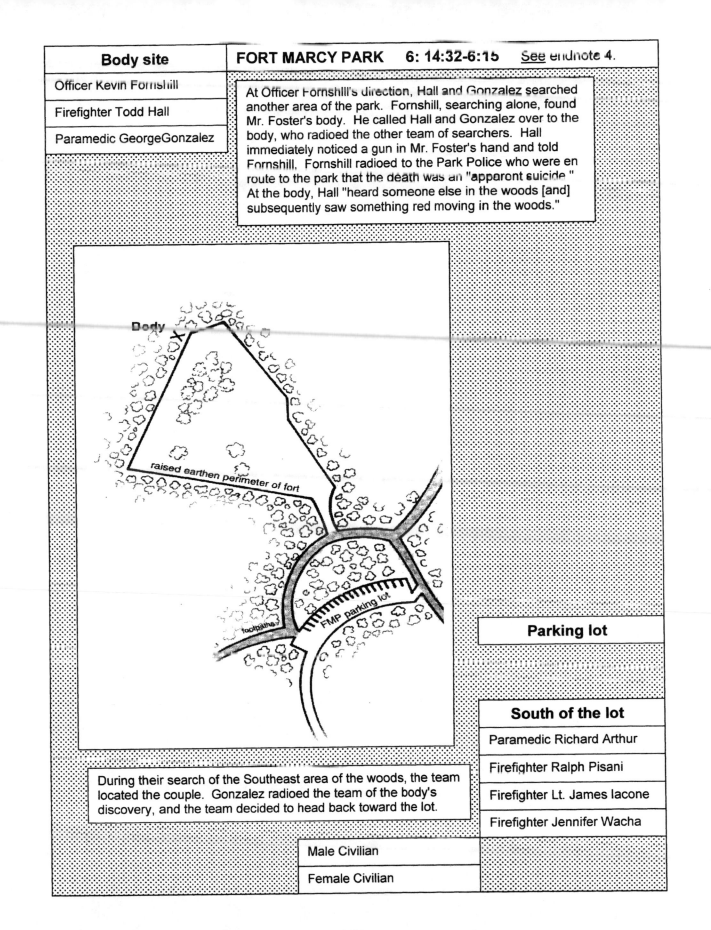

During their search of the Southeast area of the woods, the team located the couple. Gonzalez radioed the team of the body's discovery, and the team decided to head back toward the lot.

**Parking lot**

**South of the lot**

Paramedic Richard Arthur

Firefighter Ralph Pisani

Firefighter Lt. James Iacone

Firefighter Jennifer Wacha

Male Civilian

Female Civilian

| Body site |
| --- |
| Firefighter Todd Hall |
| Paramedic GeorgeGonzalez |
| Officer Kevin Fornshill |

## FORT MARCY PARK    6: 16    <u>See</u> endnote 5.

Gonzalez and Hall observed the scene.   They saw blood on the right side of Mr. Foster's shirt.  Fornshill continued communicating by radio with investigators who were driving to the park.

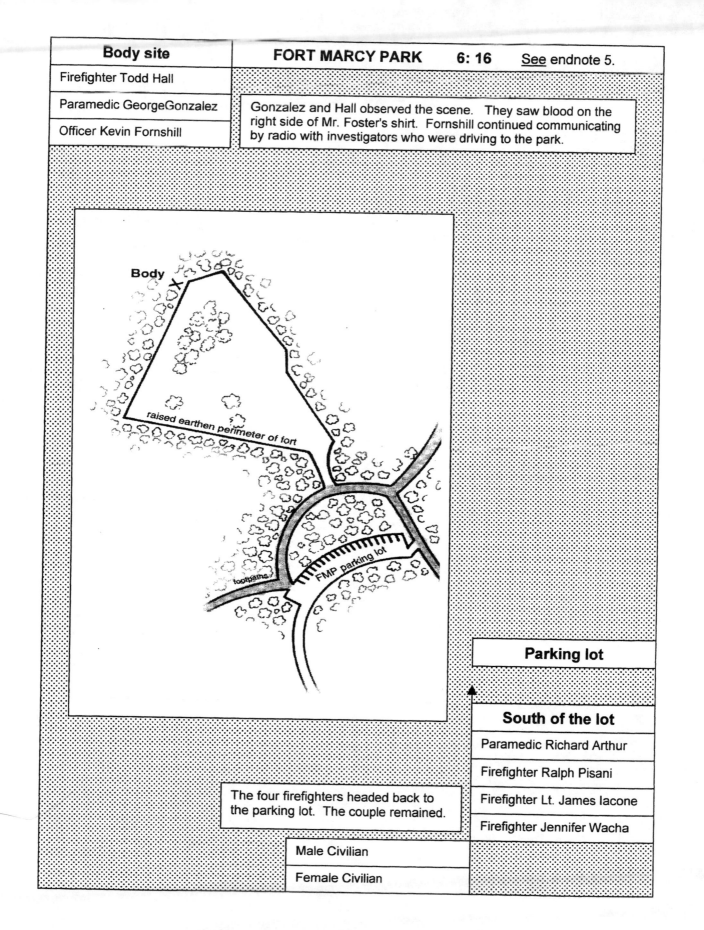

Body X

raised earthen perimeter of fort

FMP parking lot

footpaths

### Parking lot

### South of the lot

| South of the lot |
| --- |
| Paramedic Richard Arthur |
| Firefighter Ralph Pisani |
| Firefighter Lt. James Iacone |
| Firefighter Jennifer Wacha |

The four firefighters headed back to the parking lot.  The couple remained.

| Male Civilian |
| --- |
| Female Civilian |

| Body site | FORT MARCY PARK 6: 17 See endnote C. |
|---|---|
| Officer Kevin Fornshill | During Paramedic Gonzalez's evaluation, he saw a gun in Mr. Foster's right hand. He concluded that Mr. Foster was obviously dead, had been for "two to four hours," and made no attempt at resuscitation. Because of the straight position of the body and the lack of blood, both Hall and Gonzalez concluded that the death appeared suspicious. Hall reportedly saw a female Park Police officer before leaving the site, possibly Hodakievic. |
| Firefighter Todd Hall | |
| Paramedic GeorgeGonzalez | |

**Body**

raised earthen perimeter of fort

FMP parking lot

footpaths

**Parking lot**

Paramedic Richard Arthur

Firefighter Ralph Pisani

Firefighter Lt. James Iacone

Firefighter Jennifer Wacha

Officer Franz Ferstl

Officer Franz Ferstl, who had received the first call to respond to the park, reached the parking lot and headed up to the body site.

**South of the lot**

Male Civilian

Female Civilian

| Body site | FORT MARCY PARK | 6: 18 | <u>See</u> endnote 7. |
|---|---|---|---|

**Body site**

Officer Kevin Fornshill

Officer Franz Ferstl

Firefighter Todd Hall

Paramedic GeorgeGonzalez

Hall and Gonzalez decided to return to the parking lot. Officer Ferstl arrived at the body and observed the scene.

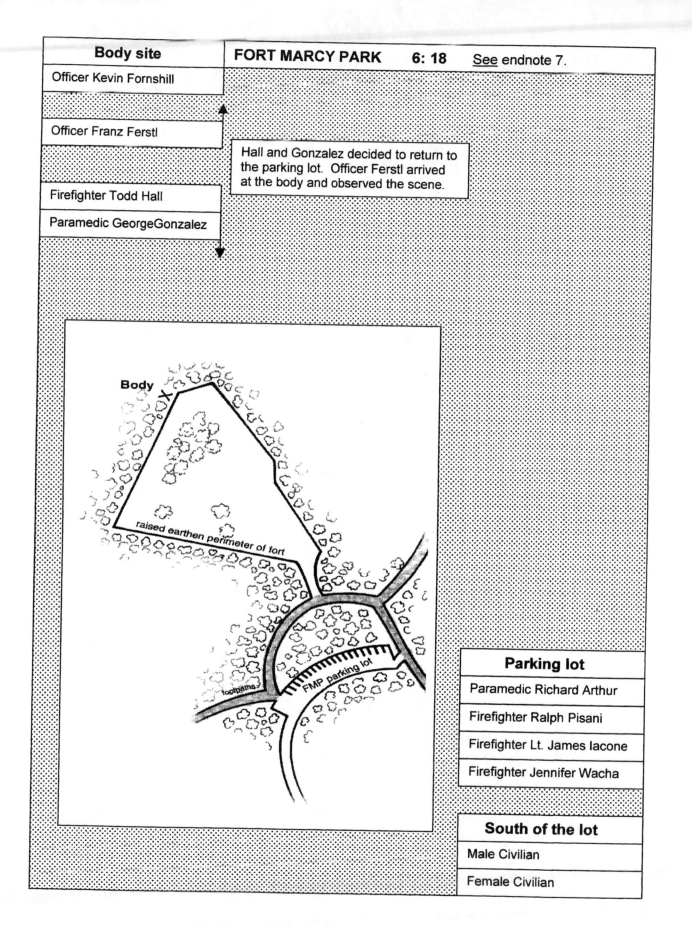

**Body**

raised earthen perimeter of fort

footpaths

FMP parking lot

### Parking lot

Paramedic Richard Arthur

Firefighter Ralph Pisani

Firefighter Lt. James Iacone

Firefighter Jennifer Wacha

### South of the lot

Male Civilian

Female Civilian

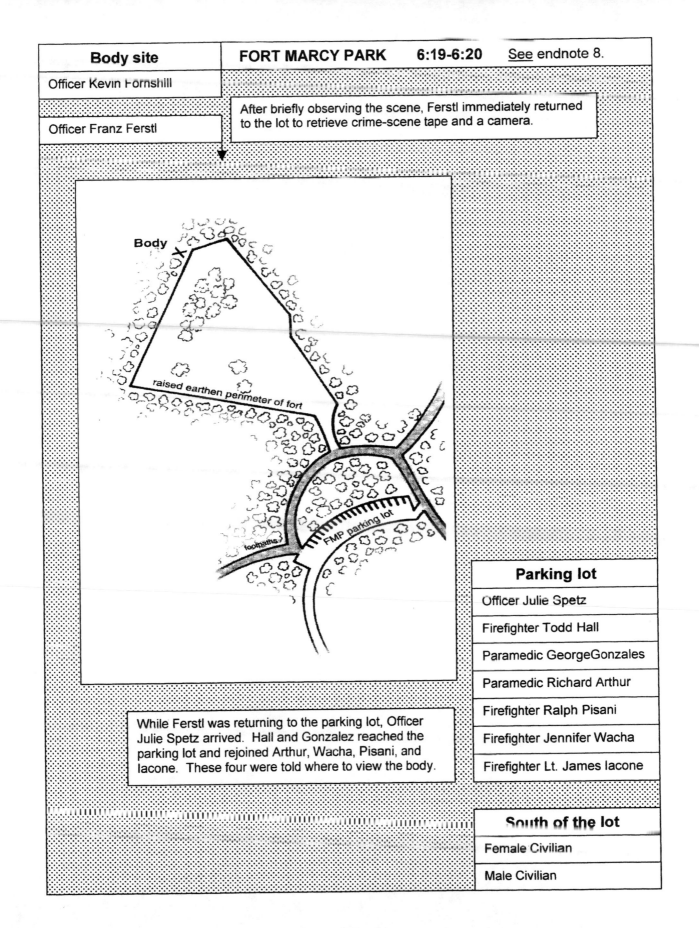

| Body site | FORT MARCY PARK | 6:19-6:20 | See endnote 8. |

Officer Kevin Fornshill

Officer Franz Ferstl

After briefly observing the scene, Ferstl immediately returned to the lot to retrieve crime-scene tape and a camera.

Body
X

raised earthen perimeter of fort

footpaths

FMP parking lot

While Ferstl was returning to the parking lot, Officer Julie Spetz arrived. Hall and Gonzalez reached the parking lot and rejoined Arthur, Wacha, Pisani, and Iacone. These four were told where to view the body.

### Parking lot

Officer Julie Spetz

Firefighter Todd Hall

Paramedic GeorgeGonzales

Paramedic Richard Arthur

Firefighter Ralph Pisani

Firefighter Jennifer Wacha

Firefighter Lt. James Iacone

### South of the lot

Female Civilian

Male Civilian

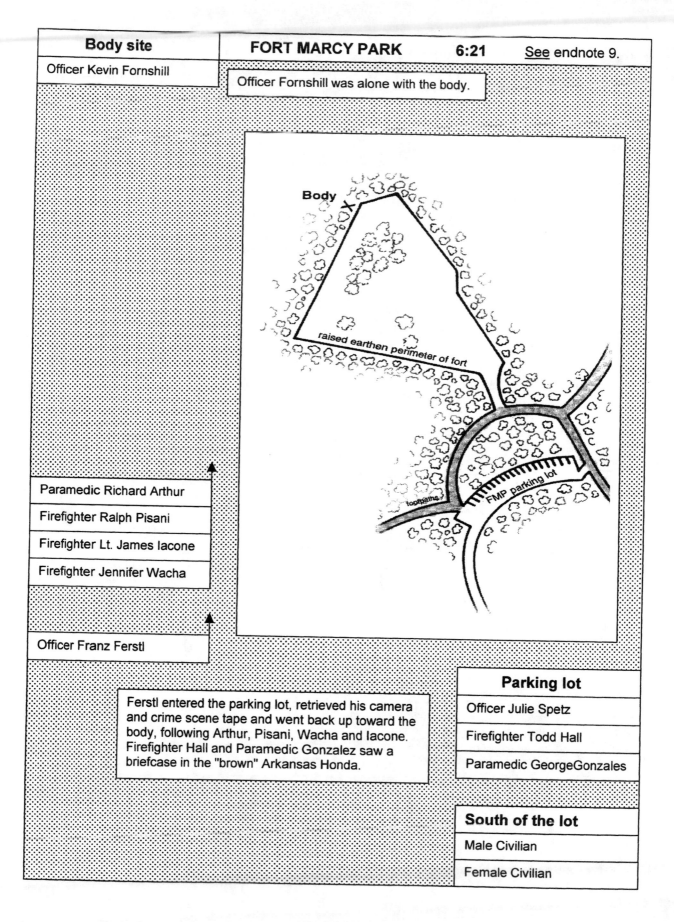

**Body site**

Officer Kevin Fornshill

**FORT MARCY PARK**     6:21     <u>See</u> endnote 9.

Officer Fornshill was alone with the body.

Body

X

raised earthen perimeter of fort

FMP parking lot

top paths

Paramedic Richard Arthur

Firefighter Ralph Pisani

Firefighter Lt. James Iacone

Firefighter Jennifer Wacha

Officer Franz Ferstl

Ferstl entered the parking lot, retrieved his camera and crime scene tape and went back up toward the body, following Arthur, Pisani, Wacha and Iacone. Firefighter Hall and Paramedic Gonzalez saw a briefcase in the "brown" Arkansas Honda.

**Parking lot**

Officer Julie Spetz

Firefighter Todd Hall

Paramedic GeorgeGonzales

**South of the lot**

Male Civilian

Female Civilian

| Body site | **FORT MARCY PARK**    6:22 | See endnote 10. |
|---|---|---|

**Body site**

Officer Kevin Fornshill

Paramedic Richard Arthur

Firefighter Ralph Pisani

Firefighter Lt. James Iacone

Firefighter Jennifer Wacha

Officer Franz Ferstl

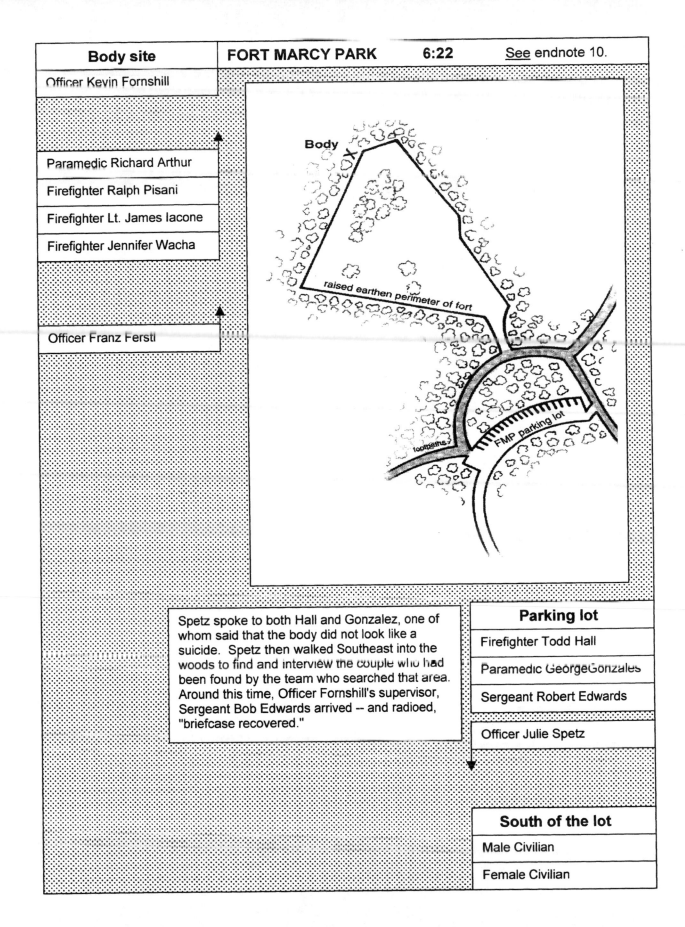

Body

raised earthen perimeter of fort

footpaths

FMP parking lot

Spetz spoke to both Hall and Gonzalez, one of whom said that the body did not look like a suicide. Spetz then walked Southeast into the woods to find and interview the couple who had been found by the team who searched that area. Around this time, Officer Fornshill's supervisor, Sergeant Bob Edwards arrived -- and radioed, "briefcase recovered."

**Parking lot**

Firefighter Todd Hall

Paramedic George Gonzales

Sergeant Robert Edwards

Officer Julie Spetz

**South of the lot**

Male Civilian

Female Civilian

| Body site | FORT MARCY PARK    6:23    See endnote 11. |
|---|---|

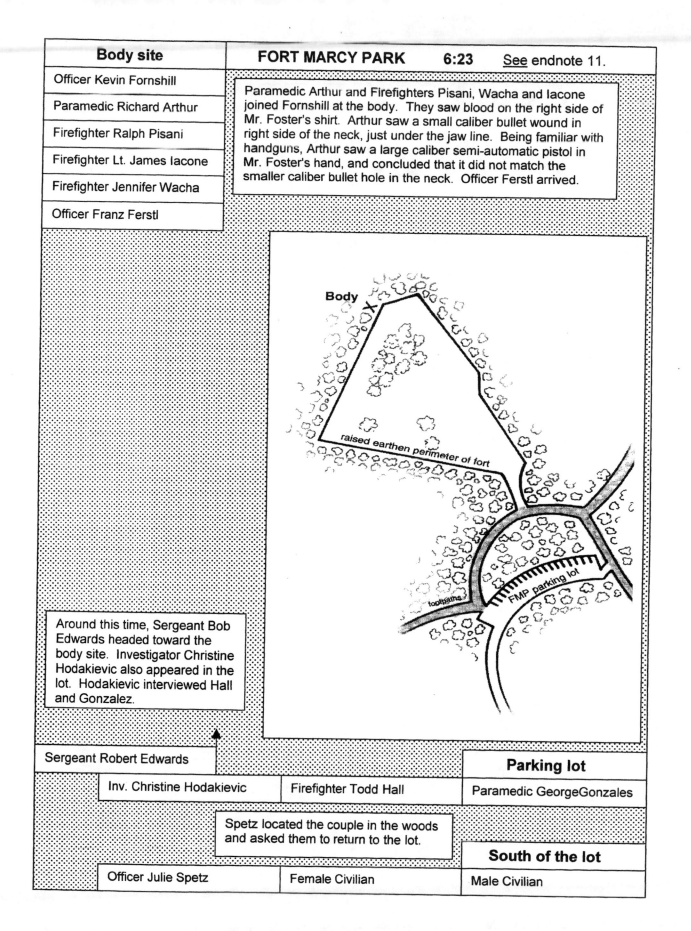

**Body site**

Officer Kevin Fornshill

Paramedic Richard Arthur

Firefighter Ralph Pisani

Firefighter Lt. James Iacone

Firefighter Jennifer Wacha

Officer Franz Ferstl

Paramedic Arthur and Firefighters Pisani, Wacha and Iacone joined Fornshill at the body. They saw blood on the right side of Mr. Foster's shirt. Arthur saw a small caliber bullet wound in right side of the neck, just under the jaw line. Being familiar with handguns, Arthur saw a large caliber semi-automatic pistol in Mr. Foster's hand, and concluded that it did not match the smaller caliber bullet hole in the neck. Officer Ferstl arrived.

Body

raised earthen perimeter of fort

footpaths

FMP parking lot

Around this time, Sergeant Bob Edwards headed toward the body site. Investigator Christine Hodakievic also appeared in the lot. Hodakievic interviewed Hall and Gonzalez.

Sergeant Robert Edwards

**Parking lot**

| Inv. Christine Hodakievic | Firefighter Todd Hall | Paramedic GeorgeGonzales |
|---|---|---|

Spetz located the couple in the woods and asked them to return to the lot.

**South of the lot**

| Officer Julie Spetz | Female Civilian | Male Civilian |
|---|---|---|

| **Body site** | **FORT MARCY PARK** 6:24 | See endnote 12. |
|---|---|---|

When Officer Ferstl returned and began to tape off the crime scene, Officer Fornshill left the body site. Fornshill had been at the body site for about 10 minutes. He maintained that he never saw the gun, even after straining to see it. Officer Ferstl finished taping off the body site and began photographing the body. Arthur and his team did not see an exit wound or a bloody mess. Officially, there was a half-dollar size hole out of the top of Mr. Foster's head. The blood these fire & rescue workers saw on the right side of the shirt was dry.

Officer Franz Ferstl

Paramedic Richard Arthur

Firefighter Ralph Pisani

Firefighter Lt. James Iacone

Firefighter Jennifer Wacha

Officer Kevin Fornshill

Sergeant Robert Edwards

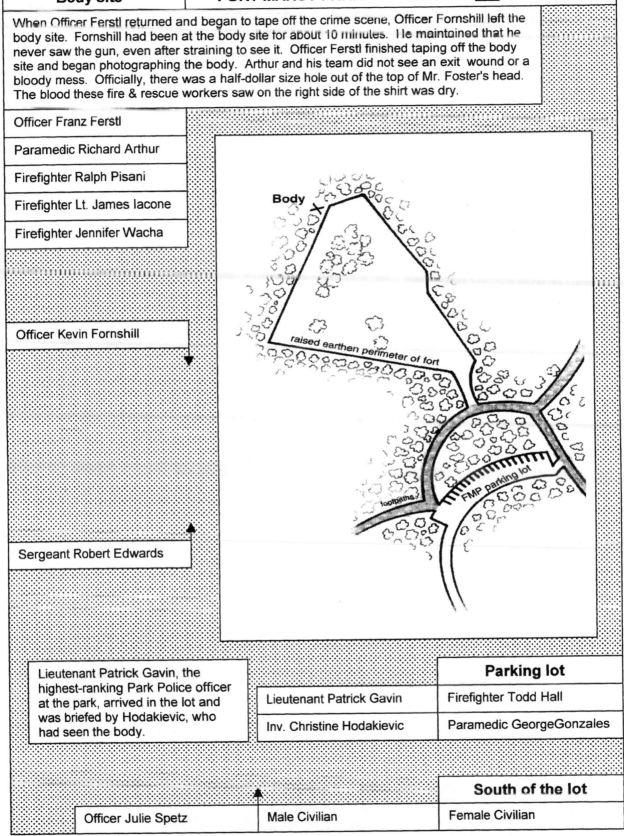

Lieutenant Patrick Gavin, the highest-ranking Park Police officer at the park, arrived in the lot and was briefed by Hodakievic, who had seen the body.

| | **Parking lot** |
|---|---|
| Lieutenant Patrick Gavin | Firefighter Todd Hall |
| Inv. Christine Hodakievic | Paramedic GeorgeGonzales |

| | | **South of the lot** |
|---|---|---|
| Officer Julie Spetz | Male Civilian | Female Civilian |

| Body site | FORT MARCY PARK    6:25    <u>See endnote 13.</u> |
|---|---|

**Officer Franz Ferstl**

Officer Ferstl continued photographing the body with the semi-automatic pistol in the hand. He saw a small amount of "not fresh" blood around the mouth. Arthur and his group left the body, returning to the lot.

**Paramedic Richard Arthur**

**Firefighter Ralph Pisani**

**Firefighter Lt. James Iacone**

**Firefighter Jennifer Wacha**

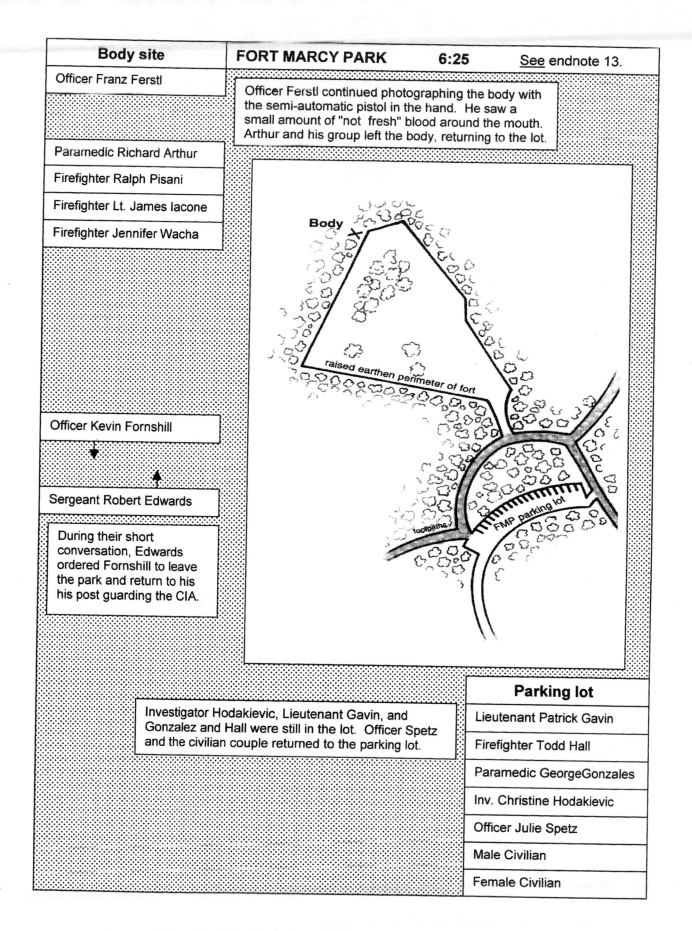

Body
X

raised earthen perimeter of fort

footpaths

FMP parking lot

**Officer Kevin Fornshill**

↓
↑

**Sergeant Robert Edwards**

During their short conversation, Edwards ordered Fornshill to leave the park and return to his his post guarding the CIA.

Investigator Hodakievic, Lieutenant Gavin, and Gonzalez and Hall were still in the lot. Officer Spetz and the civilian couple returned to the parking lot.

### Parking lot

Lieutenant Patrick Gavin

Firefighter Todd Hall

Paramedic GeorgeGonzales

Inv. Christine Hodakievic

Officer Julie Spetz

Male Civilian

Female Civilian

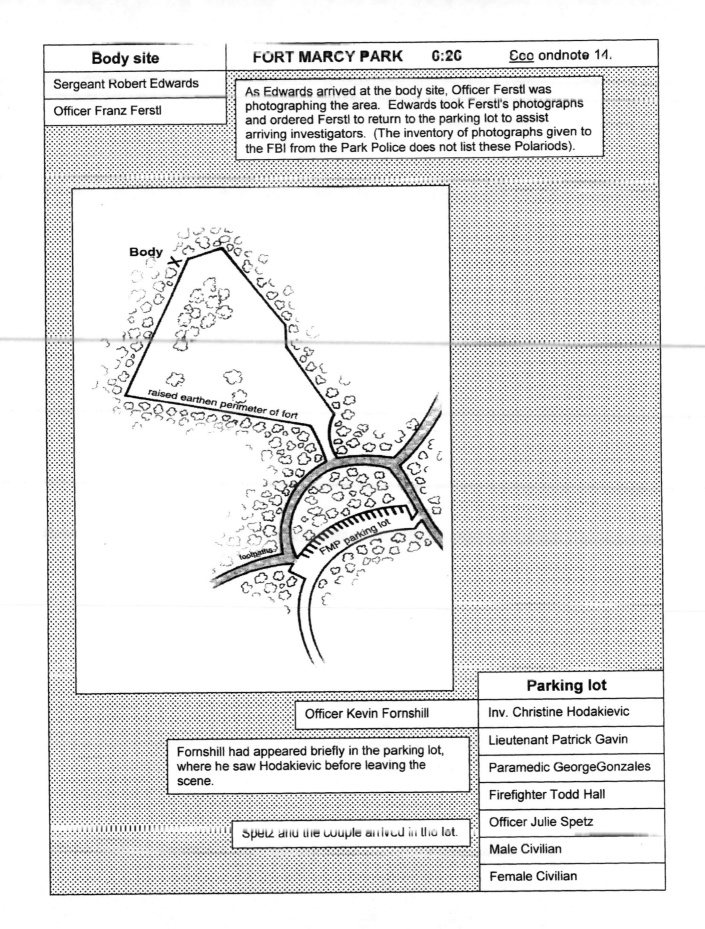

**Body site**

Sergeant Robert Edwards

Officer Franz Ferstl

As Edwards arrived at the body site, Officer Ferstl was photographing the area. Edwards took Ferstl's photographs and ordered Ferstl to return to the parking lot to assist arriving investigators. (The inventory of photographs given to the FBI from the Park Police does not list these Polariods).

Body

raised earthen perimeter of fort

footpaths

FMP parking lot

Officer Kevin Fornshill

Fornshill had appeared briefly in the parking lot, where he saw Hodakievic before leaving the scene.

Spetz and the couple arrived in the lot.

**Parking lot**

Inv. Christine Hodakievic

Lieutenant Patrick Gavin

Paramedic GeorgeGonzales

Firefighter Todd Hall

Officer Julie Spetz

Male Civilian

Female Civilian

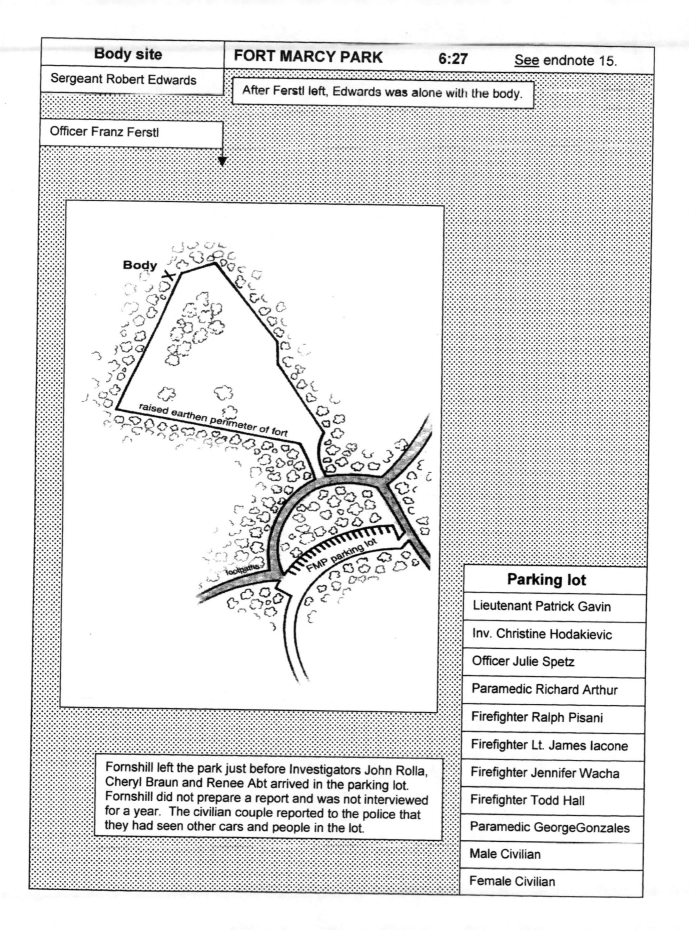

| | |
|---|---|
| **Body site** | **FORT MARCY PARK**　　6:27　　<u>See</u> endnote 15. |

Sergeant Robert Edwards

After Ferstl left, Edwards was alone with the body.

Officer Franz Ferstl

**Body** ✗

raised earthen perimeter of fort

footpaths

FMP parking lot

Fornshill left the park just before Investigators John Rolla, Cheryl Braun and Renee Abt arrived in the parking lot. Fornshill did not prepare a report and was not interviewed for a year. The civilian couple reported to the police that they had seen other cars and people in the lot.

### Parking lot

Lieutenant Patrick Gavin

Inv. Christine Hodakievic

Officer Julie Spetz

Paramedic Richard Arthur

Firefighter Ralph Pisani

Firefighter Lt. James Iacone

Firefighter Jennifer Wacha

Firefighter Todd Hall

Paramedic GeorgeGonzales

Male Civilian

Female Civilian

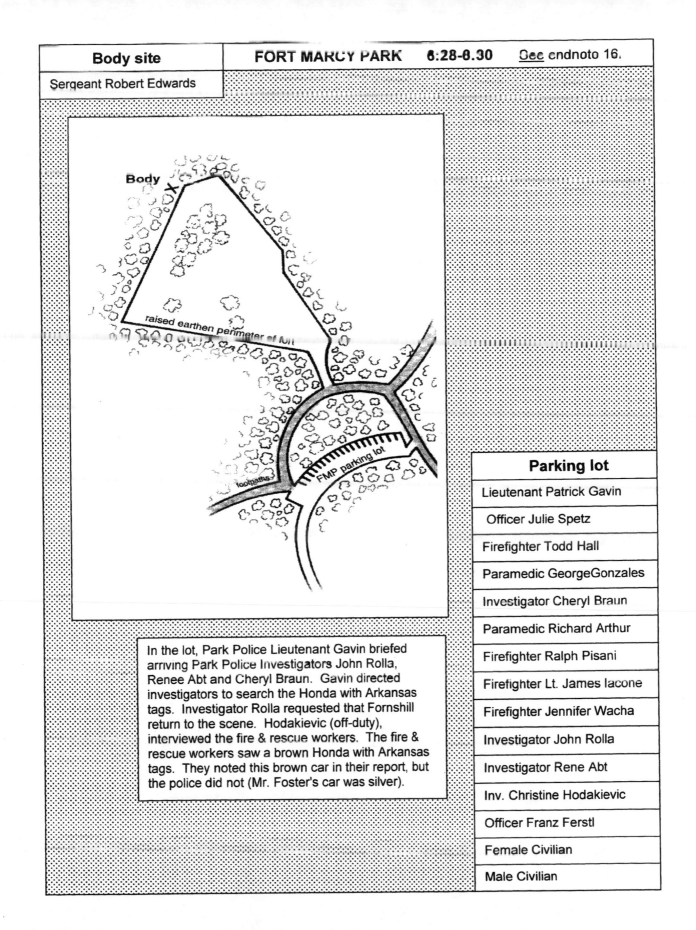

| Body site | FORT MARCY PARK 6:28-8.30 | See endnote 16. |

**Sergeant Robert Edwards**

Body

X

raised earthen perimeter of fort

footpaths

FMP parking lot

In the lot, Park Police Lieutenant Gavin briefed arriving Park Police Investigators John Rolla, Renee Abt and Cheryl Braun. Gavin directed investigators to search the Honda with Arkansas tags. Investigator Rolla requested that Fornshill return to the scene. Hodakievic (off-duty), interviewed the fire & rescue workers. The fire & rescue workers saw a brown Honda with Arkansas tags. They noted this brown car in their report, but the police did not (Mr. Foster's car was silver).

## Parking lot

| Parking lot |
|---|
| Lieutenant Patrick Gavin |
| Officer Julie Spetz |
| Firefighter Todd Hall |
| Paramedic GeorgeGonzales |
| Investigator Cheryl Braun |
| Paramedic Richard Arthur |
| Firefighter Ralph Pisani |
| Firefighter Lt. James Iacone |
| Firefighter Jennifer Wacha |
| Investigator John Rolla |
| Investigator Rene Abt |
| Inv. Christine Hodakievic |
| Officer Franz Ferstl |
| Female Civilian |
| Male Civilian |

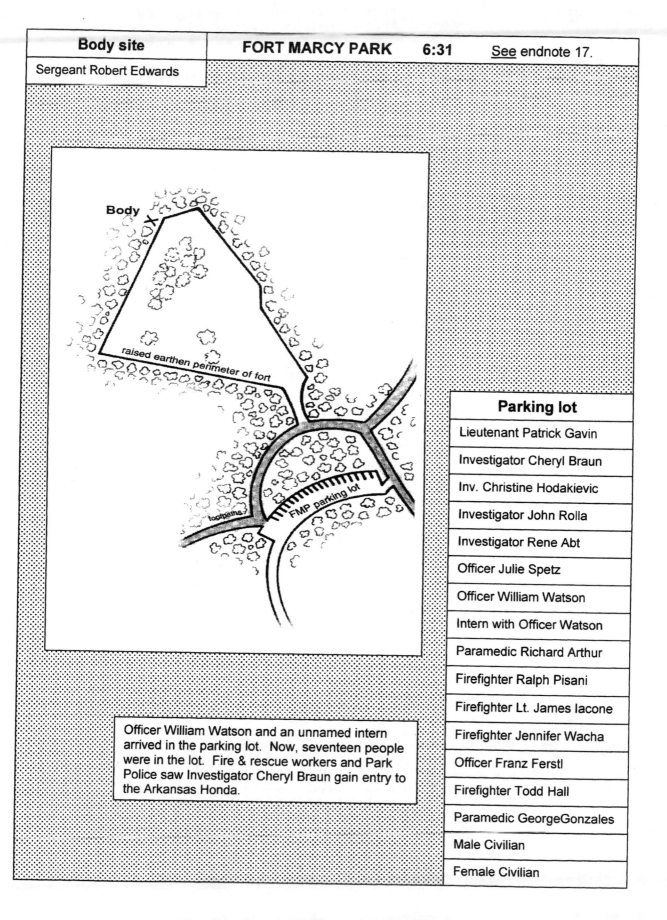

**Body site**     **FORT MARCY PARK**    **6:31**     <u>See</u> endnote 17.

Sergeant Robert Edwards

Body

raised earthen perimeter of fort

footpaths

FMP parking lot

Officer William Watson and an unnamed intern arrived in the parking lot. Now, seventeen people were in the lot. Fire & rescue workers and Park Police saw Investigator Cheryl Braun gain entry to the Arkansas Honda.

| Parking lot |
| --- |
| Lieutenant Patrick Gavin |
| Investigator Cheryl Braun |
| Inv. Christine Hodakievic |
| Investigator John Rolla |
| Investigator Rene Abt |
| Officer Julie Spetz |
| Officer William Watson |
| Intern with Officer Watson |
| Paramedic Richard Arthur |
| Firefighter Ralph Pisani |
| Firefighter Lt. James Iacone |
| Firefighter Jennifer Wacha |
| Officer Franz Ferstl |
| Firefighter Todd Hall |
| Paramedic GeorgeGonzales |
| Male Civilian |
| Female Civilian |

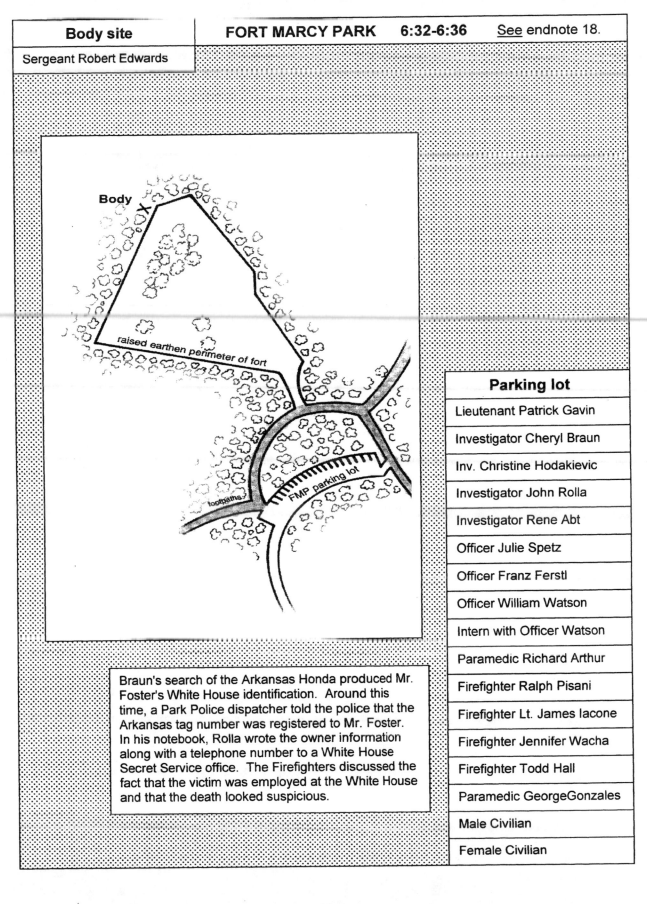

**Body site**

**FORT MARCY PARK**   6:32-6:36   <u>See</u> endnote 18.

Sergeant Robert Edwards

Body

raised earthen perimeter of fort

footpaths

FMP parking lot

Braun's search of the Arkansas Honda produced Mr. Foster's White House identification. Around this time, a Park Police dispatcher told the police that the Arkansas tag number was registered to Mr. Foster. In his notebook, Rolla wrote the owner information along with a telephone number to a White House Secret Service office. The Firefighters discussed the fact that the victim was employed at the White House and that the death looked suspicious.

| Parking lot |
| --- |
| Lieutenant Patrick Gavin |
| Investigator Cheryl Braun |
| Inv. Christine Hodakievic |
| Investigator John Rolla |
| Investigator Rene Abt |
| Officer Julie Spetz |
| Officer Franz Ferstl |
| Officer William Watson |
| Intern with Officer Watson |
| Paramedic Richard Arthur |
| Firefighter Ralph Pisani |
| Firefighter Lt. James Iacone |
| Firefighter Jennifer Wacha |
| Firefighter Todd Hall |
| Paramedic GeorgeGonzales |
| Male Civilian |
| Female Civilian |

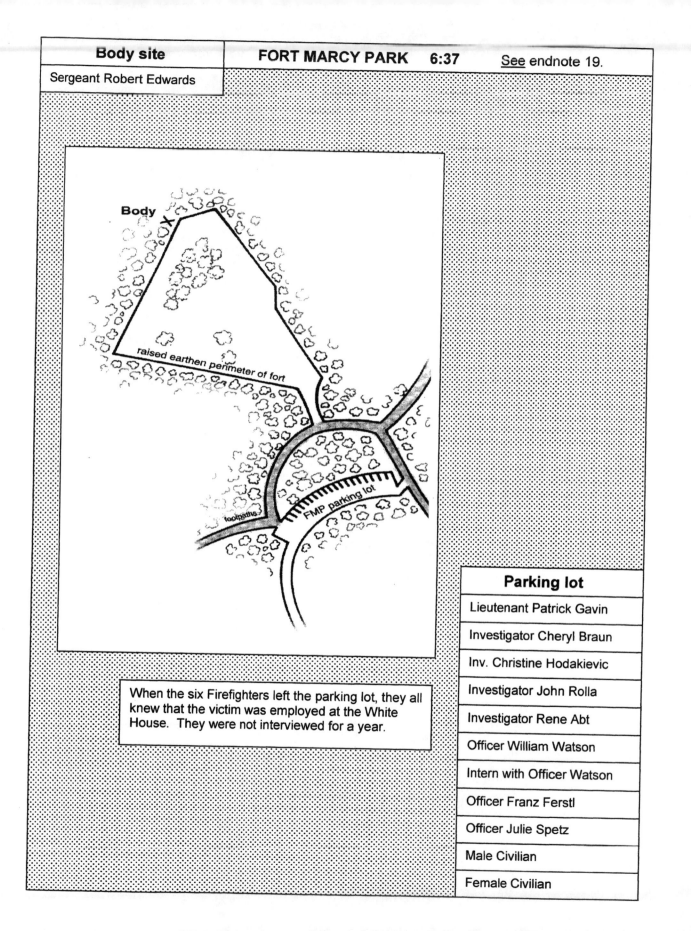

Sergeant Robert Edwards

Body

X

raised earthen perimeter of fort

footpaths

FMP parking lot

When the six Firefighters left the parking lot, they all knew that the victim was employed at the White House. They were not interviewed for a year.

**Parking lot**

Lieutenant Patrick Gavin

Investigator Cheryl Braun

Inv. Christine Hodakievic

Investigator John Rolla

Investigator Rene Abt

Officer William Watson

Intern with Officer Watson

Officer Franz Ferstl

Officer Julie Spetz

Male Civilian

Female Civilian

Sergeant Robert Edwards

Hodakievic directed Gavin to the body.

Inv. Christine Hodakievic

Lieutenant Patrick Gavin

### Parking lot

| Lieutenant Ronald Schmidt | Officer William Watson | Officer Julie Spetz |
|---|---|---|
| Investigator John Rolla | Intern with Officer Watson | Male Civilian |
| Officer Franz Ferstl | Investigator Cheryl Braun | Female Civilian |

In the parking lot, police questioned the civilian couple. Lieutenant Ronald Schmidt arrived, offered assistance, and Braun reportedly told him it was a suicide and that they "had not found the credentials yet." Schmidt left. While Rolla, Abt, and Braun awaited the arrival of Evidence Technician Peter Simonello, Braun finished questioning the civilian couple and Abt walked to the front gate to investigate the Mercedes that had broken down.

Investigator Rene Abt

| Body site | FORT MARCY PARK 6:42-6:43 <u>See</u> endnote 21. |
|---|---|

| Body site |
|---|
| Sergeant Robert Edwards |
| Lieutenant Patrick Gavin |
| Inv. Christine Hodakievic |

Gavin looked at the scene, saw blood trickling out of Mr. Foster's mouth, and thought he had been mugged. Because Ferstl remained in the lot, Hodakievic was the only witness who saw the body both before and after Edwards had been alone with it. Hodakievic's report addressed only the activities in the parking lot. When she later saw photographs of the body, she said the appearance of the body had changed from when she had seen it.

Sometime during the over 15 minutes that Sergeant Edwards was alone with the body, an untraceable .38 caliber black revolver replaced the automatic pistol in Mr. Foster's hand. Edwards also moved Mr. Foster's head to the right side, causing blood to flow out of the mouth onto his right side (and leaving a stain on the right cheek from its contact with the bloody right shoulder). This made it appear that the blood already on the right side, which had in fact drained from the right side neck wound, had come from the mouth. He thus concealed the existence of the neck wound (inconsistent with suicide), and made it appear as if Mr. Foster may have been shot in the mouth (consistent with suicide). The official explanation for the contact blood stain on the right cheek is that it had appeared when an unknown fire and rescue worker checked the pulse.

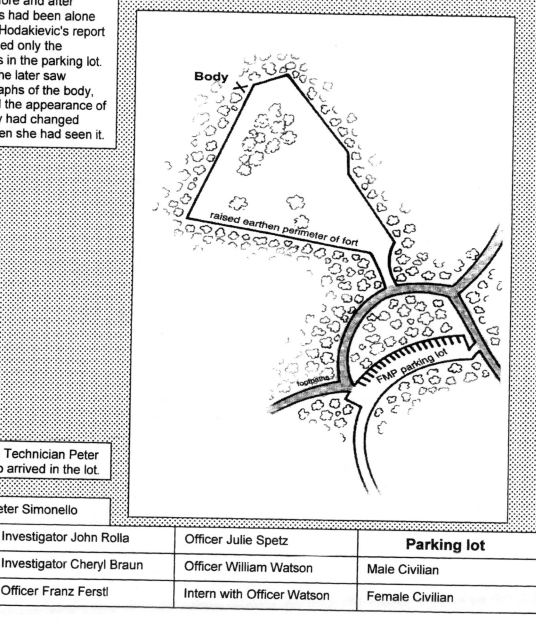

Evidence Technician Peter Simonello arrived in the lot.

Ev Tech Peter Simonello

| Investigator John Rolla | Officer Julie Spetz | **Parking lot** |
|---|---|---|
| Investigator Cheryl Braun | Officer William Watson | Male Civilian |
| Officer Franz Ferstl | Intern with Officer Watson | Female Civilian |

| Body site | FORT MARCY PARK | 6:44 | <u>See</u> endnote 22. |
|---|---|---|---|

| Body site |
|---|
| Sergeant Robert Edwards |
| Lieutenant Patrick Gavin |
| Inv. Christine Hodakievic |

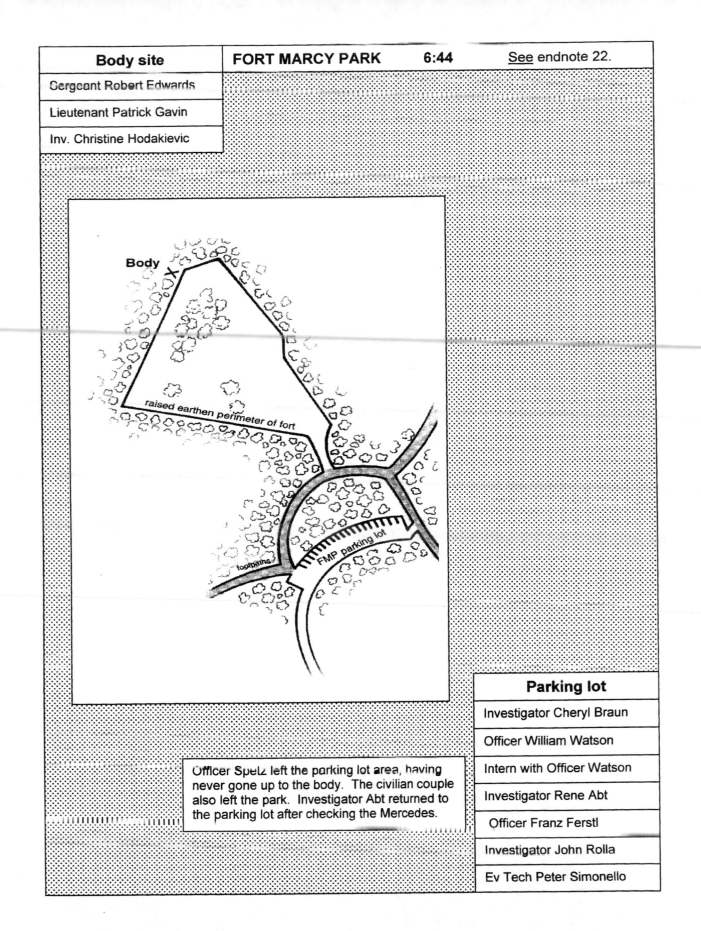

Body

raised earthen perimeter of fort

footpaths

FMP parking lot

| Parking lot |
|---|
| Investigator Cheryl Braun |
| Officer William Watson |
| Intern with Officer Watson |
| Investigator Rene Abt |
| Officer Franz Ferstl |
| Investigator John Rolla |
| Ev Tech Peter Simonello |

Officer Spetz left the parking lot area, having never gone up to the body. The civilian couple also left the park. Investigator Abt returned to the parking lot after checking the Mercedes.

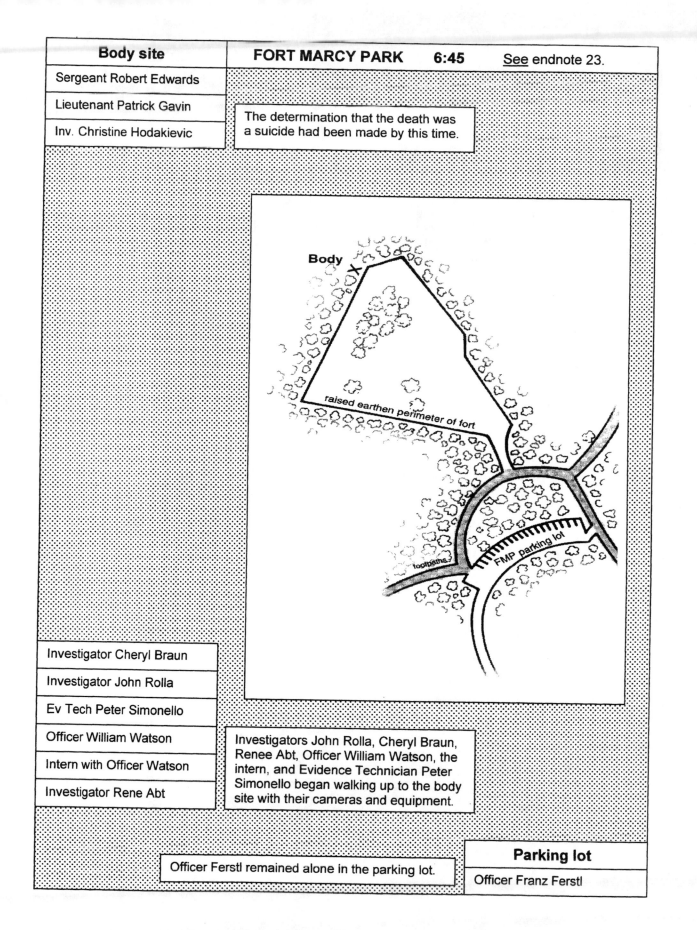

| **Body site** | **FORT MARCY PARK** 6:45 <u>See</u> endnote 23. |
| --- | --- |
| Sergeant Robert Edwards | |
| Lieutenant Patrick Gavin | |
| Inv. Christine Hodakievic | |

The determination that the death was a suicide had been made by this time.

Body
X

raised earthen perimeter of fort

FMP parking lot

footpaths

| Investigator Cheryl Braun |
| --- |
| Investigator John Rolla |
| Ev Tech Peter Simonello |
| Officer William Watson |
| Intern with Officer Watson |
| Investigator Rene Abt |

Investigators John Rolla, Cheryl Braun, Renee Abt, Officer William Watson, the intern, and Evidence Technician Peter Simonello began walking up to the body site with their cameras and equipment.

Officer Ferstl remained alone in the parking lot.

| **Parking lot** |
| --- |
| Officer Franz Ferstl |

| **Body site** |
| --- |
| Sergeant Robert Edwards |
| Lieutenant Patrick Gavin |
| Inv. Christine Hodakievic |
| Investigator Cheryl Braun |
| Investigator John Rolla |
| Ev Tech Peter Simonello |
| Investigator Rene Abt |
| Intern with Officer Watson |
| Officer William Watson |

When the investigators arrived at the body site, they observed Sergeant Edwards taking photographs. Braun was told that the death was a suicide. According to Rolla, although Gavin was the senior officer present, Braun and Hodakievic were in charge of the scene and did the "decision making." Rolla was in charge of the body scene. Rolla said it was his first "suicide" investigation.

Body

raised earthen perimeter of fort

footpaths

FMP parking lot

| **Parking lot** |
| --- |
| Officer Franz Ferstl |

| Body site |
|---|
| Sergeant Robert Edwards |
| Lieutenant Patrick Gavin |
| Intern with Officer Watson |
| Investigator Cheryl Braun |
| Inv. Christine Hodakievic |
| Ev Tech Peter Simonello |
| Investigator John Rolla |
| Investigator Rene Abt |
| Officer William Watson |

**FORT MARCY PARK**    6:49-6:53    <u>See</u> endnote 25.

The Investigators observed the wet, flowing, fresh blood, as well as the contact stain on Mr. Foster's face, all caused when Edwards moved the head. They also saw the older, dark, dried blood that the earlier witnesses had seen. There are no reports of anyone who saw the body having seen the official entrance or exit wounds. No one saw blood spatter, bone or brain matter. Rolla and Simonello photographed the scene, Rolla taking Polaroids (the "backside" photographs vanished) and Simonello using his 35-mm camera (reportedly "underexposed"). Those who recalled the gun in Mr. Foster's right hand described it as a revolver. Rolla emptied Mr. Foster's pockets, found nothing, and Braun, Hodakievic and Rolla realized that there were no keys in Mr. Foster's pockets.

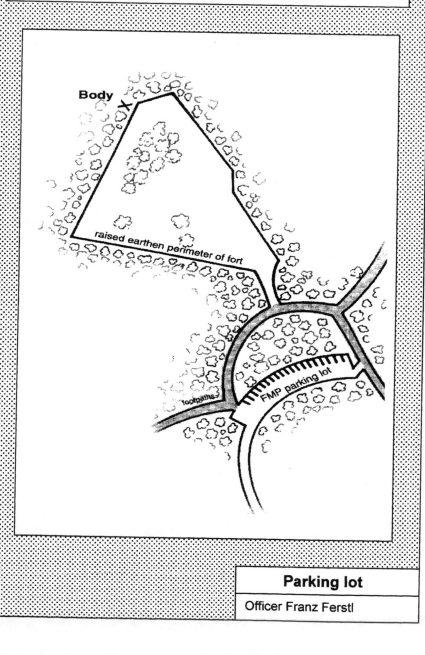

| Parking lot |
|---|
| Officer Franz Ferstl |

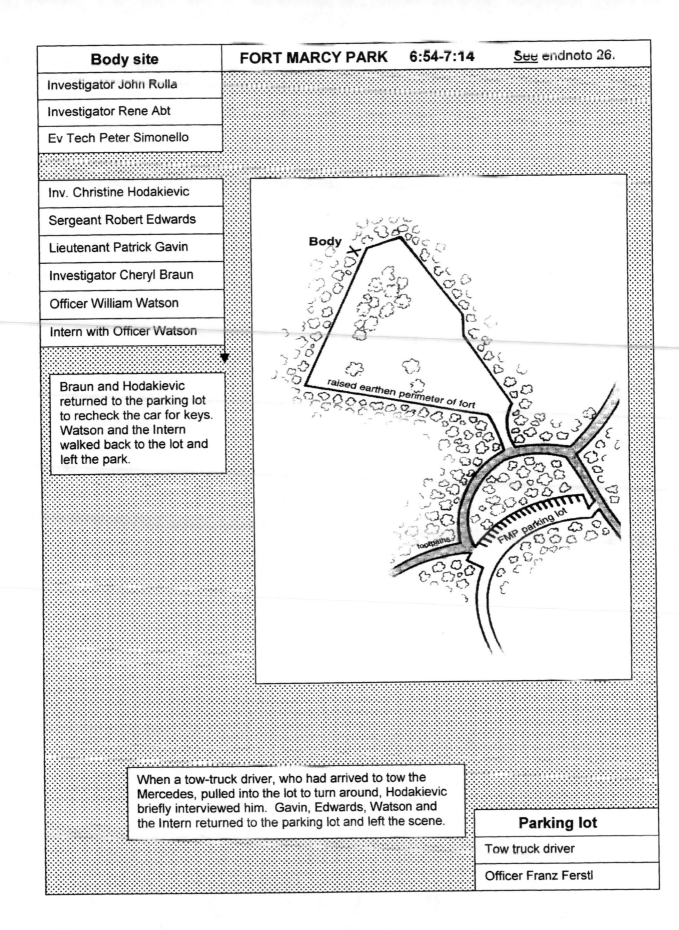

| Body site | FORT MARCY PARK | 6:54-7:14 | See endnote 26. |
|---|---|---|---|

**Body site**

Investigator John Rolla

Investigator Rene Abt

Ev Tech Peter Simonello

Inv. Christine Hodakievic

Sergeant Robert Edwards

Lieutenant Patrick Gavin

Investigator Cheryl Braun

Officer William Watson

Intern with Officer Watson

Braun and Hodakievic returned to the parking lot to recheck the car for keys. Watson and the Intern walked back to the lot and left the park.

**Body**

raised earthen perimeter of fort

footpaths

FMP parking lot

When a tow-truck driver, who had arrived to tow the Mercedes, pulled into the lot to turn around, Hodakievic briefly interviewed him. Gavin, Edwards, Watson and the Intern returned to the parking lot and left the scene.

**Parking lot**

Tow truck driver

Officer Franz Ferstl

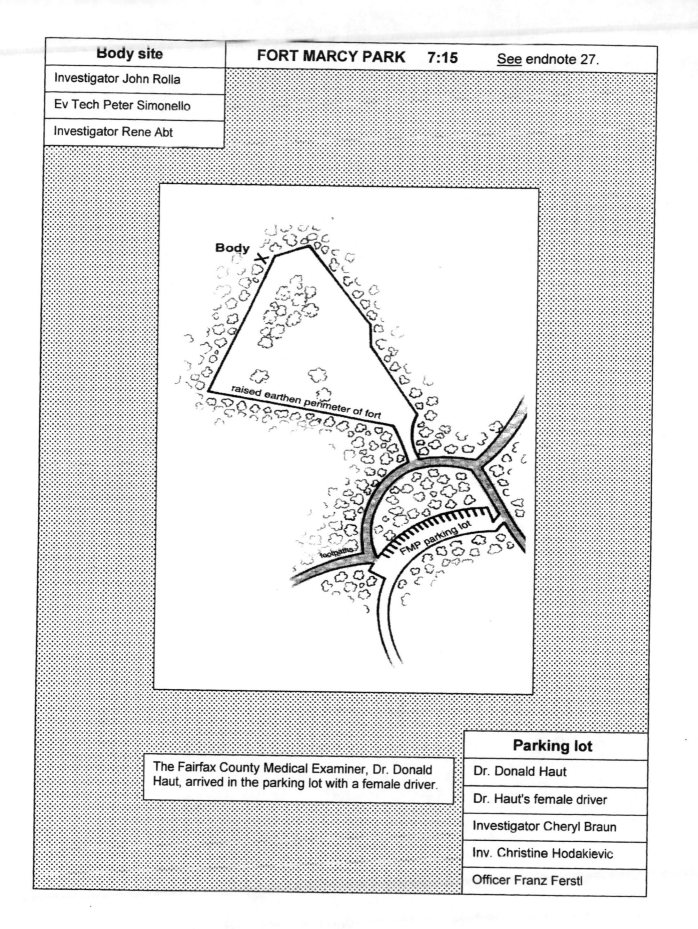

**Body site**

Investigator John Rolla

Ev Tech Peter Simonello

Investigator Rene Abt

**FORT MARCY PARK   7:15   See endnote 27.**

Body
X

raised earthen perimeter of fort

FMP parking lot

footpaths

The Fairfax County Medical Examiner, Dr. Donald Haut, arrived in the parking lot with a female driver.

**Parking lot**

Dr. Donald Haut

Dr. Haut's female driver

Investigator Cheryl Braun

Inv. Christine Hodakievic

Officer Franz Ferstl

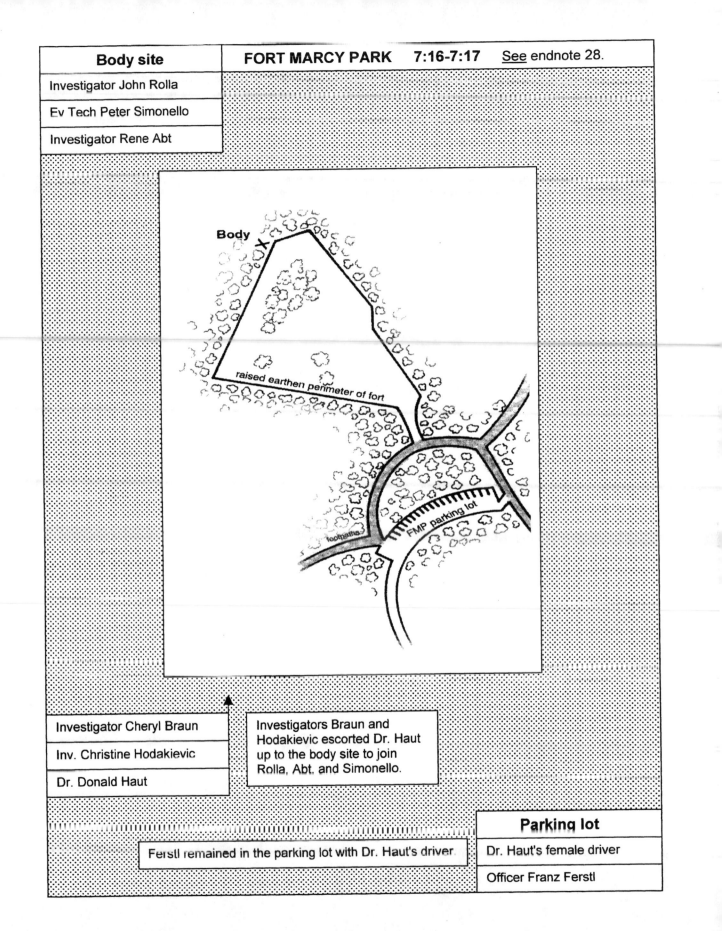

| Body site | FORT MARCY PARK   7:16-7:17   <u>See</u> endnote 28. |
| --- | --- |
| Investigator John Rolla | |
| Ev Tech Peter Simonello | |
| Investigator Rene Abt | |

Body

raised earthen perimeter of fort

FMP parking lot

footpaths

| Investigator Cheryl Braun |
| --- |
| Inv. Christine Hodakievic |
| Dr. Donald Haut |

Investigators Braun and Hodakievic escorted Dr. Haut up to the body site to join Rolla, Abt, and Simonello.

Ferstl remained in the parking lot with Dr. Haut's driver.

| Parking lot |
| --- |
| Dr. Haut's female driver |
| Officer Franz Ferstl |

| Body site | |
|---|---|
| **Body site** | **FORT MARCY PARK**    7:18-7:43    <u>See</u> endnote 29. |
| Investigator Cheryl Braun | |
| Ev Tech Peter Simonello | By the time Hodakievic, Braun, and Haut arrived at the body, Simonello had removed the black .38 revolver from Mr. Foster's right hand. Mr. Foster's fingerprints were not on the gun. Dr. Haut examined the body. He observed a small bullet hole in Mr. Foster's neck and noted it in his report. Rolla gloved up and probed the back of Mr. Foster's head. He felt a "mushy spot," but no exit wound. At 7:43, Dr. Haut pronounced the body dead and ordered it transported. Rolla later described to the FBI his inspection of the back of Mr. Foster's head, but that portion of the FBI agent's handwritten notes of that interview is redacted. |
| Inv. Christine Hodakievic | |
| Dr. Donald Haut | |
| Investigator Rene Abt | |
| Investigator John Rolla | |

Body

raised earthen perimeter of fort

footpaths

FMP parking lot

| **Parking lot** |
|---|
| Officer Franz Ferstl |
| Dr. Haut's female driver |

| Body site | FORT MARCY PARK 7:44 See endnote 30. |
|---|---|
| Investigator Rone Abt | |
| | |
| Investigator Cheryl Braun | Dr. Haut, Technician Simonello, and Investigators Rolla, Braun, and Hodakievic returned to the parking lot, leaving Investigator Renee Abt alone with the body. |
| Dr. Donald Haut | |
| Inv. Christine Hodakievic | |
| Ev Tech Peter Simonello | |
| Investigator John Rolla | |

Body

raised earthen perimeter of fort

footpaths

FMP parking lot

| Parking lot |
|---|
| Officer Franz Ferstl |
| Dr. Haut's female driver |

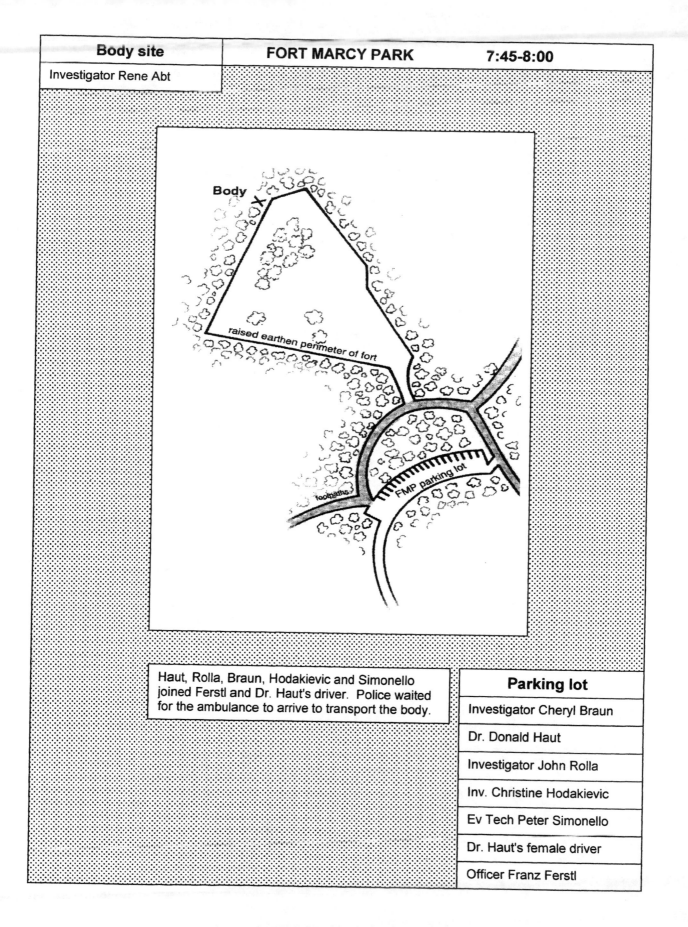

| Body site | FORT MARCY PARK | 7:45-8:00 |

Investigator Rene Abt

**Body** X

raised earthen perimeter of fort

footpaths

FMP parking lot

Haut, Rolla, Braun, Hodakievic and Simonello joined Ferstl and Dr. Haut's driver. Police waited for the ambulance to arrive to transport the body.

| Parking lot |
| --- |
| Investigator Cheryl Braun |
| Dr. Donald Haut |
| Investigator John Rolla |
| Inv. Christine Hodakievic |
| Ev Tech Peter Simonello |
| Dr. Haut's female driver |
| Officer Franz Ferstl |

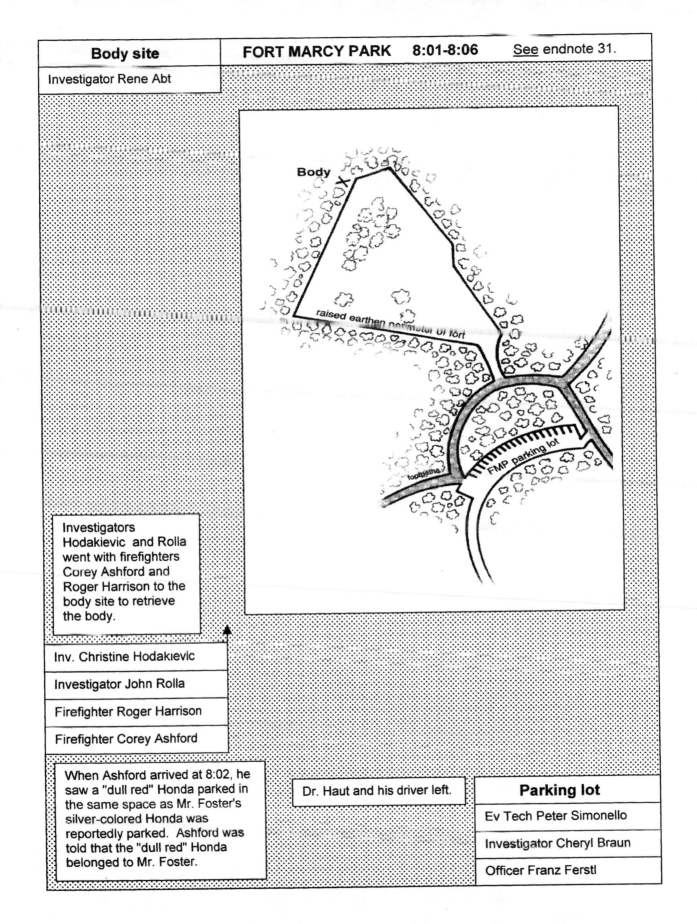

**Body site**  |  **FORT MARCY PARK**  8:01-8:06  <u>See</u> endnote 31.

Investigator Rene Abt

Body

X

raised earthen perimeter of fort

footpaths

FMP parking lot

Investigators Hodakievic and Rolla went with firefighters Corey Ashford and Roger Harrison to the body site to retrieve the body.

Inv. Christine Hodakievic

Investigator John Rolla

Firefighter Roger Harrison

Firefighter Corey Ashford

When Ashford arrived at 8:02, he saw a "dull red" Honda parked in the same space as Mr. Foster's silver-colored Honda was reportedly parked. Ashford was told that the "dull red" Honda belonged to Mr. Foster.

Dr. Haut and his driver left.

**Parking lot**

Ev Tech Peter Simonello

Investigator Cheryl Braun

Officer Franz Ferstl

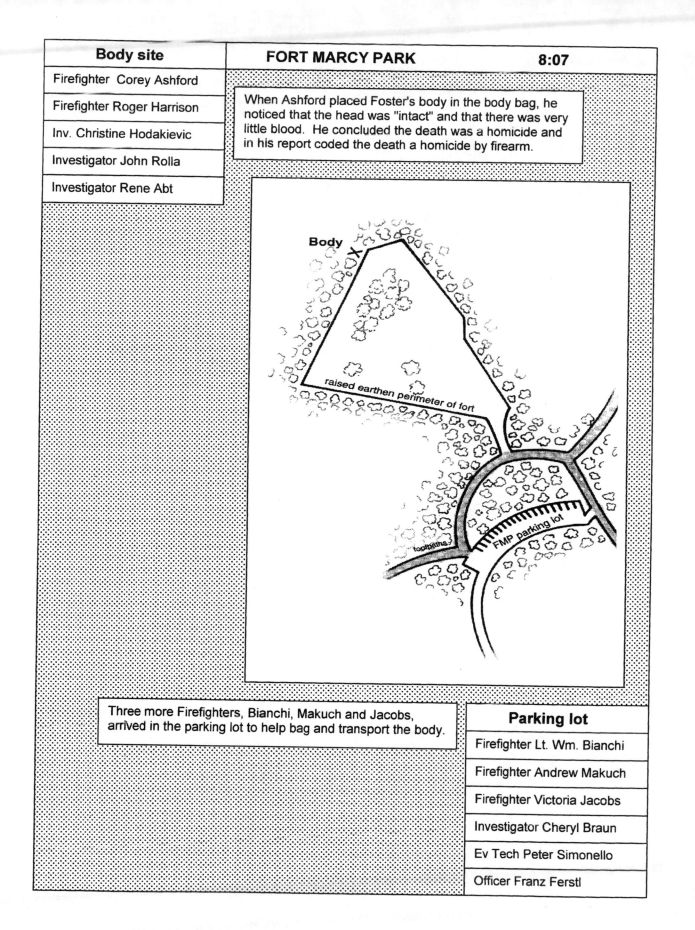

| Body site |
| --- |
| Firefighter Corey Ashford |
| Firefighter Roger Harrison |
| Inv. Christine Hodakievic |
| Investigator John Rolla |
| Investigator Rene Abt |

**FORT MARCY PARK**  8:07

When Ashford placed Foster's body in the body bag, he noticed that the head was "intact" and that there was very little blood. He concluded the death was a homicide and in his report coded the death a homicide by firearm.

Body X

raised earthen perimeter of fort

footpaths

FMP parking lot

Three more Firefighters, Bianchi, Makuch and Jacobs, arrived in the parking lot to help bag and transport the body.

| Parking lot |
| --- |
| Firefighter Lt. Wm. Bianchi |
| Firefighter Andrew Makuch |
| Firefighter Victoria Jacobs |
| Investigator Cheryl Braun |
| Ev Tech Peter Simonello |
| Officer Franz Ferstl |

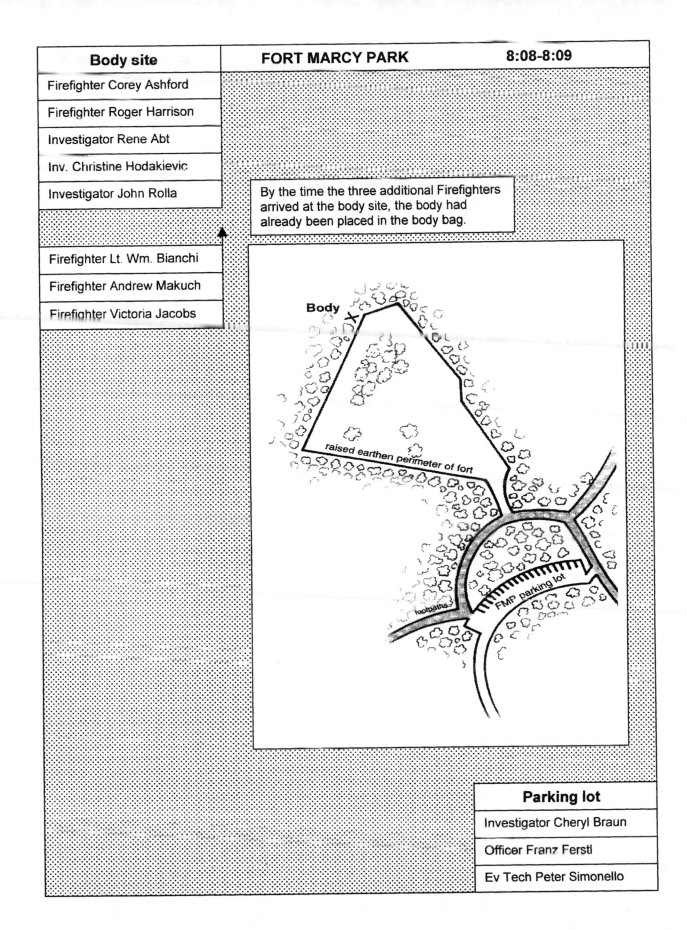

| Body site |
|---|
| Firefighter Corey Ashford |
| Firefighter Roger Harrison |
| Investigator Rene Abt |
| Inv. Christine Hodakievic |
| Investigator John Rolla |
| Firefighter Lt. Wm. Bianchi |
| Firefighter Andrew Makuch |
| Firefighter Victoria Jacobs |

**FORT MARCY PARK**          8:08-8:09

By the time the three additional Firefighters arrived at the body site, the body had already been placed in the body bag.

**Body**

raised earthen perimeter of fort

FMP parking lot

footpaths

| Parking lot |
|---|
| Investigator Cheryl Braun |
| Officer Franz Ferstl |
| Ev Tech Peter Simonello |

| **Body site** | **FORT MARCY PARK** | **8:10-8:15** |

The five Firefighters and Investigators Hodakievlc, Rolla, and Abt returned to the parking lot with Mr. Foster's body.

| |
|---|
| Firefighter Corey Ashford |
| Firefighter Roger Harrison |
| Firefighter Lt. Wm. Bianchi |
| Firefighter Victoria Jacobs |
| Firefighter Andrew Makuch |
| Inv. Christine Hodakievic |
| Investigator John Rolla |
| Investigator Rene Abt |

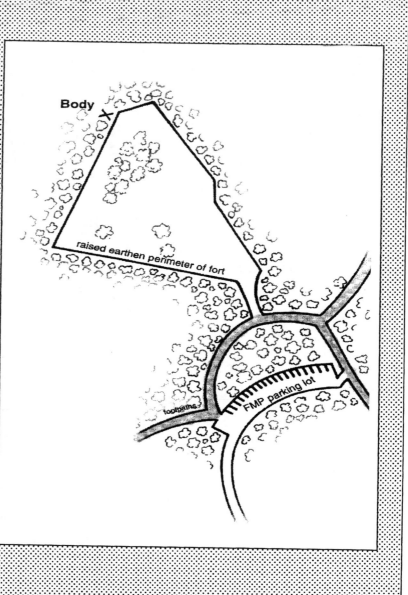

Body

raised earthen perimeter of fort

footpaths

FMP parking lot

Firefighters transported the body from the park to the morgue, and Investigators remained in the lot.

| **Parking lot** |
|---|
| Investigator Cheryl Braun |
| Officer Franz Ferstl |
| Ev Tech Peter Simonello |

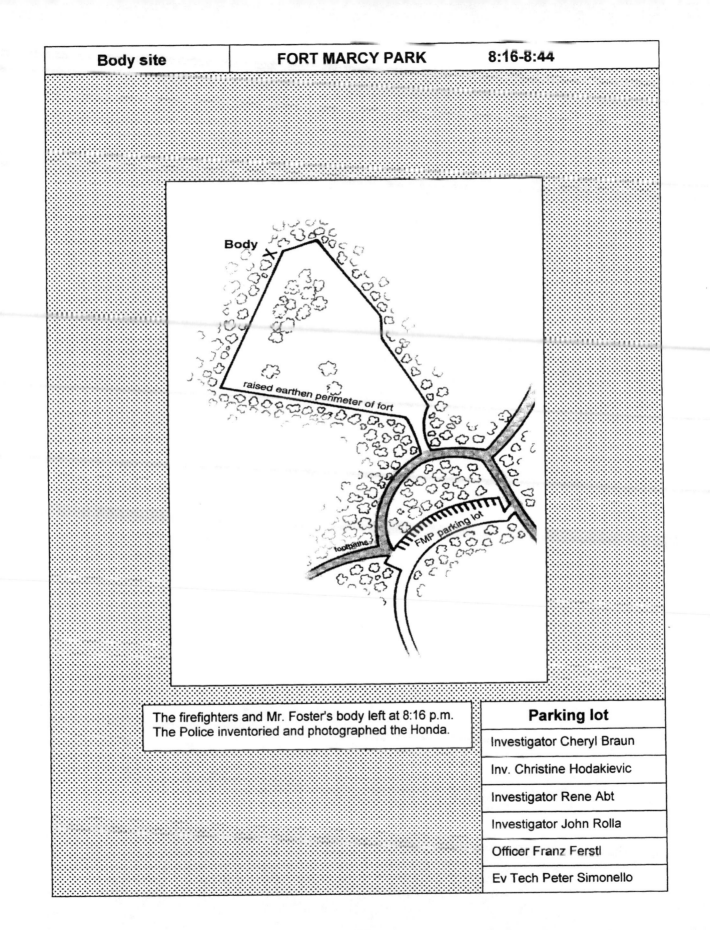

| Body site | FORT MARCY PARK | 8:16-8:44 |

**Body**

raised earthen perimeter of fort

footpaths

FMP parking lot

The firefighters and Mr. Foster's body left at 8:16 p.m. The Police inventoried and photographed the Honda.

### Parking lot

| Parking lot |
|---|
| Investigator Cheryl Braun |
| Inv. Christine Hodakievic |
| Investigator Rene Abt |
| Investigator John Rolla |
| Officer Franz Ferstl |
| Ev Tech Peter Simonello |

| Body site | FORT MARCY PARK | 8:45-9:30 |
|---|---|---|

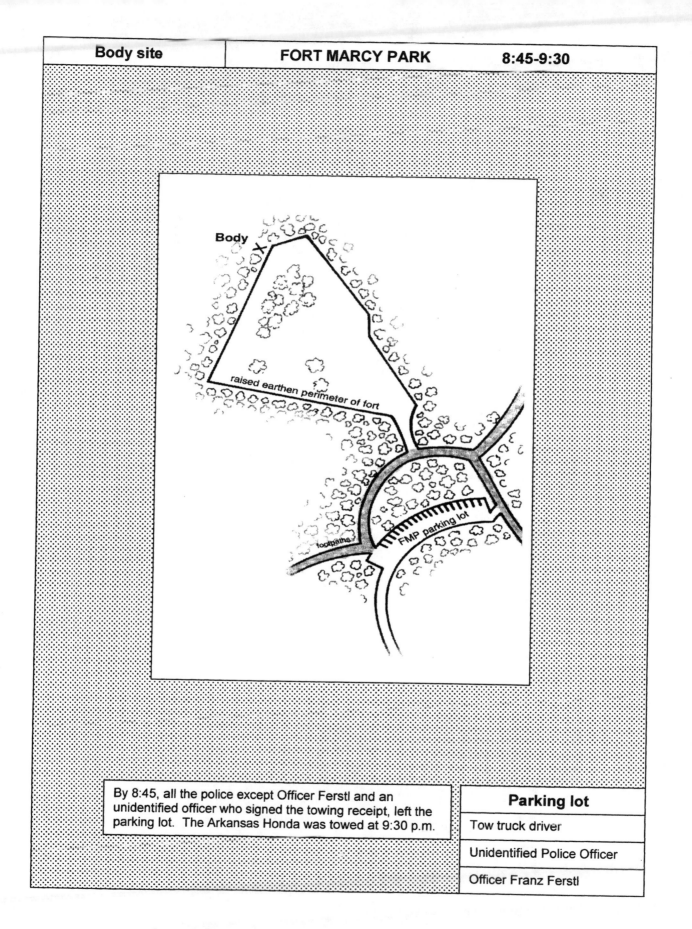

**Body**

raised earthen perimeter of fort

footpaths

FMP parking lot

By 8:45, all the police except Officer Ferstl and an unidentified officer who signed the towing receipt, left the parking lot. The Arkansas Honda was towed at 9:30 p.m.

### Parking lot

Tow truck driver

Unidentified Police Officer

Officer Franz Ferstl

## III. OVERVIEW OF THE COMPARISON OF THE PUBLICLY AVAILABLE EVIDENCE TO THE OIC'S REPORT

On July 15, 1997, Mr. Starr filed, under seal, with the United States Court of Appeals for the DC Circuit, Special Division for the purpose of Appointing Independent Counsels, its Report on the Death of Vincent W. Foster, Jr. Eighty-six days later, on October 10, 1997, the Court ordered it unsealed and released to the public. The OIC's interim Report is 114 pages long, exclusive of its twenty-four page Appendix, which it bound separately. It is double-spaced and has 353 footnotes. Its authors are unknown.[146]

The available records, from which the exhibits below are drawn, include reports of various kinds, testimony, depositions, FBI and Park Police witness interview reports, photographs, laboratory reports, investigators' memos, and handwritten notes.

Of the 184 exhibits cited below, 134 of them are drawn from the volumes assembled by the 1994 Senate Banking Committee.[147] Except for those documents which are withheld or redacted (the most controversial), these volumes contain most of the records generated by the FBI under the Fiske probe, and many of the records generated under the first FBI/Park Police investigation. They were released in January of 1995. Of the 52 remaining exhibits, 25 were provided through Freedom of Information Act lawsuits. Fourteen exhibits are taken from the volumes assembled by the 1995 Senate Whitewater Committee, released in 1997.[148]

---

[146] OIC, p. 15: "The OIC legal staff in Washington, D.C., and Little Rock, Arkansas, participated in... preparing this report."

[147] S. Hrg. 103-889. HEARINGS RELATED TO MADISON GUARANTY S&L AND THE WHITEWATER DEVELOPMENT CORPORATION – WASHINGTON, DC PHASE, Committee on Banking, Housing, and Urban Affairs, United States Senate, (redacted) Volumes I, II & XIV, available from the Senate Banking Committee clerk in January, 1995.

[148] S. HRG. 104-869. INVESTIGATION OF WHITEWATER DEVELOPMENT Corporation and Related Matters, SPECIAL COMMITTEE TO INVESTIGATE WHITEWATER DEVELOPMENT CORPORATION AND RELATED MATTERS, ADMINISTERED BY THE COMMITTEE ON BANKING, HOUSING AND URBAN AFFAIRS UNITED STATES SENATE.

Four exhibits are taken from the U.S. House of Representatives investigation into the Travel Office matter.[149] The five exhibits denoted with an asterisk* were not obtained from any official investigative records. The remaining four exhibits are the Clinger Report, a photograph released by ABC News, a report found in the National Archives, and the Fiske Report (*Report of the Independent Counsel In Re Vincent W. Foster, Jr.*). The Fiske Report, 58 double-spaced pages, was released to the public on June 30, 1994.

The OIC hides FBI agents' participation in its death probe by citing reports conducted during its tenure as "OIC." Because references to the term "OIC" could be to grand jury testimony, or to reports prepared by FBI agents, or to reports prepared by other investigators, there is no way to tell which of these reported witnesses' accounts are the interviewing FBI agents' version of the facts described.

OIC, p. 18-19, fn. 26:

"*...As used in citations herein, the term 'OIC' refers to a transcript of either an interview or a grand jury appearance by a witness...*"

In its footnotes, the OIC refers its readers to documents that purport to prove the conclusions it makes. Of these 353 footnotes, 265, or 75% of them, refer the reader to documents that are unavailable.

| Description of withheld documents | Footnote references | Percentage of secret references |
|---|---|---|
| "OIC" documents | 88 | 33% |
| FBI documents | 62 | 24% |
| Dr. Henry Lee's Report | 60 | 23% |
| Dr. Alan Berman's Report | 30 | 11% |
| Dr. Brian Blackbourne's Report | 16 | 6% |
| Other documents and sources | 7 | 3% |
| Total number of secret sources | 265 | 100% |

---

[149] H.R. 104-849. INVESTIGATION OF THE WHITE HOUSE TRAVEL OFFICE FIRINGS AND RELATED MATTERS, available September, 1996.

## Overview

The OIC hired Dr. Henry Lee, a renowned forensic scientist, Dr. Brian Blackbourne, a forensic pathologist, Dr. Alan Berman, a "suicidologist," and a handwriting expert, Gus R. Lesnevich. All experts' reports remain withheld from public view, so that we do not even know their completion dates. The OIC claims to have provided its experts with all the relevant evidence to review. As you will see, it did not. All experts are confident in their opinions, apparently undaunted by the admitted scarcity of evidence.[150]

Contrary to the impression given in its Table of Contents, the evidence in support of the Report's various conclusions are largely scattered throughout its 114 pages. Therefore, to analyze any given issue, one must peruse the entire Report in search of citations to evidence bearing on that issue. Consider looking in the OIC's 114-page Report to see its analysis of five important issues.

---

[150] OIC, p. 14, fn. 20: As Dr. Lee explained, a perfect reconstruction of the circumstances of Mr. Foster's death was not possible at the time of the OIC's investigation. The reasons include the lack of complete documentation of the original shooting scene; the lack of subsequent records and photographs of each item of physical evidence prior to examination; the lack of x-rays of Mr. Foster's body from the autopsy; the lack of documentation of the amount of blood, tissue, and bone fragments in the areas at the scene under and around Mr. Foster's head; the lack of close-up photographs of any definite patterns and quantity of the blood stains found on Mr. Foster's clothing and body at the scene; and the unknown location of the fatal bullet, which makes complete reconstruction of the bullet trajectory difficult. Lee Report at 485.

OIC, p. 114: "Dr. Berman concluded that '[i]n my opinion and to a 100% degree of medical certainty, the death of Vincent Foster was a suicide. No plausible evidence has been presented to support any other conclusion.'"[fn353]

Exhibit 12, Fiske Report, June 30, 1994: "On the afternoon of Tuesday, July 20, 1993, in Fort Marcy Park, Fairfax County, Virginia, Vincent W. Foster, Jr., committed suicide by firing a bullet from a .38 caliber revolver into his mouth. As discussed below, the evidence overwhelmingly supports this conclusion, and there is no evidence to the contrary."

| Wound | Gunshot Residue | Gun | Blood | Photographic Evidence |
|-------|-----------------|-----|-------|-----------------------|
| 1,8,26, 27,29, 30,31, 32,33, 34,61, 63,64, 75,76, 111 | 1,26,28, 30,32,33, 42,43,44, 45,46,53, 58,62,63, 64,65,78, 79,112 | 25,26,27, 28,36,37, 38,39,40, 41,43,45, 54,61,62, 77,79,80, 81,82,83, 84,85, 110,112 | 11,14,25, 26,28,29, 36,38,39, 40,46,47, 48,49,57, 59,60,61, 63,64,65, 66,67,68, 112,113 | 16,17,21,24,25, 26,27,29,30,31, 32,33,35,42,43, 45,46,47,49,52, 59,60,61,62,63, 64,65,66,67,72, 73,78,79,81,82, 87,90,93,111, 113 |

The autopsy is the cornerstone of both the OIC's and the Fiske probe's reports. Officially, six experts have relied on its findings, four hired by the Fiske probe and two by Starr's. All of these experts agree that there was no neck wound. And none of them reported having found anything about the amount or configuration of blood at the scene that refutes or even calls into question the official conclusion of suicide in the park.

In the next 250 pages, for all the issues except depression, we will review most of the available evidence and compare it with the OIC's representations of the evidence, as well as the OIC's conclusions. We will also examine issues that the OIC omitted from its Report. Then, in Chapter X, we will explore the reasonable inferences to be drawn from the facts. As you review the evidence, keep in mind that our goal is to prove to you the existence of a cover-up, and please remember to keep an open mind until you have reviewed all the evidence.

## IV. EVIDENCE OF KNOWLEDGE OF THE DEATH BEFORE THE OFFICIAL TIME OF NOTIFICATION

Summary: The OIC conceals that the FBI's Violent Crime Squad claimed it did not learn of the death until press accounts appeared the next day, that Fire & Rescue workers learned from Park Police by 6:37 that Mr. Foster was employed at the White House, and that William Kennedy learned of the death by 8:00. The OIC addresses only the time when Helen Dickey learned of the death. In doing so, it purportedly relies on telephone records to dismiss Arkansas Troopers' accounts that Dickey notified them of the death before 8:30, while claiming that the telephone record of the call to the Trooper is "not available."

## Notification

In its three-page section entitled Notification (p. 91-94), the Report claims that *"The Secret Service was notified of Mr. Foster's death at about 8:30 p.m..."*

### 1. FBI's Violent Crime Squad

In addition to the White House, Mr. Foster's family, and the Secret Service, the FBI was notified. The OIC does not reveal who notified the FBI or when this notification took place. The FBI's Report of its initial death investigation[151] may set forth when the FBI was notified. The OIC does not reveal the existence of this Report, and it too is not publicly available.

The record demonstrates that on the evening of the death, the Park Police had been fully apprised, all the way up to its Regional Director. Park Police Lieutenant Patrick Gavin called Park Police Chief Robert Langston between 9:00 and 10:00 on the evening of the death.[152] Chief Langston in turn called Park Police Regional Director Robert Stanton.[153]

When Secret Service Agent Dennis Martin was notified of Foster's death by his Watch Commander around 8:30 or 9:00 p.m. on the evening of the death, Martin called his White House liaison Paul Imbordino.[154] Imbordino told Martin

---

[151] Exhibit 65, Deposition of FBI Agent Scott Salter, June 30, 1995: "[I]t's basically a summary of events from the 21st through the conclusion of, through August 4th or 6th or whatever it was, through the conclusion of the investigation that we did."

[152] Exhibit 83, Deposition of Park Police Chief Robert E. Langston, June 27, 1995: "Q. Do you recall what time it was that you were contacted? A. It was dark so I would imagine it was somewhere around 9:00 or 9:30, 10:00, somewhere in that area."

[153] Exhibit 83, Deposition of Park Police Chief Robert E. Langston, June 27, 1995: "Q. Did you make any phone calls? A. Yes. Q. Who did you call? A. I notified Bob Stanton, who was the regional director."

[154] Exhibit 84, Deposition of Secret Service Agent Dennis Martin, June 22, 1995: "A. Maybe between 8:30 and 9:00, something like that. *** Q. I think we can go quickly through your conversation with Mr. Imbordino. Did you call him at home? A. Yes, I am not sure if I reached him by pager or direct. I can't recall that, but I did speak to him."

to meet FBI and Park Police investigators at the southwest
gate on the next morning, July 21,[155] to facilitate their
entry into the White House to meet with David Watkins and
other White House officials.[156]   Between 8:30 and 8:40
Wednesday morning, before the arrival of Park Police at the
southwest gate,[157] two FBI agents[158] appeared at the southwest
gate, and Martin knew at least by then that Mr. Foster's
death "was the investigation of the FBI and the U.S. Park
Police."[159]

---

[155]   Exhibit 84, Deposition of Secret Service Agent Dennis
Martin, June 22, 1995:   Q.  And what if anything, did you
do in connections with Mr. Foster's death when you arrived
at the White House on the morning of the 21st?  A.  I was
to meet investigators at the southwest gate.  Q.  Did you
know that before you arrived at the White House that
morning?  A.  Yes, I did.  Q.  How did you know that?  A.
That's per a telephone conversation with Paul Imbordino the
night before.  Q.  On the evening of the 20th, Mr.
Imbordino told you to meet investigators the next morning?
A.  He said I would help facilitate getting the
investigators in, yes.

[156]   Exhibit 84, Deposition of Secret Service Agent Dennis
Martin, June 22, 1995:  A.  ...I had gone into the west
wing earlier with another group of investigators that were
there.  Q.  Well I missed that.  Let me come back to that.
What group of investigators were already there?  A.  As I
went down to the gate to meet the Park Police, I observed
the unmarked vehicle pull up to the southwest gate, which I
recognized as the chief of the Park Police.  Q.  Is that
Mr. Langston?  A.  Yes.  Q.  Was anyone with Mr. Langston?
A.  Major Hines.  Q.  Before 8:00 in the morning?  A Yes.

[157]   Exhibit 84, Deposition of Secret Service Agent Dennis
Martin, June 22, 1995:  Q.  How much longer did you wait?
A.  With the FBI agents with me?  Q.  Yes.  A.  I was maybe
standing with the FBI agents maybe 10, 15 minutes.  Q.  And
then Captain Hume and Detective Markland arrived; is that
right?  A.  Yes, they arrived on foot.  Q.  What time,
approximately, do you think they arrived?  A.  It seemed
like it was before 9:00.

[158]   Exhibit 84, Deposition of Secret Service Agent Dennis
Martin, June 22, 1995:  "The first two investigators who came
were FBI agents."

[159]   Exhibit 84, Deposition of Secret Service Agent Dennis
Martin, June 22, 1995:  "[B]asically it wasn't our investigation.
It was the investigation of the FBI and the U.S. Park Police."

## Notification

According to the testimony of FBI agent Scott Salter, one of the agents who had responded to the southwest gate of the White House before 9:00 a.m., he did so at the request of FBI agent John K. Danna[160] of the FBI's Violent Crime Squad. The Violent Crime Squad is responsible for investigating assaults under "the Presidential assassination statute."[161]

Yet Danna's story was decidedly different from Salter's. According to Danna, his first official participation was when Captain Hume called him on Wednesday, July 21 around 10:00 a.m. from the Old Executive Office Building, and requested FBI support. According to Danna's testimony, he didn't learn of the death until the media reported it on Wednesday, July 21.

> Q. Prior to that call from Captain Hume of the Park Police, what information, if any, did you have regarding Mr. Foster's death?
>
> A. I don't recall specifically what I observed or heard in the media. My only source of information was what I heard on TV or read in the paper that morning. I had no other information.
>
> Q. You had no official information about it?
>
> A. Absolutely not.[162]

---

[160] Exhibit 65, Deposition FBI Agent Scott Salter, June 30, 1995: "John Danna called us in my car and told us to go to the southwest gate of the White House and meet him there and that we were to, that we were going to be working on a death investigation involving Mr. Foster's death."

[161] Exhibit 85, Deposition of FBI Agent John Danna, June 28, 1995: "Q. ...What generally are the responsibilities for [sic] the violent crime squad? A. ...Included also in that area are assault cases on members of Congress, Supreme Court, and we also have the Presidential assassination statute on my squad, which is Title 18, section 1751."

[162] Exhibit 85, Deposition of FBI agent John K. Danna, June 28, 1995: That morning after Mr. Foster -- the 20th, the morning of the 21st, around 10:00 I got a call from Captain Hume, H-u-m-e, in the Park Police, and he had called and told me that he was in the White House, in fact, in the Old Executive Office Building, investigating the suicide of Mr. Foster. And he requested that I come over and hook up with him and provide him some assistance in a cooperative effort. And because of that I told him I would, and also called two of my agents that were out on the street on

Danna was the FBI agent who worked in the very FBI office which was charged with complying with the federal statute mandating that the FBI investigate Mr. Foster's death (discussed below). According to his sworn testimony, he received word of the death only after the Secret Service, the White House, Mr. Foster's family, and press had all been apprised of the death. And he decided to investigate only after the Park Police "requested that [he]... provide... some assistance in a cooperative effort." Prior to that time, Danna testified, he had "absolutely" no "official information about" the death.

## 2.    Fire & Rescue workers and Park Police

The Fairfax County Fire and Rescue workers knew that Mr. Foster was a White House employee before they left Fort Marcy Park. That was at 6:37 p.m.[163] Firefighter Lieutenant William Bianchi related this to the FBI on March 17, 1994.

"Bianchi also heard from the returning FCFRD personnel that the victim was deceased and had been employed at the White House... When Bianchi learned that the victim was a White House employee, he instructed Hall and Iacone to make their reports on the incident very detailed."[164]

The Fairfax County Fire & Rescue workers learned, of course, from the Park Police. Their 6:37 departure time is accurate. (We believe that the official version (p. 23,

---

other matters and asked them to meet me over there. Q. Prior to that call from Captain Hume of the Park Police, what information, if any, did you have regarding Mr. Foster's death? A. I don't recall specifically what I observed or heard in the media. My only source of information was what I heard on TV or read in the paper that morning. I had no other information. Q. You had no official information about it? A. Absolutely not.

[163]   Exhibit 34, Electronic log of McLean Fire Station Engine 1, July 20, 1993

[164]   Exhibit 87, Report of FBI interview of Firefighter Lieutenant William Bianchi, March 17, 1994. Exhibit 88, Handwritten notes of FBI interview of Firefighter Lieutenant William Bianchi, March 17, 1994: "One of Clinton's buddies has killed himself."

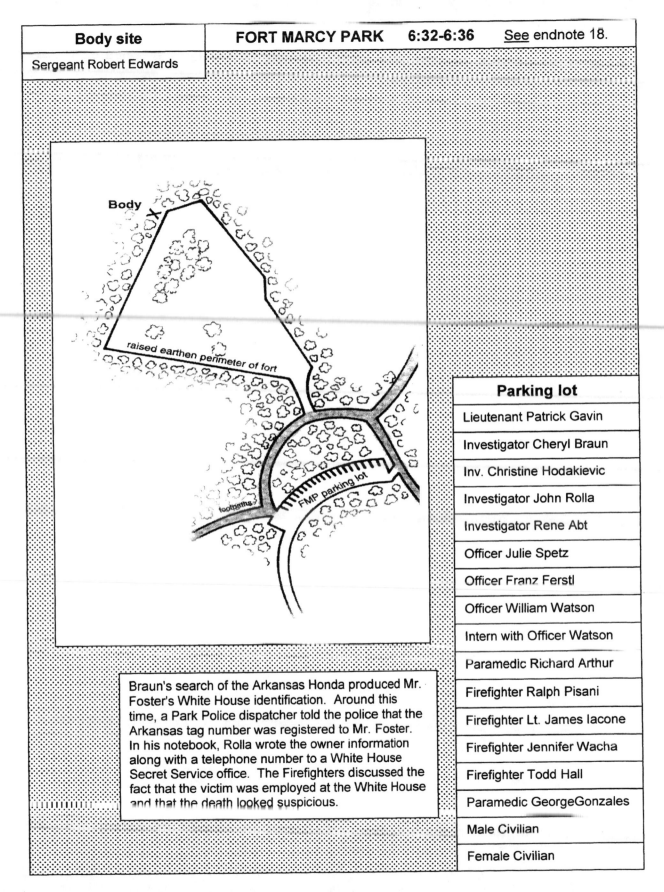

Braun's search of the Arkansas Honda produced Mr. Foster's White House identification. Around this time, a Park Police dispatcher told the police that the Arkansas tag number was registered to Mr. Foster. In his notebook, Rolla wrote the owner information along with a telephone number to a White House Secret Service office. The Firefighters discussed the fact that the victim was employed at the White House and that the death looked suspicious.

### Parking lot

Lieutenant Patrick Gavin

Investigator Cheryl Braun

Inv. Christine Hodakievic

Investigator John Rolla

Investigator Rene Abt

Officer Julie Spetz

Officer Franz Ferstl

Officer William Watson

Intern with Officer Watson

Paramedic Richard Arthur

Firefighter Ralph Pisani

Firefighter Lt. James Iacone

Firefighter Jennifer Wacha

Firefighter Todd Hall

Paramedic GeorgeGonzales

Male Civilian

Female Civilian

fn. 45) that *"Officer Fornshill of the Park Police arrived at 6:11:50 p.m."* is inaccurate, as discussed above.)

Perhaps the Park Police did not know that the abbreviation, "WHCA" on the Motorola pager they found attached to Mr. Foster's belt stood for White House Communications Agency.[165] And perhaps they didn't see the White House parking sticker, which presumably would have been on the windshield of the car he parked daily in slot 16 on West Executive Avenue.[166]

But they would have known that Mr. Foster was employed at the White House upon their inspection of his laminated White House Communications Center identification, with his photograph on it, which they found on the front passenger's seat of the Arkansas Honda at the park. (They also found a White House Federal Credit Union card in his wallet). Paramedic Richard Arthur saw police gaining access to the Arkansas Honda[167] before he left the park at 6:37.[168] Park Police Investigator John Rolla testified that it was he who searched the Arkansas Honda and found in it Mr. Foster's White House identification, whereupon he thought he had "better call [the] Secret Service."[169] Rolla's handwritten notes, made at the scene, reveal that he knew the telephone number of the Secret Service office to call.

---

[165]     Exhibit 89, Park Police Evidence Property Control Receipt, July 20, 1993.

[166]     Exhibit 16, Report of FBI interview of Lisa Foster, May 9, 1994.

[167]     Exhibit 71, Report of FBI interview of Paramedic Richard Arthur, March 16, 1994: "He observed them gaining access to a cream colored car with a suit jacket and tie in it, looking for identification of some sort."

[168]     Exhibit 34, Electronic log of McLean Fire Station Engine 1, July 20, 1993

[169]     Exhibit 6, Deposition of Park Police Investigator John Rolla, July 21, 1994: "I retrieved the jacket, retrieved the wallet, there was identification, under the jacket on the seat was a White House Identification thing with a photo ID on it. It wasn't until then I knew that this was a White House guy. We better call Secret Service."

**Notification**

> "Vincent Foster, Jr...
> Lt. Walter
> 395-4366"[170]

The telephone number, 395-4366, rings in Room 058 in the basement of the White House, a Secret Service office. "Lt. Walter" is Lieutenant Danny Walter of the United States Secret Service.

According to the FBI's report of its April, 1994, interview with Park Police Investigator Cheryl Braun, it was she who found the White House Communications Center identification in the car. (Under its *Fort Marcy* section, the OIC skims over this discrepancy by reporting that both *"Braun and Rolla... found Mr. Foster's White House identification."*[171]) The FBI interviewed Police Investigator Cheryl Braun on April 28, 1994.

> Braun found a White House identification on the front passenger seat. Braun stated that she advised another officer to call the Shift Commander and inform him of this new development... She advised that approximately thirty minutes passed whereupon she learned that the Commander had never been notified and then she, herself, advising him [sic] of the White House identification at approximately 7:30-7:45 p.m.[172]

The corresponding handwritten notes of Braun's FBI interview reveal that she told the FBI that she made the call at "7:30," not the "approximately 7:30-7:45" that made its way into the corresponding typed FBI interview Report. The notes of this FBI interview of Braun also reveal that William Watson was the "officer" who Braun had told to notify the Shift Commander.[173] (Watson was a member of the

---

[170] Exhibit 90, Handwritten notes of Park Police Investigator John Rolla, July 20, 1993.

[171] OIC, p. 26: "The two lead Park Police investigators (Braun and Rolla) photographed and examined the car and, during examination, found Mr. Foster's White House identification.[fn54]"

[172] Exhibit 91, Report of FBI interview of Park Police Investigator Cheryl Braun, April 28, 1994.

[173] Exhibit 92, Handwritten notes of FBI interview of Park Police Investigator Cheryl Braun, April 28, 1994.

Park Police SWAT team, who did not prepare any report and was never interviewed by the FBI or Park Police investigators, but had reportedly responded to the scene before anyone knew of Mr. Foster's White House connection.) Because the Shift Commander that Braun is said to have "called" at 7:30 was Lieutenant Patrick Gavin, who had been at the park at from 6:24 p.m. until about 7:10 p.m., Braun's account is problematic. But even if it were true, it would still leave one hour before the White House was notified.

The OIC addressed only when Helen Dickey learned of the death, discussed below.

### 3. William Kennedy and Craig Livingstone

According to Associate White House counsel William Kennedy, Chief of White House Personnel Security Craig Livingstone told him of Mr. Foster's death "around 8:00."[174]

### 4. White House telephone records

The OIC explains away Arkansas State Trooper Roger Perry's account of having received a call from the personal assistant of the Clintons, Helen Dickey, notifying him of the death, before the White House was officially notified at 8:30 p.m. Eastern time. (Upon learning of the death, Perry called former Arkansas State Police commander Lynn Davis and trooper Larry Patterson, who recalled that Perry called him with the news around 7:00 p.m. Eastern time.[175])

The discrepancy between the troopers' account and Ms. Dickey's had been the subject of some publicity, having been the only issue regarding the Foster death investigation which was addressed by Senator D'Amato's Committee. (D'Amato had called only Dickey to testify, not Perry, Patterson, or Davis.)

---

[174] Exhibit 46, Deposition of Associate White House Counsel William Kennedy, July 11, 1995: "It was around 8:00 or so. I got a call from Craig Livingstone telling me that he had a report that Vince was dead."

[175] OIC, p. 92, fn. 284: "Another Arkansas trooper stated that the first trooper called him soon after the Dickey call. This second trooper 'placed the time of this telephone call at approximately 6:00 PM' Arkansas time. 302, 11/9/95, at 1."

Photographs

The OIC's version is that Troopers Perry and Patterson were wrong[176] (former Arkansas State Police commander Davis' account is not mentioned), Ms. Dickey's account is accurate, and long distance White House telephone records which could prove it are *not available.*[177]

## V.  EVIDENCE THAT THE OIC CONCEALED THE DISAPPEARANCE OF PHOTOGRAPHS

Summary: Edwards took charge of the scene and took possession of Ferstl's approximately seven photographs taken of the body site. He absconded with them. The OIC conceals that Ferstl's Polaroids vanished by falsely claiming that (1) Ferstl's Polaroids are inventoried as being Edwards', and (2) Edwards took no photographs. The OIC conceals that Edwards did, in fact, take photographs by claiming that he did "not recall" whether he photographed Mr. Foster's body. Abt recalled that Edwards had taken photographs, as did Rolla and Braun.

The OIC conceals that the Polaroids that Rolla had taken had vanished by falsely reporting that Rolla was mistaken when he testified that he took at least two Polaroids of the back of Mr. Foster's head. Rolla testified that he was certain that he shot "backside" photographs, he inspected his Polaroids as they came out, he remembered what pictures he had taken, and that the "backside" photographs were in his office the night of the death, but he never saw them again. The OIC falsely reports that Rolla did not have a camera when the body was rolled.

---

[176]  OIC, p. 94, fn. 292: Precise recollections of time, if not tied to a specific event that can be documented as having occurred at an exact time, can, of course, be imprecise or inaccurate. Here, the recollection is tied neither to a specific event nor to an exact time. The recollection instead is of a general three-hour period of time in which the call might have been received. The recollection is not reflected in a contemporaneous document.

[177]  OIC, p. 93, fn. 288: White House Residence phone records indicate that a call was placed to the number of Dickey's father at 10:06 p.m. OIC Doc. No. DC-95-7; Dickey 302, 2/7/96, at 2. A call to the Arkansas Governor's Mansion is not reflected on these records. As indicated, the call may have been made from a phone in the White House not on the floors of the White House Residence: The Usher's Office employee who notified Dickey recalls Dickey making a call, but not in the Residence, soon after he notified her. 302, 5/21/96, at 2. Complete records for such calls are not available.

## Photographs

The OIC concealed that the roll of 35-mm film produced usable photographs. It claims that the 35-mm film was "underexposed," but offers no explanation. The FBI Lab falsely claimed that the "underexposed" negatives produced "limited detail." Three witnesses said that these photographs were clear, including the photographer who had shot the roll of film.

On May 2, 1994, Park Police Captain Charles Hume provided the FBI with all of the Polaroid photographs of the body site and parking lot that officially exist. The FBI's *Receipt for Property Received* inventories these photographs.[178] Officially, only thirteen Polaroids of the body site were taken[179] (fourteen according to an FBI Laboratory Report[180]), two of which have been released.

The *Receipt for Property Received* denotes that of these thirteen, five, marked on the back "from... Sgt. [Robert] Edwards 7/20/93 on scene,"[181] are listed as depicting:

1 - Rear of Cannon
2 - Heavily foliated area
3 - VF's body - looking down from top of berm
4 - VF's body - focusing on the face
5 - VF's body - focusing on right shoulder/hand

The other eight are marked on the back with Park Police Investigator John Rolla's initials, "JCR 7/20/93."[182] They are inventoried as depicting:

---

[178]   Exhibit 94, FBI Receipt for Property Received, Inventory of Polaroid photographs, May 2, 1994.

[179]   OIC, p. 73:  "Thirteen of the Polaroids provided to Mr. Fiske's Office and the OIC are of the body scene, and five are of the parking lot scene."

[180]   Exhibit 95, FBI Laboratory Report, May 9, 1994:  "Q73-Q86 Copies of fourteen death scene photographs of Vincent Foster."

[181]   OIC, p. 73:  "The backs of the other five say 'from C202 Sgt. Edwards 7-20-93 on scene.'[fn213]"

[182]   OIC, p. 73:  "Of the 13 Polaroids of the body scene, eight are initialed by Investigator Rolla."

## Photographs

1 - Right hand showing gun & thumb in guard
2 - Glasses on ground
3 - VF's body taken from below feet
4 - VF's body focusing on right side & arm
5 - VF's - focusing on top of head thru heavy foliage
6 - VF's body - focus on head and upper torso
7 - VF's face - looking directly down on face
8 - VF's face - taken from right side focusing on face

The photograph marked "JCR" on the back, inventoried as "Right hand showing gun & thumb in guard," is in the public domain, having been released to and broadcast by ABC News in January of 1994, and subsequently printed in Newsweek. Another of Rolla's photographs, inventoried as depicting "glasses on ground," was released in the summer of 1998 pursuant to a Freedom of Information Act lawsuit.

The inventory does not evidence any of "approximately seven"[183] Polaroids taken by Park Police Officer Franz Ferstl. The OIC sought to explain this anomaly in its two-paragraph *Photographs* section of its Report.

### 1.   Sergeant Edwards absconded with Officer Ferstl's Polaroids

Officer Franz Ferstl, the beat man for the area, was dispatched from Glen Echo Park Police Station. Following in a separate car was Park Police Officer Julie Spetz. Ferstl arrived at the park around 6:17 p.m., whereupon Ferstl immediately went to the body site. Spetz arrived around 6:19 and searched other areas of the park for witnesses. When Ferstl arrived at the body site, already present were firefighters Hall and Gonzalez and Park Police Officer Kevin Fornshill. Firefighters had already determined that "there would be no effort to resuscitate."[184]

---

[183]   Exhibit 96, Report of FBI interview of Park Police Officer Franz Ferstl, May 2, 1994: "Ferstl advised that he also took several Polaroid photos of the crime scene... Ferstl stated that to the best of his recollection, he took approximately seven..."

[184]   Exhibit 78, Report of FBI interview with Firefighter Lieutenant James Iacone, March 11, 1994: "Gonzalez provided directions to the body over the radio to Iacone. After Iacone's group arrived at the  location of the body, the medics confirmed that there would be no effort to resuscitate the patient. As the officers on the medic unit, Gonzalez would have been responsible for pronouncing the patient deceased."

| Body site |
| --- |
| Officer Franz Ferstl |
| |
| Paramedic Richard Arthur |
| Firefighter Ralph Pisani |
| Firefighter Lt. James Iacone |
| Firefighter Jennifer Wacha |

Officer Ferstl continued photographing the body with the semi-automatic pistol in the hand. He saw a small amount of "not fresh" blood around the mouth. Arthur and his group left the body, returning to the lot.

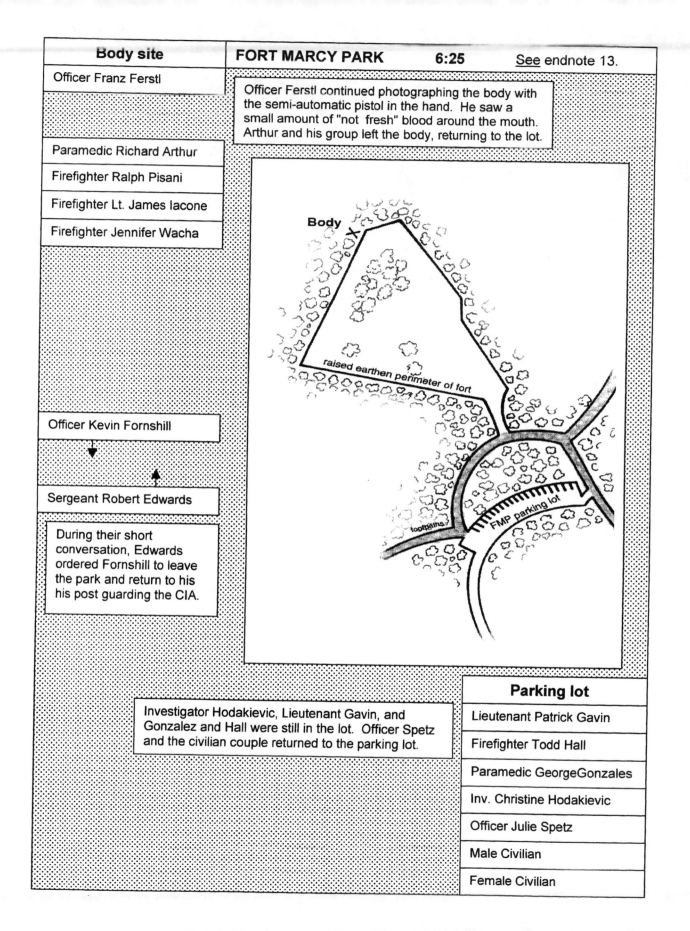

Officer Kevin Fornshill

Sergeant Robert Edwards

During their short conversation, Edwards ordered Fornshill to leave the park and return to his his post guarding the CIA.

Investigator Hodakievic, Lieutenant Gavin, and Gonzalez and Hall were still in the lot. Officer Spetz and the civilian couple returned to the parking lot.

| Parking lot |
| --- |
| Lieutenant Patrick Gavin |
| Firefighter Todd Hall |
| Paramedic GeorgeGonzales |
| Inv. Christine Hodakievic |
| Officer Julie Spetz |
| Male Civilian |
| Female Civilian |

## Photographs

After observing the body, Ferstl returned to his cruiser to retrieve crime-scene tape and a Polaroid camera. On his return to the body site, Ferstl noticed that the "body appeared to be in the identical position it was when he first observed it."[185] Fire and Rescue workers, along with Officer Fornshill, then left the area of the body. Ferstl then photographed the body.

As Officer Fornshill was walking back to the parking lot, he met Park Police Sergeant Robert Edwards, who was walking toward the body site carrying a Polaroid camera.[186]

It was clear to Fornshill and Ferstl that Edwards had taken charge of the scene.[187] Edwards did not compose any

---

[185] Exhibit 96, Report of FBI interview of Park Police Officer Franz Ferstl, May 2, 1994: ...He stated that to the best of his recollection, on returning a second time to the death scene, the body appeared to be in the identical position it was when he first observed it. Ferstl stated that to the best of his recollection, he took approximately seven photos; he cannot recall if he initialed or dated them, but he does not believe he did so. Ferstl advised that at some point, Sergeant Edwards arrived at the death scene.

[186] Exhibit 79, Deposition of Park Police Officer Kevin Fornshill, July 12, 1994: Q. Did you talk with any of these guys later? A. I passed — you mean later on? Q. I mean later that day? Next week? A. I passed Sergeant Edwards on the hill. Q. The hill being? A. In Fort Marcy, there's a bit of an incline. I was going down, he was coming up. He was carrying a Polaroid camera to take some pictures of the crime scene. Q. Who was this? A. Sergeant Edwards. Q. Okay. Is he a technician? A. No. But some of the cars have Polaroids; some don't.

[187] Exhibit 79, Deposition of Park Police Officer Kevin Fornshill, July 12, 1994: Q. After you got the call did you go straight to Fort Marcy Park?... A. ...I requested permission from my sergeant to respond and assist. Q. That would be Sergeant Edwards? A. Yes. Q. What happened then? A. He authorized me to respond, and I went directly to Fort Marcy Park to assist Fairfax County Fire and Rescue.

Exhibit 96, Report of FBI interview with Park Police Officer Franz Ferstl, May 2, 1994: "...Sergeant Edwards instructed him to go back to the parking lot and see if they needed any assistance..."

131

report. Neither the FBI or Park Police investigators interviewed him during the course of the first 17-day investigation, nor did the FBI interview him during the Fiske probe.

The FBI's May 2, 1994, report of its interview with Officer Ferstl reveals that he and Sergeant Edwards were up at the body site before Park Police Lieutenant Patrick Gavin and Investigators Rolla, Braun and Abt arrived at the Fort Marcy parking lot. During this time that only Edwards and Ferstl were at the site, Edwards took possession of the seven Polaroids that Ferstl had taken before Edwards' arrival. Edwards then ordered Ferstl to return to the parking lot to assist other investigators, as memorialized in the FBI's report of its interview with Ferstl.

> [F]erstl was not sure who he gave the Polaroid photos to, stating that it was either Sergeant Edwards or one of the investigators. Ferstl advised that USPP Investigators Cheryl Braun and John Rolla also arrived on the scene, adding that at that point in time, Sergeant Edwards instructed him to go back to the parking lot and see if they needed any assistance there.[188]

When Edwards ordered Ferstl back to the parking lot, he may have known that Park Police Investigators Braun and Rolla were arriving at the scene from monitoring his hand-held radio. When Ferstl left, Edwards was alone at the body site.

The OIC admits that Ferstl gave his Polaroids to Edwards. But if Sergeant Edwards told the OIC's FBI agents what he did with Officer Ferstl's photographs, it is indiscernible from the OIC's Report. (The first and only report of interview with Edwards was generated under the OIC's probe, and is still secret.) The OIC chose to relate

---

[188]     Exhibit 96, Report of FBI interview of Park Police Officer Franz Ferstl, May 2, 1994.

only what Ferstl reportedly understood, from sources
unknown, of what Edwards did with the Polaroids.

OIC, p. 73:

*Officer Ferstl said that he took Polaroids, and
without initialing or marking them, gave them to
Sergeant Edwards, who gave them to investigators.*[fn214]

When Park Police Lieutenant Patrick Gavin arrived at
the park, Officers Hodakievic and Ferstl were in the
parking lot. Hodakievic and Gavin later walked up to the
body site together.[189] When Hodakievic arrived at the body
site, Sergeant Edwards briefed her and showed her only one
of the photographs in his possession.[190]

Recall that Ferstl's photographs are not inventoried.
The OIC's excuse is that they are inventoried, but bear the
initials of Sergeant Edwards. Ferstl, explains the OIC,
left the backs of the Polaroids he took blank, then gave
them to Edwards.[191] Sergeant Edwards, in turn, also without
writing anything on the back of Ferstl's Polaroids, gave
them to Park Police Investigator Renee Abt.[192] Abt then

---

[189] Exhibit 98, Report of FBI interview of Park Police
Lieutenant Patrick Gavin, April 28, 1994: To the best of
his recollection, the following U.S. Park Police officers
were present at the park when he arrived. Officer Kevin
Fornshill, Sergeant Bob Edwards, Officer Franz Ferstl,
Investigator Christine Hodakievic. He stated that
Investigator Hodakievic met him at the parking lot and
later directed him up to where the body had been
discovered...

[190] Exhibit 81, Report of FBI interview with Park Police
Investigator Christine Hodakievic, May 2, 1994: "[O]fficer
Hodakievic... does recall being initially briefed by Sergeant
Edwards, which included being informed that the decedent had a
revolver in his right hand, as well as being shown a Polaroid
photograph of decedents position at the death scene."

[191] OIC, p. 73: "The backs of the other five say 'from C202
Sgt. Edwards 7-20-93 on scene.'[fn213] Officer Ferstl said that he
took Polaroids and, without initialing or marking them, gave them
to Sergeant Edwards..."

[192] OIC, p. 73: "...Sergeant Edwards... gave them to the
investigators.[fn214]"

133

wrote on the backside of Ferstl's Polaroids *"from... Sgt. Edwards 7/20/93 on scene."*[193]  Because Sergeant Edwards did not himself take any photographs, according to the OIC, Ferstl's Polaroids are not missing.

The OIC reports its version of Edwards' account, that he *"does not recall taking any Polaroids himself"* (p. 73-74).  If Edwards knew he did not photograph the body, he would have said so and the OIC surely would have quoted him.  The OIC claims that Edwards does not *"recall"* whether he photographed Mr. Foster's body, and conceals the accounts of others who did recall Edwards having photographed the body.

The OIC addresses Park Police Investigator Renee Abt's recollection that Edwards, not Ferstl, had taken the Polaroids that Edwards gave to her.  She too, the explanation continues, was mistaken.

OIC, p. 74, fn. 215:

*OIC, 1/12/95, at 7, 199-203.  Investigator Abt recalled Sergeant Edwards taking Polaroids, OIC, 1/12/95, at 11, but Sergeant Edwards said he only carried the Polaroid camera and the Polaroids taken by Ferstl, but does not recall taking any Polaroids himself, OIC, 1/12/95, at 7, 199-203.*

The Report chose to discount only Investigator Abt's observation that Sergeant Edwards took Polaroid photographs.  Yet the OIC does not quote Abt, stating only that *"Investigator Abt recalled Sergeant Edwards taking Polaroids."*  It then rebuts Abt's reported account with Edwards; *"but Sergeant Edwards... does not recall taking any Polaroids himself."*  To give Edwards' account more credence, the OIC repeats it, once in the body of the Report and once in a footnote.[194]

---

[193]  OIC, p. 73, fn. 213:  "The handwriting on these photographs is that of Investigator Abt."

[194]  OIC, p. 73-74:  "Sergeant Edwards does not recall taking Polaroids himself."  OIC, p. 74, fn. 215:  "...Sergeant Edwards... does not recall taking any Polaroids himself, OIC, 1/12/95, at 7, 199-203.

## Photographs

The FBI's May 2, 1994, report of its interview with Abt reflects that she "specifically observed" Edwards taking Polaroid photographs.

> Upon arriving at the death scene, she specifically observed Sergeant Edwards in the process of completing Polaroid photography of the body and to the best of her recollection believes that contemporaneous with Edwards finishing his Polaroid photography, Investigator John Rolla commenced taking a series of Polaroid photographs. Upon Investigator Rolla completing his Polaroid photography, she believes that Officer Peter Simonello commenced taking 35mm photographs of the body and the surrounding environs.[195]

The OIC chose to relate only what Abt said, one officer's word against another. The OIC thus conceals that Rolla also saw Edwards photographing the body, as Rolla testified on deposition.

> Q. Did anyone else take photographs that you are aware of?
> A. I think that Edwards, Sergeant Edwards took a couple of Polaroids, I told him to give them to me... I didn't know who this guy was, nobody [knew] who this guy was...[196]

---

[195] Exhibit 99, Report of FBI interview of Park Police Investigator Renee Abt, May 2, 1994.

[196] Exhibit 6, Deposition of Park Police Investigator John Rolla, July 21, 1994: Q. Did you use a Polaroid camera? Yes. I used Polaroid. He used a 35 millimeter and apparently, for what ever reason, bad film or whatever, it came out too light or too dark. Q. Those are his photographs? A. Right. Q. Did anyone else take photographs that you are aware of? A. I think that Edwards, Sergeant Edwards took a couple of Polaroids, and I told him to give them to me, not having a collection –– you know, I didn't know who this guy was, nobody [sic] who this guy was, but we are not going to have a collection of dead body photographs, and I don't think there was an attempt, but lots of times –– I just wanted to make sure I had everything, and there wasn't anything walking around out there. Q. Did you use the same camera that he used? A. No.

| Body site |
|---|
| Sergeant Robert Edwards |
| Lieutenant Patrick Gavin |
| Inv. Christine Hodakievic |
| Investigator Cheryl Braun |
| Investigator John Rolla |
| Ev Tech Peter Simonello |
| Investigator Rene Abt |
| Intern with Officer Watson |
| Officer William Watson |

**FORT MARCY PARK**     **6:46-6:48**     <u>See</u> endnote 24.

When the investigators arrived at the body site, they observed Sergeant Edwards taking photographs. Braun was told that the death was a suicide. According to Rolla, although Gavin was the senior officer present, Braun and Hodakievic were in charge of the scene and did the "decision making." Rolla was in charge of the body scene. Rolla said it was his first "suicide" investigation.

raised earthen perimeter of fort

footpaths

FMP parking lot

| Parking lot |
|---|
| Officer Franz Ferstl |

## Photographs

And, according to the FBI's report of its April 27, 1994 interview with Rolla, the Polaroids of the body site consisted of a combination of the Polaroids that he and Edwards had both taken.

> "[The] Polaroid photographs were a combination of the photographs he and Sergeant Edwards took at the scene..."[197]

Park Police Investigator Cheryl Braun also testified that Sergeant Edwards had taken Polaroids, and that Edwards showed her his Polaroids before turning them over to Park Police Investigators.

> Q. Who did you say briefed you when you arrived at Fort Marcy Park?
> A. Well, initially I went and spoke with Officer Spetz, and then when we got to where the body was Sergeant Edwards had taken a few Polaroids and he gave those to us and just, you know, basically told us briefly, you know, what we had. And then we — I mean we were right there, so we went and looked ourselves.[198]

According to Park Police Investigator John Rolla's July 21, 1994 testimony, it is standard operating procedure for detectives (investigators) on a crime scene to take complete control of the scene.

> Q. Would you ordinarily work closely with a field commander in the course of your investigation?
> A. No... When the detectives come on the scene, the detectives are in charge of that crime scene. They are the ones responsible, sergeants, lieutenants, doesn't matter...[199]

---

[197] Exhibit 100, Report of FBI interview of Park Police Investigator John Rolla, April 27, 1994.

[198] Exhibit 101, Deposition of Park Police Investigator Cheryl Braun, July 23, 1994.

[199] Exhibit 6, Deposition of Park Police Investigator John Rolla, July 21, 1994: Q. Would you ordinarily work closely with the field commander in the course of your investigation. A. No, in fact, probably a lot of police departments, you have good police officers and stuff, but when the detectives come on the scene, the detectives are

Upon the arrival of the Park Police Investigators, Sergeant Edwards should have given all the Polaroids to the investigators then in charge of the body site. But Edwards did not turn over Officer Ferstl's Polaroids. Investigator Rolla testified that Sergeant Edwards had given him two Polaroids.

> Q. Did you say that you also saw some Polaroids that Sergeant Edwards might have taken at the scene?
>
> A. They had at least two Polaroid photographs.
>
> Q. They had photographs?
>
> A. Photographs, two Polaroid photographs that I requested, and I'm not sure which ones they are, they may be in the -- I may have just put them in the -- I think I told them to mark the -- to initial the photographs. I don't know if this is my fault, but I believe all the photographs were put in there and they don't show anything different. I looked at them, they don't show anything different than my photographs.
>
> Q. But you say you only remember two photographs from Sergeant Edwards?
>
> A. Yes.[200]

(Rolla's observation that other photographs "don't show anything different" than his did implies that there

---

in charge of that crime scene. They are the ones that are responsible, sergeants, lieutenants, doesn't matter. Unless we are specifically relieved of duty, we say what goes, you know, we are supposed to be in charge and tell people -- control access to the crime scene. You know, I have never had a problem with a field commander, working with him, when we need people, fielding people for interviews, but they try not to get involved because it's not their job. Q. So Lieutenant Gavin wasn't telling you to do anything at the scene? A. No. Q. Was he participating at all in your conversations or decision making? A. No. Q. So, it was Detective Abt and Detective Braun? A. Braun and Christine Hodakievic, who was an investigator at the time, has since left. She wanted to go back on patrol. She got off work, took a couple hours leave, lives out that way. On her way, she stopped to assist. Q. Because she heard something on the radio? A. Right. She was there before us.

[200] Exhibit 6, Deposition of Park Police Investigator John Rolla, July 21, 1994.

138

## Photographs

were duplicates -- no duplicates appear on the inventory.)
The OIC reports, probably accurately, that Edwards gave
investigators five Polaroid photographs that were unsigned.
Because they were not initialed, their origin could not be
determined.  There is no record of Officer Ferstl ever
having been asked to describe the state of the body when he
first saw it, or to describe the photographs he had taken.

Edwards' removal of Ferstl from the body site before
the arrival of other Park Police permitted Edwards to
tamper with the body unhindered by the presence of
witnesses.  Because Edwards obtained Ferstl's Polaroids,
which were the only crime scene photographs taken before
Edwards' arrival, he was able to conceal the existence of
the only documentation that could have exposed his having
tampered with the crime scene.  And, being a Sergeant who
had taken charge of the scene, he would not have to answer
to Ferstl, who was just an Officer, regarding what he had
done with Ferstl's Polaroids.

With Ferstl absent from the crime scene, and after
tampering with the body, Edwards photographed the body and
replaced Ferstl's seven Polaroids with the series of
Polaroids Edwards had taken with his own camera.  Other
Park Police investigators who subsequently arrived at the
body site saw Edwards taking photographs.

In short, Edwards gave the Polaroids he took to Park
Police Investigator John Rolla and absconded with the
photographs that Ferstl had taken -- photographs that would
have revealed that the body had been tampered with.

Officer Christine Hodakievic walked up to the body in
the company of Park Police Lieutenant Patrick Gavin.  While
at the body site, Sergeant Edwards showed Hodakicvic one of
the Polaroids in his possession.  When the FBI showed
Hodakievic a photograph when in interviewed her in May,
1994, she reported that blood appeared on the face and
shirt that were not there when she saw the body.

In order to further clarify her observations at the
death scene, a series of enlarged Polaroid photographs
provided by the USPP were shown to her.  Hodakievic,
after viewing these Polaroid photographs, stated that
in her opinion they were not identical to the Polaroid
photograph that was initially shown to her by Sergeant
Edwards.  She reiterated the fact that the photograph

Sergeant Edwards had showed to her was consistent with her observations, specifically that there was no blood on the face...[201]

Hodakievic's reported observation of the absence of blood on the face likely refers to when she first viewed the body, before escorting Gavin to the body.[202] Gavin saw a trickle of blood running down the face.[203]

## 2. Rolla's two Polaroids of the back of the head vanished

Also publicly known is that Park Police Investigator John Rolla testified on deposition that at least two Polaroids that he remembered taking of the back of Mr. Foster's head had vanished. The OIC also sought to explain this anomaly in its two-paragraph *Photographs* section. The OIC posits, in a footnote, that Rolla was wrong. He was simply mistaken about having taken these photographs.

According to the OIC, on April 17, 1996, three years after the death, and two years after having given sworn testimony to the contrary, Rolla recanted.

---

[201]    Exhibit 81, Report of FBI interview with Park Police Investigator Christine Hodakievic, May 2, 1994.

[202]    Exhibit 102, Handwritten notes of FBI interview of Lieutenant Patrick Gavin, April 28, 1994: "Inv. Christine Hodakievic met him in Pk [parking] Lot, took up to scene, she'd been there."

[203]    Exhibit 98, Report of FBI interview of Park Police Lieutenant Patrick Gavin, April 28, 1994: Lt. Gavin advised that he took a cursory look at the body and his only recollections are that there was a trickle or what appeared to be blood coming out of the mouth, running down the right side of the face. He stated that the face was pointing up toward the sky. He did not recall seeing blood coming from the nose, nor does he recall any blood or blood stains on the shirt. Lt. Gavin stated that there could have been more blood present on the shirt or face, but that he does not recall seeing it.

## Photographs

OIC, p. 72, fn. 214:

*"...Investigator Rolla initially suggested in a Senate deposition that he had taken photographs of the back of Mr. Foster's body... [H]e intended to take such Polaroids but he believes Investigator Braun took the Polaroid camera back to the parking lot... 302, 4/17/96, at 4..."*

The OIC does not quote Rolla's deposition. Rather, the OIC characterizes Rolla's testimony as having *"suggested"* that he had taken backside photographs. This is decidedly different from Rolla's sworn account given two years earlier.

Q. When you turned the body over with Dr. Haut, did you or anyone else take photographs of the area under the body?

A. You know, we rolled the body and I took Polaroids of the body rolled... I know I took Polaroids of that. I am not sure exactly how many I took, but I don't recall seeing those again. I mean, I had them in the office that night, I did reports, and I don't know what happened.

Q. Do you remember how many Polaroids you would have taken?

A. Unless there was something significant.

Q. I'm sorry.

A. Unless there was something significant. Again the shirt... back of his shirt and back of his head...[204]

\*　　\*　　\*

Q. Do you recall taking a specific picture of the pooled blood that had been under his head?

A. I don't recall that, I recall taking a picture of his head and around it, and I recall looking at that Polaroid...[205]

\*　　\*　　\*

Q. Did you have more than one packet of Polaroid film with you that day?

---

[204] Exhibit 6, Deposition of Park Police Investigator John Rolla, July 21, 1994

[205] Exhibit 6, Deposition of Park Police Investigator John Rolla, July 21, 1994.

141

A. I think I had more than one packet... I may have reloaded because I know I took some on the backside. I don't have those photos. I put them in a jacket, God knows how many people looked through those, and I don't know what happened.

Q. It's those pictures that you don't remember being in the jacket or the files afterwards?

A. I don't remember seeing backside photos and I know I would have taken...

　　　　　　　*　　*　　*

Q. Is it those pictures that you don't remember being in the jacket or in the file afterwards?

A. [I] had at least one from a way [sic] from him, after rolling him, and probably at least two more, or at least one more. I would say there has to be two, because I would have taken -- since a lot of times investigators won't take too many Polaroids, they will leave it to me, and I wanted to have photographs... I may have taken a close-up of the back of the head...[206]

　　　　　　　*　　*　　*

Q. When did you first notice they [Polaroids] weren't around?

A. I don't recall until being interviewed by the FBI about it. I know I took pictures.[207]

Rolla testified that he viewed all of his Polaroids as they developed and had a clear memory of what pictures he had taken.

Q. Polaroids come out right as you are taking the pictures, right?

A. Yes, right.

Q. Do you remember as you were taking the pictures looking at the pictures right then?

A. Right.

Q. What was the quality of the pictures?

A. I think the Polaroids were fine.[208]

---

[206] **Exhibit 6**, Deposition of Park Police Investigator John Rolla, July 21, 1994.

[207] **Exhibit 6**, Deposition of Park Police Investigator John Rolla, July 21, 1994.

[208] **Exhibit 6**, Deposition of Park Police Investigator John Rolla, July 21, 1994.

## Photographs

                    *     *     *

Q. Do you remember being shown photographs when you were interviewed by the FBI?

A. Yes.

Q. What kind of photographs were they?

A. They were my Polaroid photographs.

Q. Were they yours?

A. Yes.

Q. How could you tell they were yours?

A. I remember taking them. I remember what pictures I took...[209]

The OIC tells us that Rolla gave his camera to Investigator Braun and that Braun took the camera to the parking lot to photograph the car. Implicit in the OIC's claim that Rolla *"believes [that]... Braun took the camera"* is that the two investigators shared the one camera. This is false.

> OIC, p. 73, fn. 214:
>
> *"...Investigator Rolla initially suggested in a Senate deposition that he had taken photographs of the back of Mr. Foster's body. 7/21/94, at 89-90. After reviewing the Polaroids, Investigator Rolla stated that he intended to take such Polaroids, but believes Investigator Braun took the camera back to the parking lot..."*[210]

Braun testified that before she left the body site to go to the parking lot to photograph the car, she instructed

---

[209]   Exhibit 6, Deposition of Park Police Investigator John Rolla, July 21, 1994.

[210]   OIC, p. 73, fn. 214: OIC, 1/11/95, at 85, 87. Investigator Rolla initially suggested in a Senate deposition that he had taken photographs of the back of Mr. Foster's body. 7/21/94, at 89-90. After reviewing the Polaroids, Investigator Rolla stated that he intended to take such Polaroids, but he believes Investigator Braun took the Polaroid camera back to the parking lot before Dr. Haut arrived and the body was turned. 302, 4/17/96, at 4. The records are consistent with Investigator Rolla's statement, as the time "1930" is indicated on the back the Polaroids taken by Investigator Braun at the parking lot scene, and Dr. Haut appears not to have arrived at the park until approximately 7:40 p.m.

Rolla how to photograph the body, and left him to conduct the body site photography while she photographed the car. So each had a camera and Braun did not take Rolla's camera, contrary to the OIC's claim.

> Q. Okay. What were you doing while they were taking the photographs?
>
> A. I was basically directing Investigator Rolla what to do because he was new in the office. I wanted him to get the experience of handling a crime scene. So I was directing him what to do, and then I gave him some instructions. And to help save time, I went down to the car to start going through the car to look for identification and a suicide note.[211]

*      *      *

> Q. Did you interview anyone else out at the scene that night?
>
> A. At the scene? No. Just the couple when we initially got there, and then from there we went up to the body and I, you know, got Investigator Rolla started on the photos and what needed to be done on that particular scene...[212]

*      *      *

> Q. Was the car photographed before or after you went through it?
>
> A. It was photographed, I would take [a] picture of an area and then go through that area, and then — so it was photographed prior.[213]

The OIC notes that Braun marked the Polaroids she took of the car as having been taken at 7:30, and the OIC states that *"Dr. Haut appears not to have arrived at the park until approximately 7:40 p.m."* These facts, according to the OIC, corroborate Rolla's new account because *"Braun took the Polaroid camera back to the parking lot before Dr. Haut arrived and the body was turned."*

---

[211]  <u>Exhibit 101</u>, Deposition of Park Police Investigator Cheryl Braun, July 23, 1994.

[212]  <u>Exhibit 101</u>, Deposition of Park Police Investigator Cheryl Braun, July 23, 1994.

[213]  <u>Exhibit 101</u>, Deposition of Park Police Investigator Cheryl Braun, July 23, 1994.

## Photographs

OIC, p. 73, fn. 214:

*...Rolla stated that he intended to take such
Polaroids, but he believes Investigator Braun took the
Polaroid camera back to the parking lot before Dr.
Haut arrived and the body was turned." 302, 4/17/96,
at 4. The records are consistent with Investigator
Rolla's statement, as the time "1930" is indicated on
the back the Polaroids taken by Investigator Braun at
the parking lot scene, and Dr. Haut appears not to
have arrived at the park until approximately 7:40 p.m.*

The OIC's claim that "*[t]he records are consistent*" is
false. The records do not corroborate the OIC's version of
Rolla's revised account. In the *Report of Investigation by
Medical Examiner*, Dr. Haut reported that he viewed the body
at "7:15 p.m.,"[214] 25 minutes before the "*approximately 7:40
p.m.*" time the OIC claims he pulled into the Fort Marcy
lot. (Dr. Haut's *Report of Investigation by Medical
Examiner* was discovered at the National Archives on July
19, 1997, four days after the OIC filed its Report.)

Park Police Identification Technician Peter Simonello
and investigator Rolla photographed the body site in
tandem, Simonello using his 35-millimeter camera and Rolla
using his Polaroid camera. According to Simonello's
testimony, Rolla took what Simonello referred to as "backup
[Polaroid] photographs" of his 35-mm photographs.

Q. Do you remember about how many photographs you
took?
A. I believe I took the whole roll, which would be 24
photographs.
Q. Do you know if anyone else was taking photographs
out there?
A. John Rolla was taking Polaroids.
Q. Did he take any photographs of the body?
A. He took Polaroids of the body, yes. I would take
a photograph with the 35 and he would take what we
call a backup photograph with a Polaroid...[215]

---

[214] Exhibit 103, Report of Investigation by Medical Examiner,
July 20, 1993.

[215] Exhibit 104, Deposition of Park Police Evidence Technician
Peter Simonello, July 14, 1994.

### 3. OIC concealed that the roll of 35-mm film produced usable photographs

Park Police Identification Technician Peter Simonello shot an entire roll of 35-millimeter photographs at Fort Marcy Park. Later that night, back at the Park Police Anacostia Station, Simonello left the film in an envelope. The film was reportedly picked up to be processed at another location. Officially, we are simply told that the entire roll was *"underexposed."* The OIC fails to explain how or why this happened.

The OIC failed to interview those with access to the film and does not tell its readers whether the problem was the film, the camera, or error by the photographer or the developer. The Report's entire discussion of the roll of 35-millimeter film is as follows.

OIC, p. 72-73:

*Park Police Identification Technician Simonello took 35-millimeter photographs of Mr. Foster's body and of the scene.[fn211] Park Police investigators also took a number of Polaroids of Mr. Foster's body and of the scene. Polaroids taken at a crime or death scene develop immediately, and thus are useful in the event that problems occur in developing other film (as occurred here[fn212]).*

OIC, p. 73, fn. 212:

*"The 35-millimeter photographs were underexposed; thus, the Polaroids were of greater investigative utility."*

The Report relies heavily on photographic evidence while downplaying the importance of the 35-millimeter photographs. The OIC's vague and perfunctory reference that the *"35-millimeter photographs were underexposed"* hides that these photographs, even if in fact underexposed, were enhanced. When the FBI interviewed Peter Simonello, the photographer who shot the roll of 35-millimeter film, the interviewing agents showed him some of these 35-millimeter photographs, printed to a size of 8" x 10." The photograph "looked good," according to Simonello.

## Photographs

Simonello was assigned to the Park Police Anacostia Operations Facility.[216] He testified during his July 14, 1994 deposition that, although he was not sure, he believed that Park Police Evidence Technician Larry Romans took the undeveloped film to another facility for processing.

Q. Ordinarily, what happens? You leave the scene. You have film with you. What's the sequence of events to get it developed?

A. We have a film envelope that we use and I place it in there, fill out the envelope and give it to... Larry Romans, and I believe he has a -- we have a darkroom at the Brentwood facility... I believe he's the one that developed this roll.[217]

Because there is no record of Romans ever having been interviewed, we do not know whether the film was in fact

---

[216] Exhibit 105, Report of FBI interview of Park Police Identification Technician Peter Simonello, May 5, 1994: "Mr. Peter J. Simonello, Identification Technician, United States Park Police (USPP), Anacostia Operations Facility, Washington, D.C. (telephone number 690-5192) was interviewed..."

[217] Exhibit 104, Deposition of Park Police Identification Technician Peter Simonello, July 14, 1994: Q. You said earlier you thought the camera might have been malfunctioning? A. After I got the results back, I figured the camera was malfunctioning. Q. Was the camera ever sent off site to be looked at or to see if there was anything wrong with it? A. I don't believe so, no. I don't know how long it was after I took the shots that they were developed. And of course, I didn't realize until they were developed that the camera malfunctioned that day. I may have malfunctioned. I don't know. Q. Ordinarily, what happens? You leave the scene. You have film with you. What's the sequence of events to get it developed? A. We have a film envelope that we use and I place it in there, fill out the envelope and give it to Technician Romans, Larry Romans, and I believe he has a — we have a darkroom at the Brentwood facility that he uses and he develops film there, and I believe he's the one that developed this roll. Q. And generally, how soon after you provided the film are the prints developed? A. If it's a rough job, he can do it immediately, the next day when he comes in, the next shift he's working. On average, if it's not a rush job, it would be a week, maybe more, depending on how backed up he is.

delivered to, and processed by, the Brentwood Park Police facility.

Simonello testified that the Anacostia station had its own darkroom. And he testified that, because of the "importance of the case," he "wanted to keep" track of the evidence.

Q. Where would you lay the clothes out?
A. These clothing were laid out in the floor of the photo darkroom in the rear of the processing lab.
Q. So the photo darkroom, is that typically where the clothing would be put to dry?
A. That's where we typically put it.[218]

\* \* \*

Q. How would a choice be made between your evidence locker -- this is Anacostia --
A. Yes.
Q. - and Brentwood?
A. Again, that's up to the individual. In this case, I knew of the importance of the case, and I wanted to keep it where I knew exactly what was going on with it, so I kept it in our facility...

\* \* \*

Q. Is that the usual time to leave clothes to dry?
A. It varies... However, they probably left them there, awaiting my return, because I was the technician handling the original.[219]

Because the Park Police Anacostia station, to which Simonello was assigned, had a darkroom, the film did not need to leave that location to be processed. Its removal precluded Simonello from seeing the negatives or prints. The last time Simonello saw the roll of film was on the evening he shot it, when he placed it in an envelope.

Simonello testified that he was surprised to receive a note simply informing him that the negatives were underdeveloped, without "whatever prints were made," which,

---

[218] Exhibit 104, Deposition of Park Police Identification Technician Peter J. Simonello, July 14, 1994.

[219] Exhibit 104, Deposition of Park Police Identification Technician Peter Simonello, July 14, 1994.

he said, would have been "usual [because he was] the
technician in the case."

Q. How long did it take [to develop the film] in this
case?

A. I believe they were probably done by the time I
got back Sunday. I had a note that they were
underdeveloped... I can't remember if he left the
negatives on my desk or not, but he had left a
note...

* * *

Q. But you think that prints were made from the
negatives originally?

A. From our department, I don't think they were. I
never saw them. It's usual that I, as the
technician in the case, would receive copies of
whatever prints were made and I didn't receive
any.[220]

In 1994, Simonello assembled evidence to turn over to
the Fiske probe's FBI agents, but he could not remember
whether this evidence included the negatives of the roll of
film he shot.[221]

In its May 25, 1994 report, the FBI Lab uses the term,
"limited detail" to describe the results of its enhancement
efforts.

The 35mm color negatives (Q32) were examined to locate
frames for photographic enhancement. The selected
frames (5, 6, 7, 8, 9, 10, 17, 18) were printed using
Kodak Ultra print paper to produce maximum image
detail. Due to the negatives having been underexposed

---

[220] Exhibit 104, Deposition of Park Police Identification
Technician Peter Simonello, July 14, 1994.

[221] Exhibit 104, Deposition of Park Police Identification
Technician Peter Simonello, July 14, 1994: Q. When you
were putting together the package to go to the FBI, do you
recall putting in a package of prints? A. We didn't make
any -- you mean negatives? Q. No. Do you remember
putting the -- sending the negatives to the FBI? A. I
know they requested them. Again, there's so much material
I handed over, I can't specifically remember handing over
the negatives.

during the photographic process, limited detail could be extracted from each of the selected frames.[222]

Absent from this FBI Lab report is what detail may have been extracted from the other sixteen frames (1-4, 11-16 & 19-24). There is no reference to these frames anywhere else in the public record.

Simonello testified on deposition that the FBI Lab enhanced the 35-millimeter photographs so they did not appear underexposed. According to Simonello, these photographs "looked good."

Q. Have you subsequently become aware of any information [from the FBI] that would contradict anything in your report?

A. The only thing I read in there that I was wondering about is they said my 35 millimeter roll of film was overexposed [sic] and they weren't able to get any prints from it. But I recall that I was in the office there when they took a statement from me that day. I guess that was that date in May, and they showed me some 8-by-10 color photographs, and they indicated they were able to, in fact, enhance the photographs which I took, and I saw several of those 8-by-10s and I commented on what a good job they did because they looked good to me. They didn't look underexposed. They were able to enhance them and in the report they indicate they were not able to get anything from them.[223]

The second time the FBI interviewed Patrick Knowlton, May 11, 1994, FBI Agent Larry Monroe showed Patrick one of the 35-millimeter photographs that Simonello had taken. The photograph was of two cars in the parking lot of Fort Marcy Park. While trying to convince Patrick that the photographed car was the one Patrick had seen at the park, Monroe stated that the photograph's having been underexposed, along with the shade from the trees hitting it, made it appear darker than it really was. Monroe's

---

[222]   Exhibit 95, FBI Laboratory Report, May 9, 1994.

[223]   Exhibit 104, Deposition of Park Police Identification Technician Peter Simonello, July 14, 1994.

Photographs

report of that interview reflects Patrick's having seen the photograph, which appeared dark but otherwise clear.

> "[H]e was also exhibited a 35mm photograph (partially underexposed) which was taken by Officer Peter Simonello, USPP at Fort Marcy parking lot on July 20, 1993. The photograph of Mr. Foster's Honda when viewed next to a light colored USPP vehicle appears extremely dark in color..."[224]

Richard Arthur testified that the FBI showed him what appeared to be 35-millimeter photographs of the body scene.

> Q. I do have another question for you. Do you recall being shown photographs by the FBI?
> A. Yes..
> Q. What kind of pictures were they, if you know?
> A. They were pictures of the body scene.
> Q. Were they Polaroid pictures?
> A. No, they weren't. They didn't appear to be Polaroid pictures. They appeared to be pictures that the Park Police took on the scene, 35-millimeter, I would say.
> Q. Were they clear?
> A. They appeared to be pretty clear.[225]

## VI. EVIDENCE THAT THE OIC COVERED UP THE ABSENCE OF THE OFFICIAL MOUTH ENTRANCE WOUND & HEAD EXIT WOUND, AND THE EXISTENCE OF A NECK WOUND

Summary: Officially, there was an entrance wound in the soft palate and an exit wound about the size of a half-dollar about three inches below the top of the back of the head.

*Witness accounts of a bullet wound in Mr. Foster's neck and the absence of the official mouth entrance wound and skull exit wounds*: The Medical Examiner reported a gunshot wound to the neck, Paramedic Arthur was certain he saw a small caliber entrance wound on the neck, and there is

---

[224] Exhibit 106, Report of FBI interview of Patrick Knowlton, May 12, 1994.

[225] Exhibit 107, Deposition of Paramedic Richard Arthur, July 14, 1994.

no record of any of the 26 persons who viewed Mr. Foster's body before the autopsy having seen either official entrance or exit wounds.

*The autopsy:* Three officials claimed that, on their own initiative and without prior discussion, each was responsible for rescheduling the autopsy from Thursday to Wednesday, July 21. Because the autopsy was moved up to 15 hours after the body's discovery, the two investigating police officers did not attend, in violation of standard operating procedure (SOP), having worked all night. Dr. Beyer began the autopsy before the police arrived, in violation of SOP, during which time he removed the soft palate and tongue, the only evidence of both the actual and official entrance wounds. Dr. Beyer refused to tell the attending police the identity of the man who assisted him in the autopsy. He did not know the caliber of weapon, so he left that portion blank on his Report of Autopsy. He and he alone reported that gunpowder was on the soft palate. But Dr. Beyer's own laboratory could find no traces of gunpowder on the tissue from the soft palate. The day of the autopsy, the FBI was apprised that its "preliminary results" showed "no exit wound." The attending police reported that Dr. Beyer told them results of the x-rays. Dr. Beyer later claimed there were no x-rays. There was no official estimate of time of death. The evidence of the bullet trajectory is conflicting.

*Bloodstains consistent with the neck wound:* The OIC conceals that the bloodstains are consistent with the neck wound, but not with the official mouth wound. Blood present on Mr. Foster's neck, in his mouth, collar, right-side and back-side of his shirt is consistent with its having drained from the neck wound.[226]

*Official excuse for blood on Mr. Foster's right side is that it drained from his mouth when an "early observer" moved the head to check for a pulse,*

---

[226] Officer Fornshill claimed he could not recall the appearance of the blood at the scene. Paramedic Gonzalez saw blood on the right side. Firefighter Hall saw blood on the right collar. Paramedic Arthur saw the neck wound and blood coming from it. Pisani saw blood on the right shoulder. Wacha saw it in mouth and on the shirt. Ferstl saw blood around the mouth. Edwards' observations are unknown. Hodakievic saw blood under the head on the ground. Gavin saw blood out the mouth. Officers Rolla and Braun saw blood on right shoulder. Simonello saw blood close to the jawline and right shoulder. Abt saw it on the shirt and right collar. There is no record of what Watson and the "intern" may have seen. Dr. Haut reported that blood on the back of the head was "matted," trauma to the neck, and that the wound looked like it was caused by a "low velocity weapon." Ashford coded the death homicide and he did "not recall getting blood on his uniform."

Wounds

*then repositioned it -- but Edwards did it to obscure or camouflage the existence of the neck wound:* The OIC posits that (because no neck wound existed) the blood on Mr. Foster's right side had drained from his mouth when an "early observer" moved the head to check for a pulse, then repositioned it. The OIC conceals that no one admitted to having moved the head or seeing it being moved, and that no one tried resuscitation because Mr. Foster clearly appeared to have been dead for some time.[227]

The OIC conceals that the blood on the right shoulder and shirt could not have been caused by an "early observer" because all early observers saw these stains as they arrived.[228]

The OIC conceals that the blood was dry until after Edwards had been alone at the site.[229] Edwards moved the head to cause blood to drain from

---

[227]    Dale testified that there was "no doubt he was dead." Fornshill denied having moved the head and related that neither Gonzalez nor Hall had moved the head. Gonzalez said that no one checked for a pulse because Mr. Foster was clearly deceased and had been for "2-4 hours." Hall saw no one touch the body and he "backed off" because he was not a "medic." Arthur "did not check for a pulse" because Mr. Foster "was obviously dead." Iacone said that "medics confirmed there would be no efforts to resuscitate."

[228]    Dale saw a "stain on his right shoulder." Gonzalez testified that he saw the bloodstain "on the right shoulder... [in the] clavicle area." Hall said it was soaked into the collar. Arthur saw it on the right shoulder of the shirt. Pisani saw blood on Mr. Foster's right shoulder. Wacha saw blood on the shirt. Pisani saw "blood on Mr. Foster's right shoulder."

[229]    Fornshill testified that the blood was "dried... dark in color... [and] flaking." Gonzalez testified that the blood he saw was "dry." Hall saw blood on the collar but not on face or shirt, and said that the photos showed blood that he did not see. Arthur testified the blood was not running. Pisani saw no blood on the face and said that the photographs showed more blood than he saw. Ferstl saw a small amount of blood around the mouth, which was "not fresh." Edwards, interviewed only in 1995, ordered Fornshill to leave the park, took Ferstl's photos and ordered him back to the parking lot, leaving Edwards alone at the site -- after which time the blood was wet. Hodakievic (perhaps at the site before and after Edwards) did "not recall" seeing any blood. Gavin saw blood "trickling out of the mouth and running down the right side

153

the mouth to the neck to obscure and camouflage the existence of the neck wound.

The OIC conceals that the only witnesses who saw the blood transfer contact stain arrived at the site after Sergeant Edwards had been alone with the body.[230]

*Blood quantity insufficient:* The OIC conceals that the blood quantity observed was consistent with death caused by a small-caliber low-velocity bullet, and inconsistent with a point-blank shot to the mouth with .38 caliber high-velocity ammunition.[231]

---

of the face." Rolla saw wet blood coming out of the nostril and mouth and down the face and also wet on the shirt and shoulder and ground. Abt saw both "dried and liquid" blood on the face. Simonello saw "blood running from the nose" and on the cheek near the jawline. Braun saw it in the nose and mouth area of the chin near the right shoulder and running down the right side of the face.

[230] Rolla saw a transfer stain on the face. Abt saw a blood transfer stain on lower right cheek. Evidence Technician Simonello testified that he saw the transfer bloodstain "around the shirt collar, shoulder area."

[231] Dale said there was no blood around the head. Fornshill saw a "slight trail of blood" from the mouth and could not "recall any other blood." Gonzalez testified that the scene did not fit the usual .38 caliber gunshot head wound. Hall saw blood on the shirt and noticed no other blood. Arthur saw some around the mouth and nose but mostly on the right shoulder of the shirt. Pisani did not recall seeing any blood around the body. Wacha saw blood only on the mouth and shirt. Iacone did not recall seeing any blood. Ferstl saw a "small amount" of blood around the mouth and did not recall any from the nose or on the shirt. Hodakievic, who apparently viewed the body both before and after Edwards had been alone with it, said "she did not notice any blood on the decedent's face or on his shirt." Lieutenant Gavin saw a "trickle... out of the mouth" and did not recall blood from nose nor on the shirt. Rolla said blood "was not all over the place, it was directly under his head." Abt said that aside from the blood on the shirt, there was no evidence in "immediate vicinity of [the] death scene." Simonello said there "wasn't a great deal" of blood. There is no record of Braun's having commented on the quantity of blood. Dr. Haut did "not see blood on Foster's face..., [the] volume of blood [on the back of the head was] small and he did not recall seeing blood on... [the] shirt." Harrison did "not recall

## Neck wound

The OIC's claim of "blood-like stains" on the vegetation is contradicted by the accounts of witnesses at the body site.[232]

Officially, Mr. Foster placed the barrel of the .38 caliber revolver loaded with two high-velocity cartridges against his soft palate. Officially, the exit wound, about three inches below the top of the back of the head, was about the size of a half-dollar. The absence of these wounds, as well as the existence of the bullet wound in Mr. Foster's neck, explains many of the anomalies in the case.

1. **Witness accounts of a bullet wound in Mr. Foster's neck and the absence of the official mouth entrance wound and skull exit wounds**

   a. **Reports of Medical Examiner Haut and Paramedic Richard Arthur of the existence of a neck wound**

On July 19, 1997, four days after the OIC filed with the Court its interim Report on Mr. Foster's death, a researcher perusing Foster case documents at the National Archives found the *Report of Investigation by Medical Examiner.*[233] Dr. Donald Haut, the only doctor to see the body at the park, wrote it. He listed 7:15 p.m. as being the time he viewed the body.

It was a lucky find. Haut's Report was found with documents that had been released by the Senate Banking Committee in January of 1995. There were forty-seven boxes of such records. There had been a great deal of speculation as to why Dr. Haut's *Report of Investigation by*

---

observing any blood" and filed no hazardous material (blood) report.

[232] Fornshill did not relate having seen any blood on the vegetation. Gonzalez testified that the scene was unusual in appearance for a gunshot wound to the head. Pisani did not notice any blood around the body. Rolla reported "no blood on the plants or trees surrounding... [the] head." Abt observed no evidence in the "immediate vicinity of death scene." Dr. Haut remembered "no blood... on vegetation around the body." Ashford saw no blood on the ground.

[233] Exhibit 103, Report of Investigation by Medical Examiner, July 20, 1993.

*Medical Examiner*, as well as the *Death Certificate*, also authored by Haut, was not in Senate Hearings volumes.

The "Cause of Death" section on the first page of the Report appears below.

| CAUSE OF DEATH: PERFORATING GUNSHOT WOUND MOUTH- HEAD | MANNER OF DEATH: (check one only) ☐ Accident ☒ Suicide ☐ Homicide ☐ Natural ☐ Undetermined ☐ Pending | AUTOPSY: AUTHORIZED I Pathologist _ Autopsy No. _ |
|---|---|---|

I hereby declare that after receiving notice of the death described herein I took charge of the body an regarding the cause and manner of death in accordance with the Code of Virginia as amended; and that the tained herein regarding such death is correct to the best of my knowledge and belief.

| July 20, 1993 | Fairfax County | *[signature]* |
|---|---|---|
| Date | City or County of Appointment | Signature of Medical Exa |

Because the word "head" is not centered and there are some black marks to the left of it, it looks as if a different word had initially been typed in, but later whited out. In all likelihood, the falsifier decided not to center the word "head" because that would have required him to type over a whited-out word, and that would have been apparent on the photocopy. But the falsifier had failed to cover all of the original word, and we see what appears to be the bottom of a four-letter word.

That was not his only mistake. Because Haut's signature appeared on the front, maybe he didn't know that the Report has a backside. Under "Narrative Summary of Circumstances Surrounding Death," the following appears:

> July 20, 1993  After anonymous call was received at 18:04 hours US Park Police officers found 48 yrs Caucasian male with self-inflicted <u>gunshot wound mouth to neck</u> on a foot path in Marcey [sic] Park... (emphasis supplied).

The OIC didn't provide an excuse for Dr. Haut's having reported the neck wound because Haut's Report was not in the public domain when the OIC filed its Report. We don't know what Dr. Haut wrote as the cause of death on the *Death Certificate*. Perhaps the OIC was as dishonest in revealing the contents of the *Death Certificate,* as it was about the *Report of Investigation by Medical Examiner.*

## Neck wound

OIC, p. 27, fn. 27:

> ...Dr. Haut completed a "Report of Investigation
> by Medical Examiner" after the incident; the report is
> stamped with the date July 30, 1993.  OIC Doc. No. DC-
> 106A-1 to DC-106A-2.  The report states that the cause
> of death was "perforating gunshot wound mouth-head"
> and the means of death was a "38 caliber handgun."
> Id.  It states that the manner of death was "suicide."
> Id.  Dr. Haut signed the death certificate.  It states
> that the cause of death was "perforating gunshot wound
> mouth - head" and that the manner of death was
> "suicide" by "self-inflicted gunshot wound mouth to
> head."

The OIC even hides the date that the Report of
Investigation by Medical Examiner was written, reporting
only that "the report is stamped with the date July 30,
1993." Actually, it was stamped, "Jul 30 Received No Va
Medical Examiner," evidencing when Dr. Beyer's office
received it.  Dr. Haut wrote it the night of the death.
Written above "July 20, 1993," and Dr. Haut's signature, is
the following declaration.

> I hereby declare that after receiving notice of the
> death described herein I took charge of the body and
> made inquiries regarding the cause and manner of death
> in accordance with the Code of Virginia as amended;
> and that the information contained herein regarding
> such death is correct to the best of my knowledge and
> belief.

Dr. Haut was not the only medical personnel to report
the existence of a bullet wound in Mr. Foster's neck.
Richard Arthur is one of those observant witnesses who
knows what he saw, no matter how many times he's told he
didn't see what he remembered seeing.  His account of the
wound (and gun) has been quite problematic for the FBI.
He's been interviewed five times.  Each time, the FBI's
report of his observations is a little more watered down.

At the time of Mr. Foster's death, Arthur had been a
paramedic in the employ of Fairfax County for nine years.
Luckily, we have his Senate deposition a year after the
death, the only record of what Arthur saw which the FBI
could not edit.  He refused to alter his account of having
seen the bullet hole in Mr. Foster's neck.  He seemed

certain, and a little exasperated, when asked a year after
Mr. Foster's death, July 14, 1994.

> Q.    Let me ask you this:  If I told you that
>       there was no gunshot wound in the neck, would
>       that change your view as to whether it was a
>       suicide or not?
>
> A.     No...  What I saw is what I saw.  I saw blood
>       all over the right side of the neck, from here
>       down, all over the shoulder, and I saw a small –
>       what appeared to be a small gunshot wound here
>       near the jawline.  Fine, whether the coroner's
>       report says that or not, fine.  I know what I
>       saw.[234]

According to the OIC's account of the fourth FBI
interview with Arthur, in April of 1996, three years after
the death, Arthur finally recanted.

OIC, p. 34, fn. 77:

> ...Another of the FCFRD personnel, Richard Arthur,
> initially said he saw what appeared to be a bullet
> wound on the neck.  OIC, 1/5/95, at 63.  After

---

[234]    Exhibit 107, Deposition of Paramedic Richard Arthur, July
14, 1994:  Q.   Let me ask you this: If I told you that
there was no gunshot wound in the neck, would that change
your view as to whether it was a suicide or not?  A.  No,
because I mean -- I've read the reports and all that stuff
and the report from Fiske came out and he says there's no
gunshot wound to the neck and there was no sign of struggle
and that it was definitely, from what I understand -- let
me see if I can remember this right -- he used an old-style
revolver, put it in his mouth upside down and pulled the
trigger.  What I saw is what I saw.  I saw blood all over
the right side of the neck, from here down, all over the
shoulder, and I saw a small -- what appeared to be a small
gunshot wound here near the jawline.  Fine, whether the
coroner's report says that or not, fine. I know what I saw.
*** A.  I saw what appeared to be a bullet hole, which was
right around the jawline on the right side of the neck.  Q.
About how big?  A.  It looked like a small-caliber entrance
wound, something with -- I don't want to say a .22 or
whatever, but it was a small caliber.  It appeared to be a
smaller caliber than the gun that I saw.  Q.  Can you
estimate how big it was?  A.  I can't say for sure about
how big the hole was.  I can't really estimate.  There was
blood all around it, blood down the side of the neck.

## Neck wound

*examining autopsy photos, which he said were taken
from a better angle and a better view, he said he may
have been mistaken about such a wound.   302, 4/24/96,
at 1...*

In 1994, Arthur testified he saw a "small gunshot
wound here near the jawline...   I know what I saw."   In
1996, according to the OIC's FBI agents, *"he said he may
have been mistaken about such a wound."*

No investigator interviewed Arthur before the first
investigation was closed as a suicide.   The FBI interviewed
him the first time in March of 1994, during their second
death investigation.   From what we can tell of the FBI
agent's handwritten notes of that interview, Arthur did not
equivocate about having seen the bullet wound in Mr.
Foster's neck.

"small caliber gunshot wound to neck right side near
jaw line"[235]

According to the typed version of that March 16, 1994
FBI interview, Arthur "noted" only "what appeared" to be a
bullet hole in the neck.

"He noted what appeared to be a small caliber bullet
hole in Foster's neck on the right side just under the
jaw line..."[236]

---

[235]   Exhibit 109, Handwritten notes of FBI interview with
Paramedic Richard Arthur, March 16, 1994.

[236]   Exhibit 71, Report of FBI interview of Paramedic Richard
Arthur, March 16, 1994:  The deceased's clothes were not
disheveled, the hill area was clean and there was nothing
that struck him as unusual, except for the following
things, which make him doubt that it was a suicide:  the
straight attitude of the body, the apparent caliber of the
gun appeared bigger than the hole he thought he had
observed just under the jawline, and that he remembered the
barrel of the gun as being under Foster's thigh (possibly
half-way)...  He noted what appeared to be a small caliber
bullet hole in Foster's neck on the right side just under
the jaw line about half way between the ear and the tip of
the chin.  He did not note anything else he thought might
be a bullet hole.

The FBI took another crack at Arthur five weeks later, on April 29, 1994. The handwritten interview notes of that FBI interview similarly reflects that Arthur saw the neck wound.

> "It was a small caliber gun shot wound to neck right side near jaw line. High caliber weapon in hand."[237]

Again, the FBI watered down Arthur's account in its typed version of that interview, reporting that he "believed... was of the impression... was struck by his recollection... could not say for certain... the mark... was definitely a wound."

> He believed that he saw a wound on the right side of Foster's neck near the jaw line. He was of the impression that this wound was caused by a small caliber gun shot and was struck by his recollection that the weapon in Foster's hand was a high caliber weapon. Arthur could not say for certain whether the mark he had seen on Foster's neck was definitely a wound.[238]

The history of Arthur's interviews with the FBI repeated itself under the OIC's investigation, during which time he was interviewed two more times, in January of 1995 and again in April of 1996. Finally, according to the FBI's still-secret report of the fifth interview with him, after viewing the *"autopsy photos,"* which, the OIC claims, Arthur said were taken from a *"better angle and a better view,"* he admitted *"he may have been mistaken."*

Typically, the underlying record contradicts the OIC's claim that Arthur said the autopsy photographs were taken from a *"better angle and a better view."* When he testified under oath years earlier that he knew what he saw, "whether the coroner's report says that or not," he also said that

---

[237]   Exhibit 180, Handwritten notes of FBI interview with Paramedic Richard Arthur, April 29, 1994.

[238]   Exhibit 82, Report of FBI interview of Paramedic Richard Arthur, April 29, 1994.

he examined the "small caliber entrance wound" at the scene from "two [to] three feet" away.[239]

### b. No record of any of 26 persons who viewed the body before the autopsy having seen the official entrance and exit wounds

Of the twenty-six persons known to have seen Mr. Foster's body on July 20, 1993, ten were trained medical personnel (two medical doctors, two paramedics, and six fire & rescue workers). Of the remaining sixteen, ten were Park Police, one was a Fairfax County Police officer, one citizen, an unnamed intern, an unnamed morgue guard, and two White House officials.

There is no record of nineteen of these twenty-six witnesses having commented upon their observation of having seen any entrance wound. Another said "[i]t seemed like" he had seen an entrance wound because the "teeth had black marks on it." Another said he did not observe an entrance wound in the mouth and did not believe any photographs of a wound to the mouth exist. As we saw, Paramedic Arthur was sure he had seen a bullet hole on the neck on the right side. Another witness remembered a wound on the right side of the head. And the report of another witness's account is still secret. Not even one of these officials was

---

[239] Exhibit 107, Deposition of Paramedic Richard Arthur, July 14, 1994: Q. Where was the blood coming from? A. To me it looked like there was a bullet hole right here. Q. In the neck? A. Yes, right around the jawline. Q. The neck and jawline underneath the right ear? A. Somewhere there. I would have to see a picture to point it out exactly where but there was a little bit of blood coming out of the mouth, too, and a little out of the nose but the main was right here. I didn't see any on the left side. I didn't see any on the chest or anything. *** Q. With respect to the bullet wound you think you saw in the - at the scene could you describe in some detail exactly what you thought you saw? A. I saw what appeared to be a bullet hole, which was right around the jawline on the right side of the neck. Q. About how big? A. It looked like a small-caliber entrance wound, something with -- I don't want to say a .22 or whatever, but it was a small caliber. It appeared to be a smaller caliber than the gun I saw. *** Q. How close to the body were you when you saw this? A. 2, 3 feet.

interviewed until months after the initial 17-day death investigation was closed.[240] There is no record of the entrance wound until Dr. Beyer performed the autopsy and, as we shall see, his account is highly suspicious and appears to be contradicted by the scientific evidence.

Not one of the twenty-six eyewitnesses who had viewed Mr. Foster's body described seeing the official inch-and-a-quarter exit wound described by the OIC.

You wouldn't know any of this from reading the OIC's Report.

OIC, p. 20:

*"Thirty-one witnesses, 19 of whom observed Mr. Foster's body, have provided relevant testimony about their activities and observations in and around the Fort Marcy Park area on July 20, 1993."*

OIC, p. 24:

*"Later, five of the Park Police personnel prepared typed reports:  the responding beat officer (Ferstl), the two lead investigators (Rolla and Braun), Officer Hodakievic, and the identification technician..."* (Simonello).

The OIC claims that there was an exit wound in the back of Mr. Foster's head about the size of a half-dollar.

OIC, p. 30-31:

*"It [the autopsy report] describes exit wound as a wound of 1 1/4" x 1"*

---

[240]  Exhibit 101, Deposition of Investigator Cheryl Braun, July 23, 1994:  "Q.  Do you know if anyone ever followed up with the EMS or fire fighting personnel in terms of taking statements from them?  A.  I am not aware if they did."  Exhibit 79, Deposition of Park Police Officer Kevin Fornshill, July 12, 1994:  "[T]here was no official debriefing in regards to me being interviewed by the detectives or the investigators."  Exhibit 74, Report of FBI interview of EMT Corey Ashford, February 23, 1994:  "Ashford has not been interviewed by any other law enforcement agency regarding his actions surrounding the emergency response call related to Foster."

**No record of official wounds**

OIC, p. 31:

*"The exit wound is depicted [in the autopsy report] as being present three inches from the top of the head, approximately in the midline, and there is an irregular wound measuring one and one quarter inch by one inch."*[fn68]

OIC, p. 31:

*With respect to the wound, Dr. Beyer stated: "The entrance wound was in the back of the mouth, what we call the posterior oropharynx, where a large defect was present. There was also a soft palate tissue defect, and powder debris could be identified in the area of the soft palate and the back of the mouth."*

### Civilian Dale

Dale testified that there were "No signs of" Mr. Foster's having been shot. Dale surmised that "he had been hit in the head."[241]

### Officer Kevin Fornshill

Reportedly the first official to view Mr. Foster's body was Park Police Officer Kevin Fornshill. According to the testimony of two Park Police on the scene, it would have been SOP for him to file a Report.[242] He did not.

---

[241]   Exhibit 51, Deposition of Dale by Congressmen Burton, Mica and Rohrabacher, July 28, 1994: A. You see somebody laying there dead, you go what happened here, did somebody shoot him? No signs of it. Was he in a fight? Was he hit in the head. Q. What did you think happened? What did it look like? A. Well, when I started looking to see if he had anything in his hands, he had been hit in the head, what does that tell you?

[242]   Exhibit 104, Deposition of Park Police Officer Peter Simonello, July 14, 1994: "Q. In your experience, is it usual for the first officer on the scene to file a report? A. He has to file it." Exhibit 6, Deposition of Park Police Investigator John Rolla, July 21, 1994: "Yes. First officer on the scene would take the original case number and do the original case report and everything we do is under that number on subsequent..."

In fact, as he testified on deposition less than a year later, Fornshill was inexplicably not even interviewed about his observations at the scene.

> Q. Did any of the detectives on the scene come and talk to you?
> A. No...
> Q. None of these guys ever talked to you about the crime scene?
> A. No, not that I know of.[243]

On April 29, 1994, the FBI interviewed Fornshill for the first time. In the interviewing FBI agent's eleven pages of notes taken during the interview, there is no mention of any wounds observed by Fornshill. The notes only state that "Kevin was unaware of death cause."[244]

### Firefighter Todd Hall
### Paramedic George Gonzalez

Paramedic Todd Hall was deposed on July 20, 1994 and was interviewed by the FBI March 18, and again on April 27, 1994. On the first anniversary of the death, when Hall was asked, "Did you see any entrance or exit wounds?" he was uncertain, testifying only that "[i]t seemed like I seen one, the mouth, the teeth had black marks on it when I found it."[245] This description is consistent with a number

---

[243] Exhibit 79, Deposition of Park Police Officer Kevin Fornshill, July 12, 1994:  Q.  Did any of the detectives on the scene come and talk to you?  A.  No.  Q.  Do you know who the detectives were?  A.  I'm drawing a blank on that one...  Q.  None of these guys ever talked to you about the crime scene?  A.  No, not that I know of...  Q.  Did you ever talk to any of the other officers or people out there about what had happened?  A.  There was some conversation the next day after the news had announced whose body it was at Fort Marcy, and there was some conversation about that, but there was no official debriefing in regards to me being interviewed by the detectives or the investigators. [930]

[244] Exhibit 108, Handwritten notes of FBI interview of Park Police Officer Kevin Fornshill, April 29, 1994.

[245] Exhibit 67, Deposition of Paramedic Todd Hall, July 20, 1994.

of witnesses who reported seeing dried blood in the mouth and on the teeth. Moreover, there was no gunpowder on the teeth (see below) and Hall told Paramedic Arthur that Hall doubted that Mr. Foster's death was a suicide.[246]

Paramedic George Gonzalez, the third official to view Mr. Foster's body, related on deposition that he only "assume[d] there's an entrance wound from the mouth, because there was a lot of blood within the mouth,"[247] although Gonzalez expressed doubts whether enough blood had emanated from the mouth to justify the conclusion that there was, in fact, an entrance wound there.[248]

Gonzalez told the FBI that he recalled a bullet wound on the upper right side of the head.[249] Five months later, Gonzalez testified that he discussed the wound with another witness because he "was just wondering if he had the same recollection" of seeing a wound "on the side of the head."[250]

---

[246]   Exhibit 109, Handwritten notes of FBI interview with Paramedic Richard Arthur, March 16, 1994: "Todd thought odd - doubtful suicide"

[247]   Exhibit 110, Deposition of Paramedic George Gonzalez, July 20, 1994: Q. Did you ever see an entrance wound or an exit wound? A. I can only assume there's an entrance wound and that was from the mouth, because there was a lot of blood within the mouth, you could see that. It was dark and some of it had clotted already. I didn't see an exit wound.

[248]   Exhibit 110, Deposition of Paramedic George Gonzalez, July 20, 1994: Q. What about two paragraphs below that. "Gonzalez said he was surprised to find so little blood at the death scene of someone who appeared to have placed a 38 in his mouth and pulled the trigger." A. That's true. Q. But you didn't say a 38 though, because you didn't know what type of gun it was? A. No. I just said that there was very little blood for an accident such as this that occurred, such as this to occur. Q. That would be? A. A gunshot to the mouth. I said there wasn't a lot of blood.

[249]   Exhibit 111, Handwritten notes of FBI interview of Paramedic George Gonzalez, February 23, 1994: "Recalls seeing a hole in upper right front portion of head."

[250]   Exhibit 110, Deposition of Paramedic George Gonzalez, July 20, 1994: A. I think we were trying to -- I was trying to recall whether there was a gunshot wound on the side of the

Gonzalez testified that he "didn't see an exit wound,"[251] that the head was unusually intact,[252] and that it was peculiar that Mr. Foster's body was "laid out straight." He had never seen a body in that position as a suicide.[253]

---

head. I could not remember. I was just wondering if he had the same recollection. Q. So you were trying to remember where the entrance wound was? A. Yes, for some reason, I was trying to recall. Something in my mind said it was on the side of the head. There could have been a spot of blood or a run of blood. I couldn't remember at that time. That's why I was asking him.

[251] Exhibit 110, Deposition of Paramedic George Gonzalez, July 20, 1994.

[252] Exhibit 110, Deposition of Paramedic George Gonzalez, July 20, 1994: Q. If every time you'd gone to a suicide scene with a gunshot. [sic] It had been a mess, would you have said always, or every time I've had a gunshot wound suicide to the mouth, it's been a mess? A. Please repeat your question. Q. If your experience had been that every time you'd gone to a scene like this, it had always been a mess. Would you have said that to him? Would you have said, every time I've been to a scene like that, it's been a mess? (Pause). A. Let me describe a few situations that you'll maybe better understand the word "usually." Sometimes the head is either gone, decapitated. Okay, from say the mouth all the way up. Sometimes you have the whole frontal part of your face but with the back portion, the occipital region gone. Sometimes it's the side of the face if it's an angle or approach the gunshot from the side, this side of the face is usually gone. I guess when I say usually. I'm thinking of numbers and the majority of the numbers, to describe your question, as far as usually.

[253] Exhibit 110, Deposition of Paramedic George Gonzalez, July 20, 1994: A. You have to understand when you say it's possible, it's almost like filling a void in our report, filling in a category in our department to describe the incident. It does not mean it's concretely, it just means it's a possible situation that may occur to our best knowledge. We can describe the situation in this category. Q. What might be some things that would cause that preliminary determination to change. A. I guess finding a scene that's unfamiliar or different than what you're accustomed to finding. It does not usually fit a normal call, not a normal call, but back to this word "usual" call, a suicide or something. Q. Actually, I've got some

No record of official wounds

**Officer Franz Ferstl**

The report composed by the second police officer at the body site, Evidence Technician Franz Ferstl, does not mention any wounds he may have seen.[254] If the FBI asked Ferstl to describe the wounds he saw during its 1994 interview with him, it is not reflected in the report of that interview, nor anywhere else in the publicly available record.

**Paramedic Richard Arthur**
**Firefighter Ralph Pisani**
**Firefighter Lieutenant James Iacone**
**Firefighter Jennifer Wacha**

Paramedic Richard Arthur testified that he "didn't see the entrance wound in the mouth,"[255] and that the entrance wound he saw in the neck looked like a "small sized bullet hole."[256] Arthur concluded, "it just didn't look like a suicide."[257] He also testified that he "didn't see" any exit wound.

---

other articles here we can talk about but, one, you've been quoted as saying that you noticed some peculiar aspects to the scene. Did anything strike you as peculiar or unusual about the scene? A. The fact that he was straight, laid out straight, yes. That's peculiar. Q. Have you ever seen a body in that position as a suicide? A. No.

[254] Exhibit 112, Park Police Report of Officer Franz Ferstl, July 20, 1993.

[255] Exhibit 107, Deposition of Paramedic Richard Arthur, July 14, 1994: "I didn't see the entrance wound in the mouth."

[256] Exhibit 107, Deposition of Paramedic Richard Arthur, July 14, 1994: And from what I saw, a gunshot wound here looked like a small sized bullet hole, small caliber, and from the gun that I saw, it appeared to be a larger caliber like an automatic or something. It just didn't match up. *** [887] It just seems weird. And the bullet hole, the caliber from what I saw and that just didn't match up. Like I said, I'm not a forensic expert. Maybe he used a lower caliber bullet or somebody used a low cal bullet and low cal gun.

[257] Exhibit 107, Deposition of Paramedic Richard Arthur, July 14, 1994: Q. Let me ask you one more question about that. If I told you that they found an entrance wound in the

167

Q. What about the exit wound at the back of the head?
A. Is there one? I didn't know there was one...
   I didn't see the exit wound.[258]

Based on his experience, Arthur was surprised by the absence of an exit wound.

> And I don't know -- I heard a .38 revolver was
> reported and to me, a .38 would have an exit
> wound. I've seen .38 gunshot wounds before to
> the head, and they've had exit wounds before. I
> don't know, maybe just out of some weird
> coincidence or something, this one didn't, but
> from what I saw in past things, .38s usually have
> an exit wound.[259]

There is no record of firefighters Ralph Pisani or Jennifer Wacha ever having been asked what wounds they may have seen. Lieutenant James Iacone "didn't look for or see wounds," according to the FBI's handwritten notes of its March 11, 1994 interview with him.[260]

### Sergeant Robert Edwards

See Sergeant Edwards' movements in the maps above. Edwards never wrote any report of his involvement at the

---

upper part of his mouth -- A. That's what I remember from the reports. Q. -- and that was in a straight line to the exit wound in the back of the head, would that change your view as to whether it's a homicide or suicide? A. If that's what they found, and that's what they say they found, then fine. That's what they found. I know what I saw. Now, if I saw that, and that's what was there and that's what I saw and I saw the exit -- if it appeared that the man shot himself in the mouth or something, then fine, maybe he shot himself in the mouth and it was a suicide. But to me, from the positioning of the body and the gun that I saw and stuff, it just didn't look like a suicide.

[258] Exhibit 107, Deposition of Paramedic Richard Arthur, July 14, 1994.

[259] Exhibit 107, Deposition of Paramedic Richard Arthur, July 14, 1994.

[260] Exhibit 77, Handwritten notes of FBI interview of Firefighter Lieutenant James Iacone, March 11, 1994.

scene, he was not interviewed during the first investigation, there is no record of the FBI having interviewed him during the Fiske probe, and there is no public record of what he may have observed.

### Lieutenant Patrick Gavin
### Investigator Christine Hodakievic

Park Police Officer Christine Hodakievic's report does not mention any wounds she may have seen,[261] nor is there any record of her observations in the FBI's 1994 interview report, or anywhere else in the record. She only recalled being "informed" there was an exit wound.[262]

Lieutenant Patrick Gavin, the highest-ranking official at the body site, did not write a report. There is no mention of his observations of any wound in the FBI's Report of its 1994 interview with him, or anywhere else in the public record.

### Investigator John Rolla
### Investigator Cheryl Braun
### Evidence Technician Peter Simonello
### Investigator Renee Abt
### Officer William Watson
### Intern with Officer Watson

John Rolla, the lead Park Police Investigator at the body site, did not mention any observations of an entrance wound in his report.[263] He testified on deposition on July 21, 1994, that he did not look or see for an entrance wound.

---

[261] Exhibit 76, Park Police Report of Investigator Christine Hodakievic, July 21, 1993.

[262] Exhibit 81, Report of FBI interview of Park Police Investigator Christine Hodakievic, May 2, 1994: "She recalls the medical examiner inquiring about an exit wound and being informed by investigator John Rolla that he, Rolla, had found an exit wound at the back of the head."

[263] Exhibit 113, Park Police Report of Investigator John Rolla, July 21, 1993.

Q. What about his mouth, his teeth or whatever?
A. I didn't look at the teeth that closely. I knew the medical examiner would and the medical examiner's report [reported that] there were no broken teeth.[264]

(It is questionable whether a .38 revolver, with a relatively high sight and firing the official high caliber ammunition, would not have damaged teeth from the recoil.)

Rolla seemed uncertain of the exit wound, testifying only that there "appeared to be an exit wound"[265] and that "the skull appeared to be fractured from the inside out."[266] Rolla's description of a "mushy spot" stands in sharp contrast to Dr. Beyer's description of a one-and-a-quarter inch hole.

Q. Was there any attempt to find bone fragments or anything in the ground?
A. They searched the area... I still can't believe that the hole -- it's a small hole. They may put their finger through it, that's a big hole. His head was not blown out... I probed his head and there was no big hole there. There was no big blowout. There weren't brains running all over the place. There was blood in there. There was a mushy spot. I initially thought the bullet might still be in his head. Could have been the brain pushed up against that hole. There's no big hole

---

[264] Exhibit 114, Deposition of Park Police Investigator John Rolla, June 20, 1995: "Q. What about his mouth, his teeth or whatever? A. I didn't look at the teeth that closely. I knew the medical examiner would and the medical examiner's report there were no broken teeth."

[265] Exhibit 114, Deposition of Park Police Investigator John Rolla, June 20, 1995: "No trauma to the body other than what appeared to be an exit wound in the center rear portion of his head, blood under his head. There is no other trauma... it wasn't brains blown all over the place..."

[266] Exhibit 113, Park Police Report of Investigator John Rolla, July 21, 1993: "I rolled the decedent over and observed a large blood stain three quarters down the back of the decedent's shirt. I observed trauma to the center portion of the back of the decedent's head. The skull appeared to be fractured from the inside out."

No record of official wounds

or big blowout in his head.[267]

\*     \*     \*

[Dr. Haut] looked at the back of his head.  I
looked at the back of his head, and I was wearing
gloves, I probed his head and I could feel -- what
I felt in his head was mushy here.  I did not, you
know, there was hair, blood and other matter
there, and I did not observe any blowout, like his
brains had been blown out all over the place.  It
just appeared it was mushy there.[268]

Of the two pages of the handwritten interview notes of
the FBI's 1994 interview with Rolla, immediately above the
only redaction are the words "back of head."[269]

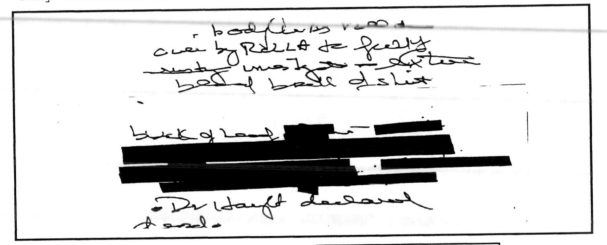

Handwritten notes
of FBI interview of
Park Police Investigator John Rolla:

Body was rolled
over by Rolla to fully
investigate – extensive
blood back of shirt
back of head [redacted]
[line redacted]
[line redacted]
[line redacted]
Dr. Haut declared
dead

---

[267]  Exhibit 6, Deposition of Park Police Investigator John
Rolla, July 21, 1994.

[268]  Exhibit 6, Deposition of Park Police Investigator John
Rolla, July 21, 1994.

[269]  Exhibit 115, Handwritten notes of FBI interview of Park
Police Investigator John Rolla, April 27, 1994.

171

Park Police Investigator Cheryl Braun did prepare a two-page typed Report.[270] It too does not mention any observation of any wounds, and there is similarly no record of her ever having commented on her observations of any wounds.

Park Police Evidence Technician Peter Simonello's Report does not mention any wounds,[271] nor does the FBI's Report of its April, 1994 interview with him.[272] Simonello testified on deposition that he did not observe any entrance wound in the mouth and added that he did not believe any photographs of a mouth wound existed.

> Q. Did you come to realize at some point that there was a wound in the mouth of Mr. Foster?
> A. I never observed that personally...
> Q. Did you see any photographs? Do you know if anybody from the Park Police took photographs inside the mouth?
> A. I saw the autopsy photographs, and I do not believe there's any that actually show the interior of the mouth.[273]

Simonello looked, saw what he testified he thought was an exit wound, but failed to describe what he saw.

> Q. You said you saw the wound after the body was moved. Where did you see these wounds or wound?
> A. What I saw was the wound to the back of the head.
> Q. How close were you to the body when it was moved?
> A. I was right up on it, within a foot or two.[274]

---

[270]    Exhibit 116, Park Police Report by Investigator Cheryl Braun, July 20, 1993.

[271]    Exhibit 117, Park Police Report by Park Police Evidence Technician Peter Simonello, July 25, 1993.

[272]    Exhibit 105, Report of FBI interview of Park Police Evidence Technician Peter Simonello, April 28, 1994: "[W]hen the decedent's body was turned on its stomach he observed a large pool of blood where the head had been situated. Simonello stated that he photographed his particular area and checked for the expended round with negative results."

[273]    Exhibit 104, Deposition of Park Police Evidence Technician Peter Simonello, July 14, 1994.

## No record of official wounds

Park Police Investigator Renee Abt did not write a report and there is no public record of her having observed an entrance or exit wound.

Neither SWAT Team Officer William Watson, nor the intern who reportedly accompanied him,[275] wrote any reports, and there are no comments regarding any observations by either of them anywhere in the public record.

### Dr. Donald Haut

The two Reports of the FBI's interviews with Dr. Donald Haut, the only doctor to view the body at the park, are silent on Haut's observations of the wounds he saw, although he wrote in his *Report of Investigation of Medical Examiner* that the wound was "mouth to neck."

The FBI's Report of its interview with him repeatedly refers to his having looked for an exit wound, but fails to relate whether he found one.

> The purpose of lifting the right shoulder of the body was to check for an exit wound... Haut and a USPP officer raised Foster to look at the back of the head. The reason for looking at the back of the head was to locate an exit wound. He recalls seeing blood around the back of Foster's head... In examining the back of the head Haut describes the blood being clotted.

---

274     Exhibit 104, Deposition of Park Police Evidence Technician Peter Simonello, July 14, 1994: Q. Did you see any wounds on the body? A. At first observation I did not. I just saw the blood. Q. Did you ever see any wounds on the body? A. When the body was turned over, there was a wound to the back portion of his skull... Q. You said you saw the wound after the body was moved. Where did you see these wounds or wound? A. What I saw was the wound to the back of the head. Q. How close were you to the body when it was moved? A. I was right up on it, within a foot or two. Q. Was there blood in the area? A. Yes. Q. Where was the blood? A. Pooling of blood directly underneath where his head had been, and then there was some blood along the back of his shirt, top portion of his shoulders, upper half of his back there was blood.

275     Exhibit 118, Handwritten notes by Investigator Renee Abt, July 20, 1993: "Post arrival Watson + intern"

Although the volume of blood was small, Haut did recall that the blood was matted and clotted under the head. Haut pulled on Foster's right shoulder turning him to the left in order to conduct his examination.[276]

The FBI's Report of its interview with Haut also notes that whatever wound he observed did not appear to be consistent with the official .38 caliber weapon.

"Haut believed that the wound was consistent with a low velocity weapon."[277]

## Firefighter Corey Ashford
## Firefighter Roger Harrison

Firefighter Roger Harrison helped Corey Ashford lift Mr. Foster's body into the body bag. Ashford coded the death a homicide. The FBI's Report of its 1994 interview is silent on what Ashford saw, so there is no public record of why he saw fit to code the death a homicide. Arthur testified that Ashford told him the head was intact, meaning that there was no exit wound.

I talked to Corey who put the body into the body bag. He classified it as a homicide... but I asked him if there was an exit wound, and he said no. He said the

---

[276] Exhibit 181, Report of FBI interview of Dr. Donald Haut, April 14, 1994: The purpose of lifting the right shoulder of the body was to check for an exit wound... Upon arriving at the body, Haut recalls that the decedent was located on a foot path over a hill. Haut and a USPP officer raised Foster to look at the back of the head. The reason for looking at the back of the head was to locate an exit wound. He recalls seeing blood around the back of Foster's head...

[277] Exhibit 73, Report of FBI interview of Dr. Donald Haut, April 12, 1994: "After examination of the back of Foster's head, Haut believed that the wound was consistent with a low velocity weapon. Haut recalled a separate case in which a .25 caliber rifle caused a much more devastating wound to the victim." Exhibit 119, Handwritten notes of FBI interview of Medical Examiner Dr. Donald Haut, April 12, 1994: "To look at back of head lifted with officer. Looking for wound of exit... Wound may be consistent w/low velocity weapon Haut recalls seeing .25 cal rifle [inserted] weapon wound that had much more devastating impact."

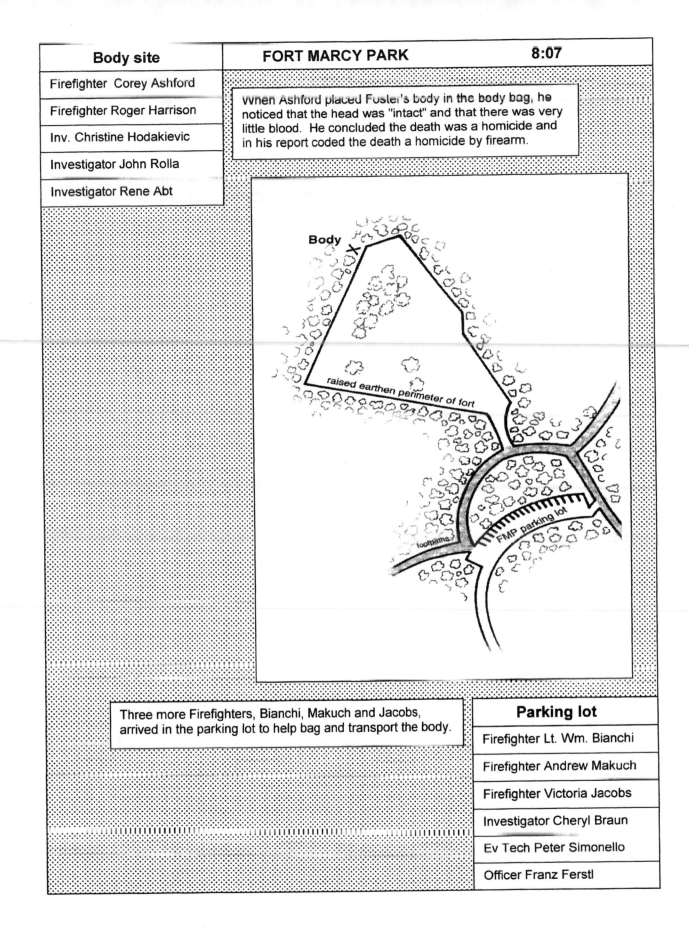

| Body site |
|---|
| Firefighter Corey Ashford |
| Firefighter Roger Harrison |
| Inv. Christine Hodakievic |
| Investigator John Rolla |
| Investigator Rene Abt |

**FORT MARCY PARK** 8:07

When Ashford placed Foster's body in the body bag, he noticed that the head was "intact" and that there was very little blood. He concluded the death was a homicide and in his report coded the death a homicide by firearm.

Body
X

raised earthen perimeter of fort

FMP parking lot

footpaths

Three more Firefighters, Bianchi, Makuch and Jacobs, arrived in the parking lot to help bag and transport the body.

| Parking lot |
|---|
| Firefighter Lt. Wm. Bianchi |
| Firefighter Andrew Makuch |
| Firefighter Victoria Jacobs |
| Investigator Cheryl Braun |
| Ev Tech Peter Simonello |
| Officer Franz Ferstl |

head was intact when he picked it up.  So that's just another thing that led me to believe that it could have been a homicide...  Like I said, I asked him [Corey Ashford] if the head was intact and he said yeah.  I asked him how he coded it as a homicide, and he said that's what he thought it was.[278]

The FBI's Report of its March 11, 1994 interview with Firefighter Roger Harrison also contains no reference to any wounds.

**Morgue witnesses -**
**Dr. Julian Orenstein**
**County Police Officer David Tipton**
**unidentified guard**
**William Kennedy**
**Craig Livingstone**

Dr. Julian Orenstein examined Mr. Foster's body twice on the evening of July 20, at Fairfax County Hospital. According to the FBI's Report of its April, 1994 interview with him, he examined the body once in the ambulance shortly after its arrival, and, when he learned that the body was a White House official, he went to the morgue and examined the body a second time.[279]  It was the first time Orenstein had ever gone to the morgue to examine a body.[280] The second time he examined the body, in the morgue, he specifically looked for an exit wound.[281]  The FBI's Report

---

[278]  Exhibit 107, Deposition of Paramedic Richard Arthur, July 14, 1994.

[279]  Exhibit 121, Report of FBI interview of Dr. Julian Orenstein, April 14, 1994:  Orenstein later went back to the morgue area of the hospital after hearing a discussion that the decedent was from The White House.  He recalled that members of the Secret Service were coming to the hospital to view the body...  At the morgue, Orenstein and Police Officer Dave Tipton, Fairfax County Police Department, lifted the body by the shoulders.  Orenstein pulled the body forward noting that it had...

[280]  Exhibit 121, Report of FBI interview of Dr. Julian Orenstein, April 14, 1994:  "Orenstein noted that this was the first instance he could recall where he went to the morgue to look at a decedent."

[281]  Exhibit 121, Report of FBI interview Dr. Julian Orenstein,

176

of its interview with him does not relate what he may have seen on either occasion.

When Orenstein viewed the body the second time in the Morgue, Fairfax County Police Office David Tipton accompanied him and, according to the FBI's Report of its interview with Orenstein, Tipton helped Orenstein lift the body.[282] According to that same FBI Report of its interview with Orenstein, an unidentified morgue guard[283] also viewed the body. There is no public record of Fairfax County Police Office David Tipton's having been interviewed,[284] or of the unknown guard at the morgue, who also viewed the body.[285]

White House Officials Associate Counsel William Kennedy and Chief of Personnel Security Craig Livingstone both testified that they went to the hospital morgue where they viewed Foster's body. There is no record of what they observed.

## 2.    The autopsy

All experts and both the Starr and Fiske reports depend primarily on Dr. Beyer's Report of Autopsy in concluding suicide in the park. The OIC cites the autopsy over eighty times, but reveals very little about it.

---

April 14, 1994:  "Orenstein pulled the body forward noting that it had become rigid. The purpose for lifting the body by the shoulders was to locate and observe the exit wound on the decedent's head."

[282]    Exhibit 121, Report of FBI interview Dr. Julian Orenstein, April 14, 1994.

[283]    Exhibit 121, Report of FBI interview of Dr. Julian Orenstein, April 14, 1994:  "Dr. Orenstein was not aware of anyone else who saw Foster at the hospital other than himself, Officer Tipton and the morgue guard."

[284]    Exhibit 121, Report of FBI interview of Dr. Julian Orenstein, April 14, 1994.

[285]    Exhibit 121, Report of FBI interview of Dr. Julian Orenstein, April 14, 1994.

The autopsy

OIC, p. 34:

*"Dr. Beyer's conclusions were reviewed by two sets of experts, one set retained by the OIC and the other by Mr. Fiske's Office. Their analyses of Dr. Beyer's findings and of the relevant laboratory analyses are outlined below. They confirm the conclusions reached at the autopsy."*

## a. Rescheduled

The body was discovered at 6:00 p.m. on Tuesday, July 20. The autopsy was initially scheduled for Thursday, July 22. But Dr. Beyer began the autopsy just thirteen hours after the body had been removed from the park. He had begun the autopsy sometime before 10:00 a.m. on Wednesday, July 21.

As of Tuesday evening, the White House understood that the autopsy was to be performed on Thursday, a day-and-a-half after the body had been discovered. Deputy Assistant to the President Bill Burton wrote that the autopsy had been scheduled for "7:00 a.m." Thursday morning.[286]

Captain Hume,[287] Major Hines[288] and Dr. Beyer each claim that they were responsible for rescheduling the autopsy.

---

[286] Exhibit 122, Deposition of Deputy Assistant to the President Bill Burton, July 5, 1995: Q. Who wrote those notes? A. They're in my handwriting. Q. Now, directing your attention to 450, are those notes or writings that you took down on the evening of July 20 as you were getting basic information and phone numbers from various people regarding discovery of Mr. Foster's body? A. I can't tell from looking at them if I wrote them that evening or the next day. *** Q. Now it says here at the bottom, "autopsy 7:00 a.m., 7-22-93, two to three hours." A. I do not remember where I got that information. I do not remember where I got that information.

[287] Exhibit 123, Deposition of Park Police Captain Charles Hume, July 22, 1994: "The only thing I asked Dr. Beyer if he could move the autopsy up to get that done as soon as possible."

[288] Exhibit 124, Deposition of Park Police Major Robert Hines, July 25, 1994: "Q. But this was something that you initiated?

## The autopsy

The investigators on the case, Rolla and Braun, were told from two different sources that it was moved up "at the request of the White House."[289]

According to Sergeant Rule, Captain Hume moved the autopsy up at Chief Langston's request. Hume testified he moved it up to that morning at the request of the White House.[290]

As Rule, Rolla, Braun and Abt discussed the probable timing of the autopsy at the police station at 6:00 Wednesday morning, the autopsy had already been scheduled to occur just hours later at 10:00 a.m. And when Dr. Beyer's office told Rolla at 6:30 Wednesday morning that the autopsy would not be performed until the next day,[291] it had already been scheduled to be performed three and a-half-hours later.

On Wednesday morning at 10:00, Major Hines and Chief Langston met with White House staff at the White House to brief them on the case. The meeting lasted about "30

---

A. I initiated it, yes. Q. And no one suggested this to you?
A. Yes. And I've done that before."

[289] Exhibit 101, Deposition of Park Police Investigator Cheryl Braun, July 23, 1994: A. Did someone tell you explicitly that the autopsy was being moved up because the White House had requested it? A. Yeah. Q. Who told you that? A. I believe I was speaking to Detective Squires. Q. Who is that? A. He is another detective in the office. But I am fairly certain that's who I was speaking to. But I am not positive on that. And yeah, I had been told that at the request of the White House the autopsy was moved up.

Exhibit 6, Deposition of Park Police Investigator John Rolla, July 21, 1994: "[The reschedule had been] specifically at the request of the White House."

[290] Exhibit 123, Deposition of Park Police Captain Charles Hume, July 22, 1994: "Q. Okay. And do you recall who asked you to move the autopsy date? A. I believe it was Major Hines asked me... that request came from the White House."

[291] Exhibit 6, Deposition of Park Police Investigator John Rolla, July 21, 1994.

minutes."[292]    During that 10:00 a.m. White House briefing, according to Hines, the subject of funeral arrangements came up.  According to Hines, he told White House personnel that an autopsy would have to be performed.  Hines testified that, without being asked to do so, he volunteered to "try and get it scheduled [for] that day." Hines testified that "sometime after" that 10:00 a.m. meeting, he had his first discussion about the "timing or scheduling" of the autopsy.  Hines claimed that after his White House briefing, he "asked the investigators to talk to the doctor to see if they would do the autopsy faster."[293]

Major Hines' account that he asked that the autopsy be moved up after the White House briefing obviously cannot be true.  The autopsy had begun before 10:00 a.m., when Hines and Langston met at the White House for the briefing.

Dr. Beyer testified before the Senate that both the White House and the Park Police were wrong.  Dr. Beyer insisted that it was his idea to change the scheduled time of the autopsy.

> Q.  Officer Rolla, you asked earlier about this
> question of moving up the autopsy.  It is agreed

---

[292]    Exhibit 124, Deposition of Park Police Captain Robert Hines, July 25, 1994:  "Q.  How long was the presentation at the White House?  A.  I would say about 30 minutes, 25, 30 minutes."

[293]    Exhibit 124, Deposition of Park Police Major Robert Hines, July 25, 1994:  Q.  You mentioned something about scheduling the autopsy.  When did you first have any discussions about the timing or the scheduling of the autopsy?  A.  Well, at some time after that, you know.  I said I would arrange for the autopsy, to try to get it scheduled that day if we could.  Q.  You said that at the White House?  A.  At the White House meeting, yes.  Q.  Why did it come up?  A.  I think they were talking about funeral arrangements.  I don't recall who said what about it or what exactly was said.  And I said we would have an autopsy.  They asked when.  And I said, well, I don't know, I'd try to find out.  It was later I found out that it was scheduled for sometime later.  And I asked the investigators to talk to the doctor to see if they would do the autopsy faster.  Q.  But did anyone at the White House specifically ask you to move the autopsy up?  A.  They did not.  They did not.

that the autopsy was moved up by a day. Is that correct, doctor?

A. Well, as soon as I heard about the case, I had the body transported over, and we make every effort to do an autopsy within less than 24 hours if possible. Therefore, once I could get the body over, we proceeded with the autopsy.

Q. But did you receive a message, doctor, asking you to try to proceed faster than normal?

A. No, sir.

Q. It is my understanding that Major Hines, who is sitting behind you but not at the table, that his recollection is different, and that he believes that the request to move it up was in order to facilitate the transfer of the body to Arkansas. Is that accurate, Mr. Rolla? Do you remember that, Ms. Braun?

A. (Ms. Braun). That was my understanding, when we left that morning, the autopsy was set for the day after the 22nd, and then I found out later on in the day that it had gotten moved up and that they did the post on the 21st.

Q. And it was your understanding that that was in order to facilitate the transfer of the remains to Arkansas?

A. (Ms. Braun). Yes, that is my recollection.

Q. Now, doctor, whether or not there was any request to move the time of the autopsy up, this would obviously call into question whether or not there was any reason for so doing. And I ask you, sir, whether or not, in the course of any of the 20,000 autopsies you have performed, you have ever altered, changed, or adjusted the outcome of your autopsy to fit anybody's requirements or schedule?

A. Not anybody else's schedule to me. We may alter it to fit our own schedule.[294]

The Report's entire discussion of the timing of the autopsy appears below.

OIC, p. 28:

*"The autopsy occurred on July 21, 1993..."*

---

[294]    Exhibit 125, Senate Testimony of Dr. James Beyer, July 29, 1994.

OIC, p. 29, fn. 63:

*Id.* at 9. *Dr. Beyer had no conversations with members of the White House, the Foster family, or Foster family attorneys in connection with the autopsy.* *Id.* at 6.

### b. Failure of investigators to attend

After Park Police Sergeant Robert Rule learned that the autopsy had been moved up, he "called Investigator Rolla at home and told him they are going to do the autopsy today [Wednesday]." Rule said he wanted to give Rolla the opportunity to attend because "the investigators that actually worked the crime scene" should "go to the autopsy whenever possible."[295] When Rolla "got the call [at home] at 8:30 a.m.," he had been asleep, having worked all night,[296] and declined to attend the autopsy.

The OIC fails to address the issue of why Dr. Beyer performed the autopsy without the attendance of any of the investigating officers. That would have been standard operating procedure so investigators and the doctor can exchange information, according to Park Police Investigators Rolla[297] and Braun.[298] The OIC omits this fact.

---

[295] Exhibit 126, Deposition of Park Police Sergeant Robert Rule, July 26, 1994: "You know, it is nice to have the investigators that actually worked the crime scene go to the autopsy whenever possible but it is not essential. So I called Investigator Rolla at home and told him that they are going to do the autopsy today."

[296] Exhibit 6, Deposition of Park Police Investigator John Rolla, July 21, 1994.

[297] Exhibit 6, Deposition of Park Police Investigator John Rolla, July 21, 1994: Q. Is it SOP to have someone who was at the scene of the death attend the autopsy? A. Yes. That would be normal operating procedure. As I say, there may be nothing - there may be questions, you like to explain the scene, and the doctor likes to hear besides reading the report and looking at the photographs. He can explain things if you have questions. The investigator may have questions that he needs to ask the doctor.

[298] Exhibit 101, Deposition of Park Police Investigator Cheryl Braun, July 23, 1994: "Q. Is it standard operating procedure

## The autopsy

### c. Entrance wound evidence removed

The OIC hides the fact that the autopsy began before the police arrived, in violation of the requirements of the Medical Examiner's Office.[299]

The OIC tells us (p. 28) that *"[t]he autopsy occurred on July 21, 1993, in the presence of six persons"* and (p. 64) that *"six persons who attended the autopsy, and who therefore were able to examine the body itself, confirmed that there were no wounds on Mr. Foster's body other than the mouth-head bullet wound."*

Park Police Detective James Morrissette attended the autopsy, and wrote a report regarding it. The OIC misrepresents the contents of that report.

OIC, p. 28:

*"Officer Morrissette's report on the autopsy states: 'After briefing him with the available information surrounding the crime scene and the victim he started the autopsy on the victim.'"*

The OIC deceptively omits the next sentence of Morrissette's Report.

*"Prior to our arrival the victim's tongue had been removed as well as parts of the soft tissue from the pallet."*[300]

_____

for an investigator or someone who was at the death scene to attend the autopsy? A. Yes."

[299] Exhibit 128, Deposition of Dr. James C. Beyer, July 13, 1994: Q. Doctor, did you personally make the decision that the Park Police should be present during the autopsy? A. That's a requirement of my office. Any time you have a gunshot wound and particularly one that might be of a suspicious character, the police have to be present during the autopsy.

[300] Exhibit 127, Park Police Report of Park Police Detective James Morrisette, July 21, 1993.

## The autopsy

Thus, the OIC implies that the Park Police Officers who attended the autopsy examined the body and confirmed that the only wound was the official mouth-head wound.

The function of the officers who attended the autopsy, Evidence Technicians Hill and Johnson, was to photograph the autopsy and collect and preserve evidence such as the clothing. Detective Morrissette's knowledge of the entrance and exit wounds came from what Dr. Beyer told him.[301] The other two people who attended the autopsy were Sergeant Rule[302] and Dr. Beyer's assistant.

### d. Refusal to identify autopsy assistant

Normally, an associate pathologist in the Medical Examiner's Office, Dr. Field, would assist Dr. Beyer in performing the autopsy.[303] But for Mr. Foster's autopsy, an "assistant" aided Dr. Beyer.[304] The OIC did not identify him, only telling us (p. 28) that *"Dr. James Beyer, Deputy Chief Medical Examiner, conducted the autopsy, aided by an assistant."*[305]

---

[301] <u>Exhibit 128</u>, Deposition of Dr. James Beyer, July 13, 1994: "I indicated to him [Detective Morrissette] where the entrance wound was, where the exit wound was, and I thought there was a strong suspicion of powder debris around the entrance site."

[302] <u>Exhibit 126</u>, Deposition of Park Police Sergeant Robert Rule, July 26, 1994.

[303] <u>Exhibit 128</u>, Deposition of Dr. James Beyer, July 13, 1994: "If there's an autopsy to be done, normally we [Dr. Beyer & Dr. Field] do them together."

[304] <u>Exhibit 128</u>, Deposition of Dr. James Beyer, July 13, 1994: "Q. As the deputy chief medical examiner, are there other medical personnel that work under you? A. I have an associate pathologist who works with me... Q. Did Dr. Field participate in this autopsy in any way? A. No."

[305] <u>See</u> <u>also</u>, OIC, p. 31: "Dr. Beyer's assistant confirmed that Dr. Beyer inserted a probe through the path of the bullet... The assistant recalled that after the brain was removed and visually inspected, Dr. Beyer dissected it... and that no bullet fragments were located in the brain. 302, 9/11/95, at 2-3." <u>OIC, p. 33</u>: "Dr. Beyer's assistant, for example, said he did not see any other wounds..."

## The autopsy

The OIC is not alone in its refusal to identify this man. Dr. Beyer refused to identify his assistant to the Park Police who attended the autopsy, as Sergeant Robert Rule related under oath.

> "I asked just the name of his assistant and Dr. Beyers [sic] is kind of an older guy and very experienced and he put me in my place very quickly, he says you are dealing with me here, you don't need his name."[306]

### e.    Caliber of weapon unknown

Although Dr. Haut had not indicated to Dr. Beyer whether the death resulted from suicide or homicide,[307] Dr. Beyer was unconcerned whether the sizes of the wounds were consistent with the official .38 revolver. He did not know what caliber the weapon was until after he had completed his Report of Autopsy,[308] so he left that portion of the Report requesting the weapon's caliber blank.[309] The only information Dr. Beyer did have going into the autopsy was that Mr. Foster "was found with a weapon in close vicinity to the body."[310]

---

[306]    Exhibit 126, Deposition of Park Police Sergeant Robert A. Rule, July 26, 1994:  Q.  Do you remember any of conversations you had during the autopsy.  A.  One.  I asked just the name of his assistant and Dr. Beyers (sic) is kind of an older guy and very experienced and he put me in my place very quickly, he says you are dealing with me here, you don't need his name.  So we kind of knew who he was -- Dr. Beyers (sic) is a very nice guy but he is all business.

[307]    Exhibit 128, Deposition of Dr. James C. Beyer, July 13, 1994:  "What did Dr. Haut tell you [on July 21st] was the probable cause of death?  A.  It appeared to be a gunshot wound.  Q.  Did he say it was a suicide?  A.  Not at that time, no."

[308]    Exhibit 128, Deposition of Dr. James C. Beyer, July 13, 1994:  "Q.  Doctor, do you know what type of cartridge was involved in this case?  A.  At the time of the autopsy, no, sir."

[309]    Exhibit 23, Report of Autopsy, Gunshot Wound Chart.

[310]    Exhibit 128, Deposition of Dr. James C. Beyer, July 13, 1994:  "Q.  What other information [besides no signs of struggle] did you look to in this case?  A.  The police telling me that he was found with a weapon in close vicinity to the body.  Q.  Any other information?  A.  No."

### f.    Lab Report may contradict the existence of the official entrance wound

The gun could not have been shot without the discharge of gunshot residue, and there was none found on Mr. Foster's face,[311] eye area,[312] nose,[313] lips,[314] teeth,[315] or hard palate.[316]

Two of the Fiske probe's four pathologists interviewed Dr. Beyer on March 31, 1994, then wrote a report of that interview. That Report evidences that Beyer told these doctors that he had found "large quantities" of gunpowder when he viewed sections of the soft palate under a microscope.

"5 slides... [containing] 13 sections of [the] soft palate... demonstrate large quantities of black foreign material... consistent with gunpowder residue".[317]

This information was a cornerstone of the pathology panel's Report.

---

[311]    Exhibit 129, Fiske's pathologists' Report of interview with Dr. Beyer, March 31, 1994:  "Face:  ...No evidence of gunpowder residue, soot or stippling..."

[312]    Exhibit 129, Fiske's pathologists' Report of interview with Dr. Beyer, March 31, 1994:  "Conjunctivae:  No evidence of... gunpowder residue..."

[313]    Exhibit 129, Fiske's pathologists' Report of interview with Dr. Beyer, March 31, 1994:  "Nose:  Unremarkable."

[314]    Exhibit 129, Fiske's pathologists' Report of interview with Dr. Beyer, March 31, 1994:  "Lips:  ...No gunpowder residue identified."

[315]    Exhibit 129, Fiske's pathologists' Report of interview with Dr. Beyer, March 31, 1994:  "Teeth:  Intact... No gunpowder residue identified."

[316]    Exhibit 129, Fiske's pathologists' Report of interview with Dr. Beyer, March 31, 1994:  "Hard palate:  Intact and without evidence of gunpowder residue."

[317]    Exhibit 129, Pathologists' Report of interview with Dr. Beyer, March 31, 1994.

## The autopsy

"The large quantity of gunpowder residue present on
microscopic sections of the soft palate indicates that
Mr. Foster placed the barrel of the weapon into his
mouth with the muzzle essentially in contact with the
soft palate when he pulled the trigger."[318]

The pathologists' Report was, in turn, a cornerstone
of the Fiske Report, released to the public on June 30,
1994.

"Microscopic sections of Foster's soft palate...
taken during Foster's autopsy reveal large quantities
of gunpowder..."[319]

The Fiske Report informs its readers that its
"Pathologist panel was able to examine" these sections of
the soft palate, implying that it had.

The pathology panel had apparently submitted their
undated Report to the authors of the Fiske Report without
having seen the FBI Lab's May 9, 1994 Report.  That FBI Lab
Report refers to an earlier report by Dr. Beyer's own
laboratory.

"No ballshaped gunpowder was identified on the tissue
samples from the inside of Foster's mouth, when
examined at the Office of the Medical Examiner for
Northern Virginia."[320]

That was a problem.  So on June 13, 1994 the FBI
issued another Lab Report attempting to explain why no
ballshaped gunpowder was found on the tissue samples.

It was previously reported that no ball-shaped
gunpowder was identified on the tissue samples from
the inside of Foster's mouth... [but] these tissue

---

[318]  Exhibit 130, Forensic Pathology and Medical Examiner-
related Findings and Conclusions pertaining to the Investigation
of the Death of Vincent W. Foster, Jr., undated.

[319]  Exhibit 12, Fiske Report, June 30, 1994:  "The Pathologist
panel was able to examine microscopic sections of Foster's soft
palate obtained during the autopsy.  These sections reveal large
quantities of gunpowder..."

[320]  Exhibit 95, FBI Lab Report, May 9, 1994.

samples were prepared in a way which is not conducive to retaining unconsumed gunpowder particles... [so] [t]he FBI Laboratory findings are not inconsistent with the pathologists' Report... in which the firearm was in Foster's mouth.[321]

In short, the "large quantity of gunpowder residue [which was] present on microscopic sections of the soft palate" had vanished between the time that Dr. Beyer observed it and "when [it was] examined [by someone else] at the Office of the Medical Examiner for Northern Virginia."

The OIC killed this scientific anomaly with silence.

OIC, p. 32:

*The [autopsy] report states that '[s]ections of the soft palate' were 'positive for powder debris,' and Dr. Beyer said that the gunpowder debris in the mouth was 'grossly present,' meaning that it could be seen with the naked eye, and was 'present in a large amount.'"[fn72]*

### g. FBI apprised of "preliminary results" of "no exit wound"

A heavily redacted Teletype from the FBI's Washington Metropolitan Field Office to the FBI's Director (the acting FBI Director at the time was Floyd Clarke), confirmed that the FBI was apprised of the autopsy results on July 21, 1993, the same day it was performed. Far from what the OIC related, the Teletype reported the absence of an exit wound.

"[P]reliminary results include the finding that a .38 caliber revolver, constructed from two different weapons, was fired into the victim's mouth with <u>no exit wound</u>."[322] (emphasis supplied)

---

[321] <u>Exhibit 27</u>, FBI Lab Report, June 13, 1994.

[322] <u>Exhibit 131</u>, Teletype from the FBI's Washington Metropolitan Field Office to the Director of the FBI, July 23, 1993: "[T]o confirm referenced telcalls, on 7/21/93 [the day Dr. Beyer performed the autopsy]... preliminary results include the finding that a .38 caliber revolver, constructed from two

## The autopsy

At the time the Teletype was sent from the FBI's Washington Metropolitan Field Office, Robert Bryant served as its Agent-in-Charge.  He has since been promoted to Deputy Director, second in command to Mr. Freeh.

### h.    X-rays vanished

There are several conflicting reports regarding the x-rays.  These include that x-rays were taken and readable, x-rays were taken but unreadable, that no x-rays were taken, that the x-ray machine was broken, and that it worked sometimes, but not for Mr. Foster's autopsy.  Dr. Beyer could not explain how he told the Park Police the results of the x-rays he claimed not to have taken.

The OIC reports that x-rays had in fact been taken, but were unreadable.  Yet, Detective Morrissette, who attended part of the autopsy, wrote that Dr. Beyer explained the results of the x-rays.

> "Dr. Beyers [sic] stated that x-rays indicated that there was no evidence of bullet fragments in the head."[323]

The OIC's excuse is simply that Dr. Beyer somehow stated what the x-rays showed without having taken readable x-rays.

OIC, p. 76, fn. 224:

> "...Dr. Beyer made that statement and reached that conclusion without x-rays..."

The OIC recounts that Dr. Beyer's unnamed "assistant recalled... taking the x-ray" with the "recently obtained new x-ray machine."

---

different weapons, was fired into the victim's mouth with no exit wound."

[323]    Exhibit 127, Report of Park Police Detective James Morrisette, July 21, 1993.

## The autopsy

OIC p. 75-76:

*The assistant stated that the machine sometimes would expose the film and sometimes would not. In this case, the assistant recalled moving the machine over Mr. Foster's body in the usual procedure and taking the x-ray. He said he did not know until near the end of the autopsy that the machine did not expose the film.[fn222] In addition, like Dr. Beyer and the assistant, the administrative manager of the Medical Examiner's Office recalled "numerous problems" with the x-ray machine in 1993 (which, according to records, had been delivered in June of 1993).[fn223]*

The OIC offers no explanation of why the x-rays were not inspected *"until near the end of the autopsy,"* as opposed to the beginning. (The Fiske Report had reported that x-rays had not been taken at all.[324]) The FBI's check of the records did not include a review of the service records for the new multi-thousand-dollar x-ray machine, according to an affidavit of an individual who did check.

[T]he technician who was responsible for installing and servicing this machine, Mr. Jesse Poore... denied that there had been any trouble with the machine, which he had installed in June 1993. He checked his records and reported that the machine was installed on June 15, 1993 and that the first service call was on Oct. 29, 1993 to make an adjustment to make the pictures darker.[325]

Thus, the OIC posits that the new x-ray machine had *"numerous problems"* making the pictures too dark. Yet, service was not requested for four months after its purchase, three months after Mr. Foster's autopsy, at which time service was requested because the pictures were too light.

On July 29, 1994, Dr. Beyer testified before the United States Senate Banking Committee.

---

[324]    Exhibit 12, Fiske Report, June 30, 1994: "The office X-ray machine was inoperable at the time of Foster's autopsy, and as a result no X-rays were taken."

[325]    *Exhibit 132, Affidavit of Reed Irvine re interview with Mr. Jesse Poore.

## The autopsy

Senator FAIRCLOTH. Dr. Beyer, your autopsy report indicates that you took x-rays of Mr. Foster.

Dr. BEYER. I had anticipated taking them, and I had so stated on one of my reports.

Senator FAIRCLOTH. Your autopsy report says you took x-rays of Mr. Foster. Did you?

Dr. BEYER. No, sir.

Senator FAIRCLOTH. Why did you say you did if you didn't?

Dr. BEYER. As I indicated, I made out that report prior to actually performing the autopsy. We'd been having difficulty with our equipment, and we were not getting readable x-rays. Therefore, one was not taken.

Senator FAIRCLOTH. What was wrong with the x-ray machine?

Dr. BEYER. We had a new machine; we had new grids; and we had a new processor. We were having a number of problems.

Senator FAIRCLOTH. Why didn't you call Fairfax Hospital and arrange for a portable x-ray machine to be brought in for your use in such an important occasion?

Dr. BEYER. Because this was a perforating gunshot wound. If it had been a penetrating one, I would have gotten an x-ray of the head.

\* \* \*

Senator FAIRCLOTH. Did you or the Medical Examiner's office have your servicing company come in and fix the x-ray machine?

Dr. BEYER. We were trying to remedy our problems. At that particular time we were not getting readable x-rays.

Senator FAIRCLOTH. When was it repaired?

Dr. BEYER. I have no x-rays in my files between July 6 to the 26. After July 26, 1993, we were getting x-rays.

Senator FAIRCLOTH. You mean for 20 days you ran a coroner's office and did autopsies without an x-ray machine?

Dr. BEYER. We don't take x-rays on very many cases. Primarily only gunshot cases.

Senator FAIRCLOTH. The Park Police officers who were present at the autopsy said you told them not only was an x-ray taken, you also told them the results of the x-ray. How do you account for the contradiction?

191

## The autopsy

Dr. BEYER. I have no explanation because I did not take an x-ray.

Senator FAIRCLOTH. How did you tell the Park Police the results of an x-ray that you didn't take?

Dr. BEYER. I don't recall telling --

Senator FAIRCLOTH. Well, they do.

Dr. BEYER. I have no explanation.

         *     *     *

Dr. BEYER. The equipment was not working, and I saw no need to take an x-ray.

Senator FAIRCLOTH. You saw no need to take an x-ray?

Dr. BEYER. No, sir.[326]

According to the OIC, Dr. Beyer *"checked the box [reporting that x-rays were made] before the autopsy."*

OIC, p. 76:

*"With respect to the check of the x-ray box on the report, Dr. Beyer stated that he checked the box before the autopsy while completing preliminary information on the form and that he mistakenly did not erase that check mark when the report was finalized.[fn224]"*

The OIC's excuse does not address why Dr. Beyer would have checked "Yes" in anticipation of taking x-rays if "the equipment" had not been "working" for the last two weeks, particularly if he "saw no need to take an x-ray."

The Medical Examiner reported a gunshot wound to the neck, Paramedic Arthur was certain he saw a small caliber wound on the neck, and there is no record of any of the 26 persons who viewed Mr. Foster's body before the autopsy having seen either the official entrance or exit wounds. Because Dr. Beyer removed the evidence of the entrance wound before the police arrived, and the x-rays vanished, we have only Dr. Beyer's word on which to rely.

---

[326] Exhibit 125, Testimony of Dr. James C. Beyer before the United States Senate Banking Committee, July 29, 1994. Compare H. Schneider, *Senate Banking Panel Turns To Foster Death; No New Evidence Emerges In Testimony*, Wash. Post, July 30, 1994.

The autopsy

In another case in which Dr. Beyer performed the autopsy, he is alleged to have ruled a homicide as being a suicide. Robert Bryant, while Agent-in-Charge of the FBI's Washington Metro Field Office, supported his conclusion.[327]

### i.    No official estimate of time of death

Dr. Beyer was unconcerned with the time of death at the autopsy, as he testified at his July 13, 1994, deposition.

Q.    Is it your practice never to provide a time of death analysis in your autopsy reports?

A.    We may assist them if it appears to be of a critical nature. Other than that, we don't put anything in the autopsy report.

Q.    What is your definition of a critical nature?

A.    If one had a case where a body -- there was no definite information concerning when the individual had last been seen, who had contact with him, who had a phone call with him. Any indication about the last time they had intake of food and they were found under suspicious circumstances. Then there might be some indication for attempting to make an estimate of time of death.

Q.    Do you think any of those factors were present in this case?

A.    Not that I was aware.

Q.    Did you subsequently become aware of whether any of those factors were present in this case?

A.    I made no determinations.[328]

The Fiske Report's brief reference to the time of death was in a footnote.

"As stated in the Pathologist Report, the available information is insufficient to determine the precise time of death during that afternoon. Pathologist Report, at paragraph 4."[329]

---

[327]    See website of Parents Against Corruption & Cover-up, http://www.clark.net/pub/tburkett/pacc.

[328]    Exhibit 128, Deposition of Dr. James C. Beyer, July 13, 1994.

**The autopsy**

The OIC followed suit.

OIC, p. 30, fn. 66:

*"Officer Morrissette's report also indicates that Dr. Beyer stated at the autopsy 'that it appeared that the victim had eaten a 'large' meal which he [Dr. Beyer] believed to have occurred within 2-3 hours prior to death.' USPP Report (Morrissette) at 1. An exact time of death has not been established."*

There are indications in the record from which the time of death can be approximated. The OIC chose to omit the sentence of Officer Morrissette's report following the one it chose to quote.

"He [Dr. Beyer] was unable to state positively what type of food was consumed but stated that it might have been meat and potatoes."[330]

By all accounts, Mr. Foster had a cheeseburger and French-fries between 12:30 and 1:00. So, according to Dr. Beyer's approximation from the digestion of his lunch, Mr. Foster died between 2:30 and 4:00 p.m.

Paramedic George Gonzalez in his Incident Report estimated that based upon the "pooling of blood in the extremities," Mr. Foster had been dead "2-4 hrs"[331] at 6:15 p.m., similarly putting the time of death between approximately 2:15 and 4:15 p.m.

### j. Conflicting evidence of bullet trajectory

Dr. Beyer's Report of Autopsy reported a defect in the soft palate.[332] Fiske's pathology panel concluded, "Mr. Foster placed the barrel of the weapon into his mouth with the muzzle essentially in contact with the soft palate when

---

[329]   Exhibit 12, Fiske Report, June 30, 1994.

[330]   Exhibit 127, Park Police Report by Detective James Morissette, August 2, 1993.

[331]   Exhibit 133, Incident Report of Paramedic George Gonzalez, July 20, 1993.

[332]   Exhibit 23, Report of Autopsy, July 21, 1993.

## The autopsy

he pulled the trigger."[333]  Yet, Beyer's Autopsy Report
claimed that the "entrance wound is in the posterior
oropharynx."[334]  These accounts cannot both be true.  A
single bullet could not have pierced both the soft palate
and the oropharynx and exited the top of the head, as the
drawing below illustrates.

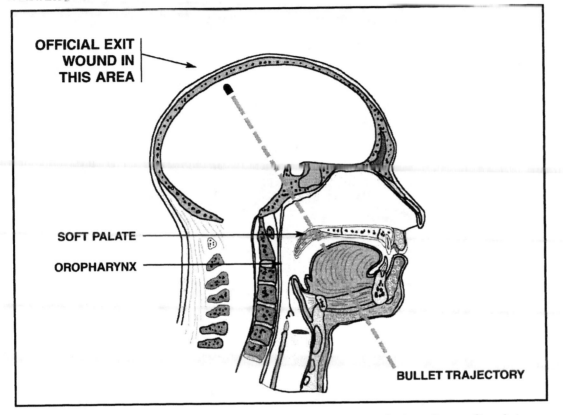

The posterior oropharynx is the back wall of the throat below the soft palate.
The soft palate is the tissue that forms the aft portion of the roof of the mouth.
The Report of Autopsy stated that the entrance wound was in the oropharynx.
Fiske's pathologists concluded that the muzzle was placed against the soft
palate.  Both cannot be true.  An entrance wound in the oropharynx could not
have resulted in the reported official exit wound because the trajectory of an
intra-oral gunshot wound entering the oropharynx would have been too low.
BULLET TRAJECTORY:  Much of the evidence presented in this filing is
offered to prove the trajectory shown above.

---

[333]    Exhibit 130, Forensic Pathology and Medical Examiner-
related Findings and Conclusions pertaining to the Investigation
of the Death of Vincent W. Foster, Jr., undated.

[334]    Exhibit 23, Report of Autopsy by Dr. James C. Beyer, July
21, 1993.

## 3.    Bloodstains consistent with the neck wound

All six official experts (Fiske's four pathologists[335] and the OIC's pathologist and forensic scientist) found nothing in any of the bloodstains on Mr. Foster's clothing or body repudiating the official conclusion. These experts opined that the way the blood was configured was consistent with how and where Mr. Foster officially died, from firing a high-velocity .38 caliber bullet into his mouth where his body lay.[336]

Not one of the twenty-one witnesses who viewed Mr. Foster's body at Fort Marcy Park described bloodstains consistent with the official mouth-entrance and head-exit wounds. Blood was present on the right side of Mr. Foster's neck, on his right collar, on his right shoulder, down his right shirtsleeve, and in his mouth.

It is logical that the blood that had soaked into the back of his shirt, and pooled on the ground under his head, had drained from the small caliber bullet hole observed in his neck. Blood on the right side of the front of the shirt would have drained from the neck wound, rather than from the official wound in the mouth. Blood absorbed into the back of the shirt could have drained from the neck wound as well as from a wound in the back of the head. And the blood that had accumulated in the mouth could have emanated from the wound caused by the small caliber bullet that had entered from under the jaw line.

---

[335]    Charles S. Hirsch, M.D., James L. Luke, M.D., Donald T. Reay, M.D., and Charles J. Stahl, M.D.

[336]    Exhibit 12, Fiske Report, June 30, 1994:  The blood on Foster's right cheek and jaw is a "contact stain typical of having been caused by a blotting action, such as would happen if a blood-soaked object was brought in contact with the side of his face and taken away, leaving the observed pattern behind."  Lab Report, at 9

OIC, p. 65:  "Dr. Blackbourne concluded that 'Vincent Foster committed suicide on July 20, 1993 in Ft. Marcy Park by placing a .38 caliber revolver in his mouth and pulling the trigger.'" OIC, p. 65, fn. 190:  "The panel of pathologists reached the same conclusion.  Pathologists' Report at 4."

## Bloodstains consistent with the neck wound

Fifteen of the twenty-one witnesses who observed Mr. Foster's body at the park saw blood consistent with there being a wound in the right side of the neck. Of the other six witnesses, three could not recall the blood they saw, and there is no record of what the other three might have seen.

### Officer Kevin Fornshill

Park Police Officer Kevin Fornshill, the first official at the body site, reportedly could not remember the amount or configuration of the blood he saw. But he did remember that there was no change in either "the amount or the texture of the blood on the face"[337] between the time he first saw it and after the first two rescue personnel on the scene had inspected the body. As set forth below, those men, Gonzalez and Hall, saw blood on the right side, consistent with where one would expect it to have drained from the neck wound.

### Firefighter Todd Hall
### Paramedic George Gonzalez

The only record of Firefighter Hall's observations, from the first time the FBI interviewed him in the spring of 1994, was that "Hall sighted blood on the right collar area of the decedent's shirt,"[338] which was inches below where the neck wound was reported to have been.

---

[337]   Exhibit 79, Deposition of Park Police Officer Kevin Fornshill, July 12, 1994:  Q.  You testified early on this afternoon that your view of the head of the body was momentarily obstructed while the paramedic person performed some sort of assessment, correct?  A.  Yes.  Q.  Prior to the obstruction, you had an opportunity to observe the position of the head?  A.  Yes. I did.  Q.  And immediately after the obstruction, you had an opportunity to view the position of the head?  A.  Yes.  Q.  Was there any change, in your opinion, in the position of the head at that point?  A.  Not that I could see.  Q.  Was there any change, at that point, in the amount of blood or the texture of blood on the face?  A.  No.

[338]   Exhibit 179, Report of FBI Interview of Firefighter Todd Hall, April 27, 1994:  "Hall sighted blood on the right collar area of the decedent's shirt."

Paramedic George Gonzalez testified that "there was blood on the right side of the body, the shirt area."[339] He reportedly told the FBI that there was also blood in the mouth.[340]

### Officer Franz Ferstl

The second police officer at the scene, Franz Ferstl, "did not recall" whether there was blood on Mr. Foster's shirt, according to the FBI's report on its May, 1994 interview with him. He did see a "small amount of blood around the mouth,"[341] consistent with what one would expect had the bullet entered from the neck.

### Paramedic Richard Arthur
### Firefighter Ralph Pisani
### Firefighter Lieutenant James Iacone
### Firefighter Jennifer Wacha

Paramedic Richard Arthur's account of the blood, provided in his deposition testimony less than a year after the death, was consistent with its having drained from the bullet wound he was certain he had seen in Mr. Foster's neck.

Q.  Did you see any blood?
A.  Yes.
Q.  Where was the blood?
A.  All down the right side neck, all down the right

---

[339]   Exhibit 110, Deposition of Paramedic George Gonzalez, July 20, 1994:  "Q.  Can you describe any blood you saw on the body?  A.  Yes.  There was some about the face.  There was blood on the right side of the body, the shirt area."

[340]   Exhibit 135, Report of FBI interview of Paramedic George Gonzalez, February 23, 1994:  "The visual inspection of Foster also included a look into Foster's mouth which revealed the presence of blood."

[341]   Exhibit 96, Report of FBI interview of Park Police Officer Franz Ferstl, May 2, 1994:  Ferstl advised that he observed a small amount of blood around the mouth, adding that the blood did not appear fresh.  Ferstl did not recall any blood coming from the nose, nor did he recall any blood on the shirt...  He stated that the shirt was very clean and he does not recall any blood stains or dirt stains on the shirt.

shoulder all the way to about here.

Q. Where was the blood coming from?

A. To me, it looked like there was a bullet hole right here.

Q. In the neck?

A. Yes, right around the jawline.

Q. The neck and jawline underneath the right ear?

A. Somewhere there. I would have to see a picture to point it out exactly where, but there was a little bit of blood coming out of the mouth, too, and a little out of the nose but the main was right here. I didn't see any on the left side. I didn't see any in the chest or anything.

Q. For the record, when you say in the main right here --

A. It was all from here, the neck all the way down to the right.

Q. Down the right shoulder?

A. Yeah, down to the right shoulder to about here.

Q. And so was it pooled blood or was the shirt just damp with blood?

A. Pooled meaning -- what do you mean? Was he lying in a pool of blood?

Q. Was there standing blood or was it just --

A. Was it going down the arm?

Q. Was it pooled there or dripping?

A. I didn't see any blood dripping...[342]

According to the FBI's April 1994 report of its interview with Firefighter Ralph Pisani, he saw "blood on Foster's right shoulder..."[343]

Firefighter Lieutenant James Iacone did "not recall observing any blood," according to the FBI's March, 1994 interview with him.[344]

---

[342] Exhibit 107, Deposition of Paramedic Richard Arthur, July 14, 1994.

[343] Exhibit 136, Report of FBI interview of Firefighter Ralph Pisani, April 27, 1994: "Pisani was located in a position where he was looking over the left side of the body and was able to see blood on Foster's right shoulder... Pisani did not recall seeing any blood located around the body."

[344] Exhibit 78, Report of FBI interview of Firefighter Lieutenant James Iacone, March 11, 1994: "Iacone does not recall observing any blood."

The FBI reported in March of 1994 that Firefighter Jennifer "Wacha thought blood may have been on the victim's mouth as well as on his shirt."[345]

### Lieutenant Patrick Gavin
### Investigator Christine Hodakievic

Lieutenant Patrick Gavin, the highest ranking official at the body site, told the FBI he saw a "trickle" of what appeared to be blood "coming" out of the mouth, according to the FBI's report of its April 1994 interview with him. That report relates that Gavin did not "recall any blood or blood stains on the shirt," but that blood "could have been" on the shirt although he did "not recall seeing it."[346]

The OIC recites that Officer Hodakievic told the FBI on February 7, 1995 that she *recalls 'lot of blood' underneath the decedent's head."* A week later, according to the OIC, she was *"describing blood on the ground and on the back of head and shirt when body moved."*

Absent from the OIC's rendition of Officer Hodakievic's observations, from its secret reports, is any description of where on the body Hodakievic saw the blood.

---

[345] Exhibit 74, Report of FBI interview of Firefighter Jennifer Wacha, March 11, 1994: "Wacha thought blood may have been on the victim's mouth as well as on his shirt. She could not recall the volume."

[346] Exhibit 98, Report of FBI interview of Park Police Lieutenant Patrick Gavin, April 28, 1994: Lieutenant Gavin advised that he took a cursory look at the body and his only recollections are that there was a trickle or what appeared to be blood coming out of the mouth, running down the right side of the face. He stated that the face was pointing up toward the sky. He did not recall seeing blood coming from the nose, nor does he recall any blood or blood stains on the shirt. Lt. Gavin stated that there could have been more blood present on the shirt or face, but that he does not recall seeing it.

Exhibit 80, Handwritten notes of FBI interview of Park Police Lieutenant Patrick Gavin, April 28, 1994: "Only blood he recalls is trickle coming out mouth - can't recall blood coming from nose - nor does he recall blood on shirt. Only made a cursory look - doesn't mean blood wasn't there. Could have."

## Bloodstains consistent with the neck wound

OIC, p. 67, fn. 192:

*...Hodakievic 302, 2/7/95, at 4 (recalls "lot of blood underneath the decedent's head); Hodakievic OIC, 2/14/95, at 16, at 16 (describing blood on the ground and on the back of head and shirt when body moved)...*

**Investigator John Rolla**
**Investigator Cheryl Braun**
**Evidence Technician Peter Simonello**
**Investigator Renee Abt**

Park Police investigator John Rolla testified that he saw blood on the ground directly under the head.[347] In his report composed after midnight on the evening of the death, Rolla wrote that he saw blood on the "right shoulder area" of the shirt.[348] These observations are consistent with blood having flowed from the neck wound.

Park Police investigator Cheryl Braun testified that she saw blood "[i]n the nose area and in the mouth area."[349]

---

[347]  Exhibit 6, Deposition of Park Police Investigator John Rolla, July 21, 1994:  A.  I observed a pool of blood under his head that was wet and beginning to dry and clot, and it was directly under his head.  It was not all over the place, it was directly under his head, running down this way.  *** Q.  What about on the ground?  A.  I believe there was some blood mark on the ground, I don't remember. But most of the blood under his head, where his head was, yes, there was blood on the ground, but most of the blood that had run down was absorbed in his clothes.

[348]  Exhibit 113, Report by Park Police Investigator John Rolla, July 21, 1993:  "I observed blood in his nose and mouth area, on his right shoulder area and underneath his head.  The blood on the ground and on his shirt appeared to still be wet.  There was no blood on the plants or trees surrounding the decedent's head." Exhibit 100, Report of FBI interview of Park Police Investigator John Rolla, April 27, 1994:  "Rolla also observed a deposit of blood on the decedent's shirt in the area of the right upper shoulder which also appeared to be wet but drying."

[349]  Exhibit 101, Deposition of Park Police Investigator Cheryl Braun, July 27, 1994·  Q.  Was there blood on the body?  A. Yes, there was.  Q.  Where?  A.  In the nose area and in the mouth area.  And there were lots of flies in the eyes, nose, and mouth.  There was also the blood in the -- on his shirt in the area of his right shoulder.

## Bloodstains consistent with the neck wound

Park Police Evidence Technician Peter Simonello testified that "[t]here was some blood on the right shoulder, and there was some blood, I believe, near the right rib cage."[350]

Park Police investigator Renee Abt recorded in her contemporaneous notes that there was a "large blood pattern [on the] right shoulder and right collar of [the] shirt."[351]

### Dr. Donald Haut

Dr. Donald Haut's account, memorialized in the FBI's report of its 1994 interview with him, is that he had seen "matted" blood on the back of the head.[352] Dr. Haut's *Report of Investigation of Medical Examiner* did not record any wound in the skull, but did note trauma to the neck.[353]

According to the FBI's handwritten notes of the interviewing agent's interview with him, Dr. Haut opined that the "[w]ound may be consistent [with a] low velocity weapon [and that] Haut recalls seeing .25 cal. (rifle) weapon that had much more devastating impact."[354] The FBI's typed report of that interview is in accord.[355]

---

[350] Exhibit 104, Deposition of Park Police Evidence Technician Peter Simonello, July 14, 1994.

[351] Exhibit 118, Handwritten contemporaneous notes of Park Police Investigator Renee Abt, at 7:10 p.m., July 20, 1993: "Large blood pattern Rt shoulder + collar of shirt dried and liquid."

[352] Exhibit 73, Report of FBI interview of Dr. Donald Haut, April 12, 1994: "Although the volume of blood was small, Haut did recall that the blood was matted and clotted under the head."

[353] Exhibit 103, Medical Examiner Report of Investigation by Dr. Donald Haut, July 20, 1993.

[354] Exhibit 119, Handwritten notes of FBI interview of Dr. Donald Haut, April 12, 1994: "Wound may be consistent w/ low velocity weapon. Haut recalls seeing .25 cal. (rifle) weapon that had much more devastating impact."

[355] Exhibit 73, Report of FBI interview of Dr. Donald Haut, April 12, 1994.

## Firefighter Corey Ashford

Firefighter Corey Ashford was not interviewed during the initial investigation.[356]  In his July 20, 1993, narrative report, Ashford coded the death as a homicide by assault with a firearm.  According to the FBI's February 1994 interview with him, it was "believed by Ashford that Foster was the victim of murder," and he "did not recall getting blood on his uniform."[357]

**4.    Official excuse for blood on Mr. Foster's right side is that it drained from his mouth when an "early observer" moved the head to check for a pulse, then repositioned it -- but Edwards did it to obscure or camouflage the blood evidence of the existence of the neck wound**

Because the neck wound did not officially exist, the experts hired by Mr. Fiske's probe set forth their theory of why blood was found on Mr. Foster's right side, yet the head was observed and photographed facing straight up.

All official experts agree on how the blood ended up on the right collar, right shoulder, and right front shirt. They all concluded, each relying in large part on their predecessors,[358] that there was no wound on the neck,[359] so it had to have come from his mouth.

---

[356]    Exhibit 74, Report of FBI interview of Corey Ashford, February 23, 1994:  "Ashford has not been interviewed by any other law enforcement agency regarding his actions surrounding the emergency response call related to Foster."

[357]    Exhibit 74, Report of FBI interview of Paramedic Corey Ashford, February 23, 1994:  Ashford did not recall seeing any blood on Foster's body, noting that he was not looking for it at the time.  It was initially believed by Ashford that Foster was the victim of a murder...  Ashford did not recall seeing any blood while placing Foster in the bag. Ashford did not recall any blood getting on his uniform or on the disposable gloves he wore while handling the body.

[358]    OIC, p. 64, fn. 188:  ...Similarly, Dr. Hirsch, an expert pathologist retained during the Fiske investigation, examined the autopsy photographs and stated that he saw flecks of dried blood depicted on the neck and that he saw "nothing in the photographs", and there certainly is nothing described in the autopsy to make me suspect that

All these retained experts agree on how this must have occurred. Blood had accumulated in the mouth postmortem while the head was in a straight-up[360] position, an "early observer" turned Mr. Foster's head to the right,[361] the blood

---

there is in any way any trauma to the side of his neck." OIC, 2/16/95, at 43, 45. The panel of pathologists further stated that, apart from the wound through the back of the head, "there was no other trauma identified." Pathologists' Report at 1...

OIC, p. 64, fn. 188: "...The scene and autopsy photographs were reviewed during Congressman Clinger's probe and the Senate's inquiry into Mr. Foster's death, both of which concluded that he committed suicide by gunshot through the back of the mouth out the back of the head..."

[359] OIC, p. 64, fn. 188: "Dr. Beyer, who conducted the autopsy, was shown an enlarged autopsy photograph of the side of the neck and said, "I see blood, but I don't see any trauma." OIC, 2/16/95, at 15..." OIC, p. 64, fn. 188: "...Dr. Blackbourne stated that a mark on the side of the right upper neck, just below the jawline, seen in autopsy photographs, represents small fragments of dried blood and does not represent any form of injury. Id...." OIC, p. 64, fn. 188: "...Dr. Lee reviewed the scene and autopsy photographs and evidence and indicated that there was only an entrance wound through the back of the mouth and an exit wound out the back of the head. Lee Report at 89-92, 486..."

[360] OIC, p. 66: "The Polaroids... [and] witnesses... describe the position of the head as facing virtually straight, not tilting noticeably to one side or the other."

[361] Exhibit 130, Forensic Pathology and Medical Examiner-Related Findings and Conclusions Pertaining to the Investigation of the Death of Vincent Foster. Jr., undated: "The finding of the head facing forward and the right sided blood stains are mutually exclusive. We conclude that a rightward tilt of his face was changed to a forward orientation by one of the early observers before the scene photographs were taken." OIC, p. 64: "Dr. Blackbourne concluded that the blood... suggests that an early observer may have caused movement of the head.[fn188]" OIC, p. 66: "[T]he expert pathologists and Dr. Lee... concluded... that the head made contact with the right shoulder... [when] rescue personnel at the scene handled the decedent's head..." OIC, p. 65, fn. 189: "...For obvious reasons, the head must have been facing to the right when the body was found or have been turned to the right when the body was examined at the scene..."

drained out onto the right collar, right shoulder, and right front shirt, after which this early observer repositioned the head in the same straight-up position.

This excuse was first offered on May 9, 1994 by the FBI Lab. It claimed "that the head moved or was moved..." although it claimed not to know the "specific manner" of how it happened.

> The contact stain on the right cheek and jaw of the victim is typical of having been caused by a blotting action, such as would happen if a blood-soaked object was brought in contact with the side of his face and taken away, leaving the observed pattern behind. The closest blood-bearing object which could have caused this staining is the right shoulder of the victim's shirt. The quantity, configuration and distribution of the blood on the shirt and the right cheek and jaw of the victim are consistent with the jaw being in contact with the shoulder of the shirt at some time. The available photographs depict the victim's head not in contact with the shirt and therefore indicate that the head moved or was moved after being in contact with the shoulder. The specific manner of this movement is not known.[362]

The Fiske probe's panel of pathologists (Drs. Hirsch, Luke, Reay, and Stahl) noted that "[t]he finding of the head facing forward and the right sided blood stains are mutually exclusive." It offered the same excuse of the head having been moved in its undated, three-and-a-half page report, entitled *Forensic Pathology and Medical Examiner-Related Findings and Conclusions pertaining to the Investigation of the Death of Vincent W. Foster Jr.*

> According to multiple observers at the scene, the head was facing forward when Foster's body was found, an observation confirmed in scene photographs. There were linear blood stains coursing across the right side of the face, emanating from the nose and mouth. A broad transfer type blood smear was present at the right side of the chin and neck, precisely corresponding to a similar blood stain of the right collar area of the shirt. For obvious reasons, the

---

[362]   Exhibit 95, FBI Lab report, May 9, 1994.

head must have been facing to the right when the body was found or have been turned to the right when the body was being examined at the scene. In either circumstance, blood accumulated in the nose and mouth from the bullet defect of the soft palate and base of the skull would have spilled over the face and soiled the right shoulder and collar of the shirt. The finding of the head facing forward and the right sided blood stains are mutually exclusive. We conclude that a rightward tilt of his face was changed to a forward orientation by one of the early observers before the scene photographs were taken.[363]

The OIC joins this conclusion and relies on Dr. Beyer to dismiss evidence of the neck wound.

OIC, p. 33:

*"Dr. Beyer said that observation of Mr. Foster's body revealed no wounds on the neck..."*

The official explanation, that the head was turned to the right then repositioned, is correct. But it was Sergeant Robert Edwards who turned then repositioned the head, not an "early observer" and not to check for a pulse.

Before Edwards was alone at the body site, there was already blood on the right collar, right shoulder and right shirtsleeve, as well as a small amount of blood on the face. Blood had also accumulated in the mouth. The blood on the skin was dry. The blood on the right side of the body had drained from the wound in the right side of the neck.

In order to hide the existence of the neck wound (which would be inconsistent with suicide), Sergeant Edwards provided an excuse for the blood being on the right side of the body -- it should have been on the front if the death were suicide by intra-oral gunshot. Edwards turned Mr. Foster's head to the right, his chin rested on his shoulder and the blood that had accumulated in the mouth spilled onto the right shoulder, joining the blood that was already there. A trickle of blood also drained laterally

---

[363]    Exhibit 130, Forensic Pathology and Medical Examiner-Related Findings and Conclusions pertaining to the Investigation of the Death of Vincent W. Foster Jr., undated.

206

from Mr. Foster's mouth and nose across the right side of
his face. Edwards then repositioned the head in the
"straight up" position. The chin being in contact with the
bloody shoulder resulted in the presence of a contact blood
stain on the chin.

In spilling the blood toward the small caliber bullet
wound in Mr. Foster's neck, and down onto his right
shoulder and collar, Edwards obscured and camouflaged the
existence of the bullet wound in Mr. Foster's neck. By
moving the head to the right, Edwards sought to make it
appear that the blood on Mr. Foster's right side collar and
right shoulder, which had in fact drained from the neck
wound, had emanated from his mouth when the head was
turned. As we shall see, among the evidence of Edwards'
wrongdoing is that before he was alone at the body site,
the blood was dry. After Edwards' actions, the blood
appeared wet.

In a lengthy footnote, the OIC implies that either
Firefighter Todd Hall or James Iacone was probably the
"early observer" who moved the head to the right (whereupon
the blood drained out) and then repositioned it. The
strongest evidence the OIC offers to support its hypothesis
is Hall's statement, *"I recall attempting to check the
carotid pulse,"* and Iacone's still-secret FBI interview
Report relating that *"Iacone checked for pulse."*

The balance of this footnote states that Fornshill
described the paramedics' movements *"around head of body"*
(without providing that description - the referenced report
is secret),[364] that one paramedic *"believe[s]"* that a
Firefighter did check the pulse,[365] that another Park Police
officer was *"notified"* by a paramedic that he and another
paramedic had checked for vital signs,[366] that a Park Police

---

[364]    OIC, p. 66, fn. 191:  "...Fornshill OIC, 1/11/95, at 92-93,
104-105 (describing movements of FCFRD personnel Hall and
Gonzalez around head of body)..."

[365]    OIC, p. 66, fn. 191:  "...Gonzalez Senate Deposition,
7/20/94, at 19 ('I believe Todd [Hall] did' check the pulse);
Gonzalez OIC, 1/10/95, at 56-57 (Hall may have checked for
pulse)..."

[366]    OIC, p. 66, fn. 191:  "...USPP Report (Hodakievic) at 1
(Gonzalez [sic] notified me that . . . Gonzalez [sic] and Hall
checked the body for vital signs and found none)..."

officer *"advised"* another Park Police officer that *"a medic checked the subject's neck for a pulse,"*[367] and that yet another Park Police officer *"learned"* that personnel *"felt for a pulse in the carotid artery."*[368]

In sum, upon a close reading of the following lengthy footnote, it is obvious that the FBI could find no one to report they moved the head or saw anyone else move it.

OIC, p. 67, fn. 191:

*Fornshill OIC, 1/11/95, at 92-93, 104- 105 (describing movements of FCFRD personnel Hall and Gonzalez around head of body); Hall Senate Deposition, 7/20/94, at 22 ("I recall attempting to check the carotid pulse."); Gonzalez Senate Deposition, 7/20/94, at 19 ("I believe Todd [Hall] did" check the pulse); Gonzalez OIC, 1/10/95, at 56-57 (Hall may have checked for pulse); USPP Report (Hodakievic) at 1 (Gonzalez [sic] notified me that...Gonzalez [sic] and Hall checked the body for vital signs and found none."); Iacone OIC, 1/10/95, at 22 (Iacone checked for pulse); USPP Report (Ferstl) at 1 ("Ofc. Fornshill advised that a medic checked the subjects [sic] neck for a pulse"); Gavin OIC, 2/23/95, at 15, at 15 (learned at scene that FCFRD personnel "felt for a pulse in the carotid artery and got none."). The action of checking for vital signs and an airway may have caused some spillage of blood and may have caused the head to make contact with the right shoulder.*

The last sentence of this footnote makes yet another wholly unsupported claim, which is that this unknown individual also checked for an airway.

---

[367]     OIC, p. 66, fn. 191:   "...USPP Report (Ferstl) at 1 ('Ofc. Fornshill advised that a medic checked the subjects [sic] neck for a pulse')..."

[368]     OIC, p. 66, fn. 191:   "...Gavin OIC, 2/23/95, at 15, at 15 (learned at scene that FCFRD personnel 'felt for a pulse in the carotid artery and got none.')..."

blood flow

**Before**

These illustrations show Mr. Foster's body as it appeared to the early observers who saw the body before Sergeant Edwards was alone at the body site. There was very little blood on Mr. Foster's face, and it all appeared dark and dry. Illustrations clockwise from the bottom: (1) this close-up view shows very little blood on the face and some inside his mouth and nose. Also shown is blood on the right collar and shoulder of the shirt. (2) This illustration shows a bird's-eye view of the dried blood soaked into the right collar, shoulder and down the sleeve. (3) This side view depicts the body lying straight, face up on an incline with the arms straight at the sides [a gun in his right hand is not shown].

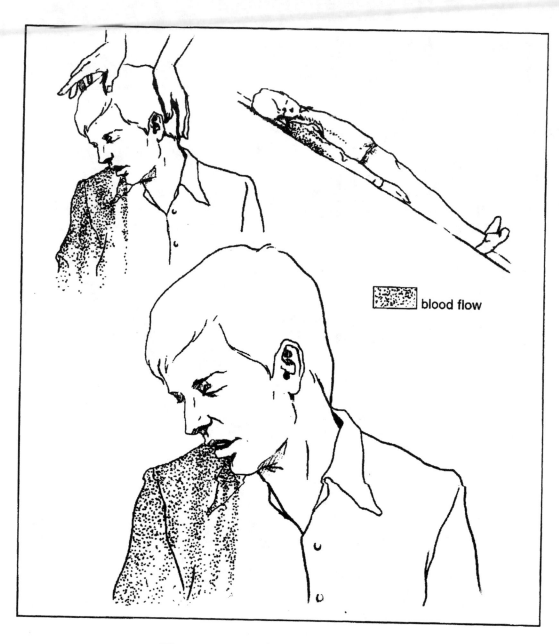

**The movement of Mr. Foster's head**

The OIC and its experts concluded that Mr. Foster's head was moved at the scene. We agree.

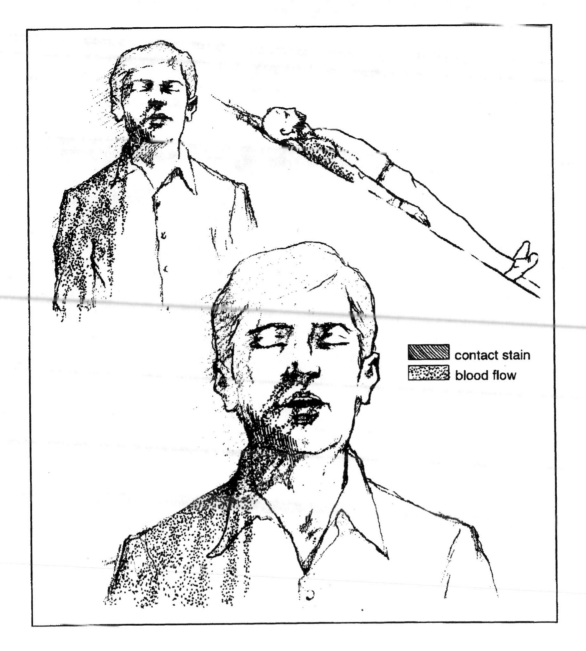

**After**

These illustrations show Mr. Foster's body as it appeared to observers who viewed the body after Sergeant Edwards was alone at the body site. There was now more blood on Mr. Foster's face, and a blood contact stain. The blood was now both dry and wet. Clockwise from the bottom, illustrations show: (1) additional wet blood on the face and shirt, some of which is flowing from the nose and mouth. A contact stain is also now on the right chin from its contact with the bloody shoulder of the shirt. (2) This bird's-eye view shows the additional blood on the face and shirt, and shows the new contact stain on the face. (3) This side view depicts the bloodstains on the right side of the shirt. It also shows the additional blood on the face and the contact stain.

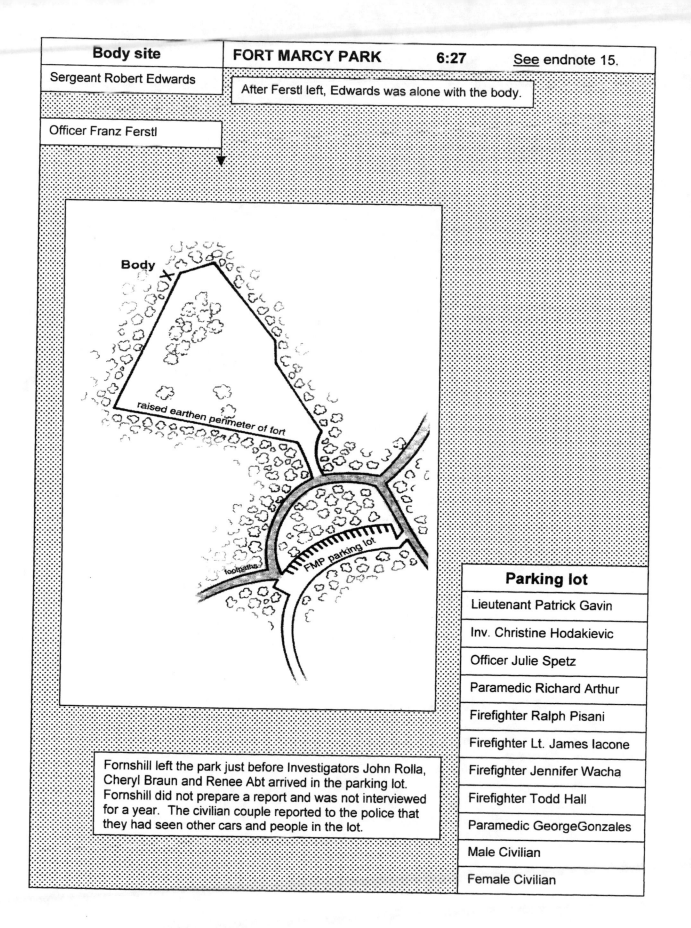

**Body site** | **FORT MARCY PARK** 6:27 See endnote 15.

Sergeant Robert Edwards

After Ferstl left, Edwards was alone with the body.

Officer Franz Ferstl

**Body** X

raised earthen perimeter of fort

footpaths

FMP parking lot

Fornshill left the park just before Investigators John Rolla, Cheryl Braun and Renee Abt arrived in the parking lot. Fornshill did not prepare a report and was not interviewed for a year. The civilian couple reported to the police that they had seen other cars and people in the lot.

**Parking lot**

Lieutenant Patrick Gavin

Inv. Christine Hodakievic

Officer Julie Spetz

Paramedic Richard Arthur

Firefighter Ralph Pisani

Firefighter Lt. James Iacone

Firefighter Jennifer Wacha

Firefighter Todd Hall

Paramedic GeorgeGonzales

Male Civilian

Female Civilian

| **Body site** | |
|---|---|
| Sergeant Robert Edwards | Sometime during the over 15 minutes that Sergeant Edwards was alone with the body, an untraceable .38 caliber black revolver replaced the automatic pistol in Mr. Foster's hand. Edwards also moved Mr. Foster's head to the right side, causing blood to flow out of the mouth onto his right side (and leaving a stain on the right cheek from its contact with the bloody right shoulder). This made it appear that the blood already on the right side, which had in fact drained from the right side neck wound, had come from the mouth. He thus concealed the existence of the neck wound (inconsistent with suicide), and made it appear as if Mr. Foster may have been shot in the mouth (consistent with suicide). The official explanation for the contact blood stain on the right cheek is that it had appeared when an unknown fire and rescue worker checked the pulse. |
| Lieutenant Patrick Gavin | |
| Inv. Christine Hodakievic | |

Gavin looked at the scene, saw blood trickling out of Mr. Foster's mouth, and thought he had been mugged. Because Ferstl remained in the lot, Hodakievic was the only witness who saw the body both before and after Edwards had been alone with it. Hodakievic's report addressed only the activities in the parking lot. When she later saw photographs of the body, she said the appearance of the body had changed from when she had seen it.

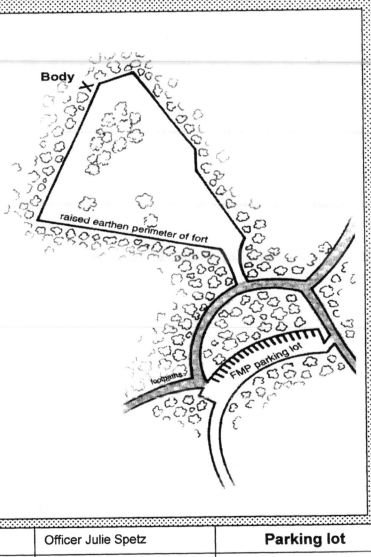

Evidence Technician Peter Simonello arrived in the lot.

Ev Tech Peter Simonello

| Investigator John Rolla | Officer Julie Spetz | **Parking lot** |
|---|---|---|
| Investigator Cheryl Braun | Officer William Watson | Male Civilian |
| Officer Franz Ferstl | Intern with Officer Watson | Female Civilian |

### a. No reports of "early observers" having moved the head or seen it being moved and resuscitation was not attempted

The OIC's conclusion is unsupported. The first nine observers of the body, Dale, Fornshill, Hall, Gonzalez, Arthur, Pisani, Wacha, Iacone and Ferstl, all of *the "early observers,"* denied moving the head or seeing anyone else move it.

Additionally, all witnesses testified that the body clearly appeared to have been dead for some time, so it would have been obviously uncalled-for to move the victim in an attempt to try to resuscitate him.

Moreover, contrary to the OIC's implication, logic dictates that neither Hall nor Iacone would have even examined the body. They were not paramedics, but were each accompanied by a paramedic.

### Civilian Dale

Dale, the first person to officially view the body at around 5:45 p.m., would not have attempted to revive Mr. Foster because, as he testified, there "was no doubt he was dead."[369]

### Officer Kevin Fornshill

Park Police Officer Kevin Fornshill denied having moved the head. The handwritten notes taken on April 29, 1994 by the FBI of its interview of Fornshill related that neither Gonzalez nor Hall moved the head. Those notes state that Fornshill reported that there was "no blood on shirt or head [and that the head was in the] same position after EMTs [examined the body, and that there was] nothing different after EMTs [examined the body]."[370]

---

[369] Exhibit 51, Deposition of Dale by Congressman Dan Burton July 28, 1994: "Q. Now you found the body and you realized -- you thought he was dead? A. Well, there was no doubt he was dead."

[370] Exhibit 108, Handwritten notes of report of FBI interview of Park Police Officer Kevin Fornshill, April 29, 1994.

| Body site | FORT MARCY PARK 6: 17 See endnote 6. |
| --- | --- |
| Officer Kevin Fornshill | During Paramedic Gonzalez's evaluation, he saw a gun in Mr. Foster's right hand. He concluded that Mr. Foster was obviously dead, had been for "two to four hours," and made no attempt at resuscitation. Because of the straight position of the body and the lack of blood, both Hall and Gonzalez concluded that the death appeared suspicious. Hall reportedly saw a female Park Police officer before leaving the site, possibly Hodakievic. |
| Firefighter Todd Hall | |
| Paramedic George Gonzalez | |

Body
X

raised earthen perimeter of fort

FMP parking lot

footpaths

### Parking lot

Paramedic Richard Arthur

Firefighter Ralph Pisani

Firefighter Lt. James Iacone

Firefighter Jennifer Wacha

### South of the lot

Male Civilian

Female Civilian

Officer Franz Ferstl

Officer Franz Ferstl, who had received the first call to respond to the park, reached the parking lot and headed up to the body site.

## Firefighter Todd Hall
## Paramedic George Gonzalez

Todd Hall, a firefighter, would not have provided any medical treatment to Mr. Foster, as he testified in 1994.

Q. Did anybody else touch him that you recall seeing?
A. The medics, George and Arthur, when they got there.
Q. They touched him?
A. I assume they did. That's their job.
Q. Did you see them touch him?
A. No. I pretty much backed off and let them take over.
Q. Why is that?
A. Because they are the medics.[371]

On the first anniversary of the death, in response to the question whether anyone checked to see if Mr. Foster was alive, Paramedic Gonzalez perfunctorily testified, "He was dead."

Q. What did you see when you got to the body?
A. I saw a dead male. He'd obviously been dead for some time. His skin color was pale. He had a white shirt on, his mouth was open. His eyes were slightly open, and he had flies about his eyes, nose, mouth...
Q. Did anyone check to see if he was alive or dead, check the pulse or anything?
A. He was dead.[372]

---

[371] Exhibit 67, Deposition of Firefighter Todd Hall, July 14, 1994: Q. Who was the driver, who was the medic? A. I was the driver. George Gonzalez was the officer in charge, and Richard Arthur was the second man... Q. Did you hear anyone say, well, he's dead? A. I don't remember hearing it. I pretty much assumed he was. Q. Did anybody else touch him that you recall seeing? A. The medics, George and Arthur, when they got there. Q. They touched him? A. I assume they did. That's their job. Q. Did you see them touch him? A. No. I pretty much backed off and let them take over. Q. Why is that? A. Because they are the medics.

[372] Exhibit 110, Deposition of Paramedic George Gonzalez, July 20, 1994.

216

Gonzalez had opined in his report composed the evening of the death that the body appeared to have been dead for two to four hours.[373]

### Officer Franz Ferstl

Officer Ferstl did not move Mr. Foster's head because he did not get closer than "three to five feet from the head."[374]

### Paramedic Richard Arthur
### Firefighter Lieutenant James Iacone

Richard Arthur, the only paramedic in the group of four that arrived at the site minutes after Fornshill, Hall and Gonzalez, testified that Mr. Foster "was obviously dead."[375] According to the FBI's report of its interview with him, "in Arthur's judgement, Foster was obviously dead and so he did not check for a pulse."[376]

The FBI reported that Iacone told the interviewing agent that upon his arrival at the body site, after Mr. Foster had been examined, "the medics confirmed there would be no efforts to resuscitate the patient."[377] Paramedic

---

[373] Exhibit 133, Narrative report of Paramedic George Gonzalez, July 20, 1993: "Had been approx dead 2-4 hrs"

[374] Exhibit 96, Report of FBI interview of Officer Ferstl, May 6, 1994: "Ferstl stated that he did not see Officer Fornshill or the medical technicians touch or move the body in any manner. Ferstl advised that he did take a look at the body from a position at the top of the berm, looking down at the body from approximately three to five feet from the top of the head."

[375] Exhibit 107, Deposition of Paramedic Richard Arthur, July 14, 1994: "[F]rom what I saw and from what it looked like, he was obviously dead."

[376] Exhibit 110, Report of FBI Interview with Paramedic Richard Arthur, March 16, 1994.

[377] Exhibit 78, Report of FBI Interview of Firefighter James Iacone, March 11, 1994: "After Iacone's group arrived at the location of the body the medics confirmed there would be no efforts to resuscitate the patient."

Arthur explained in his testimony that Iacone's unit came as "extra personnel just in case for carrying equipment, if CPR is needed, the medics can do the IVs and stuff, they [Iacone's unit] can do the manual labor."[378]

Firefighters would not have checked for a pulse or have cleared Mr. Foster's airway after the paramedics had concluded that Mr. Foster was obviously dead.  So, the OIC's theory that one of the "*early observers*" moved then repositioned the head is clearly without foundation.

OIC, p. 66:

*The testimony and contemporaneous reports point to the conclusion that rescue personnel at the scene handled the decedent's head to check for vital signs and an open airway.*

---

[378] Exhibit 107, Deposition of Paramedic Richard Arthur, July 14, 1994:   Q.  Who went out to Fort Marcy Park with you? A.  On the medic unit, the driver was Todd Hall.  The officer was Sergeant George Gonzalez and Richard.  I was in the back.  On the fire engine I want to say it was Ralph Pasany [sic] driving.  At the time I think he was a sergeant but he's now a lieutenant.  I should remember his name -- Icahn [sic].  Jay Icahn [sic], and then in the bucket of the engine. --  Q.  The bucket being the middle? A.  Well, you've got the driver, the officer and the two firefighters sit backwards and stuff, they're called buckets.  In the bucket it was Jennifer Walker [sic], firefighter Jennifer Walker [sic].  Q.  Why does the fire truck go --  A.  On certain dispatches, they're automatically dispatched, such as if there's a broken arm, it would just be a medic unit or an ambulance. If it's a shooting, heart attack, stabbing, something that calls for lots of work, lots of manpower where you may need to do a lot, they automatically send an engine just for assistance. The call came in as a -- if I remember correctly, it was a body lying next to a cannon, unknown situation, don't know if the patient is alive, dead, don't know if a hanging, whatever. We had no idea, so they automatically sent a medic unit and an extra personnel just in case for carrying equipment, if CPR is needed, the medics can do the IVs and stuff, they can do the manual labor.

b. **No "early observer" could have caused right side bloodstains because they all saw these stains as they arrived**

### Civilian Dale

Dale, the first witness to officially discover the body, testified that there was a "stain on his right shoulder... that could have been blood."[379]

### Firefighter Todd Hall
### Paramedic George Gonzalez

Firefighter Todd Hall, who accompanied Gonzalez, remembered blood on the collar of Mr. Foster's shirt.[380]

Paramedic George Gonzalez, in the group of the third and fourth *"early observers,"* saw the blood stain on the shirt before the head was moved.

Q. Can you, be a little more specific, where on the face or how much?

A. There wasn't that much on the face. There was some like I would say either a stream of blood. Primarily blood around the lip and inside the mouth was the contained area of blood. And just on the right shoulder, it looked like the blood was under the shirt because it had stained through

---

[379] Exhibit 51, Deposition of Dale by Congressmen Burton, Rohrabacher, and Mica, July 28, 1994: A. On his right shoulder. It was a stain -- the stain on his shoulder was-- Q. Was it red? Or was it blood? A. No. It was light purple, almost the identical to the color of the wine cooler. Q. So you don't think it was blood. A. I do not think it was blood. In the very center of -- it looked like he had thrown up on his right shoulder. In the very center there was one small spec area, probably no larger than a silver dollar that was black, that could have been blood in the very center of it.

[380] Exhibit 67, Deposition of Paramedic Todd Hall, July 20, 1994: "Q. Did you notice any of this pooling of blood, cyanotic, or something? A. All I recall is a couple of drops on his collar." Exhibit 179, Report of FBI interview of Firefighter Todd Hall, April 27, 1994: "Hall sighted blood on the right collar area of the decedent's shirt."

the white shirt.

\*     \*     \*

Q. Did you see any wet blood on the shirt?

A. I just saw a stain, a blood stain.

Q. Can you estimate about how big it was on the shirt?

A. It can be deceiving.  It was just in this area right in here, right about in this area of the clavicle area.

\*     \*     \*

Q. Was the blood in that phase dry or what?

A. Dry.[381]


**Paramedic Richard Arthur**
**Firefighter Ralph Pisani**
**Firefighter Jennifer Wacha**


Richard Arthur, the only paramedic in the group of four who arrived at around 6:22 p.m., testified on deposition that he saw blood all down the right shoulder area of Mr. Foster's shirt.[382]  The FBI's report of its interview with Firefighter Ralph Pisani notes that he saw "blood on Foster's right shoulder..."[383]  Firefighter Jennifer Wacha told the FBI that she "thought blood may have been on the victim's... shirt."[384]

---

[381]  Exhibit 110, Deposition of Paramedic George Gonzalez, July 20, 1994.

[382]  Exhibit 107, Deposition of Paramedic Richard Arthur, July 14, 1994.  Exhibit 82, Report of FBI interview of Paramedic Richard Arthur, April 29, 1994:  "Arthur recalls seeing blood on the decedent's right shoulder."  Exhibit 180, Handwritten notes of FBI interview of Paramedic Richard Arthur, April 29, 1994: "Blood on right shoulder."

[383]  Exhibit 136, Report of FBI interview of Firefighter Ralph Pisani, April 27, 1994.

[384]  Exhibit 72, Report of FBI interview of Firefighter Jennifer Wacha, March 11, 1994:  "Wacha thought blood may have been on the victim's mouth as well as on his shirt.  She could not recall the volume."

### c. The blood was dry until after Edwards had been alone at the body site

**Civilian Dale**

Dale, the witness who discovered the body, testified that "the blood was dried hard and black"[385] and that there were "not streams of blood on the side of his face."[386]

**Officer Kevin Fornshill**

The handwritten notes taken by the FBI of its interview with Park Police Officer Kevin Fornshill, taken April 29, 1994, state that Fornshill saw a "trickle of dried dark blood corner of right side of mouth and possibly flake, spotty not flowing."[387]

According to Fornshill's testimony, the blood he saw was "dried... dark in color... [and] flaking... like paint on a wall."[388] Fornshill did not mention any wet or flowing blood.

---

[385] Exhibit 51, Deposition of Dale by Congressmen Burton, Mica and Rohrabacher, July 28, 1994.

[386] Exhibit 51, Deposition of Dale by Congressmen Burton, Mica and Rohrabacher, July 28, 1994.

[387] Exhibit 108, Handwritten notes of report of FBI interview of Park Police Officer Kevin Fornshill, April 29, 1994: "Trickle of dried dark blood corner of right side of mouth and possibly flake, spotty not flowing No other blood on face... No blood on shirt or head same position after EMTs. No change in body etc after his initial observation."

[388] Exhibit 79, Deposition of Park Police Officer Kevin Fornshill, July 12, 1994: A. The lips were slightly parted and I do recall flies coming in the area of the lips, perhaps even entering the mouth itself because the lips were parted. Again, I didn't tilt the head enough, but slightly resting to one side and there was a trail of blood coming down the corner of the mouth, down to the chin. *** Q. Did you say you could see blood on the face? A. Yes. The blood would have been a trail of dried blood because I remember it was flaking too. It was dark in color. The texture was flaking up, you know, kind of curling like paint on a wall sometimes. It was trailing down from the lip or the corner of the lip on down.

## Firefighter Todd Hall
## Paramedic George Gonzalez

Hall testified that the pictures he had been shown by the FBI did not depict what he had seen when he viewed the body. He speculated that the head had been moved after he had viewed the body, before the photographs had been taken.

Q. Did you notice any of this pooling of blood, cyanotic, or something?
A. All I recall is a couple of drops on his collar. That's all I recall.
Q. Do you remember seeing any blood on his face?
A. No, I remember his face being straight when I was going to check because whatever turned his head, from the pictures I saw, there was more blood than I recall seeing. And that may be because, in the pictures, his head had been turned and that may have caused the bleeding, the blood to flow.[389]

---

[389] Exhibit 67, Deposition of Paramedic Todd Hall, July 20, 1994: Q. Tell me again, what was the position of the head when you first saw the body? A. I'd say it was in a line, looking up into the sky. Q. In the pictures you saw with the FBI? A. Yes. It was turned to the side, and blood was coming out of its mouth. Q. It was turned to? A. I think it was turned to the right. Q. So when you saw it, it was straight up. Did you notice blood off the side? A. No, All I noticed was a couple of drops on the collar. *** Q. Did you notice any of this pooling of blood, cyanotic, or something? A. All I recall is a couple of drops on his collar. That's all I recall. Q. Do you remember seeing any blood on his face? A. No, I remember his face being straight when I was going to check because whatever turned his head, from the pictures I saw, there was more blood than I recall seeing. And that may be because, in the pictures, his head had been turned and that may have caused the bleeding, the blood to flow. *** Q. And you said you saw some blood on the face? A. I recall seeing a couple of drops of blood on his collar and that's it. Q. Do you recall if it was wet or dry? Could you tell? A. It had pretty much soaked into his collar. Q. When you say his collar, on the right, which side? A. I recall it being over here. Q. Which side are you indicating? A. My left, his left. Q. His left side. Do you remember seeing any other blood on any other part of the clothes? A. No. Q. What about on the face? A. No.

# The blood was dry until after Edwards had been alone with the body

When asked if the blood he saw was wet or dry, Hall responded that the blood "had pretty much soaked into the collar." And Hall did not observe any contact stain on the face.

When Paramedic George Gonzalez testified on the first anniversary of the death, in response to the question, "Was the blood in that phase dry or what?" answered, "Dry."[390]

## Officer Franz Ferstl

Park Police Officer Franz Ferstl, the second police officer at the body site, related to the FBI that his "primary responsibility was to secure the crime scene." Ferstl first looked at the body, returned to his police cruiser to retrieve police crime scene tape, and then returned to the body site where he saw that the Fire & Rescue personnel had left. "He stated that to the best of his recollection, on returning a second time to the death scene, the body appeared to be in the identical position it was when he first observed it."[391]

According to the FBI's report of its interview with him, Ferstl "advised that he observed a small amount of blood around the mouth, adding that the blood did not appear fresh."[392]

## Paramedic Richard Arthur
## Firefighter Ralph Pisani

Paramedic Richard Arthur described the blood he saw as dry, not running. He also saw the blood on the shirt.

---

[390]   Exhibit 110, Deposition of Paramedic George Gonzalez, July 20, 1994.

[391]   Exhibit 96, Report of FBI interview of Officer Franz Ferstl, May 2, 1994.

[392]   Exhibit 96, Report of FBI interview of Park Police Officer Franz Ferstl, May 2, 1994: Ferstl advised that he observed a small amount of blood around the mouth, adding that the blood did not appear fresh. Ferstl did not recall any blood coming from the nose, nor did he recall any blood on the shirt... He stated that the shirt was very clean and he does not recall any blood stains or dirt stains on the shirt.

A.  I took a quick look, saw what appeared to be a
    bullet hole, saw the blood on the side of the
    neck, so I guess I assumed it was a bullet hole.
Q.  Was the blood dry?
A.  It wasn't running...

                    *      *      *

Q.  How big would you say the blood stain was on the
    shirt that you observed?
A.  Well, from -- maybe an inch or so up from the
    elbow on the right elbow up the sleeve and like
    from the collar bone all the way around.  It was
    like all around here.[393]

According to the FBI's April 27, 1994 interview with
Firefighter Ralph Pisani, he observed "blood on Foster's
right shoulder... [but] did not recall seeing any blood on
Foster's face."[394]  According to the FBI's handwritten notes
of that interview, Pisani's recollection of the blood he
saw on the face differed from that depicted in the
photograph the FBI showed him.[395]

### Sergeant Robert Edwards

No one reported having observed anyone move the head.
Only Sergeant Edwards was alone with the body.  Edwards did
not write a report and there is no record of the FBI having
interviewed him during the Fiske probe.  The only record of
Edward's having been interviewed is a reference to a secret

---

[393]    Exhibit 107, Deposition of Paramedic Richard Arthur, July
14, 1994.

[394]    Exhibit 136, Report of FBI interview of Firefighter Ralph
    Pisani, April 27, 1994:  Pisani was located in a position
    where he was looking over the left side of the body and was
    able to see blood on Foster's right shoulder.  Pisani did
    not recall seeing any blood on Foster's face.  Pisani
    further noted that he did not approach closer than ten feet
    to the body.  Pisani did not see anyone touch the body
    while he was at the scene.

[395]    Exhibit 137, Handwritten notes of FBI interview of
Firefighter Ralph Pisani, April 27, 1994:  "From photos: didn't
recall blood on face."

report in a footnote in the OIC's Report regarding Edwards' apparent denial that he had photographed the body.[396]

### Lieutenant Patrick Gavin
### Investigator Christine Hodakievic

Lieutenant Patrick Gavin told the FBI that when he arrived at the park, "Investigator Hodakievic met him at the parking lot and later directed him up to where the body had been discovered." Gavin told the FBI he saw "a trickle" of what appeared to be blood "coming" out of Mr. Foster's mouth and "running down" his face.[397]

Hodakievic did not report any observations of blood in the report she wrote on July 20, 1993. We believe that she saw Mr. Foster's body before and after Edwards was alone with the body. According to the FBI's report of its interview with her, "[s]he advised that she did not notice any blood on the decedent's face or on his shirt but recalls his arms being straight at his side."[398]

### Investigator John Rolla
### Investigator Cheryl Braun
### Evidence Technician Peter Simonello
### Investigator Renee Abt

Investigator Rolla testified that the "blood coming from the right nostril and the right corner of his mouth down the side of his face... appeared to still be wet."[399]

---

[396]    OIC, p. 74, fn. 215: "OIC, 1/12/95, at 7, 199-203. Investigator Abt recalled Sergeant Edwards taking Polaroids, OIC, 1/12/95, at 11, but Sergeant Edwards said he only carried the Polaroid camera and the Polaroids taken by Ferstl, but does not recall taking any Polaroids himself, OIC, 1/12/95, at 7, 199-203."

[397]    Exhibit 98, Report of FBI interview of Park Police Lieutenant Patrick Gavin, April 28, 1994.

[398]    Exhibit 81, Report of FBI interview with Christine Hodakievic, May 2, 1994.

[399]    Exhibit 6, Deposition of Park Police Investigator John Rolla, July 21, 1994: I noticed blood coming from the right nostril and the right corner of his mouth down the side of his face. It appeared to still be wet, but drying. Flies were buzzing around his face, starting to -- no eggs

The blood was "trickling from his right nostril and the right side of his mouth."[400]  Since Rolla observed the face "straight up" in the same position as observed by Officer Ferstl, who reported that earlier "the head was pointed straight up toward the sky,"[401] the head had been moved and returned to the straight up position.

Rolla testified that "[t]he blood on the ground and on his shirt appeared to still be wet."[402]  The FBI's report of its April 27, 1994 interview of Rolla similarly reports that the "[f]acial blood... emanating from the right side of the decedent's mouth... was still wet..., [the] blood under the decedent's head... appeared wet, [and that] blood on the decedent's shirt in the area of the right upper shoulder... also appeared to be wet..."[403]

---

were laid yet, I think they were just making their way to do that.

[400]     Exhibit 6, Deposition of Park Police Investigator John Rolla, July 21, 1994:  "[T]he blood was still wet. Q. The blood on the body? A. The blood under his head was just starting to gel. It was still wet. The edges, I think the edges where there was less blood were starting to gel."

[401]     Exhibit 96, Report of FBI interview of Park Police Officer Franz Ferstl, May 2, 1994.

[402]     Exhibit 6, Deposition of Park Police Investigator John Rolla, July 21, 1994:  "I observed blood in his nose and mouth area, on his right shoulder area and underneath his head. The blood on the ground and on his shirt appeared to still be wet. There was no blood on the plants or trees surrounding the decedents head."

[403]     Exhibit 100, Report of FBI interview of Park Police Investigator John Rolla, April 27, 1994:  Facial blood consisted of blood leading from the right nostril to the right side of the face and blood emanating from the right side of the decedent's mouth. He further advised the facial blood was still wet but starting to dry. He also observed a pool of blood under the decedent's head which appeared wet, but was also in the process of drying. Rolla also observed a deposit of blood on the decedent's shirt in the area of the right upper shoulder which also appeared to be wet but drying.

# The blood was dry until after Edwards had been alone with the body

Park Police Investigator Cheryl Braun testified that she saw blood "[i]n the nose area and in the mouth area... [and] on his chin in the area of his right shoulder."[404] The FBI reported that Braun stated that she "clearly recalls blood in the area of the nose running down the right side of the face."[405]

Park Police Evidence Technician Peter Simonello also testified that he observed "blood running from the nose... on the lower part of the cheek towards the chin, the jawline..."[406]

An entry in Park Police Investigator Renee Abt's notes, written at the scene at 7:10 p.m., notes that she saw both "dried and liquid" blood.[407] The FBI's report of its May 1994 interview with Abt is in accord.

> Investigator Abt advised that upon arriving at the scene she took personal responsibility for taking notes on the death scene and as such observed the decedent from a series of vantage points... She stated that... portions of the facial blood appeared

---

[404] Exhibit 101, Deposition of Park Police Investigator Cheryl Braun, July 23, 1994: Q. Was there blood on the body? A. Yes, there was. Q. Where? A. In the nose area and in the mouth area. And there were lots of flies in the eyes, nose, and mouth. There was also the blood in the -- on his shirt in the area of his right shoulder.

[405] Exhibit 91, Report of FBI interview of Park Police Investigator Cheryl Braun, April 28, 1994: "Braun states that she clearly recalls blood in the area of the nose running down the right side of the face; she can't say for sure, but she vaguely recalls some trace of blood around the mouth and also traces of blood on the right shoulder of the shirt."

[406] Exhibit 104, Deposition of Park Police Evidence Technician Peter Simonello, July 14, 1994: "There was some blood running from the nose. There was some blood on the lower part of the cheek towards the chin, the jawline. There was some blood on the right shoulder, and there was some blood, I believe, near the right rib cage."

[407] Exhibit 118, Handwritten contemporaneous notes of Park Police Investigator Renee Abt, at 7:10 p.m., July 20, 1993: "Large blood pattern Rt shoulder + collar of shirt. Dried and liquid"

dry while other portions appeared to be liquid in nature.[408]

### d. The only witnesses who saw the blood transfer contact stain arrived at the site after Sergeant Edwards had been alone with the body

Edwards' movement of the head, causing blood to flow from the mouth and nose to conceal that blood had drained from the neck onto the collar and shirt, caused the contact stain. Witnesses who viewed the body before Edwards' arrival did not see it. Rolla, Simonello, and Abt did.

Rolla testified that he saw a transfer stain "on his face" and that it was "pretty apparent" that Mr. Foster's head had touched his shoulder.[409]

Park Police Evidence Technician Peter Simonello reportedly told the FBI that he saw a "blood transfer pattern on the right cheek."[410] The transfer bloodstain

---

[408] Exhibit 99, Report of FBI interview of Park Police Investigator Renee Abt, May 2, 1994: Investigator Abt advised that upon arriving at the scene she took personal responsibility for taking notes on the death scene and as such observed the decedent from a series of vantage points. She advised that after viewing a series of enlarged Polaroid photographs obtained from USPP that these photographs were a true and accurate depiction of the decedent's body and the surrounding area which she personally observed on July 20, 1993. She stated that in her opinion, portions of the facial blood appeared dry while other portions appeared to be liquid in nature.

[409] Exhibit 6, Deposition of Park Police Investigator John Rolla, July 21, 1994: A. There was blood on his shoulder, possibly like a transfer stain. Q. What's a transfer stain? A. A transfer stain is -- blood wasn't initially in one location or another. It was on his face -- or on his shirt, not his face. One touched the other. But at this point his face was up, straight up, when I saw him... Q. In your opinion, at some point, the right side of his head touched with the right side of his shoulder? A. Yes. I think it's pretty apparent.

[410] Exhibit 105, Report of FBI interview of Park Police Evidence Technician Peter Simonello, April 28, 1994: He specifically recalls blood staining around the chin area

228

was, according to Simonello's sworn testimony, on the "lower cheek near the jawline."

Q. You had mentioned a transfer stain on the shirt is that correct?

A. Yes.

Q. Could you describe that, as you first saw it.

A. Well, the transfer stain I saw, there was blood on his lower cheek near the jawline. The lower edge was very clean -- the blood stain and the lower edge appears to be a straight sharp edge, and I saw blood on the part of his shirt which I believe is around the shirt collar, shoulder area. I deduced that the stain was made because his face was against there at one time. The sharp edge, therefore, coming from the edge of the shirt not allowing the blood to get below that point on his face, and that's what I felt was a transfer stain.

\* \* \*

Q. Do you know if the head was moved before you saw it?

A. I can only deduce that it was because of the stain I saw, but no one told me it was, and I have not been able to find -- no one ever said anything since that that it has been, but I felt it had to have been sometime in contact with that shirt prior to my arrival.[411]

Park Police Investigator Abt reported to the FBI that she observed a contact transfer blood stain on the "lower right cheek."[412]

---

and from the nose down the right cheek. Simonello also observed blood along the right side of the decedent's mouth and specifically recalls what he labeled as a blood transfer pattern on the right cheek as well as noticing the presence of a few flies around the decedent's nostrils.

[411] Exhibit 104, Deposition of Park Police Evidence Technician Peter Simonello, July 14, 1994.

[412] Exhibit 99, Report of FBI interview of Park Police Investigator Renee Abt, May 2, 1994: Additionally she did observe a segment of blood on the decedent's lower right cheek which appeared to be transferred blood and specifically mentioned observing a number of flies on the decedent's face to include flies in the mouth and in the

## 5.    Blood quantity insufficient

All six official experts (Fiske's four pathologists[413] and the OIC's pathologist and forensic scientist) posit that the amount of blood was consistent with how and where Mr. Foster officially died, from firing a high-velocity .38 caliber bullet into his mouth where his body lay.[414]

The OIC concludes its two-page *Quantity of Blood* discussion with a mischaracterization of skeptics' opinions regarding the lack of blood at the scene.  The OIC claims that skeptics opine that *"blood must already have drained from the body elsewhere."*[415]  That is decidedly not the basis of the skepticism.  The skepticism is based on insufficient blood at the scene to justify the conclusion that Mr.

---

nostrils with numerous other flies swarming around the body.

[413]   Charles S. Hirsch, M.D., James L. Luke, M.D., Donald T. Reay, M.D., and Charles J. Stahl, M.D.

[414]   OIC, p. 65:  "Based on all of the above evidence, analysis, and conclusions, Dr. Blackbourne concluded that 'Vincent Foster committed suicide on July 20, 1993 in Ft. Marcy Park by placing a .38 caliber revolver in his mouth and pulling the trigger.  His death was at his own hand.'[fn190]  OIC, p. 65, fn. 190: "Blackbourne Report at 5.  The panel of pathologists reached the same conclusion.  Pathologists' Report at 4..."

[415]   OIC, p. 68:  There has been occasional public suggestion, premised on the supposedly low amount of blood observed at the Fort Marcy scene, that blood must already have drained from the body elsewhere and the fatal shot therefore must have been fired elsewhere.  As revealed by the foregoing descriptions of the evidence, the underlying premise of this theory is erroneous:  A quantity of blood was observed at the park under the body and on the back of the head and shirt.  Moreover, the suggestion fails to account for the blood that subsequently drained from Mr. Foster's body during movement to the autopsy.  The blood-quantity evidence, even when considered in isolation from other evidence, does not support (and indeed contravenes) a suggestion that the fatal shot was fired at a place other than where Mr. Foster was found at Fort Marcy Park.[fn197]

OIC, p. 68, fn. 197:  "There are also a number of other items of evidence that contradict any such suggestion, as noted elsewhere in this report."

## Blood quantity insufficient

Foster died there by a shot directly into the mouth from the official high-velocity .38 caliber ammunition. How much blood may have drained elsewhere is not relevant.

Not one observer saw a quantity of blood consistent with the official .38 caliber gunshot wound to the mouth.

The accounts of the body scene witnesses the OIC uses to support its blood-quantity claim are embodied in its two-page discussion under the heading *Quantity of Blood.*

OIC, p. 66-67:

*"Many who saw the body at Fort Marcy Park <u>after</u> it was lifted and rolled over at the scene described a quantity of blood behind Mr. Foster's head, under his body, and on the back of his shirt.*[fn192]*"*

The lengthy footnote to this passage sets forth the OIC's version of the accounts of five of the twenty-one witnesses who saw the body; Park Police Investigator Abt, Medical Examiner Haut, Park Police Investigator Hodakievic, Park Police Investigator Rolla and Park Police Identification Technician Simonello.[416]

---

[416]   <u>OIC, p. 67, fn. 192:</u>  Abt OIC, 2/9/95, at 30 ("We noted that there was a good amount of blood again on the back portion of the shirt and the collar, things like that."); Haut OIC, 2/16/95, at 13 ("[o]n the ground, underneath his head, there was a pool of congealed blood"); Hodakievic 302, 2/7/95, at 4 (recalls "lot of blood underneath the decedent's head); Hodakievic OIC, 2/14/95, at 16, at 16 (describing blood on the ground and on the back of head and shirt when body moved); USPP Report (Rolla) at 1-2 ("I observed blood... underneath his head... I rolled the decedent over and observed a large blood stain three quarters down the back of the decedent's shirt."); Rolla 302, 4/17/96, at 4 ("When Rolla rolled the body he observed new, wet blood pouring out of the nose and possibly the mouth of the decedent.  Rolla also observed a pool of blood, approximately 4 inches across, which had been under the head and neck area.  Rolla also observed the back of the shirt was soaked with blood from the collar to the waist."); USPP Report (Simonello) at 1 ("When the body was turned onto its stomach I observed a large area of blood where the head had been resting. . . . I also observed a larger area of blood where the victim's back had been, coinciding with blood stains on the back of shirt."); Simonello 302, 2/7/95 at 3 ("after the body was rolled,

231

The OIC reports that a large quantity of blood was found under Mr. Foster's body when it was rolled over. Yet, according to those who were present, the quantity of blood at the scene was insufficient to support the official conclusion that he died from a point-blank shot to the mouth with .38 caliber high-velocity ammunition.

Additionally, the Report relates (p. 58[417]) that *"Dr. Lee stated that one photograph of the scene 'shows a view of the vegetation in the areas where Mr. Foster's body was found. Reddish-brown, blood-like stains can be seen on several leaves of the vegetation in this area.'[fn170]"* The footnote to this passage tells us that this finding would be consistent with the official version "[i]f these stains are, in fact, blood spatters," but does not tell us whether Dr. Lee opined that the *"blood-like"* substance depicted in the Polaroid is blood.

OIC, p. 59, fn. 171:

*"Dr. Lee said that '[i]f these stains are, in fact, blood spatters, this finding is consistent with the shot having been fired at the location where Mr. Foster's body was found.' Id."*

### Civilian Dale

When Congressman Burton asked Dale, the civilian who officially discovered the body, whether there was any blood around the head, Dale replied, "None."[418]

---

Simonello observed a large blood pool under the head of the decedent and on the back of the decedent's shirt").

[417] OIC, p. 59: Dr. Lee stated that one photograph of the scene "shows a view of the vegetation in the areas where Mr. Foster's body was found. Reddish-brown, blood-like stains can be seen on several leaves of the vegetation in this area."[fn170] He also noted that "[a] close-up view of some of these blood-like stains can be seen in [a separate] photograph."[fn171]

OIC, p. 112-113: "Dr. Lee observed blood-like spatter on vegetation in the photographs of the scene."

[418] Exhibit 51, Deposition of Dale taken by Congressmen Burton, Mica & Rorabacher, July 28, 1994: "Q. But you didn't

**Blood quantity insufficient**

## Officer Kevin Fornshill

Park Police Officer Kevin Fornshill testified that he "saw only a slight trail of blood coming out of the mouth," and that he did not "recall any other blood."[419]

The FBI's report of its interview with Fornshill notes only that he saw a trickle of dried blood in Mr. Foster's mouth.

> At this position, he noticed a trickle of dried, dark blood at the corner of the right side of the decedent's mouth but did not view any other blood on the face or for that matter on the decedent's shirt or trousers.[420]

---

see any blood as close as you got around the head or anything like that? A. None."

[419] Exhibit 79, Deposition of Park Police Officer Kevin Fornshill, July 12, 1994: Q. Did you see any blood on the body? A. Yes. Q. Where did you see the blood? A. There was a slight trail of blood coming out of the mouth on the right hand side over the lips and down the chin. Q. Any other blood? A. Not that I could see, no, sir. *** Q. Did you see any other blood on the body? A. No, I don't recall any other blood.

[420] Exhibit 138, Report of FBI interview of Park Police Officer Kevin Fornshill, April 29, 1994: According to Private Fornshill, his initial observation of the body was from the body's left side at a distance of approximately 6 feet, moving in a 180 degree arc, viewing the body from both the top looking down directly at the body, as well as moving to the right side of the body. While admitting that his initial observation of the body was probably less than 15 seconds, he does recall that while to the left hand side of the body, that the hair on the head was neatly in place, the mouth was slightly open and he could observe the top teeth. He indicated from this position, he also viewed flies moving around the lips and around the mouth area and specifically recalls that the decedent's shirt was white in color, clean and apparently starched with the collar open. He further observed that the decedent's trousers were in his opinion extremely neat and devoid of any dirt, debris or soil. Fornshill then recalls moving to the right of the body on the top of the crest of the hill where he noticed that the decedent's complexion was grayish in color and that the head was slightly tilted to the right. At this

The handwritten notes of that interview similarly relate that Fornshill reported seeing a "trickle of dried dark blood [on the] corner of [the] right side of [the] mouth... [and] no other blood on [the] face... [and] no blood on [the] shirt."[421]

There is no record of Fornshill's having seen blood on the ground. When asked what he observed on the ground, he testified that he was looking but "didn't see anything."[422]

---

position, he noticed a trickle of dried, dark blood at the corner of the right side of the decedent's mouth but did not view any other blood on the face or for that matter on the decedent's shirt or trousers.

[421] Exhibit 108, Handwritten notes of report of FBI interview of Park Police Officer Kevin Fornshill, April 29, 1994: "Trickle of dried dark blood corner of right side of mouth and possibly flake, spotty not flowing. No other blood on face... No blood on shirt or head same position after EMTs. No change in body etc. after his initial observation."

[422] Exhibit 79, Deposition of Park Police Officer Kevin Fornshill, July 12, 1994: Q. Was there anything unusual about the ground around the body that you noticed? A. It's funny you should ask that, because I even went so far, I sort of strained. I remember shifting my weight again and looking down the embankment. If I was here on the top of the embankment, I looked down to check and see if there was anything else, any items, any ground disturbed, any twigs broken, leaves disturbed, anything like that. I didn't see anything. Perhaps there may have been. I don't know. I was looking for luggage, clothing, anything at all like that. Q. Was there any trash or human debris? A. Nothing like that at all, because I made a point of visually looking for that. Q. The ground appeared to you to be undisturbed? A. Yes. Q. Was is [sic] still light outside around this time? A. Yes, it was. Q. Do you wear glasses or contact lenses? A. No. Q. Did you say you could see the hands from your vantage point? A. No, I didn't see the hands. Q. You could see the feet and the face but not the hands? A. Yes. Q. How long were you looking at the body before you were joined by the EMS personnel? A. Geez, a matter of seconds, 15, 20 seconds perhaps. Q. Did you look for a gun in the vicinity of the body? A. No. I didn't. Q. Did you notice anything unusual about the body or the vicinity? A. No, other than the fact that there was a body in the park. Q. Based on this scene, you determined that this was a suicide? A. When the EMS personnel came up and they said, there's a gun

## Blood quantity insufficient

Officer Fornshill testified that he "viewed the grass and foliage around the death scene,"[423] but saw blood only around the mouth of the victim.

### Firefighter Todd Hall
### Paramedic George Gonzalez

Firefighter Todd Hall reportedly saw blood on the collar of the shirt and nowhere else.[424] He testified that he did not see any blood on the decedent's face.[425]

Paramedic George Gonzalez noted that the condition of Mr. Foster's head did not fit what he had "usually" observed in prior occasions of a .38 caliber gunshot to the head.

> Q. If your experience had been that every time you'd gone to a scene like this, it had always been a

---

in his right hand, do you see the gun. Then I'm straining and looking for the gun. I couldn't see the gun. But when they told me that. I made the assumption, which I shouldn't have, and made a broadcast and said it appeared to be an apparent suicide.

[423] Exhibit 79, Deposition of Park Police Officer Kevin Fornshill, July 12, 1994: "Q. You had an opportunity to view the grass and foliage around the death scene and in particular around the location of the body? A. Yes."

[424] Exhibit 66, Report of FBI interview of Firefighter Todd Hall, March 18, 1994: "Hall thought there were only a couple of drops of blood on Foster's shirt collar. Foster's body was further described to have had flies moving in and out of the mouth. No other blood was noticed on the body."

[425] Exhibit 67, Deposition of Paramedic Todd Hall, July 20, 1994: Q. Do you remember seeing any blood on his face? A. No, I remember his face being straight when I was going to check because whatever turned his head, from the pictures I saw, there was more blood than I recall seeing. And that may be because, in the pictures, his head had been turned and that may have caused the bleeding, the blood to flow.

Exhibit 67, Deposition of Paramedic Todd Hall, July 20, 1994: "Q. Do you remember seeing any other blood on any other part of the clothes? A. No. Q. What about on the face? A. No."

235

mess. Would you have said that to him? Would you have said, every time I've been to a scene like that, it's been a mess? (Pause).

A. Let me describe a few situations that you'll maybe better understand the word "usually." Sometimes the head is either gone, decapitated. Okay, from say the mouth all the way up. Sometimes you have the whole frontal part of your face but with the back portion, the occipital region gone. Sometimes it's the side of the face if it's an angle or approach the gunshot from the side, this side of the face is usually gone.[426]

## Officer Franz Ferstl

The FBI's report of its May, 1994 interview with Franz Ferstl, the second police officer at the scene, states that he "observed a small amount of blood around the mouth... [and that he] did not recall any blood coming from the nose, nor did he recall any blood on the shirt [and that] the shirt was very clean and he does not recall any blood stains... on the shirt."[427]

## Paramedic Richard Arthur
## Firefighter Ralph Pisani
## Firefighter Lt. James Iacone
## Firefighter Jennifer Wacha

Paramedic Richard Arthur testified that he saw blood "[a]ll down the right side neck [and] shoulder... coming from... a bullet hole... [i]n the neck... [and] a little bit of blood coming out of the mouth... and nose." He saw no blood "on the left side... [or] chest."[428]

The FBI's report of its interview with Firefighter Ralph Pisani notes that he "did not recall seeing any blood

---

[426] Exhibit 110, Deposition of Paramedic George Gonzalez, July 20, 1994.

[427] Exhibit 96, Report of FBI interview of Park Police Officer Franz Ferstl, May 2, 1994.

[428] Exhibit 107, Deposition of Paramedic Richard Arthur, July 14, 1994.

## Blood quantity insufficient

located around the body."[429]   The FBI's report of its
interview with Firefighter Lieutenant James Iacone recounts
that he did not "not recall observing any blood."[430]   The
only blood Firefighter Jennifer Wacha observed was on the
mouth and shirt.[431]

### Sergeant Robert Edwards

See Sergeant Edwards' movements in the maps above.   He
never wrote any report of his involvement at the scene.   He
was not interviewed during the first investigation.   There
is no record of the FBI having interviewed him during the
Fiske probe.   There is no record of what he may have
observed.

### Lieutenant Patrick Gavin
### Investigator Christine Hodakievic

Lieutenant Patrick Gavin, the highest ranking official
at the body site, reportedly told the FBI he saw "a trickle
or what appeared to be blood coming out of the mouth...
[and that] [h]e did not recall seeing blood coming from the
nose, nor does he recall any blood or blood stains on the
shirt."[432]

The OIC recites that Officer Hodakievic told the FBI
on February 7, 1995 that she *recalls 'lot of blood'*

---

[429]   Exhibit 136, Report of FBI interview of Firefighter Ralph
Pisani, April 27, 1994.

[430]   Exhibit 78, Report of FBI interview of Firefighter
Lieutenant James Iacone, March 11, 1994:   "Iacone does not recall
observing any blood."

[431]   Exhibit 72, Report of FBI interview of Firefighter Jennifer
Wacha, March 11, 1994:   "Wacha thought blood may have been on the
victim's mouth as well as on his shirt.   She could not recall the
volume."

[432]   Exhibit 98, Report of FBI interview of Park Police
Lieutenant Patrick Gavin, April 28, 1994.   Exhibit 80,
Handwritten notes of FBI interview of Park Police Lieutenant
Patrick Gavin, April 28, 1994:   "Only blood he recalls is trickle
coming out mouth - can't recall blood coming from nose - nor does
he recall blood on shirt.   Only made a cursory look - doesn't
mean blood wasn't there.   Could have."

*underneath the decedent's head."* A week later, according to the OIC, she was *"describing blood on the ground and on the back of head and shirt when body moved,"* although the OIC does not provide that description.

> OIC, p. 67, fn. 192:
>
> *"...Hodakievic 302, 2/7/95, at 4 (recalls 'lot of blood' underneath the decedent's head); Hodakievic OIC, 2/14/95, at 16, at 16 (describing blood on the ground and on the back of head and shirt when body moved)...*

In the spring of 1994, Hodakievic reportedly told the FBI that she "did not notice any blood on the decedent's face nor any blood on the decedent's shirt."[433] It is unknown whether these reported observations of Hodakievic refer to the first time she viewed the body or when she returned to the body with Lieutenant Gavin.

### Investigator John Rolla
### Investigator Cheryl Braun
### Evidence Technician Peter Simonello
### Investigator Renee Abt

Besides Haut and Hodakievic, the Report's footnote 192 cites Investigator Rolla, Evidence Technician Simonello, and Investigator Abt.

The FBI's version of Rolla's April 1996 account is that *"[w]hen Rolla rolled the body he observed new, wet blood pouring out of the nose and possibly the mouth of the decedent. Rolla also observed a pool of blood, approximately 4 inches across, which had been under the head and neck area. Rolla also observed the back of the shirt was soaked with blood from the collar to the waist."*

Rolla had testified that the blood "was not all over the place, it was directly under his head on the ground."[434]

---

[433]  Exhibit 81, Report of FBI interview of Park Police Investigator Christine Hodakievic, May 2, 1994.

[434]  Exhibit 6, Deposition of Park Police Investigator John Rolla, July 21, 1994:  A.  I observed a pool of blood under his head that was wet and beginning to dry and clot, and it

## Blood quantity insufficient

His report, prepared on the evening of the death, specifically notes that "[t]here was no blood on the plants or trees surrounding the decedents (sic) head."[435]

Park Police Investigator Cheryl Braun's two-page typed report, prepared hours after viewing the body at the park, inexplicably failed to include any mention of the wounds or blood she may have observed.[436] She later testified before the Senate that "everything was consistent with a suicide,"[437] but she was not asked why she had earlier testified that the determination of suicide was made before she looked at the body.[438]

---

was directly under his head. It was not all over the place, it was directly under his head, running down this way. *** Q. What about on the ground? A. I believe there was some blood mark on the ground, I don't remember. But most of the blood under his head, where his head was, yes, there was blood on the ground, but most of the blood that had run down was absorbed in his clothes.

[435] Exhibit 113, Report by Park Police Investigator John Rolla, July 21, 1993.

[436] Exhibit 116, Report of Park Police Investigator Cheryl Braun, July 20, 1993.

[437] Exhibit 177, Senate testimony of Park Police Investigator Cheryl Braun, July 29, 1994: Q. Let me just stop you there. My time is up. I want to, if I may, just ask one question, and then I will yield because I do not want to trespass on the time either. Did either of you see anything at the time that caused you to think that this might not be a suicide or the way it apparently would have appeared to you? In other words, when you arrived, saw the scene, and saw the body, was there anything that struck either of you that would have caused you to say, maybe this was not a suicide. Was there anything that stuck out at that time that you recall now, or that you made a point of at the time? Ms. Braun. A. No. When we arrived at the scene and I went up to the scene, everything was consistent with a suicide.

[438] Exhibit 101, Deposition of Park Police Investigator Cheryl Braun, July 23, 1994: Q. Did he [Edwards] say he thought that the death was by suicide? A. I don't recall exactly how he did it, and he did show the pictures to it that he had snapped. Q. Was it your understanding that a determination had been made as to the cause of death? A. I think we more made that determination. You know, like I

According to the OIC, in February of 1995, Park Police Evidence Technician Peter Simonello told the FBI that *"after the body was rolled, Simonello observed a large blood pool..."* The OIC fails to relate that, less than a year after the death, Simonello testified that he expected more blood patterns than he observed.

Q. In the interview with the FBI, however, it appears you did see some blood on the shirt, and I'll hand you that. You might want to look at the top paragraph of that page.

A. Okay.

Q. Do you have any explanation for that inconsistency?

A. No. I remember seeing a teeny droplet of blood. One time I thought it was on his finger but it may have been on his shirt or vice versa. There wasn't a great deal of it which I would have wanted to see, a patterning.[439]

---

said, when we first got the call. It was for a dead body. Then I asked if it was natural or of suspicious nature. And I was told suspicious, so I had them close the gate. Then once we got there, maybe actually I do remember speaking to Lieutenant Gavin. So maybe it was Lieutenant Gavin who might have -- it might have been Lieutenant Gavin then who actually initially explained what the scene was, because I had some knowledge of it when I went to speak with the couple and ask them if they had heard anything or seen anything and ask them about other vehicles that were in the area. Yeah, I would say it was Lieutenant Gavin actually. Q. Did Lieutenant Gavin mention anything about suicide? A. I can't recall. I don't -- I don't recall if he or if that was what we -- it seems to me that we had made that determination prior to going up and looking at the body.

[439] Exhibit 104, Deposition of Park Police Evidence Technician Peter Simonello, July 14, 1994: Q. In that report you indicate that you saw one droplet of blood on the right index finger and no blood splatter on the shirt sleeves. Do you see that? A. Uh-huh. Q. In the interview with the FBI, however, it appears you did see some blood on the shirt, and I'll hand you that. You might want to look at the top paragraph of that page. A. Okay. Q. Do you have any explanation for that inconsistency? A. No. I remember seeing a teeny droplet of blood. One time I thought it was on his finger but it may have been on his

## Blood quantity insufficient

The OIC reported that the entrance wound in the soft palate was a contact wound.[440] Yet, Simonello testified that there was no tissue or blood on the gun, and that "[i]n a contact wound type of situation... [w]hen the gas expands and withdraws, it sometimes pulls material into the barrel..."[441]

Simonello's report, composed July 26, 1993, recounted that there was "no discernible forward or back spatter blood evidence on the victim's shirtsleeves."[442] The questions raised by the appearance of the scene were not limited to the absence of blood spatter, as he testified less than a year after the death.

---

shirt or vice versa. There wasn't a great deal of it which I would have wanted to see, a patterning.

[440]   OIC p. 62 fn. 183:  "Mr. Foster placed the barrel of the weapon into his mouth with the muzzle essentially in contact with the soft palate when he pulled the trigger."

[441]   Exhibit 104, Deposition of Park Police Evidence Technician Peter Simonello, July 14, 1994:  Q.  Did you see any blood on the gun when you recovered it?  A.  I recall seeing one small speck or droplet of blood on the barrel.  Q.  Is there any type of chemical analysis that would be typically done on a gun?  A.  Analysis for what?  Q.  Other than blood.  I guess, maybe DNA or something like that.  A.  You can do DNA.  In a contact wound type of situation with a gun, from my readings, there can be a drawback into the barrel of tissue or blood.  When the gas expands and withdraws, it sometimes pulls material into the barrel in a contact wound or suicide type.

[442]   Exhibit 134, Park Police Report Supplement by Evidence Technician Peter Simonello, July 26, 1993:  There was blood staining around the chin area and from the nose down the right cheek.  Blood stains also were found on the right shoulder and neck area as well as the right ribcage area of the shirt...  A cursory examination of the victim's hands for blood spatter evidence revealed one droplet on the right index finger, above the second joint.  No discernible forward or back spatter blood evidence on the victim's shirtsleeves.

A.   Then, upon closer observation of everything that we had there. I started filing away certain questions I wanted to have answered, things that didn't -- I didn't have immediate answers to before I came to a conclusive -- an opinion that was conclusive. And those things were transfer blood stain, how did that happen? Is this gunpowder on his hand, went through my head and that cylinder blast I'm talking about, to have that checked out. Why was there a spot of blood down here... on his shirt... near the lowest rib, in that area of the rib cage on the right side. These are things that I couldn't answer immediately and so we wouldn't come to a conclusion until we had all these questions as far as we could to get them answered. I wondered about the fact that I didn't see a lot of blood spattered on his white shirt -- his arms of his white shirt. Spatters -- when a high-velocity bullet hits, blood is turned in teeny, tiny droplets. I saw one or two drops, but not indicative of a pattern.

Q.   Where did you see those drops?

A.   I think one drop was on his finger, his right hand. I think there was a very small drop. And there may have been one on his chin, but not -- I thought why isn't there more? That was my thinking there. The other thing is how did he shoot the gun. I saw his thumb trapped in there, but I wonder how you -- why would you want to shoot a gun that way? I wondered about the glasses. Are those his glasses? If they're not his glasses, whose glasses are they? And I also played the guessing in my head, how could this have been done? If he didn't do it, could it be done by somebody else and if so, how? Those are my general impressions of the scene.[443]

Simonello's puzzlement as to why he did not see "a lot of blood spatter[s]," but only "one or two" from the "high-velocity bullet" stands in sharp contrast to the OIC's claim.

---

[443]   Exhibit 104, Deposition of Park Police Evidence Technician Peter Simonello, July 14, 1994.

## Blood quantity insufficient

According to the OIC, in February of 1995, Investigator Renee Abt said, *"we noted that there was a good amount of blood again on the back portion of the shirt and the collar, things like that."* The FBI's report of its interview with Abt relates that she noted blood in the area of the right shoulder, "checked out the immediate vicinity of the death scene but did not observe any items of an evidentiary nature."[444] This would include blood.

### Dr. Donald Haut

Dr. Donald Haut, the only doctor to view Mr. Foster's body at the scene, had written on the back page of his Report (if not the front) that the Police "found... [a] gunshot wound mouth to neck." He told the FBI ten months after the death that the volume of blood was small.

> [H]e did not see blood on Foster's face... Haut believed that the wound was consistent with a low velocity weapon. Haut recalled a separate case in which a .25 caliber rifle caused a much more devastating wound to the victim... [and the] volume of blood [on back of the head] was small.[445]

According to the FBI's report of its interview with him in April of 1994, "Haut did not recall seeing blood on the decedent's shirt or face and no blood was recalled on the vegetation around the body."[446]

Yet the OIC ignores Haut's earlier accounts and quotes their FBI agents as reporting that in February of 1995, Dr. Haut said he saw *"[o]n the ground, underneath his head, there was a pool of congealed blood."*

---

[444]   Exhibit 99, Report of FBI interview of Park Police Investigator Renee Abt, May 2, 1994.

[445]   Exhibit 73, Report of FBI interview with Dr. Donald Haut, April 12, 1994.

[446]   Exhibit 181, Report of FBI interview of Dr. Donald Haut, April 14, 1994.

### Firefighter Corey Ashford
### Firefighter Roger Harrison

Firefighters Cory Ashford and Roger Harrison lifted Mr. Foster's corpse into a body bag. In Ashford's July 20, 1993, report, he coded the death as a "96," which stands for homicide by assault with a firearm.[447] The FBI's report of its February 1994 interview with him contains at least some of his observations. The interviewing agent wrote "it was initially believed by Ashford that Foster was the victim of a murder...," implying that he later changed his opinion.

> Ashford did not recall seeing any blood on Foster's body, noting that he was not looking for it at the time. It was initially believed by Ashford that Foster was the victim of a murder... Ashford did not recall seeing any blood while placing Foster in the bag. Ashford did not recall any blood getting on his uniform or on the disposable gloves he wore while handling the body... Ashford lifted Foster from behind the shoulder, cradling the victim's head... Ashford did not recall seeing any blood while placing Foster in the bag...[448]

The FBI interviewed Ashford again in April of 1994. That report also relates that Ashford did not recall seeing any blood.

> "Ashford did not recall seeing any blood on the ground at the location of Foster's body during this evaluation."[449]

Harrison was interviewed when the FBI contacted him in March of 1994. That report notes that "[h]e did not notice any blood at the scene."[450] The FBI's report of its March,

---

[447]　Exhibit 120, Incident report of Firefighter Corey Ashford, July 20, 1993.

[448]　Exhibit 74, Report of FBI interview of Firefighter Corey Ashford, February 23, 1994.

[449]　Exhibit 139, Report of FBI interview of Firefighter Corey Ashford, April 27, 1994.

[450]　Exhibit 140, Report of FBI interview of Firefighter Roger

The guns

1994, interview with Harrison recounts that there was not
enough blood to warrant his filing of a hazardous material
report.

"If there was a quantity of blood present on Foster's
body, a hazardous material report would have been
filed noting the condition and amount of blood."[451]

## VII. EVIDENCE THAT THE OIC COVERED UP THAT MR. FOSTER DID NOT FIRE OR OWN THE GUN FOUND AT THE PARK

Summary: The OIC hides that the gunshot residue patterns on Mr.
Foster's hands prove that he did not fire the weapon.

The OIC conceals that Remington, the manufacturer of the ammunition
found in the gun, has never used "ball smokeless powder," the type of
ammunition found on the body and clothing. Gunpowder and blood on the
eyeglasses proves he was wearing them when the shot was fired, but they
could not have landed where they were found. The OIC claims that Dr.
Lee found "gunpowder like" particles in the soil at the park over a year
after the death. The OIC mentions that the FBI lab found two types of
powder on Mr. Foster's clothing, but offers no explanation.

The OIC conceals that a semi-automatic handgun was in Mr. Foster's
hand before the official revolver was placed in his hand. The OIC
misrepresents that Mr. Foster owned the gun found in his hand.

### 1. Impossibility of gunshot residue patterns on hands having been caused by self-inflicted wound

The official death weapon is a black 1913 .38 Colt
Army Special six-shot revolver, with a four-inch barrel.[452]

---

Harrison, March 11, 1994: Harrison did not recall if there
was any blood on body... He did not notice any blood at
the scene... Harrison did not recall seeing any blood on
Foster and did not recall seeing any blood on individuals
handling the body. If blood had been present on Foster's
body, a hazardous materials report would have been filed
noting the condition and the amount of blood. Harrison did
not recall anyone at the scene getting blood on them from
the wounds associated with the death of Foster.

[451]   Exhibit 140, Report of FBI interview with Firefighter Roger
Harrison, March 11, 1994.

[452]   Exhibit 142, Park Police Evidence Control Receipt, by
Evidence Technician Peter Simonello, July 20, 1993.

Its having been found with the right thumb in the trigger guard mandates a finding that if Mr. Foster had fired the gun, it would have been with his right thumb. This has been the official conclusion from day one.

A close look at this claim proves that it too is false.

When a revolver is fired and the bullet leaves the cylinder and enters the barrel, the internal pressure expels gasses, burning and unburned powder, and particulate and vaporized lead, referred to as smoke or gunshot residue (GSR). The blast results in GSR being vented through the "barrel-cylinder gap" at high speed, forming a ring perpendicular to the gun's barrel. Since the weapon's frame prevents the GSR from emanating from the top, and the crane cylinder shaft deflects it at the bottom, it is expended out at an angle and forms two triangles, one to the left of the weapon and one to the right.

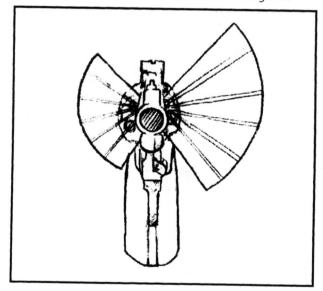

**As the GSR escapes at an angle,
it separates like spokes of a wheel.**

When these black soot-like escaping particles deposit themselves on a surface they strike, they form, roughly speaking, a visible line, directly in line with the barrel-cylinder gap, like the lines of deposits left on both of Mr. Foster's index fingers and the web between his right

Gunshot residue

thumb and index finger.  Dr. Beyer drew the GSR deposit on
Mr. Foster's hands in his Autopsy Report's "body diagram."

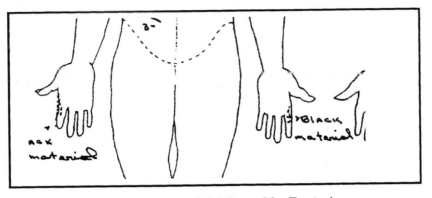

**Dr. Beyer's drawing of GSR on Mr. Foster's
hands in the body diagram of the Autopsy Report**

We want to approximate the length of the GSR line that
Dr. Beyer drew.  To do so, we first review what exists of
the public record of where exactly the GSR began and ended.
Simonello reported that the GSR was "between the thumb's
joint (web area) and the fingertip"[453] (of the forefinger),
and Fiske's pathologists' similarly reported that it
"extended from the distal joint to the web area of the
thumb."[454]  It began at the first joint of the forefinger,
and extended down into the web area.  Since the proportions
of everyone's hands are about the same, if we can
approximate the length of Mr. Foster's hands from the tip
of the forefinger down into the web area, we can
approximate the length of line of GSR.

Because Mr. Foster, who was 6'4" inches tall, could
hold a basketball palm-down with one hand, the length of
his right index finger approached six inches in length from
the top of his fingertip to the web area, and the third
(last) phalange of his index finger was around an inch
long, the length of the gunshot residue deposit was over
five inches long.

---

[453]    Exhibit 134, Park Police Report Supplement by Evidence
Technician Peter Simonello, July 26, 1993.

[454]    Exhibit 130, Forensic Pathology and Medical Examiner-
related findings and Conclusions pertaining to the Investigation
of the Death of Vincent Foster, Jr., undated.

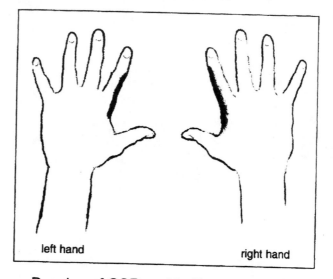

Drawing of GSR on Mr. Foster's hands

Because we know the approximate length of the GSR, let's have a closer look at those two triangles. (Remember that since the weapon's frame prevents the GSR from emanating from the top and bottom of the weapon, it is expended out at an angle and forms two triangles, one to the left of the weapon and one to the right.) By looking at a replica of the official death weapon, we know the approximate angle at which the "spokes of a wheel" emanate from the weapon. If you know the angle, or degrees, of one corner of a triangle, and you know that the two sides which emanate from this corner meet the third side of the triangle, and you know the length of that third side of the triangle, you can figure out the length of the other two sides.

Now, to see where Mr. Foster's hands were in relation to the weapon when it was fired, we need only put the triangles where they go. The GSR lines on Mr. Foster's hands are the third side of the triangle. We know the position of his hands when the gun was fired.

The closer his hands were to the cylinder, the shorter the length of the GSR deposit. The minimum distance that Mr. Foster's right hand could have been from the center of the barrel when cylinder blast occurred, using the five-inch arc, is calculated as over two inches away, perpendicular from the barrel.

### Gunshot residue

This exercise is telling. When the shot was fired,
the web between his right thumb and index finger, and both
of his index fingers, were in the gunshot residue
trajectory of the cylinder-blast from the cylinder-barrel
gap -- and that puts the right thumb too far away from the
trigger to have pulled it. It would have been impossible
for Mr. Foster's right thumb to reach the trigger at the
same time as his right thumb-index finger web was in the
trajectory of the GSR from the cylinder-blast.

Contrary to the official version, he did not pull the
trigger of the official death weapon with his right thumb.
The only possible way to have gunshot residue deposited on
the right index finger and web area and left index finger,
a sufficient distance from the barrel-cylinder gap to
provide the five-inch length of the residue pattern, is if
the weapon was fired by the hand of another. The residue
patterns were made when Mr. Foster held his hands with the
palms facing the revolver's cylinder, consistent with his
hands being in a defensive posture.

Although the FBI Lab had earlier concluded that "it
cannot be concluded that the... revolver produced these
gunshot residues,"[455] its May 9, 1994 Report reached the
opposite conclusion.

> Apparent gunshot residue (smoke) was noted... on the
> side of the right forefinger and web area of the
> victim's right hand. These residues are consistent
> with the disposition of smoke from the... cylinder
> blast when the K1 revolver is fired...

---

[455]   Exhibit 27, FBI Lab Report, June 13, 1994: "It cannot be
concluded that the K1 revolver produced these gunshot
residues..."

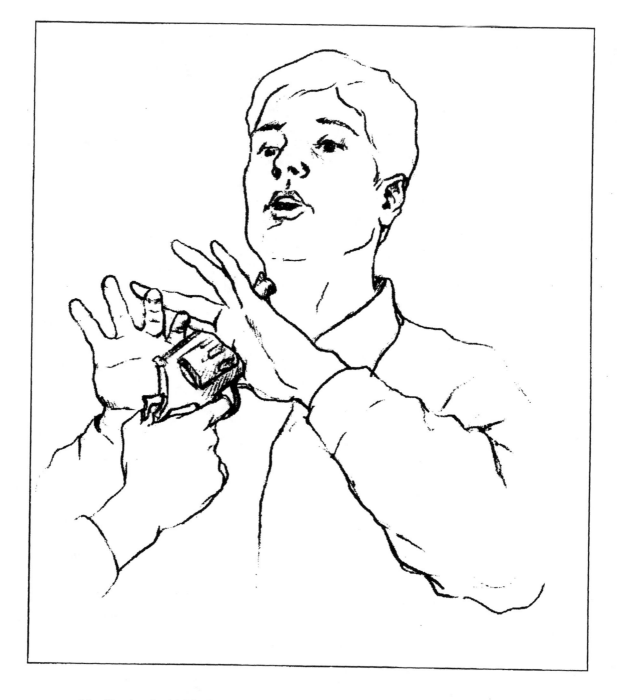

Mr. Foster held his hands with the palms facing the revolver's
cylinder -- consistent with his hands being in a defensive posture

## Gunshot residue

The position of the victims [sic] hand... is consistent with, but not limited to, the following position of the right hand during firing: Pulling the trigger of the K1 revolver with the right thumb...[456]

There is no record of any of the investigators ever having considered the possibility of Mr. Foster having positioned his hands in a defensive posture.

OIC, p. 26:

"They [Park Police] observed no signs of a struggle.

OIC, p. 28:

"Nonetheless, the evidence from the scene — including the gun, the apparent residue, the nature of the wound, the blood, the lack of any signs of struggle -- points to the conclusion that death resulted from suicide by gunshot."

The OIC reports Dr. Lee's conclusion that the gunshot residue on Mr. Foster's hands "indicated that Mr. Foster held the weapon when it was fired."

---

[456] Exhibit 95, FBI Lab Report, May 9, 1994: Apparent gunshot residue (smoke) was noted in the Q60, Q112, Q125, Q126, photographs on the side of the right forefinger and web area of the victim's right hand. These residues are consistent with the disposition of smoke from the muzzle blast or cylinder blast when the K1 revolver is fired using ammunition like that represented by specimens Q1 and Q2 when this area of the right hand is positioned near the front of the cylinder or to the side of and near the muzzle.

\* \* \*

The position of the victims [sic] hand in the Q77, Q79 and Q97 photographs relative to the revolver and the apparent disposition [sic] of gunshot residue (smoke) visible in the Q60, Q112, Q125, Q126 and Q127 photographs is consistent with, but not limited to, the following position of the right hand during firing: Pulling the trigger of the K1 revolver with the right thumb single or double action, or having the right thumb inside the trigger guard with the web area and side of the right forefinger near the front of the cylinder.

## Gunshot residue

OIC, p. 44:

*Dr. Lee concluded, "[b]ased on laboratory
observations and the examination of the scene
photographs," that "the revolver . . . is consistent
with the weapon which resulted in the death of Mr.
Vincent Foster. The barrel of this weapon was likely
in Mr. Foster's mouth at the time the weapon was
discharged. Gunshot residue noted on Mr. Foster's
right hand and the lesser amounts of deposits on his
left hand indicated that Mr. Foster held the weapon
when it was fired.* [fn117]

The footnote to this passage refers the reader to Dr.
Lee's secret report.

OIC, p. 44, fn. 117:

*"Lee Report at 488."*

Thus, there is no way of learning how Dr. Lee could
have concluded that Mr. Foster could have fired the gun
with his right thumb, and have gunshot residue deposited on
the web area between it and his right index finger,
contrary to the demonstration above.

Ignoring the absence of gunpowder on Mr. Foster's
face,[457] the OIC also reports Dr. Blackbourne's concurrence.

OIC, p. 62:

*Finally, Dr. Blackbourne stated that "[w]hen a
revolver is fired, smoke issues out of the space
between the cylinder and the barrel. This smoke will
be deposited on skin, clothing or other objects close
to the cylinder gap. The autopsy report documents
that smoke deposits were noted on the radial aspect of
both right and left index fingers."*

---

[457]   Exhibit 129, Fiske's pathologists' Report of interview with
Dr. Beyer, March 31, 1994:  "Face:  ...No evidence of gunpowder
residue, soot or stippling..."

## 2. Gunpowder

The authors of the Report use the terms gunshot residue and gunpowder interchangeably, which is inaccurate. Gunshot residue is expelled from the weapon. It may include gasses, burning and unburned gunpowder, and particulate and vaporized lead, and is sometimes simply referred to as "smoke."

Forty-four times in its 114 page Report, the OIC uses one of the following terms, "black gunshot residue-like material," "gunpowder residue," "gunpowder debris," "unburned and partially burned gunpowder," "partially burned gunpowder particles," "gunpowder," "gunshot residue," "powder debris," "ball smokeless powder" and "black material residue."

### a. Type found not used by Remington

Only once, under its *Glasses* section, does the report identify the type of gunpowder found.

OIC, p. 58:

*"The FBI Laboratory found one piece of ball smokeless powder on the eyeglasses, and it was 'physically and chemically similar to the gunpowder identified in the cartridge case.*[fn164]*"*

Remington manufactured the two cartridge cases, labeled .38 Sp HVL. "HV" stands for high velocity.

The official version is that Mr. Foster put the bullets in the revolver recovered from his hand, and fired the gun. Because Remington has never used ball smokeless powder in the manufacture of any of its HV .38 caliber cartridges,[458] for the official version to be true, the bullets would have to have been "reloads." (Reloading is done to save money or obtain particular firing

---

[458] *Exhibit 141, Letter from Sporting Arms and Ammunition Manufacturers Institute, Inc., (SAAMI), February 23, 1998: "In its ammunition, Remington used propellants mostly manufactured by Dupont and Hercules. Both Dupont and Hercules manufactured flake type propellants. Winchester Western manufactured a flattened, spherical propellant which was named 'Ball Powder.'"

characteristics.)  The OIC does not reveal whether reloaded ammunition was found in the gun.

Another curious finding was the existence of two types of gunpowder which were dissimilar.  The FBI Lab found two such particles, one on the "debris collected from the clothing," and one on "a piece of paper used to dry Foster's clothes."  The Fiske Report excused the finding of two types of gunpowder on Mr. Foster's clothing by explaining that "[i]t is possible that the clothes were contaminated while in this [Park Police station] room."[459] OIC may have felt it necessary to mention this anomaly.  It did so in a footnote, but proffered no explanation, merely repeating the FBI Lab's perfunctory conclusion that the finding was irrelevant.

OIC, p. 46, fn. 125:

*FBI Lab Report, 6/13/94, at 2.  In debris collected from the clothing, the FBI Laboratory found approximately 20 gunpowder particles that were similar to the gunpowder in the fired cartridge case of the gun found in Mr. Foster's hand, and two that were not. The Laboratory stated that one of the two dissimilar particles was "not consistent with having originated from a fired cartridge" and the other one was found "on a piece of paper used to dry Foster's clothes." Id. at 3.  From these facts, the Laboratory stated that these two particles are "not likely associated with this investigation."  Id.*

### b.    Present on broken eyeglasses found 17 feet uprange

Mr. Foster's eyeglasses were found in a densely foliated area at least thirteen feet from his feet and nineteen feet from his head, with gunpowder on them, up-

---

[459]    Exhibit 12, Fiske Report, June 30, 1994:  The FBI Lab found that these particles did not originate from the fired cartridge in Foster's gun.  These particles are believed to be the result of contamination some time after the clothing was removed from Foster's body... Foster's clothes were laid out to dry for four days on the floor... adjacent to the laboratory... equipped with an exhaust fan...  It is possible that the clothes were contaminated while in this room.

range (in the opposite direction from the bullet trajectory). The FBI Lab did not attempt an explanation of this anomaly.

"No determination can be made as to the position of the Q3 glasses at the time of death."[460]

The Fiske Report did. The glasses flew off Mr. Foster's head and "bounced" through dense foliage, up-range, "down the hill."

One obvious scenario is that the eyeglasses were dislodged by the sudden backward movement of Foster's head when the gun was fired, after which the glasses bounced down the hill.[461]

The OIC killed this anomaly with silence.

OIC, p. 58:

*"The analyses and conclusions of the experts and investigators in this and prior investigations reveal that the location where the glasses were found is consistent with the conclusion that Mr. Foster was wearing the glasses at the time the shot was fired.[fn166]"*

The footnote to that sentence refers the reader to Dr. Lee's (still secret) report.

OIC, p. 58, fn. 166:

*"E.g., OIC Investigators' Memorandum (Lee)."*

In the photograph of the eyeglasses as found below the body,[462] a stick shields the view of where the stem appears to be broken away from the frame, and the stems are inexplicably closed.

---

[460] Exhibit 27, FBI Lab Report, June 13, 1994.

[461] Exhibit 12, Fiske Report, June 30, 1994.

[462] Exhibit 143, Photograph of eyeglasses found at scene.

### c.    Reportedly found in soil over a year later

The OIC implies that Dr. Lee found evidence corroborating the official version of events from his discovery of *"gunpowder-like particles"* in the soil from *"the berm on which Mr. Foster's body was found."*

OIC, p. 58-59:

*As part of his examination, Dr. Lee went to Fort Marcy Park with OIC investigators and obtained soil and other materials from the berm on which Mr. Foster's body was found.[fn167] Dr. Lee examined the soil samples; he reported that "[a] few unburned and partially deformed gunpowder-like particles were recovered from the soil in the area where Vincent Foster's body was found."[fn168] It cannot be determined "whether these particles were deposited on the ground at the time of Mr. Foster's death or at any other period of time."[fn169]*

The OIC admits that Dr. Lee could not determine when these particles might have been deposited on the berm.  But it does not tell us whether these particles were, in fact, gunpowder, and if so, whether it was ball shaped.  Moreover, the Report tells us that, if there was a search during the initial FBI/Park Police investigation, it was not "intensive."

OIC, p. 58, fn. 167:

*"Lee Report at 422.  [N]o intensive review of the area under and around Mr. Foster's body occurred on July 20 or during the 1993 Park Police investigation."*

But the OIC fails to apprise its readers that, according to the Fiske Report, the FBI did conduct an intensive search.

"The area immediately beneath where Foster's body was found was searched by... FBI lab personnel [who] excavated to a depth of approximately eighteen inches, searching the soil through various screening methods."[463]

---

[463]    Exhibit 12, Fiske Report, June 30, 1994.

This sort of dishonesty, as we have and will continue to see, pervades the OIC's Report.

### 3. The guns at the park

The OIC's claim (p. 79) that *"the descriptions provided by the first two persons to observe the gun, as well as of numerous others, are consistent with the gun retrieved from the scene,"* is not true.

### Civilian Dale

The civilian witness who officially discovered the body, Dale, did not see a gun in Mr. Foster's hand. The majority of the OIC's discussion of the observations of a gun officially retrieved from Mr. Foster's hand (77-79) is devoted to explaining that the gun was there but that Dale had simply missed seeing it. The Report tells us that the gun was hard to see from the view depicted in the *"Polaroids taken from above the head,"* and according to *"several witnesses."* The OIC concludes that, based on its *"careful evaluation,"* the gun was, in fact, in Mr. Foster's hand.

OIC p. 78:

*"The totality of the evidence leads to the conclusion that the gun recovered from Fort Marcy Park was in fact in Mr. Foster's hand when C5 happened upon the body, but that C5 simply did not see it.*[fn227]*"*

OIC, p. 77-78:

*That is supported, moreover, by the testimony of several witnesses establishing that the gun was difficult to see in Mr. Foster's hand when standing in a position above the head on the top of the berm.*[fn226] *That is further confirmed by Polaroids taken from above the head that reveal the difficulty of seeing the gun from that angle.*

The majority of what we know of Dale's version is in the transcript of his sworn statement, given before Congressmen Burton, Mica and Rohrabacher, on July 28, 1994, at Dale's home. The OIC's explanation wholly ignores that testimony. Dale repeatedly and unequivocally testified that Mr. Foster's hands were "palms up,"[464] the opposite of the "palms down" depiction in the Polaroid photographs taken long after Dale had left the scene. In an obvious attempt to hide from him that the crime scene had surely been tampered with, FBI agents Larry Monroe and Bill Columbell (the same agents who interviewed Patrick Knowlton) "led [him] to believe that the hands were [palms] up."[465] The agents refused all of Dale's four requests to let him see the scene photographs[466] to verify what he had seen, each time explaining that it would "jeopardize their investigation."[467]

---

[464] Exhibit 51, Sworn testimony given by CW before Congressmen Burton, Mica and Rohrabacher, July 28, 1994: I looked to see if he had anything in his hands and that's when I saw his hands both palms up... His -- both palms were face up, thumbs out to the side... The palms were face up... Right beside him neatly... Q. But in the report they say you believed that the palms were up but you say there is no doubt? A. I never said -- I said I believe it. I mean I know it... Both palms, neatly at his side and they were just like that... Nothing in the hands... The palms were up... Absolutely. Q. How sure are you that the palms were up? A. As sure as I'm standing right here. I am absolutely and totally unequivocally, the palms were up. I looked at both palms. There was nothing in his hands. I didn't look at one and assume the other. I looked at both of them. Q. How long did you spend over the body? Five seconds? 10 seconds? A. Oh, no. Two minutes.

[465] Exhibit 51, Sworn testimony given by CW before Congressmen Burton, Mica and Rohrabacher, July 28, 1994: After having seen the photo of the hand and the gun I'm sure the hand had been moved because the palms were both face up when I saw Mr. Foster's body... That is not a picture of what I saw. The man's palms were straight up... they wouldn't show me the pictures and led me to believe that the hands were up and the gun was concealed on other side... There was no gun in his hand.

[466] Exhibit 51, Sworn testimony given by CW before Congressmen Burton, Mica and Rohrabacher, July 28, 1994: Q. You -- the FBI -- you asked the FBI what, about the picture... A. Numerous times... If you will show me the picture of... his hands that you said there was no gun in -- that I said there was no gun in and you said there was, then I could tell you point blank if somebody had tampered with it, with Mr. Foster's body.

[467] Exhibit 51, Sworn testimony given by CW before Congressmen

## Guns at the park

The FBI showed Dale its April, 1994 report of its interview with him, which states *"the possibility does exist that there was a gun on rear of hand [sic] that he might not have seen,"*[468] and had him sign it.

OIC, p. 77, fn. 225:

*"OIC, 2/23/95, at 52-53. C5 also had previously reviewed and adopted the interview report containing that statement. See 302, 4/14/94, at 4 (reviewed and initialed by witness)."*

### Officer Kevin Fornshill

The OIC's discussion of Officer Fornshill's involvement under its *Observations of Gun at Scene* section is limited to parenthetically noting that he did not the gun.

OIC, p. 77:

*"...([A]lthough Officer Fornshill himself did not see or look for it, but rather was told of it by the others)."*

Fornshill's explanation for being incurious, offered in a lengthy footnote under its *Fort Marcy* discussion, thirty-three pages before its *Observations of Gun at Scene* section, is that Paramedic Todd Hall told him there was a gun in the hand.

---

Burton, Mica and Rohrabacher, July 20, 1994: <u>Id.</u>: Q. What did they say when you asked to see the pictures? A. Well, it will jeopardize our investigation, I can not show it to you at this time... that was the common answer I got from them every time... four, five times I directly and inquired, let me see the picture...

[468] <u>OIC, p. 77</u>: First, when questioned by the OIC, C5 agreed with a statement attributed to him in an interview that "there was extreme dense and heavy foliage in the area and in close proximity to the body, and the possibility does exist that there was a gun on rear of hand [sic] that he might not have seen."[fn225]

OIC, p. 25, fn. 48:

*...According to Officer Fornshill, as Hall was examining the body, Hall said words to the effect that "we've got a gun here" and pointed in the general direction of the decedent's right hand. Fornshill 302, 4/29/94, at 3; Senate Deposition, 7/12/94, at 21; OIC, 1/11/95, at 93, 114. Fornshill did not see the gun, however. 302, 4/29/94, at 3; OIC, 1/11/95, at 79. He said that he could not see the gun either because of his position or the vegetation around the hand. 302, 4/29/94, at 3; Senate Deposition, 7/12/94, at 21; OIC, 1/11/95, at 114. As to why he did not move into position to confirm the existence of the gun, Fornshill said, "I'm not the investigator. I let the investigator do that. I'm maintaining the scene. If there's a gun at the scene, I'm making sure nobody touches the gun, I'm making sure nobody disturbs the gun... If the EMT [emergency medical technician] tells me there's a gun there then I'll go with that." OIC, 1/11/95, at 115.*

Fornshill's story, primarily revealed in his Senate deposition, was that he abandoned his duty guarding the CIA entrance[469] to respond to the dead body call. He and two "rescue workers went into the park to locate the body..." He "instructed the paramedics to go one direction" and "check[ed] this [opposite] way..."[470]

After he called the two paramedics, Gonzalez and Hall, over to the body, Fornshill said he "could see the feet and

---

[469]    Exhibit 79, Deposition of Park Police Officer Kevin Fornshill, July 12, 1994:  "I was at the entrance, the parkway to the CIA."

[470]    Exhibit 79, Deposition of Park Police Officer Kevin Fornshill, July 12, 1994:  Originally, when the broadcast went over the air, it made reference to a second cannon in the park area.  I wasn't familiar with the location of the second cannon so myself and the rescue workers went into the park to locate the body...  I instructed the paramedics to go one direction, had them check that direction.  I said I would check this way...

the face but not the hands" because one of the paramedics, "bent over, obstructing [his] view..."[471]

Fornshill testified that he radioed that the death was an "apparent suicide,"[472] without having seen the weapon from "within five feet away,"[473] "[b]ased on the determination the person was dead... [and his] assumption from the paramedic... that the gun was found in his hand."[474]

There is no explanation how Fornshill could have remained at the body site for over ten minutes, sometimes alone with an unobstructed view, without having seen the gun. He never made a report of his involvement.[475] No investigator debriefed him or even spoke to him about what he saw.[476] "Nothing unusual had occurred,"[477] Fornshill

---

[471] Exhibit 79, Deposition of Park Police Officer Kevin Fornshill, July 12, 1994.

[472] Exhibit 79, Deposition of Park Police Officer Kevin Fornshill, July 12, 1994: [W]hen he showed the gun, or tried to show me the gun, saying there's a gun there, I advised communications that it appeared to be a suicide... Q. And you said that it appeared to be a suicide based on what? A. Based on the determination the person was dead. Again, my assumption from the paramedic and that the gun was found in his hand, which is what the paramedic told me.

[473] Exhibit 79, Deposition of Park Police Officer Kevin Fornshill, July 12, 1994: "Q. How many feet were you from the body? A. Five perhaps... From my switching from the area from the left, the majority of my visual inspection was from the right hand side of the body..."

[474] Exhibit 79, Deposition of Park Police Officer Kevin Fornshill, July 12, 1994.

[475] Exhibit 79, Deposition of Park Police Officer Kevin Fornshill, July 12, 1994: I went back to the station, I engaged in a conversation with Officer Hedakovic [sic] whose name I gave you earlier, and I asked if there was any need for me to document anything, just being the first one to respond to the body. And it was felt that there was really no need for me to document anything...

[476] Exhibit 79, Deposition of Park Police Officer Kevin Fornshill, July 12, 1994: Q. Did any of the detectives on the scene come and talk to you? A. No... Q. Not one of these guys [detectives on the scene] ever talked to you about the crime scene? A. No, not that I know of... Q.

testified, so he did not read the newspaper accounts of the death until January of the following year.

### Firefighter Todd Hall
### Paramedic George Gonzalez

Paramedic Todd Hall testified in the summer of 1994 that he could not remember specifically what the gun looked like, but that he recalled seeing "just a gun."

> Q. But you couldn't tell what kind of gun it was?
> A. No. I seen it was a gun. I just didn't try to determine what type it was.
>
> \*     \*     \*
>
> Q. When you say the hand that you saw at the scene, was it holding the gun, gripping the gun?
> A. I couldn't tell. I didn't get that close. All I know is that I saw the gun.[478]

Notwithstanding that Hall, one of the first two persons to observe the gun, couldn't tell what kind of gun it was, the OIC claims that his *"description... [is] consistent with the gun retrieved from the scene."*

OIC, p. 79:

*There are discrepancies in the descriptions of the color and kind of gun seen in Mr. Foster's hand. However, the descriptions provided by the first two persons to observe the gun, as well as of numerous others, are consistent with the gun retrieved from the scene and depicted in the on-the-scene Polaroids.[fn229]*

---

Did you ever talk to any of the other officers or people out there about what happened? A. There was some conversation the next day... but there was no official debriefing in regards to me being interviewed by the detectives or the investigators...

[477] Exhibit 79, Deposition of Park Police Officer Kevin Fornshill, July 12, 1994: "[N]othing unusual had occurred, to my knowledge... I think I looked at it [the beat officer's Report] sometime after the incident, perhaps a month or so after the incident..."

[478] Exhibit 67, Deposition of Paramedic Todd Hall, July 20, 1994.

## Guns at the park

Besides Hall, Paramedic George Gonzalez is the other of the *"first two persons to observe the gun"* on whom the OIC relies in its claim that these two men described seeing a gun a *"consistent with the gun retrieved from the scene."*

Gonzalez testified in the summer of 1994 that the position of the gun he saw at the park, before Sergeant Edwards had been alone with the body, was different than the position of the gun as it was photographed in Mr. Foster's hand at the park.

> Q.　Apparently you recall the gun being in a different position than what was photographed?
> A.　That's correct.[479]

Gonzalez testified that he "looked at the gun at a glance,"[480] that he "didn't know the size of the gun nor the type of gun,"[481] and that "as time goes on, I remember less and less."[482]

But, according to the OIC, Gonzalez is said to have remembered more as time went on. The unknown type of gun that he had seen at a glance was a *"black or dark revolver."*

---

[479]　Exhibit 110, Deposition of Paramedic George Gonzalez, July 20, 1994.

[480]　Exhibit 110, Deposition of Paramedic George Gonzalez, July 20, 1994: "Q.　Did you study the gun for any other kind?　A. No, I just looked at the gun at a glance as my visual approach assessment, standing on the right side of the body and looking at the head, and on down."

[481]　Exhibit 110, Deposition of Paramedic George Gonzalez, July 20, 1994: "Q.　Do you remember what type of gun it was?　A.　All I could say, like I said to you, it's a revolver.　I don't know the size gun nor the type gun, or anything like that."

[482]　Exhibit 110, Deposition of Paramedic George Gonzalez, July 20, 1994:　"I'll have to go with that statement [regarding observations of contents of car] because, as time goes on, I remember less and less."

# Guns at the park

OIC, p. 79, fn. 229:

"*See* Gonzalez 302, 5/15/96, at 4; Gonzalez OIC, 1/10/95, at 43 (saw black or dark revolver in hand)..."

## Officer Franz Ferstl

Park Police Officer Franz Ferstl arrived on the scene to relieve Officer Kevin Fornshill. Ferstl photographed the body site with a Polaroid camera. He filed an Incident Report, but that Report does not mention his seeing any gun.[483] The FBI's Report of its interview with him in May of 1994 does report that he saw a gun, yet it does not provide any description of that gun.

"Ferstl advised that he did see a weapon in the victim's right hand."[484]

## Paramedic Richard Arthur
## Firefighter Ralph Pisani
## Firefighter Lieutenant James Iacone
## Firefighter Jennifer Wacha

The FBI did not interview Paramedic Richard Arthur during the course of its first investigation, but has since interviewed him on four separate occasions. The FBI interviewed him twice during the Fiske probe, once on March 16, 1994, and again on April 29, reportedly to "clarify" his account. The OIC's FBI agents interviewed him again in January of 1995. But again, his account was not satisfactory to the FBI, so Starr's FBI agents interviewed him a fourth time in April of 1996, three years after the death.

Arthur's account of the neck wound (see above) was not the only controversial part of his testimony. His observations of the gun at the scene were also problematic. The FBI's final account of these observations bear little resemblance to the first such Report, particularly when

---

[483] Exhibit 112, Park Police Report of Officer Franz Ferstl, July 20, 1993.

[484] Exhibit 96, Report of FBI interview of Park Police Officer Franz Ferstl, May 2, 1994.

compared to the interviewing agent's' handwritten notes of that first FBI interview.

This first interview had been conducted eight months after Arthur had inspected the body around 6:22 p.m. on July 20, 1993. Those handwritten notes, taken in April of 1994, reflect that he unequivocally remembered what he had seen.

> "Barrel end tucked under right leg. 100% sure automatic weapon (was in Army look at gun magazines Knows the diff between automatic & revolver) Appeared like .45 automatic."[485]

The corresponding typed version of that interview does not reflect his "100%" certainty, reporting only that "[he] did not believe the gun was a revolver."[486]

The Report of Mr. Arthur's second FBI interview, conducted in April of 1994, states that the gun "appeared... he thought... to the best of his memory, he recalls..." was not a revolver.

> "Arthur saw what appeared to be a gun that he thought was a 9 - millimeter pistol... to the best of his memory, he recalls the handle on the weapon being square in shape."[487]

According to the OIC's FBI agents, in January of 1995 (his third FBI interview), Paramedic Arthur opined that the gun was not a revolver because *he did not recall seeing a cylinder.*

---

[485]　Exhibit 109, Handwritten notes of FBI interview with Paramedic Richard Arthur, March 16, 1994.

[486]　Exhibit 82, Report of FBI interview with Paramedic Richard Arthur, April 29, 1994: "Foster had a gun located under his right hand... did not believe the gun was a revolver... stood on the right side near the head, approximately 2-3 feet away from Foster's right hand."

[487]　Exhibit 82, Report of FBI interview with Paramedic Richard Arthur, April 29, 1994.

## Guns at the park

OIC, p. 79, fn. 228:

*...Arthur states that the gun was black-brownish but not a revolver (based on the fact that he did not recall seeing a cylinder).  OIC, 1/5/95, at 46-47. After viewing a photograph of the weapon in the decedent's hand, Arthur stated, according to the interview report, "My memory is, I saw a semi-automatic, however, I must have been mistaken."  302, 4/24/96, at 2...*

Arthur's deposition testimony before Senate investigators provides his account in its pristine form, without the opportunity for the FBI to filter or spin it. Arthur testified that he saw Foster's hand on "the clip portion" of the "automatic... not a revolver."[488]

He demonstrated that he knew the difference by drawing pictures. [489]

---

[488]    Exhibit 107, Deposition of Paramedic Richard Arthur, July 14, 1994.

[489]    Exhibit 107, Deposition of Paramedic Richard Arthur, July 14, 1994.

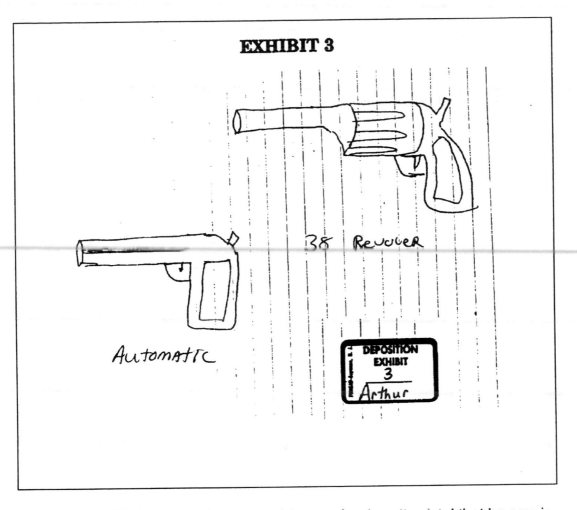

**EXHIBIT 3**

38 Revolver

Automatic

DEPOSITION
EXHIBIT
3
Arthur

Paramedic Richard Arthur's drawing of the semi-automatic pistol that he saw in Mr. Foster's hand, and of a revolver to demonstrate that he knew the difference between the two types of guns.

Thus, according to the FBI's fourth interview with Arthur, he admitted that he *"must have been mistaken"* when he was "100% sure" years earlier that the gun which he saw from "2 to 3 feet away," and later drew a picture of, was not a revolver.

By referring to the semi-automatic and the revolver as "the" gun, the OIC does not confront the existence of the semi-automatic.

| Body site |
| --- |
| Officer Kevin Fornshill |
| Paramedic Richard Arthur |
| Firefighter Ralph Pisani |
| Firefighter Lt. James Iacone |
| Firefighter Jennifer Wacha |
| Officer Franz Ferstl |

**FORT MARCY PARK**   **6:23**   <u>See</u> endnote 11.

Paramedic Arthur and Firefighters Pisani, Wacha and Iacone joined Fornshill at the body. They saw blood on the right side of Mr. Foster's shirt. Arthur saw a small caliber bullet wound in right side of the neck, just under the jaw line. Being familiar with handguns, Arthur saw a large caliber semi-automatic pistol in Mr. Foster's hand, and concluded that it did not match the smaller caliber bullet hole in the neck. Officer Ferstl arrived.

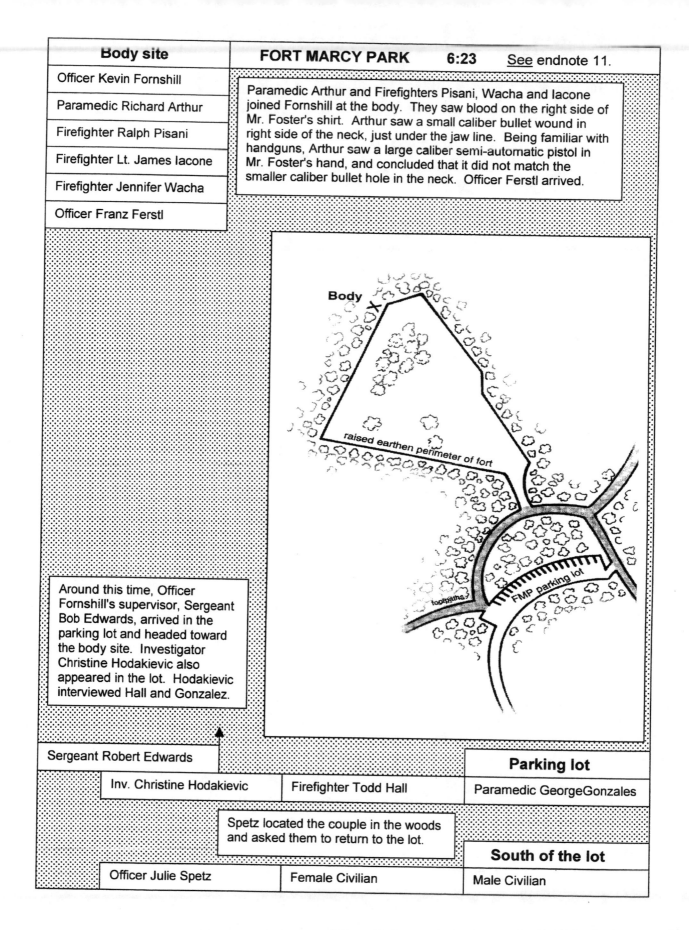

Around this time, Officer Fornshill's supervisor, Sergeant Bob Edwards, arrived in the parking lot and headed toward the body site. Investigator Christine Hodakievic also appeared in the lot. Hodakievic interviewed Hall and Gonzalez.

| Sergeant Robert Edwards | | | |
| --- | --- | --- | --- |
| | Inv. Christine Hodakievic | Firefighter Todd Hall | **Parking lot** Paramedic GeorgeGonzales |

Spetz located the couple in the woods and asked them to return to the lot.

| | | | **South of the lot** |
| --- | --- | --- | --- |
| | Officer Julie Spetz | Female Civilian | Male Civilian |

## Guns at the park

There is no record of Firefighters Ralph Pisani or Jennifer Wacha ever having opined on the type of gun they may have seen.

In claiming that the "*discrepancies are created by statements of FCFRD personnel Arthur and Iacone...,*" and that "*Iacone stated that the gun was a silver-colored revolver-type weapon,*" the OIC cites a 1994 FBI Report, which is public, and a January, 1995 OIC interview, which is not.

OIC, p. 79, fn. 228:

> ...*Iacone stated that the gun was a silver-colored revolver-type weapon.  302, 4/27/94, at 3; OIC, 1/10/95, at 27.*[490]

Contrary to the OIC's claim, page 3 of the above-referenced April 1994, FBI interview report does not mention the gun.  Page 2 notes that Iacone saw "what appeared to be a revolver... but did not look closely..."[491] (The OIC reports that Iacone saw a silver gun.  As we shall see, the official death weapon was black.)

### Sergeant Robert Edwards

There is no publicly available record of the gun Sergeant Robert Edwards saw.  Although he was "in charge of

---

[490]  OIC, p. 79, fn. 228:  These discrepancies are created by statements of FCFRD personnel Arthur and Iacone, which themselves are not consistent.  Arthur states that the gun was black-brownish but not a revolver (based on the fact that he did not recall seeing a cylinder).  OIC, 1/5/95, at 46-47.  After viewing a photograph of the weapon in the decedent's hand, Arthur stated, according to the interview report, My memory is, I saw a semi-automatic, however, I must have been mistaken."  302, 4/24/96, at 2.  Iacone stated that the gun was a silver-colored revolver-type weapon.  302, 4/27/94, at 3; OIC, 1/10/95, at 27.

[491]  Exhibit 78, Report of FBI Interview of James Iacone, March 11, 1994:  "Iacone does not recall observing any blood.  He saw what appeared to be a revolver in Foster's right hand, but he did not look closely enough to see an entrance or exit wound."

the scene,"[492] he did not write a report.  The Senate did not depose him and the FBI did not interview him until 1996, so Edwards' account of the gun he saw, if one exists, is still secret.

### Lieutenant Patrick Gavin
### Investigator Christine Hodakievic

The senior Park Police at the scene, Lieutenant Patrick Gavin, also did not write a report.  Gavin told the FBI he saw "the gun," but there is no record of his having described it.[493]

We believe that Park Police Officer Christine Hodakievic viewed the body before and after Edwards had been alone at the body site.  Hodakievic wrote an Incident Report on July 20, 1993 that does not mention any gun[494] (or wounds or blood).  She, too, never saw the weapon, as is apparent from the FBI's May, 1994, report of its interview with her.  The FBI reported that based on "Sergeant Edwards... [having] informed [her] that the decedent had a revolver in his right hand," she "briefed... officers [Braun and Rolla]... includ[ing] informing them that a weapon had been located in the decedent's right hand."

The FBI explained her having failed to see the weapon (that Gonzalez had seen after "a few seconds"[495]) after "five

---

[492]    Exhibit 81, Report of FBI interview of Park Police Officer Christine Hodakievic, May 2, 1994:  "Officer Hodakievic advised to the best of her recollection, upon arriving at the death scene, Sergeant Edwards (USPP) was basically in charge of the death scene and believes that Officer Franz Ferstl was also present."

[493]    Exhibit 98, Report of FBI interview Park Police Lieutenant Patrick Gavin, April 28, 1994.

[494]    Exhibit 76, Park Police Criminal Incident Report, by Christine Hodakievic, July 21, 1993.

[495]    Exhibit 110, Deposition of Paramedic George Gonzalez, July 20, 1993:  "Q.  And the gun issue.  Did you see a gun right away? A.  Yes.  I mean right away, it took me a few seconds.  When I looked down -- when we do our assessment, on my assessment I recognized a gun present."

to ten minutes" at the body site by explaining that she said "it was difficult to actually see the weapon."

> She does recall being initially briefed by Sergeant Edwards, which included being informed that the decedent had a revolver in his right hand, as well as being shown a Polaroid photograph of decedent's position at the death scene. She further maintained that after being briefed, she initiated a cursory look at the body from the top of the berm, moving from the left of the decedent's body to the right of the body. She related that in spite of being informed that decedent had a gun in his right hand, it was difficult to actually see the weapon...[496]

**Investigator John Rolla**
**Investigator Cheryl Braun**
**Evidence Technician Peter Simonello**
**Investigator Renee Abt**
**Unidentified Intern**
**Officer Watson**

Investigator John Rolla, the thirteenth person to see the body, was the first to report that he "observed a dark colored revolver in Mr. Foster's right hand."[497]

Investigator Braun reported "seeing a revolver in the right hand."[498]

Park Police Identification Technician Peter Simonello noted in his Report, written on July 26, six days after the incident, that he had removed a black .38 revolver from Mr. Foster's hand.[499] His Senate deposition is in accord.[500]

---

[496]  Exhibit 81, Report of FBI interview of Park Police Officer Christine Hodakievic, May, 2, 1994.

[497]  Exhibit 113, Park Police Incident Report, by Park Police Investigator John Rolla, July 21, 1993.

[498]  Exhibit 91, Report of FBI interview of Investigator Cheryl Braun, April 28, 1994: "Braun stated that she recalls seeing a revolver in the right hand, pointing out that she was looking for the gun as she had already been told that it was a suicide."

[499]  Exhibit 134, Park Police Report Supplement by Evidence Technician Peter Simonello, July 26, 1993.

Park Police Investigator Renee Abt's contemporaneous notes state that a "revolver & 2 rounds" were recovered at the park.[501] Officer Watson and the unnamed intern did not file reports, and there are no known reports of their having been interviewed.

## 4. Ownership of gun and ammunition

### a. Gun

The Report declares (p. 79) that *"[v]irtually all theories that the manner of death was not suicide rest on the assumption that the gun did not belong to Mr. Foster."* The OIC concludes (p. 84) that the *"combination of testimonial, circumstantial, and forensic evidence supports the conclusion that the gun found in Mr. Foster's hand belonged to Mr. Foster."*

In sum, the testimonial and circumstantial evidence upon which the OIC purportedly relies in dismissing *"all theories"* is that family members recall that Mr. Foster owned a silver .38 revolver,[502] that it was brought from Little Rock when he moved to Washington, and that this gun was missing from his home the day he died.[503] Let us see.

---

[500]    Exhibit 104, Deposition of Park Police Evidence Technician Peter Simonello, July 14, 1994.

[501]    Exhibit 118, Handwritten notes of Park Police Investigator Renee Apt, July 20, 1993.

[502]    Exhibit 98, Report of FBI interview with Lieutenant Patrick Gavin, April 28, 1994:  "Mr. Burton first inquired about whether the U.S. Park Police had checked the registration on the gun that was used, asking if they knew whose gun it was..."

[503]    OIC, p. 80-81:  Mrs. Lisa Foster similarly recalls that her husband took possession of several handguns from his parents' house near the time of his father's death.[fn233] She recalled that, after they moved to Washington in 1993, some guns were kept in a bedroom closet.[fn234] She recalled what she described as a silver-colored gun[fn235] (she also referred to it as a "cowboy gun"[fn236]), which had been packed in Little Rock and unpacked in Washington. She also recalled a .45 caliber semi-automatic pistol. She said she found one gun in its usual location on July 20, 1993,[fn237] the .45 caliber semi-automatic pistol.[fn238] She did not find the other gun on or after July 20, 1993.[fn239]

272

## Ownership of gun

Tho Report tells us that of Mr. Foster's three children, one saw *"a handgun"* in Washington,[504] another observed *"one or two handguns,"*[505] and the third saw *"an old .38 caliber revolver"* but *"was unable to conclusively identify"* it[506] as being the same gun which was found in Mr. Foster's hand.

The OIC also tells us of a letter written by a family friend who, after showing a photograph of the gun to Mr. Foster's sister, Sharon, wrote that she said the gun *"looked like"*[507] a gun given to Mr. Foster by his mother[508]

---

[504] OIC, p. 84: "Mr. Foster's daughter stated she recalled someone unpacking a handgun at the house when they initially moved to Washington, although she never saw any other guns in their Washington, house."[fn254]

[505] OIC, p. 83-84: Mr. Foster's younger son stated that he saw one or two handguns in a shoebox along with a number of loose bullets while unpacking in Washington. The younger son stated that these items came from his grandfather's house. He described his grandfather's guns as a small, pearl handled gun, and one or two revolvers. He believes his father placed the guns in a closet in Washington.[fn253]

[506] OIC, p. 83: Mr. Foster's older son said he knew his father had an old .38 caliber revolver. He saw it being unpacked at their house in Washington when they moved there. Mr. Foster told his son that he had received this gun from his father (Vincent Foster, Sr.). The older son did not know where the gun was kept in Washington. The son was unable to conclusively identify the gun recovered on July 20, 1993, from Mr. Foster's hand as the one he had previously seen.[fn252]

[507] OIC, p. 82-83: Sharon Bowman, one of Mr. Foster's sisters, recalled that her father kept a black revolver in a drawer of his bedside table.[fn246] She said that she had retrieved various handguns from her parents' house, placed them in a shoebox, and put them in her mother's closet (and Ms. Bowman said they later were given to Mr. Foster, Jr.).[fn247] During the 1993 Park Police investigation, John Sloan, a family friend of the Fosters, wrote a letter to Captain Hume of the Park Police, stating that he had shown Sharon Bowman a photograph of the gun. According to the letter, Ms. Bowman stated that it "looked like a gun she had seen in her father's collection," and particularly pointed out the "'wavelike' detailing at the base of the grip."[fn248] Ms. Bowman was later shown the revolver recovered from Fort Marcy Park. She indicated that it looked like one that her

(who also could not identify it[509]). Regarding the sister's statements, the OIC recounts that the letter related that it looked like a gun her father had owned.

OIC, p. 82:

"[I]t 'looked like a gun she had seen in her father's collection,' and particularly pointed out the 'wavelike' detailing at the base of the grip."

This quote is accurately excerpted, but dishonest without the inclusion of the two sentences of the letter appearing immediately after the one that it chose to quote.

"I asked if she remembered any other features. She did not."[510]

The OIC omits any mention of the FBI's interview of Lee Bowman, Mr. Foster's nephew and the family member who was most familiar with the subject gun collection. Bowman had become familiar with the gun collection from hunting with his grandfather. After the death of Mr. Foster, Sr., in 1991, Mrs. Alice Mae Foster gave the handguns to Mr.

---

father kept in the house in Hope, but she could not positively identify it.[fn249]

508   OIC, p. 80: Mrs. Alice Mae Foster, Mr. Foster's mother, stated that Mr. Foster, Sr. died in 1991. He had kept a revolver in a drawer of his bedside table, in addition to other guns in the house.[fn231] In 1991, when Mr. Foster, Sr. had been ill and bedridden for a period of time, Mrs. Alice Mae Foster had all the handguns in the house placed in a box and put into a closet. Subsequent to the death of Mr. Foster, Sr., in 1991, Mrs. Alice Mae Foster gave Mr. Foster, Jr., the box of handguns.[fn232]

509   OIC, p. 80, fn. 232: "302, 5/2/95, at 1-2. Mrs. Alice Mae Foster and her long-time housekeeper viewed the gun recovered from Mr. Foster's hand, but they could not specifically identify it as one of the guns previously possessed by Mr. Foster, Sr. Id. at 2, 4."

510   Exhibit 145, Letter from John Sloan to Park Police, undated: "Ms. Bowman said it [the photograph] looked like a gun she had seen in her father's collection. She particularly pointed out the 'wavelike' detailing at the base of the grip. I asked if she remembered any other features. She did not."

## Ownership of gun

Foster. Bowman's knowledge further attests that a black revolver was not among the guns in the collection. The FBI's Report of its June 28, 1994, interview with Bowman waters down the significance of his account, but it is still there.

> Bowman recalled seeing that his grandfather possessed about three pistols/revolvers; about four shotguns; and two or three rifles... [He said] the gun does not ring a bell particularly. Bowman said the '.38 caliber nature of the weapon was familiar, but that he didn't remember the black handle and the dark color of the metal.[511]

According to Bowman, there was a .38 caliber revolver in the collection, but it was silver, not black.[512]

According to the OIC's version of a May, 1994, report of an FBI interview with Mrs. Foster, an FBI agent showed Mr. Foster *the actual gun* found in Mr. Foster's hand, whereupon she said it may have been the same gun she had seen in her Washington home.

OIC, p. 81:

> *On May 9, 1994, she was shown the actual gun that was recovered and said, according to the interview report, that the gun "may be a gun which she formerly saw in her residence in Little Rock, Arkansas" and that "she may have seen the handgun . . . at her residence in Washington.* [fn241]*"*

---

[511]  Exhibit 146, Report of FBI interview with Lee Bowman, June 28, 1994.

[512]  Compare A. Devroy, *Clinton Finds No Explanation to Aide's Death*, Wash. Post, July 23, 1993: "The [Park Police] chief said Foster owned a gun described being like the one found." S. Labaton, *Justice Dept. to Stay on Case of Aide's Death*, N.Y. Times, July 22, 1993: "In clarifying an account they had provided Wednesday, Federal officials said today that only one 38-caliber Army Colt revolver had been recovered in the case, not two." M. Carlson, *Where Hope Ends*, Time Magazine, August 2, 1993: "Last Tuesday afternoon, six months to the day since his boyhood friend had taken the oath of office... put his father's antique .38-cal. Colt revolver in his mouth and ended his life..."

275

The FBI (and the Fiske Report) had recounted the same version of events after its FBI agents interviewed Mrs. Foster in the Spring of 1994.

> Lisa Foster then examined a revolver which had been brought to the interview by the interviewing agents. Foster examined the revolver, which had also been found at Fort Marcy Park on July 20, 1993, and stated that she believed it may be a gun which she formerly saw in her residence in Little Rock... Lisa Foster recalls... she found a handgun inside a travel trunk which had been packed by Foster prior to his departure for Washington. Specifically, as Lisa Foster was packing in Little Rock, she came across a silver colored gun, which she then packed in with her other property... Lisa Foster believes that the gun found at Fort Marcy Park may be the silver gun which she brought up with her other belongings when she permanently moved to Washington.[513]

But there is a flaw in this long-standing official conclusion that the silver gun brought from Little Rock, reportedly missing (OIC, p. 82) from the Foster residence on the evening of the death, was the one found at the scene: The official death weapon is entirely black,[514] not silver.

The only plausible explanation of why the FBI showed Mrs. Foster a "silver colored" handgun is as follows. The interviewing FBI agents knew from the Park Police case file turned over to them that when shown a photograph of the black official death gun, she could not identify it because the only .38 revolver she knew of was silver. The Park Police handwritten interview notes of an interview with Mrs. Foster, taken nine days after Mr. Foster's death, reflects that when she was shown a photograph of the gun,

---

[513]   Exhibit 16, Report of FBI interview with Mrs. Foster, May 9, 1994.

[514]   Exhibit 147, Photograph of black revolver.  Exhibit 148, ABC News photograph of black weapon in hand.  Exhibit 134, Park Police Report Supplement by Evidence Technician Peter Simonello, July 26, 1993:  "[T]he victim had on his right hand a black revolver."

## Ownership of gun

Mrs. Foster could not identify it because the only Foster family gun with which she was familiar was silver.

> "Not the gun she thought it must be, silver, six gun, large barrel."[515]

The OIC skims over the obvious discrepancy of the color of the gun by recounting that when shown the gun in November of 1995, Mrs. Foster stated *"it was the gun she unpacked in Washington,"* but that *"she seemed to remember the... gun looking lighter in color."*

OIC, p. 81-82:

> *She stated to the OIC in November of 1995, when viewing the gun recovered from Mr. Foster's hand, that it was the gun she unpacked in Washington but had not subsequently found,*[fn242] *although she said she seemed to remember the front of the gun looking lighter in color when she saw it during the move to Washington.*[fn243]

The revolver found in Mr. Foster's hand was black. By all accounts, the revolver Mr. Foster owned was silver. The OIC attempts to confuse the issue by reporting that Mrs. Foster *"seemed to remember the front of the gun looking lighter in color."*

The FBI's suicide conclusion would have been undercut by the knowledge that the weapon found in Mr. Foster's hand was unknown to the family. So the Report hides the color of the weapon found in Mr. Foster's hand (as Fiske had) and baldly asserts (p. 84) that the gun *"which was missing when she looked in the closet after Mr. Foster's death... was the one found at the scene."* The OIC's claim that the death weapon was missing from the home is new.

---

[515]   Exhibit 149, Handwritten notes of Park Police interview with Mrs. Foster, July 29, 1993. Exhibit 144, Park Police Report by Park Police Detective Peter Markland, July 29, 1993: "She was presented with a photograph of the weapon found with Mr. Foster's body but was unable to identify it." Exhibit 6, Deposition of Park Police Investigator John Rolla, July 21, 1994: "No. The only real question I got to ask was about the gun, did Vincent own a gun. She asked me what does it look like, you know. To me, right away I am thinking oh, he does, well, it's a black-colored revolver, .38 revolver. She cut me off..."

277

## Ownership of gun

OIC, p. 82:

*Webster Hubbell stated that, on the night of Mr. Foster's death, Lisa Foster went upstairs in the Foster house with him. While there, she looked into the top of a closet, pulled out a "squared-off" gun, and said, according to Hubbell, that one of the guns was missing.*[fn244] *To Hubbell's knowledge, the "other gun" was never found at the Foster house.*[fn245]

OIC, p. 84:

*"Mrs. Lisa Foster said that she recalls two guns in a bedroom closet in Washington, one of which was missing when she looked in the closet after Mr. Foster's death..."*

But, again, the FBI reported a year after Mr. Foster's death that there was one gun, not two, and that it was in "its usual location" after the death.

"Lisa Foster was aware of the location of one gun inside her residence in Washington and she found that gun still in its usual location on the night of July 20, 1993."[516]

---

[516] Exhibit 16, Report of FBI interview with Mrs. Foster, May 9, 1994.

Ownership of gun

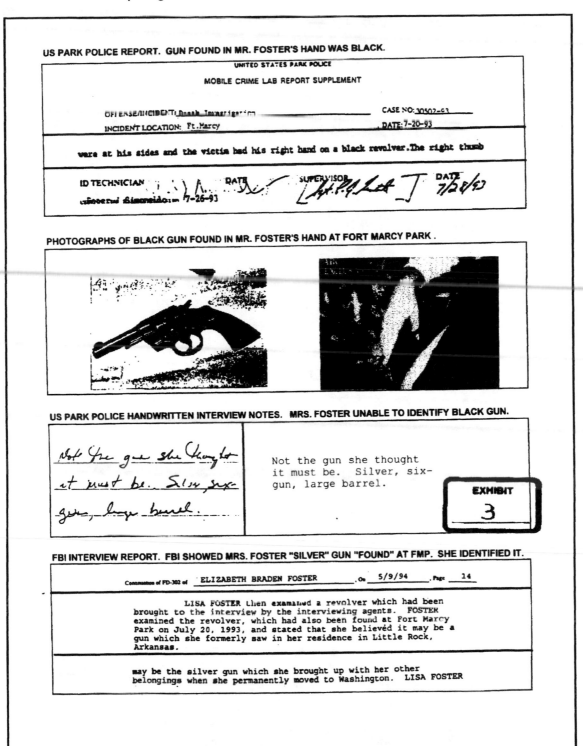

US PARK POLICE REPORT. GUN FOUND IN MR. FOSTER'S HAND WAS BLACK.

UNITED STATES PARK POLICE

MOBILE CRIME LAB REPORT SUPPLEMENT

OFFENSE/INCIDENT: Death Investigation     CASE NO: 30502-93

INCIDENT LOCATION: Ft. Marcy     DATE: 7-20-93

were at his sides and the victim had his right hand on a black revolver. The right thumb

ID TECHNICIAN Vincent Simonelio on 7-26-93     DATE     SUPERVISOR     DATE 7/28/93

PHOTOGRAPHS OF BLACK GUN FOUND IN MR. FOSTER'S HAND AT FORT MARCY PARK.

US PARK POLICE HANDWRITTEN INTERVIEW NOTES. MRS. FOSTER UNABLE TO IDENTIFY BLACK GUN.

Not the gun she thought
it must be. Silver, six-
gun, large barrel.

EXHIBIT
3

FBI INTERVIEW REPORT. FBI SHOWED MRS. FOSTER "SILVER" GUN "FOUND" AT FMP. SHE IDENTIFIED IT.

Continuation of FD-302 of   ELIZABETH BRADEN FOSTER     .On   5/9/94     .Page   14

    LISA FOSTER then examined a revolver which had been
brought to the interview by the interviewing agents. FOSTER
examined the revolver, which had also been found at Fort Marcy
Park on July 20, 1993, and stated that she believed it may be a
gun which she formerly saw in her residence in Little Rock,
Arkansas.

    may be the silver gun which she brought up with her other
belongings when she permanently moved to Washington. LISA FOSTER

Exhibit 3 of Appendix to the OIC's Report on the Death of Vincent
Foster, Jr., submitted September 23, 1997, released to the public
on October 10, 1997

### b.    **Ammunition**

The .38 caliber ammunition found in Mr. Foster's Arkansas home did not match that found in the official death weapon.  From this fact, instead of drawing the inference that the ammunition recovered from the weapon did not belong to Mr. Foster, the OIC infers *"[t]hat is further evidence suggesting that Mr. Foster, Sr., possessed a .38 caliber gun."*[517]

The Report's other reference implying that Mr. Foster may have owned ammunition similar to that found in the official gun is that *"Mr. Foster's younger son stated that he saw... a number of loose bullets while unpacking in Washington."* (p. 83).  Had the number of these bullets been two (the same number found in the park), or had any matching ammunition ever been recovered, the Report surely would have said so.

In 1975, Remington discontinued the manufacture of the ammunition found at the park.  From this fact, the OIC draws the inference that the gun was located in the home of Mr. Foster's parents when Remington still made the ammunition.

OIC, p. 38:

*Dr. Lee noted that the ammunition found in this weapon was type "RP .38 SPL HV," manufactured by Remington Peters.  Dr. Lee stated that information from the manufacturer indicated that this ammunition was discontinued in 1975, and that the cartridge therefore would have been manufactured prior to that time.*[fn93]

---

[517]    OIC, p. 80, fn. 231:  In August 1994, Sharon Bowman (the sister of Vincent Foster, Jr.) found five .38 caliber cartridges at the family home in Hope.  302, 12/1/94, at 1-2.  That is further evidence suggesting that Mr. Foster, Sr., possessed a .38 caliber gun or guns.  FBI Laboratory examination revealed that four of the cartridges were of the same manufacture (Remington) as in the revolver found in Mr. Foster's hand; they were manufactured at a different time than the cartridge and casing recovered from Mr. Foster's gun.  FBI Lab Report, 2/21/95, at 2.

## Ownership of gun

OIC, p. 38, fn. 93:

*Lee Report at 488-89. That finding is consistent with the fact that, as is explained below, the gun at one time likely was located in the home of Mr. Foster's parents in Hope, Arkansas.*

But Remington has never used the ball smokeless powder in the ammunition found at the park. If the official ammunition found had been used to fire the fatal shot, the cartridge would have to have been a "reload." The ammunition could have been reloaded at any time. These facts undermine the OIC's conclusion that "*the gun at one time likely was located in the home of Mr. Foster's parents in Hope, Arkansas.*"

### c.    Oven mitt

OIC, p. 54:

*"Apart from a variety of other compelling circumstantial and testimonial evidence (discussed below) that the gun belonged to Mr. Foster, the evidence regarding the pants pocket and oven mitt also tends to link Mr. Foster to the gun."*

The OIC claims (p. 52-55) that Dr. Henry Lee found new trace evidence in an oven mitt[518] found in Mr. Foster's car, consistent with the conclusion that Mr. Foster transported the official death weapon to the park in the mitt. The OIC posits that this finding, along with another new finding of the same type of trace evidence in Mr. Foster's pants pocket,[519] supports its hypothesis. According to the OIC,

---

[518]  OIC, p. 53:  As noted, Dr. Lee also examined the oven mitt recovered from Mr. Foster's car. He reported: "Dark particle residues were located inside the oven mitt. Instrumental analysis revealed the presence of the elements lead and antimony in these particles; this finding could indicate that an item which had gunshot residue on it, such as the revolver . . . came in contact with the interior of [the oven mitt]"[fn150]  Dr. Lee further stated that "[s]unflower-type seed husks were located on the inner surfaces of this oven mitt..."

[519]  OIC, p. 53-54:  Dr. Lee reported that "[m]acroscopic and microscopic examination of the inside of the front pants pockets revealed the presence of fibers and other

Mr. Foster carried the gun from his home to the park in the mitt, then to where his body was found in his pants pocket.

The record also contradicts the OIC's conclusion that this evidence *"tends to link Mr. Foster to the gun"* because there was, by all previous accounts, no oven mitt in the car at the park.

Park Police Investigator Rolla testified that he found "[n]othing out of the ordinary" in the glove compartment of the car at the park. He "found normal stuff in the car, sunglasses, photos, registration...".[520] Park Police Investigator Braun testified that when viewing "the glove compartment [she found] nothing out of the ordinary."[521]

---

materials, including a portion of a sunflower seed husk in the front left pocket. Instrumental analysis of particles removed from the pocket surface revealed the presence of lead. These materials were also found inside the oven mitt located in the glove compartment of Mr. Foster's vehicle... The presence of these trace materials could indicate that they share a common origin. These materials in the pants pocket clearly resulted from the transfer by an intermediate object, such as the Colt weapon."[fn149] ***These sunflower seed husks found in Mr. Foster's front, left pants pocket."[fn151] Dr. Lee stated that "[t]his finding suggests that the sunflower seed husk found inside the pants pocket could have been transferred from the oven mitt through an intermediate object, such as the revolver."[fn152]

[520] Exhibit 6, Deposition of Park Police Investigator John Rolla, July 21, 1994: Q. What about on [sic] the glove compartment? A. Nothing out of the ordinary. I think the vehicle registration was in the glove compartment. I took that for the time being. *** Q. What about [what you found] in the glove compartment? A. Nothing out of the ordinary... I looked through the whole car. I looked at everything... Trust me, I looked. I looked under the seats, I looked in the trunk. I looked at every piece of paper I could find. *** Q. What did you do, what would you describe what your search of the car was... [sic]? A. I went through the car looking - again looking for anything that could lead me to believe that it was other than a suicide or it was a suicide, anything that could help confirm one way or the other...

[521] Exhibit 101, Deposition of Park Police Investigator Cheryl Braun, July 23, 1994: Q. What do [sic] you find in the car? A. I went through the car. I found normal stuff in the car, sunglasses, photos, registration... *** Q. What

## Ownership of gun

But again, according to the OIC's (still secret) reports of reinterviews conducted years later, both of these Investigators suddenly remembered the presence of an oven mitt on July 20, 1993.

OIC, p. 52, fn. 148:

*"Investigators Rolla and Braun also recalled the oven mitt in the glove compartment of the car on July 20. Braun OIC, 2/9/95, at 95-96; Rolla 302, 4/17/96, at 6."*

According to the detailed description by Park Police of all items found in the car at the park (including, for example, the dates on coins, a "large Fender" guitar pick, and the brand names on the empty cigarette packs), the oven mitt was not in the car at the park.[522] One page of this list specifically itemizes the contents of the glove compartment -- no oven mitt. (The available photographs show an oven mitt in the glove compartment of Mr. Foster's car at the impound lot -- not at Fort Marcy Park.)

The OIC claims that associate White House counsel William Kennedy kept this oven mitt for six or more months before giving it to Mr. Fiske's FBI agents.

OIC, p. 52:

*William Kennedy, Associate White House Counsel, eventually took possession of Mr. Foster's car on behalf of the Foster family after the Park Police released it on July 28, 1993. Mr. Kennedy maintained contents of the car that had not been taken into evidence by the Park Police, and he produced those contents to investigators from Mr. Fiske's Office.[fn147]*

---

else did you see in the car? A. As I was saying earlier, the jacket with the wallet and credentials. There was [sic] pictures in the glovebox, and sunglasses, a couple of cigarette boxes...

[522] Exhibit 143, Park Police Evidence/Property Control Receipt, July 20, 1993.

Aside from being a break in the chain-of-custody, the record contradicts this claim. The FBI's report of its May, 1994, interview with William Kennedy recounts that Mr. Kennedy did not pick up the car from the Police for at least six weeks (well after *"July 28"*), after which time Chief of White House Personnel Security Craig Livingstone "got the car and parked it on the West Executive Avenue for about two weeks. Thereafter, it was moved for a two-month period of time to the New Executive Office Building basement..."[523] When the car was disposed of, Mr. "Kennedy retrieved... [mostly] junk such as M&Ms, plastic cups... [and] threw most of these items away but still has some items in his possession."

Kennedy had not given any of the items he *"maintained"* to the FBI as of the time it interviewed him in May of 1994,[524] nor is there any publicly available record of his ever having produced any items to FBI *"investigators from Mr. Fiske's Office."*

---

[523]   Exhibit 7, Report of FBI interview with William Kennedy, May 6, 1994: [H]e [Kennedy] retrieved Foster's car from the U.S. Park Police approximately one and one-half to two months after Foster's death. Livingstone got the car and it was parked on the West Executive Avenue by the White House for about two weeks. Thereafter, it was moved for a two-month period of time to the New Executive Office Building basement, while a dialogue continued with Lisa Foster regarding the final disposition of the car. It was agreed that the car would be sold to Mrs. Foster's brother.

[524]   Exhibit 7, Report of FBI interview with William Kennedy, May 6, 1994: When the brother and his wife came to Washington to pick up the car, Kennedy retrieved miscellaneous items from the vehicle. He described the car as being 'trashed' with family junk such as M&Ms, plastic cups, class notes, CD player, shoes, Ray Ban sunglasses, books, etc. Kennedy said he threw most of these items away but still has some items in his possession.

## VIII. EVIDENCE CONTRADICTING THE OFFICIAL CLAIM THAT MR. FOSTER DROVE TO THE PARK

Summary. Mr. Foster was dead by 4:20 p.m. The OIC conceals that at 4:20 p.m. Mr. Foster's Arkansas Honda was not in the Fort Marcy Park parking lot.

The OIC's claim that "only [two] cars... were known to law enforcement and the OIC" is false. Civilian witnesses saw the older brown Arkansas Honda, not Mr. Foster's 1989 silver Honda.

Patrick Knowlton saw the mid-1980s brown Arkansas Honda in the same spot as Mr. Foster's 1989 silver Honda car was later found, and a man acting suspiciously in a car backed in three spots from the Arkansas car. Patrick suffered witness tampering.

*Summary of car keys not at the park:* The OIC conceals that Mr. Foster's car keys were not at Fort Marcy Park by falsely reporting (1) that Rolla had "simply missed" the keys when he "patted" the pockets at the park, (2) that Kennedy and Livingstone could not have later placed the keys in the pocket because they visited the morgue after police had retrieved the keys, and (3) that Kennedy and Livingstone were not allowed in the same room as the body.

The OIC's claim that Rolla had "simply missed" two sets of keys when he "patted" Mr. Foster's pockets at the park is contradicted by the accounts of Rolla and at least two other Park Police. The OIC falsely claims that Kennedy and Livingstone could not later have placed the keys in the pocket because they visited the morgue after Braun had retrieved the keys at the morgue. The OIC's chronology is contradicted by the accounts of Park Police, Secret Service, Kennedy, Livingstone, and other White House personnel. The OIC relies on falsified or nonexistent hospital logs and failed to obtain records that would prove whether Kennedy and Livingstone visited the morgue before Rolla and Braun.

### 1. The other Arkansas Honda at the Park

The Report hides that Mr. Foster's car was not at the park when he was dead. As we saw in the *Preface*, that is why Patrick Knowlton was targeted for harassment. It also hides that another Arkansas Honda was parked in the same spot as Mr. Foster's car was reportedly later found.

The record of whether the 1983 or 1984 brown Honda left the lot, as well as whether Mr. Foster's 1989 Honda arrived, is confusing and unsettled, for several reasons. First, many of the statements of the witnesses' accounts, memorialized by the Park Police and later the FBI, are unclear. Second, some of these accounts may be referring to a broken-down Mercedes on the parkway, near the driveway into the lot, or maybe to Officer Hodakievic's car. Third, some of the officials reportedly saw a briefcase in a car, Patrick saw a briefcase in the older brown Honda, and in Mr. Foster's car there was, officially, no briefcase. Fourth, evidence suggests that Mr. Foster's car was not in the park at 8:00 p.m. In any event, the OIC's claim, that only two cars were *positively identified and known to law enforcement and the OIC,"* is not true.[525]

---

[525] Exhibit 79, Deposition of Park Police Officer Kevin Fornshill, July 12, 1994: "[Saw] two to three cars at the far end of the lot... and officially a Honda parked closer to the parkway entrance." Exhibit 66, FBI Report of interview with Todd Stacey Hall, March 18, 1994: "Upon arriving at Fort Marcy Park, Hall noticed an unoccupied brown car with the engine running parked in the lot. He noticed that the car was not parked in a space... Also contained in the car was a briefcase..."

Exhibit 67, Deposition of Paramedic Todd Hall, July 20, 1994: Q. Do you remember seeing an unoccupied car with the engine running in the parking lot? A. Yes. It was speculation between all of us that it was the car in the lot running. Q. That it was running? A. Well, I did hear it running... Q. But you remember seeing a car there? A. Yes, there was one parked yes. There was [sic] two or three cars there... I can't say whether it was there when we left or not...

Exhibit 133, Incident Report by Paramedic George Gonzalez, July 20, 1993: "Two other Veh. Brwn Honda AR Tags and White Nissan" Exhibit 71, Report of FBI interview of Paramedic Richard Arthur, March 16, 1994: "[T]here was a red car with hazard lights blinking... this vehicle had departed Fort Marcy prior to the departure of Arthur and his unit." Exhibit 78, Report of FBI interview of Firefighter Lieutenant James Iacone, March 11, 1994: "Iacone had observed three or four automobiles in the lot. Among the vehicles, Iacone noted a Honda Accord which was either red or maroon in color and which displayed Arkansas registration plates." Exhibit 72, Report of FBI interview of Firefighter Jennifer Wacha, March 11, 1994: "[I]n the parking area... the engine was running... also a third car in the lot."

## The time of death

### a.   Mr. Foster was dead before 4:20 p.m.

As discussed above, Dr. Beyer testified that he was unconcerned with the time of death.  The OIC's Report only briefly mentions time of death in a footnote, wherein it gives a clue by including the reported account that Dr. Beyer said, "*'that it appeared that the victim had eaten a 'large' meal which he believed to have occurred within 2-3 hours prior to death.*"[526]  Because Dr. Beyer also reportedly said the meal "might have been meat and potatoes,"[527] and because by all accounts, Mr. Foster had a cheeseburger and French-fries between 12:30 and 1:00, according to Dr. Beyer's approximation from the digestion of his lunch, Mr. Foster died between 2:30 and 4:00 p.m.  Paramedic George Gonzalez in his Incident Report estimated that based upon the "pooling of blood in the extremities," Mr. Foster had been dead "2-4 hrs"[528] at 6:15 p.m., similarly putting the time of death between approximately 2:15 and 4:15 p.m..

### b.   Patrick Knowlton and the absence of Mr. Foster's car at the park at 4:30

The Special Division of the United States Court of Appeals for the District of Columbia Circuit ordered the OIC to include Patrick Knowlton's submission to its Appendix to its Report on Mr. Foster's death.  We saw excerpts from it in the Preface.  The first exhibit to that Appendix appears again below, followed by some more excerpts from the Appendix.

---

[526]   OIC, p. 30, fn. 66:  Officer Morrissette's report also indicates that Dr. Beyer stated at the autopsy 'that it appeared that the victim had eaten a 'large' meal which he believed to have occurred within 2-3 hours prior to death.'  USPP Report (Morrissette) at 1.  An exact time of death has not been established.

[527]   Exhibit 127, Park Police Report by Detective James Morrissette, August 2, 1993.

[528]   Exhibit 133, Incident Report by Paramedic George Gonzalez, July 20, 1993.

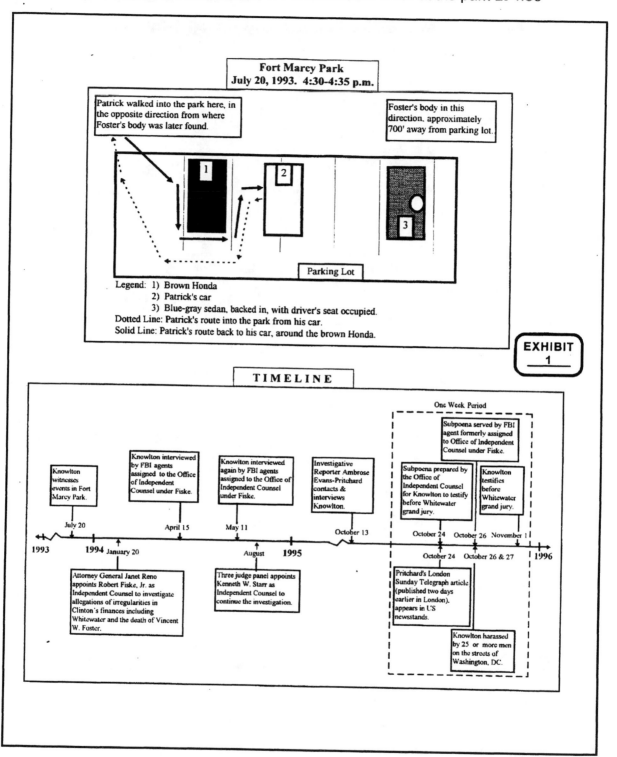

**Fort Marcy Park**
**July 20, 1993. 4:30-4:35 p.m.**

Patrick walked into the park here, in the opposite direction from where Foster's body was later found.

Foster's body in this direction, approximately 700' away from parking lot.

1

2

3

Parking Lot

Legend: 1) Brown Honda
2) Patrick's car
3) Blue-gray sedan, backed in, with driver's seat occupied.
Dotted Line: Patrick's route into the park from his car.
Solid Line: Patrick's route back to his car, around the brown Honda.

**EXHIBIT 1**

**TIMELINE**

One Week Period

Subpoena served by FBI agent formerly assigned to Office of Independent Counsel under Fiske.

Knowlton interviewed by FBI agents assigned to the Office of Independent Counsel under Fiske.

Knowlton interviewed again by FBI agents assigned to the Office of Independent Counsel under Fiske.

Investigative Reporter Ambrose Evans-Pritchard contacts & interviews Knowlton.

Subpoena prepared by the Office of Independent Counsel for Knowlton to testify before Whitewater grand jury.

Knowlton testifies before Whitewater grand jury.

Knowlton witnesses events in Fort Marcy Park.

July 20        April 15        May 11        October 13        October 24    October 26   November 1

1993   1994 January 20              August   1995              October 24   October 26 & 27   1996

Attorney General Janet Reno appoints Robert Fiske, Jr. as Independent Counsel to investigate allegations of irregularities in Clinton's finances including Whitewater and the death of Vincent W. Foster.

Three judge panel appoints Kenneth W. Starr as Independent Counsel to continue the investigation.

Pritchard's London Sunday Telegraph article (published two days earlier in London), appears in US newsstands.

Knowlton harassed by 25 or more men on the streets of Washington, DC.

Exhibit 1 of Appendix to the OIC's Report on the Death of Vincent Foster, Jr., submitted September 23, 1997, released to the public on October 10, 1997

Appendix to the OIC's Report on the Death of Vincent Foster, Jr., September 23, 1997:

Upon review of those excerpts of the Report provided by the OIC, it is manifest that the Report omits the information Patrick provided which refutes the FBI's repeated official conclusion of suicide in the park. Even though our review is limited by the fact that we were provided only the passages reprinted below and so the context is unclear, it is apparent that the Report also omits evidence Patrick provided which indicates that the FBI obstructed justice in this matter.

For example, the Report's first reference notes that at 4:30 p.m., Patrick saw in the Fort Marcy lot a rust-brown Honda with Arkansas license plates. Although this information is correct, it deceptively omits that Patrick is certain that this older car was not Mr. Foster's 1989 silver-gray colored car. Forensic evidence strongly indicates that Mr. Foster was dead by the time Patrick was in the park. Therefore, Mr. Foster could not have driven to the park in his Honda.

> Page 21 of the OIC's Report:
> Another citizen (C2) drove his rental car into Fort Marcy parking lot at approximately 4:30 p.m. While there, C2 saw one unoccupied car which he describes as a "Rust brown colored car with Arkansas license plates."[fn35] C2 also saw another nearby car; that was occupied by a man who exited his car as C2 exited his own car.[fn36] C2 described this man as having "a look like he had a -- an agenda, although everything I based my observation of this guy, was from the gut," "more than anything else.:" C2 and the man did not speak to one another.
> [fn35] OIC 11/1/95 at 22, 28
> [fn36] Id at 25

This first passage also notes that the other car in the lot was occupied by a man who exited his car as Patrick exited his own car (the man exited his car after Patrick walked toward the park). The excerpt omits any other details of the man's behavior. Mr. Foster's body was located about

700 feet away from the area where: (1) the man's car was backed in to its parking spot giving him full view of the driveway leading into the lot; (2) the man gave Patrick a menacing stare; and (3) the man returned to his own car only when Patrick chose to walk in the opposite direction from where Mr. Foster's body was found about 70 minutes later.

The Report goes on at page 22 to tell us that the "man had reentered his car by the time" Patrick had "returned to the parking lot," and at 69 that he saw "a man in a car next to him." We do not know of the context in which these passages appear.

> Page 22 of the OIC's Report:
> went into the park to urinate, and the other man had reentered his car by the time C2 returned to the parking lot.[fn39] C2 then left the park in his car.[fn40]
> [fn39] Id at 38
> [fn40] Id at 61-62

> Page 69 of the OIC's Report:
> During the afternoon, before Park Police and FCFRD personnel were called to the scene at Fort Marcy Park, C2 saw a man in a car next to him;

Twenty pages later, the Report notes that Patrick "saw a briefcase" in the Arkansas car along with a "jacket... [and two] wine coolers." This statement again deceptively implies that the car was Mr. Foster's even though Mr. Foster's car reportedly did not contain wine coolers or a briefcase.

> Page 89 of the OIC's Report:
> C2 testified that he saw a briefcase -- as well as wine coolers in a car with Arkansas plates that was parked in the parking lot. He stated: "I looked and saw the briefcase and saw the jacket, saw the wine coolers it was two of them. I remember exactly how they were laying in the back seat of the car."[fn274]
> [fn274] C2 OIC, 11/1/95, at 34

This final passage omits that Patrick testified (and repeatedly told the FBI) exactly where these

items were in the rust-brown Honda. The suit
jacket Patrick saw in that car was draped over
the back of the driver's seat. The suit jacket
later found in Mr. Foster's car [sic] was folded
and lying on the front passenger's seat.

Moreover, the Report's purported reliance on
grand jury testimony is an attempt to give the
Report more credibility. Indeed, the catalyst
for Patrick's grand jury testimony was the
appearance in U.S. newsstands of the October 22nd
issue of the *London Sunday Telegraph,* in which
Ambrose Evans-Pritchard described Patrick's
reaction when he was shown the FBI report of his
interview with two FBI agents detailed to Mr.
Fiske's probe. It was the first time Patrick had
seen the report of the interview, which had been
conducted eighteen months earlier. Evans-
Pritchard wrote that Patrick "was stunned."
Referring to the FBI's assertion that Patrick
stated he "would be unable to recognize the man"
he had seen at the park, Patrick is quoted as
saying "That's an outright lie."

Evans-Pritchard's article also states:

"They showed him a photograph of [Foster's]
Honda... 'They went over it about 20 times,
telling me that this was Foster's car,' said
Knowlton. 'But I was quite adamant about
it. I saw what I saw, and I wasn't going to
change my story'... Starr's investigators
have never talked to Knowlton. The federal
grand jury has never summoned him to give
sworn testimony."

On October 24, the same day that this newspaper
reached U.S. newsstands, the OIC prepared a
subpoena summoning Patrick to testify before the
Whitewater grand jury. The secret grand jury
subpoena was served two days later by an FBI
agent who was formerly detailed to Mr. Fiske's
probe, whereupon Patrick was harassed and
intimidated by 25 or more men -- during which
time the FBI ignored his repeated pleas for help.
The Report omits all of this, even though Patrick
submitted a report detailing the harassment to

the OIC in March of 1996, which included reports of a polygraph examination, a psychiatric examination, witnesses' affidavits, photographs of two members of the harassment team and the names and addresses of two others.

Patrick was harassed beginning October 26, 1995, the same day he received his subpoena to appear before Mr. Starr's Whitewater grand jury. The fact that Patrick was subpoenaed was known only to the OIC and the FBI.

The report referred to in the Appendix that Patrick submitted to the OIC in March, 1996, detailing the harassment he suffered is his *Report of Witness Tampering*. Excerpts appear below.

*Report of Witness Tampering*, March 4, 1996.

The authors wrote this Report of Witness Tampering primarily to:

(1)   Protect Knowlton from further harm by publicizing the harassment, and

(2)   Establish that Knowlton is credible and stable.

Two persons besides Knowlton, a journalist and a Ph.D. consultant and educator, witnessed the events of October 26 and 27. Each witness states unequivocally that what they observed was willful harassment. On October 26, Knowlton's girlfriend wrote down the license plate number of the car driven by one of the perpetrators. Evans-Pritchard provided disturbing evidence regarding that plate:

> [T]he license plate Knowlton noted from Thursday had checked out with a law en-forcement source... as being a federal gov-ernment vehicle... suggested Knowlton was "being warned, or there was an attempt being made to destabilize him before he appeared before the grand jury."

It is a crime to harass a witness for the purpose of dissuading him from assisting in a grand jury probe.    Title  18  US  Code,  Section  1512, "Tampering  with  witness,  victim  or  informant," states in part:

> (c)  Whoever intentionally harasses another person and hinders, delays, prevents or dissuades any person from—
>
>         *    *    *
>
> (4)  causing a criminal prosecution... to be sought or instituted, or assisting in such prosecution or proceeding;
>
> or attempts to do so shall be fined under this title or imprisoned...

It is a civil rights violation for two or more persons to conspire to deter by intimidation anyone from testifying freely, fully, and truthfully before a grand jury.  Title 42 US Code, Section 1985(2),  "Conspiracy to interfere with civil rights," part (2), "Obstructing justice; intimidating party, witness, or juror," states in part:

> If two or more persons in any State or Territory *conspire to deter, by* force, *intimidation,* or threat, *any* party *or witness in any court of the United States* from attending such court, or *from testifying to any matter pending therein, freely, fully, and truthfully...*

This case is important.  The facts of the harassment is telling.  It begs that a mystery be solved:  Why did someone commit a crime to try to obstruct the investigation into the death of Vincent Foster?

        *    *    *

This document presents the entire sequence of events in chronological order.  Section I describes the unwittingly crucial five minutes Knowlton spent in Fort Marcy Park through when he unexpectantly received a subpoena to testify before the grand jury over two years later. Section II details the initial harassment, suspect by suspect, a total of 25 encounters in two days.  Section III describes further harassment, both before and after the grand jury testimony, and the testimony itself.

$$* \quad * \quad *$$

## SECTION I

## KNOWLTON'S OBSERVATIONS AT FORT MARCY PARK, VIRGINIA

## July 20, 1993:

While heading home in heavy traffic on the George Washington Memorial Parkway, Patrick Knowlton pulled into Fort Marcy Park to urinate. He noticed the clock on his car read 4:30. There were only two cars in the parking lot. An unoccupied 1983 or 1984 rust brown four-door Honda was parked close to the southern footpath entrance. Knowlton noticed the distinctive Arkansas license plate on the brown Honda. A metallic blue-gray four-door sedan was backed in three or four spaces to the right of the brown Honda. In the driver's seat of the blue-gray sedan was a lone man. Knowlton parked between the two cars, closer to the brown Honda.

Immediately after Knowlton parked, the man in the blue-gray sedan lowered the passenger side electric window and gave him a menacing stare. The look made Knowlton feel like he was intruding, and appeared to him to communicate "Get the hell out of here." The man appeared to be Hispanic or Middle Eastern. Knowlton thought he may have been there for some sort of criminal activity. Before getting out of his car, Knowlton took his wallet and checkbook from the front passenger's seat and hid them under the driver's seat.

As he started towards the park's footpath, Knowlton heard the blue-gray sedan's door open. Apprehensive of being victimized, Knowlton walked to the information sign bordering the foot path entrance to the park, and looked to his right to see if the man was approaching. Knowlton observed the man leaning on the roof of the driver's side of the blue-gray sedan, watching him intently. After pausing for about a minute

feigning to read the sign to make sure the man
was not approaching, Knowlton quickly proceeded
75 feet down the footpath to a nearby tree.

As he relieved himself, Knowlton watched the
trail to see whether the man approached. From
where he stood, he could see the brown Honda, the
front of his own car, and the back of the blue-
gray sedan. He heard the man close the door of
the blue-gray sedan, and figured the man may have
gotten back in his car, or maybe was approaching
him.

As Knowlton returned to his own car with a
heightened sense of awareness, he scanned the
parking lot. He walked directly toward the
driver's side door of the brown Honda, and then
around the back of that car, thinking that maintaining his distance from the man might provide
an additional margin of safety.

After getting back in his car, he looked to his
right as he locked his driver's side car door,
and observed the man seated in the driver's seat
of the blue-gray sedan still staring at him.

The way he maneuvered back to his car enabled
Knowlton to view the interior of the brown Honda.
He noticed a man's dark suit jacket hung over the
back of the driver's seat, a briefcase (darker in
color than the interior of the car) lying flat on
the front passenger seat, and two full bottles of
wine cooler lying flat on the back seat. As he
walked around the rear of the brown Honda, he
again saw the Arkansas license plate. As he left
the park, after seeing the items in the brown
Honda, it occurred to Knowlton that he might have
interrupted the man from rifling that car.

*     *     *

## KNOWLTON'S STATEMENT BY TELEPHONE TO US PARK POLICE

### July 22, 1993:

The following evening, Knowlton saw on the 11:00
news in Etlan, Virginia, that Vincent Foster,

Deputy White House Counsel and financial confidant of the Clintons, was found dead at Fort Marcy Park. At 12:23 a.m., he called the US Park Police and reported over the phone to an officer. That officer told him that a detective on the case would call him at 6:00 a.m. When no officer called, Knowlton called the Park Police before he left for work at 7:30 a.m., and again reported what he had witnessed.

Over the course of the next two years, Knowlton told friends, family and acquaintances what he had witnessed at Fort Marcy Park, and even told the story at a few parties.

### KNOWLTON'S INTERVIEWS WITH INVESTIGATORS ASSIGNED TO THE OFFICE OF SPECIAL COUNSEL UNDER ROBERT FISKE

Almost nine months later, FBI Special Agent Larry Monroe called Knowlton and asked him to come by the Office of Special Counsel for an interview.

### April 15, 1994:

Knowlton was interviewed for approximately two and one half hours at the Office of Special Counsel by Agent Monroe, with FBI Special Agent William Colombell present in the room intermittently. The agents were friendly and made Knowlton feel at-ease. When Knowlton entered Monroe's office, he was seated next to Monroe's desk. Knowlton immediately noticed on Monroe's desk an autopsy report, autopsy sketches, Polaroids, and witness statements. Monroe then left the room to get coffee. Knowlton glanced at the documents on Monroe's desk.

After Knowlton gave his statement, Monroe had him repeat it while Monroe took notes. Monroe reviewed his notes as Knowlton gave his statement a third time. During the interview, Monroe and Knowlton engaged is some small talk about Knowlton's Etlan, Virginia residence, and Monroe's home in Manassas, Virginia.

Afterwards, Monroe showed Knowlton six to eight photographs of a car, one by one, while questioning him 15 to 20 times in various ways whether the photographs were of the brown Honda he saw. During this phase of the interview, Monroe repeatedly stated that he did not want to influence Knowlton in any way. Knowlton consistently responded that the car in the photograph was not the brown Honda he saw.

Monroe then became irritated, stood up, tossed the photographs on the desk, called in Agent Colombell, and asked Colombell whether the Park Police photographed the wrong car. Colombell assured Monroe that the photographs were of Foster's car. Monroe stated that the Park Police made many mistakes. Monroe then told Colombell that "Knowlton doesn't think these photographs are of the right car."

Monroe again showed the photographs to Knowlton and asked whether the photographs were of the car he saw. While stating that he did not want to influence Knowlton's answers, Monroe explained that the sunlight may have altered the photographs.

At the end of the interview, Monroe, in Colombell's presence, stated to Knowlton that since Foster's death, the Foster family has had a very difficult time, especially the children. Monroe then suggested to Knowlton that he not talk to the Press for the sake of the Foster family. Soon thereafter Knowlton was invited to appear on the G. Gordon Liddy Show. Knowlton declined.

## May 11, 1994:

About a month later, Monroe interviewed Knowlton a second time at the Office of Special Counsel, primarily about the brown Honda he saw at Fort Marcy Park. This interview took about two hours. Knowlton again felt the atmosphere was friendly. Monroe reviewed the notes he took the first time he interviewed Knowlton. He then said he should not show Knowlton statements of other witnesses, but that he would. He then showed Knowlton statements of other witnesses who had seen a different car at Fort Marcy Park, a later model Honda, grayish-brown or taupe in color.

Monroe explained the Honda Knowlton saw may have looked darker to him because of the way the shade from the trees was hitting it. He then showed Knowlton an under-exposed photograph of a car parked next to a police cruiser. The car in this photograph looked black. Knowlton again stated that the car he saw was not the one shown in the photographs.

Monroe then escorted Knowlton to the FBI laboratory in the Hoover Building, where he showed Knowlton brochures for 1988 through 1990 Hondas, and asked that he pick out the car. Knowlton said the cars depicted in the brochures were too new, and asked for brochures of older cars. As none were available, Knowlton looked through car color panels. The lab technician, Frederic Whitehurst, said he was familiar with the dull finish Knowlton described. Knowlton picked out two panels, both of which turned out to be of early 1980s Hondas.

Agent Whitehurst suggested to Agent Monroe that he run through the Arkansas DMV every Honda of the year and color that Knowlton had picked. Monroe responded curtly, and said not to worry because they were "on top of all this."

## SUNDAY TELEGRAPH ARTICLE

### October 13, 1995:

Eighteen months later, Knowlton was located and interviewed by Ambrose Evans-Pritchard, the Washington Bureau Chief of the *Sunday Telegraph*, a London newspaper. Evans-Pritchard was interested in Knowlton because Evans-Pritchard has been writing about the Foster death since it occurred, and has for the last year been investing considerable time and resources investigating events concerning Foster's death, and various other Whitewater probes.

Knowlton was not easy to find. Evans-Pritchard located him with the help of a private investigator.

Evans-Pritchard provided Knowlton with copies of the FBI Reports FD-302 ("302"), which were reports of Knowlton's April and May, 1994 interviews with FBI Agents Monroe and Colombell. The reports misrepresented what Knowlton had said to the agents. Knowlton pointed out the most blatant inaccuracies to Evans-Pritchard.

Knowlton told Evans-Pritchard that he told Monroe he could in fact identify the man in the blue-gray sedan. The 302 states just the opposite. Within a week, Evans-Pritchard retained a police artist, who with Knowlton's help, made a composite sketch of the man.

**October 22, 1995:**

An article written by Evans-Pritchard appeared in the London Sunday Telegraph, "*Death in the Park: Is this the killer?*" The article reported some of the inaccuracies in the FBI reports, stated that Knowlton had not been subpoenaed to testify before the grand jury, and that two other witnesses who arrived at Fort Marcy Park 30 minutes after Knowlton left had also not been subpoenaed. Accompanying the article was the police artist's composite sketch of the man in the blue-gray sedan who gave Knowlton a "threatening look" at Fort Marcy Park. The article stated in part:

\* \* \*

The *Sunday Telegraph* asked if he would be willing to help with an artist's sketch of the suspect...

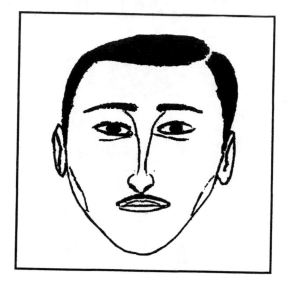

\*     \*     \*

"They went over it about 20 times,
telling me that this was Foster's car,"
said Knowlton.  "But I was quite
adamant  about it.  I saw what I saw,
and I wasn't going to change my
story..."

Starr's investigators have never talked
to Knowlton.  The federal grand jury
has never summoned him to give sworn
testimony.

Not included in either the Appendix to the OIC's
Report, or the *Report of Witness Tampering*, is a
description of the incident the night of May 10, 1994, the
evening before the second interview.  The events of that
night, recounted in Patrick's lawsuit, appear below.

Patrick Knowlton v. Robert Edwards et al., US District
Court for the District of Columbia, Civil Action No.
96-2467:

65.   In early May of 1994, Monroe telephoned
Plaintiff at his Virginia residence and requested a
second in-person interview.  Plaintiff agreed.  The
two scheduled a meeting for 10:00 a.m., May 11th,
1994.

66.   On May 10, 1994, the night before his second interview with Monroe, Plaintiff was driving his 1979 refurbished Peugeot 504 eastbound on Constitution Avenue, NW, accompanied by three adult passengers, one gentleman and two ladies.  It was about 10:30 p.m.  Defendant Scott Jeffrey Bickett drove a 1988 Oldsmobile with Illinois license plates, accompanied by adult two male passengers, and was tailgating Plaintiff for about three blocks. Plaintiff, driving slowly and looking for a parking space, approached the intersection of 21st Street, saw a vacant parking spot, put on his directional, and stopped just past the spot.  Bickett pulled into the spot.  Plaintiff got out of his car and said to Bickett, "I was gonna park there."  Bickett said two words, then walked away, accompanied by the two other males who were passengers in the Oldsmobile.  There was no other conversation between the occupants of Plaintiff's car and the occupants of Bickett's car.

67.   Plaintiff parked his car in front of Bickett's, then left with his companions.

68.   Immediately upon Plaintiff's vacating the area, Bickett returned to the scene, took a tire iron from his Oldsmobile, smashed the Peugeot's four headlights, both taillights and struck the radiator with sufficient force to put a hole in it, causing over $3,700 in damages to Plaintiff's Peugeot.

69.   About fifteen minutes after he had left his Peugeot, Plaintiff returned to where it was parked.  A limousine driver, who is a retired District of Columbia Metropolitan Police Department Captain, who had witnessed the incident, told Plaintiff and Park Police Officers Hammond and McIntyre who had arrived by that time what Bickett had done, and provided the Oldsmobile's license plate number.  Park Police assigned the case incident number 021327.

70.   Plaintiff reasonably believes and therefore avers that Bickett is employed by the Department of Defense with a Sensitive Compartmented Information security clearance, and that Bickett has been briefed at FBI headquarters and has served at the direction of FBI personnel, as alleged above.  Accordingly, Plaintiff alleges that Bickett's wrongful conduct was at the direction of FBI personnel.  The purpose of Bickett's having committed these violent actions toward Plaintiff late in the evening before the morning of Plaintiff's second scheduled interview with

301

Monroe was to cause Plaintiff to be in a deteriorated emotional state while being interviewed by Monroe. The conspirators sought to make Plaintiff more vulnerable to being manipulated by Monroe's haranguing to obtain from Plaintiff the sought-after admission that the Arkansas Honda Plaintiff saw in the park could have been Mr. Foster's 1989 year model Honda.

71.   Monroe interviewed Plaintiff a second time on the morning following Bickett's malicious attack on Plaintiff's car, while Plaintiff was still jarred and distressed...

75.   In the weeks following Bickett's malicious conduct, Park Police told Plaintiff that the vandal could not be identified or located.  On October 18, 1995, this license plate number was provided to a private investigator.  The next day, the investigator called and provided the Oldsmobile owner's name, address, home telephone number, employer, and wife's name.  Plaintiff provided this information to the Park Police, whereupon Bickett confessed to Park Police Detective Frank A. Barwinzak.  Despite repeated requests to do so, the Office of the United States Attorney for the District of Columbia failed and refused to prosecute Bickett.

Further excerpts from the March, 1996 *Report of Witness Tampering* appear below.

## KNOWLTON SUBPOENAED BY WASHINGTON OFFICE OF INDEPENDENT COUNSEL UNDER KENNETH STARR

### Thursday morning, October 26, 1995:

Four days after Evans-Pritchard's article was published, on Thursday, at 10:30 a.m., Knowlton was served a subpoena to testify before the Washington, DC federal grand jury on the following Wednesday, November 1, 1995.  FBI Special Agent Russell Bransford, assigned to Starr's Office of Independent Counsel in Washington, personally served Knowlton the subpoena at Knowlton's home.  Knowlton had never had any contact with the court system and asked Bransford several questions about what to expect. Bransford was helpful and cordial.  He explained that Knowlton was not a target, but simply a witness.  He gave Knowlton his business card, and suggested that Knowlton call him if he had any more questions.

Agent Bransford was formerly assigned to the Office of Special Counsel under Fiske, and worked with Agents Monroe and Colombell.

Harassment began later that same evening.[529]

---

[529]    See also Patrick Knowlton v. Robert Edwards et al., US District Court for the District of Columbia, Civil Action No. 96-2467, Plaintiff's Opposition to... Defendants' Alternative Motion for Summary Judgment, notes 2 & 3:

Affidavit of Mr. Gene Wheaton:  "I have... over 40 years in the criminal justice system, including... security projects related to intelligence.  I have qualified as an expert witness...  In part because of my close association with the Chief, Assessment Branch, CIA, I became extremely knowledgeable of psychological operations (PsyOps) and techniques of the intelligence community... there are various methods and purposes in conducting surveillance... Intimidation is one purpose of a close, obvious surveillance... This case appears to be the misuse of surveillance techniques to scare and intimidate the witness or to destroy his credibility...  could be expected in the area of illegal intelligence operations  ...to make him appear paranoid and thus destroy credibility as a witness... I have used this technique...  Mr. Clarke has asked me to render an opinion on the following question: Was one of the purposes of the actions described in the Amended Complaint to intimidate Mr. Knowlton to try to prevent him from testifying freely, fully, and truthfully? In my opinion, provided the events reported in the Amended Complaint are accurately portrayed, my answer is yes."

Affidavit of Mr. Ted L. Gunderson:  "Since my retirement in 1979 as Senior Special Agent in Charge of the FBI, Los Angeles Division, I have testified many times as an expert witness in both civil and criminal matters...  Mr. Knowlton's allegations of harassment... is a technique that I am both aware of and knowledgeable about which is used by government agents and law enforcement officers.  This technique is used for intimidation and to prevent a witness from testifying and/or testifying truthfully and/or cooperating with officials out of fear of harm to the witness or his loved ones. I have knowledge of this tactic and know of instances when it has been used."

# United States District Court

FOR THE ——————— DISTRICT OF ————— COLUMBIA

TO: PATRICK KNOWLTON

## SUBPOENA TO TESTIFY
## BEFORE GRAND JURY

SUBPOENA FOR:

☒ PERSON ☐ DOCUMENT(S) OR OBJECT(S)

YOU ARE HEREBY COMMANDED to appear and testify before the Grand Jury of the United States District Court at the place, date, and time specified below.

| PLACE | COURTROOM |
|---|---|
| United States District Court for the District of Columbia Third & Constitution Avenue, N.W. Washington, D.C. | Grand Jury, Third Floor |
| | DATE AND TIME |
| | November 1, 1995/12:00 Noon |

YOU ARE ALSO COMMANDED to bring with you the following document(s) or object(s):°

☐ *Please see additional information on reverse.*

This subpoena shall remain in effect until you are granted leave to depart by the court or by an officer acting on behalf of the court.

| U.S. MAGISTRATE OR CLERK OF COURT | DATE |
|---|---|
| Nancy M. Mayer-Whittington, Clerk | October 24, 1995 |
| (BY) DEPUTY CLERK | (D331) (FD) |

This subpoena is issued upon application of the United States of America

NAME, ADDRESS AND PHONE NUMBER OF ASSISTANT U.S. ATTORNEY

John D. Bates, Deputy Independent Counsel
Office of the Independent Counsel
1001 Pennsylvania Avenue, N.W., Suite 490 North
Washington, D.C. 20004

Front of Subpoena for Patrick Knowlton to testify before the Whitewater Grand Jury.  Prepared October 24, 1995, served October 26, 1995.

CO 293 (Rev. 9/91)  Subpoena to Testify Before Grand Jury

## RETURN OF SERVICE [1]

| | DATE | PLACE |
|---|---|---|
| **RECEIVED BY SERVER** | | |
| **SERVED** | 10-26-95 | 2424 Pennsylvania Ave. N.W. Apt. 910 |

**SERVED ON (PRINT NAME)**

Patrick James Knowlton

| SERVED BY (PRINT NAME) | TITLE |
|---|---|

## STATEMENT OF SERVICE FEES

| TRAVEL | SERVICES | TOTAL |
|---|---|---|

## DECLARATION OF SERVER [2]

I declare under penalty of perjury under the laws of the United States of America that the foregoing information contained in the Return of Service and Statement of Service Fees is true and correct.

Executed on ___10/26/95___
_Date_

_Russell T. Bransford_
_Signature of Server_
OIC, 1001 Pennsylvania Ave., N.W., Suite 490
Washington, D.C. (202) 307-0443
_Address of Server_

**ADDITIONAL INFORMATION**

BRETT M. KAVANAUGH (ASSOCIATE COUNSEL)
(202) 514-8688

(1) As to who may serve a subpoena and the manner of its service see Rule 17(d), Federal Rules of Criminal Procedure, or Rule 45(c), Federal Rules of Civil Procedure.
(2) "Fees and mileage need not be tendered to the witness upon service of a subpoena issued on behalf of the United States or an officer or agency thereof (Rule 45(c), Federal Rules of Civil Procedure; Rule 17(d), Federal Rules of Criminal Procedure) or on behalf of certain indigent parties and criminal defendants who are unable to pay such costs (28 USC 1825, Rule 17(b) Federal Rules of Criminal Procedure)".

Back of Patrick Knowlton's Whitewater Grand Jury subpoena.

SECTION II

HARASSMENT

**Thursday evening and Friday early afternoon, October 26 & 27, 1995:**

At around 7:20 p.m., Knowlton and his girlfriend, Kathy, walked from his home in the Foggy Bottom neighborhood to Dupont Circle, and back to Bertucci's Restaurant in Foggy Bottom. Although pedestrian traffic was light, he was continuously followed and repeatedly harassed. During the time Knowlton spent in public that evening, eleven or more men walked towards him, or came from behind, and gave him purposeful, intimidating, timed stares. The men followed him on the street, into a drug store, and into a restaurant. He was also trailed by car.

In her sworn affidavit, Kathy stated that she "has never witnessed anything like this before or since. It was intentional, coordinated, intimidating, and extremely unnerving." Kathy holds a Ph.D. in Organizational Development, and is employed as a consultant and educator.

At Kathy's suggestion and with her help, Knowlton wrote down and tape recorded the details of the harassment shortly after each occurrence. On Thursday, October 26, the descriptions of the men who harassed Knowlton were hand written within 90 minutes of their being observed. Tapes of what occurred were recorded later that afternoon, and again that evening.

The activities of the men who harassed Knowlton, as well as the descriptions of these men, are reported in great detail. The authors retained the services of a psychiatrist and psychologist to prove that Knowlton has a superior power of recall and that he is stable. Prior to writing his report, Harvard trained psychiatrist Thomas C. Goldman referred Knowlton to psychologist Lanning E. Moldauer, who administered tests of visual reproduction (memory tests). The doctors reported that Knowlton placed in the 90th percentile of

306

what the general population would be expected to score. Dr. Goldman reports, "This result domonstrates Mr. Knowlton has unusually good powers of delayed recall of visually-presented stimuli and would be consistent with his ability to report accurately on the events of late October 1995."

After separately interviewing Knowlton and Kathy, reading this Report, and reviewing Dr. Moldauer's findings, Dr. Goldman reported that Knowlton "showed no indication of a paranoid process or of any other pathological process that would tend to undermine Mr. Knowlton's credibility in this instance."

Dr. Goldman relays the following in regard to the plausibility of Mr. Knowlton's recalling the descriptions as set forth in this Report:

> Nothing in the descriptions of any of these individuals suggests anything so far outside the realm of the possible as to seem incredible...
>
> You had asked me to opine on whether it was possible for an ordinary person to make such a large number of detailed observations given the short period of time... First, Mr. Knowlton was clearly in a state of high alert from perceived danger. In such a state, perceptions are generally heightened in intensity and powers of concentration and recall can be greatly enhanced.... Secondly, Mr. Knowlton tends naturally to be a person who is attentive to details in his environment... Thirdly, Mr. Knowlton was administered the Wechsler Memory Scale, Revised, by Dr. Moldauer. This is a standardized, widely used and well respected instrument. The results indicated that while Mr. Knowlton scored in the average range overall, his performance on Visual Reproduction subtests 1 and 2, was quite superior. These are the tests closest in form to the actual situation that occurred on October 26 and the days following... In these tests... [Mr. Knowlton placed] in the 90th percentile (that is, he scored better than nine out of ten people in the general population would be expected to score). This test result demonstrates Mr. Knowlton has unusually good powers of delayed recall of visually-presented

stimuli and would be consistent with his ability to report accurately on the events of late October 1995.

The authors also retained the services of a very well respected polygraph expert, Paul K. Minor. Knowlton passed.

---

### AMERICAN INTERNATIONAL Security Corporation

10805 Main Street • Suite 600 • Fairfax, Virginia 22030
(703) 691-1110

Paul K. Minor
President

#### POLYGRAPH EXAMINATION REPORT

**CLIENT:**
John H. Clarke

**EXAMINATION DATE:**
12-21-95

**TIME IN:**
2:00 PM

**TIME OUT:**
3:30 PM

**EXAMINEE NAME:**
Patrick J. Knowlton

**DATE AND PLACE OF BIRTH:**
[Deleted]   New York

**HOME ADDRESS:**
[Deleted]

**SOCIAL SECURITY NUMBER:**
[Deleted]

**PRESENT EMPLOYER AND POSITION:**
Self-employed

**CITIZENSHIP/ALIEN REG. # :**
U.S.

**PURPOSE OF EXAMINATION:**

_____ Pre-employment screening     __XX__ Specific Issue

**CONCLUSION:**

__XX__ No deception indicated     _____ Deception indicated     _____ Inconclusive
(see information)

---

**INFORMATION:** Prior to the polygraph pre-test interview and examination, the examinee read and voluntarily signed the consent/waiver form, which with all other examination material, is retained in our files. Should you need further information, please do not hesitate to contact our office.

Mr. Patrick Knowlton claims he entered Ft. Marcy Park about 1630 hours, July 20, 1993. He requested this examination to verify what he saw there, and to verify what he claims to be subsequent harassment. During the first testing phase the following relevant questions were asked of Knowlton:

A. Have you deliberately lied about what you saw at Ft. Marcy Park on July 20, 1993? No.
B. Are you lying about seeing a bluish car and a brown Honda with Arkansas plates? No.
C. Are you lying about seeing a man sitting in the blue car? No.
D. Had you been to Ft. Marcy Park on only one prior occasion? Yes.
E. Did you lie about anything in your Grand Jury testimony of Nov. 1, 1995? No.

During the second phase, the following relevant question was asked:

A. Is the account of harassment true as stated in the report of witness tampering? Yes.

Deception was not indicated to any relevant question.

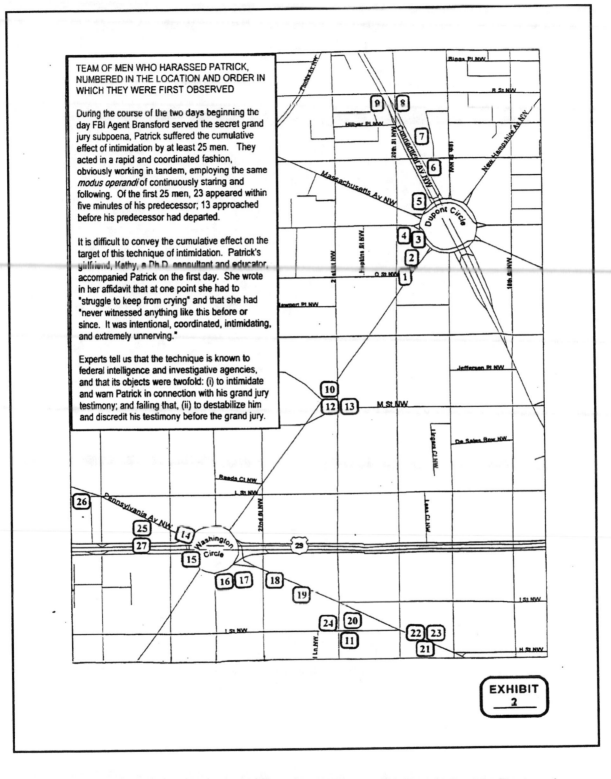

TEAM OF MEN WHO HARASSED PATRICK,
NUMBERED IN THE LOCATION AND ORDER IN
WHICH THEY WERE FIRST OBSERVED

During the course of the two days beginning the
day FBI Agent Bransford served the secret grand
jury subpoena, Patrick suffered the cumulative
effect of intimidation by at least 25 men. They
acted in a rapid and coordinated fashion,
obviously working in tandem, employing the same
*modus operandi* of continuously staring and
following. Of the first 25 men, 23 appeared within
five minutes of his predecessor; 13 approached
before his predecessor had departed.

It is difficult to convey the cumulative effect on the
target of this technique of intimidation. Patrick's
girlfriend, Kathy, a Ph.D. consultant and educator,
accompanied Patrick on the first day. She wrote
in her affidavit that at one point she had to
"struggle to keep from crying" and that she had
"never witnessed anything like this before or
since. It was intentional, coordinated, intimidating,
and extremely unnerving."

Experts tell us that the technique is known to
federal intelligence and investigative agencies,
and that its objects were twofold: (i) to intimidate
and warn Patrick in connection with his grand jury
testimony; and failing that, (ii) to destabilize him
and discredit his testimony before the grand jury.

**EXHIBIT 2**

Exhibit 2 of Appendix to the OIC's Report on the Death of Vincent Foster, Jr.,
submitted September 23, 1997, released to the public on October 10, 1997.

## Suspect 1

*Description: White male. Approximately 5'10", 180 lbs, mid-40s. Light colored hair, balding, rounded face, light complexion, brown suit, white shirt, red & gold striped tie, black soft-soled shoes.*

Patrick and Kathy walked up New Hampshire Avenue. Kathy walked on Patrick's left. A man walked toward them while constantly glaring directly at Patrick's face. The man directed his stare into Patrick's eyes as he approached. As he passed on their left, he turned his head toward Patrick and ignored Kathy. The man then crossed O Street, where he stopped and watched them. When Kathy and Patrick stopped and looked back, they saw the man still standing and looking at them. The man raised his wrist to his mouth and spoke into his coat sleeve.

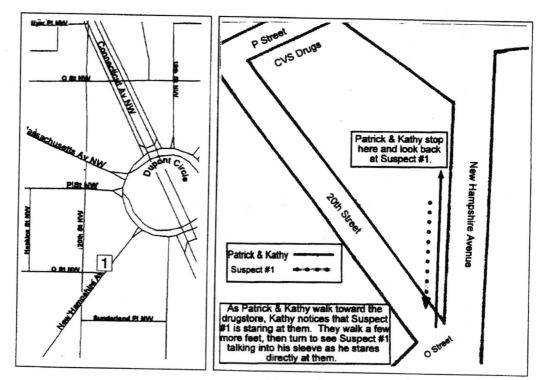

This contact with the first man lasted for approximately three minutes.

> *Patrick's reaction:* *Kathy noticed this man, and mentioned to me that the man was staring at me. I glanced at him and noticed his stare. I thought the man's behavior was bizarre. I laughed when the man talked into his sleeve, and I mentioned to Kathy "this guy is acting very strange."*

## Suspect 2 - within five seconds later

*Description: White male. Approximately 5'10", 190 lbs, 40s. Light brown hair, well-groomed, fair-skinned, clear complexion, navy blue suit jacket, dark gray slacks, maroon tie.*

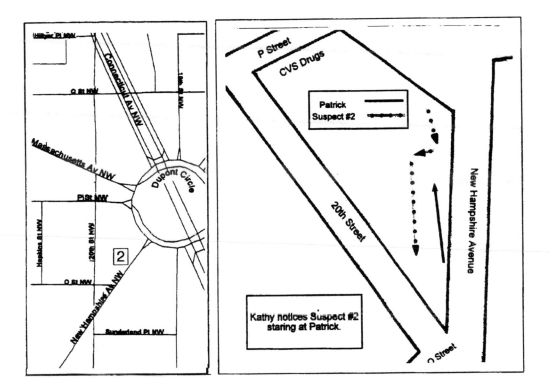

This man directed a constant glare at Patrick's face as he approached Patrick and Kathy on New Hampshire Avenue just below Dupont Circle. While continuing to glare, the man walked directly towards Patrick, then cut to Patrick's left. As he passed, he turned his head toward Patrick, past Kathy, while continuously glaring into

Patrick's eyes.  This contact lasted about 15 seconds.

> *Patrick's reaction:*  As the man approached, Kathy interrupted our conversation and mentioned that this man was also staring at me.  I thought it was very weird.

\*     \*     \*

Suspect 4 - about four or five minutes later
*Description:  Black male.  Approximately 6'1",  190 lbs, mid 30s. Military-style haircut, clear complexion, dark eyes, oval face, small features, Bluejays baseball cap, blue & gray*

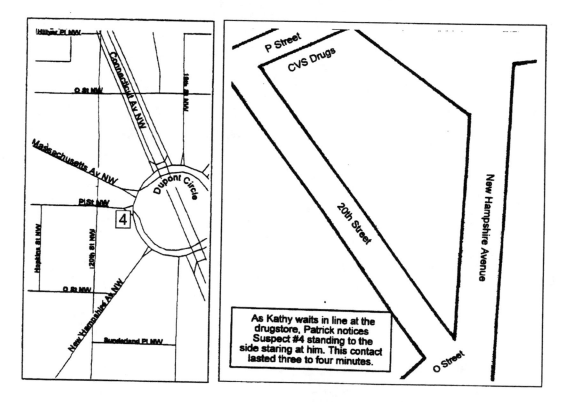

As Kathy waits in line at the drugstore, Patrick notices Suspect #4 standing to the side staring at him. This contact lasted three to four minutes.

As Patrick sat in a nearby chair while Kathy waited in line at the CVS pharmacy counter, a man got in line behind Kathy.  While in line, the man did not face forward.  Rather he stood facing Patrick, and glared at him.  This glare continued as the man moved up in line, for a period of three to four minutes. When Kathy handed her prescription to the pharmacist, the man walked away.

> *Patrick's reaction*: I looked away from the man, but every time I glanced up I saw the man still glaring. I thought maybe the glare was racially motivated, and the man was trying to start a confrontation. As Kathy and I left CVS, Kathy mentioned that she was getting scared. I said I was too, but we shouldn't get carried away. It was probably just our imagination.

*     *     *

### Suspect 6 - about one minute later - same as 21

*Description:     White male.     Approximately 6'4", 225 lbs, mid-40s. Clean shaven, light-colored hair, light-colored eyes, clear complexion, physically fit, beige baseball cap, beige jacket, wire-rim glasses, dark bluejeans, white sneakers.*

Patrick and Kathy were walking north on Connecticut Avenue towards Q Street when Patrick noticed Suspect 6 standing at Q Street and Connecticut Avenue, standing military "at-ease" style, staring directly at them. As they approached the corner, the man focused a glare at Patrick's face. As they reached the corner, the man pivoted on one foot, keeping his military-type stance, all the while glaring at Patrick's head. Kathy and Patrick crossed the street against the light. The man followed behind Patrick, at a distance of about three feet.

While walking the length of the block, Patrick periodically looked back. (At about the middle of the block, Patrick and Kathy noticed Suspect 7.) Suspect 6 continued to follow, at a distance of about three feet as they walked toward R Street. (As they approached the intersection, Suspect 8 crossed R Street, walking directly towards Patrick while glaring constantly at him.) Patrick and Kathy approached the intersection of R Street and Connecticut Avenue. When Suspect 6 was about eight feet away from Patrick and Kathy, he veered to the right of them, while continuing to glare. Suspect 6 then again assumed the military-type "at-ease" stance. The contact Suspect 6 lasted approximately four minutes.

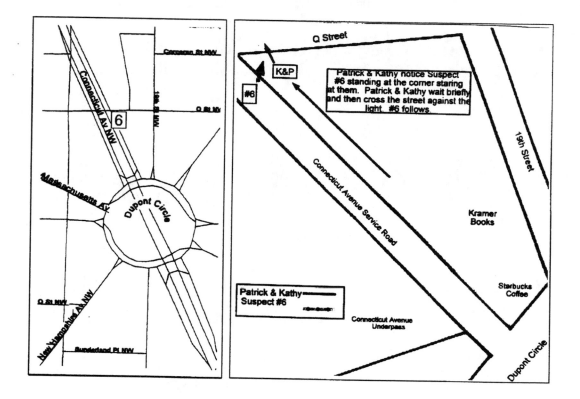

_Patrick's reaction_: I asked Kathy if the guy was staring just at me or at her too. She said that it was only me. As we approached I realized he was staring at me. I became very nervous. It was then that it occurred to me that it may have something to do with the subpoena I received that morning. As he followed us against the light, my legs became rubbery, and I thought we were in trouble. As we walked, we discussed trying to remember what everyone was wearing and what they looked like.

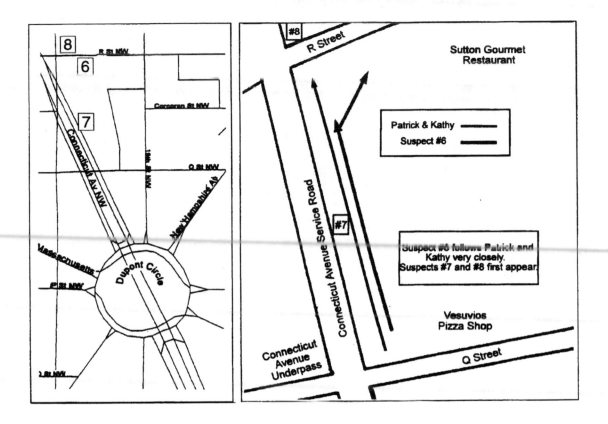

\*     \*     \*

### Suspect 9 - no time elapsed between contacts

*Description:    Male,   Middle   Eastern   features.
Approximately 5'8", 190, 40s.   Short dark wavy
hair,  mustache,  clear complexion,  olive-colored
skin, stocky upper build, physically fit, brown
tweed jacket, open light-colored shirt, olive-
colored pants, black soft-soled shoes.*

Patrick   and   Kathy   walked   to   the   median   strip
between   the   northbound   and   southbound   lanes   of
Connecticut  Avenue,  waiting  for  a  break  in  the
traffic  to  reach  the  west  side.   Patrick  noticed
a  man  standing  on  the  northwest  corner  of  R
Street  and  Connecticut  Avenue,  staring  directly
at  them.    Patrick  directed  Kathy's  attention  to
this  man.     As   soon   as   they   began   to   cross
Connecticut   Avenue,   this   man,   continuing   to
stare,  began  to  cross  R  Street,  so  that  the  man

reached the southwest corner of Connecticut and R Street at the same time as Patrick and Kathy. After reaching the corner, Patrick and Kathy walked arm-in-arm southbound on Connecticut Avenue. The man also walked southbound, to the left and three feet abreast of Kathy. He looked over Kathy and directly at Patrick's face for approximately 15 seconds as the three walked.

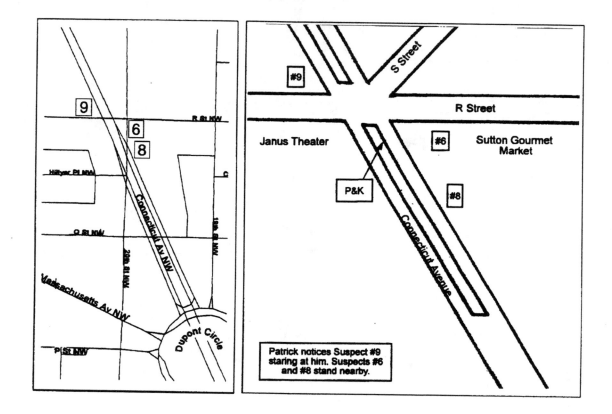

Patrick notices Suspect #9 staring at him. Suspects #6 and #8 stand nearby.

Patrick and Kathy were now in fear for their safety. In an effort to escape the man's glare, Patrick and Kathy, still walking arm-in-arm, increased their pace. Patrick looked back and noticed that the man was walking faster, but that they had separated themselves from the man by a distance of about 15 feet. Kathy and Patrick decided to try and regain their composure by stopping and acting as if they were reading a menu displayed in a restaurant window. As they stopped, the man passed by slowly while continuing to glare at Patrick's face. The man

walked until he reached a real estate office
three doors down, where he stopped and looked in
that window. During the two or three minutes that
they all were stopped, the man intermittently
looked to his right at Patrick and Kathy.
Patrick and Kathy began to walk back toward
Patrick's home and the man. As they began to
walk southbound, the man began to walk
southbound, looking back every few seconds.
Patrick and Kathy slowed their pace, almost to a
stop. The man did the same. Patrick and Kathy
stopped and looked at another restaurant menu
display. The man also stopped, and again looked
at Patrick and Kathy every few seconds. Patrick
and Kathy decided to walk at a brisk pace, back
to the CVS drugstore, then home, without looking
or paying attention to anyone on the streets.
The man watched intently as they departed. This
contact lasted for about seven minutes.

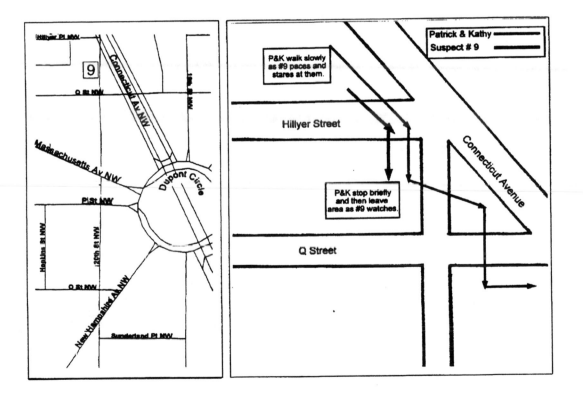

*Patrick's reaction*: *When the man looked at me, I really became panicked. My legs were like rubber. All these men were making it very obvious. So I said let's walk back. I didn't want to take a cab or the metro. I just wanted to walk back to our neighborhood very briskly and not look at anybody.*

\*     \*     \*

## Early Friday afternoon, October 27, 1995:

Suspects 16 & 17 - about thirty seconds later
*Description 16 (driver[530]): Male, Middle Eastern features. Approximately early-30s. Short neatly cut wavy hair, mustache, dark eyes, glasses, open-collared white shirt, healthy looking.*

*Description 17 (passenger[531]): Male, Middle Eastern features. Approximately early-30s. Straight neatly cut dark hair, dark eyes, mustache, healthy looking.*

Chris [journalist Christopher Ruddy] and Patrick continued walking around Washington Circle. As they walked around the Circle, they observed a white Honda stopped in a no-parking zone in the northbound lane of 23rd Street, at Washington Circle. The car was occupied by two men, both of whom were staring in their direction. The two men glared at Patrick

---

[530]  See Knowlton v. Edwards, et al., US District Court CA No. 96-2467:

22. Defendant Ayman Alouri (hereinafter "AYMAN ALOURI") is an individual whose residence address is 2300 Pimmit Drive, Apartment 704 West, Falls Church, Virginia. AYMAN ALOURI was born in the country of Jordan and is a naturalized citizen of the United States.

[531]  See Knowlton v. Edwards, et al., US District Court CA No. 96-2467:

23. Defendant Abdel Salem Alouri (hereinafter "ABDEL ALOURI") is an individual whose last known residence address is 5800 Quantrell Avenue, Apartment 1511, Alexandria, Virginia. ABDEL ALOURI was born in the country of Jordan. His citizenship is unknown to Plaintiff.

and Chris as they crossed in front of them at 23rd Street. When they got about twenty feet past the intersection, both Chris and Patrick glanced back. The two men were still staring. The car started, and proceeded very slowly onto the circle. As the car proceeded past them, the passenger gave Patrick a continuous glare. The car went around the circle, out of sight.

After Patrick and Chris walked for about another thirty seconds, the car approached them again from behind, and as it drove slowly past, both occupants glared at Patrick. The car slowed about sixty feet ahead, then stopped. Chris and Patrick stopped walking. Both occupants then adjusted the car mirrors so as to watch Chris and Patrick.

> *Patrick's reaction:* At first, I didn't want to believe that these guys were there watching me. When they drove away, I thought I was right, they weren't there watching me. But when they drove around the circle and slowly came back staring at me, and stopped their car, I realized that they were involved, and I was again scared that we may be in danger.

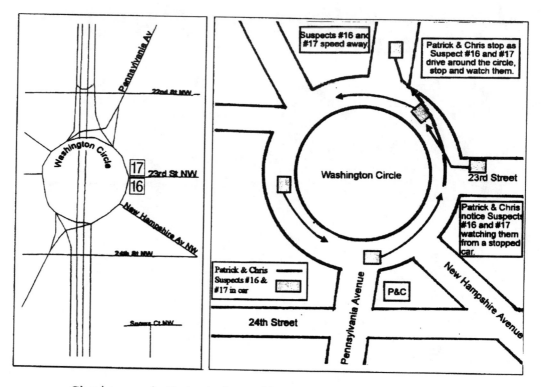

Chris and Patrick walked in the direction of the car, observed the license plate, whereupon the car ran a light and sped away.[532]

---

[532]  See Ambrose Evans-Pritchard, *Death mystery plot thickens*, London Sunday Telegraph, November 5, 1995:

> Knowlton and Ruddy snapped some photos and wrote down the registration numbers of two cars that were engaged in an obvious attempt to intimidate. It turns out that both cars are owned by young Arabs living in the Washington suburbs of Northern Virginia.
>
> Just to be certain we found the right people, we paid a midnight visit to one of the owners at his rented house near Largely. Two Arabs came to the door and Ruddy recognized them instantly as the driver and the passenger of a white Honda that had trailed them. Knowlton, further back in the shadows, said he recognized the driver at once. To our surprise, the license plates were clearly displayed in the parking spot in front of the house, but they were attached to a different car... We chatted on the doorstep. One of the Arabs - let us call him Aymen - did all the talking. The other just stared at us... He denied any involvement in

Suspects 18 (about thirty seconds later), 19, 20, 21(6), 22, & 23

*Description 18:* Male, Middle Eastern features. Approximately 5'8", 170 lbs, early-30s...

As Suspect 18 passed and changed direction eastbound, he gave Patrick a continuous blank stare. Suspect 18 walked ahead of Patrick and Chris, so they slowed their pace. For the next half block, every few seconds Suspect 18 looked back at Patrick's face.

As Chris and Patrick approached the middle of the block, Suspect 19 passed them on Chris' left, while staring at Patrick's face. When Suspect 19 got about five paces in front of them, Chris approached him and tried to speak to him, whereupon the man walked into the building then to his right, the Humana Health Clinic. Patrick and Chris stood outside the door and watched Suspect 19, who was clearly out of place surrounded by a roomful of mostly juvenile patients.

As Patrick and Chris continued to walk eastbound, they noticed Suspect 18 standing on the sidewalk about 60 feet ahead looking in their direction. Suspect 18 then resumed walking eastbound ahead of them. Suspect 18 turned right on 21st Street, toward Eye Street. He crossed Eye Street and walked eastbound in front of the 2000 Penn Mall. Patrick and Chris followed. As Chris and Patrick entered that block, Suspect 20 walked directly toward Patrick, giving Patrick a purposeful glare. Suspect 20 passed Patrick on his right, continuously glaring at him. Patrick and Chris then entered the 2000 Penn Mall.

---

the surveillance of Knowlton. But he paled when we told him that we had photos of the goon squad.

Ayman had the air of a man who had been contracted to do some low level harassment and had now found himself way out of his depth...

Five minutes later, Patrick and Chris left through the main exit. Standing about 50 feet to their right were Suspect 18 and Suspect 20, conversing. Suspect 20 looked toward Chris and Patrick, and began walking toward them. Suspect 18 then talked into his shirtsleeve and crossed 20th Street...

*Description 21(6)* *(Same man as Suspect 6): White male. Approximately 6'4", 225 lbs, 45. Clean-shaven, light-colored hair, slightly balding, light-colored eyes, clear complexion, physically fit, blue suit, white shirt, red tie, wire-rim glasses.*

As Patrick neared the steps into the Deli, he saw Suspect 21(6) staring down at him from the top of the steps. Patrick recognized him as Suspect 6 from the previous evening. As Patrick climbed the steps, Suspect 21(6) descended the steps, staring constantly at Patrick.

*Patrick's reaction: When I recognized him from the night before, I was overcome with fear. I froze at the bottom of the stairs, not knowing whether to walk past him for fear that he would do something to me.*

*Description 22: White male. Approximately 5'10", 190 lbs, late-40s. Dark hair graying on the sides, clean shaven, very clear complexion, black-rimmed glasses, broad shoulders, black suit, white shirt, tie, soft-soled shoes, carrying newspaper, very healthy looking.*

*Description 23: White male. Approximately 6', 190 lbs, late-40s. Rounded face, grayish-light hair, glasses, clean-shaven, gray sport coat, blue dress shirt, tie, healthy looking.*

Patrick exited the building and sat down alone at a sidewalk table. Approximately three minutes later, Suspect 22 bumped his chair from behind, and walked past him while glaring.

As Chris exited the building, Patrick stood up, approached Chris, and pointed out Suspect 22, who was looking in a bank window and peering at Patrick. Suspect 23 then walked past Patrick while glaring at him.

Chris again wanted to approach one of these men. Patrick insisted that they head back to Patrick's home.

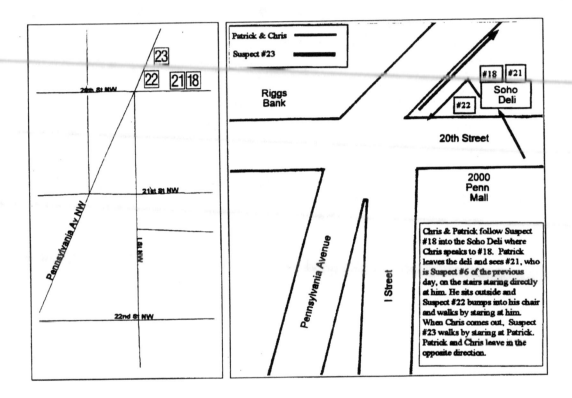

*Patrick's reaction:* I just felt like this was totally unbelievable. It seemed to have escalated beyond what it was the night before. It was more intense. I thought it was so calculated. I felt overwhelmed. By this time I could feel my body shaking. I wanted to go home and be in a safe place, and to call the FBI.

\*　　　\*　　　\*

**KNOWLTON VISITED BY FBI SPECIAL AGENT RUSSELL BRANSFORD, ASSIGNED TO THE OFFICE OF INDEPENDENT COUNSEL**

**Monday afternoon, October 30, 1995:**

Knowlton's lawyer left several messages on FBI Special Agent Russell Bransford's voicemail over the weekend to notify the FBI about the harassment and to request protection. Bransford had given his business card to Knowlton when he served the subpoena the previous Thursday. On Monday, at around noon, Bransford telephoned Knowlton regarding the harassment, and agreed to visit Knowlton at his apartment later that day. Knowlton asked Bransford to call in advance of his visit so Knowlton's lawyer could be present.

Bransford agreed to call in advance, but that afternoon called from his car phone while parked in front of Knowlton's building. Knowlton asked for a few minutes to call his lawyer. Bransford told Knowlton he did not need an attorney, and that he just wanted to talk to him. Knowlton replied that after what had happened to him, he didn't want to talk to anybody without his lawyer present. Knowlton hung up, located his lawyer's number, and picked up the telephone. The telephone line was dead. Knowlton's telephone line had never before (or since) gone dead.

Bransford arrived at Knowlton's door two or three minutes later as Knowlton was checking both his telephone extensions. Knowlton let Bransford in and asked whether he had hung up his phone. Bransford answered that he had hung up his phone, confirmed that the phone was dead, and stated, unsolicited, "If there was a phone tap on there, you'd never know it, they're totally undetectable."

Knowlton told Bransford about the harassment, and asked for protection. Bransford asked several times, "What do you want us to do?" Knowlton consistently responded that he wanted the FBI to do whatever it is that they customarily do for

324

someone in Knowlton's position. Bransford offered to take Knowlton to a hotel where "hopefully no one would follow us," and if harassed to call 911 and then Bransford's pager number. Knowlton asked whether they would leave an agent with him. Bransford said no.

Knowlton was distraught about being harassed. He was unhappy with the FBI because he felt that FBI agents were somehow responsible for his being harassed by falsely recording his information. He also thought the FBI should have responded earlier to his requests for protection.

Frustrated, Knowlton asked Bransford why he was sent there if he wasn't going to do anything for him. Knowlton asked Bransford, "What's your role?" Bransford explained that he worked under Fiske and that he was kept on under Starr. Bransford said he worked with Agents Monroe and Colombell. Knowlton complained that Bransford should not have been selected to come over to Knowlton's home, since his problems stemmed from Monroe's misrepresentations of Knowlton's statements to the FBI. Knowlton asked Bransford whose side he was on, to which Bransford replied he was on Kenneth Starr's side.

Knowlton asked if he should trust Bransford. Bransford answered, "I don't know Mr. Knowlton, that's a good question." Knowlton said, "Get the hell out of my house. I want you to leave now."

\*    \*    \*

## KNOWLTON TESTIFIES BEFORE THE WHITEWATER GRAND JURY

**Wednesday, November 1, 1995:**

"On the morning of the first, I awoke from a very restless sleep. I believe I went to bed nervous and woke up the same way. I felt overwhelmed by events of the past week. The night before I had plenty of phone calls, all kinds of advice on how to handle myself, telling me what to expect, even a fax about grand jury proceedings. I received a great deal of support."

Knowlton arrived at the courthouse with his lawyer and Kathy a few minutes before noon, when he was scheduled to testify. The grand jury took their lunch break at noon. The prosecutor who later conducted all the questioning introduced himself and excused Knowlton until after lunch.

Before entering the grand jury room, Knowlton's lawyer again suggested that Knowlton try and stay as calm as he could, to go slowly and concentrate on exactly what was being asked, to answer as best he could only what was being asked, and not to argue. His lawyer emphatically told Knowlton not to hesitate to request a break whenever he needed one.

Only the witness, the prosecutors, the jurors, and the court reporter are allowed into the grand jury room. Kathy and Knowlton's lawyer waited in the hallway while Knowlton testified.

When Knowlton entered the grand jury room, he was seated facing a majority of the jurors, who were seated sparsely at classroom type desks affixed to chairs on a tiered platform. In front of the jurors were conference tables, with Knowlton at one end and three more jurors at the other (two men and one woman).

The prosecutor who had excused him for lunch was also seated at the conference table to Knowlton's right, in front of the three grand jurors. Another prosecutor, Starr's Washington, D.C. deputy, sat slightly behind and to Knowlton's right. He never introduced himself to Knowlton. Having an unknown person seated behind him made Knowlton feel uneasy. During Knowlton's appearance, this prosecutor never spoke, and passed notes to the questioner.

Witnesses, unlike prosecutors and grand jurors, are not prohibited by law from discussing the proceeding. Knowlton remembers a good deal of what occurred in the grand jury room.

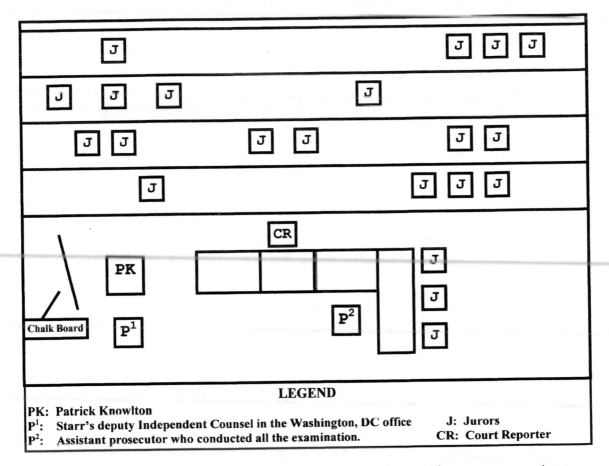

**LEGEND**

PK: Patrick Knowlton
P¹: Starr's deputy Independent Counsel in the Washington, DC office
P²: Assistant prosecutor who conducted all the examination.

J: Jurors
CR: Court Reporter

After Knowlton was sworn in, the prosecutor obtained some background information from him, including his address, birthdate, social security number, age, education and work history. He was then asked when and why he moved to the District of Columbia, when he moved from Washington to Etlan, Virginia, and when he moved back to Washington. The prosecutor asked him to identify and explain his relationship with the two other men who lived in the Etlan residence. Knowlton responded that they were friends and that the Etlan property was a joint real estate venture.

Knowlton then asked to step out of the room into the hallway to briefly ask Kathy if she could remember the dates he moved from Washington to Etlan, and back to Washington. When Knowlton returned, the prosecutor asked him who currently lived in the house in Etlan, whether he owned the house, and to again explain his relationship with the men at the house in Etlan.

Knowlton was asked how he knew about Fort Marcy Park, whether someone told him about the park, how many times he had been there, whether he had ever been there alone before July 20, 1993, and why he stopped at the park that day. After he was asked to tell all his activities from the time he left Etlan through the time he returned, he was asked what he saw at Fort Marcy Park.

The prosecutor asked him to again identify and explain his relationship with the other men who owned the house in Etlan, Virginia. When asked why he waited so long to come forward, Knowlton responded that he reported what he saw in July of 1993, and believed it was up to investigators to get back to him if they needed him. The prosecutor sat resting his head on his hand, as if the testimony was of little or no importance. Knowlton felt his character was being attacked.

Knowlton asked for a short break, whereupon he stepped into the hallway and briefly complained to his lawyer that "they are trying to discredit" him.

When he returned, the prosecutor asked whether Knowlton still went to the house in Etlan, and whether he was listed in the telephone book in either Washington or Etlan. Knowlton answered that he still went to Etlan on weekends, that he was not listed in the phone book at either residence.

The prosecutor reviewed the relevant portion of the US Park Police Report. He stated that the Park Police reported that Knowlton had said that the blue-gray sedan had Virginia tags, and that the FBI reported the same thing. The prosecutor then asked Knowlton if he told investigators that the car had Virginia tags. Knowlton responded that he had not.

When the prosecutor asked Knowlton why he waited two days before calling the police, he responded that he called on the same day he saw the news report that Mr. Foster's body was found, which was the day after the body was discovered. (The police report was dated July 22 because Knowlton called after midnight.)

The prosecutor again questioned Knowlton about how long he had been at Fort Marcy Park on July 20, 1993. He asked why Knowlton did not leave the park upon his arrival if the man who stared at him scared him so much. Knowlton responded that he urgently needed to urinate, and that he was only in the park for four or five minutes. Regarding the brown Honda, he was asked whether he saw the date on the license plates and whether he was aware that diplomatic plates were red, white and blue, as are Arkansas plates. Knowlton answered that he did not see the date on the plate, and that he was aware that diplomatic plates are red, white, and blue.

Regarding the items in the brown Honda, he was asked where the jacket was placed, did he see a folder, and what color was the folder. Knowlton responded that he never used the word folder, and that he did not see a folder in the car, but rather a briefcase. The prosecutor then asked Knowlton why he now says he saw wine coolers in the brown Honda, when they are not mentioned in the FBI report, and whether he heard that evidence showed wine cooler traces on Mr. Foster's clothes. He responded that he told the FBI and the Park Police that he saw two wine coolers in the back of the brown Honda, and that he never heard any reports of wine cooler traces on Foster's clothes.

The prosecutor then asked Knowlton about his involvement with the press, including who had contacted him, whether he had contacted any reporters, and whether he had been paid for his story. Knowlton responded that his first contact with the Press occurred on October 13, 1995. He also said that a number of reporters had contacted him since that time, that he had not contacted the Press, that he had not been offered money for his story. He was asked whether he had been contacted by anyone on Capitol Hill, including House members, Senators, or their staff, to which he responded that he had not.

Knowlton was briefly asked about the "alleged misquotes" in the FBI 302 reports of his statements. He was not given a copy to review. Knowlton suggested that the prosecutor look at the hand written notes taken by Agent Monroe. The prosecutor responded that there were "no notes available." [The notes were later produced under a Freedom of Information Request.]

The prosecutor asked whether there was anything unusual about the front seat of the brown Honda, and whether it was positioned forward or back. He read the portion of the FBI report which states that Knowlton "could not further identify this particular individual (the man in the blue-gray sedan) nor his attire," and asked him whether he had said that. Knowlton responded that he had not.

The prosecutor next asked with whom Knowlton spoke in preparing his testimony and when those conversations took place. He was specifically asked to include all reporters, and the times those conversations took place. After answering, Knowlton asked to take a short break.

When the testimony recommenced, he again told Knowlton to identify everyone to whom he had related his story since July of 1993. Knowlton responded that he had told many people, including family and friends, and that he had even told the story at dinner parties. Then he asked Knowlton to again state his contacts with the Press and Capitol Hill. He replied that he already answered that question.

The prosecutor then focused on Evans-Pritchard's October 22 *Sunday Telegraph* article, asking whether Knowlton really felt threatened, whether he thought the man in the park was really going to kill him, and did the FBI badger him.

Knowlton responded that Evans-Pritchard's article was accurate except that Knowlton didn't use the words "kill" or "badger." Knowlton said that after he read the article, he called Evans-Pritchard and asked him to change the statements, and that Evans-Pritchard agreed.

The prosecutor followed up by questioning Knowlton about the frequency of his contacts with Evans-Pritchard. Knowlton answered that he had frequent contacts with Evans-Pritchard. He said he called Evans-Pritchard and the FBI when he was harassed, but only Evans-Pritchard responded that weekend. He was then asked what advice he received from journalists and whether he received a call or fax from Evans-Pritchard the previous day. Knowlton answered he had received a fax from Evans-Pritchard about grand jury procedure the previous day. At this point, Knowlton had testified for about an hour and 45 minutes. He was very irritated.

The prosecutor asked when Knowlton first spoke with an attorney, the name of the attorney, and whether his attorney was at the courthouse that day. Why did he need an attorney, the prosecutor queried. Knowlton replied that he felt he needed representation due to the harassment he had suffered and to deal with members of the Press who were contacting him.

He asked if he knew "CW" (the "confidential witness" who discovered the body). Knowlton said he did not know CW, whereupon the prosecutor asked Knowlton whether he had ever talked to or met CW. He answered no. Knowlton was then asked whether he had received any information that wine coolers were found next to Foster's body. Knowlton responded that his lawyer's office received a fax about the wine coolers, but that Knowlton had not seen it.

Toward the end of the questioning, the prosecutor said, "Tell us about the alleged harassment, Mr. Knowlton." Knowlton responded that it "was not alleged, it happened." He then repeatedly asked that the prosecutors tell him who sent agent

331

Bransford to his house.  The prosecutor responded twice that they were not there to answer Knowlton's questions.  When Knowlton adamantly asked again, the prosecutor seated behind him said that they ("we") sent Bransford to his home. Knowlton explained what Bransford had said to him two days earlier, and that Knowlton considered Bransford's actions further harassment.  Knowlton then summarized the harassment which occurred the previous Thursday and Friday [October 26 & 27].

At this point in the proceeding, Knowlton was infuriated.  He asked for a break.  He was angry about not being believed about the harassment and the fact that the prosecutors had sent Bransford to his home.

When the proceeding resumed, Knowlton was asked why he came forward with his story at this time. Knowlton replied that he was approached by Evans-Pritchard.

The prosecutor asked, "Why did you call the police?  Why didn't you wait for someone to call you?"  Knowlton responded that if nobody knew who he was, they would not know to call him. Knowlton then asked whether the prosecutor was suggesting that the man in the blue-gray sedan took down his license plate number.  The prosecutor responded no and asked sarcastically if Knowlton came forward because he is a "good citizen" and a "good Samaritan?"  Knowlton said he came forward because at the time he thought what he saw might have been relevant.

At this point, the prosecutor asked Knowlton to step out of the room so the prosecutors could ask the grand jurors what questions they wanted asked.  After a short break, the lead prosecutor passed a paper to the questioner, who then asked Knowlton a series of questions about the man in the Park in the blue-gray sedan.  Did the man talk to Knowlton?  Did he pass Knowlton a note? Did he approach Knowlton in any way?  Did the man point a gun at him?  Did the man touch him? Knowlton answered no to each of these questions about the man in the blue-gray sedan.

Finally, the prosecutor said he had some questions that the grand jurors wanted asked. Were the wine coolers empty or full? Knowlton said full. Were the doors in the brown Honda locked or unlocked? Knowlton responded he didn't notice. How did he know someone other than the man in the blue-gray sedan hadn't seen him at Fort Marcy Park? Knowlton answered that he didn't know whether someone other than that man had seen him, but he hoped someone else had seen him to verify his actions and the time he was there.

Knowlton began testifying at 1:00 p.m., and was excused at approximately 3:45 p.m. Knowlton was asked about his account of what occurred at Fort Marcy Park and his statements to the FBI for about an hour. Based upon the demeanor of the prosecutors, the questioning, and the fact that one of the prosecutors sat behind him, Knowlton believes that the OIC was trying to rattle and discredit him before the grand jury.

* * *

## HARASSMENT

**Thursday afternoon, November 2, 1995:**

Suspect # 27
*Description: Male, Middle Eastern features. Approximately 5'8", 160 lbs, 30s. Short, black neatly-cut hair, dark eyes, clear complexion, mustache, carrying black canvass bag open at the top, black-rimmed glasses, army issue green three-quarter length coat, light beige pants, black shoes.*

At about 3:30 p.m., Patrick went down to the lobby of his apartment building. As he exited the elevator, he noticed a man standing outside the building with his back to the building. As Patrick walked toward the front door, another tenant entered, and the man followed into Patrick's building. As soon as the man made eye contact with Patrick, he became startled, and immediately turned around, walked out the door, and stood looking at the newspaper box to the left of the entrance with his back to Patrick. With his back to the building, he took short steps, side to side, as if he was nervous.

Patrick walked out the door, turned right, walked about 20 feet, looked back and saw the man walking behind him about 15 feet slightly to his left. Patrick continued about another 80 feet to the corner to another newspaper box. As he retrieved the paper, he looked up and to his left, and saw the man looking down and reaching into his bag with his right hand. The man looked up, made eye contact with Patrick, and quickly pulled his hand out of the bag and dropped the bag to his side.

Seconds after Patrick started walking toward his building, they walked past each other. About ten feet after they passed, Patrick looked behind him and saw the man standing on the corner looking back at Patrick.

Patrick then turned around and walked toward the man. The man turned and ran. He ran diagonally across 24th Street, across K Street, and onto Washington Circle.

> *Patrick's reaction:* As the man reached into his bag, I was scared. I thought he was reaching for a gun. Then the fear turned into anger. I felt fed-up and decided to confront the guy. I thought if the guy was going to shoot me, he better shoot me. When he ran away, the reality of being in danger sunk in, and the anger turned back to fear.

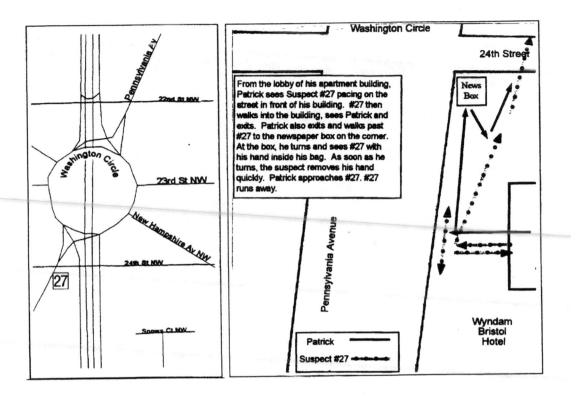

From the lobby of his apartment building, Patrick sees Suspect #27 pacing on the street in front of his building. #27 then walks into the building, sees Patrick and exits. Patrick also exits and walks past #27 to the newspaper box on the corner. At the box, he turns and sees #27 with his hand inside his bag. As soon as he turns, the suspect removes his hand quickly. Patrick approaches #27. #27 runs away.

Patrick ——————

Suspect #27 ●—●—●—●—●

*Friday afternoon, November 3, 1995:* When he went out the next day at around 2:00 p.m., Patrick walked from his apartment building to the Crestar Bank at 1925 K Street, then to Riggs Bank on Pennsylvania Avenue at 20th Street.

Suspect 28
*Description: White male. Approximately 6', 190 lbs, late-30s or early-40s. Healthy appearance, clean shaven...*

\*       \*       \*

c.     **The civilian couple at the park**

The OIC begins its seven page *Briefcase* discussion by posing five questions to prove that a briefcase was not in Mr. Foster's Honda.

OIC, p. 85:

*To determine whether a briefcase (and perhaps that black briefcase) was in Mr. Foster's car at Fort Marcy Park, five related questions must be considered: 1. Did those who saw Mr. Foster leave the White House on July 20 see him with a briefcase? 2. Was a briefcase observed in Mr. Foster's car at Fort Marcy Park? 3. Did the Park Police return a briefcase to the Secret Service that evening? 4. Was a briefcase in Mr. Foster's office at the White House after his death? 5. How many briefcases did Mr. Foster use?*

None of these questions discloses the existence of the brown Arkansas Honda in which, according to at least four witnesses, there was a briefcase -- "recovered" by Sergeant Edwards.[533]  So the OIC's conclusion, that *"neither it nor another briefcase was in his car at Fort Marcy Park,"* is accurate.  But it deceptively omits the existence of the other Arkansas Honda in the lot.[534]

---

[533]     Exhibit 135, Report of FBI interview of Paramedic George Gonzalez, February 23, 1994:  "[T]he Honda contained a necktie, suit-coat, and a black briefcase / attache case."  Exhibit 66, Report of FBI interview of Firefighter Todd Hall, March 18, 1994: "Also contained in the car was a briefcase...  Hall noted that the aforementioned vehicle with the suit coat and briefcase bore Arkansas tags."  Exhibit 79, Deposition of Park Police Officer Kevin Fornshill, July 12, 1994:  "Q. Did you see a briefcase?  A. Possibly."  Exhibit 173, Report of FBI interview of Patrick Knowlton, April 15, 1994:  "He further stated that he observed in this Honda a leather briefcase or leather folder on the passenger side seat."  Exhibit 58, Transcript of radio transmission, Park Police:  "[B]riefcase recovered."

[534]     See also Exhibit 12, Fiske Report, June 30, 1994:  Another man stated that he drove into Fort Marcy Park between 4:15 and 4:30 p.m.  He observed two cars in the parking lot of the Park at that time.  He described one as a brown Japanese made car with an Arkansas license plate.  When shown photographs of Foster's car, he stated that the car he saw appeared darker in color and more compact.  He stated that nobody was in the car, but there was a man's

### The civilian couple at the park

The descriptions of the car provided by two other civilians also generally fits the description of the car Patrick saw, not Mr. Foster's. This couple arrived at the park between 5:15 and 5:30, 40 to 55 minutes after Patrick had left the park at 4:35. (Their names are withheld in deference to their privacy.)

The couple pulled into the lot, sat in their car a while, then went into the woods. When they walked from the lot, this car, at the time the only one in the lot besides theirs, was parked in the very spot where Mr. Foster's car was later recovered. The couple was still there when police arrived. Officer Julie Spetz brought them back to the parking lot for questioning.

The FBI reported that the lady said the car was a mid-1980's model and that a man, possibly bare-chested, had been sitting in the driver's seat.

> [T]he only vehicle in the parking area was a relatively old (mid-1980's) Honda, possibly a Honda Accord, either tan or dark in color, parked... adjacent to a path leading to the northern section of the park... believes a white male was seated in the driver's seat of this particular vehicle... had dark hair and could have been bare chested.[535]

According to the FBI's report of its interview with her gentleman friend, he noticed the hood of this car was up and a man standing around it.

> The hood of the [brownish-colored] vehicle was up and a white male was standing in the vicinity of the vehicle. He described the white male as in his mid-to late 40's, approximately six feet in height, medium

---

> suit jacket folded over the passenger seat of the car. He recalls that the car was parked in one of the first spaces on the left side of the lot, which is where the Park Police found Foster's car following his death. The Park Police also found Foster's suit jacket draped over the front passenger seat of his car.

[535] Exhibit 150, Report of FBI interview with Female Civilian, April 7, 1994.

build, long blonde hair and beard, appeared unclean and unkempt."[536]

The OIC simply reports (p. 69) that the couple *"did "not see anyone in or touching Mr. Foster's car."* This is true because Foster's car was not in the lot, and dishonest without mentioning that the couple saw men in and around another Arkansas car in the lot, before they walked into the woods.

Park Police Investigator Cheryl Braun reported that the couple saw a third car which parked alongside "the deceased's car," and that this car "left shortly after their arrival."[537] But the gentleman said the car was still parked there when they went into the woods,[538] and the female reported that the Park Police report of her interview "was untrue."[539]

### d.    Other evidence that Mr. Foster's car may not have been at the park

The OIC's discussion of the cars at the scene is spread out under the three sections of its Report.[540] The Report tells us that two cars were in the Fort Marcy parking lot when authorities arrived.[541] The Report falsely

---

[536]    Exhibit 151, Report of FBI interview with Male Civilian, April 5, 1994.

[537]    Exhibit 116, Park Police Report by Investigator Cheryl Braun, July 20, 1993.

[538]    Exhibit 116, Park Police Report by Investigator Cheryl Braun, July 20, 1993.

[539]    Exhibit 150, Report of FBI interview of Female Civilian, April 7, 1994:  "In recalling this particular [Park Police] interview, [Female Civilian] stated that she is positive that her initial comments that a vehicle that she observed as a light-colored older model pulling in next to the Honda was untrue."

[540]    See OIC, p. 21, *Fort Marcy* section; p. 68-69, *Unidentified Persons and Cars* section; and p. 87-89, *Mr. Foster's car at Fort Marcy* subsection under seven-page *Briefcase* discussion (85-91).

[541]    OIC, p. 68-69:  "[T]hree cars belonging to civilians were in and around the Fort Marcy parking lot area when the first Park Police and FCFRD personnel arrived: (1) Mr. Foster's gray Honda Accord with Arkansas tags; (2) the

states that one of these cars was Mr. Foster's, and that these cars are the *"only cars positively identified and known to law enforcement and the OIC."*

In fact, the OIC ignores evidence that suggests that Mr. Foster's silver-gray Honda still may not have arrived in the park when the ambulance crew responded around 8:00 p.m. to transport the body. The FBI's report of its interview with Firefighter Corey Ashford relates that he observed a "black Cadillac," a "dark red" Honda, and police cars including an "unmarked White Ford Crown Victoria."[542] Ashford drew a diagram depicting where these cars were parked. Ashford drew a "dull red Honda" in the parking spot where Mr. Foster's Honda was officially parked.

## 2. Car keys not at the park

The Fiske Report had deceptively implied that Mr. Foster's car keys were found at Fort Marcy Park.

> Park Police investigators observed a suit jacket that matched the pants worn by Foster, neatly folded over the passenger seat of the car. In the jacket was Foster's White House identification. The keys to the car were located in Foster's pants pocket. The car was impounded and searched, but nothing significant to the investigation was found.[543]

But police had searched Mr. Foster's pants pockets, as well as the Honda at the park, and found no keys. This fact was problematic for the official version that Mr. Foster had driven his car to the park. Park Police Investigator John Rolla had testified that he and Investigator Cheryl Braun "were puzzled why [they] found no keys to the car,"[544] yet police disregarded this obvious evidence of foul play.

---

white Nissan... and (3) the broken-down blue Mercedes... [outside the lot on the parkway entrance] ...only cars positively identified and known to law enforcement and the OIC..."

[542]  Exhibit 139, Report of FBI interview of Firefighter Corey Ashford, April 27, 1994.

[543]  Exhibit 12, Fiske Report, June 30, 1994.

[544]  Exhibit 6, Deposition of Park Police Investigator John

## Car keys not at the park

The keys were not located until hours later at the hospital morgue, when Police investigators again searched the same pants pockets, without having first searched anywhere else.

Investigator Rolla, who searched the pockets, would have had to have missed two sets of key rings, both found later in Mr. Foster's right pants pocket at the morgue. One ring, containing Mr. Foster's personal keys, contained at least four keys and a tab marked "Vince's Keys." Also in Mr. Foster's right front pants pocket was a second key ring with his White House keys. On this ring were two tabs (a plastic tab and a large metal inscribed tab) and four keys (two door keys, a cabinet drawer type key, and an inscribed high security key with Medeco-type cuts[545]). Had these two sets of key rings been in Mr. Foster's pocket, the chances of Rolla's having missed them are not good.

The OIC does not tell its readers that there were two sets of keys and does not describe them. It simply claims that the keys were there but that Rolla had missed finding them.

OIC, p. 74:

*Investigator Rolla said he felt into Mr. Foster's pants pockets at the scene in looking for personal effects.[fn216] Later, when it became apparent to Investigators Rolla and Braun that they did not have the keys to the car, they went to the hospital to check more thoroughly for keys.[fn217] The hospital logs indicate that Investigators Rolla and Braun were at the morgue at 9:12 p.m.[fn218] Investigator Braun*

---

Rolla, July 21, 1994: Q. Did you get any keys? A. I searched his pants pockets. I couldn't find a wallet or nothing in his pants pockets. Later on Investigator Braun and myself searched the car... We searched the car and we were puzzled why we found no keys to the car... As it turned out Investigator Braun and myself went to the morgue in Fairfax hospital, after we made a death notification to recheck him.

[545] Exhibit 95, FBI Lab Report, May 9, 1994. See also Exhibit 152, Park Police Evidence/Property Control Receipt, July 20, 1993.

*thoroughly searched the pants pockets by pulling the pockets inside out, and she found two sets of keys.*[fn219]

A footnote to this passage cites a still secret report of an April 1996 FBI interview report of Investigator Rolla.

OIC, p. 74, fn. 216:

*...Investigator Rolla has said that he did not reach to the bottom of the suit pants pockets at the time he took personal effects into evidence at the scene. 302, 4/17/96, at 3.*

Another footnote relates that Rolla did not really search the pants pockets at the park, but had simply *"patted the pants."*

OIC, p. 74, fn. 220:

*USPP Evidence/Property Control Receipt (Braun) at 1-2. The evidence indicates that no persons other than police, rescue, medical, and hospital personnel had access to the body from the time when Investigator Rolla patted the pants at the park until the time when Investigator Braun recovered the keys in the pants pocket at the hospital.*

This version is at odds with the account Rolla had earlier provided to the FBI, with Rolla's sworn testimony on deposition, his sworn testimony before the Senate, as well as the accounts of Park Police Investigators Cheryl Braun and Christine Hodakievic.

When he testified before the Senate Banking Committee in June of 1994, Rolla testified that he had "emptied the pockets."

Q.  You didn't search his person at the scene did you?
A.  After it was pronounced, we emptied his pockets. Yes, I did remove his personal property and search them.[546]

---

[546]  Exhibit 171, Senate testimony of Park Police Investigator John Rolla, July 20, 1995.

**Car keys not at the park**

During his July 21, 1994, deposition, Rolla testified that police were perplexed by the absence of Mr. Foster's car keys.

"I searched his pants pockets. I couldn't find a wallet or nothing in his pants pockets... we searched the car and we were puzzled why we found no keys to the car."[547]

The FBI's report of its April 27, 1994, interview with Rolla also reflects that he was looking for the keys when he searched the pockets.

"Rolla advised that he specifically recalled searching the decedents (sic) front pants pockets in an attempt to locate the keys to the decedent's 1989 Honda, advising that he was unsuccessful in locating the car keys."[548]

Rolla's search was thorough enough to exclude the existence of a suicide note, according to the FBI's report of its April, 1994, interview of Park Police Investigator Cheryl Braun.

"She observed Officer Rolla check the pants pockets, both front and rear, in an effort to find identification or a possible suicide note."[549]

The FBI's report of its May, 1994, interview with Christine Hodakievic states that she "does recall Investigator John Rolla checking the decedent's body for identification specifically the decedent's front and rear pockets."[550]

The absence of the keys at the park presented another problem for the FBI. Associate White House Counsel William

---

[547] Exhibit 6, Deposition of Park Police Investigator John Rolla, July 21, 1994.

[548] Exhibit 100, Report of FBI interview of Park Police Investigator John Rolla, April 27, 1994.

[549] Exhibit 91, Report of FBI interview of Park Police Investigator Cheryl Braun, April 28, 1994.

[550] Exhibit 81, Report of FBI interview of Park Police Investigator Christine Hodakievic, May 2, 1994.

Kennedy and Chief of White House Personnel Security Craig Livingstone had visited Mr. Foster's body at the morgue. The issue, then, is whether one of these men planted the keys. To solve this problem, the OIC claims that Kennedy and Livingstone visited the morgue after Braun had retrieved the keys at the morgue. And the OIC posits that, in any event, these White House personnel were not allowed in the same room as the body.

OIC, p. 74-75, fn. 220:

> *USPP Evidence/Property Control Receipt (Braun) at 1-2. The evidence indicates that no persons other than police, rescue, medical, and hospital personnel had access to the body from the time when Investigator Rolla patted the pants at the park until the time when Investigator Braun recovered the keys in the pants pocket at the hospital. Two White House officials (William Kennedy and Craig Livingstone) viewed the body at the hospital, but the hospital logs reflect that they viewed the body near 10:30 p.m., OIC Doc. No. DC-108-13 -- well <u>after</u> Investigators Braun and Rolla had retrieved the keys. Moreover, a Fairfax County Police officer stationed on regular assignment at the hospital that evening and a nursing supervisor escorted Mr. Kennedy and Mr. Livingstone, and allowed them to see the body only through a glass window. Officer 302, 2/10/95, at 2.*

The OIC's version that Kennedy and Livingstone visited the morgue after Investigators Rolla and Braun did can be true only if these Investigators visited the morgue before proceeding to the Foster residence, where they made a death notification. The times of these events are seldom found in the record. But witnesses' accounts of events do appear in the record relative to the known times of when the body was transported to the hospital morgue, of witnesses' arrival at the Foster home, and the time that the President began and completed his *Larry King Live* interview.

Rolla testified that "Braun and myself went to the morgue in Fairfax hospital after we made a death notification... [and that] [a]fter we left the [Fort Marcy] scene, myself and Investigator Braun were heading to Mr. Foster's residence in Georgetown to make death notification... [when] Lieutenant Gavin called us... [and]

343

said to call this guy named David Watkins [while they were] in the car on the way to make the death notification."[551]

The FBI's account in the report of its interview with Rolla puts these events in the opposite sequence.

Investigator Rolla departed the Fort Marcy Park... and in the company of Investigator Braun traveled to Fairfax County Hospital where they located in the right front trouser pocket of the decedent the keys... subsequent to the discovery of these keys... he [Rolla] and Investigator Braun picked up Mr. David Watkins... and proceeded to the Foster residence.[552]

Rolla testified that Kennedy and Livingstone obtained permission to view the body before David Watkins had requested that he accompany the Park Police to the Foster home to notify the family.[553] Because the Park Police arrived at the Foster home by 10:00 p.m.,[554] Kennedy had to have obtained permission to view the body before this time.

The testimony of both Rolla and Braun corroborate that after they picked up Watkins and his wife, they arrived at the Foster home at the same time as Web Hubbell and Sheila Anthony.[555] The only contact Rolla and Braun had with

---

[551] Exhibit 6, Deposition of Park Police Investigator John Rolla, July 21, 1994.

[552] Exhibit 100, Report of FBI interview of Park Police Investigator John Rolla, April 27, 1994.

[553] Exhibit 6, Deposition of Park Police Investigator John Rolla, July 21, 1994: Q. After you okayed them [Kennedy and Livingstone] to go identify the body at the hospital, then you were told to call Watkins; is that right? A. Somewhere around there. I mean, I talked to Livingstone, I did at least three phone calls in the car. In between I was told to call this guy Watkins a personal friend.

[554] Exhibit 176, Senate testimony of Park Police Investigator Cheryl Braun, July 20, 1995: "Q. Is it fair to say you arrived there sometime between 10:00 and 10:30 in the evening? A. As my recollection serves me, it was around 10:00 p.m."

[555] Exhibit 6, Deposition of Park Police Investigator John Rolla, July 21, 1994: A. Unfortunately everybody showed up as we were walking up to the door, so it was a circus-like atmosphere. And -- who's that big guy -- I think he

Kennedy and Livingstone was by car telephone as Rolla was
on the way to David Watkins' home.[556]

Secret Service Agent Dennis Martin testified that when
Livingstone called him from his car telephone "between 8:30
[and] 9:00 p.m.," Livingstone was "enroute... to the
location of the body in the morgue."[557]

---

was a member of the Rose Law Firm also, I forget his.  Q.
Is it in your conversation with the FBI?  A.  It might be.
He was just in the news recently.  He was there, I think it
was Sheila Anthony.  I am not sure if his elder sister was
there.  There were two sisters, two women, one being Sheila
Anthony and this other guy, just a huge guy.  I know he is
in the limelight.  Q.  Webster Hubbell?  A.  Webster
Hubbell, right, Web Hubbell.  And there were a couple of
other -- we had David Watkins, his wife, Web Hubbell,
Sheila Anthony and I think another woman which I think was
the other sister, I am pretty sure.

Exhibit 101, Deposition of Park Police Investigator Cheryl Braun,
July 23, 1994:  "Mr. Watkins was with us, and at the same time we
were walking up to the front steps of Mr. Foster's house, a whole
entourage, which included Web Hubbell... got there at about the
same time we did."

[556]   Exhibit 114, Deposition of Park Police Investigator John
Rolla, July 20, 1995:  "I got a call on the car phone from
Lieutenant Gavin...  [W]e were rerouted en route to the Watkins
house... to pick up a close friend to make the notification
with...  There was another phone call.  Bill Kennedy and Craig
Livingston... they wanted... to see the body."

[557]   Exhibit 153, Deposition of Secret Service Agent Dennis
Martin, June 22, 1995:  Q.  Roughly what time was it when
you reached Mr. Livingstone?  A.  It was before 9:00 in the
evening.  I received a call -- maybe it was about 20
minutes after I received the initial call.  Q.  And if the
initial call was around 8:30, your guess, therefore it was
before 9:00?  A.  Yes.  Q.  Where did you reach Mr.
Livingstone?  A.  It seemed like it was a portable phone or
car phone...  Q.  So your best impression is that it was on
a cell phone.  What makes you think that?  A.  Because it
was static, and I think it was discussed.  I think he
mentioned that he was on the car phone, that we might get
lost.  Q.  He was physically in his car?  A.  Yes...  ***
Because I figured he was en route.  Since he was in his
vehicle, he would be en route from there [home].  Q.  To
where?  A.  To the location of the body in the morgue.

Kennedy testified that he went "straight to the hospital" and that he called the Foster home from the Hospital and spoke to Hubbell, who had arrived simultaneously with Rolla and Braun.

> Q. So you called Mr. Foster's home and coincidentally spoke with Mr. Hubbell?
>
> A. Yeah, I don't recall exactly how I got there.   I don't know who answered the phone, but I got to Web, which is not surprising...
>
> Q. What do you recall about your conversation with Mr. Hubbell?
>
> A. I just told him -- I know now that a lot of stuff had occurred while I was at the hospital, such as the Park Police going to notify them and like that, but I, of course, didn't have any idea that had gone on, because I had gone straight to the hospital.  So I just passed on the information that I was at the hospital, and I had seen the body, and I told him -- I told Web I was coming to the house.[558]

The FBI's report of its interview with William Kennedy reflects that between "8:15 and 8:30 p.m.," Kennedy learned that the body was on its way to the morgue, whereupon Kennedy said that he "had to go to the hospital."[559]   Because

---

[558]   Exhibit 46, Deposition of Associate White House Counsel William Kennedy, July 11, 1995.

[559]   Exhibit 7, Report of FBI interview of Associate White House Counsel William Kennedy, May 6, 1994:  [William Kennedy] received a telephone call between 8:15-8:30 p.m. from Craig Livingstone, Director of White House Personnel Security.  Livingstone worked for Kennedy at that time. Livingstone had gotten a call from "an inspector" that Foster was dead.  Kennedy said he was "stunned" at the news...  The body was enroute to a hospital (name not recalled by Kennedy).  Kennedy said that he (Kennedy) had to go to the hospital.  Kennedy did not notify anyone else at the time.  Shortly after his arrival at the hospital, Livingstone also arrived.  They confirmed with a policeman on duty at the hospital that the Foster body was there and that the matter involved the U.S. Park Police.

Exhibit 98, Report of FBI interview of Park Police Lieutenant Patrick Gavin, April 28, 1994, transcribed notes made by Gavin:  --Christina Tea who said White House people were at the hospital to view the body and should she permit

the body was on its way to the hospital between 8:17 and 8:30 p.m., when Kennedy learned of the death, and Kennedy testified that it took him "20 to 25" minutes to get to the hospital,[560] he probably arrived at the hospital before 9:00 p.m. Because the computerized ambulance log demonstrates that the body was deposited in the morgue at 9:00 p.m.,[561] Kennedy likely arrived at the morgue before the body did.

Livingstone's handwritten chronology of the events of the evening of the death, written three days later, July 23, states that he and Kennedy were at the Hospital by 9:30 and viewed the body by 9:45.[562]

Livingstone testified that after he left the Hospital, he and Kennedy drove in the same car to the Kennedy home (in Alexandria, Virginia) to pick up Mrs. Kennedy, and then to the Foster residence. Because these three arrived at the Foster residence, according to Kennedy, between "10:30 and 11:00,"[563] Kennedy and Livingstone had visited the morgue well before 10:30.

---

this. --Officer Tipton Fairfax County Police Department - he talked to Tipton also re White House staffers wanting to see the body and informed Tipton to "let them see the body but make sure they don't disturb or take any effects." -- Craig Livingstone and William Kennedy, identified as White House officials - both these men were at the hospital and wanted to see the body.

[560] Exhibit 46, Deposition of Associate White House Counsel William Kennedy, July 11, 1995: Q. Before you left for the hospital, did you call anyone else in the White House to convey any information of any kind? A. I did not. Q. And I take it you met Mr. Livingstone at the hospital? A. I got there before he did, so it would be better to say he met me there. The answer is yes. Q. How far is Fairfax Hospital from your home? A. Pretty good ways. I couldn't tell you in miles. I mean I could show you on a map where I live, and you could figure it out. It's a pretty good ways. Q. Do you have any estimates in minutes how long it may have taken you? A. 20 to 25 maybe.

[561] Exhibit 154, Electronic log of McLean Fire Station, Ambulance 1, July 20, 1993: "20:59:28"

[562] Exhibit 47, Deposition of Chief of White House Personnel Security Craig Livingstone, July 10, 1995.

[563] Exhibit 47, Deposition of Chief of White House Personnel

The OIC's claim that Kennedy and Livingstone arrived at the morgue at 10:30 p.m. is also contradicted by the accounts of White House Special Counsel Jane Sherburne, Deputy Assistant to the President Bill Burton, White House Chief of Staff Mack McLarty, Webster Hubbell, and David Watkins.

A memorandum written by White House Special Counsel Jane Sherburne sets forth the chronology of events on the evening of July 20, 1993.  It reflects that Kennedy and Livingstone viewed the body at the morgue while the President was appearing on *Larry King Live*.  The President ended that interview at 10:00 p.m.  This memorandum evidences that when David Watkins was notified around 9:00 p.m., Kennedy and Livingstone were "on their way to the hospital."

"Watkins... was told that Kennedy and someone else were on their way to the hospital to identify the body.  He [Watkins] also learned that two people were on their way to the Foster house to notify Mrs.

---

Security Craig Livingstone, July 10, 1995:  Q.  What's the next thing that happened?  A.  We left the hospital.  Q. We meaning who?  A.  Mr. Kennedy and I left the hospital. Q.  Okay.  I neglected to ask you, did you drive to the hospital?  Q.  Alone?  A.  Correct.  Q.  And did you and Mr. Kennedy leave the hospital together?  A.  Yes we did. Q.  Did you get in the same cars or separate cars?  A.  As I recall it, I drove -- as I recall it, I drove Mr. Kennedy in my car to his house.  Q.  Do you know how Mr. Kennedy got to the hospital?  A.  He drove his car.  Q.  So you left Mr. Kennedy's car at the hospital?  A.  Correct.  He was pretty upset.  Q.  Okay then you drove to the Foster residence; is that correct?  A.  No, sir, we drove to Mr. Kennedy's house.  Q.  Okay.  What was your purpose in going to Mr. Kennedy's home?  A.  We picked up his wife.  Q. Okay.  A.  And we switched cars.  Q.  Moving from your car to another of Mr. Kennedy's cars?  A.  Correct.  Q.  And then what happened?  A.  We drove to Mr. Foster's house. Q.  When you arrived at the Foster home that evening, your estimate -- and I realize it's an estimate -- was around 10:30 or 11:00.  Who was there -- 11:00.  Who was there? A.  The President had just arrived.  His vehicles were parking.

Foster. Watkins wanted to go with them. This was
arranged."[564]

This memorandum also relates that Kennedy had viewed
the body before the President had ended his appearance on
*Larry King Live* at 10:00 p.m.

"After viewing the body, Kennedy called McLarty at the
White House and spoke with him briefly. McLarty
already knew about the death; the President was still
on Larry King."[565]

Deputy Assistant to the President Bill Burton testified
that he learned of Foster's death "10 to 15 minutes prior
to" the 9:00 p.m. start of *Larry King Live*. Burton added
that "either Craig Livingstone or Bill Kennedy... were out
at the hospital... [a]nd they confirmed it... [d]uring the
approximately 30-40 minutes..." since the time that Burton
had learned of the death.[566] So that puts Kennedy and

---

[564] Exhibit 44, The White House Sherburne Memo Chronology, May,
15, 1996.

[565] Exhibit 44, White House Sherburne Memo Chronology, May 15,
1996: Kennedy -- left work at 7 p.m. Livingstone called
him at home between 8 and 8:30 and said that Foster was
dead, Craig said he had spoken with the Park Police,
Kennedy was aghast and asked Craig to confirm the
information. Craig called back later and said he had
confirmed that Foster was dead, and said that it had been a
suicide and that the body was found in a park. Craig also
said he had learned from the Park Police that the body was
en route to a hospital. Kennedy was familiar with the
hospital and said he would meet Livingstone there. Kennedy
arrived first. It took 45 minutes before they could get
confirmation that the body was there. Finally, they were
permitted to see the body. After viewing the body, Kennedy
called McLarty at the White House and spoke with him
briefly. McLarty already knew about the death; the
President was still on Larry King.

[566] Exhibit 122, Deposition of Deputy Assistant to the
President Bill Burton, July 5, 1995: Q. Do you remember
approximately when [you learned of Foster's death]? A. It
was approximately before the President's broadcast of the
Larry King show from the residence of the White House
started [9:00]. I would guess 15 to 10 minutes prior to
that... Q. And do you remember how you learned that it
was Mr. Foster's body who had been discovered? A. Later

Livingstone at the morgue by 9:40 p.m., consistent with the White House Sherburne Memo chronology of confirmation by Kennedy and Livingstone before the President's appearance on *Larry King Live* ended at 10:00 p.m.

Testimony of Mr. Burton indicated that shortly after 9:00 p.m., he told White House Chief of Staff Mack McLarty that Kennedy and Livingstone had confirmed that it was Mr. Foster who had died.  McLarty's testimony corroborates Burton's account.[567]

Webster Hubbell's account also supports that Kennedy and Livingstone were at the morgue well before 10:30 p.m. Hubbell testified that he spoke with George Stephanopoulos "around 8:30-9:00," whereupon he learned of the death and "that Bill Kennedy was going to identify the body."[568]

---

in the evening I talked to either Craig Livingston [sic] or Bill Kennedy.  Both were out at the hospital where Mr. Foster's body was.  And they were the ones who said it was Vince, told me, and that confirmed it.  During the approximately 30-40 minutes when I was on the phone with these police officers and [Kennedy & Livingstone], I came to understand that it was Mr. Foster's body that had been found.

[567]  Exhibit 156, Deposition of White House Chief of Staff Thomas F. McLarty, July 6, 1995:  Q.  Do you recall when the show began?  A. I think it began at 9:00 Eastern Time. Q.  Was there a brief period of preparation before the beginning of the show?  A.   There was a brief period as I remember.  Q.  And you were present for that?  A.  I believe I was.  Q.  Did there come a time while you were in the residence that you learned that a body of someone who was believed to be employed at the White House had been found at Fort Marcy Park?  A.  Yes, at some point during this period.  How did you learn that?  A.  Mr. Burton informed me, as I was leaving the White House, that there had been a body discovered, that they thought -- the authorities thought it to be Vince Foster, although they were not certain at that point, and it had been an apparent suicide.  Q.  You say you were leaving the White House. About what point were you leaving the White House relative to the filming of this interview with Larry King?  A.  The interview, as I remember it, Mr. Chertoff, had just begun. They had several minutes of interview; it seemed to be going quite well.

[568]  Exhibit 157, Deposition of Associate Attorney General

## Car keys not at the park

David Watkins lived near the Foster home. Park Police Investigators Braun and Rolla picked up Watkins and his wife on their way to the Foster home to notify the family. According to Watkins' testimony, they arrived at the Foster home at about the same time as Web Hubbell, Sheila Anthony and Sharon Foster Bowman.[569]

That was shortly after 9:00 p.m. Hubbell was having dinner at the Lebanese Taverna when Stephanopoulos contacted him. Hubbell proceeded to Sheila Anthony's home, who "lives almost directly across the street from" Hubbell's home. Then Hubbell, and Mr. Foster's sisters Sheila and Sharon "drove to the Foster residence and got there just at the same time that David Watkins and [his wife]... and the Park Police."[570] According to Hubbell's chronology,[571] because all of these people, including Braun

---

Webster Hubbell, July 13, 1995: Q. Who called you regarding Mr. Foster's death. A. George Stephanopoulos called me at the restaurant. I was having dinner at a restaurant. I'm sorry... Q. Do you have any recollection about what time of evening Mr. Stephanopoulos called you? A. No, I really -- I mean, it was probably around 8:30 to 9:00... [George] told me that it was true, that Bill Kennedy was going to identify the body. Obviously I was in shock. He said that David Watkins was on his way with the Park Police to advise Lisa [Foster] and I should get there as soon as possible.

[569]     Exhibit 93, Deposition of Director of White House Personnel David Watkins, July 11, 1995: "Q. [D]id the officers drive you to the Foster home? A. Yes. Q. Do you recall anyone else arrived shortly after you did at the Foster home... A. Web Hubbell, Beryl [sic] Anthony, Sharon Bowman. Beryl [sic] Anthony and Sharon Bowman were sisters of Vincent Foster."

[570]     Exhibit 157, Deposition of Associate Attorney General Webster Hubbell, July 13, 1995: A. Yes. I reminded George that Sheila Anthony was just right -- Sheila Anthony lives almost directly across the street from me, that Sheila, we would need to notify Sheila as well and that she was across the street... I walked across to tell Sheila... Vince's other sister was visiting Sheila that night, Sharon. Her name is Sharon Bowman... [W]e drove to the Foster residence and got there just at the same time that David Watkins and Eileen got there, Eileen Watkins, and the Park Police.

[571]     Exhibit 157, Deposition of Associate Attorney General

and Rolla, arrived at the Foster residence shortly after 9:00 p.m., Braun and Rolla could not have recovered the keys at 9:12 p.m. at the morgue, as the OIC claims.

Several reports relate that Rolla and Braun left the park around 8:45 p.m.,[572] and one relates that it was around 8:30.[573] According to Braun's testimony, Rolla was handling the telephone calls during their drive.[574] There were at least five such calls.[575] The last call was to hospital

---

Webster Hubbell, July 13, 1995: "[A]round 8:30 to 9:00... [Stephanopoulos] told me that it was true, that Bill Kennedy was going to identify the body... He said that David Watkins was on his way with the Park Police to advise Lisa [Foster] and I should get there as soon as possible."

[572] Exhibit 175, Addendum to July 20 Park Police Report authored by Investigator John Rolla, August 5, 1993: "Cleared the scene [Fort Marcy Park] at approximately 2045 hours." Exhibit 100, Report of FBI interview of Park Police Investigator John Rolla, April 27, 1994: "Investigator Rolla departed the Fort Marcy Park at approximately 8:45 p.m. and in the company of Investigator Braun..."

[573] Exhibit 174, Deposition of Park Police Investigator Cheryl Braun, July 19, 1995: "Q. What time did you clear the death scene? A. I don't recall specifically. Is it - I think it was somewhere in the neighborhood of like 8:30, but I don't recall the specific time."

[574] Exhibit 174, Deposition of Park Police Investigator Cheryl Braun, July 19, 1995: "Q. And you then called Watkins as you were driving to the hospital? A. John did. I was driving."

[575] Exhibit 91, Report of FBI interview of Park Police Investigator Cheryl Braun, April 28, 1994: [W]hile she and Officer Rolla were in [sic] route to the hospital in an attempt to retrieve the keys from the body, she was contacted... with instructions to call... David Watkins... who wanted to accompany the officers to the Foster home when the family was notified of his death. Sergeant Braun stated that she and Officer Rolla did telephonically contact Watkins, agreeing to pick him up at his home prior to going to the Foster residence... [Braun] and Rolla were again contacted by the Shift Commander... with instructions to call a White House Official named Kennedy... [U]pon calling Kennedy, he requested that he and a Mr. Livingston [sic] of the White House be permitted to view the body... [S]he or John Rolla called the hospital identifying themselves as Park police and instructing the hospital

personnel to instruct them to let Kennedy and Livingstone
view the body but not to allow them to "remove any
objects." If, during this fifteen-minute drive, they were
headed to the hospital, as the OIC claims, they would have
been at or near the hospital by the time they finished the
five telephone conversations. If so, they could have asked
hospital personnel to have Kennedy and Livingstone await
their impending arrival instead of instructing them to let
these White House personnel see the body but not to let
them "remove any objects."

Braun and Rolla left Fort Marcy Park as early as 8:30
p.m.[576] If they had proceeded directly to the hospital,
about a 15-minute drive from the park, they would have
arrived at the morgue at around 8:45 p.m., while the body
was still in the ambulance at the emergency room awaiting
Dr. Orenstein to pronounce it dead.[577] Yet, according to the
OIC's version of events, this 15-minute drive took over 40
minutes.[578]

To further support its claim that Kennedy and
Livingstone could not have planted the keys, the OIC cites
a secret interview report with an anonymous *"officer,"* whom
is said to have reported that Kennedy and Livingstone were
*"allowed to see the body only through a glass window."*

---

officials to let a Mr. Kennedy and Livingston [sic] view
the body but not to disturb or remove any objects.

[576] Exhibit 176, Senate testimony of Park Police Investigator
Cheryl Braun, July 20, 1995: "Q. Approximately how long did you
remain at the scene that evening? A. Until approximately 8:30
in the evening."

[577] OIC, p. 28 fn. 58: The body arrived at the hospital at
approximately 8:30 p.m., according to logs of the FCFRD.
Hospital and morgue logs show that Dr. Julian Orenstein
viewed the body at the hospital in the ambulance at 8:49
p.m., and that the body was received at the morgue at 9:00
p.m. OIC Doc. Nos. DC-108-12 to DC-108-16.

[578] OIC, p. 74: "Later, when it became apparent to
Investigators Rolla and Braun that they did not have the keys to
the car, they went to the hospital to check more thoroughly for
keys.[fn217] The hospital logs indicate that Investigators Rolla and
Braun were at the morgue at 9:12 p.m.[fn218]"

OIC, p. 74-75, fn. 220:

"*...Moreover, a Fairfax County Police officer stationed on regular assignment at the hospital that evening and a nursing supervisor escorted Mr. Kennedy and Mr. Livingstone, and allowed them to see the body only through a glass window. Officer 302, 2/10/95, at 2.*"

Yet Rolla testified that Kennedy and Livingstone were let into the same room as the body.

They have to be let into the morgue room to view it. Many times when you view a body, you are in a separate room and view it through glass. This time, I don't think that happened. They were in the morgue in the hospital, they were let in, the room attendant unzipped the body bag, they looked at it, he zipped it back up.[579]

As Rolla testified that Kennedy and Livingstone "were in the morgue in the hospital, they were let in, the room attendant unzipped the body bag," somebody surely told him this. The "room attendant" is a likely candidate, which would put Rolla in the morgue after Kennedy and Livingstone.

The FBI's reports of its interviews with Investigator Braun and Lieutenant Gavin do not sound as if Kennedy and Livingstone viewed the body through a glass window.[580]

The OIC cites "*hospital logs*" in support of its position that Kennedy and Livingstone viewed the body "*well after Investigators Braun and Rolla had retrieved the keys.*" (emphasis in original). The Evidence Receipt

---

[579] Exhibit 6, Deposition of Park Police Investigator John Rolla, July 21, 1994.

[580] Exhibit 91, Report of FBI interview of Park Police Investigator Cheryl Braun, April 28, 1994: "[S]he or John Rolla called the hospital identifying themselves as Park police and instructing the hospital officials to let a Mr. Kennedy and Livingston [sic] view the body but not to disturb or remove any objects." Exhibit 98, Report of FBI interview of Park Police Lieutenant Patrick Gavin, April 28, 1994: "[L]et them see the body but make sure they don't disturb or take any effects."

reflects that Braun reported logging in the keys at 8:45 p.m.[581] If Police did, in fact, retrieve the keys at the morgue, this time is wrong. The body was not placed in the morgue until after Dr. Orenstein viewed the body at 8:49.[582]

Rolla testified that he and Braun drove from the park to the Foster home and not directly to the morgue.[583] Braun testified that she and Rolla went to the hospital first,[584] contradicting the accounts of virtually every other witness.

The OIC's claim, that *[t]he hospital logs indicate that Investigators Rolla and Braun were at the morgue at 9:12 p.m..."* and that the *"hospital logs reflect that they*

---

[581]    Exhibit 152, United States Park Police Evidence Control Receipt, July 20, 1993.

[582]    OIC, p. 28, fn. 58:  The body arrived at the hospital at approximately 8:30 p.m., according to logs of the FCFRD. Hospital and morgue logs show that Dr. Julian Orenstein viewed the body at the hospital in the ambulance at 8:49 p.m., and that the body was received at the morgue at 9:00 p.m. OIC Doc. Nos. DC-108-12 to DC-108-16.

[583]    Exhibit 6, Deposition of Park Police Investigator John Rolla, July 21, 1994:   [A]fter we left the scene, myself and Investigator Braun were heading to Mr. Foster's residence in Georgetown to make death notification...  We also got a call to -- Lieutenant Gavin said to call this guy named [David] Watkins...  in the car on the way to make the death notification.

[584]    Exhibit 176, Senate testimony of Park Police Investigator Cheryl Braun, July 20, 1995:  A.  After we left the scene, we went to the hospital briefly to retrieve some property. Q.  And after you were at the hospital, did you get a call to go pick somebody up?  A.  Yes, we did.  Q.  Who was that?  A.  We were requested to pick up Mr. David Watkins to allow him and his wife to assist us with the notification to the Foster family.

See also Exhibit 91, Report of FBI interview of Park Police Investigator Cheryl Braun, April 28, 1994:  "[W]hile she and Officer Rolla were in route to the hospital in an attempt to retrieve the keys from the body, she was contacted... with instructions to call... David Watkins..."

[Kennedy and Livingstone] viewed the body near 10:30
p.m.",[585] is untrue.

The records of cellular telephone calls would likely
settle whether Kennedy and Livingstone visited the morgue
before the police, as would have interviews with the
hospital administrator, the morgue guard, or Fairfax County
Officer David Tipton, whose responsibility included
admitting visitors into the morgue. If the OIC obtained
these records or interviewed these witnesses, it declined
to reveal the results.

The OIC never resolved a number of conflicts in the
testimony of William Kennedy, Craig Livingstone and the
police investigators. Livingstone testified that he and
Kennedy left Kennedy's car at the hospital, drove to
Kennedy's home in Livingstone's car, left Livingstone's car
at Kennedy's house, and that they took another of Kennedy's
cars to the Foster home.[586] Livingstone also testified that

---

[585]   OIC, p. 75, fn. 220:  "...Two White House officials
(William Kennedy and Craig Livingstone) viewed the body at the
hospital, but the hospital logs reflect that they viewed the body
near 10:30 p.m., OIC Doc. No. DC-108-13 -- well after
Investigators Braun and Rolla had retrieved the keys."

[586]   Exhibit 47, Deposition of Chief of White House Security
Craig Livingstone, July 10, 1995:  Q.  What's the next
thing that happened?  A.  We left the hospital.  Q.  We
meaning who?  A.  Mr. Kennedy and I left the hospital.  Q.
Okay.  I neglected to ask you, did you drive to the
hospital?  Q.  Alone?  A.  Correct.  Q.  And did you and
Mr. Kennedy leave the hospital together?  A.  Yes we did.
Q.  Did you get in the same cars or separate cars?  A.  As
I recall it, I drove -- as I recall it, I drove Mr. Kennedy
in my car to his house.  Q.  Do you know how Mr. Kennedy
got to the hospital?  A.  He drove his car.  Q.  So you
left Mr. Kennedy's car at the hospital?  A.  Correct.  He
was pretty upset.  Q.  Okay then you drove to the Foster
residence; is that correct?  A.  No, sir, we drove to Mr.
Kennedy's house.  Q.  Okay.  What was your purpose in going
to Mr. Kennedy's home?  A.  We picked up his wife.  Q.
Okay.  A.  And we switched cars.  Q.  Moving from your car
to another of Mr. Kennedy's cars?  A.  Correct.  Q.  And
then what happened?  A.  The three of us drove to Mr.
Foster's house.

he and Kennedy later returned to Kennedy's home, and then to the hospital to get Mr. Kennedy's car.[587]

Kennedy's account differed. The handwritten notes of Kennedy's FBI interview state, "CL [Craig Livingstone] lvs [leaves] his car at Hosp."[588] He testified that from the Foster home, he and Livingstone went directly to the hospital to pick up Livingstone's, not Mr. Kennedy's, car, whereupon Kennedy returned home.[589]

Rolla testified that when Livingstone and Kennedy sought permission to view the body, they were already together, not in separate cars.

Q. Okay. So did you call Livingstone or did you speak to Livingstone or Kennedy or both.

A. I think it was Bill Kennedy, he just said Craig Livingstone is right here with me.[590]

Braun's account also seems to be that Kennedy and Livingstone were together before they went to the

---

[587] Exhibit 47, Deposition of Chief of White House Security Craig Livingstone, July 10, 1995: A. We left Mr. Foster's home and went directly to Mr. Kennedy's home. Q. Okay. And then what happened? A. I suggested to him that I could take my car and drive him out to the hospital to get his car so that he wouldn't have to deal with it in the morning. Q. And is that what you did? A. And that's what we did.

[588] Exhibit 184, Handwritten notes of FBI interview of Associate White House Counsel William Kennedy, May 6, 1994.

[589] Exhibit 46, Deposition of William H. Kennedy, July 11, 1995: "Q. Mr. Kennedy, what did you do when you left the Foster residence that evening? A. Got in the car with my wife and Mr. Livingstone and we drove back to the hospital where his vehicle was, and then I went home."

[590] Exhibit 114, Deposition of John Rolla, June 20, 1995: Q. Okay. So you called Livingstone or did you speak to Livingstone or Kennedy or both. A. I think it was Bill Kennedy, he just said Craig Livingstone is right here with me. They identified themselves and basically stated they wanted to see the body, asked if they could see the body.

hospital.[591]   Kennedy's testimony also seems to reflect that they were traveling in one, not two, cars.[592]

## IX.   OTHER ANOMALIES

### 1.   Analysis of blood on eyeglasses and gun

The OIC claims that blood was visible to the naked eye on both sides of both lenses of the eyeglasses found at the scene, apparently claiming that it had emanated from the contact entrance wound in the soft palate.[593]

OIC p. 57:

*"Dr. Lee stated that '[b]loodstains were found on both sides of the lenses' of Mr. Foster's eyeglasses. These bloodstains 'were less than or equal to 1 mm in size.'"*

This finding conflicts with the FBI lab's May 9, 1994 Lab Report, reporting that the results of its serological analysis on the glasses was, "no blood."

"No blood was identified on Q3 [eyeglasses]."[594]

Regarding the gun, we find the same anomaly.  In 1994, the FBI lab reported that "limited areas on the outer and inner surfaces of the barrel were selected and subjected to chemical testing for the presence of blood with negative

---

[591]   Exhibit 174, Deposition of Cheryl Braun, July 19, 1995: "Q.  At the hospital did you meet someone named Kennedy?  A.  No, we spoke to them on the phone.  Q.  You spoke to them?  A. Right."

[592]   Exhibit 46, Deposition of William Kennedy, July 11, 1995: "As I say, I was in pretty bad shape, but I got back in the car to go get my wife so that we could go to the Fosters."

[593]   OIC p. 62, fn. 183:  Id.  Similarly, the panel of pathologists concluded that the large quantity of gunpowder residue on the soft palate "indicates that Mr. Foster placed the barrel of the weapon into his mouth with the muzzle essentially in contact with the soft palate when he pulled the trigger."  Pathologists' Report at 1...

[594]   Exhibit 95, FBI Lab Report, May 9, 1994.

results."[595]   Similarly, the Fiske Report, relying on that probe's pathologists, explained that the absence of blood on the gun did not refute the official conclusion.

The Pathologist Panel found that "[t]he absence of visible blood on the revolver is not inconsistent with the self-inflicted bullet wound [he] sustained. Visual or chemical identification of blood on the weapon in gunshot wound suicides is a common but by no means universal finding."  Pathologist Report, ¶ 2.[596]

According to the OIC, the Fiske Report's explanation was unnecessary.  Dr. Lee reported finding blood on the gun.

OIC, p. 39:

*"Dr. Lee examined the gun and reported that '[s]mall specks of brownish-colored deposits were noted.'[fn96] Dr. Lee found that '[s]ome of these deposits gave positive results with a chemical test for blood' although the 'quantity of sample present was insufficient for further analysis.'"[fn97]*

OIC, p. 78:

*"As explained by... Dr. Lee... traces of blood evidence were derived from the gun..."*

## 2.   Missing bullet

In its two page section entitled *Search for Bullet,* the OIC relates that the fatal bullet could not be found in during the initial 17-day FBI/Park Police investigation (*"Park Police... investigation"*[597]) or during the FBI probe

---

[595]   Exhibit 27, FBI Lab Report, June 13, 1994.

[596]   Exhibit 12, Fiske Report, June 30, 1994.

[597]   OIC, p. 94:  During the Park Police, Fiske, and OIC investigations, searches were conducted of Fort Marcy Park for the bullet that caused Mr. Foster's death.  On July 22, 1993, four Park Police personnel (Hill, Johnson, Rule, and Morrissette) searched with a metal detector the immediate area where the body was found.  Their search for the bullet was unsuccessful.

under Fiske ("[i]nvestigators in Mr. Fiske's Office"[598]).
The OIC relates that it conducted a *"broader search...
utilizing information obtained through ballistics tests
[but that it too] did not locate a bullet fired from the
recovered gun from Mr. Foster's hand."*

But, the OIC concludes, its failure to find the bullet
*"does not affect the conclusion that Mr. Foster committed
suicide in Fort Marcy Park"* because *"the bullet could
have... landed well outside the park..., there is a
distinct possibility... [that] the bullet... ricochet[ed],
[and] [a]nother variable is that 'Foster's head could have
been turned to one side or the other when the shot was
fired.'"[599]*

---

[598]     OIC, p. 95: "Investigators in Mr. Fiske's Office conducted
a search in the area where Mr. Foster's body was found.  Their
search for the bullet fired from Mr. Foster's gun was
unsuccessful."[fn293]  See also Exhibit 12, Fiske Report, June 30,
1994:  "On April 4, 1994, sixteen individuals from the FBI Lab
went to Fort Marcy Park to conduct a search...  In an attempt to
locate the bullet, FBI Lab personnel surveyed and marked out a
grid in what the FBI Lab determined was the most likely area..."

[599]     OIC, p. 95-96:  With the assistance of Dr. Lee, the
National Park Service, and a large number of investigators,
the OIC organized a broader search of Fort Marcy Park for
the fatal bullet.  The search was led by Richard K. Graham,
an expert in crime scene metal detection.  The search plan
was devised utilizing information obtained through
ballistics tests performed by the Army Research Laboratory,
Aberdeen Proving Grounds, Maryland.  The search did not
locate a bullet fired from the recovered gun from Mr.
Foster's hand.  That the search did not uncover the fatal
bullet does not affect the conclusion that Mr. Foster
committed suicide in Fort Marcy Park.  Because a search
covering the maximum range estimates "would have included a
vast area..., a search which was limited in scope to the
highest probability area, closer to the minimum range
estimates, was undertaken."[fn294]  In other words, while the
OIC covered a broader area than previous searches, "the
maximum range estimates" predicted the possibility that
"the bullet could have cleared the tree tops in Ft. Marcy
and landed well outside the park."[fn295]  Moreover, although
lines ultimately were laid out within the park along the
outer limits of a 90 degree arc to a distance of 175
meters,[fn296] which represented the highest probability
areas,"[fn297] a full search of even 90 degree-175 meter range
would have included areas outside the park that were not
searched.[fn298]  In addition, because dense foliage and trees

360

## Other anomalies

A condition precedent to the OIC's conclusion that the bullet could have *"landed well outside the park"* would, of course, be the existence of an exit wound in the top of the back of the head.

The authors of the Fiske Report almost seemed to know that the bullet was not in the park.

"It would have been enormously time-consuming, costly, and in all likelihood unproductive, to have searched the entire park for the bullet."[600]

### 3.    Reported lack of dragging-type soil patterns

The OIC's claim that Dr. Lee found no evidence that would indicate that the body was dragged is another example of the unreliability of Dr. Lee's conclusions.

OIC, p. 51:

*"Dr. Lee reported that '[n]o dragging-type soil patterns or damage which could have resulted from dragging-type action were observed on these pants.'[fn143]"*

Yet, the police dragged the body up a steep, dirt embankment, according to Rolla's testimony.

---

surround the area where Foster's body was discovered, and since there is a...cannon approximately 12.5 feet directly behind the location where the body lay, there is a distinct possibility the bullet's trajectory was altered due to its striking or ricocheting off a natural or man-made obstruction.[fn299] Another variable is that "Foster's head could have been turned to one side or the other when the shot was fired."[fn300]

See also OIC, p. 14, fn. 20: "As Dr. Lee explained, a perfect reconstruction of the circumstances of Mr. Foster's death was not possible at the time of the OIC's investigation. The reasons include... the unknown location of the fatal bullet, which makes complete reconstruction of the bullet trajectory difficult. Lee Report at 485."

[600]    Exhibit 12, Fiske Report, June 30, 1994.

## Other anomalies

"[I] rolled that body... and he began sliding down the hill... to keep him from sliding all the way down the darn embankment... I pulled him, he slid down..."[601]

And, according to the FBI's report of its interview with Park Police Officer Christine Hodakievic, she "recall[ed] the decedent's body starting to slide down the hill..."[602]

### 4. Analysis of dirt on shoes

The OIC's analysis of the dirt on the shoes, when compared to Fiske's, provides another example of the facts having changed, but the conclusion remaining the same.

*Dr. Lee reported that examination of a photograph of Mr. Foster's shoes taken by the FBI Laboratory at the time of its initial examination revealed brownish smears on the left heel.[fn136] Dr. Lee further stated that his own macroscopic and microscopic examinations of the shoes revealed the presence of soil-like debris.[fn137] (The FBI Laboratory photo of the shoes, taken in 1994 at the time of the Laboratory's examination of the clothing, shows traces of soil visible to the naked eye.) Dr. Lee found that "[t]race materials were located embedded in the grooves of the sole patterns at the heel of [the left shoe]. A portion of this material subsequently was removed. Microscopic and macroscopic examination showed this material to contain mineral particles, including mica, other soil materials, and vegetative matter." [fn138] Dr. Lee stated that this fact "indicates the sole of the shoe had direct contact with a soil surface containing these materials."[fn139]*

In a footnote to this passage, the OIC explains that the FBI Lab's *"earlier"* report of the absence of soil on the shoes was simply a *"misunderstanding."* When the FBI reported that there was *"no coherent soil,"* according to the OIC, it really meant that it in fact found soil on Mr.

---

[601]     Exhibit 6, Deposition of Park Police Investigator John Rolla, July 21, 1994.

[602]     Exhibit 81, Report of FBI interview of Christine Hodakievic, May 2, 1994.

## Other anomalies

Foster's shoes, but that its amount was insufficient for comparison.

OIC, p. 50, fn. 139:

*...There has been misunderstanding of the statement in an earlier FBI Lab Report that no "coherent soil" was found in the samples. FBI Lab Report, 5/9/94, at 12 (emphasis added). The FBI Lab Report's statement regarding a lack of coherent soil simply means, as explained in the preceding paragraph, that there was insufficient soil to effect a comparison with soil samples from Fort Marcy Park. But a lack of coherent soil is not the same as a lack of any trace soil. And as Dr. Lee concluded, examination of Mr. Foster's shoes revealed particles of soil materials, including that the sole of the shoe did in fact have direct contact with a soil surface...*

Apparently, according to the OIC's version, the authors of the Fiske Report had neglected to look at the *"photograph of Mr. Foster's shoes taken by the FBI Laboratory at the time of its initial examination [which] revealed brownish smears on the left heel."* Had they done so, they would have seen the *"soil-like debris... visible to the naked eye,"* which was *"insufficient [in amount]... to effect a comparison with soil samples from Fort Marcy Park."* The OIC's version is that the following question and answer provided by the Fiske Report was based on the same *"misunderstanding."*

Why was no dirt found on Foster's shoes?
The FBI Lab did find mica particles on Foster's shoes and socks. These mica particles are consistent with the mica that is found at Fort Marcy Park. It was approximately 90 degrees Fahrenheit and dry on the day Mr. Foster died. Foliage leading up to and around Foster's body was dense. As a result, it is unlikely that there was a great deal of exposed moist soil in the park that would have soiled Foster's shoes.[603]

---

[603] Exhibit 12, Fiske Report, June 30, 1994.

## 5.   Hair analysis

The OIC relates that two hairs were found on Mr. Foster's clothing that did not belong to him.  The OIC declined to compare these dissimilar hairs to those of anyone in Mr. Foster's circle, offering as its excuse that any match would be to *"persons already known to have had contact with Mr. Foster."*  The OIC thus offers no sound reasoning for its decision not to determine whether Mr. Foster had contact with unknown persons.

OIC, p. 55:

*In debris collected from Mr. Foster's clothing, the FBI Laboratory reported finding two blond to light brown head hairs of Caucasian origin that were suitable for comparison purposes and dissimilar to those of Mr. Foster.[fn154]  The hairs did not appear to have been forcibly removed.[fn155]  Hair evidence can become important or relevant in a criminal investigation when there is a known suspect and a significant evidentiary question whether the suspect can be forensically linked to another person (a rape or murder victim, for example) or to a particular location.[fn156]  If the suspect is a stranger to the victim or the scene, the presence of the suspect's hair is relevant in assessing whether he or she had contact with the victim or scene.  In this case, however, the only known individuals who reasonably might have been compelled to provide hair samples were persons already known to have had contact with Mr. Foster.*

A necessary component of this reasoning would have to be the foregone conclusion of no criminal activity. Because there was criminal activity, one would want to see if that hair was dissimilar from that of known persons, to see whether Mr. Foster had contact with an unknown person. Any such person may know what happened or even be an assailant.

## 6.   Fiber analysis

The OIC declined to determine through hair analysis whether Mr. Foster may have had contact with unknown persons, but decided to explore through fiber analysis whether Mr. Foster may have been at an unknown place.  This is a change from the FBI's position in 1994, when it declined to undertake any carpet fiber analysis because it "had no way to match those particular fibers up."[604]

According to the OIC, the FBI Lab found thirty-five *"definitive carpet-type"* fibers on Mr. Foster's clothing, 23 of which were white and 12 of which were of *"various colors, including blue gray, blue, gold-brown, light brown, gray, pink, and orange."* The Report tells us that with the help of *"OIC investigators,"* the FBI Lab conducted comparisons with carpets from his *"workplace,"* car and rented Washington home. The OIC's reported results were that *"the white fibers obtained from Mr. Foster's clothing were consistent with the samples obtained from... [the] 1993... [rented] house in Washington"* and that four of the non-white fibers were consistent with samples obtained from the White House or Mr. Foster's car.[605]

---

[604]   Exhibit 178, Senate testimony of FBI Agent Lawrence Monroe, July 29, 1994:  Q.  The FBI identified carpet-type fibers of various colors... Does the FBI have any idea where that came from?  Was any attempt made to match that with any carpet in his home, car, or office?  A.  No, sir, and for the same reasons I provided in response to your first question relative to the hairs... We had no way to match those particular carpets up, outside the fact that they most likely came from his residence or from his office...

[605]   OIC, p. 56:  The FBI Laboratory reported 35 definitive carpet-type fibers in the debris collected from the clothing.  Of those fibers, 23 were white fibers.  OIC investigators sought to determine a possible source for the fibers[fn157] -- for the white fibers in particular, in light of the number of white fibers in comparison to the limited number of fibers of other colors.[fn158]  The logical known sources for possible comparison were carpets from locations with which Mr. Foster was known to have been in contact -- his car, home, and workplace.  OIC investigators obtained carpet samples from these sources, including from a white carpet located in 1993 in the house in Washington where Mr. Foster lived with his family.  The FBI Laboratory determined that the white fibers obtained from Mr. Foster's clothing were consistent with the samples obtained from that carpet.[fn159]

OIC, p. 56, fn. 158:  The remaining 12 were various colors, including blue gray, blue, gold-brown, light brown, gray, pink, and orange.  No more than three fibers of any of these colors was found.  OIC Investigators' Memorandum (FBI

OIC, p. 56-57:

*In sum, therefore, the carpet fiber evidence -- the determination that the white fibers were consistent with a carpet from the Foster's home and the variety and insignificant number of other fibers -- does not support speculation that Mr. Foster was wrapped and moved in a carpet on July 20.[fn160] Indeed, the fiber evidence, when considered together with the entirety of the evidence, is inconsistent with such speculation.*

We agree with the OIC that the FBI's fiber findings probably do not support the conclusion that Mr. Foster was wrapped and moved in a carpet (because there would probably be more fibers -- apparently unbeknownst to the OIC). No one to our knowledge has ever said that he was moved in a carpet. Moreover, the OIC's *"considered together with the entirety of the evidence"* point is wearing thin.

The OIC asks its readers to trust that the FBI retrieved a sample of carpet from Mr. Foster's car, disposed of in 1993, and from a carpet located in his rented Washington home in 1993. Yet the FBI's Lab now relates that it found pink and orange fibers, among others, but according to its 1994 Report, these colors were not among those it had earlier had found.[606] And the OIC's conclusion (p. 56, fn. 158) that *"[t]he variety of colors suggest that those fibers did not originate from a single carpet"* fails to contemplate the possibility of a multi-colored carpet, such as an Oriental.

Additionally, six different colors of carpet fibers were found on the clothing that was bagged at the autopsy on July 21,[607] and all six colors of carpet fibers were found

---

Lab Reports on Fibers). The variety of colors suggest that those fibers did not originate from a single carpet.

OIC, p. 56, fn. 159: "Id. The Laboratory also determined that four of the non-white fibers were consistent with samples obtained from the White House or Mr. Foster's car. Id."

[606] Exhibit 95, FBI Lab Report, May 9, 1994: "These colors include white, tan, gray, blue, red and green... It was also noted that a number of red/dark pink wool fibers were found."

[607] Exhibit 95, FBI Lab Report, May 9, 1994.

on his jacket and tie,[608] retrieved from his car and bagged on July 20. The OIC hides this anomaly by falsely reporting that all of the clothing was *"packaged together before trace evidence was obtained."*

OIC, p. 55, fn. 154:

*FBI Lab Report, 5/9/94, at 11; OIC investigators' Memorandum, 3/2/95, at 4 (Lab Conference). As explained above, the clothing was packaged together before trace evidence was obtained, and particular trace evidence cannot be conclusively linked to particular items of clothing that Mr. Foster was wearing at the time of his death.*

### 7.   Bone chip

The OIC claims to have found a bone chip from debris from clothing years after the FBI lab found none.

OIC, p. 51-52:

*Dr. Lee examined debris collected from Mr. Foster's clothing and reported that the debris was "found to contain a bone chip."[fn144]   Dr. Lee stated that DNA was extracted from this bone fragment and amplified, and the DNA profile generated for this bone sample was consistent with the DNA types of Mr. Foster.[fn145]   Based on his analysis of the evidence, Dr. Lee concluded that "[t]his bone chip originated from Mr. Foster and separated from his skull at the time the projectile exited Mr. Foster's head."[fn146]*

The three footnotes to this passage refer the reader to page 493 of the still-secret Lee Report. We thus have no clues as to how a bone fragment, which is said to have originated from the alleged inch-and-quarter head wound in the back of the skull, could have landed on his clothing while no other fragments were found on other clothing, or in the soil or the vegetation surrounding the body. Nor do we know whether the Lee Report purports to explain how the FBI Lab missed finding the bone fragment from the *"debris [it] collected from Mr. Foster's clothing."*

---

[608]   Exhibit 95, FBI Lab Report, May 9, 1994.

## 8.    Unusual position of body

The position of Mr. Foster's body, lying straight with his arms to his sides,[609] was unusual, according to Richard Arthur and George Gonzalez, the two paramedics who observed the body.  Arthur testified that "he was just laying perfectly straight, hands at his side."[610]  He "doubt[ed] that it was a suicide."[611]  Gonzalez similarly testified that it was so unusual that he had never seen it before.

> Q.  Did anything strike you as peculiar or unusual about the scene?
> A.  The fact that he was straight, laid out straight, yes.  That's peculiar.
> Q.  Have you ever seen a body in that position as a suicide?
> A.  No.[612]

## 9.    Other unidentified persons present at the park

In addition to the strange-acting man Patrick Knowlton saw in the park, and the man that the Male and Female civilians saw, there is a record of other witnesses having seen other unidentified individuals in the park late in the afternoon of Mr. Foster's death.  These unidentified people

---

[609]    Exhibit 81, Report of FBI interview with Christine Hodakievic, May 2, 1994:  According to the FBI's report of its interview with her, "[s]he advised that she... recalls his arms being straight at his side."

[610]    Exhibit 107, Deposition of Paramedic Richard Arthur, July 14, 1994.

[611]    Exhibit 71, Report of FBI interview of Paramedic Richard Arthur, March 16, 1994:  "[It] struck him as unusual... which make him doubt that it was a suicide: the straight attitude of the body..."  Exhibit 109, Handwritten notes of FBI interview with Paramedic Richard Arthur, March 16, 1994:  "Right side jaw line small caliber bullet hole (between ear and tip of chin) Didn't see any other bullet holes.  Didn't look like suicide - straight laying out, gun bigger than hole"

[612]    Exhibit 110, Deposition of Paramedic George Gonzalez, July 20, 1994.

include a jogger,[613] volunteers working on a park trail,[614] the driver of a white van or truck,[615] and the driver of another car.[616] Of particular interest is the account memorialized by the FBI in its interview of Firefighter Todd Hall.

> "During a cursory search of the area surrounding Foster's body, Hall thought he heard someone else in the woods. He subsequently saw something red moving in the woods."[617]

---

[613] Exhibit 151, Report of FBI interview of Male Civilian, April 5, 1994: "While in the park itself, the only person they observed was a jogger run by..."

[614] Exhibit 79, Deposition of Officer Kevin Fornshill, July 12, 1994: "I was told later that some persons on, I think it was, they were doing some repair work on a trail, they were on the opposite end of the park. There is a nature hiking trail that I imagine they were doing some work on... They were volunteers."

[615] Exhibit 150, Report of FBI interview with Female Civilian, April 7, 1994: "[T]he driver of this white van or truck was a white male, in his late 20's or early 30's who had light colored hair and was average height and weight."

[616] Exhibit 158, Report of FBI interview of civilian Jean Slade, April 11, 1994: She stated that another car, occupied by a white male, was also parked off to the right on the entrance ramp leading into the Fort Marcy parking lot... this individual proceeded up into the parking lot, turned around, and then drove off in the direction of the GW Parkway... dark hair, thick, well-groomed, summer-type shirt on, possibly plaid color, age 38-42, medium build... quite sure it was somewhere in the vicinity of 5:45-6:15 p.m... [A]t least two cars were in the parking lot and that they were both parked fairly close to one another... were situated in the beginning of the lot..."

[617] Exhibit 66, Report of FBI interview of Firefighter Todd Hall, March 18, 1994: During a cursory search of the area surrounding Foster's body, Hall thought he heard someone else in the woods. He subsequently saw something red moving in the woods... Hall noted that Ralph Pisani and one other EMS member thought they saw two males getting dressed in a wooded area adjacent to the site.

| Body site | **FORT MARCY PARK**   6: 14:32-6:15   <u>See</u> endnote 4. |
|---|---|
| Officer Kevin Fornshill | At Officer Fornshill's direction, Hall and Gonzalez searched another area of the park. Fornshill, searching alone, found Mr. Foster's body. He called Hall and Gonzalez over to the body, who radioed the other team of searchers. Hall immediately noticed a gun in Mr. Foster's hand and told Fornshill. Fornshill radioed to the Park Police who were en route to the park that the death was an "apparent suicide." At the body, Hall "heard someone else in the woods [and] subsequently saw something red moving in the woods." |
| Firefighter Todd Hall | |
| Paramedic GeorgeGonzalez | |

Body

raised earthen perimeter of fort

FMP parking lot

footpaths

During their search of the Southeast area of the woods, the team located the couple. Gonzalez radioed the team of the body's discovery, and the team decided to head back toward the lot.

| **Parking lot** |
|---|

| **South of the lot** |
|---|
| Paramedic Richard Arthur |
| Firefighter Ralph Pisani |
| Firefighter Lt. James Iacone |
| Firefighter Jennifer Wacha |

| Male Civilian |
|---|
| Female Civilian |

Other anomalies

## 10. Fingerprints

There were no fingerprints on the ammunition or gun, officially carried 700 feet in 95 degree weather, held in both hands and found clutched in Mr. Foster's right hand. The state of the official death weapon was consistent with its having been wiped clean of fingerprints. The Fiske Report suggested that there were no fingerprints on the gun (and two brass cartridges) fired by Mr. Foster by implying that heat destroyed them.

"Latent prints can be destroyed by exposure to certain elements, such as heat."[618]

The OIC informs us that the Park Police, and later the FBI Lab during the Fiske probe, could find no prints on the exterior of the gun,[619] but found one print on the underside of the pistol grip. That print was not compared until December of 1995, when the FBI Lab compared it to those of Mr. Foster and Park Police who initially handled the gun, and found that it did not match.[620] So, to this day, that print has still not been compared to those on file in the FBI database.

As to the absence of prints on the exterior of the weapon, the OIC notes that the *"determining factors in leaving latent prints are having a transferable substance,*

---

[618]   Exhibit 12:   Fiske Report, June 30, 1994.

[619]   OIC, p. 40:   "Identification Technician E.J. Smith of the Park Police examined the gun for latent fingerprints[fn103] on July 23, 1993.   The results were negative.[fn104]   The FBI Laboratory later examined the gun and similarly detected no latent prints on the exterior surface of the weapon.[fn105]"

[620]   OIC, p. 41, fn. 108:   FBI Lab Report, 6/9/94, at 2.   The FBI Laboratory, during its examinations, found one latent fingerprint on the underside of the pistol grip (that is, not on an exterior surface of the gun).   FBI Lab Report, 7/19/95, at 1.   This print has been compared to prints of Mr. Foster and of evidence technicians who initially handled the gun, but no identifications were effected.   FBI Lab Report, 12/13/95, at 1; FBI Lab Report, 8/14/95, at 1. This print would have been left by someone who assembled or disassembled the gun, for example, to repair it or to put on new grips or for some other reason.

*i.e., sweat... a clean, smooth, flat surface... and the surface of the grip handle here was textured, not smooth.* "[621]

While this is no doubt true, it does not take into account the official explanation that the gunshot residue on Mr. Foster's hands was caused by his wrapping his hands around the gun's cylinder, not the grip, and pulling the trigger with his thumb. All these surfaces are smooth, flat, and not textured.

Of all the items retrieved and fingerprinted during the course of the first brief probe, including the gun, the "miscellaneous papers" in the car at the park, the car itself, and the torn note, not one print belonged to Mr. Foster.

The absence of prints on the torn note is telling. On the billing records of Mrs. Clinton's Rose Law Firm work for a Whitewater related corporation, Castle Grande, found in the White House in 1996 (two years after they were subpoenaed), were the fingerprints of Mrs. Clinton and Mr. Foster, at least two-and-a-half years after Mr. Foster had handled them. The unsigned torn note, on which the proponents of the suicide theory have largely relied since its discovery six days after the death in the previously searched and thought to be empty briefcase (in 28 pieces with one piece missing), had only Bernard Nussbaum's palm print on it. Because the tearing process would have resulted in numerous thumb and forefinger prints on both sides of the paper, the absence of any other prints on the note mandates the conclusion that if Mr. Foster tore it up, he was wearing gloves or the pieces were wiped clean. This fact heightens the importance of the opinions of experts who opine that the note was forged (set forth in the footnotes above under *Background*).

---

[621] OIC, p. 41: The FBI Laboratory also noted that a lack of fingerprints is not extraordinary and that "[g]enerally, the determining factors in leaving latent prints are having a transferable substance, i.e., sweat, sebaceous oil or other substance on the fingers, and having a surface that is receptive to receiving the substance that forms the latent prints. A clean, smooth, flat surface is most receptive for transfer of any substance from the fingers,"[fn108] and the surface of the grip handle here was textured, not smooth.

### 11. Determination of suicide made before police investigators viewed the body

Investigator Braun testified that the "determination [of suicide was made] prior to going up and looking at the body."[622]

## X. INFERENCES TO BE DRAWN FROM THE FACTS

We told you 250 pages ago that we would review most of the available evidence, and compare it to the OIC's representations and omissions of the evidence as well as the OIC's conclusions.

The evidence of obstruction of justice or cover-up is more telling than evidence that Mr. Foster did not die at his own hand at the park. What we have seen in our review is an effort to cover up almost all the facts of the case. It is simply not possible for all the anomalies and inadequate explanations to be present without the existence of a conspiracy, a cover-up.

---

[622] Exhibit 101, Senate testimony of Park Police Investigator Cheryl Braun, July 29, 1994: Q. Did he [Edwards] say he thought that the death was by suicide? A. I don't recall exactly how he did it, and he did show the pictures to it that he had snapped. Q. Was it your understanding that a determination had been made as to the cause of death? A. I think we more made that determination. You know, like I said, when we first got the call. It was for a dead body. Then I asked if it was natural or of suspicious nature. And I was told suspicious, so I had them close the gate. Then once we got there, maybe actually I do remember speaking to Lieutenant Gavin. So maybe it was Lieutenant Gavin who might have -- it might have been Lieutenant Gavin then who actually initially explained what the scene was, because I had some knowledge of it when I went to speak with the couple and ask them if they had heard anything or seen anything and ask them about other vehicles that were in the area. Yeah, I would say it was Lieutenant Gavin actually. Q. Did Lieutenant Gavin mention anything about suicide? A. I can't recall. I don't -- I don't recall if he or if that was what we -- it seems to me that we had made that determination prior to going up and looking at the body.

**The existence of the neck wound and the absence of the official wounds.** One would expect the *Report of Investigation by Medical Examiner* to be among the thousands of pages of documents released by the Senate in 1995. Dr. Donald Haut, the only medical doctor to see the body in the park, wrote it. Above "July 20" and his signature appears:

I hereby declare that after receiving notice of the death described herein I took charge of the body and made inquiries regarding the cause and manner of death in accordance with the Code of Virginia as amended; and that the information contained herein regarding such death is correct to the best of my knowledge and belief.

It also states:

July 20, 1993  After anonymous call was received at 18:04 hours US Park Police officers found 48 yrs Caucasian male with self-inflicted gunshot wound mouth to neck on a foot path in Marcey [sic] Park...

This report was found on July 19, 1997, four days after the OIC filed with the Court its Report on Mr. Foster's death, so the OIC's Report had no reason to and did not offer an excuse for its contents.

Assume that any case generating so many thousands of pages of records would produce unexplained anomalies. But we look at all the evidence together, not separately. The *Report of Investigation by Medical Examiner* is not some stray piece of evidence, contradicted by every other piece of evidence in the case. In fact, virtually every other piece of evidence in the case points to the existence of a neck wound and efforts to cover it up. In light of this other evidence, the *Report of Investigation by Medical Examiner* was a lucky find indeed.

On July 14, 1994, Paramedic Richard Arthur, a nine-year veteran paramedic of the Fairfax County Fire & Rescue Department, testified:

Q.  Let me ask you this:  If I told you that there was no gunshot wound in the neck, would that change your view as to whether it was a suicide or not?

A.  No... What I saw is what I saw.  I saw blood

all over the right side of the neck, from here
down, all over the shoulder, and I saw a small -
what appeared to be a small gunshot wound here
near the jawline.  Fine, whether the coroner's
report says that or not, fine.  I know what I
saw.

What could possibly explain this testimony?  What is
the explanation for the OIC's claim that Arthur *said he
may have been mistaken about such a wound?*"  Ours is this:
Knowing that they could not just fail to mention Arthur's
sworn account, the FBI went back and interviewed him again.
They asked him the question, "Isn't it possible that you
could have been mistaken?"  He said, "No."  They asked him
again, and again, and again, until they got the response
they wanted.  He finally said something like, "Yes,
anything is possible."  The FBI agents left and the OIC had
what it needed -- Arthur "*said he may have been mistaken
about such a wound.*"

The FBI's use of words in its reports of witness
interviews such as "may have," "believed," "recalled," "in
his opinion," "noted," and "what appeared," is a red flag.
It usually means that the agents could not get the witness
to agree with them, necessitating the insertion of one of
these qualifying-type words.  If the issue of the accuracy
of the report ever comes up, like if the report becomes
publicly available and the witness reads it, the claim that
the agent falsified the witness's account will be more
difficult to make.  The agent would say something like, "I
said you believed you recalled that you thought it was a
brown car."

Redactions are also red flags.  In the FBI's
handwritten notes of its interview with Park Police
Investigator John Rolla, appearing immediately below the
words "back of head," four lines are redacted.  Rolla's
testimony is the only record of a description of the exit
wound before Dr. Beyer was with the body.  Rolla gloved up
and probed the head.

He did say "hole."  He said, "small hole."  He defined
his terms.  A "large hole" would be one he could have put
his finger through.  He could not put his finger through
what he found.  His conclusions were that the "mushy spot"
he felt was caused by the skull being fractured from the

inside, and that the bullet was still in the head.  By all
indications, he was right on both counts.

Q.  Was there any attempt to find bone fragments or
    anything in the ground?
A.  They searched the area...  I still can't believe
    that the hole -- it's a small hole.  They may put
    their finger through it, that's a big hole.  His
    head was not blown out...  I probed his head and
    there was no big hole there.  There was no big
    blowout.  There weren't brains running all over
    the place.  There was blood in there.  There was a
    mushy spot.  I initially thought the bullet might
    still be in his head.  Could have been the brain
    pushed up against that hole.  There's no big hole
    or big blowout in his head.

                    *       *       *

[B]ecause as we rolled him, he was starting to
slide down the hill on us, and it was very steep.
At that point, you know, he looked at the back of
his head.  I looked at the back of his head, and I
was wearing gloves, I probed his head and I could
feel -- what I felt in his head was mushy here...
It just appeared it was mushy there.

     What do you think the chances are of there being a
half-dollar sized exit wound although Rolla testified that
there was only a mushy spot he couldn't get his finger
through?  There is no record of the existence of the
official exit wound before the autopsy.  What do you think
the chances are of the existence of a half-dollar-sized
exit wound and there being no record of the 26 witnesses
who saw the body before the autopsy (two medical doctors,
two paramedics, six Fire & Rescue workers, ten Park Police,
a Fairfax County Police officer, a citizen, an unnamed Park
Police intern, an unnamed morgue guard, and two White House
officials) having seen it?

     We do have Arthur's and Haut's record of having
reporting a neck wound.  On what does the OIC rely in
relating the existence of the official wounds that nobody
could see or feel, and of the absence of the neck wound
that people did see?  Dr. Beyer's word.

     If the official exit wound had, in fact, existed, what
are the chances that the Teletype from the FBI's Washington
Metropolitan Field Office to the "Director, FBI" having

376

## Inferences

includod confirmation of the fact that there was "no exit wound"?[623]

---

[623] <u>See</u> Patrick Knowlton v. Robert Edwards et al., US District Court for the District of Columbia, Civil Action No. 96-2467:

> 56. On August 10th, 1993, eighteen days after having sent the Teletype, BRYANT, then special agent-in-charge of the FBI's Washington, DC metropolitan field office, appeared with U.S. Park Police Chief Robert Langston and Justice Department spokesman Carl Stern to announce, <u>inter alia</u>, the outcome of the FBI's investigation into Mr. Foster's death. During that press conference, BRYANT stated:
>
>> Ladies and gentlemen, I'm Bob Bryant, and I'm the special agent in charge of the Washington metropolitan field office field office of the FBI... [I]nitially, when there is a death of a high government official that's covered by the assault or assassination statutes, the FBI as a matter of course establishes liaison with the police agency that has the primary lead, in this case the United States Park Police. We followed this case from the time we were notified until we were basically of the opinion... that this was a suicide...
>>
>> \*　　\*　　\*
>>
>> Well, I think while we were with the United States Park Police, it became reasonably apparent that this was a suicide.
>>
>> \*　　\*　　\*
>>
>> I think what we were trying to do here first was trying to find out if there was a violation, if he'd been harmed, you know, assaulted or assassinated or whatever. We concluded no...
>>
>> \*　　\*　　\*
>>
>> I suggest to you that it's a very thorough investigation.
>>
>> \*　　\*　　\*
>>
>> I'd be delighted to answer that question. Any time there is an assault or death under suspicious circumstances of an official covered by the assassination or assault of a federal officer statute, we immediately put with the primary or lead agency, in this case the United States Park Police, to determine the circumstances. As we became convinced that it was, in fact, a suicide, we subsequently started to withdraw...
>
> 57. These remarks made by BRYANT were untrue and BRYANT knew them to be untrue. They were overt acts made

***The Autopsy.*** Dr. Beyer claimed responsibility for rescheduling the autopsy, and claimed that he did it on his own with no prior discussion with anyone. There is also testimony that Captain Hume did it at Chief Langston's request, which came from the White House. The third version is that Major Hines did it on his own. The OIC's discussion of the matter is that *"[t]he autopsy occurred on July 21, 1993...,"* and that *"Dr. Beyer had no conversations with members of the White House, the Foster family, or Foster family attorneys in connection with the autopsy."*

The autopsy is an important matter. It, along with the state of the body and surrounding area, supplies most of the information on which conclusions of investigations of equivocal deaths are based. In such cases, the autopsy procedure includes the exchange of information between the pathologist and scene investigators. But for this autopsy, the only information from the police to the pathologist was that a nondescript "weapon" was found "in close proximity to the body" -- that is the sum total of the information that Beyer claims to have known. Dr. Beyer left the box in his Autopsy Report requesting the caliber of the weapon blank.

Dr. Beyer checked "Yes" in his Autopsy Report next to the question, "x-rays taken?" and said that the x-rays showed there was not a trace of the bullet's lead left in the head. Later, according to Fiske, there were no x-rays taken. According to the OIC, x-rays were taken, but were unreadable. The mysterious autopsy assistant took the x-rays, according to the FBI, and didn't look at them until towards the end of the autopsy. The new x-ray machine had *"numerous problems"* making the pictures too dark, but service was not requested for three months, because the pictures were too light.

At 11:00 a.m., an hour after the police arrived to witness it, the autopsy was over. But it had begun well before 10:00 a.m., during which time, according to Morrissette's Report, "the victim's tongue had been removed

---

to further the cover-up. BRYANT's public pronouncement that the FBI "became convinced that it [Mr. Foster's death] was, in fact, a suicide," made eighteen days after the Teletype confirmed BRYANT's knowledge that there was, in fact, "no exit wound," constitutes active participation by BRYANT in the cover-up.

as well as parts of the soft tissue from the pallet." In
one of the many examples of its Report's blatant deceptions
by omission, the OIC hides that the evidence of the
entrance wound was removed before the police arrived, and
tells us only that *"Officer Morrissette's report on the
autopsy states: 'After briefing him with the available
information surrounding the crime scene and the victim he
started the autopsy on the victim.'"* We have only Dr.
Beyer's word on what evidence he saw and removed.

Dr. Beyer sent "5 slides... [containing] 13 sections
of [the] soft palate..." to his own Lab. Why? It is
reasonable to assume he did so to have his Lab test for the
"large quantity of gunpowder residue" that he saw "on
microscopic sections of the soft palate." But his Lab
could find not a trace of it. That report from the
Northern Virginia Medical Examiner's Lab is still withheld,
but an excuse for its finding is offered in a subsequent
FBI Lab report. The official finding of the "large
quantity" of GSR is the long-standing cornerstone of the
official conclusion, having been relied on by expert after
expert after expert. The OIC killed this scientific
anomaly with silence.

At his July 13, 1994, deposition, Dr. Beyer testified
why he was unconcerned with the time of death at the
autopsy.

Q. Is it your practice never to provide a time of
death analysis in your autopsy reports?

A. We may assist them if it appears to be of a
critical nature. Other than that, we don't put
anything in the autopsy report.

Q. What would your definition of a critical nature
be?

A. If one had a case where a body -- there was no
definite information concerning when the
individual had last been seen, who had contact
with him, who had a phone call with him. Any
indication about the last time they had intake of
food and they were found under suspicious
circumstances. Then there might be some
indication for attempting to make an estimate of
time of death.

Q. Do you think any of those factors were present in
this case?

A. Not that I was aware.

Q. Did you subsequently become aware of whether any of those factors were present in this case?
A. I made no determinations.

But "there was no definite information concerning when" Mr. Foster "had last been seen," or "who had contact with him." There was an "indication about the last time they had intake of food," and he was "found under suspicious circumstances." Dr. Beyer did not testify that he thought that none "of those factors were present in this case," only that he "made no determinations." This is the state of the evidence, upon which the OIC wants you to rely in taking Dr. Beyer's word on the existence of the official wounds and the absence of the neck wound.

**The car.** An estimate of time of death was unimportant to Dr. Beyer, but is an important aspect of the case. The reason Patrick Knowlton was yanked into this FBI debacle was Mr. Foster's car, or, more precisely, the absence of it in the Fort Marcy lot late Tuesday afternoon, when Mr. Foster was already dead. As it happened, had the man in the park not been acting in a strange, almost threatening way, we would not be where we are today. Patrick's senses were heightened because of the man's actions, and, having a good memory, Patrick happened to remember the color, shape and contents of the car he used as a buffer to keep his distance from the man. Twenty-seven months later, Patrick was illegally targeted to neutralize his account, and testimony, regarding the car. Only the federal government uses the *modus operandi*, or mode of operation, employed to harass Patrick. It began when he was secretly subpoenaed by the federal government.

It was obstruction of justice, or, specifically, the crime of Witness Tampering. When you finish this Chapter, we would like you to decide whether you agree with us that this crime of Witness Tampering has been solved.

We observed that there has never been any record produced or referred to corroborating the long-standing official claim that Mr. Foster left the White House compound in his own car. Senator D'Amato asked the question when FBI Agents Bill Columbell and Larry Monroe appeared before the Senate Banking Committee during its one day hearing. Typically, there was no follow-up question.

Inferences

SENATOR D'AMATO:   ...Did the FBI ever attempt to
     determine what time Mr. Foster departed the White
     House and do we know if the Secret Service keeps
     a vehicle exit log?

MR. MONROE:   Sir, all of our information right now
     suggested that Mr. Foster departed the White
     House on July 20th at approximately 1:00 p.m.
     Whether or not that departure time was based on
     interviews or a log by the Secret Service, I am
     not aware of that, sir, but we know that he left
     about that time.

SENATOR D'AMATO:   Would you be able -- I mean, this
     investigation, as it relates to the circumstances
     surrounding Mr. Foster's death, wouldn't you look
     at the vehicle departure log to determine what
     time he may have left?  Is that a routine thing?

MR. COLOMBELL:   Senator, I don't believe the vehicle
     was logged out of the White House.  I don't
     believe it was parked in an area where it would
     have been logged out of the White House.  We
     confirmed that he left around 1:00 to 1:15
     p.m...[624]

The White House security system is among the world's
most sophisticated.  If a record existed of Mr. Foster's
having driven, not walked, out of the White House compound,
in his own car, alone, around 1:00 p.m., we almost
certainly would have heard and read much about it for the
last six years.  If Mr. Foster did leave the compound,
there surely was, and still may be, a record of it.

If we deduce that the reason the record of his
departure from the campus has remained withheld is because
it is part of the cover-up, the possible reasons for that
secrecy are that (1) he walked out, (2) he drove out in his
own car accompanied by someone, (3) he occupied another's
car, or (4) he was carried and smuggled.

There also had to have been a record generated of his
car's departure.  Whoever drove the car out of the compound
knows the truth of Mr. Foster's demise and participated in
keeping it secret.  Even if the records of his car's exit
no longer exist, one or more Secret Service agents likely
knows both how Mr. Foster left the compound and who drove

---

[624]   Exhibit 17, Testimony of FBI agents Lawrence Monroe and
William Colombell, July 29, 1994.

his car out and when.  After all, Secret Service Officer
John Skyles, the last known person to have seen Mr. Foster
alive, said he "specifically remembers" Mr. Foster's having
walked out of the West Wing.

Mr. Foster asked Betsy Pond to see what was taking
Linda Tripp so long in getting his cheeseburger, so he may
have had an appointment after lunch.  Had Mr. Foster been
headed to his car, Skyles would have seen him, as claimed.
But he could also have been headed toward the Old Executive
Office Building, or OEOB, where William Kennedy and Craig
Livingstone worked in separate office suites.  FBI agent
Salter testified that he could not remember whether his
death investigation included interviewing anyone in the
OEOB when he went there the day after the death.

The FBI's report of its interview with William Kennedy
reflects that between "8:15 and 8:30 p.m.," Kennedy learned
that the body was on its way to the morgue, whereupon
Kennedy said that he "had to go to the hospital."  He did.
So did Livingstone, after which the car keys appeared in
Mr. Foster's pocket.  The keys not found at the park
consisted of two separate key rings, one with four keys and
a tab inscribed, "Cook's Jeep Sales," and another with a
tab inscribed, "Vince's Keys."  These two sets of key rings
would be virtually impossible to miss given that Park
Police Investigator Rolla testified that he searched the
pants pocket searching for, among other things, a suicide
note.

To discount the possibility that Kennedy and
Livingstone had planted the keys at the morgue, the OIC
relies on a secret interview report of an unnamed
"officer," a secret hospital log, and its reinterview of
Investigator Rolla, relating that the police visited the
morgue first.  In so doing, the OIC ignored the ambulance
logs, the White House Sherburne chronology memo, Lieutenant
Gavin's notes, and the testimonies of Secret Service Agent
Dennis Martin, Park Police Investigator Rolla, and White
House personnel Watkins, Hubbell, Stephanopolis, McLarty,
Burton, Livingstone and Kennedy.

The OIC's extraordinary effort to conceal the true
circumstances surrounding the discovery of Mr. Foster's
keys is related to the fact that the keys were not found at
Fort Marcy Park.  The absence of the car keys is to be
expected -- his car wasn't there either.

## Inferences

Conspiracy evidence is interrelated. The court in Williams v. United States, 218 F.2d 276 (1955), likened evidence of a conspiracy to a spider's web.

This evidence, which was quite voluminous and given by many witnesses, may be likened to the web of the spider. No single strand, or even several strands, would be sufficient. Yet when all these strands are considered together, and their interrelations and connections are considered, they form, we think, a complete web, which was more than sufficient to take to the jury the question of a general conspiracy among the appellants.

We have just looked at several interrelated strands of our spider web. Patrick Knowlton and the absence of Mr. Foster's Honda in the Fort Marcy lot are related to the time of death. That is related to the absence of a record of Mr. Foster's car having left the compound. He was last seen headed toward the OEOB, where William Kennedy and Craig Livingstone had offices, Kennedy and Livingstone went straight to the morgue, and the car keys appeared.

Let's look at some of the other strands of evidence in the case.

**Blood evidence**. Not one observer saw a quantity of blood consistent with the official .38 caliber gunshot wound to the mouth, leaving a half-dollar-sized exit wound.

The configuration of the blood was consistent with the neck wound, but not the official wound, so the OIC's experts concluded that an early observer moved the head, as the FBI and Fiske's experts had concluded. But, as we saw, no one moved the head until Sergeant Edwards was alone at the body site. In spilling the blood toward the small caliber bullet wound in Mr. Foster's neck, and down onto his right collar and shoulder, Edwards obscured and camouflaged the visible evidence of the bullet wound in Mr. Foster's neck. By causing the contact stain on the chin, evidencing the head having been moved to the right, Edwards sought to make it appear that the blood on Mr. Foster's right side collar and right shoulder, which had in fact drained from the neck wound, had emanated from his mouth when the head was turned. Edwards' actions may have also camouflaged the existence of the neck wound by spilling blood over that wound.

# Inferences

As we have seen, among the evidence of Edwards' wrongdoing is that before he was alone at the body site, the blood was dry. After Edwards' actions, the blood appeared wet and there was blood on the face that those who saw the body before Edwards' arrival did not see. Edwards' actions while alone with the body are also proven by the accounts of Firefighters Hall and Pisani and Investigator Hodakievic, three early witnesses who, upon viewing photographs taken after Edwards had been alone with the body, related that the photographs depicted more blood than they saw.

To obscure Edwards' actions, the OIC followed the FBI's lead and blamed the blood on the right side and the contact stain on movement of the head by an unnamed early witness, who is said to have been checking Mr. Foster's pulse. This explanation, such as it is, leaves unanswered how all of the early observers could have seen the blood on the right side upon their inspection of the body, and ignores that Mr. Foster had obviously been dead for some time and that there were therefore no efforts to resuscitate or clear an airway. Considering the importance to the OIC of this excuse for the blood on the right side of the body, it would have announced who moved the head if it could have. But it could not name any witness to the head movement, so it buried that fact in a half-page footnote. The OIC recounts what the post-Edwards witnesses had seen, but fails to recount what those who were at the body site before Edwards had seen.

Edwards' actions were necessary because at 6:00 p.m., when the call went to Fairfax County, the body had not yet been readied for its official discovery.

**Photographs.** Because Ferstl's Polaroids were the first photographs taken at the body site, they reveal the state of the body before Edwards tampered with it. Park Police Officers Ferstl, Fornshill, Hodakievic and the firefighters, the first officials to see the body, observed only dried blood around the mouth. Later witnesses saw wet blood coming from the mouth and nose and the contact bloodstain on the chin. The crime scene had been tampered with and the Polaroids that vanished can prove it. Because the body had not yet been prepped for its discovery, the photographs showing the state of the body when authorities arrived had to vanish.

## Inferences

**The Guns.** The gun presents three issues.  First, was
the official wound, and gunshot residue on the hands,
consistent with what one would expect from the official
death weapon?  Second, was the official death weapon the
only weapon in Mr. Foster's hand at the park?  And third,
did Mr. Foster own the official death weapon?  The answer
to each question is, No.

Bullet trajectories in the human body can be unusual.
But usually the bullet spins and the lead breaks up,
leaving large exit wounds.  The alleged half-dollar-sized
exit wound may have been possible from an intra-oral
gunshot with the stock .38 caliber high-velocity
ammunition, but not very likely.  In any event, the Fairfax
County personnel with the most medical training, Paramedics
Gonzalez and Arthur, as well as Dr. Haut, all the medical
experts at the scene, all expressed surprise at the
comparatively small size of the wound and paltry amount of
blood at the scene.  Additionally, because the manufacturer
of the .38 caliber high-velocity ammunition never used the
type of gunpowder found, if the official weapon had been
fired, its ammunition had been reloaded.  Mr. Foster did
not reload ammunition.  And the deposits of gunshot residue
on Mr. Foster's hands all but prove that he could not have
fired it.

Second, was the official death weapon the only weapon
in Mr. Foster's hand at the park?  No.  Like the wounds to
the body, there is a telling gap in the evidence.  Of all
the witnesses who saw the body before Edwards was alone
with it, only two saw a weapon and distinguished the type.
Two Police Officers, Fornshill at the body site for ten
minutes, and Hodakievic at the site for about 30 minutes,
never saw any weapon.  Other pre-Edwards witnesses,
including firefighter Todd Hall and Officer Ferstl, saw
some kind of weapon but we don't know whether it was a
revolver, like the official weapon, or a semi-automatic,
like the ones the Park Police carry.

The two who testified what type of weapon they saw are
Paramedics Gonzalez and Arthur.  Gonzalez did testify that
it was a revolver, but he also testified that he looked at
a glance and didn't know the type of weapon it was.
Arthur, on the other hand, told the FBI he was "100% sure"
it was a semi-automatic, and drew a picture of the
difference while under oath.  Edwards' actions were
necessary because at 6:00 p.m., when the call went to

Fairfax County, the gun, like the body, had not yet been readied for its official discovery.

Did Mr. Foster own the official death weapon?  No. The only family member who ever reportedly identified it, Mrs. Foster, was tricked into doing so by being shown a silver revolver, the same color as the gun that Mr. Foster did, by all accounts, own.  According to the family member who was most familiar with the subject gun collection, Mr. Foster's nephew Lee Bowman, Mr. Foster did not own a black revolver.  And there was no matching ammunition recovered from his Little Rock or Washington homes.  The official death weapon, being a 1913 year-model, was untraceable. First, the FBI reported that Mr. Foster's gun (singular) was in its usual location the night of the death.  Years later, there were two guns, one of which was missing, and according to Web Hubbell and the OIC, *the missing gun was the one found at the scene.*"  Where is the silver gun now? The OIC is grasping when it offers Dr. Lee's findings of the trace evidence in the oven mitt (neither inventoried nor photographed) in the car at the park.  The ownership of the weapon, as the OIC points out, is a fact of some consequence.

**Discovery of the body**.  The official version of the discovery of the body is worth scrutinizing because of some unusual aspects of the official version and because of the state of the body when authorities arrived.  As we have seen, all indications are that the wrongdoers had not yet prepared the body for authorities to inspect it when the call was placed to Fairfax County 9-1-1.  So, whoever was in the park when the body was first discovered may have seen the body, or other people, or cars in the park.

Officially, Dale discovered the body, drove to the park maintenance facility, told Swann and Stough about it, and drove off without leaving his name.  If Swann and Stough had, in fact, been drinking beer in their uniforms, as the New York Daily News reported, they more likely would have chosen to do so in the relative seclusion of Fort Marcy Park over the Park Headquarters at Turkey Run, which would have provided no seclusion from co-workers or supervisors.  If Swann had been drinking beer at Fort Marcy Park in his Park Service uniform, that would explain why he refused to provide his name to authorities.  Swann's failure to tell the Park Rangers at the Turkey Run

## Inferences

Headquarters about the dead body would also be consistent with his not wanting it known that he had been drinking.

If Swann and Stough had seen Mr. Foster's body, they may have noticed that he had been shot. That would explain why Stough knew that the body had a bullet wound in it, while Dale, who was officially Stough's only source of information regarding the state of the body, said he thought that Mr. Foster had died of a blow to the head. And, had Swann and Stough driven from Fort Marcy Park to Turkey Run, they would have seen the car accident, which Swann reported when he called the Park Police.

The Fiske Report claimed that after its "detailed analysis" of the information provided by Dale, including the "short conversation held with" the Park Service employees, Dale passed the "test" of "veracity." But virtually all the details of Dale's version of his conversation with the Park Service employees disagree with theirs.

If Dale had reported the body to Swann and Stough while they were all at Fort Marcy, that would explain why the FBI's reports of these interviews were redacted. So, perhaps Mike McAlary's March, 1994, _New York Daily News_ story, _Aide's Suicide is Confirmed by Heads-up Cops_, was accurate when it reported:

> The body was discovered by a park maintenance worker who had slipped into the area for a quiet midday drink. He reported finding the body, but then made up a story about having seen a white van. He has since recanted the white van story, admitting it was created to cover up his own behavior.

Given the state of the body site when officials began arriving, and the anomalies in the official version of events of the body's discovery, we believe that the OIC's portrayal of the discovery of the body is not completely true.

**_Notification._** Following Senator D'Amato's lead, the OIC declined to reveal when the Park Police, Fire & Rescue workers, the FBI, or White House personnel other than Helen Dickey learned of the death. Some assume that the official version, that _"the Secret Service was notified of Mr. Foster's death at about 8:30 p.m..."_, was concocted to give the White House deniability of having sanitized Mr. Foster's White House office in those first few hours of his death. Perhaps, but another motive would be to provide an excuse for the FBI's failure to respond to Fort Marcy Park.

*Review.* We have proved the existence of the neck wound and the absence of the official wounds. Had the official exit wound been there, someone would have seen it and Rolla could have put his finger through it. The pathologist refused to tell the police the name of the man who had helped remove the only evidence of the official entrance wound before the police arrived -- to see the beginning and end of the autopsy. It probably wasn't Mr. Foster who drove his car out of the White House compound, and Mr. Foster certainly didn't drive his own car to the park. (It was a year after the harassment that we figured out the import of Patrick's account.) When authorities arrived at the body (if the police were not already there - the FBI was conspicuously absent), the head was facing straight up and blood was on the right side. Had Mr. Foster's head rested on his right, blood would be on his right side. But his head would not have gone back to the straight up position as it was found. Edwards provided the excuse. We proved it and so can the missing photographs. The gun, by all accounts, did not belong to Mr. Foster, it changed from a semi-automatic model to a revolver before it was retrieved from his hand, the wounds are inconsistent with his having fired it, the ammunition would have to have been reloaded, and the gunshot residue patterns found on the hands would not have been left by Mr. Foster's having fired it. Hall seems to have heard something in the woods, seen someone running away from the body site, and the official version of the discovery of the body does not appear to be entirely true.

Other anomalies include that the official fatal bullet was never found, the conclusion of suicide was made before investigators looked at the body, the position of body was unusually straight, and there were no fingerprints found on the gun, ammunition, car, or "suicide note." There was no analysis of the two blond hairs found on Mr. Foster. First there was no blood on the eyeglasses and gun and no dirt on the shoes, then there was. The excuses for the absence of x-rays, photographs, and car keys change with time.

The OIC had its pick of pricey experts, to whom it gave the evidence supporting the official version, and

# Inferences

selectively quoted from their reports.  Dr. Lee's report
may explain what "gunpowder-like particles" are.  It may
show us the photographs of the "blood-like" stains and the
"not coherent" dirt on the shoes.  But Lee's report is
secret.  A Library of Congress clerk told us that Dr. Lee's
report would probably be available for inspection and
photocopying there in 50 years.  The OJ Simpson defense
team hired Dr. Lee to report that the crime scene appeared
to have been tampered with, and the OIC hired him to report
that the Fort Marcy crime scene appeared not to have been
tampered with.

**_Evidence of cover-up_**.  The evidence of the wounds,
autopsy, car, blood, gun, photographs, notification, and
discovery of the body do not, in and of themselves, prove
the culpability of Mr. Starr's office.  For that, we look
to see whether the OIC covered up this evidence.  Clearly
it did.

Much of the record in the case remains hidden.
Seventy-five percent of the OIC's footnotes refer the
reader to documents that are secret.  Many of the records
generated under the first two investigations, first the
FBI/Park Police and later the FBI under Fiske, are entirely
withheld or heavily redacted.  Follow-up questions in
depositions and Senate testimony are almost nonexistent.
Notwithstanding the state of the record, evidence of cover-
up pervades it.

The Report's efforts to hide the truth are easily
detected.  All sections of the Report contain numerous
examples of blatant dishonesty by omission and rely on the
secret reports generated by the OIC or its experts.  It
then ignores what it cannot explain.  Relevant evidence was
obviously withheld from its experts, whose authoritative-
sounding secret reports are quoted throughout the Report.
Evidence is largely scattered throughout the Report, making
analysis more difficult.

A significant amount of the OIC's Report is devoted to
irrelevant or misleading issues, such as whether there was
a briefcase in the Arkansas Honda without disclosing that
the car was not Mr. Foster's.  Similarly, the OIC debates
whether the quantity of blood at the scene supports the
conclusion that the body was moved, without disclosing the
one thing needed to analyze that issue, a true description
of the wounds.  Other examples include discussions of

whether Helen Dickey learned of the death too early, and the depression issue, which we look at briefly in the next Chapter.

The OIC used the autopsy as the cornerstone of its conclusion, had its experts validate its findings, and summarily dismissed evidence of there being a bullet wound in Mr. Foster's neck.

Look at examples of how new factual accounts differ from those previously memorialized, so that, according to the OIC, the facts now fit the conclusion of suicide in the park.

| Witness reference in the OIC's Report | Date new statement memorialized | New account according to the OIC |
|---|---|---|
| Park Police Investigator John Rolla, p. 26, fn. 50 | February 9, 1995 -- 19 months after death | Statement changed to "noted a wound out the back of the head" that he did not report in his deposition |
| Park Police Investigator Christine Hodakievic, p. 26, fn. 50 | February 2, 1995 -- 19 months after death | Statement changed to "noted a wound out the back of the head" that she did not report before |
| Paramedic George Gonzalez, p. 33, fn. 77 | May 15, 1996 -- 34 months after death | Deposition testimony changed, the wound he testified was on the right side of Mr. Foster's head was "not what he intended to report" |
| Paramedic Richard Arthur, p. 34, fn. 77 | April 24, 1996 -- 33 months after death | Changed his deposition to say he "may have been mistaken" about the neck wound he testified he was sure he had seen |
| Park Police Investigator John Rolla, p. 52, fn. 148 | April 17, 1996 -- 33 months after death | Changed his account of what he found in Mr. Foster's car to "recalled the oven mitt in the glove compartment" that he had not reported before |

Inferences

| Witness reference In the OIC's Report | Date new statement memorialized | New account According to the OIC |
|---|---|---|
| Park Police Investigator Cheryl Braun, p. 52, fn. 148 | February 9, 1995 -- 19 months after death | Changed her account of what she found in Mr. Foster's car and "recalled the oven mitt in the glove compartment" that she had not reported before |
| Paramedic George Gonzalez, p. 66, fn. 191 | January 10, 1995 -- 18 months after death | Changed his statement to say that firefighter Todd Hall may have checked Mr. Foster's pulse, he had testified that Mr. Foster appeared to have been "obviously dead" for 2 to 4 hours |
| Firefighter James Iacone, p. 66, fn. 191 | January 10, 1995 -- 18 months after death | For the first time stated that he "checked the pulse" after paramedics Arthur and Gonzalez concluded Mr. Foster was obviously dead for several hours |
| Investigator Renee Abt, p. 67, fn. 192 | February 9, 1995 -- 19 months after death | Changed her statement to say she remembered more blood under Mr. Foster's head |
| Park Police Technician Peter Simonello, p. 67, fn. 192 | February 7, 1995 -- 19 months after death | Changed his statement to say he saw more blood under Mr. Foster's head |
| Dr. Donald Haut, p. 67, fn. 192 | February 6, 1995 -- 19 months after death | Changed his statement to say he saw a pool of blood under Mr. Foster's head |
| Park Police Investigator Christine Hodakievic, p. 67, fn. 192 | February 7, 1995 -- 19 months after death | Changed her statement and recalled more blood |

| Witness reference in the OIC's Report | Date new statement memorialized | New account According to the OIC |
|---|---|---|
| Park Police Investigator John Rolla, p. 67, fn. 192 | April 17, 1996 -- 33 months after death | Changed his statement and recalled more blood |
| Unnamed Reporter | April 4, 1996 -- 33 months after death | New witness who recalled a blood spot on the ground |
| Park Police Officer Kevin Fornshill, p. 69, fn. 200 | January 11, 1995 -- 18 months after death | Changed his deposition testimony from reporting volunteers at Fort Marcy Park to saying there were "no volunteers" |
| Firefighter Todd Hall, p. 70, fn. 200 | January 5, 1995 & May 13, 1996 -- 18 & 34 months after death | Changed his statement from hearing and seeing someone in the woods to saying it "must have been traffic" on Chain Bridge Road |
| Park Police Investigator John Rolla, p. 73, fn. 214 | January 11, 1995 -- 18 months after death | Changed his deposition statement from saying he took photos of the back of Foster's head to say he "did not" take those photographs but only intended to take them |
| Park Police Sergeant Robert Edwards, p. 74, fn. 215 | January 12, 1995 -- 18 months after death | First and only record of being interviewed reported he said he did not take any photographs that other police officers at the scene reported seeing him shoot |
| Park Police Investigator John Rolla, p. 74, fn. 216 | April 17, 1996 -- 33 months after death | Changed his account from his testimony that he had "emptied the pockets" to he "did not reach into the bottom of the pants pocket" |

| Witness reference in the OIC's Report | Date new statement memorialized | New account According to the OIC |
|---|---|---|
| Fairfax County Officer David Tipton, p. 74-75 fn. 220 | February 10, 1995 -- 19 months after death | Contradicted the previous testimony by Investigator Rolla who said Kennedy and Livingstone were in the room with Mr. Foster's body by saying they only viewed the body through a glass window |
| Dr. James Beyer p. 76, fn. 222, fn. 223 | September 11, 1995 -- 26 months after death | Contradicted his own autopsy report that reflected x-rays were taken and the Park Police report of his comments on the x-ray results by saying the machine was "not working" |
| Paramedic Richard Arthur, p. 79, fn. 228 | April 24, 1996 -- 33 months after death | Changed his previous account that he was "100% sure" he saw a semi-automatic pistol in Mr. Foster's hand to say he "must have been mistaken" |
| Firefighter Jennifer Wacha, p. 79, fn. 229 | January 10, 1995 -- 18 months after death | Changed her account from offering no observations of a gun to saying it was consistent with the gun retrieved at the scene |

The authors of the Report are unidentified because the OIC's Report is nothing more than another layer of the same, six-year old, ongoing Justice Department cover-up. As you will see below, the OIC conceals the FBI's participation in the initial 17-day investigation, the Fiske probe, in its own probe, and deceptively implies that Congress investigated the death.

Pundits have correctly pointed out that one or two inexplicable points of evidence do not prove a cover-up. The only way to look at the evidence is to look at the big picture. In this case, the OIC's 114-page Report has evidence of cover-up on almost every page. A look at the big picture, all of the Report's claims together, cumulatively, is a look into the anatomy of the cover-up. The foregoing review of the public record of the case, made without experts or interviews of witnesses, demonstrates that not one substantive point in the OIC's Report stands up to scrutiny.  If one or two inexplicable points can be dismissed, what possible conclusion can you draw from every point in the OIC's Report being contradicted without plausible explanation?

Even though the discovery process in Patrick Knowlton's civil rights lawsuit has not yet begun, and so we have not yet exercised subpoena power, we have exposed the OIC's Report for what it is -- clear and convincing evidence of cover-up.  The government's finding of the absence of a cover-up is just not in accordance with the truth.

## XI.  STATE OF MIND

The OIC devotes fourteen pages to addressing Mr. Foster's state of mind, more pages than to any other single issue.  The issue of whether Mr. Foster was suffering from depression is irrelevant in light of the physical evidence in the case.  Although the OIC failed to prove that Mr. Foster was depressed, we will not review the record of his mental state nor compare it to the OIC's claims on the issue.  Most of the state of mind evidence is in the footnotes above under Chapter I, *Background,* should you care to review it.

First, we make some observations about the OIC's psychologist's opinion.  Then, we see that the oft-repeated verdict of depression and suicide originated in the press, and that early press accounts found their way into the final official expert opinion.

### 1.   The OIC's psychological autopsy is unreliable

The OIC quoted Dr. Alan Berman's secret, 16 or so page report 28 times.[625]  Dr. Berman[626] performed a "psychological

---

[625]   OIC, p. 98, fn. 303:  "Berman Report at 3.  Dr. Berman noted that '[r]ecent studies . . . have documented a significant relationship between perfectionism and both depression and suicidality, particularly when mediated by stress.' Id. at 13."  OIC, p. 98, fn. 304:  "Id. at 3."  OIC, p. 99, fn. 305: "Id. at 5."  OIC, p. 99, fn. 306: "Id. at 13."  OIC, p. 99, fn. 307: "Id. at 7."  OIC, p. 99, fn. 308: "Id. at 14."  OIC, p. 99, fn. 309: "Id. at 4."  OIC, p. 99, fn. 310: "Id. at 7"  OIC, p. 100,

autopsy." There is such a thing.[627] It is a research
diagnosis. Dr. Berman's conclusion, that the death was a
suicide to a "*100 degree of medical certainty*,"[628] is a

---

OIC, p. 100, fn. 315: "Id." OIC, p. 100, fn. 316: "Id. at 13."
fn. 311; "Id. at 6." OIC, p. 100, fn. 311: "Id. at 6." OIC, p.
100, fn. 311: "Id. at 13." OIC, p. 100, fn. 312: "Id. at 13."
OIC, p. 100, fn. 313: "Id. at 14." OIC, p. 100, fn. 314: "Id."
OIC, p. 100, fn. 317: "Id. at 10." OIC, p. 100, fn. 318: "Id. at
9." OIC, p. 101, fn. 319: "Id. at 6." OIC, p. 101, fn. 320:
"Id. at 14." OIC, p. 101, fn. 321: "Id. at 15." OIC, p. 101,
fn. 322: "Id. at 15." OIC, p. 101, fn. 323: "Id." OIC, p. 102,
fn. 324: "Id." OIC, p. 102, fn. 325: "Id." OIC, p. 102, fn.
326: "Id." OIC, p. 102, fn. 327: "Id."

[626]    Alan L. Berman, Ph.D., specializing in adolescent
assessment and prediction of suicide, the psychological autopsy
study. Born July 10, 1943; B.A., John Hopkins University; Ph.D.,
Clinical Psychology, Catholic University of America, 1970;
Professor of Psychology, American University 1969-1991; private
practice, 1977-present; specialty, youth suicide (assessment and
treatment), suicide prevention and the use of psychological
autopsy.

[627]    See Assessment and Prediction of Suicide, by David
C. Clark, Ph.D. and Sara L. Horton-Deutsch; edited by R.
Marris, A. Berman, J. Maltsberger, R. Yufit: *Assessment in
Absentia: The value of the Psychological Autopsy Method for
Studying Antecedents of Suicide and predicting Future
Suicides*: The phrase "psychological autopsy" refers to a
procedure for reconstructing an individual's psychological
life after the fact, particularly the person's lifestyle
and those thoughts, feelings and behaviors manifested
during the weeks preceding the death, in order to achieve a
better understanding of the psychological circumstances
contributing to a death. The essential ingredients of the
psychological autopsy method include face-to-face
interviews with knowledgeable informants within several
months of the death, review of all extant records
describing the deceased, and comprehensive case formulation
by one or more mental health professionals with expertise
in post mortem studies.

[628]    Compare OIC, p. 103: This outline is not designed to set
forth or suggest some particular reason or set of reasons
why Mr. Foster committed suicide. Rather, the issue for
purposes of the death investigation is whether Mr. Foster
committed suicide, and this outline is designed to show
that, as Dr. Berman concluded, compelling evidence exists
that Mr. Foster was distressed or depressed in a manner
consistent with suicide.[fn328]

clinical diagnosis. The psychological autopsy is an "advisory"[629] research diagnosis, not a clinical one.[630] To be a clinical diagnosis, the information upon which it would have to have been based would have to have been gathered by face-to-face interviews by Dr. Berman or another trained professional,[631] not by FBI agents untrained

---

[629]   See Assessment and Prediction of Suicide. Chap. 8, Assessment in Absentia: *The Value of the Psychological Autopsy Method for Studying Antecedents of Suicide and Predicting Future Suicides;* by David C. Clark, Ph.D.; and Sarah L. Horton-Deutsch M.S., R.N.: "Finally, we recommend that clinicians conceive of the clinical formulation and psychiatric diagnoses resulting from psychological autopsy studies as *research* formulations and research diagnoses... [T]he findings and formulations of the mental health expert have always been considered *advisory* to a medical examiner's final decisions... and not conclusive in their own right."

[630]   See Assessment and Prediction of Suicide, Chap. 8, Assessment in Absentia: *The Value of the Psychological Autopsy Method for Studying Antecedents of Suicide and Predicting Future Suicides;* by David C. Clark, Ph.D.; and Sarah L. Horton-Deutsch M.S., R.N.; under *Standard For Future Psychological Autopsy Studies*: Although the psychological autopsy method generates psychological formulations and psychiatric diagnosis that outwardly resemble clinical diagnosis... those studies have always presented their formulations and diagnosis as research diagnoses. Research diagnoses... cannot be considered equivalent to clinical diagnoses unless a clinician has validated them by means of face-to-face clinical evaluations... [and] one can never send a clinician back to interview the deceased in an attempt to validate the research diagnoses... *** [T]here is a critical limit on how much information we can construct about the person who has died by suicide, and emphasize that external validation of our formulations and diagnoses is difficult if not impossible.

[631]   See Assessment and Prediction of Suicide, Chap. 8, Assessment in Absentia: *The Value of the Psychological Autopsy Method for Studying Antecedents of Suicide and Predicting Future Suicides;* by David C. Clark, Ph.D.; and Sarah L. Horton-Deutsch M.S., R.N.; under *Assessment in Absentia, Methodological Considerations*: [U]nless data from various informants are elicited in the framework of standardized protocol, (1) the quantity and quality of data will vary as a function of the informant and the

in gathering clinical data,[632] not 8 to eleven months after death,[633] and not based on Mr. Foster's writings.[634]

---

interviewer, and (2) reconciling discrepant information from different sources will be fraught with a number of sources of bias... [T]he investigator is deprived of the means for establishing the reliability and validity of the observations."

[632] OIC, p. 98: "The OIC provided Dr. Berman with relevant state-of- mind information (the bulk of which consisted of interview reports and transcripts), which he studied and analyzed..."

[633] See Assessment and Prediction of Suicide, Chapter 8, *Assessment in Absentia: The Value of the Psychological Autopsy Method for Studying Antecedents of Suicide and Predicting Future Suicides;* by David C. Clark, Ph.D.; and Sarah L. Horton-Deutsch M.S., R.N.; under heading *Psychological Autopsy Studies for Forensic Purposes*: Police reports and other sources of information compiled shortly after a death are often more helpful than are personal interviews conducted months after the fact, when witnesses have had a chance to forget -- and conceivably alter or embellish the facts... *** [W]hen a consulting expert is not contacted until months or years after a death for an opinion about an unfamiliar case..., information available to the expert witness is usually in the form of depositions collected many months or years after the suicide. This kind of data is suspect for scientific purposes, because of the passage of time and memory decay... [T]he degree of distortion introduced cannot be quantified by any measure currently available. *** The only situation where forensic case review truly approximates the psychological autopsy method is that in which the expert undertakes a structured, independent psychological autopsy study of the death within a reasonable period of time after the death (i.e. within a year)

Compare OIC, p. 13-14: [T]he important information in assessing the cause and manner of death of death includes... testimonial and documentary evidence revealing the decedent's... state of mind in the days and weeks before his death.[fn18] In particular, the OIC obtained information gathered during the FBI and Mr. Fiske's... Experts retained by the OIC reviewed and examined the evidence.

[634] See Assessment and Prediction of Suicide; Ed. Ronald W. Maris, Ph.D.; Alan L. Berman, Ph.D.; John T. Maltsberger, M.D.;

In any event, in a paper that Dr. Berman himself wrote and published in 1993, he observed that "the psychological autopsy is speculative"[635] -- unlike an opinion to a *"100% degree of medical certainty."*[636]

## 2.    The verdict of depression

The verdict of depression is the mainstay of press reports on the matter.  It has steadfastly reported the "why" of Mr. Foster's death, but failed to report the basic information of who, what, where, when, or how.

---

Robert I. Yufit, Ph.D.; Chap. 16, *Suicide Notes Communication and Ideation*, A. Leenaars:  "The problem of the relationship between communication-written communication (including writing forms such as notes) and thought (or ideation) is a historical one...  Today the relation between communication and ideation is acknowledged to exist, but it remains complex and controversial..."

[635]   See Suicidology, Essays in Honor of Edwin S. Schneidman edited by A. Leenaar; consulting editors A. Berman, P. Cantor, R. Litman & R. Maris; 1993, Essay 14: *Forensic Suicidology and the Psychological Autopsy* by Alan L. Berman:  [F]rom this reconstruction the relationship between an individual's life-style and death style may be established (Brent 1989, Clark and Horton-Deutch 1992).  As a postdictive analysis, the psychological autopsy is speculative.  It provides a probabilistic statement, a best-bet conclusion, giving a logical understanding of the interaction between the person and events leading to that person's death. ***  The light it [the psychological autopsy] throws on its subject may be distorted by both the quality and veracity of its sources and by the pristine lens of its interpreter.

[636]   OIC, p. 3:  "Dr. Berman stated that '[i]n my opinion and to a 100% degree of medical certainty, the death of Vincent Foster was a suicide.  No plausible evidence has been presented to support any other conclusion.'"[fn3]  OIC, p. 102: "In sum, Dr. Berman, based on his evaluation of the evidence, concluded:  'In my opinion and to a 100% degree of certainty, the death of Vincent Foster was a suicide. No plausible evidence has been presented to  support any other conclusion.'"[fn327]  OIC, p.110:  "Indeed, the evidence was sufficient for Dr. Berman to conclude that 'to a 100% degree of medical certainty, the death of Vince Foster was a suicide.'"[fn350]

The official explanation for the death has appeared in the press hundreds of times in the last six years, beginning even before the first official verdict was public. These articles repeated, over and over again, that Mr. Foster had in fact committed suicide, and that he did so because of his clinical depression and perfectionist personality. Two-and-a-half years later, The American Psychologist published Dr. Sidney Blatt's The Destructiveness of Perfectionism, a study which used some of these early articles ("detailed reports") as its data. The OIC hired Dr. Berman, who apparently relied on The Destructiveness of Perfectionism in concluding that Mr. Foster took his own life because he was suffering clinical depression associated with his perfectionism. The OIC relied on Berman's conclusion in ruling that the death was, in fact, a suicide, which the media duly repeated. Thus, the psychological opinions of the reporters, based on information from unnamed sources, have come full circle. We will review this process.

But before we do, we will look at excerpts of a March 1993, speech given by former Associated Press investigative reporter Robert Parry. The subject of the speech is how the most controversial facts of the Iran-Contra affair remained largely unknown to the public. Parry's speech, given four months before Mr. Foster's death, may provide us with some insight to the media's coverage of the Foster case.

Parry said that in the seventies and early eighties, the Washington press corps was "the Watergate press corps," "fairy aggressive," "not inclined to believe... the government," and "when necessary, adversarial." During the twelve years that he worked for AP, 1974 through 1986, he saw a change, beginning with the pre-scandal denial to Congress that the Sandinistas were guilty of the human rights violations as reported by journalists in the field. Then, as the three parts of the Iran-Contra scandal broke in succession, pressure was applied to shape the media's account of the facts. Parry witnessed efforts to "discredit the journalists." The next two-and-a-half pages are taken exclusively from Parry's March, 1993, talk.

[W]hat we began to see was something that I think was unusual I think even for Washington - certainly it was unusual in my experience - a very nasty, often ad hominem attack on the journalists who were not playing along... And sadly, it worked. So, the message was quite clearly, made to those of us working on this topic that when you tried to tell the American people what was happening, you put your career at risk.

*     *     *

And what it did was escalate the pressure on journalists who were left, who were still trying to look at this in a fairly honest way and tell the American people what they could find out... In the case of NPR... Paul Allen... felt that he had no choice but to leave NPR and he left journalism altogether. These were the kind of prices that people were starting to pay, all across Washington. The message was quite clear both in the region and in Washington that you were not going to do any career advancement if you insisted on pushing these stories.

What you'll hear if you listen to the McLaughlin Group or these other shows is a general consensus - there may be disagreement on some points - but there is a general consensus of the world that is brought to bear, and often it is in absolute contradiction to the real world. It is a false reality - it's a Washington reality.

And what we have seen at the end of these twelve years, and I guess what the challenge of the moment becomes is how that gets changed. How do the American people really get back control of this - not just their government, but of their history - because it's really their history that has been taken away from them. And it's really what the Washington press corps and the Democrats in Congress as well as the Republicans are capable of, was this failure to tell the American people their history. And the reason they didn't was because they knew, or feared, that if the American people knew their real history - whether it goes back to the days of slaughters going on in El Salvador - if they had known about the little children that were put in the house and shot to death and garroted - that they wouldn't have gone along with that. And if they had known that there were felony obstructions of justice being carried out in the Oval Office they wouldn't have gone along with that either, and there would have been a real problem - there would have been a political problem I guess.

400

But it is not the role of the Washington press corps, maybe this sounds like an understatement, but it's not the role of the Washington press corps to take part in that.  Our job was supposed to be, I thought, to kind of tell people what we could find out!  We go in, we act nice, we ask a lot of questions, find some things and run out and tell you!  We're sort of like spies for the people, you know, and instead, we sort of got in there - and I guess it was real nice, we felt like we were insiders.

*      *      *

We also knew that there was a cover-up going on - which I kept insisting on even though *Newsweek* kept trying to retract it, and so I left.

*      *      *

What I think the bottom line of both books is that we are in great danger of losing our grasp of realty as a nation.  Our history has been taken away from us in key ways.  We've been lied to so often.  And important things have been blocked from us.

*      *      *

It is something that, as a democracy, we can't really allow to happen.

The main problem, at this point, is that we have a set of establishments in Washington that have failed us, as a people...  Congress failed because it didn't have the courage to stand up and do oversight and perform its constitutional responsibilities.  But what is perhaps the most shocking to Americans is that the press failed.  The press is what people sort of expect to be there as a watchdog.  What we have now, and its continuing into this new era, is the Reagan-Bush press corps.  It's a press corps that they helped to create - that they created partly by purging those, or encouraging the purging of those who were not going along, but it was ultimately the editors and the news executives that did the purging...  And this was the case all around Washington.

The people who succeeded and did well were those that didn't stand up, who didn't write the big stories, who looked the other way when history was happening in front of them, and went along whether unconsciously or just by cowardice with the deception of the American people.  And I think that's what we all have to sort of look at to see what we can do to change it.  I

think it will take a tremendous commitment by the
American people to insist on both more honest
journalism, more straightforward journalism, but also
maybe even new journalism. There has to be some other
way - some other outlets. In a way, I've grown to
despair at the possibility of reforming some of these
organizations. Maybe it can happen, but I think
ultimately, we're going to have to see a new kind of
media to replace this old one.

Parry's observations about the changes he saw in the
dynamics of the press may give us some of the explanation
of what happened in this case. Excerpts from four early
press reports of Mr. Foster's death follow. The first is
by Walter Pincus, the Washington Post's CIA beat reporter.
In his article, Pincus presented himself as a close friend
of Mr. Foster's who claimed to have known, before the
authorities had closed the first investigation, that Mr.
Foster "took his life." Pincus's article is devoid of any
discussion of the facts surrounding the death.

> Walter Pincus, Washington Post, *Vincent Foster: Out of
> His Element,* Thursday, August 5, 1993, distributed by
> Post syndication:
>
>> In the succeeding months we had him [Foster]
>> alone and his wife, Lisa when she was in tow to
>> our home for dinners. He and I met several times
>> for breakfast.
>>
>> \*       \*       \*
>>
>> In private conversations, he would handle
>> criticism of the White House in these matters
>> [nomination of Zoe Baird, Travel Office firings,
>> confirmation of Surgeon-General Jocelyn Elders]
>> calmly. He corrected critics' mistakes and
>> coolly argued the President's case. But you
>> almost could see him weighing each critical point
>> one by one, deciding which to throw away and
>> which to keep and take back with him...The travel
>> office affair was particularly vexing to him.
>>
>> \*       \*       \*
>>
>> When the [Wall Street] Journal took aim at him in
>> a lead editorial titled "Who is Vince Foster?" he
>> suddenly and surprisingly found himself
>> considered a questionable man of mystery in
>> Washington, a "crony" whose very reluctance at
>> immediately handing out a picture of himself to

an editorial page implied he had something to hide.

His composure sometimes broke when he would discuss what he considered wild assertions in one paper that would be denied but then picked up blindly by others.  He would have been amazed and extremely disturbed by the rumors that have accompanied his own suicide and found their way into print.

*　　*　　*

Near midnight that Tuesday at the Foster home in Georgetown, I sat in the garden with a few of his Arkansas friends for half an hour.  They had stories about his remarkable life in Little Rock. We then all talked - with hindsight - about how he had taken on everyone else's problems in Washington.  Each of us recalled how we had seen the little ways the pressure on him had shown through.  But none saw any sign that he would take his own life because of them and so - much too late - each voiced his own guilt about having failed Vince when he most needed help.

Similarly, a feature article appearing in the August 15, 1993 edition of Washington Post, by David Von Drehle, began by reporting that Mr. Foster drove his own "gray-brown" Honda to Fort Marcy Park and killed himself.  Von Drehle's piece is a mixture of the statistics of suicides in this country[637] and a litany of reasons for Mr. Foster to

---

[637]    D. Von Drehle, Washington Post, *The Crumbling Of A Pillar In Washington,* Aug. 15, 1993:  In America, suicide is most common among white males, with the incidence rising by age, more sharply after 45.  Most suicides leave no note.  Physicians and lawyers have unusually high suicide rates..., psychologist Robert Litman has said. *** Experts estimate that 70 percent or more of suicides are associated with depression, which has been linked to low levels of a brain chemical called serotonin.  Depression, apparently, is brought on sometimes by stressful change.  Litman has said, "I believe that suicide has a lot to do with the ideal -- often unconscious -- that one has of oneself... Suicidal people tend to believe that if they do not live up to it, their lives must be a total failure"...  People "whose sense of self-esteem is based on what others think of them" may be higher risks.  But ultimately, Colt writes,

have killed himself,[638] according to anonymous sources. It too did not discuss the facts surrounding the death. It was a preview of the OIC's Report, which would be released over four years later.

David Von Drehle, Washington Post, *The Crumbling Of A Pillar In Washington, Only Clinton Aide Foster Knew What Drove Him To Fort Marcy,* Sunday, August 15, 1993, distributed by Post syndication:

> On the afternoon of July 20, at the end of his life, deputy White House counsel Vincent Walker Foster Jr. steered his gray-brown sedan along the George Washington Memorial Parkway, up a bluff just beyond the Key Bridge.
>
> \*    \*    \*
>
> About the route to his suicide, there is no doubt. By car, this is the only way.
>
> The other road to Fort Marcy, the psychic road, is vague, mysterious and poorly marked. The map is lost - forever; it existed only in Vince Foster's mind. Some path took him -- this trusted intimate of Bill and Hillary Clinton, their "great protector," in the president's own funereal words -- to the cloistered park where, beside a cannon, he killed himself with a gunshot.
>
> \*    \*    \*
>
> "You can't have anything to hide in Washington," he told a Rose firm colleague. "If there's anything in your personal or business life that can't bear scrutiny, you shouldn't be up here."
>
> \*    \*    \*
>
> Foster somehow found time for one large nonpresidential task, addressing the graduating class of the University of Arkansas Law School,

---

"No one knows why people kill themselves... There is no single answer."

[638] D. Von Drehle, Washington Post, *The Crumbling Of A Pillar In Washington,* Aug. 15, 1993: "On May 19, Watkins fired the seven members of the [Travel Office]. *** [He and Kennedy] slowed the FBI, rather than egged it on. *** It was an enormous story, helping to drive Clinton's approval ratings to a record low for a new president... Foster was mentioned in the coverage of the report..."

his alma mater. It was his first commencement address, and he agonized over it, according to colleagues. The speech was entirely his own, and in the wake of Foster's death friends have combed it for clues.

He prized nothing more than reputation.

*   *   *

According to colleagues, Foster felt he had failed to protect the president by keeping the process under control - he, the "great protector," who once said his job was to deal with tough issues so that they do not make headlines.

*   *   *

On June 17, the *Journal's* lead editorial asked, "Who Is Vincent Foster?" a continuation of a line of attack that had begun with Hubbell. About half the essay was devoted to the *Journal's* complaint that it could not get a photograph of Foster. But woven into this puckish tale were barbs at Foster's integrity as a lawyer.

*   *   *

Another editorial appeared on July 19, the day before Foster died. Kennedy "misus[ed] the FBI's investigative powers," the editors wrote, and they concluded: "The mores on display from the Rose alumni are far from confidence-building."

To Foster, whose whole career was spent in the courtroom, the lack of evidence supporting the *Journal's* attacks was scandalous. Several friends who ventured jokes about them got a cold stare, or humorless snort, in response.

*   *   *

"It became a metaphor to him for what a snake pit this is," one top White House official said. "Yesterday's conduct judged by tomorrow's standards, with the goal being to see how many ribs you can pull out while a body's still alive."

"There was a clear sense of 'How could I let this happen? How did I let it get out of hand?'" a close Foster friend recalled. "He wasn't blaming others, at least to me. It was more introspective, along the lines of, 'Who am I? I

am an honest lawyer, wise counsel, valued for
brain and integrity.' And suddenly, that was
undermined. There was a clear sense of things
going wrong, and him at the middle of it."

*       *       *

The question that haunts his friends is this: If
he was so unhappy, why didn't he quit? It is
clear to them now that Foster felt powerless to
turn things around in the White House. "He felt
like he was running through Jell-O," one said.

But how could he go home? Picture it: Rejoin the
Rose firm after its "mores," its "view of the
law" had been attacked repeatedly (in part
because of him) by one of the most important
newspapers in America. Walk into the country
club after abandoning members as racists.
Approach new clients, having failed, in his view,
to protect the most important client a lawyer
could ever have.

And how would he live? He was, in the words of
his friends, the "tower of strength," the "rock,"
of the Arkansans. How could he leave Washington
- with the inevitable headlines: *White House Aide
Resigns in Wake of Travelgate* - and sit in Little
Rock while his friends struggled on?

"I believe he felt that way," a close friend
said. "But you go all the way around it, and it
still doesn't get to the point that you pull the
trigger."

Yet after many hours of rumination, one White
House aide thought she was beginning to
understand. "It's really easy to see how, if you
got in the tunnel, it could suck you in."

Maybe the rest of the road runs through the
tunnel.

All the anonymous sources knew that Mr. Foster
committed suicide, and why he did so, according to Von
Drehle. On the same day, also appearing in the Washington
Post, was Michael Isikoff's list of reasons for Mr. Foster
to have killed himself along with his opinion that there

406

was "no doubt that Foster was suffering from a worsening depression."

M. Isikoff, *Foster was shopping for private Lawyer, probers find*, Wash. Post, August 15, 1993:

> Foster also expressed concerns that the *Wall Street Journal* which had criticized Foster in several editorials...
>
> \* \* \*
>
> [G]iven the prospect that he might be questioned in the course of Justice Department, congressional and General Accounting Office inquiries... in connection to the travel office... Foster['s] concern about the travel office issue was evident in the handwritten note discovered in his briefcase...
>
> \* \* \*
>
> [T]he *Wall Street Journal*, which criticized Foster in several editorials, had "tarnished his reputation...
>
> \* \* \*
>
> [R]eports leave no doubt that Foster was suffering from a worsening depression...

A week later, the New York Times followed suit with Jason DeParle's feature article, also citing anonymous sources, some of whom spoke "to correct what they called misleading impressions of earlier accounts." It also used the opinions of suicide experts, as Von Drehle's piece had. DeParle claimed that Mr. Foster was "stalked by his own impossible standards of perfection."

J. DeParle, N.Y. Times, *Portrait of a White House Aide Snared by his Perfectionism  A Life Undone: A Special Report,* August 22, 1993:

> \* \* \*
>
> This account of Mr. Foster's last days is drawn from extensive interviews with White House officials, police investigators, longtime friends, and members of the extended Foster family. Some of them spoke about the situation for the first time, on the condition of anonymity, to correct what they called misleading impressions of earlier accounts.

The portrait that emerges is at least partly that of a man stalked by his own impossible standards of perfection, trapped in a world where he could no longer seem to meet them.

"This kind of perfectionism and purity is a kind of two-edged sword," said Dr. Jerome Motto, a psychiatrist at the University of California at San Francisco and an expert on suicide. "On the one hand, it makes for fantastic performance. On the other hand, it can cut you up pretty badly."

A few weeks later, the New York Times published Frank Rich's piece. Rich compared Mr. Foster's "suicide" to the subject of Calvin Trillin's book, "Remembering Denny," about Roger Denny Hansen's life and suicide. Trillin called Hansen a "golden-boy." Rich called Mr. Foster a "golden boy."

F. Rich, *Endpaper: Public Stages; Down Time*, N.Y. Times, September 5, 1993 (syndicated):

To believe that Foster's depression had no roots in Little Rock is also naïve. Recalling Foster's service as chairman of the Arkansas Repertory Theater, Sidney Blumenthal reported in the *New Yorker* that Foster "was especially proud of its performances of Broadway dramas, such as 'Night, Mother' and 'Agnes of God.'" An armchair sleuth or shrink might point out that 'Night Mother' is about a woman who shoots herself and that 'Agnes of God' tells of a nun engaged in violent martyrdom.

\*    \*    \*

The Foster and [Frank] Aller cases are echoed in another golden-boy suicide -- of another Rhodes scholar and Washington policy maker -- chronicled by Calvin Trillin this year in his book 'Remembering Denny,' Trillin had gone to Yale in the 1950's with Roger D. Hansen, a.k.a. Denny, a star athlete with a 'million dollar smile,' 'a limitless future' and a presence so potentially Presidential that his classmates pictured themselves in his cabinet...

\*    \*    \*

Trillin's baffled memoir about the demise of would-be President Hansen became a best seller this spring. Although few Americans had previously heard of Vincent Foster, his mid summer death became a national obsession. Perhaps these Capitol suicides touch the raw nerves of the country's own disillusioned mood as it lowers its expectations for a golden boy who did become President.

\* \* \*

Of course, a nation's clinical depression is as hard to gauge as an individual's. It may not be politically significant that 'Listening to Prozac," a scholarly meditation on America's current antidepressant of choice, started leapfrogging up the best-seller list just as Vincent Foster was laid to rest.

Two-and-a-half years later, The American Psychologist published Dr. Sidney Blatt's *The Destructiveness of Perfectionism*, a study which used that articles of Von Drehle, Isikoff, DeParle, and Rich, ("detailed reports") as its data. Dr. Blatt's study repeats the accounts of unnamed sources, which formed the basis of the lay opinions of Michael Isikoff, David Von Drehle, Jason DeParle, and Frank Rich. Dr. Blatt's article mentions two other suicides, but devotes most of its discussion to Mr. Foster's death.

S. Blatt, *The Destructiveness of Perfectionism,* Am. Psych. J., Vol. 50, No. 12 (Dec., 1995):

> The tragic death of Vincent Foster, a gifted and accomplished lawyer and deputy counsel to President Clinton, provides insight into how perfectionism could lead a very talented and successful individual to resort to a drastic action like killing himself - to leave family and friends at the peak of his life and career. Vincent Foster was regarded by friends and associates as a "pillar of strength" (Von Drehle, 1993, p. A21), "a rock of Gibraltar" (DeParle 1993, p.1). Rich (1993, p. 42), quoting *The Washington Post* and *The New York Times,* noted that Foster was considered "one of the golden boys
>
> \* \* \*
>
> Hillary Rodham Clinton reportedly said, "Of a thousand people who might commit suicide, I would

never pick Vince." (Rich, 1993, p. 42). Detailed reports in the public media enable us to appreciate the intensity of Vincent Foster's perfectionistic standards and his vulnerability to personal and public criticism. Extensive articles by Von Drehle (1993) in the *Washington Post* and DeParle (1993) in the *New York Times*... provided biographic materials that enable us, to some degree, to appreciate the intensity of his critical self scrutiny, his unyielding need for perfection, and the profound anguish he experienced when he felt he had failed, especially in his responsibilities to be the "great protector" (Von Drehle, 1993, p. A21) of people for whom he had felt a deep loyalty. According to DeParle (1993), "the portrait that emerges is at least partly a man stalked by his own impossible standards of perfection" (p. 22)... In a commencement address to the graduates of the University of Arkansas Law School a few months before his death, Foster stressed the importance of one's reputation... "Dents to the reputation in the legal profession are irreparable" (cited by Von Drehle, 1993, p. A20).

\*     \*     \*

Another series of events at this time involved the decision of Foster and others to resign their membership in the all-White and Christian Country Club of Little Rock, a decision that "really upset Vince... with the implication that the club and their friends were racist (Von Drehle, 1993, p. A21)...

\*     \*     \*

In this letter [note] Foster wrote... No one in the White House, to my knowledge violated any law or standard of conduct, including any action in the travel office..." (cited by Von Drehle, 1993, p. A21 [Washington Post])

\*     \*     \*

He "felt he had failed to protect the president by keeping the process under control" (Von Drehle, 1993, p. A21, [Washington Post])

\*     \*     \*

As the note written shortly before his death indicated, Foster was deeply upset by the editorials in the *Wall Street Journal*...

questioning his integrity... He believed that
they had "tarnished his reputation" (Isikoff,
1993, p. A20, [*Washington Post*]).

*        *        *

Socially prescribed perfectionism... [is] often
associated with depression and suicidal
thoughts...

*        *        *

Believing he was disgraced in Washington and
perceived as a failure in Little Rock, Foster
probably felt he had nowhere to go (Von Drehle,
1993, [Washington Post]).

*        *        *

Calvin Trillin (1993) also wrote about the
suicide at age 51 of a "golden boy" he had known
at Yale, Roger (Denny) Hansen...

*        *        *

These accounts of Vincent Foster, Alasdair
Clayre, and Denny Hansen are typical of numerous
examples of talented, ambitious, and successful
individuals who are driven by intense needs for
perfection and plagued by intense self-scrutiny,
self-doubt, and self-criticism.

*        *        *

Although **it is inappropriate to make a formal
clinical diagnosis without personal contact with
the patient,** extensive knowledge about a person's
life (Hersh & Lazar, 1993), and/or a
comprehensive psychological assessment, clearly
Foster was experiencing considerable
depression.[639]
(emphasis supplied)

The process seems to have transformed the reporters'
lay opinion into one of an expert. The OIC signed on.

OIC, p. 98, fn. 303:

*"Berman Report at 3. Dr. Berman noted that '[r]ecent
studies... have documented a significant relationship
between perfectionism and both depression and
suicidality, particularly when mediated by stress.'
Id. at 3."*

---

[639]   See S. Blatt, *The Destructiveness of Perfectionism*, Am.
Psych. J.; Vol. 50, No. 12 (Dec., 1995).

The unanimous 1993 conclusion of journalists Von Drehle, DeParle, Isikoff, and Rich is the same as the conclusion of Dr. Berman, which was released to the public in the OIC's 1997 Report.[640]  The media reported it, again.

---

[640]  OIC, p, 15:  In his report, Dr. Berman first noted that "[d]escriptors used by interviewees with regard to Vincent Foster's basic personality were extraordinarily consistent in describing a controlled, private, **perfectionist** character whose public persona as a man of integrity, honesty, and unimpeachable **reputation** was of utmost importance."[fn303]

OIC, p. 99:  "He, furthermore, faced a feared humiliation should he resign and return to Little Rock"[fn308]  OIC, p. 99:  "The torn note 'highlights his preoccupation with themes of guilt, anger, and his **need to protect others**.'[fn309]"

OIC, p. 99:  Dr. Berman reported that "[m]istakes, real or perceived, posed a profound threat to his self-esteem/self-worth and represented evidence for lack of control over his environment.  Feelings of unworthiness, inferiority, and guilt followed and were difficult for him to tolerate.  There are signs of an intense and **profound anguish**, harsh self-evaluation, **shame**, and chronic fear.

OIC, p. 100:  Dr. Berman said that Mr. Foster's "last 96 hours show clear signs of crisis and uncharacteristic vulnerability."[fn317]  Dr. Berman concluded, furthermore, that "[t]here is little doubt that Foster was **clinically depressed** . . . in early 1993, and, perhaps, sub-clinically even before this."[fn318]

OIC, p. 101:  As to why Mr. Foster was overwhelmed at that particular time, Dr. Berman explained that Mr. Foster was "under an increasing burden of intense external stress, a loss of security, a **painful scanning** of his environment for negative judgments regarding his performance, a rigid hold of **perfectionistic** self-demands..."

OIC, p. 104:  During that six-month period, certain other aspects of Mr. Foster's life also came under some scrutiny.  For example, in May 1993, a controversy arose over membership of Administration officials in **the Country Club** of Little Rock, which had no black members.  Mr. Foster was a member of that club and resigned from it that month.  On a copy of a May 11, 1993, newspaper article in Mr. Foster's office that mentioned the controversy, Mr. Foster wrote, "I wish I had done more."[fn331]

## State of mind

Micah Morrison, <u>Wall Street Journal</u>, *In Re: Vincent Foster,* November 25, 1997:

> Now Independent Counsel Kenneth Starr has compiled the results of a much more comprehensive investigation, a 114-page "Report on the Death of Vincent W. Foster Jr.," released in October by

---

<u>OIC, p. 105</u>: According to Mr. Foster's brother-in-law, former Congressman Beryl Anthony, Mr. Foster said words to the effect that he had "spent a lifetime building [his] **reputation** and was in the process of having it **tarnished.**"[fn334] As Dr. Berman noted, reputation was clearly important to Mr. Foster. Indeed, in the May 8, 1993 commencement address, Mr. Foster said that **"[d]ents to the reputation in the legal profession are irreparable"** and that "no victory, no advantage, no fee, no favor . . . is worth even a blemish on your reputation for intellect and integrity." He emphasized that the "reputation you develop for intellectual and ethical integrity will be your greatest asset or your worst enemy."

<u>OIC, p. 105</u>: At the same time, the White House staff generally was subject to media criticism during the first six months of the Administration. Some public criticism suggested incompetence, if not malfeasance, by staff members. Mr. Foster himself was mentioned several times in some of the critical editorial commentary. Numerous witnesses said that **Mr. Foster was concerned and/or upset over the press criticism.**[fn333]

<u>OIC, p. 106</u>: The **Travel Office matter**, in particular, was the subject of public controversy beginning in May 1993 and continuing through Mr. Foster's death. Criticism focused on the White House's handling of the matter before and after the May 19 firings. Legislation enacted on July 2, 1993, required the General Accounting Office (GAO) to investigate the Travel Office Firings. There was a possibility of some form of congressional review, or perhaps special counsel investigation.[fn335]

<u>OIC, p. 106-107</u>: At some point in the last week of his life, Mr. Foster wrote a note [fn337] that he had "made mistakes from ignorance, inexperience and overwork" and that he "was not meant for the job or the spotlight of public life **in Washington. Here ruining people is considered sport.**"[fn338] <u>OIC, p. 114</u>: "Dr. Berman concluded that '[i]n my opinion and to a 100% degree of medical certainty, the death of Vincent Foster was a suicide. No plausible evidence has been presented to support any other conclusion.'"[fn353] (emphasis supplied)

the Special Division of the U.S. Court of Appeals for the District of Columbia. "An evident clinical depression," was the diagnosis of Alan Berman, executive director of the American Association of Suicidology and one of the many experts Mr. Starr brought in to assist with the probe. "There are signs of an intense and profound anguish, harsh self-evaluation, shame, and chronic fear." "Mr. Foster's last 96 hours show clear signs of crisis and uncharacteristic vulnerability," Dr. Berman writes. In poignant new disclosures, Mr. Starr reports that Mr. Foster cried while talking to his wife on the Friday before his death, and in a letter to a friend wrote that "pressure, financial sacrifice, and family disruption are the price of public service at this level. As they say, "The wind blows hardest at the top of the mountain."

The wind was blowing hard at Mr. Foster from many directions. Though there was no "single, obvious triggering event" to explain the suicide, Mr. Starr writes that Mr. Foster seemed particularly plagued by the Travel Office affair. Other matters troubling him included litigation surrounding Hillary Clinton's Health Care Task Force and media criticism, led by our editorials. But also issues related to the Clinton's personal finances, their tax returns and the "1992 sale of their interest in Whitewater."

When the first investigation closed, August 5, 1993, the Washington Post had already published an article by Walter Pincus stating that Mr. Foster had "taken on everyone else's problems in Washington," that his death was a suicide, and that questions regarding that conclusion were based on "rumors." The verdict of depression, which would be repeated for the next six years, was exemplified in two articles in the Washington Post's August 15 Sunday edition, an August 22, New York Times piece, and a September 5, New York Times Magazine piece. The long summarizing Sunday Post and Times articles were widely syndicated.

These media reports are the data on which the psychological study was based, Berman almost certainly relied on the study, the OIC relied on Berman, and media reported the OIC's "*100% certain*" verdict. Thus, the psychological opinion of Michael Isikoff, David Von Drehle, Jason DeParle, and Frank Rich, based on information from unnamed sources, has come full circle,[641] and is now the OIC's psychologist's official expert opinion.[642]

---

[641] Mr. Foster was suffering from severe depression, according to Michael Isikoff, then to DeParle and Rich. Drs. Blatt and Berman agreed. Dr. Blatt accepted the accounts of Isikoff, DeParle, Von Drehle, and Rich of the importance to Mr. Foster of his reputation. Blatt said it caused him "profound anguish." Von Drehle made much of Mr. Foster's anguish over resignation from all-white Country Club. So did Dr. Blatt, Dr. Berman and the OIC. DeParle, Von Drehle, and Isikoff gave the Travel Office matter and the Wall Street Journal Editorials as the primary triggering events for Mr. Foster's demise. So did Drs. Blatt and Berman. DeParle and Von Drehle covered the unsigned torn note, discovered six days after the death in the previously searched and thought to be empty briefcase, in 28 pieces with one piece missing. Dr. Blatt's study followed suit, as did the OIC. Von Drehle called the torn note a list of his "complaints," chiefly among them being that in Washington, "ruining people is considered sport." Mr. Foster suffered from a negative self-image, according to the reporters, Dr. Blatt, Dr. Berman and the OIC. According to Von Drehle, the negative self-image was significant enough to keep Mr. Foster from returning to Little Rock. Dr. Blatt concurred. Von Drehle reported that Foster felt he had failed as the "great protector." Dr. Blatt agreed. So did Dr. Berman and the OIC. Von Drehle reported that Mr. Foster "felt powerless to turn things around." Dr. Blatt opined that he had "feelings of failure, anxiety, anger, helplessness." The OIC followed suit. Both Von Drehle and Dr. Blatt describe Mr. Foster as overwhelmed by feelings of unworthiness, failure, guilt, and disapproving self-criticism. Frank Rich compared Mr. Foster to Roger D. Hansen in Calvin Trillin's book, Remembering Denny. So did Dr. Blatt, calling Mr. Foster and Mr. Hansen perfectionists. Dr. Berman too concluded that Mr. Foster was a perfectionist.

[642] See H. Fineman & B. Cohen, *The Mystery of the White House Suicide,* Newsweek Magazine, August 2, 1993: The park Police and the Justice Department now insist that they want to know not just the "if" of suicide, but the "why" as well. If they really want to know the reason why, said Edwin Schneidman, professor emeritus of thanatology at the University of California, Los Angeles, they will have to perform what he calls a "psychological autopsy"...

## XI.  INVESTIGATIVE HISTORY

Because the initial investigation was in fact conducted jointly by the Park Police and the FBI, both agencies bear responsibility for almost all of the deficiencies that occurred during that seventeen-day period. Basic investigative procedures were ignored, both at the scene[643] and thereafter.[644] Significantly, the death was not investigated as homicide until foul play could be ruled out, the fundamental tenet of any death investigation.

### 1.  The FBI and the first 17-day probe

When more than one agency works the same case, one agency may assume the responsibility for the investigation. This assumption of the role as the lead investigative agency is called assuming primary jurisdiction.

Initially, the FBI admitted that a federal statute[645] required it to exercise primary jurisdiction over the case. Next, the Fiske Report declared that the FBI did not need to determine whether the statute covered Mr. Foster's death.  The third version, provided in the OIC's Report, is that the statute did not mandate that the FBI investigate Mr. Foster's death.

At a August 10, 1993 press conference, given to announce the results of the joint FBI/Park Police investigation, Robert Bryant, then Special Agent-in-Charge of the FBI's Washington Metropolitan Field Office,

---

[643]  For example, there was no effort made to determine the time of death, the crime scene was not secured, all persons known to have been at the park, as well as at the body site, were not interviewed, and there was no canvas of the neighborhood.

[644]  For example, the firearm was not tested for operability, Mr. Foster's handwriting was authenticated without the benefit of a certified document examiner, the police did not attend the entire autopsy, there was no effort made to determine if Mr. Foster left the White House grounds alive, and a number of persons with whom Mr. Foster spent his final 72 hours have never been interviewed.

[645]  18 U.S.C. § 1751, *Presidential and Presidential staff assassination.*

explained why the FBI investigated.

> "[T]here is a death of a high government official that's covered by the assault or assassination statute..."[646]

FBI Agent John Danna was one of the FBI agents who initially investigated the death. Agent Danna knew the statutory basis for the FBI's participation, as he later told the Senate investigators probing the removal of documents from Mr. Foster's office.

> "It was that violation... the potential violation involving a presidential staff member... Title 18, section 1751."[647]

> \* \+ \*

> "[T]he only basis we have on our squad is the 175[1] classification, which is a Presidential staff member investigation... we have to have a reason to do investigations, and the only reason we had is, again for a Presidential thing."[648]

At the August 10, 1993 press conference, then FBI Special-Agent-in-Charge Bryant explained that the FBI ruled the death a suicide.

> "We [FBI] followed this case from the time we were notified until we were basically of the opinion, along with Chief Langston's staff, that this was a suicide."[649]

---

[646]   Exhibit 162, Transcript of August 10, 1993 press conference with Deputy Attorney General Philip B. Heymann, Chief of U.S. Park Police Robert Langston, Special Agent-in-Charge of the FBI's Washington Metropolitan Field Office Robert Bryant.

[647]   Exhibit 85, Deposition of FBI Agent John K. Danna, June 28, 1995.

[648]   Exhibit 85, Deposition of FBI Agent John K. Danna, June 28, 1995.

[649]   Exhibit 162, Transcript of August 10, 1993 press conference with Philip B. Heymann, Deputy Attorney General, Robert Langston, Chief, U.S. Park Police, Robert Bryant, Special Agent-in-Charge of the Washington Metropolitan Field Office, FBI.

A year after Mr. Foster's death, on June 30, 1994, just over five months after Mr. Fiske's appointment, the *Report of the Independent Counsel In Re Vincent W. Foster, Jr.* ("Fiske Report") was released. The second page of the Fiske Report unabashedly explained that the FBI in fact conducted the probe.

> The Federal Bureau of Investigation ("FBI") provided substantial and invaluable support in this investigation. The FBI assigned seven experienced agents to the Independent Counsel's Washington office, all of whom have worked exclusively with this office for approximately the last four months. Assistance was also provided by representatives of the FBI's National Center for the Analysis of Violent Crime. In addition, experts in the FBI Laboratory performed a thorough analysis of the available evidence.[650]

Under its section entitled *Summary of Conclusions,* the Fiske Report declared that there was "no evidence" to contradict the official version of events.

> On the afternoon of July 20, 1993, in Fort Marcy Park, Fairfax County, Virginia, Vincent W. Foster, Jr. committed suicide by firing a bullet from a .38 caliber revolver into his mouth. As discussed below, the evidence overwhelmingly supports this conclusion, and there is no evidence to the contrary.[651]

The Fiske Report explained that "the FBI did not determine whether Foster was covered by this statute." It need not make this determination, it reasoned, "because the preliminary investigation by the FBI provided no indication of criminal activity."[652] Under this analysis, the case was

---

[650] <u>Exhibit 12</u>, Fiske Report, June 30, 1994.

[651] <u>Exhibit 12</u>, Fiske Report, June 30, 1994.

[652] <u>Exhibit 12</u>, Fiske Report, June 30, 1994: The FBI would have had primary investigative jurisdiction if the circumstances fell within the Presidential and Presidential Staff Assassination statute, Title 18, United States Code, Section 1751. That statute makes it a federal crime to, among other things, kill the President, Vice-President, or a specified number of persons appointed by the President or Vice-President. The statute further provides that violations shall be investigated by the FBI.* Based on a

so obviously open-and-shut that there was no need for an investigation.

The third version, that the federal statutes were inapplicable to the investigation into Mr. Foster's death, is provided by the OIC.

OIC, p. 4, fn. 4:

*See 16 U.S.C. § 1a-6(b). The FBI has mandatory jurisdiction to investigate the murders of certain high-ranking individuals employed at the White House -- those appointed under Section 105 (a)(2)(A) of title 3 employed in the Executive Office of the President. See 18 U.S.C. § 1751 (a) (defining persons covered by statute). Mr. Foster was appointed under Section 105 (a)(2)(B) and thus was not an official covered by Section 1751. OIC Doc. No. DC-210-5151.*

The Statute to which the OIC refers fixes the salaries of fifty executive branch employees. Twenty-five, appointed under 105 (a)(2)(A), were paid salaries of $133,600. The other twenty-five, appointed under 105 (a)(2)(B), were paid $123,100 per year.[653] The *Presidential and Presidential staff assassination* statute mandates that the FBI investigate assaults and assassinations of those

---

preliminary inquiry by the FBI which failed to indicate any criminal activity, the FBI's inquiry into this matter was closed... *I8 U.S.C. Section 1751 covers "any person appointed under section 105(a)(2)(A) of title 3 employed in the Executive Office of the President... Title 3, United States Code, Section 105(a)(2)(A) provides that the President may appoint twenty-five employees at a specified rate of pay. Because the preliminary investigation by the FBI provided no indication of criminal activity, the FBI did not determine whether Foster was covered by this statute.

[653] Section 105(a)(2), subparagraph (A) of Title 3 provides that "the President may appoint... 25 employees at rates... paid for level II of the Executive Schedule of section 5314 of Title 5...", whereas subparagraph (B) provides that "the President may appoint... 25 employees at rates not to exceed the rate... paid for level III... of section 5314..." Under the 1993 version of section 5314 of Title 5, level II employees were paid $133,600 annually and level III employees were paid $123,100.

top twenty-five employees appointed pursuant to 105 (a)(2)(A), paid $133,600.[654] According to the OIC, Mr. Foster's position of deputy White House counsel was in the bottom half of these fifty employees,[655] yet it offers no proof of its position.

Thus, there are three distinct official versions of whether the statute mandated that the FBI exercise primary jurisdiction over the investigation into Mr. Foster's death. But no matter which of the three versions is true (that the death was covered, that it was not, or that coverage was undetermined), the FBI had a vested interest in a finding of no criminal activity. The FBI did in fact initially investigate along with the Park Police, at which time it ruled that the death was a suicide.[656] Therefore,

---

[654] Section 1751 of Title 18 of the United States Code, *Presidential and Presidential staff assassination... and assault...,* covers "any person appointed under Section 105(a)(2)(A) of Title 3 employed in the Executive Office of the President...."

[655] Mr. Foster's salary is not public information.

[656] Compare M. Isikoff, *Park Police to Conduct Inquiry 'Routine' Probe Set On Foster's Death,* Wash. Post, July 27, 1993: The Justice Department yesterday backed off its pledge to conduct a full investigation into the death of White House senior aide Vincent Foster Jr., saying it was merely participating in a low-level "inquiry" that was being run by the U.S. Park Police. "There is no investigation being conducted by the Justice Department," chief department spokesman Carl Stern said. Because Park Police officials are convinced that Foster took his own life, the department had no authority to launch such a probe, Stern said. "There's no suspicion that a crime occurred," he said. At the same time, a Park Police official minimized that agency's inquiry, calling it a "routine" probe that was primarily aimed at assuring investigators there was a general explanation, such as depression, for Foster to have killed himself... *** Stern's comments yesterday appear to conflict with statements made by White House and Justice Department officials... *** Stern sought to minimize the apparent conflict yesterday, suggesting that some of it may result from a semantical confusion over the difference between an inquiry and "an investigation" that is launched to solve a crime... *** [A]n FBI official said yesterday the bureau

the FBI had an interest in a finding of no criminal activity in both of its subsequent investigations. Moreover, if Mr. Foster's death were not a suicide, the FBI would have violated the *Presidential and Presidential staff assassination* statute by not exercising primary jurisdiction as it requires -- another reason why the FBI has had a vested interest in a finding of no criminal activity.

The OIC concealed the breadth of the FBI's role in the initial seventeen-day death investigation, conducted jointly with the US Park Police from July 20, 1993 through August 5, 1993. The OIC's Report merely states that the FBI *"assisted the Park Police in certain aspects"* of the case, and that the FBI opened a *"separate"* investigation regarding the discovery of the alleged suicide note. There is no discussion as to why the investigation of the note was separate and apart from the investigation into the death of its author.[657] The OIC's version of the *"primary*

---

was merely "monitoring" the inquiry but not actively participating.

[657]   OIC. p. 4:  The FBI assisted the Park Police in certain aspects of the ensuing death investigation, as did other federal and Virginia agencies. Moreover, the FBI, at the direction of the Department of Justice, opened a separate investigation of possible obstruction of justice after a note was found on Monday, July 26, 1993, in Mr. Foster's briefcase at the White House. On August 10, 1993, the Department of Justice, FBI, and Park Police jointly announced the result of the death and note investigations.

OIC, p. 2:  "Two law enforcement investigations -- the initial United States Park Police investigation... concluded that Mr. Foster committed suicide by gunshot at Fort Marcy Park." OIC, p. 4:  "Because Mr. Foster's body was found in Fort Marcy Park, a park maintained by the National Park Service, the United States Park Police conducted the investigation of his death.[fn4]"

See *FBI Probes Handling of Foster Note*, Wash. Post, July 31, 1993:  The [FBI] agents were brought in to determine why 30 hours elapsed before it was turned over to U.S. Park Police investigating Foster's apparent suicide on July 20. *** Justice Department Spokesman Carl Stern said that Deputy Attorney General Philip B. Heymann requested that the FBI conduct the interviews on the handling of the note as part of an upcoming Park Police report on Foster's

*issues that have been raised*" about the case, which it sets out on page ten of its Report to define the parameters of its ensuing 104 pages, does not include the FBI's role in any investigation.[658]

The public has been told that only the US Park Police investigated from the time of the discovery of Mr. Foster's body, until the case was officially closed (the first time) sixteen days later. But publicly available federal government records demonstrate that throughout the 17-day Park Police investigation, FBI participation was considerable. This FBI participation is variously described as "investigated," "conducted interviews," "followed," "working on," "assisting" and "working leads."

On the evening of the discovery of Mr. Foster's body, the FBI arranged to send FBI Agents Scott Salter and Dennis Condon to the White House to investigate the death.[659] They were dispatched to the White House the following morning, as Agent Salter testified.

"[FBI Agent] John Danna called us in my car [on July 21] and told us to go to the southwest gate of the White House and meet him there and that we were to,

---

death. The idea was to have a "clearly disinterested party" review the matter.

[658] <u>OIC. p. 9-10</u>: The primary issues that have been raised regarding the cause and manner of Mr. Foster's death can be grouped into several broadly defined categories: (1) forensic issues; (2) apparent differences in statements of private witnesses, Park Police personnel, and Fairfax County Fire and Rescue Department (FCFRD) personnel regarding their activities and observations at Fort Marcy Park on July 20; (3) physical evidence (such as the fatal bullet) that could not be recovered; and (4) the conduct of the Park Police investigation and the autopsy.[fn15]

[659] <u>Exhibit 84</u>, Deposition of Secret Service Agent Dennis S. Martin, June 22, 1995: Q. On the evening of the 20th, Mr. Imbordino told you to meet [FBI] investigators the next morning? A. He said I would help facilitate getting the investigators in, yes... before 9:00 a.m... I had been told the night before they would be going up to Mr. Nussbaum's office to talk about Mr. Foster's death.

that we were going to be working on a death
investigation involving Mr. Foster's death."[660]

At his June 30, 1995 deposition, when handed a
memorandum and asked to identify it, Agent Salter said,
"[I]t's basically a summary of events from the 21st through
the conclusion of, through August 4th or 6th or whatever it
was, through the conclusion of the investigation that we
did."[661]  Park Police Captain Charles Hume signed Park
Police "Synopsis/Conclusion" of the investigation on August
5, 1993.[662]

Salter explained that the FBI's function was to
interview witnesses along with the U.S. Park Police:  "We
were there to assist them in conducting the investigation
which meant interviewing co-workers... [and] then proceed
as the investigation, you know, called for."[663]

Department of Interior Chief of Staff Thomas Collier
testified on deposition on June 23, 1995 that "the FBI and
the Park Police ended up working on this kind of hand in
glove."[664]  US Secret Service Agent Paul Imbordino, in
response to the question at his June 22, 1995 deposition
"Who conducted the interviews?" answered "Park Police and
FBI."[665]  Other FBI agents who conducted interviews during
the initial investigation into Mr. Foster's death included
Charles K. Dorsey[666] and Bradley J. Garrett.[667]

---

[660]    Exhibit 65, Deposition of FBI Agent Scott Salter, June 30,
1995.

[661]    Exhibit 65, Deposition of FBI Agent Scott Salter, June 30,
1995.

[662]    Exhibit 159, Park Police Report, signed by Park Police
Captain Charles Hume, August 5, 1993.

[663]    Exhibit 65, Deposition of FBI Agent Scott Salter, June 30,
1995.

[664]    Exhibit 163, Deposition of Department of Interior Chief of
Staff Thomas Collier, June 23, 1995.

[665]    Exhibit 164, Deposition of Secret Service Agent Paul
Imbordino, June 22, 1995 deposition.

[666]    Exhibit 165, Report of FBI interview of Chief of Staff for
the First Lady Margaret Williams, August 3, 1993.

During his July 30, 1994, deposition, US Park Police
Major Robert Hines testified that the FBI dominated much of
the investigation.

> Q. Did there come a time when you determined that
> [the] Department of Justice was really in charge
> of this investigation?"
> A. There came a time when I determined that they were
> calling a lot of shots, setting up a lot of
> protocols... [and that this became evident] on the
> evening of July 22."[668]

During the course of the initial investigation, FBI
agents interviewed over two dozen people regarding events
leading up to and immediately following Mr. Foster's
death,[669] far more than the Park Police interviewed.

At the August 10, 1993 press conference, Deputy
Attorney General Philip Heymann explained that "[t]he FBI

---

[667]   Exhibit 183, Report of FBI interview of Director of White
House Personnel David Watkins, August 5, 1993.

[668]   Exhibit 124, Deposition of Park Police Major Robert Hines,
July 30, 1994.

[669]   Exhibit 160, Table of Contents of reports of FBI
interviews, by FBI Agent Scott Salter, August 9, 1993:
[Assistant White House Counsel] Stephen Neuwirth, [White
House Counsel] Bernard Nussbaum, [Deputy Assistant Counsel
to the President] Charles W. Burton, [White House Chief of
Staff] Thomas McLarty, [Assistant to the President] David
Gergen, James Hamilton, [Deputy Attorney General] Phillip
Heymann, Leonard Megby, [Assistant Counsel] Clifford Sloan,
[Secret Service Agent] Donald Flynn, [Secret Service Agent]
Paul Imbordino, [Deputy Assistant Attorney General] David
Margolis, [Deputy Assistant Attorney General] Roger Adams,
[Park Police Captain] Charles Hume, [Park Police Detective]
Peter Markland, [White House executive secretary] Deborah
Gorham, Duncan Sellers, Ray Scott, Susan Purvis, Joseph
Purvis, Roger Kammerdeiner, Joseph Phillips, James Young,
[Chief of staff to the First Lady] Margaret Williams,
[Special assistant to the President] Patsy Thomasson,
[Assistant to the President] David Watkins.

See also FBI/Park Police interviews of Secretary to the White
House Counsel Betsy Pond, Executive assistant to the White House
Counsel Linda Tripp, and Staff assistant Tom Castleton.

joined the Park Police in the initial stages of the inquiry into Vince Foster's death... [and] the FBI has been assisting in that investigation..."[670]

The FBI officially closed its first investigation on August 5, 1993. But at the press conference Mr. Heymann said he had "received an FBI report this morning...",[671] four days after the FBI and Park Police had officially closed the case.

The day after the death, July 21, FBI agents met with White House Counsel Bernard Nussbaum, Assistant White House Counsel Steven Neuwirth and Assistant White House Counsel Clifford Sloan to discuss the search of Mr. Foster's office. The press focused on Mr. Nussbaum's refusal to let authorities see all the documents he reviewed during the office search on July 22 in the presence of the FBI and the Park Police, and later, to allegations that White House personnel searched the office before Nussbaum's official search.

No press account has ever mentioned the FBI's prior search, memorialized by a US Secret Service Report, written by a TSD (Technical Security Division) officer of the US Secret Service. On August 3, 1993, that officer wrote that on July 31, 1993, eleven days after the death, an FBI agent told him of the FBI's involvement in the case.

> "[The agent]... and some other agents (five) were working on the Foster suicide... working... leads on some info they had received..."[672]

This Report also recounts that another Secret Service Officer told the author that, by the time the locks to Mr. Foster's office had been changed, FBI agents had already removed "evidence" from Mr. Foster's office.

---

[670]   Exhibit 162, Transcript of August 10, 1993 press conference with Philip B. Heymann, Deputy Attorney General, Robert Langston, Chief, U.S. Park Police, Robert Bryant, Special Agent-in-Charge of the Washington Metropolitan Field Office, FBI.

[671]   Exhibit 162, Transcript of August 10, 1993 press conference with Philip B. Heymann, Deputy Attorney General, Robert Langston, Chief, U.S. Park Police, Robert Bryant, Special Agent-in-Charge of the Washington Metropolitan Field Office, FBI.

[672]   Exhibit 166, US Secret Service Memorandum, August 3, 1993.

The reason for the Officer there and the lock request [was] to seal the office for the investigation. The [Uniformed Secret Service] officer then told us [the author and another T.S.D. officer] that the FBI had removed evidence from Mr. Foster's desk, never inferring [sic] what the evidence was.[673]

The source of the information that "the FBI had removed evidence" was the Officer who was there to change the locks on Wednesday, July 21 at 10:30 p.m.[674] So, we know that the FBI had to have removed evidence from Mr. Foster's office before the locks were changed. The FBI was later charged with determining who had secretly ferreted out documents from Mr. Foster's office in the aftermath of his death,[675] and determining what was removed.

### 2. Publicity of the removal of Whitewater documents from Mr. Foster's office on the eve of the Fiske probe

The Independent Counsel Statute expires every five years, unless reenacted. Congress let it expire on December 15, 1993. It was not until August of 1994 that Congress reenacted the statute and the three-judge panel of the United States Court of Appeals for the DC Circuit regained its power to appoint a special prosecutor.

---

[673] Exhibit 166, US Secret Service Memorandum, August 3, 1993.

[674] Exhibit 167, Federal Security Systems Work Orders for lock change in Mr. Foster's White House Office, July 21, 1993.

[675] See Exhibit 178, Senate testimony of FBI Agent Lawrence Monroe, July 29, 1994:

> Senator Faircloth: As a professional law enforcement Officer, would you infer from the removal of these documents the evening of Mr. Foster's death after the office was supposed to have been secured, would that constitute obstruction of justice?
> Mr. Monroe: I can make no inference there, and that is going to be, and is, part of our continuing investigation, sir.

[Senate Report 104-280 (June 17, 1996), which specifically addressed the issue of the removal of documents from Mr. Foster's office in the aftermath of his death, fails to address the prospect of culpability of any FBI agents.]

In late 1993, federal regulations did, however, authorize Attorney General Janet Reno to appoint what is know as a "regulatory" Independent Counsel. Six months to the day after Mr. Foster died, January 20, 1994, Ms. Reno appointed Robert B. Fiske, Jr., to serve as regulatory Independent Counsel. His mandate was to investigate whether there were violations of criminal law relating to the Clintons' "relationship with:

(1)  Madison Guaranty Savings and Loan Association;
(2)  Whitewater Development Corporation; or
(3)  Capital Management Services."[676]

Mr. Foster's name was linked to Whitewater and to the failed Madison Guaranty Savings & Loan in two articles that appeared in the Washington Post in early November, 1993.[677] On December 18, 1993, the Washington Post published an article by Michael Isikoff, *Probe Pursues White House Aide's Undisclosed Diary*.[678] It reported that in December, an anonymous "Park Police investigator has said he recalls seeing 'paperwork' related to McDougal in the pile of documents he inspected at Hamilton's office" five months earlier, in July of 1993.[679] According to the next day's New York Times, anonymous sources were "trying to

---

[676]  28 CFR § 603.1 (1993) (Code of Federal Regulations).

[677]  See M. Isikoff & S. Schmidt, *Clinton's Former Real Estate Firm Probed*, Wash. Post, Nov. 2, 1993. "[T]he late Vincent Foster, the Clintons' personal attorney and later Deputy White House counsel, met McDougal to execute the sale of the Clintons' interest in Whitewater to McDougal." See also S. Schmidt, *Regulators Say They Were Unaware Of Clinton Law Firm's S&L Ties*, Wash. Post, Nov. 3, 1993. "Madison Guaranty Savings and Loan, failed in 1989, costing taxpayers... According to FDIC records, however, the late Vincent Foster, a Rose partner before joining the Clinton White House..."

[678]  See M. Isikoff, *Probe Pursues White House Aide's Undisclosed Diary*, Wash. Post, December 18, 1993: "One Park Police investigator has said he recalls seeing 'paperwork' related to McDougal in the pile of documents he inspected at Hamilton's office."

[679]  Exhibit 6, Deposition of Park Police Investigator John Rolla, July 21, 1994: "Myself and Lieutenant Russ, K a s s, went to Hamilton's office. This was, again, a couple days after the initial search of his office at the White House."

determine" whether Whitewater files were removed from Mr. Foster's office, "no such file was listed in the inventory," but "it was possible that the file... had been... given to James Hamilton, the family lawyer."[680]

The next day, Jerry Seper's Washington Times piece, *Clinton papers lifted after aide's suicide*,[681] reported that Whitewater documents were, in fact, ferreted out of Mr. Foster's White House office by "two Clinton political operatives... less than three hours" after the discovery of the body. It credited the account to "two U.S. Park Police investigators who asked not to be publicly identified," who said it was "not clear who took the documents," but that they were "turned over to Mr. Foster's attorney, James Hamilton."

Three days later, on December 23, 1993, the Washington Post reported White House confirmation of the removal of a file, but that attorney David Kendall, not James Hamilton, had it. A "file on Whitewater" was in the possession of "the Clinton's personal attorney, David E. Kendall," having been given to Kendall by Bernard Nussbaum.[682]

---

[680] See D. Johnston, *Missing White House File Is Sought*, N.Y. Times, December 19, 1993: Federal investigators are trying to determine whether a file relating to a failed Arkansas savings-and-loan owner and his investment firm was taken from the White House office of Vincent W. Foster Jr. after he committed suicide in July, law-enforcement officials said today... But the law enforcement officials said no such file was listed in the inventory of items in Mr. Foster's office that was conducted by Bernard W. Nussbaum, the White House Counsel, in the presence of Federal agents on July 22...

[681] See J. Seper, *Clinton papers lifted after aide's suicide*, Wash. Times, December 20, 1993: White House officials removed records... [during] a clandestine visit July 20 to Mr. Foster's office - less than three hours after his body was found... by two Clinton political operatives, according to two U.S. Park Police investigators who asked not to be publicly identified... The investigators said the existence of the Whitewater records came to light when Park Police visited Mr. Hamilton's office "about a week after the death" to review a personal diary that also was taken during one of the searches...

[682] See S. Schmidt, *Hill Seeks Probe of Land Deal*, Wash. Post, December 23, 1993: "A file on Whitewater was discovered in

The <u>Washington Times</u>'s claim, that the Park Police knew in July of 1993 that Whitewater documents were removed, is suspect. Even if the Park Police did, in fact, see the papers in July of 1993, it is unlikely that they would have known at that stage what they were viewing. The term "Whitewater," as well as Mr. McDougal's name, appeared only once as of July, 1993, in an April <u>Washington Post</u> article concerning the President's tax returns. Indeed, if the Whitewater documents had been turned over to Hamilton or Kendall, the person who took them would likely be known. That person, if he or she exists, has not yet materialized.

The OIC recounts this dubious version of events.

OIC, p. 6:

> *On December 20, 1993, the White House confirmed that Whitewater-related documents had been in Mr. Foster's White House Office at the time of his death. On January 12, 1994, President Clinton asked Attorney General Reno to appoint an independent counsel, and on January 20, 1994, the Attorney General appointed Robert B. Fiske, Jr....*

The report of the removal of Whitewater documents appeared to have provided a rationale, or pretext, for the FBI, working under the auspices of Mr. Fiske's office of the regulatory Independent Counsel, then planned and established a month later, to have its FBI agents investigate Mr. Foster's death, again.

### 3. Reports generated by Fiske's FBI probe

Most of the evidence cited in this work was generated during the Fiske probe. As we have seen, evidence that the FBI under the auspices of the Fiske probe concealed the facts surrounding Mr. Foster's death pervades the publicly available federal government record in the case.

---

Foster's office after his July 20 suicide and was turned over to the Clinton's personal attorney, David E. Kendall, by White House Counsel Bernard Nussbaum."

OIC, p. 2:

*"[The] law enforcement investigation... under the
direction of regulatory Independent Counsel Robert B.
Fiske, Jr. — concluded that Mr. Foster committed
suicide by gunshot in Fort Marcy Park."*

The Report's description of the Fiske probe as *"a new
investigation of Mr. Foster's death"* misleads the reader.
Given the FBI's significant participation in the first
probe, the Fiske probe was new in name only.

OIC, p. 6-7:

*"Mr. Fiske also opened a new investigation of Mr.
Foster's death, utilizing FBI resources and a panel of
distinguished and experienced pathologists."*

The OIC omits that Fiske's *"panel of distinguished and
experienced pathologists"* had significant ties to the FBI,
as well as to each other. Dr. James L. Luke, who headed
Fiske's pathology panel at the same time as the FBI
employed him,[683] co-authored publications with two of the
other three of the pathologists on the panel, Drs. Donald
Reay[684] and Charles Stahl.[685]

The FBI's *Law Enforcement Bulletin* published an
article by Dr. Reay.[686] Dr. Stahl held a faculty position at

---

[683]    Exhibit 12, Fiske Report, June 30, 1994:  "Employment...
Present  Forensic Pathologist, Investigative Support Unit,
Federal Bureau of Investigation, FBI Academy, Quantico,
Virginia."

[684]    Exhibit 12, Fiske Report, June 30, 1994:  "J.L. Luke, D.T.
Reay... *Correlation of Circumstances with pathological findings
in asphyxial Deaths by Hanging...*"   "J.L. Luke and D.T. Reay.
*The perils of investigating and certifying deaths in police
custody...*"

[685]    Exhibit 12, Fiske Report, June 30, 1994:  "Stahl, C.J...
Luke, J.L. *The effect of Glass as an Intermediate Target on
Bullets...*"

[686]    Exhibit 12, Fiske Report, June 30, 1994:  "D.T. Reay and
Mathers, R.L.: *Physiological effects of neck holds,* FBI Law
Enforcement Bulletin..."

the FBI Academy in Quantico, Virginia.[687] He also served on the faculty of a seminar given by the Office of the Chief Medical Examiner of Virginia, which is the office that performed the autopsy on Mr. Foster.[688]

The OIC's pathologist, Dr. Brian Blackbourne, worked for the District of Columbia Medical Examiner's Office at the same time as Dr. Stahl and Dr. Luke, the Fiske probe's lead pathologist.[689] Dr. Blackbourne also co-authored at least one publication with Dr. Luke.[690]

## 4. The FBI and the OIC

Under the heading *OIC Personnel*, the Report tells us that its investigators included three FBI agents.[691] The OIC

---

[687]    Exhibit 12, Fiske Report, June 30, 1994: "Teaching Appointments: Faculty, Advanced Forensic Pathology Course, Armed Forces Institute of Pathology, FBI Academy, Quantico, VA"

[688]    Exhibit 12, Fiske Report, June 30, 1994: "Teaching Appointments... Faculty, Medico-Legal Seminar, Office of the Chief Medical Examiner, Commonwealth of Virginia..."

[689]    Exhibit 12, Fiske Report, June 30, 1994: "Employment... 1971-1983 Chief Medical Examiner, District of Columbia Office of the Chief Medical Examiner, 19th Street and Massachusetts Ave, S.E. Washington, D.C." Exhibit 12, Fiske Report, June 30, 1994: "Faculty, Inservice Training Program in Homicide Investigation, Criminal Investigations Division, Metropolitan Police Department, District of Columbia, May 1969; October 1969; May 1970; April 1971; September 1972; March 1973; September 1973"

[690]    Exhibit 12, Fiske Report, June 30, 1994: "J.L. Luke, B.D. Blackbourne and W.J. Donovan, *Bed-Sharing Deaths Among Victims of Sudden Infant Death Syndrome - A Riddle within a Conundrum...*

[691]    OIC, p. 2-3: "The OIC's conclusion is based on analyses and conclusions of a number of experienced experts and criminal investigators retained by the OIC. They include... several experienced investigators with extensive service in the Federal Bureau of Investigation (FBI)..."

OIC, p. 12: OIC investigators who worked with these outside, independent experts included an FBI agent detailed from the FBI-MPD[fn16] Cold Case Homicide Squad in Washington, D.C. Agents with the Cold Case Squad work with MPD homicide detectives in reviewing and attempting to solve homicides that have remained unsolved for more than one

notes (p. 12) that *"these [three] investigators did not work on previous investigations of Mr. Foster's death."* It fails, however, to reveal that during the course of its three-year Foster death probe, it did use FBI agents other than the three it mentioned, and that some of these agents had been detailed to the Fiske investigation. FBI agent Russell T. Bransford, who served the grand jury subpoena on Patrick Knowlton, was one such agent.

As we have seen, the FBI Laboratory served a major role in the OIC's Report.

## 5.   Congress never conducted a probe of the death

The OIC declares on the second page of its Report that *"[t]wo inquiries in the Congress of the United States reached the same conclusion."*[692] This is not true. Not one congressional committee has ever investigated the circumstances of Mr. Foster's death.

> OIC, p. 8:
>
> [T]he [Senate Banking] Committee concluded its inquiry with a report issued on January 3, 1995, stating that "[t]he evidence overwhelmingly supports the conclusion of the Park Police that on July 20, 1993, Mr. Foster died in Fort Marcy Park from a self-inflicted gun shot wound to the upper palate of his mouth."[12]

The OIC omits that this conclusion, which it recounts under its *Congressional Inquiries* section, was outside the scope of the Committee's limited investigative jurisdiction. Senate Resolution 229, *Section 1, Scope of the Hearings*, adopted in June of 1994 by a Democratic controlled Congress, confined the Foster death inquiry to

---

year. Another OIC investigator has extensive homicide experience as a detective with the MPD in Washington, D.C., for over 20 years. Two other investigators assigned to the Foster death matter have experience as FBI agents investigating homicides of federal officials and others.[fn17]

[692]   See also OIC, p. 114:   "In sum, based on all of the available evidence, which is considerable, the OIC agrees with the conclusion reached by every official entity that has examined the issue:   Mr. Foster committed suicide by gunshot in Fort Marcy Park on July 20, 1993."

whether the White House was guilty of "improper conduct" during the course of "the Park Service Police Investigation into the death."[693] Mr. Fiske had supported the adoption of Resolution 229.

The OIC accurately excerpts the Senate Banking Committee Report which states that "[t]he evidence overwhelmingly supports the conclusion," but actually, the 1994 Banking Committee had no jurisdiction to consider the matter. Because lines of inquiry exploring the issue of how and where Mr. Foster died were beyond the Committee's limited investigative jurisdiction, the Senate Banking Committee's having included those statements in its Report was misleading.

Although most Committee members plainly disavowed having considered the issue,[694] Senator Orrin Hatch in his opening statement spoke as if the Committee had thoroughly investigated the issue and had independently determined the manner and place of the death, and that there was "is absolutely no credible evidence to contradict the Fiske Report's conclusion that Vincent Foster took his own life and it happened at Fort Marcy Park."[695]

---

[693]    Exhibit 161, *Resolution 229* states in pertinent part:

> SECTION 1.  SCOPE OF HEARINGS.
>     The Committee on Banking, Housing, and Urban Affairs (referred to as the "committee") shall—
>         (1)    conduct hearings into whether improper conduct occurred regarding —
>                     *    *    *
>         (B)    the Park Service Police investigation into the death of White House Deputy Counsel Vincent Foster;

[694]    Exhibit 26, Senate Banking Committee opening statements, July 29, 1994: Senator Carol Moseley-Braun, "Our investigation is only into the propriety of the investigation surrounding his tragic and untimely death;" Senator Robert F. Bennett, "I will be happy to stipulate that Vincent Foster committed suicide;" Senator Pete Domenici:  "I don't think anyone on our side is challenging whether or not it was a suicide."

[695]    Exhibit 26, Senate Banking Committee opening statement of Senator Orrin Hatch, July 29, 1994.

When the 1994 Senate Banking Committee had its one day hearing in July, the only representatives who appeared to represent Mr. Fiske's office were Dr. Charles Hirsch and FBI Agents Larry Monroe and William Columbell. These two agents interviewed some of the more problematic witnesses in the case, including Patrick Knowlton and the civilian who was officially the first to discover the body and who requested anonymity. We do not know who else Agents Monroe and Columbell may have of interviewed.

The other Report cited by the OIC under its *Congressional Inquiries* section is the "Summary Report," authored by Congressman William Clinger.

OIC, p. 7:

> *On February 24, 1994, Congressman William F. Clinger, Jr., then the ranking Republican on the Committee on Government Operations of the United States House of Representatives, initiated a probe into the death of Mr. Foster. Mr. Clinger's staff interviewed emergency rescue personnel, law enforcement officials, and other persons involved in the Park Police investigation of Mr. Foster's death.[fn9] Mr. Clinger's staff obtained access to the Park Police reports and to photographs taken at the scene and at the autopsy.[fn10] Mr. Clinger issued a report on August 12, 1994, concluding that "all available facts lead to the conclusion that Vincent W. Foster, Jr. took his own life in Fort Marcy Park, Virginia on July 20, 1993."[fn11]*

OIC, p. 7, fn. 9:

> *Summary Report by William F. Clinger, Jr., Ranking Republican, Committee on Government Operations, U.S. House of Representatives, on the Death of White House Deputy Counsel Vincent W. Foster, Jr., at 1 (Aug. 12, 1994)*

The OIC omitted that this Report is not a Government Operations Committee report, and that it was only six pages long (plus two pages of endnotes), and that the FBI or people associated with it supplied the information upon which it was largely based.[696]

---

[696]   Exhibit 168, Summary Report by William F. Clinger, Jr.,

## XIII.  CONCLUSION

We hope you have kept an open mind as you reviewed the evidence.  The acceptance of the existence of a conspiracy in this case challenges the views that many of us have about our government, the news media, and Mr. Starr.  Some of us may not want to learn the truth, and we have the right to ignore it.  But we also have the right to learn the truth, should we choose to, and to decide whether knowing it is important.

If the Court grants Patrick Knowlton's motion, this document will forever be available from any government printing office.  This filing is for the public.

The object of the Constitution's separation of the governmental power into three branches is to keep government honest.  Each branch pursues different interests.  Each oversees the others.  And each is adversarial when necessary.  James Madison described this constitutional technique of protecting against government corruption as an "auxiliary precaution."

We have all been told that the Congress, the media, and independent counsels have repeatedly scrutinized Mr. Foster's death, and that there was no criminal wrongdoing. Yet, this filing proves the existence of an obvious, six-year old cover-up.  Something is wrong.

The Independent Counsel statute, or Ethics in Government Act (or "Act") expires June 30, 1999, one week from the date of this filing.  Opponents of the Act argue

---

August 12, 1994:  As part of our probe, my staff or I interviewed... law enforcement officials... review FBI lab reports... a comparison of CW's statements to FBI agents... special thanks to... Office of Special Counsel Robert B. Fiske, Jr. for their assistance... the New York Post reports that former FBI director William Sessions said... Dr. James L. Luke - forensic Pathology Consultant, FBI Investigative Support Unit, FBI Academy... Isikoff reports that DOJ and FBI agents... The DOJ had earlier planned to release reports...  The autopsy was performed by Dr. Beyer... The Forensic Pathologist Panel included...  Dr. Charles Hirsch... Small traces of an anti-depressant... [were] found in Mr. Foster's bloodstream.  Fiske report at 30...  Fiske report at 30...

that, because our Constitution already provides its citizens with a system of oversight, we do not need another precaution against government corruption. In theory, they are right. But this argument assumes that the separate components of the system effectively exercise oversight over one another, and that the press acts somewhat like a watchdog.

**The Executive.** The public has been told that the US Park Police investigated from the time of the discovery of Mr. Foster's body, until the case was officially closed the first time, 17 days later. But publicly available federal government records demonstrate that throughout this first 17-day probe, FBI participation was considerable.

For the six months after the first brief probe, August through January 1994, the case was closed. At the end of January, Attorney General Reno appointed Robert Fiske to serve as regulatory Independent Counsel, and the FBI under the auspices of the Fiske probe generated most of the proof of cover-up that we reviewed above.

Six months into Mr. Fiske's tenure, in August of 1994, Mr. Starr took over, and three years later, in July, 1997 he announced the conclusion of his Foster death probe.

Technically, the Independent Counsel's investigative jurisdiction remains open until the OIC files its final Report and closes down. Therefore, the Foster case is still open. This purportedly simple case of suicide has been open for all but six months of the last six years, under the jurisdiction of the executive branch.

"The Justice Department has been near the center of almost every major political scandal of the twentieth century."[697] The term, "Independent Counsel," is short for "Counsel who is Independent from the Justice Department." In 1993, on the eve of the expiration of the last five-year term of the Independent Counsel statute, then Senator William Cohen stressed the importance under the Act of investigations being independent from the Justice

---

[697] Robert E. Palmer, *The Confrontation of the of the Legislative and Executive Branches: An Examination of the Balance of Powers and the Role of the Attorney General*, 11 Pepp. L. Rev. 331, 353-54 (1984).

## Conclusion

Department in ensuring that justice appears to have been done.

> The appearance of justice having been done is equally important as justice having been done. We can see this over a period of years where an investigation has been conducted by the Justice Department... questions have remained. They say, "Well, was it really an independent investigation or was it a cover-up, a whitewash?" When those questions tend to linger... the cloud of doubt remains, and the cynicism remains... The law, however, serves two ends, both equally important in our democratic society. One is that justice be done, and the other is that it appear to be done. The appearance of justice is just as important as justice itself, in terms of maintaining public confidence...[698]

The point of the law is to have an entity other than the Justice Department investigate allegations of, among other things, Justice Department wrongdoing. Mr. Starr seems to have missed the point.

> [I]f it's understood by the American people, [the OIC] will be understood as essentially a microcosm of the Justice Department. *** [T]he creation of that culture of the microcosm of the Justice Department has been so important to me in terms of my sense of what my obligations are as independent counsel.[699]

The creation of an OIC that is a microcosm of the DOJ, with all the attributes of the big Justice Department, is self-defeating. It is not "Independent." The need for independence from the DOJ is all the more evident in the expansions of jurisdiction of Mr. Starr's OIC. Travelgate[700] involves the administration's illegal use of

---

[698] See 139 CONG. REC. S15846-01 & S15847-01 (daily ed, Nov. 17, 1993) (statement of Sen. Cohen).

[699] Statements of Kenneth Starr at press conference, February 21, 1997.

[700] By Order entered March 22, 1996, the Court ordered: ...[T]he investigative and prosecutorial jurisdiction of Independent Counsel Kenneth W. Starr be expanded to investigate whether any violations of federal criminal law were committed by William David Watkins, former Assistant

the FBI to investigate the White House Travel Office.
Filegate[701] involves the White House's illegal use of FBI
files. The OIC is also charged with determining whether
Bernard Nussbaum, White House Counsel at the time of Mr.
Foster's death, violated the law when he testified before
Congress on June 26, 1996.

Of all of Mr. Starr's various investigations, the one
in which the necessity of maintaining independence from the
Justice Department is the most obvious is his probe of Mr.
Foster's death. Before Mr. Starr's appointment to head the
statutory OIC in August of 1994, the only substantive
investigations into Mr. Foster's death, including the first
probe, were conducted by the FBI. Yet, Mr. Starr chose to
use FBI agents and the FBI Lab to investigate Mr. Foster's
death.[702] The use of a federal investigative agency to
investigate a case that it had twice closed as a simple
suicide presents an obvious conflict of interest and
defeats the purpose of the Ethics in Government Act.
Congress cautioned against this type of conflict:

> Because independent counsels are appointed to handle
> politically sensitive investigations for the primary
> purpose of avoiding any appearance of partiality or
> bias, it is particularly important that they and their

---

to the President for Management and Administration, in
connection with his December 1993 interview with the
General Accounting Office concerning the firing of the
White House Travel Office employees and to determine
whether prosecution is warranted..."

[701] By Order entered June 21, 1996, the Court ordered:
...[T]he investigative and prosecutorial jurisdiction of
Independent Counsel Kenneth W. Starr be expanded to
investigate whether any violations of federal criminal
law... committed by Anthony Marceca... relating to requests
made by the White House between December 1993 and February
1994 to the Federal Bureau of Investigation for background
investigation reports and materials...

[702] Independent Counsel Leon Silverman, who investigated
allegations that President Reagan's Secretary of Labor Raymond
Donovan had ties to organized crime, noted that he "hired private
investigators so that the investigation would not appear to be
federally controlled." K. Harringer, Independent Justice, 1992.

# Conclusion

investigations be above any suspicion or allegation regarding conflict of interest.[703]

Because the cover-up is obvious, the OIC's attempt at maintaining the appearance of justice having been done will eventually fail. Mr. Starr's OIC will go down in history as having perpetuated a fraud on the American people, and as having joined the very corruption it was supposed to have exposed and prosecuted.

**The Congress.** The 1994 Senate Banking Committee was the only Committee that claimed to have looked into the death. Its limited investigative jurisdiction precluded it from investigating the facts of Mr. Foster's death, and only Senator Lauch Faircloth saw fit to cross-examine any of the witnesses, who were limited to FBI agents Monroe and Columbell, Park Police, Dr. Beyer, and Dr. Hirsch, one of Fiske's four pathologists. Dr. Beyer's testimony revealed that the x-rays vanished and that the witnesses had not gotten their story straight on who was responsible for rescheduling the autopsy to occur just 16 hours after the body's discovery. The determination of how or where Mr. Foster died was not an issue before the Committee and Senators from both sides of the aisle stipulated to Fiske's conclusion in opening statements. Senator Orin Hatch took a more aggressive approach, acting as if the Committee had determined the manner and location of the death. Network news broadcast it to millions.

> There is absolutely no credible evidence to contradict the Fiske Report's conclusion that Vincent Foster took his own life and it happened at Fort Marcy Park. There is no evidence to the contrary. I suspect conspiracy theorists will always differ with this conclusion...

Senator D'Amato's 1995 Committee had the requisite jurisdiction, but declined to probe the death. Our efforts to apprise the Congress of the facts have been steadfastly ignored.[704]

---

[703] Act of Dec. 15th 1987, Pub. L. No. 100-191, 1987 U.S.C.C.A.N. (101 Stat. 1293) p. 2172.

[704] See endnote 32.

439

***The news media***.  This is what happened.  Patrick was
harassed beginning October 26, 1995, and the harassment
obviously involved the FBI.  Five months later, we
completed Patrick's *Report of Witness Tampering*, detailing
and proving the harassment (which you read portions of
above), and gave it to almost all the major newspapers.[705]
No articles appeared.

On October 24, 1996, just under a year after the
harassment (before the one-year statute of limitations for
the assault count expired), Patrick filed his civil rights
lawsuit.  Because the timing was on the eve of the
Presidential election, the suit was filed under seal in
anticipation of attacks that the suit was politically
motivated.  On November 12, 1996, one week after the
election, it was unsealed and distributed at a press
conference held on the steps of the federal courthouse in
Washington.  Many representatives of the press attended.[706]
There was almost no coverage.

A year later, October 10, 1997, Patrick's 20-page
submission was attached as an Appendix to Mr. Starr's
Report on Mr. Foster's death, by order of the Special
Division for the Purpose of Appointing Independent Counsels
of the United States Court of Appeals.  The media received
the Report and its Appendix, much of which is reprinted
above.  Despite the obvious historical significance of
evidence of the FBI cover-up in the case being ordered
attached to the Independent Counsel's Report, the media
suppressed its existence.  Some of the articles even
mentioned Patrick's name, but not his Court-ordered
Appendix.[707]  On the evening of October 10, 1997, Peter
Jennings announced that Starr's report should "satisfy even
the most ardent conspiracy theorists."  (Only three out of
ten Americans believed him.[708])

---

[705]   See endnote 33.

[706]   See endnote 33.

[707]   See endnote 33.

[708]   According to a Zogby International Poll conducted in
January 1998, three months after the release of Mr. Starr's
report on Mr. Foster's death, 21.9 percent of those polled
believe that Mr. Foster was murdered, while only 31.9
percent accept the official suicide story.  By nearly two
to one, 44.4 percent to 23.2 percent, respondents agree

## Conclusion

In October of 1998, Patrick's Amended Complaint was filed (before the expiration of the three-year statute of limitations period for the civil rights violation). It names as defendants United States Park Police Sergeant Robert Edwards, Deputy Chief Medical Examiner James Beyer and his unknown assistant, Deputy Director of the FBI Robert Bryant, FBI agents Lawrence Monroe and Russell Bransford, unknown FBI Lab technicians, Scott Bickett, and the group of men who harassed Patrick: Ayman Alouri, Abdel Alouri, and 24 John Does. The press ignored it.

Those are the developments in the case, each of which occurred in October of the last four years. They were the harassment in October of 1995, the filing of the suit in October of 1996, the Court-ordered Appendix to the OIC's Report in October of 1997, and the filing of the Amended Complaint in October of 1998. The media still fails to apprise the public of these facts.

We cannot explain it, but, despite the fact that evidence of the cover-up is obvious, no major news organization has ever assigned a single reporter to the case. Our efforts to apprise members of the press have been steadfastly rebuffed.[709] The press has acted mostly as a conduit for the official announcements and conclusions of the executive branch, like a public relations department, or the press in countries that do not enjoy the same guarantees of free speech as we do. By its attacks on doubters as conspiracy theorists, the media has a record of turning questions of fact in the case into questions of the motives of those who question the official conclusion, and even into questions of mental stability.[710]

Besides repeating the official conclusions, the media's reporting of the facts of the case is generally limited to the verdict of depression. In light of the

---

that there was a government cover-up involving the facts and circumstances of Mr. Foster's death, while 32.4 percent are not sure. 43.5 percent of the participants felt that politicians and the media were too willing to accept the findings in Mr. Foster's death. 27.6 disagreed and 28.9 percent were unsure.

[709] See endnote 33.

[710] See endnote 33.

physical evidence in the case, the facts of which the press has yet to report, the print on the depression verdict could be the basis of a study on the role of the press during the progress of the cover-up.[711]

Here we simply point out what is now manifest. After six years of an obvious cover-up under the nose of the Washington press corps, the media has a powerful interest in keeping the facts of the case from public view. Mike Wallace remarked on *60 Minutes* that some people even accused him of being "a part of the conspiracy." He is not. But his most valuable professional asset, his credibility, as well as the credibility of his industry, will be diminished when the existence of the conspiracy is no longer a secret. Today, suppressing the truth of Mr. Foster's death is a matter of professional self-preservation for numerous members of the news media.

Immediately after this filing is unsealed, it will have been delivered to every major news organization in America. Every day that goes by without its being reported makes the point that much stronger. The media just will not inform the public what it knows of the truth in the case.

*The Independent Counsel Statute.* The Independent Counsel statute has a five-year "sunset." It expires every five years, unless reenacted. The current Act expires June 30, 1999, one week from the date of this filing, five years since it was reenacted, and five years since Mr. Starr was appointed. The five-year term of the Act has coincided with Mr. Starr's tenure. Congress must decide whether to let it lapse permanently and return to pre-independent counsel law, or to reauthorize it. Congress may reauthorize it with amendments, or even try to devise a new system of handling cases of apparent violations of the law by high government officials. Congress will not decide whether to renew it by its expiration date, June 30, 1999, and we will be without our Independent Counsel statute at least until Congress decides.

The issue has a way of going away for five years at a time. What happens at reauthorization will depend on the experience of the five years in between. What

---

[711]    *See* endnote 33.

happens in the last year before reauthorization is the key to it all.[712]

Those who are sensitive to the Justice Department's image resent the Independent Counsel statute because it is a form of institutionalized distrust of the Justice Department, "a clear enunciation by the legislative branch that we [DOJ] cannot be trusted on certain species of cases," an "insult."[713]

On February 24, March 3, 17 & 24, and April 14, Senator Thompson's Committee on Governmental Affairs held Hearings, *The Future of the Independent Counsel Act*. Most of the Committee's witnesses suggested that Congress let the law lapse, including Mr. Starr, who "respectfully recommend[ed] that the statute not be reenacted."[714] Starr argued that the Act impinges on Congress's oversight role[715] and that it is "constitutionally dubious."[716] He noted that

---

[712]   Remarks of Mary Gerwin, counsel to the 1984 Senate Subcommittee for Oversight of Government Management, K. Harringer, Independent Justice, 1992, p. 90.

[713]   New York Times Magazine, July 6, 1997, quoting Lee Radek: "Institutionally, the Independent Counsel statute is an insult. It's a clear enunciation by the legislative branch that we cannot be trusted on certain species of cases;" see also Joseph E. DiGenova, *The Independent Counsel Act: A Good Time to End a Bad Idea*, 86 Georgetown U. Law Rev. 2305 (1998): "[W]e need to restore confidence in the DOJ and its ability to handle cases of this nature..."; and see Cass R. Sunstein, *Bad Incentives and Bad Institutions,* 86 Georgetown U. Law Rev. 2267, 2276 (1998): "But the more important point is that the Act breeds distrust of government..."

[714]   Compare Testimony of Lawrence E. Walsh, March 24, 1999: Senate Committee on Governmental Affairs, Hearings, *The Future of the Independent Counsel Act*: "Should a statute which presently protects against such an apparent conflict of interest be abandoned without something better to take its place?"

[715]   Testimony of Kenneth Starr, Senate Committee on Governmental Affairs, Hearings, *The Future of the Independent Counsel Act,* April 14, 1999: "[T]he law also may have the effect of discouraging vigorous oversight by the Congress, in a departure from our traditions."

the Act fosters tension with the Justice Department[717] and invites media criticism of the appointing Court.[718]  Mr. Starr believes that attempts to give the appearance of justice are unattainable under the Act.[719]  Other criticisms of the Act include the length of the investigations,[720] the ability of Independent Counsels to employ substantial

---

[716]  Compare the Supreme Court's decision in Morrison v. Olson, 487 U.S. 654 (1988), upholding the constitutionality of the Ethics in Government Act by vote of seven to one.

[717]  Testimony of Kenneth Starr, Senate Committee on Governmental Affairs, Hearings, *The Future of the Independent Counsel Act,* April 14, 1999:  The tension is an institutional one, which exists regardless of the particular Administration or Independent Counsel.  As Attorney General Reno testified in 1993, "the relationship between the Department and Independent Counsels [is] difficult at times," characterized by "undue suspicion and resistance, on both sides."

[718]  Testimony of Kenneth Starr, Senate Committee on Governmental Affairs, Hearings, *The Future of the Independent Counsel Act,* April 14, 1999:  "The law may have the unfortunate effect of eroding respect for the judiciary, through attacks -- unanswered and institutionally unanswerable -- on the Special Division.  It is one thing to turn the political attack machine on a prosecutor; it is quite another to turn it on the judiciary."

[719]  Testimony of Kenneth Starr, Senate Committee on Governmental Affairs, Hearings, *The Future of the Independent Counsel Act,* April 14, 1999:  Because the Independent Counsel is vulnerable to partisan attack, the investigation is likely to be seen as political.  If politicization and the loss of public confidence are inevitable, then we should leave the full responsibility where our laws and traditions place it, on the Attorney General (or, where she deems it appropriate, her appointee as special counsel) and on the Congress.

[720]  Compare 139 CONG. REC. S15846-01 & S15847-01 (daily ed, Nov., 1993) (statement of Sen. Levin):  Another criticism has been the length of the investigations.  Some of them have taken a long time, some of them have not.  Complex federal criminal cases often take years to investigate.  I think you [Attorney General Reno] would concur.  The McDade case [Pennsylvania Congressman charged with bribery] -- there were four years of investigation before indictment; Ill Wind [Pentagon procurement fraud], six years so far.

resources in pursuing targets,[721] and the imposition of expense upon those who are investigated.[722]

We review three provisions of the Independent Counsel statute. If the Act is renewed, Congress plans to keep one of these three provisions, the one that has to do with the statute's efforts to keep the costs of Independent Counsel investigations down. The second provision we review is the requirement that Independent Counsels file a final Report. As of the date of this filing, the reporting requirement has almost no chance surviving any renewed statute. We also look at current law's provision that the Court appoints Independent Counsels, which also appears to have little chance of making it into any renewed statute.

*The Act's method of saving costs.* The Independent Counsel statute seeks to create an office independent and separate from the Department of Justice ("DOJ"), even though all costs of running the OIC are paid by the DOJ.[723] A significant tie between the two entities under the Act is that "[a]t the request of an independent counsel, ...the Department of Justice shall provide... resources and personnel... [to] be detailed to the staff of the independent counsel."[724] "This provision enables independent

---

[721]    Compare 139 CONG. REC. S15846-01 & S15847-01 (daily ed, Nov., 1993) (statement of Sen. Cohen): "And so I would say that when the Justice Department focuses upon an individual, be it a member of Congress or not a member of Congress, there are substantial resources brought to bear against that individual."

[722]    Compare 139 CONG. REC. S15846-01 & S15847-01 (daily ed, Nov. 1993) (statement of Sen. Cohen): I would also point out... [that] this notion that somehow we impose greater expense upon those who are investigated by independent counsels is so far greater than imposed by the Justice Department. I daresay, as Senator Levin's pointed out, Joseph McDade was investigated for four years prior to the bringing of an indictment. Six years for the prosecution of Noriega. Ill Wind and Abscam took years.

[723]    28 U.S.C. §594(d)(2): "The Department of Justice shall pay all costs relating to the establishment and operation of any office of independent counsel."

[724]    28 U.S.C. § 594(d)(1) states in part: An independent counsel may request assistance from the Department of Justice... and the Department of Justice shall provide that assistance, which may include... the use of the resources

counsels to use, for example, the laboratory resources and investigative agents of the FBI."[725] For the first ten years of the Act, the DOJ billed a number of OICs for their use of DOJ resources. But this seemed pointless, since the OIC in turn billed these costs back to the DOJ. The DOJ was, "in effect, demanding reimbursement for itself."[726] So in 1988, Congress directed the DOJ to stop billing OICs for their use of DOJ resources.[727]

The Act directs the Special Division to appoint an Independent Counsel who will conduct his activities in a "cost effective manner,"[728] and requires the OIC to conduct its activities with "due regard for expense."[729] Therefore, the Act provides an incentive for the OIC to use FBI agents and the FBI laboratory. The more the OIC relies on the FBI, as opposed to independent investigators and laboratories, the less the reported cost of the investigation.

But the Independent Counsel's incentive to use FBI agents and the FBI Lab is antithetical to the way the Act is supposed to work -- to be independent from the DOJ and its FBI. It is a flaw in the statute. Congress's consideration of whether and how to reenact the law has not included any consideration of making OICs more autonomous from the very entity they are supposed to be independent

---

and personnel necessary to perform such independent counsel's duties. At the request of an independent counsel, prosecutors, administrative personnel, and other employees of the Department of Justice may be detailed to the staff of the independent counsel.

[725] Senate Report No. 100-123. Act of Dec. 15th 1987, Pub. L. No. 100-191, 1987 U.S.C.C.A.N. (101 Stat. 1293) p. 2172.

[726] Senate Report. No. 100-123. Act of Dec. 15th 1987, Pub. L. No. 100-191, 1987 U.S.C.C.A.N. (101 Stat. 1293) p. 2172.

[727] Senate Report No. 100-123. Act of Dec. 15th 1987, Pub. L. No. 100-191, 1987 U.S.C.C.A.N. (101 Stat. 1293) p. 2172: "Congress intended the Justice Department to provide independent counsels with the same assistance it provides to its other high-priority, federal criminal cases... [and are] instructed to discontinue the practice of requiring reimbursement agreements."

[728] 28 U.S.C. § 593(b)(2).

[729] 28 U.S.C. § 594(1)(1)(A)(i).

from, the Justice Department. In fact, Congress is considering ways to somehow fold OICs into the Justice Department, to save more money.

We agree with Donald Smaltz, the Independent Counsel *In re Espy*, who observed that executive branch officials control hundreds of billions of dollars in governmental programs.

> Independent Counsel investigations are expensive and, because of the initial start-up costs, probably more expensive than the average DOJ investigation (although we don't know how much more because the DOJ does not report its figures). However, the question "How much more expensive?" is less important than "Is the expense justifiable?" In answering the question, the public must appreciate that Independent Counsels investigate corruption at the highest levels of government by individuals who hold the public trust. These guardians of the public trust deserve the closest of scrutiny in the performance of their public duties as provided for in the Independent Counsel Act. The President, his cabinet, and their immediate staffs, oversee substantial sections of our economy and control hundreds of billions of dollars in governmental programs and subsidies. When we begin to evaluate the costs in monetary terms whether to investigate and root out the corruption of officials in charge of these programs, we start down a dangerous path. Any investigation of criminal acts, whether they are conducted by the DOJ, Congress, or an Independent Counsel, will be expensive and time consuming. But when compared to insuring the safety and welfare of the people and upholding the rule of law by holding our leaders accountable, the costs are a small price to pay.[730]

Smaltz's investigation has yielded 14 guilty pleas and convictions and over $6 million in fines.

*The requirement that Independent Counsels file a final Report.* Today, the statute requires independent counsels to file a final Report setting forth "fully and completely

---

[730] Donald C. Smaltz, *The Independent Counsel: A View From Inside*, 86 Georgetown U. Law Rev. 2366 (1998).

a description of the work of the independent counsel."[731]
The main reason for this provision is to ensure that the
special prosecutor does not whitewash the investigation, in
keeping with the purpose of the Act of maintaining the
appearance of justice having been done. If the Act is
reenacted, all indications are that the reporting
requirement has little chance of surviving, as Mr. Starr
pointed out to the Senate during his April 14 testimony:

> The witnesses before this Committee have been
> virtually unanimous in their opposition to final
> reports.[732] I concur. If the statute is reauthorized,
> I respectfully recommend that Congress eliminate the
> report requirement. Compiling the report and (as the
> statute dictates) seeking comments from persons named
> in it are burdensome and costly tasks. And, as Mr.
> Fiske said in his testimony here, the requirement may
> encourage Independent Counsels to continue turning

---

[731]   28 U.S.C. § 594(h)(1)(B).

[732]   See, e.g., Testimony of Samuel Dash, Senate Committee on
Governmental Affairs, Hearings, *The Future of the
Independent Counsel Act*: In addition, I have developed
serious doubts about the usefulness and fairness of a final
report to the special division of the court. Regular
federal prosecutors do not file such reports after an
investigation, whether they decide to prosecute or not. It
is basically unfair for an Independent Counsel to spell out
why a target who was not been indicted still is believed to
be guilty. The 1994 reauthorization act made some changes
here, but it is still permissible for an independent
counsel to label a target as guilty, even though the
evidence was insufficient for an indictment. Further, the
requirement to file a final report tends to lengthen the
investigation. It leads the independent counsel to want to
show in the report that substantial work was done and that
he has dotted every "i" and crossed every "t." An example
of this was Starr's conclusions on the Foster suicide,
which could have been publicly released at least two years
before the written report was filed. The need for the
written report and the controversy over Fiske's findings
compelled Starr to continue to make an exhaustive
investigation, piling up evidence... *** When Starr...
redid the Foster investigation, and filed a report agreeing
with Fiske that Foster's death was a suicide, that
conclusion was generally accepted publicly, except for some
die hard conspiracy theorists.

# Conclusion

stones after they have concluded that no prosecutable criminal case exists. We should leave to others -- to Congress, journalists, and, ultimately, the people -- the task of making broader judgments about matters under investigation.[733]

The unknown authors of Mr. Starr's Foster death Report are guilty of willful, premeditated acts of deception. Yet, without Mr. Starr's having filed his Report on Mr. Foster's death, the foregoing comparison of its work to the underlying investigative record would not have been possible, and it would have been impossible to prove the OIC's participation in the cover-up.

The obligation of OICs to file Reports explaining their work facilitates the Ethics in Government Act's purpose of ensuring that justice is done, which is the only way of maintaining the appearance that justice has been

---

[733]   See also Brett M. Kavanaugh, *The President and the Independent Counsel*, 86 Georgetown U. Law Rev. 2133, 2137, 2155 (1998):

> Congress should eliminate the reporting requirement. The reporting requirement adds time and expense to independent counsel investigations, and the reports are inevitably viewed as political documents. The ordinary rules of prosecutorial secrecy should apply. *** The most illogical part of the current independent counsel statute is its final report requirement. The provision was originally designed to ensure that the special prosecutor did not "whitewash" the investigation. The rationale does not justify a report; the fear of whitewashing is the reason that a special counsel is appointed in the first place.

See also ABA, April, 1997, *Report and Recommendations, The Independent Counsel Statute: The Need for Limitations* [reversing prior position], by Nancy Luque, Saul M. Pilchen & Lee Radek, pp. 23-24: "[supporting] elimination of the reporting requirement."

> Compare Lawrence E. Walsh, *The Need for the Renewal of the Independent Counsel Act*, 86 Georgetown U. Law Rev., 2379, 2388 (1998). A public officer who spends millions of dollars should be required to explain his actions to the reporting court and particularly why the subject was not prosecuted... In any event, the public is entitled to know why, when the Attorney General decided an expensive investigation was necessary, no prosecution followed.

done.  What we see in the Foster case is an attempt at the appearance of justice being done but without its really being done.  In other words, it is a cover-up.  The reporting requirement is a safeguard against cover-ups.  If Congress reenacts the Act with no reporting requirement, the public will have no way of knowing whether the Justice Department is using the Act to perpetuate more FBI cover-ups, as it did in the Foster case.

The Act also provides for the inclusion of comments and factual information as an appendix to the OICs' Reports.[734]  The objects of allowing persons named in final Reports to attach facts and comments to OIC's reports are to further the goals of the Act -- so that final reports are full and complete, to hold the Independent Counsel accountable, and to ensure that justice is done.

This section of the law's final Report provision is also designed to afford a measure of fairness to targets and others named in final Reports.  Although it did not seek to indict him, Starr's grand jury probe targeted Patrick Knowlton.  He was targeted illegally, not legally.  If the Court grants Patrick Knowlton's motion, this filing will be attached to the Independent Counsel's Report.  The OIC's Foster death Report may have been the last such report ever filed with the Court.

*Selection of Counsels by the Court.*  Under the current Independent Counsel statute, the Court, as opposed to the Attorney General, selects and appoints independent counsels.  The last time there was no Independent Counsel statute, late 1993 into the summer of 1994, Attorney General Reno appointed Robert Fiske to serve as regulatory Independent Counsel, resulting in the second layer of the FBI cover-up into Mr. Foster's death.  Mr. Starr posits that we should leave it to the news media to inform us whether a regulatory independent counsel does a good enough job.  But today, the view of the press as willing to keep the public informed is wishful thinking, a fiction.  In the 1990s, we heard nothing of Mr. Fiske's prosecutorial record.  Apparently, we would have had it been the same press that we had in the 1980s.

---

[734]    28 U.S.C. § 594(h)(2).

## Conclusion

W. Barret, *Freedom to Steal, Why Politicians Never go to Jail*, New York Magazine, February 4, 1980.

> Crooked politicians have nothing to fear in New York. Contrary to much of the post-Watergate anti-corruption ballyhoo... As astounding as it may seem, not since the legendary Carmine DeSapio was convicted back in 1969 for bribery has a top politician or any of the thousands of public officials in the Southern District's territory -- Manhattan, the Bronx, and Westchester -- found himself in handcuffs. It is uncertain whether this pattern of timidity on the part of the politically appointed prosecutors will change [with the] replace[ment of] Robert B. Fiske in the prestigious post... *** The end of Fiske's term, in March will, in fact, conclude a ten-year period which... [has brought] the transformation of the Southern District into a red-light district for political corruption. *** The price we all pay for these relationships and priorities is a federal jurisdiction where official corruption appears legally impenetrable.[735]

In any event, the appointment by the executive of special counsel to investigate the executive is obviously antithetical to the appearance of justice having being done.

**Conclusion.** The obvious Justice Department cover-up of the facts of Mr. Foster's death is approaching its sixth anniversary. Its secrecy has spanned two special counsels, two sets of Congressional hearings, and the appearance of hundreds of newspaper articles reporting that there was no foul play. What Associated Press reporter Robert Parry had to say six years ago applies today.

> What you'll hear if you listen to the McLaughlin Group or these other shows is a general consensus way -- there may be disagreement on some points -- but there is a general consensus of the world that is brought to bear, and often it is in absolute contradiction to the real world. It is a false reality -- it's a Washington reality... How do the American people really get back

---

[735] See endnote 33.

451

control of this - not just their government, but of their history - because it's really their history that has been taken away from them. And it's really what the Washington press corps and the Democrats in Congress as well as the Republicans are capable of, was this failure to tell the American people their history. And the reason they didn't was because they knew, or feared, that if the American people knew their real history... they wouldn't have gone along with that. *** [W]e sort of got in there - and I guess it was real nice, we felt like we were insiders.

An insider mentality pervades Washington's institutions -- the press, the Congress and the administration and its Justice Department. Many of its members have an "inside-the-beltway" mentality. The reasoning is "no more Watergates," and "the economy is good." Those of this ilk generally go farther in Washington. There is an aspect of elitism to this mentality; gentlemen do not wash their colleague's dirty linen in public -- and there is a great deal of dirty linen in the Foster case. The mentality is that publicizing very serious wrongdoing would simply not be worth the anguish that it would cause the country, much less the woe to the press and government that would ensue from public knowledge of the scarcity of oversight.

The record of Mr. Starr's OIC is one of inactivity in matters implicating the Justice Department, and of efforts to prosecute the President regarding an aspect of his personal life. In following this course of action, Mr. Starr's OIC has turned the public against the Independent Counsel statute, so that now the public's opinion of the law is the same as that of the Justice Department's and Mr. Starr's -- one of opposition to its reenactment. The more Mr. Starr's OIC is seen as partisan, expensive and unnecessary, the less likely the law is to be reenacted.

Today, inside the beltway, the separate branches of government and the press are largely pursuing the same goal -- credibility -- and are not always adversarial when necessary. The more serious the wrongdoing, the more painful it would be for Washington to exercise oversight, and the less likely the truth is to surface. But this state of affairs is hidden. It would seem that the federal government effectively oversaw itself. The impeachment proceedings are over. The charges were not serious enough

## Conclusion

to warrant the President's removal.  There was not another
Watergate.  The Independent Counsel statute may never be
renewed.  Calls for more civility in government have been
made.  In short, corruption in the Justice Department and
its FBI is becoming more and more impenetrable.

Under the Act, a majority of members of either party
of the Judiciary Committees of either House of Congress
could ask Janet Reno to apply to the Court for appointment
of an Independent Counsel to investigate Mr. Foster's
death.[736]  Because Ms. Reno's Justice Department generated
almost all of the evidence we reviewed above, she would not
be in a position to try to claim that the evidence of
cover-up is not, in the words of the Act, "from a credible
source."[737]  But, as long as the existence of the cover-up
remains a secret, Congress will continue to ignore the
issue.

Washington's response to an onslaught of corruption,
triggering seven Independent Counsel investigations, is to
abolish the Independent Counsel law.  One of the excuses is
that the law is institutionalized distrust of the Justice
Department.  It is; just as our Constitution is
institutionalized distrust of the separate branches of
government.  Moreover, Washington's institutions, having
failed to expose the obvious corruption in the Foster case,
are not in a position to advise the public that is does not
need the "auxiliary precaution" of the Independent Counsel
statute to protect the public from corruption.

The OIC's failure to expose the cover-up is a shame.
It is a missed opportunity for America to learn a few
things about its democratic institutions.  Its Justice
Department and FBI have become dangerously corrupt and
politicized.  We cannot trust our press to expose Justice
Department cover-ups, even when their existence is obvious.
Congress ignored all but the appearance of its having
accepted its oversight responsibility.  In short, had the
OIC prosecuted the Justice Department personnel responsible
for covering up the facts of its investigations into Mr.

---

[736]    Ethics in Government Act of 1978, As Amended, 28 U.S.C. §
592(g)(1).

[737]    Ethics in Government Act of 1978, As Amended, 28 U.S.C. §
591(d)(2).

Foster's death, we would all know of the lack of effective government oversight and the lack of integrity in the news media.

The promotion of public confidence in the integrity of the federal government is a fundamental goal of the Constitution, and of our Ethics in Government Act. The only way to maintain the appearance of justice having been done, and to foster public confidence in the integrity of the federal government, is to see to it that justice is truly done. Effective government oversight is an integral element of our democratic system. This filing proves that it is in short supply today.

Justice appears not to have been done in a number of allegations of serious FBI wrongdoing in recent years. The Alfred P. Murrah Building was blown up on the anniversary of one of the first, Waco, for which no one lost even a day's pay. Truth and accountability appear scarce. What do we gain by going further down this road of distrust of our democratic institutions, as opposed to fostering public confidence in their integrity by ensuring that justice is done? This is not the time to abolish our Ethics in Government Act.

The truth in this case is a Washington secret. Some day, it will be widely known. In the interim, those who have a personal stake in the conspiracy remaining secret will be winning their fight to keep the truth suppressed, and with it, the truth of the loss of integrity of our democracy. But there is another secret in Washington. It is that the public can learn what is wrong with our democracy -- the first step in fixing it. We do not have to go along with the cover-up because we have the power to get the facts out.[738]

The case of cover-up in the federal investigations into Mr. Foster's death is not a partisan issue. It is not about money. And it is about more than government corruption. Exposing the truth in the Foster case will shake America's confidence in the integrity of its government and press, but the disease is worse than the cure. Thomas Jefferson wrote that the three branches "shall be kept forever separate." The Constitution was

---

[738]    See Endnote 34.

# Conclusion

designed to work today.  Americans have a right to know the facts and to judge for themselves whether its separate democratic institutions have in fact accepted the responsibilities that come with the public trust -- and whether our history has been taken from us.

Respectfully submitted,


Patrick Knowlton
By Counsel

## Endnotes

| | |
|---|---|
| Endnote 1: | 6:09:58 |
| Endnote 2: | 6:10:16-6:11:00 |
| Endnote 3: | 6:12-6:14 |
| Endnote 4: | 6:14:32-6:15 |
| Endnote 5: | 6:16 |
| Endnote 6: | 6:17 |
| Endnote 7: | 6:18 |
| Endnote 8: | 6:19-6:20 |
| Endnote 9: | 6:21 |
| Endnote 10: | 6:22 |
| Endnote 11: | 6:23 |
| Endnote 12: | 6:24 |
| Endnote 13: | 6:25 |
| Endnote 14: | 6:26 |
| Endnote 15: | 6:27 |
| Endnote 16: | 6:28-6:30 |
| Endnote 17: | 6:31 |
| Endnote 18: | 6:32-6:36 |
| Endnote 19: | 6:37 |
| Endnote 20: | 6:38-6:41 |
| Endnote 21: | 6:42-6:43 |
| Endnote 22: | 6:44 |
| Endnote 23: | 6:45 |
| Endnote 24: | 6:46-6:48 |
| Endnote 25: | 6:49-6:63 |
| Endnote 26: | 6:54-7:14 |
| Endnote 27: | 7:15 |
| Endnote 28: | 7:16-7:17 |
| Endnote 29: | 7:18-7:43 |
| Endnote 30: | 7:44 |
| Endnote 31: | 8:01-8:06 |
| Endnote 32: | Correspondence with Congress. |
| Endnote 33: | The media. |
| Endnote 34: | What you can do. |

**Endnote 1, 6:09:58:** *Parking lot.* The electronic log records that a Fairfax County fire truck arrived in the Fort Marcy lot.[739] In it were firefighters Pisani, Iacone and Wacha.

**Endnote 2, 6:10:16-6:11:00:** *Parking lot.* Seconds later, the second group of rescue personnel arrived in a Fairfax County ambulance, according to the electronic log.[740] At this time, six persons were on the scene in the parking lot.

---

[739]   Exhibit 34, Electronic log of McLean Fire Station Engine 1, July 20, 1993: "6:09:58"

[740]   Exhibit 39, Electronic log of McLean Fire Station Medic 1, July 20, 1993: "6:10:16"

The six fire and rescue workers exited their vehicles, gathered their equipment, and assembled in the parking lot. At the instruction of Firefighter Lieutenant James Iacone, they split into two groups to search for the body.[741]

At this time, Officer Fornshill was not present in the parking lot.[742] (At least two reports state that Fornshill arrived on a scooter[743] and was present in the park before rescue workers arrived. Other reports state he was driving an unmarked police car,[744] and George Gonzalez reportedly told the FBI that a police officer's car entered the park "as Gonzalez's vehicle was

---

[741]   Exhibit 78, Report of interview of Firefighter Lieutenant James Iacone, March 11, 1994: "Iacone directed the crew of Engine 1 to go down one trail, possibly toward Dead Run Creek. He directed the crew of Medic 1 to another area of the park."

[742]   Exhibit 57, Report of FBI interview of Firefighter Ralph Pisani, March 11, 1994: The FCFRD personnel on the scene split into two groups to search for the scene of the possible suicide. Pisani's group was comprised of Richard Arthur from Medic 1, Jennifer Wacha, Iacone, and Pisani. A second group, comprised of George Gonzalez and Corey Ashford (sic) [Todd Hall] from Medic 1, went in another direction into the woods and eventually found the body which was later identified as that of Foster.

[743]   Exhibit 113, Park Police Report of Park Police Investigator John Rolla, July 21, 1993: "I heard scooter 261, Officer Kevin Fornshill request C.I.B. to respond to Ft. Marcy for a dead body." Exhibit 80, Handwritten notes of FBI interview of Park Police Lieutenant Patrick Gavin, April 28, 1994: "Believes Fornshill (was on scooter) was first to find it [body] (even before fire [fighters])"

[744]   Exhibit 79, Deposition of Park Police Officer Kevin Fornshill, July 12, 1994: A. Yes. I was ordered by Sergeant Edwards to return to my beat. Q. Why did he do that? A. Again, since it's basically a high priority beat that the uniform presence at the CIA, after February of last year. Q. That being the guy was shot, the guy shot people, okay. Mr. Stinson: Since then, they've maintained a uniform presence during the prime times of the day at both entrance ways and for various reasons, they don't like the cars leaving there. And typically it's a marked car. A. This day it was an unmarked car. Mr. Stinson: Because there were no more cars available.

Exhibit 76, Park Police Report of Park Police Investigator Christine Hodakievic, July 21, 1993: "car 261 Off. K.B. Fornshill"

entering the park."[745]) There is no record of Fairfax County rescue workers Wacha,[746] Iacone,[747] Pisani,[748] and Arthur[749] having reported seeing any police in the parking lot when they arrived. Firefighter Todd Hall, who was searching with paramedic George Gonzalez, specifically recalls not seeing anyone, including police, in the parking lot when he arrived. But Hall did recall meeting an officer near "a cannon" in the park.[750] Officer Fornshill reportedly told the FBI that only two rescue workers

---

[745]    Exhibit 135, Report of FBI interview of Paramedic George Gonzalez, February 23, 1994: "As Gonzalez's vehicle was entering the park, a United States Park Police (USPP) vehicle arrived and followed the EMS vehicle to the incident scene."

[746]    Exhibit 72, Report of FBI interview of Firefighter Jennifer Wacha, March 11, 1994: Upon entering Fort Marcy Park, Wacha recalls seeing one car in the parking area with its hazard lights on. She remembers that the engine was running, noting the car was unoccupied. There was also a second vehicle bearing Arkansas license plates that was parked closest to the park entrance. Contained in that vehicle was a suit jacket. There was also a third car in the lot, no details were recalled.

[747]    Exhibit 78, Report of FBI interview of Firefighter Lieutenant James Iacone, March 11, 1994: "There were no police on the scene when Iacone's crew initially arrived at the park or when they returned to the parking lot after their search of the woods was abbreviated by word that a body had been found."

[748]    Exhibit 57, Report of FBI interview of Firefighter Ralph Pisani, March 11, 1994: "There were no police on the scene when Pisani arrived, and no one was present to direct FCFRD personnel to the location of the incident."

[749]    Exhibit 71, Report of FBI interview of Paramedic Richard Arthur, March 16, 1994: "Once into the parking area, there was nobody to meet them to show them where the body was, so they split up into two groups to search down two separate paths leading off the parking lot."

[750]    Exhibit 67, Deposition of Firefighter Todd Hall, July 20, 1994: Q. Any cars there, any people there? A. Yes. There were some cars parked there. I don't recall seeing any people, no. I don't recall seeing any people. Q. What did you do after you got to the park? A. We had a call that came in, suicide in front of a cannon, so we searched the grounds for a body in front of a cannon. I think we were met there by the Park Police.

were in the parking lot when he arrived,[751] but he testified that
he saw "six or seven"[752] fire and rescue workers when he arrived
Fornshill did join the search with Todd Hall and George
Gonzalez,[753] but it is not clear when or how he appeared on the
scene.  The second[754] and third[755] police officers on the scene

---

[751]    Exhibit 138, Report of FBI interview of Park Police Officer
Kevin Fornshill, April 29, 1994:  According to Private
Fornshill, the sector or beat officer responsible for Fort
Marcy Park was not readily available and that his
instructions were to join up with Fairfax County Fire and
Rescue Squad personnel at Fort Marcy Park.  Upon entering
Fort Marcy Park, Fornshill recalls meeting at the parking
lot, two Emergency Medical Technicians (EMT), one black
male and the other a white male, names unknown, with all
three proceeding into the park, neither of them knowing the
exact location of the second cannon at Fort Marcy Park.

[752]    Exhibit 79, Deposition of Park Police Officer Kevin
Fornshill, July 12, 1994:  "Q.  Who was there when you got there?
A.  Fairfax County Engine and a rescue ambulance vehicle.  Q.
Why an engine?  A.  I don't know what their policy is.  Q.  Do
you remember how many people were there about?  A.  Perhaps six,
maybe seven Fairfax County Fire rescue personnel."

[753]    Exhibit 110, Deposition of Paramedic George Gonzalez, July
20, 1994:  Q.  Then after you parked what did you do?  A.
We got out of our units and decided to split teams.  Q.
How did you split them?  A.  Our teams were myself and Todd
Hall, along with the Park Police officer.  And as soon as
we arrived, the Park Police officer was arriving also,
right behind us.

[754]    Exhibit 96, Report of FBI interview of Park Police Officer
Franz Ferstl, May 2, 1994: To the best of his recollection,
when he arrived, the only other USPP officer present in the
park was Officer Fornshill, adding that Fornshill had
already headed up into the park itself looking for the
body.  Officer Ferstl stated that Fairfax emergency
vehicles were already on the scene and emergency personnel
were searching the park in an effort to find the body.

[755]    Exhibit 70, Report of FBI interview of Park Police Officer
Julie Spetz, May 2, 1994:  She stated that to her
knowledge, they were the second and third U.S. Park Police
officers at the scene, adding that Officer Kevin Fornshill
had already arrived.  As she drove into the park entrance,
she noted a disabled vehicle off to the right on the ramp
leading into the parking lot.  Driving into the Fort Marcy
parking lot itself, she observed two cars; one to her left
toward the front of the lot which she later learned was

reported that Fornshill was there, but did not report seeing Fornshill's vehicle.

**Endnote 3, 6:12-6:14:** *Parking lot.* No one remained in the parking lot after the rescue workers began their search for the body.[756] It is unclear exactly where Christine Hodakievic was during this time. She was not seen in the lot when firefighters arrived.[757] She reported she was there in her personal car.[758] A person who appeared to be a civilian directed searchers in the direction of the body,[759] and one witness reported a female officer near the body upon its discovery.[760]

---

Foster's vehicle. Officer Spetz cannot recall the color or make of the vehicle but does remember it had Arkansas tags on it. Officer Spetz stated that a second car, white in color, was in the rear of the parking lot, but she is unable to recall any other identifying data regarding this car. She stated that emergency vehicles (ambulance and fire truck) were also in the parking lot. Officer Spetz advised that Ferstl was in a marked car ahead of her and proceeded directly to the parking lot.

[756] Exhibit 67, Deposition of Firefighter Todd Hall, July 20, 1994: "Q. After you got there what did you do? A. We searched the grounds, we split up."

Exhibit 110, Deposition of Paramedic George Gonzalez, July 20, 1994: Q. Then after you parked what did you do? A. We got out of our units and decided to split teams. Q. How did you split them? A. Our teams were myself and Todd Hall, along with the Park Police officer. And as soon as we arrived, the Park Police officer was arriving also, right behind us. And the other team was Rick Arthur, Jay Iacone, Ralph Pisani, and Mrs. Wacha, firefighter Wacha.

[757] Exhibit 67, Deposition of Firefighter Todd Hall, July 20, 1994: "Q. Any cars there, any people there? A. Yes. There were some cars parked there. I don't recall seeing any people, no. I don't recall seeing any people."

[758] Exhibit 81, Report of FBI interview of Park Police Investigator Christine Hodakievic, May 2, 1994: "Officer Hodakievic advised that shortly after 6:00 p.m. on July 20, 1993, while in an off-duty status and while traveling North on the George Washington Memorial Parkway in her personal vehicle, heard on her police radio that a dead body had been located at Fort Marcy Park."

[759] Exhibit 77, Handwritten notes of FBI interview of Firefighter James Iacone, March 11, 1994: "Directed by citizen" Exhibit 78, Report of FBI interview of Firefighter James Iacone,

**Endnote 4, 6:14:32-6:15:** ***Body Site.*** Park Police Officer Kevin Fornshill officially discovered the body, called for rescue workers,[761] and radioed that he had found the body.[762] Fire and rescue workers Todd Hall and George Gonzalez[763] joined Officer Fornshill at the body site.

---

March 11, 1994: "Iacone now believes that the crew of Medic 1 was directed by a citizen to a body, later identified as that of Foster, but he knows no details regarding this citizen such as whether the person was a male or female."

> Exhibit 79, Deposition of Park Police Officer Kevin Fornshill, July 12, 1994: A. I went back to the parking lot. There was a lot of confusion with other cars coming in. My car, Officer Ferstl's car, the sergeant's car, and about that time the investigators would be rolling in. I believe Officer Hodakievic, who at the time was a plainclothes investigator. Q. And he's an investigator? A. She, Christine, she was an investigator at the time. She's back in uniform now. She's at the same station you can reach me at.

Exhibit 80, Handwritten notes of FBI interview of Park Police Lieutenant Patrick Gavin, April 28, 1994: "Christine Hodakievic - investigator off duty - P/C [plainclothes]"

[760] Exhibit 179, Report of FBI interview of Firefighter Todd Hall, April 27, 1994: "Hall believes that a female USPP officer was the third individual to arrive at the body. Hall remembers George Gonzalez possibly being the fourth individual to arrive at Foster's body."

[761] Exhibit 79, Deposition of Park Police Officer Kevin Fornshill, July 12, 1994: "I called out to the paramedics and had them respond over."

[762] Exhibit 169, Handwritten chronology notes of Park Police Officer J.H. Ramsden to Lieutenant Gavin, July 20, 1993: "18:14:32 - 261 found body asked for CIB"

[763] Exhibit 110, Deposition of Paramedic George Gonzalez, July 20, 1994: A. Those two looked, I followed behind them. And thoroughly to make sure that the body wasn't covered up because there's a deep embankment right past the cannon. And then, from that point on, I went to the other part of the park and about the time that I was going up the hill. Officer Fornshill and Todd Hall had already found the body at the second cannon. And I followed seconds later. Q. Did they say anything? How did you know they found the body? A. We found him, he's here. Just acknowledging the

**Endnote 5, 6:16:** *Body site.* Fornshill, Hall and Gonzalez remained at the body site.[764]

**Endnote 6, 6:17:** *Body site.* These three officials remained at the body site. (Todd Hall reportedly told the FBI that a female Park Police Officer was the third person to arrive at the body site,[765] but other witnesses do not support this, including Hall's deposition.[766] The first person to find the body, Kevin Fornshill, did not say a female officer was third at the body site.[767]) George Gonzalez stated he was the third person to arrive at the body[768] and that Officer Fornshill was the only officer present until male officer Franz Ferstl arrived.[769]

---

fact that they got a body. Q. Did you go over the body? A. Yes.

[764]   Exhibit 79, Deposition of Park Police Officer Kevin Fornshill, July 12, 1994: Q. Based on this scene, you determined that this was a suicide? A. When the EMS personnel came up and they said, there's a gun in his right hand, do you see the gun. Then I'm straining and looking for the gun. I couldn't see the gun. But when they told me that, I made the assumption, which I shouldn't have, and made a broadcast and said it appeared to he an apparent suicide.

Exhibit 58, Radio Transcript of Park Police Dispatcher and Park Police Officer Kevin Fornshill, July 20, 1993, 6:16 p.m.: "it appears to be a suicide."

[765]   Exhibit 179, FBI report of interview of Firefighter Todd Hall, April 27, 1994: "Hall believes that a female USPP officer was the third individual to arrive at the body. Hall remembers George Gonzalez possibly being the fourth individual to arrive at Foster's body."

[766]   Exhibit 67, Deposition of Firefighter Todd Hall, July 20, 1994: "Well, by the time I got to check that, I saw the gun. I stood straight up, told the police to come back. By then, George and other guys had gotten there."

[767]   Exhibit 79, Deposition of Park Police Officer Kevin Fornshill, July 12, 1994: "Q. Do you remember how many of the paramedics came over? A. Originally there were two, Gonzalez and his partner."

[768]   Exhibit 110, Deposition of Paramedic George Gonzalez, July 20, 1994: "Officer Fornshill and Todd Hall had already found the body at the second cannon. And I followed seconds later."

[769]   Exhibit 110, Deposition of Paramedic George Gonzalez, July

**Parking lot.** Based on the radio transmission, Park Police Officer Franz Ferstl arrived in the parking lot about this time. At 6:16 p.m., Ferstl radioed that he had passed an accident on the side of the parkway just below Route 123. After reporting the accident, the dispatcher stated the time as "18:17."[770] This places Ferstl less than a minute from Fort Marcy Park. After his arrival in the parking lot, Ferstl went immediately to the body site. Ferstl's FBI report reflects that when he left the lot for the body site, no one was in the lot.[771]

---

20, 1994: Q. Was Officer Fornshill the only officer present when you first discovered the body? A. Yes. Q. How long were just the three of you there? Q. Time wise? You lose track of time during those incidents. I can only guess. Q. Sure, your estimate. A. Maybe five to ten minutes maybe, when the next officer came up. Q. Do you remember the name of that officer? A. I could picture his face, a younger, Park Police officer, dark hair.

[770] Exhibit 58, Transcript of radio transmissions, Park Police Dispatcher with Park Police Officers Franz Ferstl and Kevin Fornshill, July 20, 1993:

| | |
|---|---|
| Dispatcher: | 261 [Fornshill] |
| *Fornshill:* | *261* |
| Dispatcher: | Do you copy? |
| *Fornshill:* | *10-4* |
| Dispatcher: | Also 202 [Sergeant Edwards] advises that you respond back to your post when 211 [Ferstl] arrives. |
| *Fornshill:* | *When 211 gets here have him bring some crime scene tape.* |
| Dispatcher: | 10-4, 211 you copy? |
| *Ferstl:* | *211* |
| Dispatcher: | 261 is requesting that you bring some crime scene tape on your arrival. |
| *Ferstl:* | *10-4. Also I just passed a 10-50 into the trees apparently the operator is okay standing outside the car. Saw it southbound just south of 123. Ah, have 202 assign me back to there or do you want me to stay at Fort Marcy?* |
| Dispatcher: | (inaudible) 211 that is the accident from earlier the subject is waiting (inaudible). |
| *Ferstl:* | *10-4.* |
| Dispatcher: | 18:17  [tape recording] |

[771] Exhibit 96, Report of FBI interview of Park Police Officer Franz Ferstl, May 2, 1994:  To the best of his recollection, when he arrived, the only other USPP officer present in the park was Officer Fornshill, adding that Fornshill had already headed up into the park itself

**Endnote 7, 6:18:** *Body site.* The FBI's report of Hall's interview states that firefighters (Iacone, Pisani Arthur, Wacha, Bianchi & Ashford) had responded to the body site[772] when Hall was there, but all of these firefighters were not present at the same time as Hall[773] (Bianchi & Ashford came later to transport the body). Soon after arriving at Fort Marcy Park, Officer Ferstl arrived at the body site at approximately 6:19 (based on the Police radio dispatch[774] having him pass an accident below Route 123, seconds from the park just before 6:17 p.m.)

According to Officer Ferstl[775] and Paramedic George Gonzalez,[776] when Ferstl arrived at the body site, only Officer Fornshill and

---

looking for the body. Officer Ferstl stated that Fairfax emergency vehicles were already on the scene and emergency personnel were searching the park in an effort to find the body. Ferstl stated that he made his way up to where the body had been located, stating that when he arrived, the only persons present were Officer Fornshill and one or two Fairfax County medics.

[772] Exhibit 71, Report of FBI interview of Paramedic Richard Arthur, March 16, 1994: "As Arthur returned to the parking area, Gonzalez and Hall were running back also from the left-hand path and yelled that they had found the body. Arthur went down the path to take a look."

[773] Exhibit 179, Report of FBI interview of Firefighter Todd Hall, April 27, 1994: "Hall believes he also may have spoken to Jennifer Wacha at the location of Foster's body."

Exhibit 66, Report of FBI interview of Firefighter Todd Hall, March 18, 1994: Hall was aware that the following EMS personnel were at the death scene: Jay Iacone, Heavy Rescue Squad; Ralph Pisani, Engine Driver; Richard Arthur, Medic Unit; Jennifer Wacha, Engine or Ambulance; Bill Bianchi (came to scene later/truck unit): Corey Ashford, Ambulance EMT Technician; George Gonzalez, Medic 1/Officer.

[774] Exhibit 58, Transcript of radio transmission of Park Police Dispatcher and Officer Franz Ferstl, July 20, 1993.

[775] Exhibit 69, Handwritten notes of FBI interview of Park Police Officer Franz Ferstl, May 2, 1994: "When he arr at 2nd C present were USPP Fornshill, one or two F Cty medics."

[776] Exhibit 110, Deposition of Paramedic George Gonzalez, July 20, 1994: Q. Was Officer Fornshill the only officer present when you first discovered the body? A. Yes. Q. How long were just the three of you there? Q. Time wise? You lose track of time during those incidents. I can only

the two fire and rescue workers were present. Hall and Gonzalez
left the body site and arrived at the parking lot about the same
time as Officer Julie Spetz.[777] Also arriving in the lot at that
time were the group of Arthur, Pisani, Iacone and Wacha, who had
returned from searching another area of the park.[778] Firefighter
Todd Hall recalled seeing a female officer as he was returning
his equipment to the truck,[779] possibly Spetz or Hodakievic.

---

guess.  Q.  Sure, your estimate.  A.  Maybe five to ten
minutes maybe, when the next officer came up.  Q.  Do you
remember the name of that officer?  A.  I could picture his
face, a younger, Park Police officer, dark hair.

[777]  Exhibit 170, Handwritten notes of FBI interview of Park
Police Officer Julie Spetz, May 2, 1994:  In marked car at
Glen Echo Station overheard dispatcher calling Franz Ferstl
in car 211 to respond to FMP re a D.B.  She automatically
went to FMP to assist.  She & FF [Franz Ferstl] were 2nd
and 3rd USPP to arrive...  As she arrived EMT &
firefighters were coming back to their vehicles, having
already been up to the death scene.  She spoke briefly with
firemen stating one remarked to her that he didn't think it
was a suicide and words to effect that he'd seen a number
of suicides and body was too clean.

[778]  Exhibit 71, Report of FBI interview of Paramedic Richard
Arthur, March 16, 1994:  As Arthur returned to the parking
area, Gonzalez and Hall were running back also from the
left-hand path and yelled that they had found the body.
Arthur went down the path to take a look.  He located
Foster's body somewhat off the path, located such that if
you were just walking the path you could miss it.  Police
were following Arthur to the scene.  In Arthur's judgement,
Foster was obviously dead and so he did not check for a
pulse. He noted that the body was lying perfectly straight-
-like it was "ready for a coffin."  A gun was lying on the
ground under his right hand, with the barrel partially
under Foster's thigh.  He remembers the gun as being an
automatic weapon of approximately .45 caliber.  He noted
what appeared to be a small caliber bullet hole in Foster's
neck on the right side just under the jaw line about half
way between the ear and the tip of the chin.  He did not
note anything else he thought might be a bullet hole.  He
did not touch the body and remained at a distance of two to
four feet from it.  He did not observe anybody touch the
body.  He did not observe anybody move the gun.  As he left
to return to the parking area, the U.S. Park Police were
roping off the scene.

[779]  Exhibit 67, Deposition of Firefighter Todd Hall, July 20,
1994:  "Q.  What were the Park Police officers doing?  Do you

*Parking lot.* The FBI report of its interview with Officer Julie Spetz reflects that she arrived in her squad car after Officer Ferstl.[780] Paramedic Gonzalez and Firefighter Hall were returning to the lot from the West side of the park at the same time as Arthur, Iacone, Wacha and Pisani were returning[781] to the lot from the opposite direction. They saw each other.[782] Officer Spetz arrived in the lot and saw the Park Police cars[783] and the paramedics and firefighters who were returning to the parking lot from their search.[784]

---

remember how many there were? A. I know there was the one who was with me, and then I remember a female officer arriving and I think, by then, I was starting to take equipment back to the unit."

[780]   Exhibit 70, Report of FBI interview of Park Police Officer Julie Spetz, May 2, 1994.

[781]   Exhibit 70, Report of FBI interview of Park Police Officer Julie Spetz, May 2, 1994: Officer Spetz stated that as she arrived in the parking lot, emergency medical technicians and firefighters were coming back to their vehicles and she assumed they had already been up to the death scene. She stated that she spoke briefly with the firemen, stating that one remarked to her that he did not think it was a suicide, adding words to the effect that he'd seen a number of suicides and the body was "too clean."

[782]   Exhibit 71, Report of FBI interview of Paramedic Richard Arthur, March 16, 1994: "As Arthur returned to the parking area, Gonzalez and Hall were running back also from the left-hand path and yelled that they had found the body."

[783]   Exhibit 70, Report of FBI interview of Park Police Officer Julie Spetz, May 2, 1994: "Officer Spetz stated that when first pulling into the parking lot, she did observe the Park Police vehicles but she did not see any officers and assumed that any officers on the scene, including Ferstl, were up at the death scene."

[784]   Exhibit 170, Handwritten notes of FBI interview of Park Police Officer Julie Spetz, May 2, 1994: In marked car at Glen Echo Station overheard dispatcher calling Franz Ferstl in car 211 to respond to FMP re a D.B. She automatically went to FMP to assist. She & FF [Franz Ferstl] were 2nd and 3rd USPP to arrive... As she arrived EMT & firefighters were coming back to their vehicles, having already been up to the death scene.

After regrouping in the parking lot with Hall and Gonzalez, who had just returned from the body site, Arthur, Pisani, Iacone, and Wacha went up to view the body. Spetz never went up to the body site.[785]

**Endnote 8, 6:19-6:20:** *Body site.* Ferstl left the body site seconds after his arrival to retrieve crime scene tape[786] and a camera from his patrol car. Two minutes before Ferstl's arrival at the body site, he confirmed by radio that he would bring the tape to the body site.[787] In a hurry to get to the body site, it appears Ferstl forgot to bring the tape.

**Endnote 9, 6:21:** *Body site.* Officer Fornshill remained alone at the body site.

*Parking lot.* At approximately this time, Officer Ferstl came back to get a camera and crime scene tape from his car and immediately returned to the body site.[788]

---

[785] Exhibit 170, Handwritten notes of FBI interview of Park Police Officer Julie Spetz, May 2, 1994: "Off S [Spetz] never went up to the location where the body was found and thus never saw the body of VF. After providing background info re [redacted] to Inv Randy [sic] Abt and Cheryl Braun, she left FMP, returning to her patrol."

[786] Exhibit 96, Report of FBI interview of Park Police Officer Franz Ferstl, May 2, 1994: "Ferstl pointed out his primary responsibility was to secure the crime scene. He added that as soon as he took a look at the body, he returned to his police cruiser, obtained police crime scene tape, and then returned to the death scene and taped off the area."

[787] Exhibit 58, Transcript of radio transmission of Park Police Dispatcher and Officer Franz Ferstl, July 20, 1993.

[788] Exhibit 96, Report of FBI interview of Park Police Officer Franz Ferstl, May 2, 1994: Ferstl pointed out his primary responsibility was to secure the crime scene. He added that as soon as he took a look at the body, he returned to his police cruiser, obtained police crime scene tape, and then returned to the death scene and taped off the area. In doing this, Officer Ferstl stated that he did not see any other evidentiary items in the area and did not see any signs indicating that there had been a struggle. He specifically stated that he did not see any wine bottles or other debris in close proximity to the body. Ferstl advised that when he returned to the scene a second time, Officer Fornshill was still present; to the best of his recollection, the Fairfax medical people were in the process of returning to the parking lot. Ferstl advised

**Endnote 10, 6:22:** *Parking lot.* Sergeant Edwards arrived around this time. Officer Julie Spetz stated that she briefly spoke with firemen, one of whom remarked that it did not look like suicide.[789] About this time, Spetz proceeded down the path to speak to the couple who had been found earlier by firefighters. She asked them to return to the parking lot.[790]

**Endnote 11, 6:23:** *Body site.* About this time, fire and rescue workers Arthur, Iacone, Pisani and Wacha arrived at the body site after walking up from the parking lot. Fornshill remained at the body site while fire and rescue workers viewed the body.

*Parking lot.* Sergeant Edwards proceeded to the body site. Edwards, carrying a camera, would pass Fornshill.

---

that he also took several Polaroid photos of the crime scene, adding that he is not sure if he did the photography or taping first. He stated that to the best of his recollection, on returning a second time to the death scene, the body appeared to be in the identical position it was when he first observed it.

[789] Exhibit 170, Handwritten notes of FBI interview of Park Police Officer Julie Spetz, May 2, 1994: As she arrived EMT [Emergency Medical Technicians] & firefighters were coming back to their vehicles, having already been up to the death scene. She spoke briefly with firemen stating one remarked to her that he didn't think it was a suicide and words to effect that he'd seen a number of suicides and body was too clean.

[790] Exhibit 70, Report of FBI interview of Park Police Officer Julie Spetz, May 2, 1994: Officer Spetz stated that she located a path at the rear of the lot heading down in a southerly direction, away from where the body was located. She stated that she followed this path into the woods for approximately 75 yards when she noticed a man and a woman sitting down, apparently talking. She stated that as best she recalls, they had a blanket with them and were located in a partial clearing in the woods. She remembers asking them how long they had been there but cannot recall their reply. She did ask them if they had seen any other cars or individuals in the lot when they arrived, stating that one of them remarked that they had seen a white van in the parking lot. Officer Spetz was unable to recall any other details they might have provided to her. She stated that she asked them to come up to the parking lot where they identified their car and provided background information concerning themselves.

# Endnotes

**Endnote 12, 6:24:** *Body site.* After Officer Ferstl had returned a second time to the body site,[791] Officer Fornshill turned the scene over to Ferstl. About this time, Officer Fornshill left[792] to return to the parking lot and he reportedly passed Sergeant Bob Edwards, who was on his way up to the body site.[793] Ferstl began to tape the area or photograph the body site.[794] As Ferstl

---

[791]   Exhibit 96, Report of FBI interview of Park Police Officer Franz Ferstl, May 2, 1994: "Ferstl advised that when he returned to the scene a second time, Officer Fornshill was still present; to the best of his recollection, the Fairfax medical people were returning to the parking lot."

[792]   Exhibit 79, Deposition of Park Police Officer Kevin Fornshill, July 12, 1994:  Q.  So Ferstal [sic] and Edwards come.  Did they come together or in separate cars?  A.  They came in separate cars.  Officer Ferstal [sic], Franz, he relieved me, and basically took charge of the body and the crime scene.  Q.  When you say he relieved you, what do you mean?  A.  I mean he physically --  Q.  Took charge?  A.  Yes, he physically.  There's always someone there until we're relieved by a supervisor or the investigators, so I maintained the integrity of the crime scene until I was relieved by another officer.  (discussion off the record.)  A.  Okay the death scene.  So when I was relieved by Franz Ferstal [sic], I was cleared to return back to my beat, which I did.

[793]   Exhibit 79, Deposition of Park Police Officer Kevin Fornshill, July 12, 1994:  Q.  Who was the officer in charge of the scene?  A.  At the time I was there?  That would have been Sergeant Edwards.  Q.  Were you present when the coroner arrived?  A.  No.  Q.  Did you observe any photographs taken of the body while you were at the scene?  A.  No, sir.  Q.  Did you see any personnel of any kind carrying photographic equipment?  MR. STINSON:  He already answered that earlier.  Go ahead and answer again.  Q.  Sergeant Edwards, who was my sergeant for the day, I passed him on the hill, and he was carrying a Polaroid up the hill while I was coming down.

[794]   Exhibit 96, Report of FBI interview of Park Police Officer Franz Ferstl, May 2, 1994:  Ferstl stated that to the best of his recollection, he took approximately seven photos; he cannot recall if he initialed or dated them, but he does not believe he did so.  Ferstl advised that at some point, Sergeant Edwards arrived at the death scene.  He thinks it was after he had taped off the area and taken the Polaroid shots.

was taping the crime scene,[795] fire and rescue workers Arthur, Pisani, Iacone, and Wacha returned to the parking lot. Upon returning to the lot, they gave their names to Officer Hodakievic[796] and examined Mr. Foster's car[797] before leaving at 6:37 p.m.[798]

Officer Fornshill was at the body site for about 12 minutes (and claimed not to have seen the gun, even after straining to see it[799] -- rescue workers saw it immediately).

***Parking lot.*** Shift Commander Lieutenant Patrick Gavin arrived in the parking lot about this time. Investigator Hodakievic met Gavin in the parking lot.[800] Officer Fornshill, Sergeant Edwards and Officer Ferstl were not present in the parking lot but were

---

[795]    Exhibit 71, Report of FBI interview of Paramedic Richard Arthur, March 16, 1994: "He did not observe anybody move the gun. As he left to return to the parking area, the U.S. Park Police were roping off the scene." Exhibit 136, Report of FBI interview of Firefighter Ralph Pisani, April 27, 1994: "He did recall seeing yellow tape in the area marking a police crime scene."

[796]    Exhibit 76, Park Police report of Park Police Investigator Christine Hodakievic, July 21, 1993: "Fairfax Co. EMS Medic 1: Todd Hall, George Gonzalez, Rick Arthur, Engine 1: Ralph Pisani, Jennifer Wacha, Jay Iacone" Exhibit 97, Handwritten notes of Park Police Investigator Christine Hodakievic.

[797]    Exhibit 71, Report of FBI interview of Paramedic Richard Arthur, March 16, 1994: "Once back in the parking area, the U.S. Park Police took all the EMT's names. He observed them gaining access to a cream colored car with a suit jacket and tie in it, looking for identification of some sort. Arthur was on the scene approximately 30-40 minutes."

[798]    Exhibit 34, Electronic log of McLean Fire Station Engine 1, July 20, 1993: "18:37"

[799]    Exhibit 79, Deposition of Park Police Officer Kevin Fornshill, July 12, 1994: "When the EMS personnel came up and they said, there's a gun in his right hand, do you see the gun. Then I'm straining and looking for the gun. I couldn't see the gun."

[800]    Exhibit 98, Report of FBI interview of Park Police Lieutenant Patrick Gavin, April 28, 1994: "He [Gavin] stated that Investigator Hodakievic met him in the parking lot and later directed him up to where the body had been discovered."

up toward the body site.[801]  Although Officer Christine
Hodakievic's report puts her arrival at the park at approximately
6:15, the record demonstrates that she arrived earlier (see
above).  Hodakievic interviewed Hall and Gonzalez about their
observations at the body site.[802]

**Endnote 13, 6:25:** *Parking lot.*  Officer Spetz returned to the
parking lot with the civilian couple.  Hodakievic continued her
interviews of fire and rescue workers.  Gavin did not go
immediately to the body site.  He remained in the parking lot
directing officers to check the cars and interview the witnesses
in the lot.  Hodakievic, having been to the body site earlier,[803]
did not direct Gavin to the body until later.[804]  Fornshill walked
from the body site back to the lot.[805]  They spoke.  Edwards
ordered Fornshill to return to his post.[806]

---

[801]    Exhibit 98, Report of FBI interview of Lieutenant Patrick
Gavin, April 28, 1994:  "To the best of his recollection, the
following US Park Police officers were present at the park, when
he arrived: Officer Kevin Fornshill, Sergeant Bob Edwards,
Officer Ferstl, Investigator Hodakievic."

[802]    Exhibit 76, Park Police Report of Investigator Christine
Hodakievic, July 21, 1994:  "EMS Medic 1 Supervisor George
Gonzalez notified me that they had discovered the body of a white
male in the wooded area of Ft. Marcy."

[803]    Exhibit 102, Handwritten notes of FBI interview of Park
Police Lieutenant Patrick Gavin, April 28, 1994:  "Inv. Christine
Hodakievic met him in Pk [parking] Lot, took up to scene, she'd
been there."

[804]    Exhibit 98, Report of FBI interview of Park Police
Lieutenant Patrick Gavin, April 28, 1994:  "He [Gavin] stated
that Investigator Hodakievic met him at the parking lot and later
directed him up to where the body had been discovered."  Exhibit
102, Handwritten notes of FBI interview of Lieutenant Patrick
Gavin, April 28, 1994:  "Stayed in area 40-45 minutes, insured
people in parking lot interviewed, car checked."

[805]    Exhibit 79, Deposition of Park Police Officer Kevin
Fornshill, July 12, 1994:  "Sergeant Edwards, who was my Sergeant
for the day, I passed him on the hill, and he was carrying a
Polaroid up the hill while I was coming down."

[806]    Exhibit 79, Deposition of Park Police Officer Kevin
Fornshill, July 12, 1994:  "On the way back down the hill, I
passed Sergeant Edwards who told me again to respond back to the
CIA, since that's a priority beat for us."

**Endnote 14, 6:26:** *Body site.* Sergeant Edwards arrived about this time because he passed[807] Officer Fornshill who had left the body site around 6:25 p.m. Edwards took charge of the body site, took possession of the seven photographs Officer Ferstl[808] had taken, then ordered Ferstl back to the parking lot, instructing him to assist arriving investigators.[809]

*Parking lot.* Fornshill returned to the parking lot,[810] saw Hodakievic there,[811] and left the park.[812]

---

[807]    Exhibit 79, Deposition of Park Police Officer Kevin Fornshill, July 12, 1994: "Sergeant Edwards, who was my Sergeant for the day, I passed him on the hill, and he was carrying a Polaroid up the hill while I was coming down."

[808]    OIC, p. 73: "Ferstl said that he took Polaroids and, without initialing or marking them, gave them to Sergeant Edwards."

[809]    Exhibit 96, Report of FBI interview of Park Police Officer Franz Ferstl, May 2, 1994: "Cheryl Braun and John Rolla also arrived on the scene, adding that at that point in time, Sergeant Edwards instructed him to go back to the parking lot and see if they needed assistance there."

[810]    Exhibit 79, Deposition of Park Police Officer Kevin Fornshill, July 21, 1994: Q. So Ferstl and Edwards come. Did they come together or in separate cars? A. They came in separate cars, Officer Franz Ferstl, he relieved me, and basically took charge of the body and the crime scene. Q. When you say he relieved you, what do you mean? A. I mean he physically -- Q. Took charge? A. Yes, he physically. There's always someone there until we're relieved by a supervisor or the investigators, so I maintained the integrity of the crime scene until I was relieved by another officer. So when I was relieved by Franz Ferstl. I was cleared to return back to my beat, which I did.

[811]    Exhibit 79, Deposition of Park Police Officer Kevin Fornshill, July 12, 1994: "I went back to the parking lot. There was a lot of confusion with other cars coming in. My car, Officer Ferstl's car, the sergeant's car, and about that time the investigators would be rolling in. I believe Officer Hodakievic, who at the time was a plainclothes investigator." [926]

[812]    Exhibit 79, Deposition Park Police Officer Kevin Fornshill, July 12, 1994: Q. Do you remember any of the other officers there? A. No. While I was leaving, the other officers were responding to the scene, the investigators would put themselves out over the radio as being in the area or at the scene. Q. At that point, did you leave the

**Endnote 15, 6:27:** *Body site*. After Officer Ferstl left, Sergeant Edwards remained alone at the body site for at least 15 minutes.

**Endnote 16, 6:28-6:30:** *Parking lot*. According to Investigator Abt, Fornshill was still present[813] when Investigators Braun, Abt, and Rolla arrived, but she was wrong. Investigator Braun testified that Officer Fornshill had left.[814] Investigator Rolla's report and testimony supports Fornshill's testimony -- Fornshill had left the park before investigators arrived.[815]

---

scene? A. Yes. I was ordered by Sergeant Edwards to return to my beat. *** Q. Did you talk to them before you left the scene? A. As far as who? Q. Ferstl or Edwards? A. Basically when Officer Ferstl found me. I said, you know, here you go. And again, I was told to respond back to the CIA as soon as possible. There was really no information to be exchanged because I didn't touch the body or any part of the death scene. On the way back down the hill, I passed Sergeant Edwards who told me again to respond back to the CIA, since that's a priority beat for us.

[813] Exhibit 118, Handwritten notes of Park Police Investigator Renee Abt, July 20, 1993: "1815 [6:15] requested & responding (Braun, Rolla, myself) 1835 arrival, personnel on scene Hodakievic #32 Gavin, Bob Edwards #202, 211 Ferstl, 261 Kevin Fornshill located DB w Fairfax, 213 Spetz"

[814] Exhibit 101, Deposition of Park Police Investigator Cheryl Braun, July 23, 1994: Q. Okay. And who was at the park when you got there? A. When I got there, Officer Spetz was there. Officer Fornshill was there. *** Q. All right. Then after you got this information from Spetz, what did you do? A. We -- well, we were waiting initially for Officer Simonello to get there, and he got there a couple of minutes after we did, and then we all went up with, I think it was, Officer Ferdstall [sic] who took us up to the scene. I don't recall, I don't -- for some reason I don't think Officer Fornshill was still there because I think he was working a Wolf Trap detail or something and he had to respond to that.

[815] Exhibit 6, Deposition Park Police Investigator John Rolla, July 21, 1994: Q. Did you see Fornshill when you first got into the parking lot? A. No, Fornshill was already gone. We requested him to come back because we thought it was odd, first person on the scene, to find the body. There was other things going on, he was sent to another call. We requested him to come back.

As ordered by Sergeant Edwards, Officer Ferstl was in the parking lot to assist the investigators.[816]  After Ferstl briefed[817]

---

Exhibit 6, Deposition of Park Police Investigator John Rolla July 21, 1994:  Q.  Who was there when you got on the scene?  A.  I arrived on the scene.  Christine Hodakievic was there.  She was off duty, on her way home. heard the call and stopped there.  Fornshill had already left. Sergeant Bob Edwards.  Officer Ferstl.  I don't remember his first name.  Q.  Officer, sergeant?  A.  Officer Ferstle [sic].  The EMT medical units was pulling out when we pulled in were already leaving.

Exhibit 113, Park Police Report of Investigator John Rolla, July 21, 1993:  "Upon arrival we met with Lieutenant Gavin, Off. Ferstl, car 211, Off. Spetz, car 213, and Sergeant Edwards, car 202."

Exhibit 79, Deposition of Park Police Officer Kevin Fornshill, July 12, 1994:  Q.  Do you remember any of the other officers there?  A.  No.  While I was leaving, the other officers were responding to the scene, the investigators would put themselves out over the radio as being in the area or at the scene.  Q.  At that point, did you leave the scene?  A.  Yes.  I was ordered by Sergeant Edwards to return to my beat.

[816]  Exhibit 96, Report of FBI interview of Park Police Officer Franz Ferstl, May 2, 1994:  Cheryl Braun and John Rolla also arrived on the scene, adding that at that point in time, Sergeant Edwards instructed him to go back to the parking lot and see if they needed assistance there.

[817]  Exhibit 100, Report of FBI interview of Park Police Investigator John Rolla, April 27, 1994:  Investigator Rolla advised that upon arrival at the Fort Marcy Park the above officers were briefed by USPP Officer Ferstl and informed that the decedent had apparently died of a self inflicted gunshot wound to the head and was tentatively identified as Vincent Foster, Little Rock, Arkansas.  Rolla also advised that a 1989 Honda Accord with Arkansas license plate discovered in the Fort Marcy parking lot was thought to belong to the decedent.  Rolla advised that after this orientation and in the company of Officers Apt and Ferstl and possibly Officer Hodakievic proceeded to the death scene where they joined up with Sergeant Edwards (USPP) and possibly Officer Julie Spatz [sic] (USPP).

Lieutenant Gavin, Hodakievic and the investigators,[818] Rolla requested Fornshill return to the park.[819] At 6:28 p.m., Ferstl radioed for Fornshill to return.[820] Since investigators were on the scene prior to 6:28 p.m., reports stating they arrived later are wrong.[821] Braun testified that investigators, upon their arrival, closed the gate to the park.[822]

A passerby on the Parkway saw a man fitting Investigator Rolla's description opening the gate to the park.[823] (The passerby's report that the man was driving a blue Mercedes is incorrect. The female owner of the broken-down blue Mercedes had abandoned

---

[818] Exhibit 92, Handwritten notes of FBI interview of Park Police Investigator Cheryl Braun, April 28, 1994: "Christine Hodakievic also at the Pk [parking] lot." ]

[819] Exhibit 6, Deposition of Park Police Investigator John Rolla, July 21,1994: Q. Did you see Fornshill when you first got into the parking lot? A. No, Fornshill was already gone. We requested him to come back because we thought it was odd, first person on the scene, to find the body. There was other things going on, he was sent to another call. We requested him to come back.

[820] Exhibit 58, Transcript of Park Police radio transmission, July 20,1993: Dispatcher: 18:28 211 [Ferstl]: "211 [Ferstl] could you have 261 [Fornshill] return to the crime scene..."

[821] Exhibit 118, Handwritten notes of Park Police Investigator Renee Abt, July 20, 1993: "1815 [6:15] requested & responding (Braun, Rolla, myself) 1835 [6:35] arrival" Exhibit 113, Park Police Report of Investigator John Rolla, July 21, 1993: "At approximately 1835 [6:35] hours we arrived at Ft. Marcy."

[822] Exhibit 101, Deposition of Park Police Investigator Cheryl Braun, July 23, 1994: "Q. Had the area been roped off? A. No we didn't actually because of closing the gate. That kept anybody else from coming into the area."

[823] Exhibit 86, Report of FBI interview of unknown female commuter on George Washington Memorial Parkway, March 21, 1994: On the day of Vincent Foster's death, July 20, 1994 [sic] she was traveling westbound on the George Washington Parkway (GWP) at approximately 5:30 - 6:30 p.m... On this particular night, as she was driving by the entrance to Fort Marcy Park, she noticed a well-dressed man out of his car opening the gate to the park. *** She described the man from the car as being well dressed. She further described the man as a white male, slim, dark suit, aged 30's to early 40's and average in heighth [sic].

her car at the park entrance.  It appears the man seen at the entrance was Investigator Rolla closing the gate, not opening it as reported by the passerby sometime before 6:30 p.m.)

At Gavin's direction, Officer Hodakievic interviewed the four other fire & rescue workers[824] when they returned to the parking lot.  Braun[825] had reported the rescue workers had left, Rolla reported they were leaving,[826] and Abt's notes did not comment.  All fire and rescue personnel remained in the parking lot until 6:37 p.m.[827]

All Park Police personnel but Edwards were present in the parking lot; Edwards remained alone at the body site.  Reports that Officers Spetz or Ferstl were present with Sergeant Edwards at the body site are false.[828]

---

[824]  Exhibit 76, Park Police Report of Investigator Christine Hodakievic, July 21 1993.

[825]  Exhibit 101, Deposition of Park Police Investigator Cheryl Braun, July 23, 1994:  "Q.  Any medical personnel?  A.  No medical personnel."

[826]  Exhibit 6, Deposition of Park Police Investigator John Rolla July 21, 1994:  Q.  Who was there when you got on the scene?  A.  I arrived on the scene.  Christine Hodakievic was there.  She was off duty, on her way home. heard the call and stopped there.  Fornshill had already left.  Sergeant Bob Edwards.  Officer Ferstl.  I don't remember his first name.  Q.  Officer, Sergeant?  A.  Officer Ferstle [sic].  The EMT medical units was pulling out when we pulled in were already leaving.

Exhibit 113, Park Police Report of Investigator John Rolla, July 21, 1993:  "Upon arrival we met with Lieutenant Gavin, Off. Ferstl, car 211, Off. Spetz, car 213, and Sergeant Edwards, car 202."

[827]  Exhibit 34, Electronic log of McLean Fire Station Engine 1, July 20, 1993:  "18:37"

[828]  Exhibit 96, Report of FBI interview of Park Police Officer Franz Ferstl, May 2, 1994:  "Ferstl advised that he did not return to the death scene a third time, nor was he present at the death scene when other officers took Polaroid or 35mm pictures." Exhibit 170, Handwritten notes of FBI interview of Park Police Officer Julie Spetz, May 2, 1994:  "After providing background info re:  [redacted] to investigators Renee Abt and Cheryl Braun she left FMP returning to her patrol" Exhibit 70, Report of FBI interview of Park Police Officer Julie Spetz, May 2, 1994:

Police interviews of witnesses continued while some of the fire and rescue workers gathered around the Arkansas Honda in the lot while discussing its contents.[829]  Lieutenant Gavin continued to monitor the activities in the parking lot.[830]

**Endnote 17, 6:31:**  *Parking lot.*  Officer Watson arrived with the intern in the parking lot.[831]

**Endnote 18, 6:32-6:36:**  *Parking lot.*  Before fire and rescue workers left[832] at 6:37 p.m.,[833] police searched the car[834] and

---

"Officer Spetz stated that she never did go up to the location where the body was found."

[829]    Exhibit 57, Report of FBI interview of Firefighter Ralph Pisani, March 11, 1994.  (see 6:32)  Exhibit 66, Report of FBI interview of Firefighter Todd Hall, March 18, 1994:  "By this point in time, the rest of the EMS personnel were gathered in the vicinity of the vehicle bearing the Arkansas license tags.  It was noted that USPP officers were also on scene."

[830]    Exhibit 80, Handwritten notes of FBI interview of Park Police Lieutenant Patrick Gavin, April 28, 1994:  "Stayed in area 40-45 minutes, insured people in parking lot interviewed, car checked."

[831]    Exhibit 118, Handwritten notes of Park Police Investigator Renee Abt, July 20, 1993:  "Post arrival Watson & intern"

[832]    Exhibit 87, Report of FBI interview of Firefighter Lieutenant William Bianchi, March 17, 1994:  Bianchi was at Station 1 when the FCFRD personnel who responded to the initial call returned to the station.  Bianchi heard two people who had been on the call, possibly Todd Hall and Rick Arthur, say it was a strange incident.  Bianchi also heard from the returning FCFRD personnel that the victim was deceased and had been employed at the White House.  In particular, Iacone already knew that the victim had been employed at the White House when he returned to Station 1.  When Bianchi learned that the victim was a White House employee, he instructed Hall and Iacone to make their reports on the incident very detailed.

[833]    Exhibit 34, Electronic log of McLean Fire Station Engine 1, July 20, 1993:  "18:37"

[834]    Exhibit 71, Report of FBI interview of Paramedic Richard Arthur, March 16, 1994:  "He observed them gaining access to a cream colored car with a suit jacket and tie in it, looking for identification of some sort."

found Mr. Foster's White House identification.[835]  Paramedics saw police officers "gathered in the vicinity"[836] of the Arkansas Honda "gaining access" to the car, "looking for identification."[837]  Ferstl saw Braun recover Mr. Foster's identification.[838]

The two civilians were also present[839] and did not leave until after Braun had interviewed them.[840]

---

[835]  Exhibit 101, Deposition of Park Police Investigator Cheryl Braun, July 23, 1994:  Q.  Do you remember who the registration was?  A.  Yeah.  It was to Vincent Foster.  On the front seat of the vehicle was the jacket which matched Mr. Foster's pants.  It was like folded neatly on the seat.  Inside of the jacket was -- inside pocket -- was his wallet.  And as I recall, the credentials I thought were tucked like not in a pocket but in the jacket like underneath it or inside the fold of it.  And they were the White House credentials which identified him as Vincent Foster and the picture resembled the body that we had been looking at.

[836]  Exhibit 135, Report of FBI interview of Paramedic George Gonzalez, February 23, 1994:  "Gonzalez identified the following EMS personnel as being located in the Ft. Marcy Park parking area in the vicinity of the vehicle believed to belong to Foster..."

[837]  Exhibit 71, Report of FBI interview of Paramedic Richard Arthur, March 16, 1994:  "Once back in the parking area, the US Park Police took all the EMT's names.  He observed them gaining access to a cream colored car with a suit jacket and tie in it looking for identification of some sort."

[838]  Exhibit 96, Report of FBI interview of Park Police Officer Franz Ferstl, May 2, 1994:  Cheryl Braun and John Rolla also arrived on the scene, adding that at that point in time, Sergeant Edwards instructed him to go back to the parking lot and see if they needed assistance there... Ferstl stated that Officer Cheryl Braun was in the process of searching the Foster vehicle and he recalls her finding White House identification in the front passenger seat.

[839]  Exhibit 99, Report of FBI interview of Park Police Investigator Renee Abt, May 2, 1994:  According to Investigator Apt, upon arriving at the Fort Marcy parking lot, her initial actions were to obtain necessary vehicle description and identification for a Mercedes vehicle which had been abandoned on the ramp leading up to the Fort Marcy parking lot.  Subsequent to obtaining this vehicle information, she returned to the Fort Marcy parking lot where she observed Officer Spetz (USPP), interviewing a

# Endnotes

Seventeen people have now gathered in the parking lot and <u>only</u> Sergeant Robert Edwards was with Mr. Foster's body. In Gavin's presence, fire and rescue workers saw investigators gain access to the Arkansas Honda and recover the White House identification. When Investigator Braun recovered Mr. Foster's White House identification, she reportedly told Watson to tell Lieutenant Gavin.[841] (Gavin reported that he was not present when the White House identification was recovered.[842])

**Endnote 19, 6:37:** *Parking lot.* By the time the six fire & rescue workers left the park at 6:37 p.m.,[843] they knew the victim was a White House employee.[844] Investigators Rolla, Braun, Abt,

---

middle-aged, white couple who had apparently been picnicking in an area south of the parking lot.

[840]    <u>Exhibit 116</u>, Park Police report of Park Police Investigator Cheryl Braun, July 20, 1993: "After receiving [redacted] and [redacted] information they were allowed to leave the area."

[841]    <u>Exhibit 101</u>, Deposition of Park Police Investigator Cheryl Braun, July 23, 1994: "Q. You mentioned that you asked someone to notify Lieutenant Gavin? A. Right. Q. Who do you remember you asked? A. I believe it was Officer Watson. And he had been up there, he had stopped by. He had an intern, and asked permission."

[842]    <u>Exhibit 98</u>, Report of FBI interview of Park Police Lieutenant Patrick Gavin, April 28, 1994: Lieutenant Gavin stated that he stayed in the area for approximately 30-45 minutes, insuring that witnesses in the parking lot were interviewed and the vehicles in the parking lot were checked. By the time he left, the evidence officer, Peter Simonello, had arrived on the scene. Lieutenant Gavin stated that he thought that the victim might possibly have been a government appointee because of the Arkansas tags. He noted, however, that the White House identification was discovered in the vehicle after he left the scene. To the best of his recollection, one of the detectives at the scene called him later in the evening, informing him that they had found White House identification for Foster.

[843]    <u>Exhibit 34</u>, Electronic log of McLean Fire Station Engine 1, July 20, 1993: "18:37"

[844]    <u>Exhibit 87</u>: Report of FBI interview of Firefighter Lieutenant William Bianchi, March 17, 1994: "Bianchi was at Station 1 when the FCFRD personnel who responded to the initial call returned to the station. Bianchi heard two people who had been on the call, possibly Todd Hall and Rick Arthur, say it was a strange incident. Bianchi also

Hodakievic, Watson, and the Intern waited for Identification Technician Peter Simonello to arrive before going up to the body.[845] Officer Ferstl never returned to the body site but remained in the parking lot until the tow truck arrived to pick up the Arkansas Honda.[846]

**Endnote 20, 6:38-6:41:** *Body site.* Sometime during the over 15 minutes that Sergeant Edwards was alone with the body, an untraceable .38 caliber black revolver replaced the semi-automatic pistol in Mr. Foster's hand.[847]

*Parking lot.* While Investigators waited for Technician Simonello to arrive, Investigator Rolla ran the tags on the Arkansas Honda, from which Mr. Foster's White House identification had been retrieved. The registration "came back to Vincent Foster in Little Rock, Arkansas."[848]

---

heard from the returning FCFRD personnel that the victim was deceased and had been employed at the White House. In particular, Iacone already knew that the victim had been employed at the White House when he returned to Station 1. When Bianchi learned that the victim was a White House employee, he instructed Hall and Iacone to make their reports on the incident very detailed.

[845] Exhibit 101, Deposition of Park Police Investigator Cheryl Braun, July 23, 1994: "Well we were waiting initially for Officer Simonello to get there."

[846] Exhibit 96, Report of FBI interview of Park Police Officer Franz Ferstl, May 2, 1994: Ferstl advised that he did not return to the death scene a third time, nor was he present at the death scene when other officers took Polaroid or 35mm pictures... Ferstl advised he accompanied the tow truck that removed the Foster vehicle to the USPP Anacostia station, insuring that the vehicle was properly stored and not in any way tampered with during the towing process.

[847] Exhibit 110, Deposition of Paramedic George Gonzalez, July 20, 1994: "Q. Apparently you recall the gun being in a different position than what was photographed? A. That's correct."

[848] Exhibit 6, Deposition of Park Police Investigator John Rolla, July 21, 1994: "Q. What happened after you were told that? A. We just wrote the tag down, I think I called communications on the car phone and ran the registration, it came back to Vincent Foster in Little Rock, Arkansas."

Lieutenant Ronald Schmidt stopped at the park to offer assistance. According to Investigator Braun, Schmidt did not go up to the body scene. When Schmidt asked about the victim's identification, Braun reportedly told him they "had not found the credentials yet."[849] Investigator Abt interviewed the civilian couple.[850] Lieutenant Schmidt then left the parking lot.

Hodakievic directed Gavin "up to where the body had been discovered."[851] According to Gavin, Hodakievic had been at the body site (before[852] the official discovery at 6:14). Rolla also

---

[849] Exhibit 101, Deposition of Park Police Investigator Cheryl Braun, July 23, 1994: Q. Okay. Did some of these officials come to the scene? A. No. The only official that came by other than Lieutenant Gavin was Lieutenant Schmidt, who was -- he's in charge of our narcotics and vice unit. And he stopped by. And at that time I had not found -- when he stopped by, I had not found the credentials yet, and he asked, you know, was there anything I needed, and, I said, "No, everything's fine. You know, we have a suicide. We're, you know, doing our investigation.

[850] Exhibit 99, Report of FBI interview of Park Police Officer Renee Abt, May 2, 1994: According to Investigator Apt, upon arriving at the Fort Marcy parking lot, her initial actions were to obtain necessary vehicle description and identification for a Mercedes vehicle which had been abandoned on the ramp leading up to the Fort Marcy parking lot. Subsequent to obtaining this vehicle information, she returned to the Fort Marcy parking lot where she observed Officer Spetz (USPP), interviewing a middle-aged, white couple who had apparently been picnicking in an area south of the parking lot. Ms. Apt then advised she immediately proceeded to the death scene in the company of Investigators John Rolla, Cheryl Braun with Officer Peter Simonello following them to the scene.

[851] Exhibit 98, Report of FBI interview of Park Police Lieutenant Patrick Gavin, April 28, 1994: "He [Gavin] stated that Investigator Hodakievic met him at the parking lot and later directed him up to where the body had been discovered." Exhibit 102, Handwritten notes of FBI interview of Park Police Lieutenant Patrick Gavin, April 28, 1994: "Stayed in area 40-45 minutes, insured people in parking lot interviewed, car checked."

[852] Exhibit 102, Handwritten notes of FBI interview of Park Police Lieutenant Patrick Gavin, April 28, 1994. "Inv. Christine Hodakievic met him in Pk [parking] Lot, took up to scene, she'd been there."

testified that police were on the scene earlier.[853]

Still waiting for Technician Simonello to arrive, Investigator Abt finished interviewing the couple and walked down to check out the broken down Mercedes.

**Endnote 21, 6:42-6:43:** *Body site.* When Lieutenant Gavin had arrived at Fort Marcy Park, he did not go directly to the body site,[854] first seeing to it that some of the witnesses in the parking lot were interviewed, and that the cars were checked.[855] Gavin arrived at the body about 6:42 with Investigator Hodakievic (Hodakievic is said to have recalled that Ferstl was at the body with Edwards[856] when she and Gavin arrived Edwards was alone at the time[857]). Upon Hodakievic's arrival at the body site, Sergeant Edwards spoke with her and showed her a Polaroid of the body.[858]

---

[853]   Exhibit 6, Deposition of Park Police Investigator John Rolla, July 20, 1994: I have no idea why he would -- unless he just meant the time he was pronounced. Perhaps that's what he meant, I am pronouncing him. He said, well, make that the time of death. I knew it wasn't the time of death, officers were there before 1800 hours. So if he decide [sic] at 1800 hours, somebody is in trouble.

[854]   Exhibit 98, Report of FBI interview of Park Police Lieutenant Patrick Gavin, April 28, 1994: "He [Gavin] stated that Investigator Hodakievic met him at the parking lot and later directed him up to where the body had been discovered."

[855]   Exhibit 102, Handwritten notes of FBI interview of Park Police Lieutenant Patrick Gavin, April 28, 1994: "Stayed in area 40-45 minutes, insured people in parking lot interviewed, car checked."

[856]   Exhibit 81, Report of FBI interview of Park Police Investigator Christine Hodakievic, May 2, 1994: Officer Hodakievic advised that to the best of her recollection, upon arriving at the death scene, Sergeant Edwards (USPP) was basically in charge of the death scene and believes that Officer Franz Ferstl was also present. She could not recall any other individuals being present at the time she arrived at the death scene.

[857]   Exhibit 96, Report of FBI interview of Park Police Officer Franz Ferstl, May 2, 1994: "Ferstl advised that he did not return to the death scene a third time, nor was he present at the death scene when other officers took Polaroid or 35mm pictures."

[858]   Exhibit 81, Report of FBI interview of Park Police Investigator Christine Hodakievic, May 2, 1994: "She does recall

# Endnotes

Lieutenant Gavin and Investigator Hodakievic viewed the body. Gavin thought that the victim appeared to have been mugged.[859]

**Parking lot.** Investigator Braun recalled waiting five to ten minutes for Simonello's arrival.[860] Simonello stated that he might have arrived as late as 7:00.[861] Simonello reported that he saw Officer Fornshill when he arrived.[862] According to the investigators, Fornshill had left the park before they arrived. If Officer Fornshill returned to the park, it is not reflected in the record.

The two civilian witnesses left the park after Investigator Braun had spent five to ten minutes[863] interviewing[864] them in the lot, as Abt, Spetz and Ferstl had minutes earlier.

---

being initially briefed by Sergeant Edwards, which included being informed that the decedent had a revolver in his right hand, as well as being shown a Polaroid photograph of decedent's position at the death scene."

[859]    Exhibit 102, Handwritten notes of FBI interview of Park Police Lieutenant Patrick Gavin, April 28, 1994:  "[T]hought victim could have been mugged."

[860]    Exhibit 91, Report of FBI interview of Park Police Investigator Cheryl Braun, April 28, 1994:  "She advised that as best she recalls, she, Rolla and Abt remained in the parking lot for about 5 to 10 minutes, awaiting the arrival of evidence officer Peter Simonello."

[861]    Exhibit 104, Deposition of Park Police Evidence Technician Peter Simonello, July 14, 1994:  "Q. About what time did you get to the scene?  A.  I believe it was around seven-ish. 7:00."

[862]    Exhibit 104, Deposition of Park Police Evidence Technician Peter Simonello, July    14, 1994:  "Q.  Do you remember officers' names?  A.  I believe Officer Fornshill was there, and there was a sergeant there."

[863]    Exhibit 101, Deposition of Park Police Investigator Cheryl Braun, July 23, 1994:  "Q.  So you talked to this couple that was in the park before you went over to see the body?  A.  Right.  Q. About how long were you talking to them?  A.  Probably about maybe five, ten minutes."

[864]    Exhibit 110, Park Police Report of Park Police Investigator Cheryl Braun, July 20, 1993:  "After receiving [redacted] and [redacted] information they were allowed to leave the area."

Technician Simonello arrived at the parking lot. (There, he reportedly saw Investigators Abt, Braun, Rolla, Hodakievic, and Officer Watson.[865] He also testified that he saw Abt, Braun, Rolla, Hodakievic, Fornshill, Edwards and a couple of patrol officers, probably Ferstl and Spetz.[866] Simonello was not specific about where he saw Edwards and Hodakievic, who were at the body site.)

**Endnote 22, 6:44:** *Body site*. After viewing the body, Lieutenant Gavin and Investigator Hodakievic "checked the surrounding area" for evidence.[867]

*Parking lot.* About this time, Officer Julie Spetz gave investigators information about the couple and left the park to return to her patrol.[868] Investigator Abt returned to the lot

---

[865]   Exhibit 117, Park Police Report of Park Police Evidence Technician Peter Simonello, July 25, 1993: "The undersigned responded to Ft Marcy and met with Inv. R. Abt at the entrance to the park. Inv. Abt directed me to the first parking lot inside the park where I met with the following persons: Inv. C. Braun, Inv. J. Rolla, Inv. Hodakievic, and Officer B. Watson."

[866]   Exhibit 104, Deposition of Park Police Evidence Technician Peter Simonello, July 14, 1994:  Q.  Do you remember officers' names?  A.  I believe Officer Fornshill was there, and there was a Sergeant there.  I can't remember his name right now.  Q.  Edwards?  A.  Sergeant Edwards, that's correct.  I don't remember the other officers.  I think there were a couple more patrol officers and privates, but I don't have any recollection of who they were.  I wasn't paying any attention to them at the time.  Q.  What about the investigators and detectives?  A.  Yes.  There was Investigator Cheryl Braun, Investigator John Rolla, I believe Renee Apt.  Investigator Apt, A-p-t [sic], and there's one more female investigator named Chris Hodakievic, and I don't know how to spell it.  Q.  Were there medical personnel there that you can recall?  A.  When I arrived, there wasn't.  I didn't see any.

[867]   Exhibit 81, Report of FBI interview of Park Police Investigator Christine Hodakievic, May 2, 1994:  In addition to viewing in a cursory manner the decedent's location and body description, Officer Hodakievic checked the surrounding area of the death scene, advising that she did not observe any pedestrians within the general death scene area and maintained she did not observe any trampled grass, leaves or vegetation nor any other signs of a struggle at the death scene.

after gathering information on the Mercedes. Simonello and the investigators gathered their equipment and cameras needed for their investigation of the body site.

**Endnote 23, 6:45:** *Body site.* At about this time, Sergeant Edwards began taking Polaroid photographs. Investigators observed him photographing the body site when they arrived a couple minutes later.[869] Investigator Braun testified that the "determination [of suicide was made] prior to going up and looking at the body."[870]

---

[868]   Exhibit 170, Handwritten notes of FBI interview of Park Police Officer Julie Spetz, May 2, 1994: "After providing background info re:[redacted] to investigators Renee Abt and Cheryl Braun she left FMP returning to her patrol"

[869]   Exhibit 99, Report of FBI interview of Park Police Investigator Renee Abt, May 2, 1994: Upon arriving at the death scene, she specifically observed Sergeant Edwards in the process of completing Polaroid photography of the body and to the best of her recollection, believes that contemporaneous with Edwards finishing his Polaroid photography, Investigator John Rolla commenced taking a series of Polaroid photographs.

[870]   Exhibit 101, Deposition of Park Police Investigator Cheryl Braun, July 23, 1994: Q. Did he [Edwards] say he thought that the death was by suicide? A. I don't recall exactly how he did it, and he did show the pictures to it that he had snapped. Q. Was it your understanding that a determination had been made as to the cause of death? A. I think we more made that determination. You know, like I said, when we first got the call. It was for a dead body. Then I asked if it was natural or of suspicious nature. And I was told suspicious, so I had them close the gate. Then once we got there, maybe actually I do remember speaking to Lieutenant Gavin. So maybe it was Lieutenant Gavin who might have -- it might have been Lieutenant Gavin then who actually initially explained what the scene was, because I had some knowledge of it when I went to speak with the couple and ask them if they had heard anything or seen anything and ask them about other vehicles that were in the area. Yeah, I would say it was Lieutenant Gavin actually. Q. Did Lieutenant Gavin mention anything about suicide? A. I can't recall. I don't -- I don't recall if he or if that was what we -- it seems to me that we had made that determination prior to going up and looking at the body.

***Parking lot.*** About this time,[871] Cheryl Braun,[872] John Rolla,[873] Renee Abt,[874] William Watson, the Intern, and Peter Simonello,[875] began walking up to the body site where they met Sergeant Edwards, Lieutenant Gavin, and Investigator Hodakievic.

**Endnote 24, 6:46-6:48:** ***Body site.*** When joined by more Park Police, Edwards was observed taking photographs.[876] Technician Peter Simonello,[877] Investigator Abt,[878] Investigator Braun,

---

[871]    Exhibit 92, Handwritten notes of FBI interview of Park Police Investigator Cheryl Braun, April 28, 1994: "As best recalls she and Rolla & Abt remained in P lot for 10 minutes awaiting arrival of evidence officer Peter Simonello."

[872]    Exhibit 91, Report of FBI interview of Park Police Investigator Cheryl Braun, April 28, 1994: "She stated to the best of her recollection, she, Simonello, Rolla and Abt all walked up to the death scene together."

[873]    Exhibit 100, Report of FBI interview of Park Police Investigator John Rolla, April 27, 1994: "Rolla advised that after this orientation and in the company of officers Apt and Ferstl and possibly Officer Hodakievic proceeded to the death scene where they joined up with Sergeant Edwards (USPP) and possibly Officer Julie Spetz (USPP)."

[874]    Exhibit 99, Report of FBI interview of Park Police Investigator Renee Abt, May 2, 1994: Ms. Abt then advised she immediately proceeded to the death scene in the company of Investigators John Rolla, Cheryl Braun with Officer Peter Simonello following them to the scene. She recalled that at the death scene she observed Sergeant Edwards, USPP and possibly Officers Franz Ferstl and Christine Hodakievic, USPP.

[875]    Exhibit 117, Park Police Report by Evidence Technician Peter Simonello, July 25, 1993: "I followed Investigators Rolla and Abt to the scene of the incident the location of which was referred to as "the last cannon gun at Ft. Marcy." I arrived at the scene and observed that the scene was secured with crimescene tape and that Sergeant Edwards was present."

[876]    Exhibit 99, Report of FBI interview of Park Police Investigator Renee Abt, May 2, 1994: "Upon arriving at the death scene, she specifically observed Sergeant Edwards in the process of completing Polaroid photography of the body..."

[877]    Exhibit 117, Report of Park Police Evidence Technician Peter Simonello, July 25, 1993: "I followed Investigators Rolla and Abt to the scene of the incident the location of which was referred to as 'the last cannon at Ft Marcy.' I arrived at the

Officer Watson, an Intern,[879] and Investigator Rolla[880] all arrived at the body scene about this time. (Reports that Officers Julie Spetz or Franz Ferstl were also present are incorrect.[881]) Hodakievic claims she was at the body site when investigators arrived,[882] but Abt reportedly claimed that upon her arrival at the body site, Hodakievic was not present.[883])

---

scene and observed the scene had been secured with crimescene tape and that Sergeant Edwards was present."

[878]   Exhibit 99, Report of FBI interview of Park Police Investigator Renee Abt, May 2, 1994:  Ms. Abt then advised she immediately proceeded to the death scene in the company of Investigators John Rolla, Cheryl Braun with Officer Peter Simonello following them to the scene.  She recalled that at the death scene she observed Sergeant Edwards, USPP and possibly Officers Franz Ferstl and Christine Hodakievic, USPP.

[879]   Exhibit 101, Deposition of Park Police Investigator Cheryl Braun, July 23, 1994:  "I believe it was Officer Watson.  And he had been up there, he had stopped by.  He had an intern, and asked permission.  I escorted him up to see the scene.  And then they left, came down with me when I went through the car and left shortly after that."

[880]   Exhibit 100, Report of FBI interview of Park Police Investigator John Rolla, April 27, 1994:  "Rolla advised that after this orientation and in the company of officers Apt and Ferstl and possibly Officer Hodakievic proceeded to the death scene where they joined up with Sergeant Edwards (USPP) and possibly Officer Julie Spetz (USPP)."

[881]   Exhibit 96, Report of FBI interview of Park Police Officer Franz Ferstl, May 2, 1994:  "Ferstl advised that he did not return to the death scene a third time, nor was he present at the death scene when other officers took Polaroid or 35mm pictures." Exhibit 170, Handwritten notes of FBI interview of Park Police Officer Julie Spetz, May 2, 1994:  "After providing background info re: [redacted] to investigators Renee Abt and Cheryl Braun she left FMP returning to her patrol." Exhibit 70, Report of FBI interview of Park Police Officer Julie Spetz, May 2, 1994: "Officer Spetz stated that she never did go up to the location where the body was found."

[882]   Exhibit 81, Report of FBI interview of Park Police Investigator Christine Hodakievic, May 2, 1994:  To the best of her recollection, she was at the death scene for approximately five to ten minutes when USPP John Rolla, Cheryl Braun, and Renee Abt arrived.  She immediately briefed these officers regarding her observations to

*Parking lot.* Officer Ferstl remained in the parking lot.

**Endnote 25, 6:49-6:53:** *Body site.* Lieutenant Gavin remained at the body scene until after Simonello arrived,[884] remaining at the park for "40 to 45 minutes.[885] At about this time, Edwards completed taking Polaroid photographs. Investigator Rolla stated that no one knew who Edwards was and Rolla demanded Sergeant Edwards turn over the photographs.[886]

According to Investigator Abt, when Sergeant Edwards finished taking photographs, Investigator Rolla began taking photographs,[887] reportedly at 6:50 p.m.[888] Investigator Braun then

---

include informing them that a weapon had been located in the decedent's right hand.

[883] Exhibit 155, Handwritten notes of FBI interview of Park Police Investigator Renee Abt, May 2, 1994: "Don't recall Chris Hodakievic at the scene."

[884] Exhibit 98, Report of FBI interview of Park Police Lieutenant Patrick Gavin, April 28, 1994: "By the time he left, the evidence officer, Peter Simonello, had arrived on the scene."

[885] Exhibit 80, Handwritten notes of FBI interview of Park Police Lieutenant Patrick Gavin, April 28, 1994: "Stayed in area 40-45 minutes, insured people in parking lot interviewed, car checked."

[886] Exhibit 6, Deposition of Park Police Investigator John Rolla, July 21, 1994: Q. Did anybody else take photographs that you are aware of? A. I think that Edwards, Sergeant Edwards took a couple of Polaroids, and I told him to give them to me, not having a collection -- you know, I didn't know who this guy was, nobody [knew] who this guy was, but we are not going to have a collection of dead body photographs, and I don't think that was their attempt, but a lot of times -- I just wanted to make sure I had everything, and there wasn't anything walking around out there. Q. Did you use the same camera that he used? A. No.

[887] Exhibit 99, Report of FBI interview of Park Police Investigator Renee Abt, May 2, 1994: Upon arriving at the death scene, she specifically observed Sergeant Edwards in the process of completing Polaroid photography of the body and to the best of her recollection, believes that contemporaneous with Edwards finishing his Polaroid photography, Investigator John Rolla commenced taking a series of Polaroid photographs.

instructed Rolla on how to conduct his very first homicide investigation.[889]  Rolla testified that Lieutenant Gavin was the superior officer at the scene but he did not tell Rolla what to do at the scene.  Rolla stated that Investigators Braun and Hodakievic did the "decision making."[890]

Investigators Braun[891] and Hodakievic[892] observed Rolla search Mr. Foster's pockets for a note and keys.  They found neither and were "puzzled why [they] found no keys to the car."[893]

---

[888]     Exhibit 115, Handwritten notes of FBI interview of Park Police Investigator John Rolla, April 27, 1994:  "Polaroids were taken at approx 6:50 p.m."

[889]     Exhibit 101, Deposition of Park Police Investigator Cheryl Braun, July 23, 1994.  I was basically directing Investigator Rolla what to do because he was new in the office.  I wanted him to get the experience of handling a crime scene.  So I was directing him what to do and then I gave him some instructions.  And to help save time I then went down to the car to start going through the car to look for identification and a suicide note.

[890]     Exhibit 6, Deposition of Park Police Investigator John Rolla, July 21, 1994:  Q.  But he was the superior officer on the scene.  A.  Right.  He was the superior officer on the scene.  ***  Q.  So Lieutenant Gavin wasn't telling you to do anything at the scene?  A.  No.  Q.  Was he participating at all in your conversations or decision making?  A.  No.  Q.  So, it was you, Detective Abt and Detective Braun?  A.  Braun and Christine Hodakievic, who was an investigator at the time, has since left...

[891]     Exhibit 101, Deposition of Park Police Investigator Cheryl Braun, July 23, 1994:  Q.  Did you stay with the body?  A.  I stayed with the body for probably maybe 15, 20 minutes or so, maybe half an hour, while they were taking the photos.  And I directed Investigator Rolla to check the pockets and see if he could find any identification or a suicide note or anything like that, which he didn't have any success with that.

[892]     Exhibit 81, Report of FBI interview of Park Police Investigator Christine Hodakievic, May 2, 1994:  "In regards to determining subsequent activities at the death scene, Officer Hodakievic stated that she does recall Investigator John Rolla checking the decedent's body for identification, specifically the decedent's front and rear pockets, but can't recall if any other individual might have touched or rolled the body."

**Endnote 26, 6:54-7:14:** *Parking lot.* Investigators Hodakievic and Braun decided to recheck the car and returned to the parking lot with Officer Watson and the Intern.[894] Investigator Hodakievic may have returned to the parking lot scene to telephone her daughter.[895] Investigator Braun returned to the parking lot to search the car again, looking for suicide note and car keys,[896] which were not found in the car or Mr. Foster's pockets.[897]

---

[893]   Exhibit 6, Deposition of Park Police Investigator John Rolla, July 21, 1994:  "Q.  Did you get any keys?  A.  I searched his pants pockets.  I couldn't find a wallet or nothing in his pants pockets.  Later on Investigator Braun and myself searched the car...  We searched the car and we were puzzled why we found no keys to the car."

[894]   Exhibit 101, Deposition of Park Police Investigator Cheryl Braun, July 23, 1994:  "I believe it was Officer Watson.  And he had been up there, he had stopped by.  He had an intern, and asked permission.  I escorted him up to see the scene.  And then they left, came down with me when I went through the car and left shortly after that."

[895]   Exhibit 81, Report of FBI interview of Park Police Investigator Christine Hodakievic, May 2, 1994:  "She further related that she rotated between the death scene and the parking lot, specifically recalling that on one occasion she was in the parking lot for approximately ten minutes in order to call her residence to advise her daughter of her delay."

[896]   Exhibit 6, Deposition of Park Police Investigator John Rolla, July 21, 1994:  Q.  Did you get any keys?  A.  I searched his pants pockets.  I couldn't find a wallet or nothing in his pants pockets.  Later on Investigator Braun and myself searched the car...  We searched the car and we were puzzled why we found no keys to the car.

[897]   Exhibit 171, Senate testimony of Park Police Investigator John Rolla, July 20, 1995:  "Q.  You didn't search his person at the scene did you?  A.  After it was pronounced, we emptied his pockets.  Yes, I did remove his personal property and search them."  Exhibit 101, Deposition of Park Police Investigator Cheryl Braun, July 23, 1994:  "I was basically directing Investigator Rolla what to do because he was new in the office. I wanted him to get the experience of handling a crime scene.  So I was directing him what to do, and then I gave him some instructions."

Officer Hodakievic interviewed the driver of the tow truck who had responded to tow the broken down Mercedes.[898]

**Endnote 27, 7:15:** *Body site.* Gavin stated that he remained for 40 to 45 minutes after his arrival at the park, putting his departure shortly after 7:00.[899] Sergeant Edwards left after Investigators arrived at the body site, as there were no more references to his being present.

*Parking lot.* Officer Hodakievic met the medical examiner,[900] Dr. Donald Haut, along with his driver[901] in the lot upon their arrival. Hodakievic, possibly accompanied by Braun,[902] escorted Haut to the body site. Ferstl remained in the parking lot.[903]

**Endnote 28, 7:16-7:17:** *Body site.* Investigators Hodakievic and Braun escorted Dr. Donald Haut to the body scene.[904]

[898] Exhibit 76, Park Police report of Investigator Christine Hodakievic, July 21, 1993: "At approximately 1900 hrs., a crane from Al's Towing... arrived at Ft. Marcy... to pick up the Merz."

[899] Exhibit 80, Handwritten notes of FBI interview of Park Police Lieutenant Patrick Gavin, April 28, 1994: "Stayed in area 40-45 minutes, insured people in parking lot interviewed, car checked."

[900] Exhibit 81, Report of FBI interview of Park Police Christine Hodakievic, May 2, 1994: "During one of the periods of time when she was at the Fort Marcy parking lot, Hodakievic recalls the medical examiner arriving, whom she met in the parking lot and escorted to the death scene."

[901] Exhibit 172, Handwritten notes of FBI interview of Park Police Investigator Christine Hodakievic, May 2, 1994: "M.E. eventually arrived with female driver - met in parking lot & escorted to the scene."

[902] Exhibit 73, Report of FBI interview of Dr. Donald Haut, April 12, 1994: "Upon arriving at Fort Marcy Park, USPP officers escorted Haut to the body of Vincent W. Foster, Jr., which was located approximately 150 yards into a wooded area at the park."

[903] Exhibit 96, Report of FBI interview of Park Police Officer Franz Ferstl, May 2, 1994: "Ferstl stated that he remained in the parking lot until the ambulance came and removed the body. Ferstl advised that he did not return to the death scene a third time..."

[904] Exhibit 81, Report of FBI interview of Park Police Investigator Christine Hodakievic, May 2, 1994: "During one of the periods of time she was at the Fort Marcy parking lot,

*Parking lot.* Officer Ferstl, along with Dr. Haut's female driver, remained in parking lot.

**Endnote 29, 7:18-7:43:** *Body site.* Medical Examiner Donald Haut and investigators examined the body.

**Endnote 30, 7:44:** *Body site.* Upon finishing the inspection of the body, Dr. Haut left.[905]

**Endnote 31, 8:01-8:06:** *Parking lot.* Corey Ashford arrived at the park around 8:00[906] and observed a "dull red"[907] Honda in the space where Mr. Foster's silver Honda was reported to have been. Firefighter Ashford drew and labeled this Honda, police vehicles, his ambulance, a white Ford Crown Victoria, and a Black Cadillac for FBI investigators. His drawing did not show a vehicle matching the description of Mr. Foster's silver Honda and he was later "informed that the [red] Honda belonged to the victim, Foster."[908]

---

Hodakievic recalls the Medical Examiner arriving, whom she met in the parking lot and escorted to the death scene." Exhibit 73, Report of FBI interview of Dr. Donald Haut, April 12, 1994: "Upon arriving at Fort Marcy Park, USPP officers escorted Haut to the body of Vincent W. Foster, Jr..."

[905]   Exhibit 118, Handwritten notes of Park Police Investigator Renee Abt, July 20, 1993: "1943 hours coroner Haut FFX Co. take to FFX Co. Hosp. to be pronounced rolled [sic]."

[906]   Exhibit 182, Fairfax County Fire & Rescue Department, dispatch record, July 20, 1993: "20:02 - onscne"

[907]   Exhibit 139, Report of FBI interview of Firefighter Corey Ashford, April 27, 1994: "Upon entering Fort Marcy Park, Ashford recalls seeing a vehicle believed to be a Honda Civic, that was possibly dark red in color. It was either a 1986 or a 1988..."

[908]   Exhibit 74, Report of FBI interview of Firefighter Corey Ashford, February 23, 1994: "Also recalled was a red, Honda Civic. Ashford was later informed that the Honda belonged to the victim, Foster."

LAW OFFICES
**JOHN H. CLARKE**
720 SEVENTH STREET, N.W.
SUITE 304
WASHINGTON, D.C. 20001
(202) 332-3030

June 19, 1996

ALSO ADMITTED IN VIRGINIA
AND MARYLAND

FACSIMILE
(202) 639-0999

The Honorable
United States Senate
Washington, DC  20510

Re:  Report of Witness Tampering -
*Harassment of Whitewater Grand Jury Witness*

Dear Senator        :

I am writing you to inform you of a very disturbing crime committed against my client, Mr. Patrick J. Knowlton.  Its implications are of significant interest to the public.

Mr. Knowlton was in Fort Marcy Park on July 20, 1993, within 80 minutes of the discovery of the body of deputy White House counsel Vincent Foster.  On October 22, 1995, Mr. Knowlton's story was published in a London newspaper, along with allegations that the FBI falsified reports of Mr. Knowlton's account of what he saw in the park.  Four days later, on Thursday, October 26, Mr. Knowlton was served a subpoena to testify the following Wednesday, November 1, before the Washington, DC grand jury investigating Whitewater and other matters, including Mr. Foster's death.

During the time Mr. Knowlton spent in public the same day he received the subpoena, and continuing into the following day, he was the target of an orchestrated campaign of harassment and intimidation perpetrated by 25 or more men.  We believe the harassment was an attempt to warn, destabilize and discredit Mr. Knowlton on the eve of his grand jury appearance.

The complete account of what happened to Mr. Knowlton is contained in the captioned Report.  It is available to the public (see attachment).  Mr. Knowlton and I thank you for your attention to this very disturbing crime.

Very  truly yours,

John  H. Clarke

**Personalized letter, hand delivered to all 535 members of Congress, envelope marked "Member's Personal Attention."  All seven responses follow.**

DANA ROHRABACHER
45TH DISTRICT, CALIFORNIA

WASHINGTON OFFICE:
2338 RAYBURN HOUSE OFFICE BUILDING
WASHINGTON, DC 20515-0546
(202) 225-2415  FAX: (202) 225-0145

DISTRICT OFFICE:
16132 BEACH BOULEVARD, SUITE 304
HUNTINGTON BEACH, CA 92647-2813
(714) 847-2433  FAX: (714) 847-9163

# Congress of the United States
## House of Representatives

June 19, 1996

COMMITTEES:
SCIENCE
CHAIRMAN, SUBCOMMITTEE ON
ENERGY AND ENVIRONMENT
SUBCOMMITTEE ON SPACE

INTERNATIONAL RELATIONS
SUBCOMMITTEE ON ASIA AND THE PACIFIC
SUBCOMMITTEE ON INTERNATIONAL
ECONOMIC POLICY AND TRADE

Mr. Louis Freeh
Director
Federal Bureau of Investigation
J. Edgar Hoover F.B.I. Building
Ninth Street & Pennsylvania Avenue, N.W.
Washington, D.C. 20535

Dear Director Freeh:

It has come to my attention that Patrick J. Knowlton, a Whitewater Grand Jury witness, believes he is the target of harassment by the Federal Bureau of Investigation (FBI).

Mr. Knowlton was in Fort Marcy Park the day Vincent Foster's body was found. He saw a suspicious looking man and a vehicle that are not consistent with the official version of events. The FBI interviewed Mr. Knowlton about what he saw at Fort Marcy Park. Mr. Knowlton claims that the FBI did not accurately report his testimony after the interview. Even more disturbing, Mr. Knowlton believes he was followed and harassed by a team of what he thinks may have been FBI agents after he went public with his story in order to destablize him before his grand jury appearance.

I would like to know if the FBI has conducted a surveillance of Patrick Knowlton. If so, who requested the surveillance? Most importantly, were the proper FBI procedures adhered to in the Foster case?

I appreciate your immediate attention to this request.

Sincerely,

Dana Rohrabacher
Member of Congress

DR:lw

BARNEY FRANK
4TH DISTRICT, MASSACHUSETTS

2404 RAYBURN BUILDING
WASHINGTON, DC 20615-2104
(202) 225-5931

29 CRAFTS STREET
NEWTON, MA 02158
(617) 332-3920

# Congress of the United States
## House of Representatives
### Washington, DC

558 PLEASANT STREET
ROOM 309
NEW BEDFORD, MA 02740
(508) 999-6462

222 MILLIKEN PLACE
THIRD FLOOR
FALL RIVER, MA 02721
(508) 674-3551

89 MAIN STREET
BRIDGEWATER, MA 02324
(508) 697-9403

June 20, 1996

Mr. Kenneth W. Starr
Independent Counsel
1001 Pennsylvania Avenue N.W.
Suite 490 North
Washington, DC 20004

Dear Mr. Starr,

I recently received a letter from John H. Clarke, an attorney, on behalf of his client Patrick Knowlton. He said in the letter and in a subsequent conversation which I initiated that his client has been harassed by people whom he believes are trying to prevent his testifying in the matter of Vincent Foster, and in also discrediting Mr. Knowlton with regard to the testimony he has already given. When I asked, he told me that he already reported this to your office and I told him that I had full confidence that your office would thoroughly investigate this. I did tell him that I would write to you noting that I had received this. As I told Mr. Clarke, I am fully confident that you and your office are giving this the attention it deserves.

BARNEY FRANK

BF/mg

495

JOHN D. ROCKEFELLER IV
WEST VIRGINIA

# United States Senate
WASHINGTON, DC 20510-4802

June 21, 1996

Dear Mr. Clarke:

Your letter of June 19, 1996 has been received.

We respectfully suggest you bring this matter to the attention of the proper legal authorities if you think there has been some violation of federal law with regard to your client.

Sincerely,

R. Lane Bailey
Chief of Staff


Mr. John H. Clarke
720 Seventh Street, NW
Suite 304
Washington, DC 20001

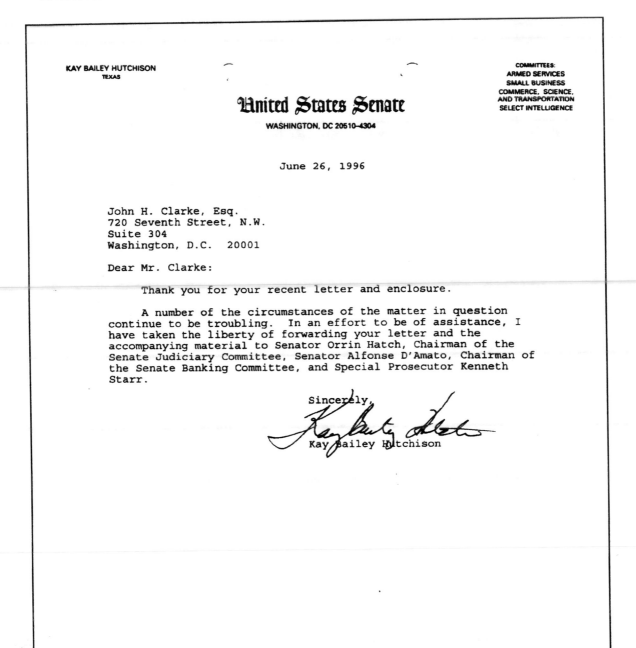

KAY BAILEY HUTCHISON
TEXAS

COMMITTEES:
ARMED SERVICES
SMALL BUSINESS
COMMERCE, SCIENCE,
AND TRANSPORTATION
SELECT INTELLIGENCE

# United States Senate

WASHINGTON, DC 20510-4304

June 26, 1996

John H. Clarke, Esq.
720 Seventh Street, N.W.
Suite 304
Washington, D.C.  20001

Dear Mr. Clarke:

Thank you for your recent letter and enclosure.

A number of the circumstances of the matter in question continue to be troubling.  In an effort to be of assistance, I have taken the liberty of forwarding your letter and the accompanying material to Senator Orrin Hatch, Chairman of the Senate Judiciary Committee, Senator Alfonse D'Amato, Chairman of the Senate Banking Committee, and Special Prosecutor Kenneth Starr.

Sincerely,

Kay Bailey Hutchison

# United States Senate
WASHINGTON, DC 20510–1004

PAUL D. COVERDELL
GEORGIA

CHAIRMAN
WESTERN HEMISPHERE SUBCOMMITTEE
FOREIGN RELATIONS COMMITTEE

June 26, 1996

Mr. John H. Clarke
Law Offices of John H. Clarke
720 Seventh Street, N.W. , Suite 304
Washington, D.C.,   20001

Dear Mr. Clarke:

Thank you for your letter of June 19, 1996, regarding your allegations of harassment of your client Patrick J Knowlton.

While I would like very much to be of direct assistance to you in this matter, there is a long-standing policy of Congressional courtesy which reserves for a Representative the privilege of handling the affairs of her constituents.  I am, therefore, taking the liberty of <u>referring your correspondence to Eleanor Holmes Norton</u>, since she represents the District of Columbia. I  am confident Representative Norton will do everything possible to assist you.

Sincerely,

Paul D. Coverdell
United States Senator

PDC/jrp

**ELEANOR HOLMES NORTON**
DISTRICT OF COLUMBIA

**COMMITTEE ON
TRANSPORTATION AND
INFRASTRUCTURE**

SUBCOMMITTEES
PUBLIC BUILDINGS AND
ECONOMIC DEVELOPMENT

WATER RESOURCES AND
ENVIRONMENT

## Congress of the United States
### House of Representatives
#### Washington, D.C. 20515

**COMMITTEE ON
GOVERNMENT REFORM AND
OVERSIGHT**

SUBCOMMITTEE
RANKING MINORITY MEMBER,
DISTRICT OF COLUMBIA

June 27, 1996

John H. Clarke, Esq.
720 Seventh Street, N.W.
Suite 304
Washington, D.C. 20001

Dear Mr. Clarke:

Thank you for your recent letter regarding your client, Mr. Patrick J. Knowlton. I have forwarded your correspondence to the House Government Reform and Oversight Committee which has jurisdiction over such matters.

Sincerely,

Eleanor Holmes Norton

DANIEL K. INOUYE
HAWAII

APPROPRIATIONS
Subcommittee on Defense

COMMERCE, SCIENCE, AND TRANSPORTATION
Subcommittee on Surface Transportation
and Merchant Marine

COMMITTEE ON INDIAN AFFAIRS

DEMOCRATIC STEERING COMMITTEE

COMMITTEE ON RULES AND ADMINISTRATION

JOINT COMMITTEE ON PRINTING

# United States Senate

SUITE 722, HART SENATE OFFICE BUILDING
WASHINGTON, DC 20510-1102
(202) 224-3934
FAX (202) 224-6747

PRINCE KUHIO FEDERAL BUILDING
ROOM 7325, 300 ALA MOANA BOULEVARD
HONOLULU, HI 96850-4975
(808) 541-2542
FAX (808) 541-2549

101 AUPUNI STREET, NO. 205
HILO, HI 96720
(808) 935-0844
FAX (808) 961-5163

July 1, 1996

John H. Clarke, Esquire
720 Seventh Street, N.W.
Suite 304
Washington, D.C.  20001

Dear Mr. Clarke:

On behalf of Senator Inouye, who is away from the office, I wish
to acknowledge receiving your letter concerning the alleged
harassment and intimidation of your client, Mr. Patrick J.
Knowlton, in conjunction with the investigation of Vincent
Foster's death and the Whitewater affair.  Before he left the
office, the Senator asked me to acknowledge your letter and <u>thank
you for sharing this information</u> with him.

Aloha,

_Margaret L. Cummisky_

MARGARET L. CUMMISKY
Legislative Director

MLC:r

500

LAW OFFICES

**JOHN H. CLARKE**
720 SEVENTH STREET, N.W.
SUITE 304
WASHINGTON, D.C. 20001

(202) 332-3030

ALSO ADMITTED IN VIRGINIA
AND MARYLAND

FACSIMILE
(202) 638-0888

July 16, 1996

<1Contact>
UNITED STATES HOUSE OF REPRESENTATIVES
Washington, DC  20515

COPY

Re:  Obstruction of Justice in the Foster investigation

Dear Congressman <65Last_Name>:

By letter dated June 19th, I informed you of a very disturbing crime committed against my client, Mr. Patrick J. Knowlton.

Last October, Mr. Knowlton's account of what he witnessed in Fort Marcy Park was published in a London newspaper, along with allegations that the FBI "falsified" their reports of his account. Four days later, Mr. Knowlton was subpoenaed to testify before Mr. Starr's Whitewater grand jury. Beginning that same day and into the following day, Mr. Knowlton was the target of a far-reaching campaign of harassment and intimidation. Only the FBI and Mr. Starr's Office of Independent Counsel (OIC) knew that Mr. Knowlton was a subpoenaed witness.

Enclosed are: (1) a journalist's account of what his sources told him regarding this case, including that "the number plates of a car seen by Knowlton... was in the computer system as a deniable plate used by the government;" (2) a summary of the facts of this case; and (3) correspondence from experts who are familiar with the type of harassment Mr. Knowlton suffered.

Congress relies on the OIC and FBI to: (1) uncover the truth behind falsified FBI reports; (2) solve crimes intended to discredit the account of those falsified FBI reports, and (3) identify FBI or OIC personnel responsible for leaking that Knowlton was subpoenaed. The facts of this case of obstruction of justice implicate the very investigators upon whom Congress and the public rely to solve the case. Mr. Knowlton as well as other good citizens of this country deserve better. Please look into this case.

Respectfully submitted,

John H. Clarke

Enclosures

Personalized letter, hand delivered to 84 members of Congress -- those members of committees having jurisdiction over the matter, envelope marked "Member's Personal Attention."  No response.

LAW OFFICES

# JOHN H. CLARKE
1730 K STREET, N.W.
SUITE 304
WASHINGTON, D.C. 20006
(202) 332-3030

ALSO ADMITTED IN VIRGINIA
AND MARYLAND

FAX (202) 822-8820

November 16, 1998

By Hand

The Honorable Henry J. Hyde
2110 Rayburn HOB
Washington, DC  20515-1306

    Re:  (1)  Patrick Knowlton v. FBI Agent Russell
                 Bransford, et al., USDC for DC, Conspiracy
                 to interfere with Civil Rights in violation
                 of 42 U.S.C. § 1985(2), Obstructing justice;
      (2)  Report on the Death of Vincent Foster, Jr.
                 By the Office of Independent Counsel
                 *In re:  Madison Guaranty*
                 *Savings & Loan Association*

Dear Chairman Hyde:

The evidence of an FBI cover-up of the facts of Mr. Foster's death is clear. The Special Division of the US Court of Appeals ordered Mr. Starr to append evidence of this FBI cover-up to the only report Mr. Starr has filed with that Court, the Report on the Death of Vincent Foster. Congress runs the risk of looking ineffective if it ignores its Constitutional responsibility to act on this matter.

Mr. Starr's repeated and accurate description of his office as a "microcosm of the Justice Department" demonstrates his failure to create a prosecutorial office independent from the Department of Justice. This explains the Office of Independent Counsel's failure to bring a single indictment regarding the Travel Office matter and FBI files matter.

Personalized letter, hand delivered to all members of the House Judiciary Committee on the eve of Mr. Starr's testimony regarding the impeachment of the President. No response.

November 16, 1998
The Honorable Henry J. Hyde
Page 2

Mr. Starr's Office of Independent Counsel being a microcosm of the Justice Department also explains the contents of its Report on Mr. Foster's death, which is nothing more than another layer of the same, ongoing Justice Department cover-up. Not one single finding in that Report can withstand scrutiny when compared to the publicly available underlying investigative record. Mr. Starr has undermined our Ethics in Government Act.

In four-and-a-half years, the Office of Independent Counsel has filed two Reports regarding its investigations. If you ask Mr. Starr only about the Lewinsky Report, you will have ignored your Constitutional responsibility to exercise oversight over the Executive. The public has a right to know Mr. Starr's answers to the enclosed questions regarding his Report on the Death of Vincent Foster.

We are informing all members of the House Judiciary Committee of the facts before filing in court the proof of the allegations in the enclosed Amended Complaint, filed October 21, 1998.

Respectfully submitted,

John H. Clarke

Enclosures:
    Appendix to Report on the Death of Vincent Foster
    Second Amended Complaint (excerpts)
        with Motion for Leave to File
    Transcript of oral argument in the trial court
        (excerpts)
    Questions prepared for Mr. Starr re the Office of
        Independent Counsel's Report on the Death of
        Vincent Foster

**Endnote 33**: The media.

***March, 1996,*** **Report of Witness Tampering** ***provided to:***
Sarah Fritz & Tom McCarthy, <u>LA Times</u>; Robert Hohler, <u>Boston Globe</u>; R.W. Apple, New York Times; Marilyn Rauber, John Crudele, & Steve Dunleavy, <u>N.Y. Post</u>; Jerry Seper, <u>Wash. Times</u>; Anne Devroy, <u>Wash. Post</u>; Michael Isikoff, <u>Newsweek</u>; Micah Morrison, <u>Wall Street Journal</u>; Lou Kilzer, <u>Denver Post</u>; editor, <u>Chicago Tribune</u>; editor, <u>Philadelphia Inquirer</u>; Jack Loftis, <u>Houston Chronicle</u>; Charles Zehren, <u>Newsday</u>; Jamie Dettmer, <u>Insight on the News</u>; Washington editor, *Reuters News Agency*; Pete Yost, *Associated Press*; Brian Gaffney, *Dateline NBC*; Ted Koppel; Julia Malone, *Cox News*; Lisa Tutman, *Cox Broadcasting*; *HardCopy*; *Unsolved Mysteries*; *Inside Edition*.

***Representatives from the following media organizations present at a November 12, 1996, press conference on the steps of federal District Court in Washington, unsealing Patrick Knowlton's civil rights lawsuit:*** CNN, *Insight on the News*, <u>Wash. Post</u>, <u>N.Y. Times</u>, <u>Wash. Times</u>, ABC News, NBC News, CBS News, Fox News, <u>Time Magazine</u>, <u>N.Y. Observer</u>, Cox News, among others.

***Media accounts of the October, 1997, release of the OIC's Report on Mr. Foster's death, mentioning Patrick Knowlton's name but failing to report the existence of his Court-ordered Appendix:***

> S. Labaton, *Report of Foster's Suicide portrays a depressed man*, <u>N.Y. Times</u>, October 11, 1997: The report also dismisses the testimony of Patrick Knowlton, a witness who says he was at the park the day Foster died and did not see his car but did see a person who stared at Knowlton menacingly. The report concludes that there is no reliable evidence that anyone at the park "had any connection to Foster's death."

> B. York, *Vince Foster, In the Park, with the Gun*, <u>The Weekly Standard Magazine</u>, October 27, 1997: Byron York is an investigative writer with the *American Spectator* \*\*\* [C]onspiracy theorists... have already begun to complain about Starr's treatment of Patrick Knowlton, a motorist who says that on July 20 he stopped in Fort Marcy to relieve himself and saw a man in a car who stared at him menacingly... But Starr found no other evidence to support Knowlton's story, and the report mentions the incident only briefly.

M. Morrison, *In Re: Vincent Foster*, Wall Street
Journal, November 26, 1997: "Most of the other
allegations, including the recollections of much-
touted witness Patrick Knowlton, represent the
confusions inevitable in any large investigation of a
dramatic event."

***Some responses from journalists when asked by the authors
whether they are interested:*** George Will, Feb., 1996:
"We're not interested in that [Foster case]; Fred Barnes,
Feb. 23, 1996: "Conservatives should ignore the death of
Vincent Foster and stick to the real issues... It was a
suicide... No, I don't want to meet Patrick Knowlton;" Tim
Russert, Feb. 29, 1996: "I appreciate your taking the
time... It is important to have your input;" James
Stewart, March 20, 1996: "Now I think it is too much of a
coincidence that he [Foster] would be that depressed and
then that somebody would somehow move in and fake some kind
of crime. Life just doesn't work like that;" Haynes
Johnson, May 28, 1996: "You have raised provocative
questions;" Ted Gest, 1996: "Our magazine [*Newsweek*] covers
consumer issues, that is not the kind of story we cover,
try one of the daily papers;" James Whalen (St. Paul
Journalism Prof.), "If there was anything suspicious about
Foster's death the Washington press would cover it;" Paul
Gigot (*Wall St. J.*), July 23, 1996: "Foster committed
suicide. Everything points to that... No, I don't want to
meet him [Patrick Knowlton] and you probably think I am
part of the conspiracy;" Michael Barone, July 30, 1996:
"I'm not going to defend the coverage of Vincent Foster by
*U.S. News & World Report*, I do not know enough about the
Foster story;" Jerry Seper (*Wash. Times*), Oct. 17, 1996:
"I don't cover Foster, I'm covering Whitewater. Ask George
Archibald, he has been assigned the Foster story;" George
Archibald, Oct. 24, 1996: "Foster is dead. I don't cover
Foster... My time is limited;" Eugene Meyer (*Wash. Post*),
Nov. 5, 1996: "No, it's not my job... I don't care about
your friend;" Karen Ballard (*Wash. Times*), Nov. 5, 1996:
"Why don't you write the story;" William Kristol, Nov. 8,
1996: "Amazing... What kind of work does Mr. Knowlton do?"
Candy Crowley (CNN), Kwame Holman, Peter Kenyon (NPR), Nov.
19, 1996: "If it was reported I would cover it... I have
to cover other news, it's not my job;" Carl Stern, Michael
McCurry, Marlin Fitzwater, & Charles Bierbauer (CNN), Feb.
13, 1997: "We don't know anything about it;" Cokie
Roberts, April 13, 1997: "Thousands of reporters have
looked into the death of Vincent Foster and everyone
including the numerous investigations have concluded that
his death was a suicide;" Paul Harvey, July 16, 1997: "The
death of White House counsel Vincent Foster has now been
investigated four times including Kenneth Starr's most

recent one and all four have reached the same conclusion. There was no conspiracy, no cover-up, it was suicide;" Mike Wallace, July 23, 1997: "Just wait until Ken Starr's report is released, then you can apologize to me;" Tom Sherwood, WRC-DC, July 31, 1997: "I can't believe there would be a cover-up... Why don't you contact Mike Isikoff;" Michael Isikoff, Aug. 13, 1997: "[I] do not have enough evidence to go with the story about Patrick Knowlton's allegations;" Martha Malan, (*St. Paul Press*), Oct. 12, 1997: "We don't have the resources to cover the Foster story... No, I don't want to talk to Patrick Knowlton;" John Crudele (*N.Y. Post*), Nov., 1997: "I don't believe there is a cover-up;" Steve Labaton, (*N.Y. Times*), Nov., 1997: "The court had to attach your submission;" Bob Zelnick, May 30, 1998: "[There isn't] any credible evidence that Vincent Foster was murdered. Can I ask to change the subject?" Harold Hostetler, June 25, 1998: "Mr. Knowlton does appear to be an honest and forthright person who is sticking up for his principles and beliefs. However, I do not see this as a potential story for *Guideposts*;" Sam Fullwood (*L.A. Times*) at Sanford Ungar AU forum (with L. Brent Bozell III, Karen DeYoung & Bill Plante), Sept. 8, 1998: "It's not my kind of story... Why don't you post it on the Internet then everyone will know... Why don't you write a book, you could make lots of money;" Matt Drudge, "I'll read this [written materials] but I was just about ready to believe the body was moved and now you're saying he was murdered;" Frank Sesno, Sept. 24, 1998: "I'll look at this;" Helen Thomas, Oct. 7, 1998: "[T]his should be reported to the American people;" Helen Thomas, April 9, 1999: "Q. I gave you the addendum to Starr's Report. Will you write about Patrick Knowlton? A. No... I don't have time. Q. Can I quote you? A. No. Q. You said then that his story should be reported. A. It is very unfair of you to do this to me. Just forget it."

**Attacks on Patrick Knowlton's mental stability**: Excerpt from <u>Knowlton v. Edwards et al</u>, USDC, DC, CA No. 96-2467:

> 170. Defendants also accomplished their object of publicly discrediting Plaintiff. On November 24, 1997, a book review entitled *The Secret Life of Ambrose Evans-Pritchard*, written by Michael Isikoff, appeared in the widely circulated <u>Weekly Standard Magazine</u>. In it, Isikoff wrote:
>
> *      *      *
>
> Evans-Pritchards' work, such as it is, consists of little more than wild flights of conspiratorial fancy coupled with outrageous and wholly uncorroborated allegations offered up by

his "sources" - largely a collection of
oddballs... and borderline psychotics.

*     *     *

Back in Washington, Evans-Pritchard breaks one of
his big stories:  Patrick Knowlton, a
construction worker who stopped to urinate at
Fort Marcy Park on the afternoon of Vince
Foster's death and -- here's the key part --
recalls seeing a mysterious "Hispanic-looking"
man lingering around the parking lot.  No sooner
has Evans-Pritchard popped this bombshell in the
*Telegraph* than, Knowlton reports,
menacing-looking men in business suits begin
following him and staring really hard at him...

*     *     *

But for the moment I prefer my own conspiracy
theory:  Evans-Pritchard doesn't believe a word
he has written... designed to discredit critics
of the Clinton White House by making them look
like a bunch of blithering idiots.

*     *     *

The next day, November 25, 1997 another book
review, entitled *Conspiracy Central*, authored by Jacob
Cohen, appeared in the widely circulated National
Review Magazine.  In it, Cohen wrote:

*     *     *

...Patrick Knowlton, who claims that he came to
the park at 4:30 on the afternoon of July 20 to
relieve himself, and at that time saw in the
parking lot a brown Honda with Arkansas plates...

*     *     *

He insists that a very sinister looking man was
hovering around the parking lot and may have
monitored his peeing...  Knowlton seems to have a
penchant for seeing the sinister in the glances
of those he meets...  Mysterious cars follow him,
he says.  Carefully organized teams of men
constantly pass him and his girlfriend on the
streets, giving them very menacing stares...
Apparently, they are present during every walk
Knowlton takes, so that any experimental stroll
will reveal them.  One wonders, is there a school
that teaches federal agents this methodology of
intimidation?

***An analysis of the use of the media during the progress of the cover-up could include:***

(1)  A comparison of the initial published accounts of Mr. Foster's demeanor (no noticeable signs of distress) to the accounts that suddenly began appearing upon the "discovery" of torn note six days after the death (rapid weight loss and other symptoms consistent with severe depression);

(2)  The alliance between the Washington press corps and the Justice Department -- permanent institutions of government;

(3)  The chilling effect on witnesses of the steady stream of press leaks that the OIC was soon to issue a report validating earlier official conclusions (see January 1995 Scripps-Howard wire reporting Starr's suicide conclusion appearing the same day that the OIC began grand jury proceedings into the death, February, 1995 *Wall Street Journal* feature quoting sources close to Starr as saying the case had been closed as a suicide, October, 1995 *60 Minutes* piece declaring that Starr's suicide report would be out shortly, December, 1995 Fox News report that Starr's Washington office was to issue a suicide report within six weeks, July, 1996 *60 Minutes* piece declaring that Starr had concluded the death was a suicide and that a report would be issued that summer, November, 1996, *Newsweek* cover story by M. Isikoff quoting unidentified sources as saying that the suicide report was to be released imminently);

(4)  Years of repeating of the official suicide conclusion in stories about other matters, like the OIC's Supreme Court litigation of its subpoena of attorney James Hamilton's notes of a consultation he had with Mr. Foster shortly before the death;

(5)  Pulitzer Prize winning journalists who misreported the Foster story: Haynes Johnson, David Broder, Bob Woodward, Anthony Lewis, Mary McGrory, James Stewart, and Mike McAlary;

(6)  The accounts of the death in virtually every book written on the Clinton Presidency:  Bob Woodward, The Agenda, Simon & Schuster, 1994; David Brock, The Seduction of Hillary Clinton, Free Press,

1996; Haynes Johnson & David Broder, <u>The System</u>,
Little & Brown, 1996; James Stewart, <u>Blood Sport</u>,
Simon & Schuster, 1996; Gary Aldrich, <u>Unlimited
Access</u>, Regnery, 1996; R. Emmett Tyrrell, <u>Boy
Clinton</u>, Regnery, 1996; Howard Kurtz, <u>Spin Cycle</u>,
The Free Press, 1998; Ann Coulter, <u>High Crimes
and Misdemeanors</u>, Regnery, 1998; Michael Isikoff,
<u>Uncovering Clinton</u>, Crown Publishing, 1999;
George Stephanopoulos, <u>All Too Human</u>, Little
Brown & Company, 1999; Lanny J. Davis, <u>Truth To
Tell</u>, Free Press, 1999; Joyce Milton, <u>The First
Partner</u>, William Morrow & Company, 1999; Helen
Thomas, <u>Front Row At The White House</u>, Scribner,
1999;

(7)   Unpublished accounts of witnesses -- in addition
      to Patrick Knowlton -- who contacted members of
      the news media to report what they know of the
      cover-up.

**W. Barret, *Freedom to Steal, Why Politicians Never go
to Jail*, <u>New York Magazine</u>, February 4, 1980:** Crooked
politicians have nothing to fear in New York.
Contrary to much of the post-Watergate anti-corruption
ballyhoo, the three United States attorneys who have
served in Foley Square for the last ten years have
failed to make a single case against a crooked
politician within their jurisdiction.  As astounding
as it may seem, not since the legendary Carmine
DeSapio was convicted back in 1969 for bribery has a
top politician or any of the thousands of public
officials in the Southern District's territory --
Manhattan, the Bronx, and Westchester -- found himself
in handcuffs.  It is uncertain whether this pattern of
timidity on the part of the politically appointed
prosecutors will change now that John S. Martin has
been designated by Senator Daniel Patrick Moynihan to
replace Robert B. Fiske in the prestigious post...
The failure on the part of the federal prosecutors in
the Southern District to involve themselves in
political-corruption cases is one of the most
fascinating, if unspoken, mysteries in city
government.  The end of Fiske's term, in March will,
in fact, conclude a ten-year period in which Nixon-
and Ford-appointed U.S. Attorneys have presided over
the transformation of the Southern District into a
red-light district for political corruption.  ***  The
description of all political-corruption cases handled
during the first three years of Fiske's term consumes
only 6 of the 187 pages enumerating major cases in the

U.S. attorney's annual reports. *** [T]he former WNEW-TV reporter who broke much of the Velez story, recalls numerous meetings with Weinberg and Fiske. "Once I know I brought them absolute, cold evidence of a crime," he said... but nothing happened. *** Charges of campaign-finance irregularities had been made [against Al DelBello] ...Fiske closed it [the grand jury] four months after he opened it... [and] sharply limited this inquiry... *** Fiske's office terminated an eight-month probe of the city's most political bank. Jack Newfield's recent piece on Staten Island Congressman Murphy in the *Village Voice* centers on an alleged $50,000 bribe *** [It] has now been quietly closed without result. *** Then U.S. Senator James Buckley delayed Fiske's appointment for several weeks because of his concern that Fiske's long-standing connections to Morgan Guaranty, one of the city's six major banks... Fiske did not "recuse" - the legal term for withdrawing... *** Nonetheless, six months after the SEC final report, Fiske released a one-page statement closing the securities case... There are a number of other cases, reported in the media, that have been covered by Southern District silence and inactivity... *** Agents from various federal departments say they prefer to work with assistants from other offices where assistants are closer to the streets and more willing to work with agents as partners... Fiske, for example, has a hard-and-fast rule that assistants are not to do field work with agents, a rule that has no parallel in other, neighboring federal districts. The price we all pay for these relationships and priorities is a federal jurisdiction where official corruption appears legally impenetrable.

Compare *Now You Know...*, Wash. Post June 22, 1998: President and Hillary Rodham Clinton fed the hands that bite them Friday night, hosting more [than] 1,000 White House reporters, spouses and progeny at a South Lawn carnival.*** But tickled reporters jammed the Ferris wheel, arcade, merry-go-round and Twister, a stomach-churning pendulum. Nothing could kill the horde's locust like appearance for children, sausages, ice cream and cotton candy.

**Endnote 34:** *What you can do.* The public has been told that the Park Police, the news media, the Congress, and independent counsels have repeatedly scrutinized Mr. Foster's death, and that there was no criminal wrongdoing. If you agree that this filing proves the existence of a cover-up, then you have concluded that two of the three branches of our government, the executive and the legislature, as well as the press, failed the public trust.

If the facts of the case do become widely known, the public will be forced to examine how far our democracy has strayed from what its founding fathers envisioned. Whether the facts of this case act as a wake-up call to the public is up to you. Only you can tell your family, friends, neighbors, acquaintances, co-workers, school, church, or synagogue about the facts of this case. You can print this filing from the Internet, link your own website to it, order copies from any bookstore, ask your library to order it, or, if the Court grants the motion, order it from any government printing office. You can decide what you can best do to get the facts into your community. Please act now and start getting the facts out.

We can improve the quality of our press and government by holding them accountable, but only if the public knows of their failure to confront the truth. We have the right to learn the facts and judge for ourselves whether America's democratic institutions have in fact accepted the responsibilities that come with the public trust -- and whether our true history is being taken from us.